1987

W

SELLING
principles and methods

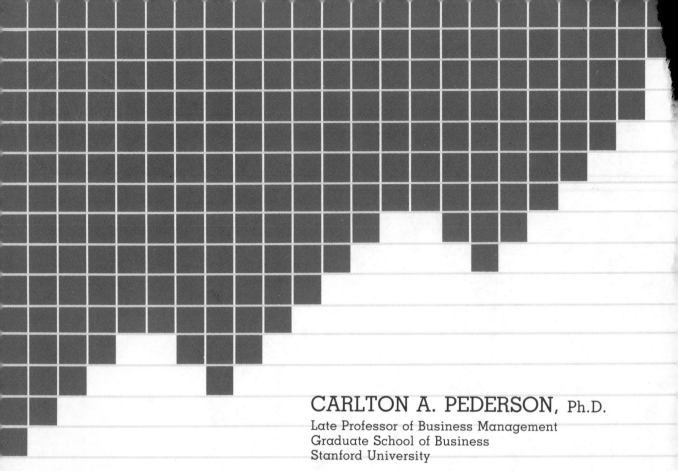

CARLTON A. PEDERSON, Ph.D.

Late Professor of Business Management
Graduate School of Business
Stanford University

MILBURN D. WRIGHT, Ed.D.

Dean Emeritus and
Emeritus Professor of Marketing
School of Business
San Jose State University

BARTON A. WEITZ, Ph.D.

Assistant Professor
Graduate School of Management
University of California, Los Angeles

SELLING

principles and methods

Seventh Edition • 1981

RICHARD D. IRWIN, INC.
Homewood, Illinois 60430

ISBN 0-256-02537-1

Library of Congress Catalog Card No. 80-84721

Printed in the United States of America

3 4 5 6 7 8 9 0 H 8 7 6 5 4 3 2

Preface

American business enterprise will be relying even more heavily upon the sales organization in the next decade. Competition will be a constant in our free enterprise economy. The very existence of many firms will depend upon the income produced through the sales organization.

With the rapid changes occurring in the marketplace, the success of sales representatives will depend upon their acquisition of new knowledges, skills, and attitudes to meet the challenges that the changing world has in store for them.

Colleges, universities, and community colleges have been excellent sources of supply for sales trainees. It is vital that our future sales representatives obtain a basic foundation of knowledge in the field of selling before they enter specific on-the-job training programs or establish their own sales organizations. The purpose of this book is to supply the educational materials and experiences which will prepare men and women for their entry into the exciting and rewarding field of selling.

Sales training materials from many successful businesses have been incorporated into this edition to provide the practical illustrations so necessary to the learning process for those who are preparing for a career in sales.

The importance of selling in the American economy is given renewed attention. Emphasis is placed throughout the book on selling as a process that provides benefits to both the buyers and the sellers.

This seventh edition has been organized into six parts. Part I, The Field of Selling, includes material on the nature, role, and rewards of personal selling and illustrations of the duties and responsibilities of sales representatives. Part II, Successful Selling Requires Knowledge plus Skill, explores the reasons why people buy, buyer characteristics and behavior patterns, and the special skills and knowledge needed for successful selling. Information also is provided on advertising and sales promotion. Part III, The Sales Process, covers the very heart of selling, beginning with prospecting and getting the right start, and continuing with planning and delivering the presentation, dramatizing, handling objections, and clos-

v

ing the sale. Part IV, Application of Sales Principles, Practices, and Techniques, provides illustrations from the business world on how different types of sales presentations are delivered and special chapters on customer relations, industrial and trade selling, and retail selling. Part V, Improving the Sales Representative's Personal Effectiveness, deals with the legal, social, ethical, and personal responsibilities of the salesperson. It includes material on how to manage yourself, your time, and your territory most effectively. Part VI, Introduction to Sales Management, treats the nature and scope of sales management. It provides an opportunity for students to gain an insight into management as the next step in their careers.

Major changes in this edition include: (1) new chapters on the management of time, territory, and self; industrial and trade selling; and the legal, social-ethical, and personal responsibilities of the sales representative; (2) the combining of the two chapters on buyer characteristics and behavior patterns and buyer motivation into one chapter in which the traditional motivational approach has been complemented with a more modern information processing approach; (3) new material on body language, the art of listening, dressing for successful selling, legal restrictions on direct selling, and selling to groups of people; (4) the revision of all chapters to include up-to-date examples, statistics, and selected references; (5) a greater emphasis upon trade and industrial selling; (6) many new end-of-chapter cases, projects, and questions; and, (7) abundant new resource material in the manual for teachers.

The authors have maintained the important features of writing style, actual business illustrations, along with the "how-to" approach which have made this text a leader in its field for 30 years.

The authors are indebted to many users of the previous editions for suggestions made to improve this revision. Special acknowledgment is due the following professors, who carefully reviewed the seventh edition and provided critiques on the text material and organization: Mary Ann Oberhaus, Orange Coast College, California; David Braun, West Los Angeles College; Edward Cotta, California State University at Long Beach; Jack McNeff, State University of New York, Farmingdale; Frank M. Falcetta, Hudson, Massachusetts; and Monroe Murphy Bird, Virginia Polytechnic Institute and State University.

Special thanks are due Ruth Zartler for her expert typing of the manuscript.

The future is becoming more uncertain at an accelerating rate. Business is becoming more complex. Salespeople will face challenges that only educated and well-trained professionals can handle. No business can survive without the successful selling of its products or services. Selling expertise is becoming more important every day!

This edition is dedicated to the memory of the late Dr. Carlton A. "Bud" Pederson, whose leadership and inspiration have helped make this a leading textbook for three decades.

Milburn D. Wright
Barton A. Weitz

Acknowledgments

The authors wish to express their sincere gratitude to the following companies for their generous contributions to the seventh edition:

AM International, Inc.
American Airlines, Inc.
American Management Association
American Telephone & Telegraph Company
Bank of America
Blyth Eastman Dillon & Co., Inc.
Bristol Laboratories
Burroughs Corporation
Carnation Company
Carter, Hawley, Hale Stores, Inc.
Chrysler Corporation
Coca-Cola Company
Colgate-Palmolive Company
Connecticut Mutual Life Insurance Company
Crown Zellerbach Corporation
The Dartnell Corporation
Dictaphone Corporation
Dow Chemical Company
Dukane Corporation
E. I. duPont De Nemours & Company
Eastman Kodak Company
The Emporium/Capwell
Federated Department Stores
Filter Queen Company
Firestone Tire & Rubber Company
FMC Corporation
Ford Motor Company
Frigidaire Division, General Motors Corporation
General Electric Corporation
General Foods Corporation
General Telephone & Electronics Corporation
General Telephone of California
The Gillette Co., Paper Mate Division
Goodyear Tire & Rubber Company
Gulf Oil Corporation
Hart Schaffner & Marx
Hewlett-Packard Company
International Business Machines Corporation
International Harvester Company
Johnson & Johnson
Kaiser Aluminum
Kelvinator Division of White Consolidated Industries, Inc.

Kroehler Furniture Company
Lever Bros. Company, Inc.
Life Insurance Agency Management Association
Lily Tulip Cup Division of Owens-Illinois, Inc.
R. H. Macy & Company
The Maytag Company
McKesson & Robbins, Inc.
Merck Sharpe & Dohme Division, Merck & Co., Inc.
Metropolitan Life Insurance Company
Mutual Benefit Life Insurance Company
N.C.R.
New York Life Insurance Company
A. C. Nielsen Company
Ortho Pharmaceutical Corporation
Otis Elevator Company
Pacific Telephone Company
Paine, Webber, Jackson & Curtis, Inc.
Penn Mutual Life Insurance Company
J. C. Penney Company
Personal Finance Company
Procter & Gamble Company
Provident Mutual Life Insurance Company
The Royal Bank of Canada
Safeguard Business Systems Corporation
Sears Roebuck & Company
SKF Industries
Sperry Remington
Standard Oil of California
Standard Register Company
State Farm Insurance Companies
Technicolor Audio-Visual Systems
3 M Company
Toledo Scale Company
U.S. Rubber Company
U.S. Steel Corporation
Wear-Ever Aluminum, Inc.
Westinghouse Electric Corporation
Xerox Corporation
Zenith Corporation

Contents

SELLING
principles and methods

Part one

THE FIELD
OF SELLING

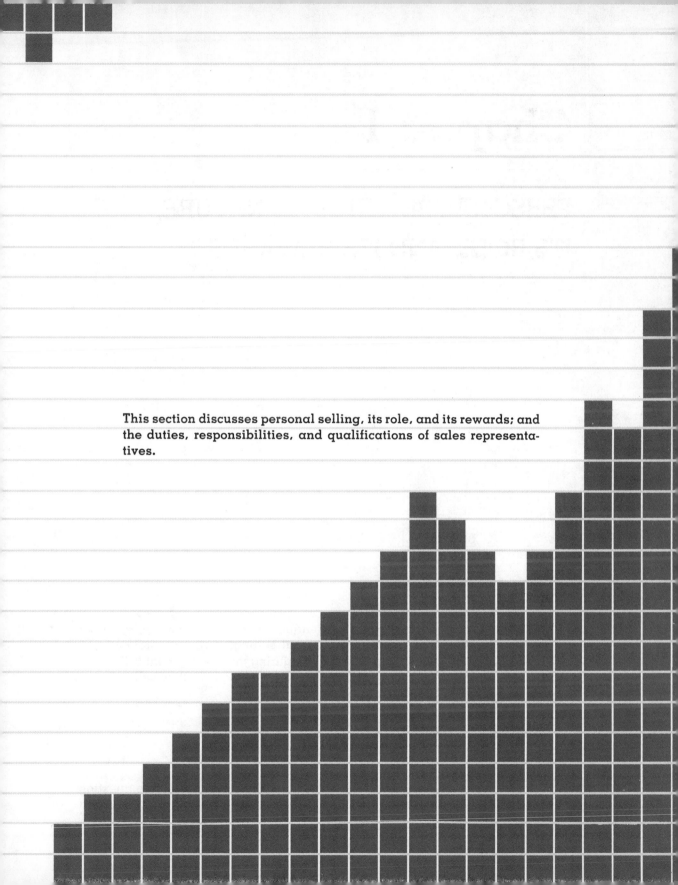

This section discusses personal selling, its role, and its rewards; and the duties, responsibilities, and qualifications of sales representatives.

Chapter 1

PERSONAL SELLING: ITS NATURE, ITS ROLE, AND ITS REWARDS

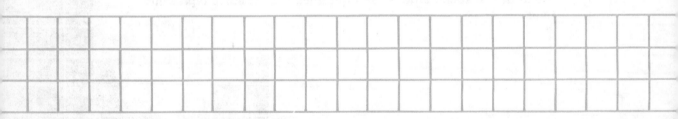

This chapter focuses attention upon the nature, role, opportunities, and rewards of personal selling. Pertinent information is included on the impact of selling during the development of the early American economy and on the importance of creative selling to the future progress of our economy.

THE NATURE OF SELLING

What is selling?

A sales executive of a large corporation was asked the question, "What is selling?" He replied, "To me, selling is the art of merchandising your goods or services at a profit." This is a direct and simple definition but perhaps it has certain shortcomings.

There has been much discussion about whether selling is an art or a science, or a combination of both. Some definitions emphasize that selling is the art of influencing or persuading people to do what the sales representative wants them to do. The Definitions Committee of the American Marketing Association has given considerable thought to defining the various terms used in the field of marketing. The committee defined "selling" as "the personal or impersonal process of assisting and/or persuading a prospective customer to buy a commodity or a service or to act favorably upon an idea that has commercial significance to the seller."[1]

It is relatively unimportant, for all practical purposes, whether selling is defined as an art or a science, or both. The above definitions, however, are incomplete. They do not emphasize sufficiently that the sales process should provide mutual, continuous satisfaction to *both* the buyer and the seller. Persuasion in which the sales representative depends upon a combination of highly emotional appeals and high-pressure tactics to force a sale has no rightful place in modern selling. Enlightened sales organizations are emphasizing selling that brings long-term satisfaction to the company, the sales representative, and the customer.

Selling, then, should be defined as *the process whereby the seller ascertains, activates, and satisfies the needs or wants of the buyer to the mutual, continuous benefit of both the buyer and the seller.*[2]

Everyone sells

Lonely hermits may be the only persons in our society whose livelihood is not dependent, to some extent, upon applying the principles of selling. A four-year-old boy soon learns the most effective techniques for selling his father on a trip to the circus. A college student may use the most convincing sales points in selling parents on the idea that he or she should have an automobile while at school.

Young graduates are faced with the most important sales job of all—the job of selling their services to an employer. If they perform this task effectively, they will go through the essential steps of mak-

[1] Ralph S. Alexander and the Committee on Definitions of the American Marketing Association, *Marketing Definitions: A Glossary of Marketing Terms* (Chicago: American Marketing Association, 1960), p. 21. This definition includes advertising, other forms of publicity, and sales promotion as well as personal selling.

[2] See also Alton F. Doody and William G. Nickels, "Structuring Organizations for Strategic Selling," *MSU Business Topics*, Autumn 1972, p. 33, for a good definition of the salesperson's role.

ing a sale. They will analyze the strong points of their personal qualifications, educational background, and work experience. They will find out everything they can about the needs of the prospective employer. They will then attempt to get the employer to satisfy its needs by purchasing their services. This is selling at the personal level.

An increasing number of young men and women are studying selling even though they do not plan to go directly into the field of personal selling. They recognize that almost everyone in business uses certain principles of selling in everyday work. Young, aspiring executives are most eager to sell themselves to associates, superiors, and subordinates; the accountant uses selling when presenting a new cost control program to the production employees; the engineer, in a sense, uses selling to present a research budget for approval; the industrial relations or personnel executive uses sales techniques in handling negotiations with the union.

Contractors, teachers, ministers, inventors, authors, politicians, and industrial engineers—all practice the art of influencing others to do what they want them to do. Those who have developed the skill of being able to influence the actions of others are usually the leaders in our society.

Is selling a profession?

Any answer to this question depends upon the exact definition and meaning of the word *profession*. The basic requirements for a true profession include the following: (1) an organized body of knowledge, (2) a relatively long and specialized preparation, (3) an organized plan or program to train individuals who plan to enter the profession, (4) an established and accepted code of ethics, (5) a set of standards for admission and disqualification, and (6) recognition that service to others comes before self-interest.

R. S. Wilson, former executive vice president and sales manager of the Goodyear Tire and Rubber Company, said that "the distinguishing mark of a professional is the constant aspiring toward perfection." He illustrated this point in the following words:

> The Professional sales representative is a person who is constantly studying to improve proficiency. I am thinking of a surgeon whom I know well who personifies to me the Professional attitude. I met him at lunch one day not long ago and he told me he was leaving by plane that afternoon for Dallas. Why? He had read in one of the Medical Journals of a surgeon in Dallas who had performed a delicate cheekbone operation in a manner that was new to him. He immediately called the Dallas surgeon on the telephone and found he was to perform such an operation the next day, so he dropped everything and left by plane to watch the operation and learn a new technique. This friend

of mine was 56 years old when this incident occurred, and to the end of his career he will go on studying and practicing to improve his proficiency. He is a true Professional.[3]

Wilson defined the professional salesperson as (1) a person who is constantly studying to improve his or her proficiency; (2) a person who recognizes that there is no substitute for hard work; (3) a person who, above all else, maintains his or her self-respect, integrity, and independence; and (4) a person who puts true value on his or her services.[4]

When one thinks of professionals in terms of the factors described above, it is obvious that many sales representatives today are not true professionals. In a number of fields of selling, however, certain sales representatives do meet all or most of the requisites of the professional. Some life insurance companies, for example, have adopted comprehensive programs for selecting and training their new sales representatives. A course of study has also been prescribed for those who are to qualify for the designation of CLU (chartered life underwriter). The American College of Life Underwriters, an independent nonprofit educational institution, awards the diploma and the registered CLU designation. This college has had a major impact upon the development of professional sales representatives in the field of life insurance.

Approximately 25 years ago the National Association of Life Underwriters, an organization of agents representing leading companies, established a code of ethics for life underwriters. In 1963, the Sales and Marketing Executives-International (SME-I) adopted a similar code of ethics for professional sales representatives. These actions were intended to raise the standards of performance among career sales representatives.

The Professional Sales Representative's Creed shown in Figure 1-1 represents the authors' views on the basic responsibilities of the professional sales representative.

It is encouraging to note that the standards of behavior have been improving rapidly during the past few years. There is greater acceptance of the concept that successful selling means providing lasting benefits to *both* the buyer and the seller.

Training a necessity in modern selling

Some individuals possess characteristics which make it easy for them to do a good job of selling. These individuals may have natural

---

[3] *Salesmanship as a Profession* (New York: Goodyear Tire and Rubber Co., 1958), p. 16. This publication is a reproduction of the Parlin Lecture given by Wilson before the Philadelphia Center of the American Marketing Association.

[4] Ibid., excerpts, pp. 16–17.

Figure 1-1
The professional sales representative's creed

✔ I will place customer and company interests above self-interest.

✔ I will be constantly alert to the concept that successful selling must bring mutual and continuous benefits to both the buyer and seller.

✔ I will maintain an optimistic and positive attitude toward my business at all times.

✔ I will maintain loyalty to my company, my associates, and my customers.

✔ I will do everything possible to support the free enterprise system based upon open competition and freedom of choice in the marketplace.

✔ I will continue to develop new knowledges, skills, and attitudes to keep pace with the changing technological and social environment.

✔ I will make every effort possible to utilize my total capacities efficiently in rendering quality service to my customers and my company.

✔ I will never violate the trust and confidence of my customers or my associates.

✔ I will maintain honesty and integrity in all of my dealings with my customers, competitors, colleagues, and company.

✔ In all of my personal activities I will attempt to do what is right and just for all parties concerned, and try to be a credit to my profession.

aptitudes for saleswork, but they must still be trained properly if they are to produce maximum results.

Many of the new products that are produced in the research and development laboratories are very complex. It is essential, therefore, that the application engineers and sales representatives be adequately trained if they are to do an effective job of matching customer needs with their products and services. During the past few years, for example, the electronics industry has brought about revolutionary changes in electronic equipment and machines, and extensive training is required for the sales representatives of the companies producing these products.

The life insurance sales representatives, if they are to do professional jobs of selling today, must have a knowledge of how Social Security, Keogh, and IRA plans affect their clients' insurance programs, and they must have a thorough understanding of tax laws. In addition to their technical or product knowledge training, they must understand the basic principles of psychology and consumer behavior.

One of the leading sales training and consulting organizations has estimated that American business spends over $500 million annually for sales training. The Caterpillar Tractor Company, for example, provides specialized factory training for all new sales trainees. Westinghouse has an extensive sales training program, including basic assignments in various manufacturing areas, assignments to sales divisions, and attendance at various sales schools. The International Business Machines Corporation has a multimillion dollar budget for sales and customer training. It is estimated that it recently cost this company approximately $20,000 to train a computer or business machines salesperson.

The importance of sales training is reflected in the expenditures per salesperson and the weeks of training per salesperson shown in Table 1-1.

All of the major automotive companies provide comprehensive sales training programs for their dealers. Sears Roebuck's recent sales training program on "Principles of Persuasion" includes records and related educational materials for use in the field. The U.S. Steel Corporation uses its own television studios and videotape operations in Pittsburgh with playback centers in 32 district sales offices throughout the United States. This new communication medium is very effective in sales training and customer education.

The recent emphasis given to training for saleswork has not been limited to the sales training programs within industry. Most large companies have shown an increasing interest in the educational backgrounds of applicants for sales positions. The Otis Elevator Company of New York, for example, puts considerable weight upon academic training as a prerequisite for saleswork. Candidates with undergraduate training in engineering and postgraduate work in business administration are preferred by this company. Other companies prefer applicants who have had academic training in the fields of marketing, sales, and the behavioral sciences. It has been estimated that over 500 of the colleges and universities in America offer basic courses in marketing and/or selling. This indicates that the schools are attempting to adapt their programs to the needs of business.

Young men and women who enter saleswork without adequate training will be at a great disadvantage in competitive selling in the years ahead. The manager of sales training for a major national

Table 1-1

Survey of selling costs

Type of salesperson	Mean training expenditure per year per person	Mean number of weeks for training per person per year
Industrial product	$15,479	24
Consumer product	11,338	16
Services	8,828	8

Source: *Sales & Marketing Management,* February 26, 1979, table 4-1, p. 66.

electric appliance company, in advising the young prospective salesperson, made this statement:

> No matter how you get that training, if you are to be a success at selling you must get it. . . . If you want to play a piano for amusement it is all right to learn to play by ear, but if you are to play a piano for a living you had better learn by note. The same advice applies to selling. If you are to make selling your lifework, better get the best training available.

ROLE OF SELLING IN THE AMERICAN ECONOMY

The United States has developed, over a relatively short span of time, the most productive economy in the history of the world. The development of this abundant economy is a tribute to the free enterprise system and to the imaginative selling which was and is today a dominant characteristic of that system.

Sales—The heart of the free enterprise system

Over the years, new products have been invented and sold in an unending procession—the steam engine, the telegraph, the reaper, the sewing machine, the cotton gin, the incandescent light, the automobile, the airplane, and the electronic computer. Sales efforts were required to introduce each of these products. The untiring efforts of thousands of sales representatives brought knowledge and understanding of products and services to customers on farms and in factories, offices, and homes.

Whether the sale was made by the owner or by a sales representative, it was the measuring stick or barometer of future success or failure for the entire free enterprise system.

Alexander R. Heron described the importance of the sale in the following words:

> The ultimate sale has become the measure of the success of every enterprise from the mine or farm to the travel bureau. That ultimate sale is the incentive for the discovery of oil, the efficient layout of the factory, the reduction of costs of extraction, conversion, and distribution. It is the all-powerful governor of the levels of profits, investments, production and employment.[5]

Heron, who spent most of his business career in the field of industrial relations, emphasized that management must carry to the workers the vital truth that if there is "no sale" there is "no job."[6]

---

[5] Alexander R. Heron, *No Sale, No Job* (New York: Harper 1954), p. ix.

[6] Ibid., p. 7.

Influence of selling in the economy

James Watt. Selling has had a potent influence upon the development of the American economy. As early as 1790, James Watt sold his new steam engine by stressing key sales features that were meaningful to his prospective customers.[7]

Cyrus McCormick. In 1831, when Cyrus McCormick first demonstrated his reaper to farmers, the farmers were skeptical. McCormick spent years educating and selling the farmers of America on the usefulness of this great invention. His early selling experiences were described as follows: "There was a great deal of uphill work about it, it must be admitted, for even out in the western region in which he had now settled, there was a great reluctance to adopt new ideas, active and enterprising as they were in that part of the country."[8] When McCormick invaded the English market by displaying his reaper at a public exhibition, the *London Times* ridiculed his invention and described it as "a cross between an Astley Charist, a wheelbarrow, and a flying machine."[9] By patient and persistent selling and demonstrating, however, McCormick finally obtained acceptance in the English market.

The reaper did much to raise the farmer from a peasant to a prosperous businessman. It was the forerunner of the millions of labor-saving machines which the International Harvester Corporation has produced and sold to farmers all over the world. The early success of this great business depended upon the selling job done by McCormick in introducing his new reaper to an uninformed and suspicious public.

Other great business leaders in many different fields of business activity have drawn upon their sales abilities to contribute to the progress of their companies. The contributions of these business leaders have had a great positive influence on the growth and development of the American economy. A few typical examples of such leaders are J. C. Penney, Harvey Firestone, Marshall Field, Henry Ford, and A. P. Giannini.[10]

J. C. Penney. When J. C. Penney was planning to open his first store in Kemmerer, Wyoming, the local banker advised him strongly against going into business. This advice did not discourage Mr. Penney, for he rented a vacant building, lived in the attic with his

---

[7] Dupont, *The Story of the Builders* (Wilmington, Del.: E. I. du Pont de Nemours and Co., 1955), p. 6.

[8] James Burnley, *Millionaires and Kings of Enterprise* (London: Harnsworth, 1901), p. 256.

[9] Ibid.

[10] *Forbes,* "60th Anniversary Year," September 15, 1977, pp. 150–57, has an exciting brief description in words and pictures of how superselling created modern mass marketing.

wife and one-year-old baby, built his own shelves, selected merchandise to meet the needs of the miners of the community, and opened his doors for business. The first day of business lasted from sunrise to sunset, with surprisingly high total cash sales of $466.59.[11] The success of the great chain organization he founded is a tribute to the merchandising and sales ability of J. C. Penney, whose genuine interest in customers and their needs has been the basis for every policy of the J. C. Penney Company. When J. C. Penney was selling behind the counter, "he considered it a sin if anyone came into the store without being waited on; he considered it a greater sin if anyone went out without making a purchase."[12] This policy has paid dividends. Today, the J. C. Penney Company has 2,134 stores, which do an annual sales volume of over $10.85 billion.[13]

Harvey Firestone.   Through his unusual ability to sell an idea, Harvey Firestone was instrumental in selling the American people on the development of highways for long-distance truck shipments. "To demonstrate the efficacy of long-distance hauling, the company sent a fleet of loaded trucks out of Akron on a tour through the South. Each arrival in town made news and provided an opportunity for an open-air lecture on the operating cost of a three-and-a-half ton truck."[14] This type of promotional selling laid the foundation for thousands of jobs in the trucking and transportation field and strengthened the economy by speeding up the building of better public highways. In 1978, the Firestone Tire and Rubber Company's sales were $4.88 billion.[15]

Marshall Field.   The contributions of Marshall Field in the department store field are known to all. Like J. C. Penney, he recognized the importance of imaginative selling and courteous service at the customer level. His most important quality was described by his brother in the following words: "If Marshall Field had anything to sell, he would sell it, if a customer came in; if a customer did not come in, he was not above going out and finding one."[16]

Henry Ford.   The pioneering years of the automotive industry provide additional evidence of the influence of selling. When Henry Ford was developing his workable horseless carriage powered by gasoline, his boss, Alex Dow, derided him and referred to his work

---

[11] Norman Beasley, *The Main Street Merchant* (New York: Whittlesey House, McGraw-Hill, 1948), p. 37.

[12] Ibid.

[13] Standard & Poor's Corp., *Standard NYSE Stock Reports*, April 1979.

[14] Alfred Lief, *The Firestone Story* (New York: Whittlesey House, McGraw-Hill, 1951), p. 120.

[15] Standard & Poor's Corp., *Standard NYSE Stock Reports*, May 1979.

[16] John Tebbel, *The Marshall Fields* (New York: E. P. Dutton, 1947), p. 27.

as a foolish obsession. This did not stop Ford, however, and finally he had the opportunity to discuss his new product with Thomas A. Edison. Edison instilled new confidence in Ford by saying: "Young man, that's the thing! You have it—the self-contained unit carrying its own fuel with it! Keep at it!"[17] Edison's faith gave Ford fresh inspiration and sent him into action. He planned a new model and made his first sale to Charles Ainsley of Detroit for $200. The economic importance of this first sale was recognized by Ford himself. "This was my first sale. I had built the car not to sell but to experiment with. I wanted to start another car. Ainsley wanted to buy. I could use the money and we had no trouble agreeing on a price."[18]

When Ford made his first sales demonstration he educated his passenger with a typical sales story: "The ignition is by electricity. Didn't you see me touch the switch up there? That fires the gas, and the puff you heard was the explosion."[19] As he passed a harness shop, he said: "His [the harness maker's] trade is doomed. Those horses will be driven from the land. Their troubles will soon be over."[20] Sales demonstrations such as this provided the lifeblood of the Ford Motor Company and filled its coffers with sufficient cash to buy new materials and labor for more and more cars. Millions of sales demonstrations have followed throughout the Ford Motor Company's history. Henry Ford expressed his sales philosophy in the following words: "It is not good business unless both buyer and seller gain by it [the sale]"[21] This positive sales philosophy and the introduction of mass production techniques, teamed together, were responsible for producing hundreds of thousands of jobs and millions of cars for the people of the whole world.

A. P. Giannini.   The principles of salesmanship were applied by A. P. Giannini to the building of the world's largest bank. Giannini's early experience in selling fruits and vegetables apparently gave him a "feel for the customer" which he successfully passed on to his entire organization. His ability to sell his concept of a "bank for the people" contributed much to the development of agriculture and industry in California.[22] In 1978, the Bank of America had over $75.7 billion in deposits.[23]

---

[17] Allan Nevins, *Ford: The Times, the Man, the Company* (New York: Scribner 1954), p. 167.

[18] Ibid., p. 167.

[19] Ibid., p. 181.

[20] Ibid., p. 183.

[21] *Ford at Fifty* (New York: Simon & Schuster, 1953), p. 21.

[22] Marquis James and Bessie Rowland James, *Biography of a Bank* (New York: Harper, 1954), chap. 1.

[23] Standard & Poor's Corp., *Standard NYSE Stock Reports*, June, 1979.

Creative sales—The key to the future

Impact of research and technological change. In the years immediately following World War II, research and development expenditures were approximately $2 billion, or less than 1 percent of the total national output. In January 1979, industrial research and development expenditures of $36.8 billion were forecast for 1979.[24] This rate of increase is likely to continue.

These expenditures will have a tremendous impact upon new and improved products and services. Some of the research-oriented companies in such fields as electronics and chemicals have predicted that over 50 percent of their sales volumes in 1980 will come from products which did not exist in 1975. The introduction of these new products will provide a tremendous opportunity for creative selling.

Need for creative selling. If it were not for the pioneering educational work of salespeople, thousands of American families would now lack such modern conveniences as the automobile, television, the vacuum cleaner, the automatic washer, the power lawn mower, or even the bathtub.

When the first bathtub was installed in the White House in 1850, there was still considerable resistance by the public to the use of bathtubs. Several states placed heavy taxes on the owners of bathtubs. The tax in New York State, for example, was $30 per year. In addition, New York passed a law prohibiting the use of bathtubs without a doctor's request.

Similar resistance has been met in the introduction of other new products. When the first metal plow was invented, farmers refused to buy it because they believed it would poison the land. People were unwilling to accept the new gas stove for fear that it would explode. The first cash registers were resisted because they were too complicated and because clerks felt that the introduction of cash registers reflected upon their honesty. These products were introduced through imaginative and constructive selling.

The need for creative selling is even greater today. The American economy is aglow with excitement. Not in decades have businesses and industry been so full of ferment. Everywhere one turns, remarkable new products—alloys, plastics, building materials, drugs, nuclear reactors, transistorized appliances and equipment, high-speed computers, and other miracles of science and industry—are being introduced. Everywhere one goes, new services, new manufacturing and merchandising methods, and fascinating new jobs are being created.

Spearheading these dramatic advances, helping vitally to expe-

---

[24] C. J. Mosbacher, "Forecast '79—$51.8 billion for R&D," *Industrial Research/Development*, January 1979, pp. 76–79.

dite and explain them, is a professional who has advanced greatly too—the salesperson. If the nation is to continue its progress toward a higher standard of living, American sales representatives must devote their best creative efforts to their profession.

The challenges ahead call for an all-out effort on the marketing and selling fronts if America is to maintain its leadership position in the world. Manufacturers in the United States are facing a worldwide economic revolution which is producing competitive conditions that are substantially different from those of the past 30 years. This change is a direct challenge to the ingenuity of the sales executives and sales representatives who are responsible for selling U.S. products in the world market.

Creative selling requires teamwork. To be effective, creative selling requires the cooperation of everyone in a business organization. Earlier in this chapter, examples were given of business owners who invented, produced, and sold products. This situation seldom arises today, for American business, to a large extent, is managed by professional managers rather than owner-managers. Furthermore, the continuous trend toward larger and more complicated business structures and more complex products has made it increasingly important for production, sales, engineering, and finance to work as a team to provide customers with the best products for their needs at the lowest possible prices.

In the present competitive market, sales representatives cannot produce optimum results unless they cooperate fully with representatives of other functions within the business organization—namely, engineering, production, finance, and research. For the same reason, it is imperative that everyone within a business recognize the importance of the customer's needs and desires when new products are being planned.

Gerald L. Phillippe, when he was chairman of the board of the General Electric Company, expressed his views on the importance of sales representatives in the marketing process as follows:

> One of the most important marketing functions is played by those unsung heroes of the business world, the salespeople. These smiling and ingenious individuals are selling more than half a trillion dollars worth of goods and services every year in this country, a major contribution to the national prosperity. They are bringing back to management—if management will listen—their direct, personal insights as to what consumers want and will pay for in the years ahead.

If product planning starts with an intimate knowledge of customers, it is obvious that the individual salesperson is in a key position to communicate customer desires and needs to product managers, market researchers, and engineers. The salespeople have a far greater awareness of the problems, plans, needs, and desires of customers than anyone else in the business organization. They have a definite responsibility, as members of the team, to keep management informed of new competition, new customer plans, market trends, and new product opportunities.

New forces and concepts in selling

The marketing concept. Considerable attention is currently being focused on the "marketing concept" in business, which emphasizes the importance of marketing in the development and growth of individual companies. The application of the marketing concept involves a growing responsibility for everyone within the marketing organization—representatives from selling, advertising, market research, product planning, sales forecasting, and sales analysis and control—to participate as a team in a coordinated effort toward the accomplishment of a common goal.

The role of the marketing executive is now undergoing rapid transition. The responsibilities of marketing executives are increasing as companies face new problems of rising costs, new products, and increased competition from domestic and foreign companies. A marketing executive must lead the way in seeing that the marketing point of view is integrated into all operations and plans of the company.

Although the marketing executive's job has taken on greater breadth, his or her primary responsibility is the management of a salesforce that sells the company's products or services at prices that generate profits. The coordinated efforts of all members of the marketing organization must be geared to getting the maximum productivity from the field sales organization. This can be accomplished most effectively by providing services, information, and technical aids for the sales representatives so that they can utilize a higher percentage of their time in face-to-face contacts with the customer. The marketing concept is discussed further in Chapter 3, Buyer Behavior and Motivation.

Great strides are being made in the development of new marketing strategies and new marketing concepts, *but the key to the success or failure of the total marketing effort is still the salesperson who awakens the desires and needs of prospects and turns these desires and needs into buying actions.*

Changing environment in business. The internal environment of business has changed significantly, and such change is likely to continue. Some of the changes which are of vital importance to the salesperson include more rigid cost control, particularly in the field of distribution costs; organizational changes; more and better information on markets, sales, and profits; better training; more time for actual selling; improved sales aids; and new concepts of reporting and data processing. A thorough understanding of these changes enables the individual salesperson to do a better job for the company, to bring greater benefits to the customer, and indirectly to produce increased personal satisfaction.

Pressure on profits. During the past two decades labor costs and other operating costs have increased steadily in almost every industry. The bargaining power of large unions has been reflected in annual cost-of-living wage increases and fringe benefits which have been partially passed on to the consumer in higher prices.

New tools and techniques for cost control. Continuous pressure on profits and expense control has caused management to concentrate its efforts on the analysis of distribution and manufacturing costs. Through the use of data processing equipment it is now possible to make significant changes in distribution methods and practices. Many companies are realizing substantial savings in distribution costs by consolidating or eliminating regional warehouses, by rearranging sales territories, and by reallocating customers.

Vastly improved communication and information systems have become powerful tools of marketing intelligence and cost control. These tools, when used effectively, will produce additional profits for the sales representatives and "plus benefits" for the customers and the company. The sales representatives who become team members in the company's total marketing strategy plan will find their jobs easier if they are provided with up-to-date information on the following questions: How many of my present customers actually add to the profit of my territory? Who are these customers? What kind of product mix will maximize profits for the different kinds of customers? Which of my customers are actually costing the company money?

With more emphasis being given to the total marketing concept, many companies have reorganized their marketing departments to include product managers. The product manager plays a vital role in planning the sales strategy to be used and in aiding the sales representative to create optimum sales of a group of products. Although the introduction of product managers in a marketing organization may alter the nature of the sales job somewhat, the primary responsibility for sales results in the territory remains with the individual salesperson.

Impact of foreign competition. During the 1960s and the 1970s, imports flooded into the United States from foreign countries. Some countries had the advantage of low labor costs, and others benefited because the latest automatic equipment and machinery had been installed in factories rebuilt after World War II. The comparative price advantages of foreign products have been reduced somewhat during the past few years because of currency revaluation, higher import taxes, and higher costs in foreign countries. Nevertheless, foreign competition for sales and services within the United States and in other markets throughout the world continues to offer significant challenges to sales representatives of U.S. companies.

New requirements for effective selling.   In order to implement the new marketing concept, all members of the marketing staff will have to acquire new knowledges, skills, and attitudes. As an important member of the marketing team, the sales representative has a responsibility for keeping informed of new developments in the areas of data processing, quantitative analysis, and the behavioral sciences.

Electronic data processing will provide live facts on the profit mix of products. This will give sales representatives a chance to alter faulty sales strategies before it is too late. Customers, in turn, will have more up-to-date information on how to maximize profits through effective inventory control. Wholesalers and retailers will be in a better position to locate slow items and to reorder fast movers. They will be able to focus attention more sharply upon profits rather than upon sales volume. If the sales representatives are to bring long-term mutual benefits to customers, they must be capable of up-to-date profit planning based upon data provided by the automated information systems.

New knowledges and skills in the behavioral sciences will provide additional opportunities for improving the effectiveness of selling. Psychologists and sociologists have been advancing the frontiers of knowledge relating to consumer motivation and buying behavior. The salesperson's skillful application of this new knowledge about the rational and irrational buying motives of customers should prove invaluable in influencing buying decisions in the marketplace.

The marketing research and sales analysis departments will supply current information on consumer motivation; sales analysis by product line and price line; geographic preference by color, size, and style; trends of sales in suburban and large city markets; the pulling power of different advertising media; and forecasts of optimum profits through the right profit mix. *All the efforts of the behavioral scientists, the market researchers, and the sales analysts will not, however, provide the persuasive leadership required to create new wants and desires and to turn these wants and desires into profitable sales. This is the responsibility of the sales reprentatives in day-to-day contacts with their prospects and customers. It is their job to close sales by convincing the buyers that their products will bring the buyers future benefits.*

OPPORTUNITIES AND REWARDS IN SELLING _____

Selling and the marketing process _____

In a broad sense, marketing includes all business activities that direct the flow of goods and services from the producer to the consumer or user. These activities include, in addition to selling, such functions as buying, transportation, storage, financing, risk bearing, and standardization.

Manufacturers, producers, and middlemen perform the various marketing functions through many types of trade channels. These channels of distribution vary for different producers and commodities. One manufacturer of household appliances, for example, may elect to sell its products directly to the consumer through direct-mail advertising; whereas a similar manufacturer may sell some of its appliances through either its own or independent wholesalers and other appliances directly through large retail stores. A company which manufacturers drug products may distribute certain products directly to hospitals, other products through chain drugstores, and still others through wholesalers.

The many variations in types of trade channels result from a number of factors, such as the kind of organization, type of products, customs and habits of the trade, channels used by competitors, margin of profit, financial position of the manufacturer, quantities in which goods are bought, amount of selling service needed by the middlemen, and location or concentration of customers.

Obviously, it is impossible to describe all of the various trade channels used by producers and middlemen. However, Figure 1–2 portrays the principal channels of distribution which are in common use today and shows the position of sales representatives within these channels. It is apparent from this illustration that the selling function plays an important part in the marketing process and that the sales representative plays an important role in each of the various channels of distribution.

Accurate information is not available on the total value of products marketed through the various channels or on the total number of salespeople at each stage of the marketing process. Figures are available, however, on the total number of salespeople by major classifications.

Employment opportunities in saleswork _____

In 1890 there were only 264,380 salesworkers in the United States.[25] The Bureau of Labor Statistics has forecast total saleswork-

---

[25] Carroll D. Wright, "American Labor," in *One Hundred Years of Commerce*, ed. Chauncey M. Depew (New York: D. O. Haynes, 1895), p. 12.

Figure 1–2
Principal channels of distribution

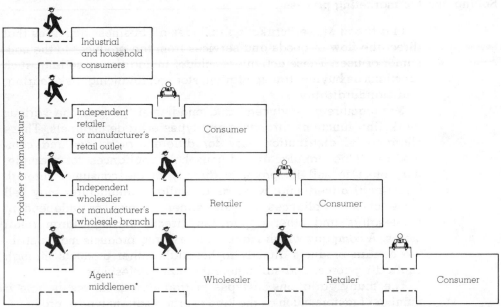

* The agent middleman is defined by the Definitions Committee of the American Marketing Association as "a middleman who negotiates purchases or sales or both but who does not take title to goods." Examples of agent middlemen include brokers, commission merchants, manufacturer's agents, selling agents, and resident buyers. A sales representative is shown between the producer and the agent middleman because, in many instances, the producer has missionary salespeople who call upon agent middlemen.

ers of 6 million by 1980. This represents a growth in salesworkers that is approximately seven times as great as the growth in population during the 90-year period from 1890 to 1980.

The estimates in Table 1–2 indicate that average annual openings are particularly plentiful for retail trade salesworkers, real estate agents and brokers, wholesale trade salesworkers, and manufacturers' salesworkers. Although insurance saleswork is not included in the table, there will always be opportunities for men and women who wish to enter this field.

Promotional opportunities for salespeople

It is impossible to generalize and say that there is one best background or spawning ground for all top executives. The chief executive of a company in the capital goods industry might well have an entirely different background than the top executive of a food manufacturing concern or a life insurance company.

Many studies have been made in an attempt to determine what qualifications are most important for success in top management positions. Some of the most important qualities are personal drive, good judgment, ability to get along with people, skill in persuasiveness, flexibility, creativeness, and intellectual capacity.[26]

In general, young people attracted to the sales field are strong in these personal traits to begin with and, because their work demands it, they develop further skills in human relations. Consequently, a large and growing number of business concerns are giving their sales and marketing executives a stronger voice in determining major company policy decisions.

The proven effectiveness of sales training as a preparation for top responsibility is perhaps best evidenced by a recent study reporting that 26 percent of the presidents of 500 leading corporations had marketing experience. The complete list of ranking corporation executives who once were sales representatives is too long to present here. A few of these leaders, however, have expressed their feelings about the importance of selling experience for promotion into top management positions. Frank Cary, chairman of the board and former president of IBM, was asked recently what advice he might give to those who had ambitions of becoming chairman and president of IBM. Cary replied as follows:

> It's hard to find a better start than sales, because you get thrown into contact with a great variety of situations and problems to solve. So I would recommend the sales track to anybody. I think it is a very good one.

Clarence J. Francis, when he was chairman of the board, General Foods Corporation, discussed "the opportunity to grow" in selling as follows:

> Is selling a good career? I answer emphatically, yes. Early in my business life, I became a salesman, and most of my active career has been concerned with selling and sales management. I know the same thing is true of many older men who have had a chance to go up the business ladder. There may have been a time when other phases of business were more important than selling. That time is past.
>
> Today the proper emphasis is on distribution—its methods, its costs, and its relation to our national economy and our national welfare. More and more, the general supervision of business enterprises must be in the hands of men who know distribution in all its phases. To have that knowledge, experience and success in actual selling is essential. I am convinced that no other area of business exceeds selling as the basis for a satisfying career for men of character, education, ability, and ambition.

Don G. Mitchell, when he was president of the General Telephone

<hr>

[26] Paul E. Holden, Carlton A. Pederson, and Gayton E. Germane, *Top Management* (New York: McGraw-Hill, 1968), chap. 2.

Table 1-2
Estimated employment and annual openings in sales occupations

Occupation	Estimated employment (000) 1976	Average annual openings, 1976–1985	Employment prospects
Automobile parts counter workers	75	4,200	Employment expected to grow faster than average due to increasing demand for new accessories and replacement parts.
Automobile sales workers	130	9,000	Employment expected to grow faster than average as demand for automobiles increases. Job openings may fluctuate, however, because sales are affected by changing economic conditions and consumer preferences.
Automobile service advisers	24	1,000	Employment expected to grow about as fast as average as automobiles increase in number and complexity. Most job openings in large dealerships in heavily populated areas.
Gasoline service station attendants	420	14,800	Employment expected to increase more slowly than average as trends toward cars with better gas mileage and toward self-service gas stations limit growth. Nevertheless, replacement needs will create many job openings.
Manufacturers' salesworkers	362	17,600	Employment expected to grow about as fast as average because of rising demand for technical products and resulting need for trained salesworkers.
Models	83	n.a.	Employment expected to grow faster than average due to rising advertising expenditures and greater sales of clothing and accessories. Nevertheless, because the occupation is so small and the glamour of modeling attracts many persons, competition for openings should be keen.

Occupation			Employment outlook
Real estate agents and brokers	450	45,500	Employment expected to rise faster than average in response to growing demand for housing and other properties. However, field is highly competitive. Best prospects for college graduates and transferees from other sales jobs.
Retail trade salesworkers	2,725	155,000	Employment expected to grow more slowly than average. However, high turnover should create excellent opportunities for full-time, part-time, and temporary work.
Route drivers	200	3,400	Employment expected to change little, but several thousand openings will result annually from replacement needs. Best opportunities for applicants with sales experience and good driving records who are seeking wholesale routes.
Securities salesworkers	90	5,500	Employment expected to grow about as fast as average as investment in securities continues to increase. Favorable job opportunities likely except during periods of economic downturn.
Travel agents	15	1,400	Employment expected to grow faster than average, but competition for jobs will be keen. Because travel expenditures often depend on business conditions, job opportunities are very sensitive to economic changes.
Wholesale trade salesworkers	808	41,000	Employment expected to grow about as fast as average, as wholesalers sell wider variety of products and improve customer services. Good opportunities for persons with product knowledge and sales ability.

Source: Occupational Outlook Quarterly, Spring 1978, pp. 15–16.

and Electronics Corporation and chairman of the board, Sylvania
Electric Products Company, in pointing the way for future sales representatives, said:

> First, and most important, there is no easy road to the top. There are
> hundreds of obstacles, thousands of difficulties, and many disap-
> pointments. But, if you have the qualifications, if you like people, if
> you are objective, and if you want to rise to high places in the business
> world, good selling is most likely to permit you to reach the top.

A survey of the membership of the Chicago Sales Executives' Club
supports this viewpoint. The members were polled to determine how
the presidents of their organizations had reached their positions;
more than half of the presidents had come up through the ranks of
the sales department.

Robert S. Wilson, former executive vice president and sales manager, Goodyear Tire and Rubber Company, described the future opportunities in selling in these words:

> It is probably true that the next quarter century will find those corpora-
> tions most successful that are most skillful in their sales divisions.
> This means opportunity for the person who enters the sales division of
> business with a truly professional training. America's leading corpora-
> tions will be avidly seeking people of that type.

A few of the many chief executives who reached their position
through sales and marketing experience include the chief executives
of the following companies: Zenith, Norton Simon, IBM, PepsiCo,
Johnson & Johnson, Xerox, Borden, Goodyear, Schering-Plough,
American Brands, Philip Morris, Procter & Gamble, Deere, Burroughs, Colgate-Palmolive, Harris, Clark Equipment, and Mon-
santo.[27]

The records of the top executives of American business who have
come up through the sales divisions of their firms attest eloquently to
the promotional opportunities for persons in the selling field. But a
sales career should not be regarded only as a stepping-stone to top
management. Many highly successful sales representatives lack the
desire or the disposition to function well in an executive capacity.
For them there are still prospects for generous recognition—personal
and financial—in lifetime careers of actual selling.

Financial rewards of selling

The financial rewards of selling vary by industry, experience,
training, and method of compensation. Consumer products sales-

---

[27] Dero A. Saunders, "The Boss' Paycheck: Who Gets the Biggest?" *Forbes*, May 29,
1978, pp. 86–111.

Table 1-3

Salespeople's annual compensation

Salesperson Level	Consumer products			Industrial products		
	1979	1978	Percent change	1979	1978	Percent change
Sales trainee:						
Straight salary..........	$12,900	$10,925	+18.1%	$13,650	$12,950	+ 5.4%
Salary plus incentive						
Salary...............	12,167	12,450	− 2.3	12,440	14,000	− 11.1
Incentive	1,200	1,300	− 7.7	3,780	1,867	+102.5
Total	13,200	14,300	− 7.7	15,700	15,400	+ 1.9
A and B salespeople:						
Straight salary..........	15,300	15,400	− 0.6	19,925	18,781	+ 6.1
Salary plus incentive						
Salary...............	16,117	14,950	+ 7.8	17,474	16,389	+ 6.6
Incentive	3,383	3,583	− 5.6	5,148	3,810	+ 35.1
Total	19,767	19,233	+ 2.8	23,079	20,700	+ 11.5
Senior salespeople:						
Straight salary..........	26,750	18,900	+41.5	25,536	23,827	+ 7.2
Salary plus incentive						
Salary...............	19,950	19,217	+ 3.8	21,871	20,710	+ 5.6
Incentive	4,383	5,617	−22.0	5,347	5,079	+ 5.3
Total	24,950	26,433	− 5.6	26,112	26,284	− 0.7
Sales supervisor:						
Straight salary..........	29,900	23,775	+25.8	28,979	28,193	+ 2.8
Salary plus incentive						
Salary...............	27,450	23,140	+18.6	25,316	24,065	+ 5.2
Incentive	4,533	4,825	− 6.1	7,426	6,506	+ 14.1
Total	32,217	29,180	+10.4	32,953	31,823	+ 3.6

Note: Some differences between years reflect changes in the organizations that reported data. It should also be noted that in the "salary plus incentive" category, the "total" compensation will not equal the sum of the "salary" and "incentive" components because not all respondents provided information for each of the components, as is the case with industrial-products senior salespeople. The AMA attributes the apparent decrease in the compensation of consumer-goods sales trainees paid on a salary-plus-incentive basis to an increased number of respondents and corresponding changes in industry categories. The 102.5 percent increase in industrial-goods sales trainee incentive payments is attributed to the increased number of industries in 1979 that were not included in 1978 because of insufficient data.

Definitions of field sales personnel:

Sales trainee: Anyone who is learning about the company's products, services, and policies, as well as proven sales techniques, in preparation for a sales assignment.

Salesperson grade A: A "regular" salesperson who has little or no selling experience except that which has been acquired in the company's sales training program. This type of salesperson makes contacts with established and prospective customers to develop interest in the company's products and to sell them.

Salesperson grade B: A salesperson who has broad knowledge of the company's products and services and sells in a specifically assigned territory. This type of salesperson maintains contact with established customers and develops new prospects.

Senior salesperson: A salesperson at the highest level of selling responsibility who is completely familiar with the company's products, services and policies. Such a salesperson usually has years of experience and is assigned to major accounts and territories.

Sales supervisor: A veteran salesperson who, because of abilities and experience, leads others. This salesperson's primary function is to direct the activities of and train salespeople and sales trainees, but he or she may also sell to selected key accounts.

Source: American Management Associations, *Executive Compensation Service.*

workers generally earn less than industrial products salesworkers. A recent study by the American Management Association shows the comparative salaries of various consumer and industrial products salesworkers for 1978 and 1979 (see Table 1-3). Further information on compensation by industry is shown in Table 1-4.

During recent years many companies have placed increasing emphasis upon the value of a broad education and/or broad experience for workers in the sales field. A marketing executive of one large company described the job of the new salesperson in the following words:

> A few years back, it was usually the salesperson out there alone, pitting his wits against the resistance of the purchasing agent. Now, more and more companies are selling on many different levels, interlocking their research, engineering, marketing, and upper management with those of their customers. This way, today's salesperson becomes a kind of committee chairperson within the company. Some manufacturers call salespersons "account managers." Their jobs are to optimize the companies' resources to serve the customers' needs.

Evidence of the importance that some companies have placed on the educational background of salesworkers may be reflected in the

Table 1-4

Compensation for three types of salespeople by industry

Industry	Experienced salesperson, 1979	Percent change, 1977–79	Semi-experienced salesperson, 1979	Percent change, 1977–79	Sales trainee, 1979	Percent change, 1977–79
Consumer goods						
Drugs/medicines	$25,500	+27.5%	$12,900	−19.4%	$15,800	+29.5%
Food	23,900	+23.2	18,500	+23.3	13,500	+ 3.8
Housewares	26,000	+12.6	19,200	+ 9.7	13,000	+21.5
Industrial goods						
Chemicals	24,000	+ 6.7	19,600	+ 4.3	16,000	+33.3
Electrical equipment/ supplies	27,000	+14.9	18,700	− 4.1	15,000	n.c.
Electronics	26,500	+12.8	18,800	− 6.0	14,500	+25.0
Fabricated metals	24,700	+ 5.6	21,500	+13.2	16,500	+12.2
General machinery	25,000	+10.6	21,400	+14.4	15,000	− 4.5
Office machines/ equipment	21,500	−13.7	20,600	n.a.	13,000	n.c.
Tools/hardware	28,400	+55.2	20,000	n.a.	14,000	+20.7

Note: Data are medians of the middle-half range of the average compensation for all salespeople reported by respondents.

n.a.—not available because of lack of 1977 data.

n.c.—no change.

Sources: S&MM calculations; Dartnell Corp., *Compensation of Salesman: 20th Biennial Survey.* Reprinted by permission.

salaries for salespersons with the bachelor's degree and those with the MBA degree. Table 1-5 shows *offers* made to 1979 and 1980 graduates, and Table 1-6 shows the median compensation earned by graduates who have been in the sales field for a few years.

The financial rewards for individuals who desire to move into sales supervision or sales management are very substantial. A recent survey of middle management sales executives portrays the comparative compensation of district sales managers, regional sales executives, national accounts managers, and product or brand sales managers for companies with different sales volumes (see Table 1-7). The figures are from 1,033 companies carefully selected by major industrial groupings.

Nonfinancial rewards of selling

The field of selling offers many nonfinancial rewards. Perhaps more than almost any other occupation, selling provides the oppor-

Table 1-5

Starting salaries of college graduates to be hired

Field	Class of 1980	Class of 1979*	Percent gain, 1979–80
Bachelor's degree			
Sales-marketing	$15,936	$13,092	21.7%
Business administration	14,100	13,464	4.7
MBA degree			
With technical BS	22,632	19,812	14.2
With nontechnical BA	21,672	18,468	17.3

Note: The salaries are what companies offered, not what they actually paid.
* Actual starting salaries paid to graduates in 1978, Northwestern University says, were $15,072 for sales-marketing graduates, $13,440 for business administration, $20,904 for MBA with technical BS, and $20,016 for MBA with nontechnical BA.

Source: Northwestern University Placement Center, *The Endicott Report, 1980;* copyright 1979.

Table 1-6

Median 1977 compensation of MBA graduates by year of graduation

Year of graduation	Marketing responsibility	Sales responsibility
1975–76	$21,000	$20,800
1967–68	37,377	37,887

Source: Abbott, Langer & Associates, Park Forest, Ill., *Compensation of M.B.A.'s,* 2d ed. copyright 1978.

Table 1-7

Median salaries of middle management sales executives

Company:

Annual sales volume	*National accounts manager*
Under $50 million	$31,000 plus 61%(14%) bonus*
Over $50 million	39,000 plus 60%(13%) bonus

Region:

Annual sales volume	*Regional sales executive*
Under $5 million	$26,100 plus 58%(17%) bonus
$5 million to $10 million	27,800 plus 66%(15%) bonus
$10 million to $20 million	30,300 plus 60%(19%) bonus
$20 million to $40 million	34,000 plus 61%(16%) bonus
Over $40 million	38,900 plus 59%(17%) bonus

District:

Annual sales volume	*District sales manager*
Under $2 million	$22,400 plus 53%(22%) bonus
$2 million to $4 million	23,800 plus 64%(14%) bonus
$4 million to $8 million	26,500 plus 71%(14%) bonus
$8 million to $16 million	28,000 plus 59%(15%) bonus
Over $16 million	30,700 plus 48%(14%) bonus

Product:

Annual sales volume	*Product or brand sales manager*
Under $10 million	$27,400 plus 52%(12%) bonus
$10 million to $20 million	29,100 plus 50%(14%) bonus
$20 million to $50 million	31,300 plus 52%(16%) bonus
Over $50 million	34,000 plus 51%(11%) bonus

* The first figure shows percentage of positions paid a bonus, and the figure in parenthesis shows the median bonus based upon the salary.

Source: American Management Associations, *Executive Compensation Service, Middle Management Report, 1979/1980,* 28th ed.

tunity of meeting and working with all kinds of people. Through these contacts, the individual builds valuable and rich experiences. By providing real and continuing service to many customers, the salesperson also builds a large group of loyal friends. Another reward of successful selling is reaped by salespersons as they establish self-confidence and prove to themselves that they will always be able to hold their own in a highly competitive economy. This feeling of security is strengthened further by the knowledge that they will never be replaced by a laborsaving machine and that they can help build their own retirement income.

Salespeople in a great many fields of selling enjoy the freedom of being their own boss. Through the right kind of investment of their abilities, time, and energy, they are likely to receive large dividends from one of the most interesting and dynamic fields of personal endeavor.

Perhaps the satisfaction that professional salesworkers can enjoy is best summed up by this quotation:

And now, as I wearily finish my last report at midnight and leave a wake-up call at the motel desk for 6:00 A.M., I am comforted by one overriding thought: the order that I must get tomorrow will be responsible for our purchasing agent ordering more material; our engineering department producing new designs; our manufacturing department producing more merchandise; our personnel department hiring more people; and for me and my family and all the other Veeco employees and their families enjoying the better life that all begins with professional salesmanship![28]

QUESTIONS AND PROBLEMS

1. Comment on the following antimarketing statement: "Only physical production has worth, while marketing is costly and worthless because it adds no tangible value to products or services."

2. This statement was overheard recently "Selling may be all right for men. They can take the hard knocks, but it is certainly no field for women. The women just can't compete." Is the statement true?

3. It is important to identify what you expect to receive from a career of work. A price must be paid for every "want" or "need" which you feel is essential in the work environment. How many of your work "wants" or "needs" are you willing to pay for?

    Prepare your own personal career "wants" and "price" analysis as follows:

"Needs" or "wants"	Price I must pay
a. $35,000 annual income	a. Hard work, long hours, etc.
b. Good social standing	b. Education, live in right neighborhood, etc.
c. Health	c. Regular hours, balanced life, etc.

    What are your conclusions?

4. What are the issues involved in the following conflicting statements? With which statement do you agree?

    a. The sovereignty of the consumer marks one of the greatest blessings of our American economy.

    b. The consumer-centered economy is a wasteful economy.

5. Would it be beneficial to society if the large life insurance companies decided to eliminate all of their sales representatives and sell life insurance by mail order at a lower quoted cost to the consumer?

6. What are the advantages and disadvantages of seeking a *beginning* job in sales as compared to accounting? banking? purchasing?

---

[28] Leonard L. Saxton. "What the Hell Am I Doing in This Business Anyway?" *Sales Management*, January 20, 1975, p. 19.

7. Sales and marketing executives are normally the highest paid functional executives in a company. What is the justification of this?

8. What are the advantages and disadvantages of the following types of selling? Life insurance? Retail selling? Selling cars? Selling real estate?

9. Do you believe that the controller of a company should have the basic knowledge of how to sell? Why?

10. To what extent should the top management of a company get involved in selling? Will the involvement differ according to the size of the company and/or the nature of the products being sold?

PROJECTS

1. Write a report on the impact of the salesperson in our free enterprise economy.

2. Review several copies of *The Wall Street Journal*, and write up a report summarizing information that appears in the *Journal* which would be useful to:

   a. A sales representative of farm equipment.

   b. An investment securities salesperson.

   c. A real estate agent.

3. Make a survey of your friends, and summarize why they have the images which they hold of selling as a career.

CASE PROBLEMS

Case 1-1

Pat Strong, choosing a sales opportunity

Pat Strong is finishing his senior year at a school of business. His work has been broad in nature, without specialization in any particular field of business. Pat's grades have been mostly B's and C's, with D's in economics and accounting. Pat spent considerable time in social, student, and fraternity activities.

While attending high school, his participation in extracurricular affairs was somewhat limited because he had a part-time job after school and on Saturdays at a gasoline service station.

Pat has always had lots of drive and energy. He has a pleasing personality and expresses himself well. He has always been handy with mechanical things. When he was in high school, he rebuilt a car, and he also did considerable mechanical work at the service station. When Pat was attending college, he spent his summers working with different companies. He spent his first summer as a route salesman for a dairy. The second summer he worked in the production department of a farm-equipment manufacturer, and during the third summer he worked with a company which was engaged in road construction work.

Pat's father is an engineer with the International Harvester Company. His older brother is a lawyer. Pat has given considerable thought to his vocational objectives. He took the Strong Vocational Interest Test, which indicated strong mechanical and sales interests and relatively low interests in music, art, law, and accounting. He had interviews with several companies and was giving serious consideration to these three job opportunities:

1. The first job offer is a position as a trainee with one of the big-three automobile manufacturing companies. The company selects 20 young college graduates each year to enter a two-year training program. During the two years the trainees obtain experience in several departments within the manufacturing division of the company. They spend most of this time at the main plant in Michigan. At the completion of the training program, the trainees are assigned to one of the company's manufacturing or production departments in a managerial capacity. The starting salary while in the training program is $1,000 per month.

2. The second job offer is a position with a large dairy company which produces and distributes dairy products in the Western and Southwestern states. The initial assignment on this job would be to learn the dairy business in one of the company's plants. After a period of one year Pat would either be assigned to a managerial position within one of the plants or, if he desires, he may transfer to the sales department. If he transfers to the sales department, he would be expected to spend a short period on one of the routes, after which time he would be given a position as direct sales manager. As district sales manager, he would be responsible for developing business within a territory. He would be in charge of selecting and supervising a number of route men in addition to calling upon some large industrial users of dairy products. The starting salary with the dairy company is $975 per month.

3. The third job offer is a position with a large national business machines and equipment company. This company manufactures a full line of electronic computers, punch-card machines, typewriters, and related office machines. The job offer with this company is in the field of sales. A new hire is expected to go to the home office for an extensive training period. After this period he or she is assigned to a

branch office as a junior sales representative. When the company feels that a new person is able to do an effective sales job, he or she is assigned to a branch with the responsibility of calling on prospective customers. If the individual is successful in sales, he or she will normally have the opportunity to accept greater responsibilities as a branch or regional manager. The starting salary with this company is $1,200 per month.

Questions

1. If you were Pat Strong, what *procedure* would you follow in evaluating the three job opportunities?
2. What factors would you consider in your evaluation?
3. Which job opportunity would you select? Why?

Case 1–2

Is planned obsolescence good?

SHALL WE SKIP MODEL CHANGES?

A few years ago a senator from a farm state proposed that the automobile industry should discontinue annual model changes. His proposal may have been based upon the following points:

1. Each year millions of dollars are spent unnecessarily to design, engineer, and tool new models. By eliminating these expenditures, the manufacturers could make substantial reductions in prices, which could be passed on to the consumers.

2. The consumers do not need the many luxuries that are included in many of our present cars. Such things as chrome, deluxe steering wheels, two-tone paint, automatic windows, expensive upholstering, power steering, streamlined fenders, fancy grilles, and muscle motors could well be eliminated.

3. Many model changes represent a face-lifting with only minor changes from the previous model.

4. Customers could get much longer use from their cars and would probably do so if there were not so many model changes.

WHY NEW MODELS ARE BEST FOR THE NATION*

I'm always surprised when people ask me: "Wouldn't it be better if you automobile manufacturers changed models less often?"

---

* Condensed and adapted from a presentation by Harlow H. Curtice, former president of General Motors.

Usually they add, "Look how successful 'X' has been without any changes at all." (And they mention by name a popular European import.)

The reason I'm surprised is that it seems perfectly obvious to me that if we hadn't started the annual model change years ago, most Americans today wouldn't be driving automobiles. And most automobiles today would look and ride and drive like 1935 models.

Let's get back to the year General Motors was organized—1908. I was a boy of 15 at the time. I remember that several men in Eaton Rapids had old buggies gathering cobwebs in their stables because by then they were driving automobiles. I am sure those men expected to keep their horseless carriages until the vehicles fell apart.

Our buying habits changed

In 1908 the automobile industry produced 63,500 passenger cars. Fewer than 200,000 were registered in all of the United States.

What would have been the future of the industry had the buying habits of the horse-and-buggy era continued to prevail?

We can get some idea by looking at countries whose buying habits have not changed to the degree that ours have.

In Europe, generally speaking, people buy only to replace what has been worn out. This is significant on two counts.

First, an automobile takes a long time to wear out. This means that a new car buyer does not come to market very often. The market, therefore, is small; volume of production is low, and price is relatively high (in terms of real purchasing power, that is). This further restricts the market.

Second, when a European owner discards his car, it is just about ready for the junk pile. As a result, the used car market is also small by our standards.

Takes longer to earn one

In Europe the problem of providing individualized transportation—self-propulsion, you might call it, or automobility—is met by offering a variety of products to fit different pocketbooks. The worker at the lathe rides a bicycle; his foreman, a motorbike; the shop supervisor, a motor scooter; the superintendent, a minicar; the plant manager, a Vauxhall or Opel; and so on up to the chairman, who, no doubt, is driven to work in a Rolls-Royce.

In this country, we handle the problem of automobility quite differently. The major new transportation we sell in volume is the automobile, and even the least expensive is a luxury car by European standards. Furthermore, we sell these new cars to only a part of the population—to an estimated 18 million households.

Then, in effect, these 18 million households "manufacture" used cars which can be sold and resold to meet transportation needs of the rest of our population.

In an average year used car sales amount to about two thirds of all cars sold.

The European system produces what we would consider inadequate individualized transportation—and the cost to the individual is high.

Our system gives us a unique automobility—and the cost to the individual is relatively low.

It is the annual model change that gives our new car buyers the incentive to trade. They want the new and the better—usually for a variety of reasons.

And it is the annual model change that puts a forced draft under our laboratories, shops, and studios. Our research men, engineers, and stylists are forever at white heat. . . . What can they invent, improve, design that will appeal to the new car buyers?

I have heard it argued that, particularly in times like these, it would be better to forgo changes and reduce price. To me this is a little like suggesting that a magazine offer the same issue two months in succession but reduce its price the second month.

Of course, I realize that even if models were not changed each year, some new car owners would continue to "trade" frequently for reasons of prestige or to avoid maintenance, but I am afraid they would be few and far between.

How much could price actually be reduced under such conditions? Hundreds of millions of dollars for annual model changes sounds like the expenditure of vast sums of money. But put these tooling costs on a "per car" basis and the picture changes. Lower tooling costs spread over fewer sales would not change unit price substantially. Furthermore, fewer sales would mean higher overhead per car and possibly higher production costs. Cars might well be more expensive, not cheaper.

It is my considered opinion that few, if any, of these changes would have occurred had not the automobile industry multiplied the use of its product by adopting the practice of the annual model change.

To our policy of what has been called "dynamic obsolescence" I also ascribe other substantial benefits. Under the spur of periodically imposed change, competition has been stimulated and technological progress speeded up.

Efficiency has been increased and the level of buying power raised. Our industry has grown and employment has mounted. Other industries have benefited, too, and whole new industries have been created.

For every man who worked in a buggy factory, a score of men now have jobs producing automobiles. For every blacksmith of yesterday, there are a hundred service stations today. Motels, supermarkets, shopping centers—all owe their existence, in the final analysis, to dynamic obsolescence in our industry.

I would go so far as to say that the policy of dynamic obsolescence is beneficial even when the product being made obsolete is immediately discarded or scrapped.

Visitors from abroad are amazed at the readiness with which we throw away things that aren't yet worn out. It seems to them that just about the time they would be getting used to an article, we discard it for something new and better. Whether it's a radio or a furnace or a set of tools or a pair of shoes or a building, we always seem to be breaking in something new.

We are always seeking an improved product that will serve us better, enable us to do more work in less time, add to our comfort, or increase our enjoyment. This is the key to increasing productivity, to producing more with less human effort.

Our critics have argued that the reason we discard things in this country is that we have so much. They accuse us of being wasteful.

Of course, the facts are exactly the opposite.

Change is essential to growth; it is responsible for our rising standard of living.

Questions

1. Evaluate the opposing views on the advantages and disadvantages of planned obsolescence in the automobile industry. With whom do you agree—the senator or Mr. Curtice? Why? Are times "different" now?
2. Who should determine whether annual model changes should be made? The customers? The manufacturers? The government? Justify your answer.
3. Is it desirable for the economy if a salesperson sells a new product, such as a new model of an automobile, by making the buyer dissatisfied with the old product—last year's model?

SELECTED REFERENCES

American Management Associations. *Executive Compensation Service, Middle Management Report, 1979/1980.* 28th ed. pp. 7–37.

Beasley, Norman. *The Main Street Merchant.* New York: Whittlesey House, McGraw-Hill, 1948.

Burnley, James. *Millionaires and Kings of Enterprise.* London: Harnsworth, 1901.

Crane, George W. "Salesmen Are the Sparkplugs of Civilization," *Sales & Marketing Management,* February 4, 1980, pp. 37–40.

Drucker, Peter. *The Age of Discontinuity.* New York: Harper & Row, 1969.

du Pont de Nemours & Co. *du Pont. The Autobiography of an American Enterprise.* New York: Scribner, 1952.

Heron, Alexander. *No Sale, No Job.* New York: Harper, 1954.

James, Marquis, and **James, Bessie Rowland.** *Biography of a Bank.* New York: Harper, 1954.

Kanter, Rosabeth Moss, and **Stein, Barry A.** "Birth of a Saleswoman." *Across the Board* (The Conference Board magazine), June 1979, pp. 14–24.

Nevins, Allan. *Ford: The Times, the Man, the Company.* New York: Scribner, 1954.

Rucks, Conway. "If Anti-Marketing Prejudice Is Rampant—It's Time for Salespeople's Lib." *Sales & Marketing Management,* March 1978, pp. 51–58.

Saunders, Dero. *"The Boss' Paycheck: Who Gets the Biggest?"* Forbes, May 29, 1978, pp. 86–111.

Scull, Penrose. *From Peddlers to Merchant Princes.* Chicago: Follett, 1967.

Slappey, Sterling G. *Pioneers of American Business.* Washington, D.C.: Grosset & Dunlap, 1974.

"60th Anniversary Year." *Forbes,* September 15, 1977.

Stern, Ethel. "Selling Charlie's Angels," *Sales and Marketing Management,* July 10, 1978, pp. 21–24.

The Story of Selling—Yesterday, Today, and Tomorrow. New York: Crowell-Collier, 1946.

"Survey of Selling Costs," *Sales & Marketing Management,* February 26, 1979, pp. 52–62

Tebbel, John. *The Marshall Fields.* New York: E. P. Dutton, 1947.

U.S. Department of Labor, Bureau of Labor Statistics. "Sales Occupations." In *Occupational Outlook Handbook,* 1978–79 ed., pp. 226–50.

Chapter 2

DUTIES, RESPONSIBILITIES, AND QUALIFICATIONS OF SALES REPRESENTATIVES

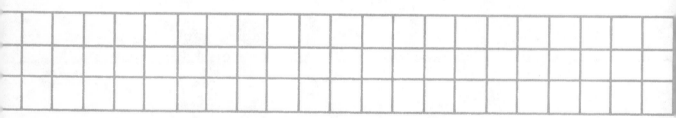

WHAT IS THE SALESPERSON'S JOB? _____

Service to the buyer _____

A salesperson's job is to get an order. However, while getting the order is the practical end result of all good selling, the real objective is to provide *service*. Selling is a two-way relationship. A sale must benefit both the buyer and the seller; otherwise a continuous, long-term relationship cannot possibly exist. "Putting over a deal" that pays off in commission to the seller but does not benefit the buyer is harmful to both.

This point of view is subscribed to by progressive sales organizations throughout the world. Sales manuals for many companies contain such statements as "High-pressure selling has no place in our steady flow of repeat orders."

One prominent computer company pays its sales representatives a straight salary without commissions—and without bonuses for exceeding quotas—because it wants the sales representatives to think more about their customers than about their next meal. "Sales representatives are encouraged to meet both the reasonable and unreasonable demands of users and their performance is measured by customer satisfaction (determined through an annual survey)."[1] This is the highest type of selling.

Of course, it should be recognized that merely because salespeople sell on a one-time basis it does not necessarily follow that they must employ high-pressure methods. For certain products, one-time selling is quite appropriate, and many good sales representatives are engaged in this activity. However, this book is concerned chiefly with the salesperson whose job is to get repeat orders.

Selling consumer goods, specialty products, and industrial lines requires a long-range plan of selling—a plan predicated on years of association between the buyer and the seller. If a sale isn't made on the first call, it may be made on the second or third visit; and after the initial sale has been consummated, the repeat business is the source of the big dividends to the company and to its sales representatives. This opportunity for repeat business is impossible unless the salesperson is honest[2] and sincere in providing service.

The salesperson's first job, then, is to serve. He or she must serve by helping the buyer, if necessary; by supplying advice on selling, merchandising, advertising, and management problems where it is called for; and by providing the kind of information or service that will further the interests of the user of the product.

Service to the company

A young salesperson who was new to the job returned to the office after a day's work and reported the sale of three office machines. This was cause for a round of congratulations until the sales manager examined the duplicate order slips. The salesperson had quoted too low a price because excessive allowances had been granted on trade-ins; the discounts had been figured incorrectly; and the new-account reports had not been filled out.

---

[1] Bro Uttal, "The Gentlemen and the Upstarts Meet in a Great Mini Battle," *Fortune,* April 23, 1979, p. 100.

[2] For a study on college students' opinions on honesty, see John S. Ewing, "Honesty, Salesmen, and College Students," *Sales & Marketing Management* May 10, 1976, pp. 73–75.

This sales representative had served the buyer, perhaps too well, but had failed to serve the company efficiently. The transaction did not prove profitable to both the buyer and the seller, and therefore it was not a satisfactory sale.

Salespeople in many companies are relied upon to gather such information as will enable the home or branch office to make intelligent decisions on sales policy. In addition, they must keep accurate records of their own activities.

Salespeople can expect to be of service to their companies by adequately representing the companies in the territories entrusted to them; by improving and expanding their companies' interests; by organizing and allocating their time and improving weak points; by making out reports accurately and on time; by following company policy and methods; and by working with supervisors, senior salespeople, or branch managers.

A large industrial firm instructs its salespeople as follows: "A salesperson's aim should be to sell: (1) Himself or herself, as a good person with whom to do business, (2) The Company, as a fair-dealing, responsible, and progressive firm, [and] (3) The Product, as the one which will do the customer's job best at the lowest possible cost."

Common duties and responsibilities

The salesperson's specific duties are determined by the type of selling he or she chooses. The choice may be to sell a tangible or an intangible product; to sell on a one-shot basis or plan to make repeat sales to the same buyer; to sell direct to the customer or to sell to a middleman. But certain basic duties and responsibilities will be found, to some extent, to be common to all types of selling, regardless of the company or the product the salesperson chooses.

Direct selling. This includes prospecting, writing orders, demonstrating, increasing sales to current users, properly quoting price and terms, and adhering to company policies and methods.

Indirect selling—Promoting company goodwill. The salesperson is the company to its customers. The salesperson's job is to maintain and further the company's good name and corporate image.

Advising and counseling. This activity involves the supplying of information to help solve the customer's merchandising, marketing, or management problems.

Handling complaints. This activity requires the salesperson to make adjustments or to recommend settlements to the home office for its consideration.

Attending sales meetings. These meetings may be held periodically to inform and instruct the salesperson on new products or policies, or to stimulate sales activities. They may be held in the branch, district, regional, or home office.

Nonselling activities—Reporting. This activity includes the preparation of daily, weekly, and monthly reports. The reports may include information on expenses, cash, calls made, sales made, miles traveled, competition, business conditions, service rendered, orders lost, and route schedules.

Collecting. Some companies require the salesperson to collect for merchandise sold before commissions are paid.

Assisting the credit department. Some companies depend upon the salesperson to collect credit information and forward it to the home office as a basis for establishing credit ratings. Other companies give the salesperson full authority and responsibility for credit.

Organizing. This activity requires the planning of routes, the proper utilization of time, and the systematizing of all sales efforts.

Working with management. This requires the ability to take orders and follow them as they are issued by the sales manager. It includes the ability to work enthusiastically without close direct supervision.

Traveling. This may be local, so that the salesperson can be home each night; or it may involve covering a district within a state, an entire state, a region including several states, or the entire nation.

Studying. Salespeople are expected to acquire new knowledge about the company, its products, and its customers' problems, and about those factors which affect business conditions in their territories.

These are representative duties and responsibilities which salespeople can expect to encounter in most fields of selling. Companies place different emphasis on certain of them, as will be seen by the job descriptions included in the latter part of this chapter.

WHAT QUALIFICATIONS ARE NEEDED TO SELL? _____

Some company requirements _____

Much has been written about the qualifications necessary to insure a successful career in selling. Most companies will disagree on the exact ranking of desirable traits or qualities.[3] Some companies

---

[3] Arthur A. Witkin. "The Myth of the Storybook Salesman," *Sales & Marketing Management,* June 14, 1976, pp. 72–73.

have prepared effective statements on what is necessary to qualify for their salesforce. One of the most successful marketing organizations has identified the following characteristics and qualities as important for success:

Impression criteria

> Appearance—neat, clean-cut.
> Dress—conservative, good taste.
> Demeanor—confident, sense of humor.
> Attitude—friendly, sincere.
> Voice and speech—talks to express not impress, knows how to listen.

"Can do" criteria

> Grades—upper 25 percent of class.
> Curriculum—tendency to take advanced and more difficult courses.
> Extracurricular activities—contributions to organizations, offices held, ability to obtain voluntary cooperation.
> Related work experience—part-time and summer jobs.
> Career goals—interest in marketing and good reasons for interest.

"Will do" criteria

> Character—integrity, self-reliance, loyalty, idealism, devout belief, principles.
> Motivation—drive, perseverance, sense of responsibility.
> Ability to get along with others—likes people, cooperative, constructive attitude, maturity.[4]

A leading automobile manufacturer believes that all good salespeople have one thing in common—a liking for people. It wants salespeople who appreciate the opportunity to meet, talk to, and work with new people every day.

A national office machine company suggests that "there is no such thing as an absolute and guaranteed pattern for the successful salesperson." This company thinks of its salespeople as educators, and describes selling for the company as follows:

> Selling in its highest form is a process of education. The successful sales representative is simply a person who knows the merits of the product and the need for it, and the salesperson's progress is in direct proportion to his or her ability to convey that knowledge to others.

The company suggests that its salespeople,

> in order to be advisors and educators—need to be sincere and honest; be able and willing to follow through; possess initiative, imagination, and resourcefulness; be neat and well groomed; have a personality

---

[4] Courtesy of General Electric Co.

that "wears well"; possess good health; enjoy meeting people; be willing to study, to follow company policy, and to put forth consistent effort.

If the salesperson is a keen observer, is mentally alert, and has sheer desire and determination to succeed, he or she has the additional qualities necessary for success. The company believes that the more formal education the salesperson has, the more rapidly he or she is likely to develop.

In its career booklet, Colgate-Palmolive Co. suggests that to be effective its salespeople need superior interpersonal skills plus the technical expertise to act as merchandising advisers to retail store managers. In addition to sales skills, they need the ability to develop and execute detailed plans. This requires the effective use of marketing programs and national advertising campaigns as well as consistent implementation of overall selling strategies.

Some sales specialists belive that they have been able to identify in rather simple terms the most important characteristics needed for selling success. "The professional salesperson recognizes that the two most important ingredients in anyone's formula for success are one's own attitude and determination, and how well he or she understands other people."[5]

According to a recent study, 44 top-ranking sales executives in some of the nation's leading corporations felt the characteristics itemized in Table 2-1 to be important when they interviewed applicants for sales positions in their firms:[6]

Table 2-1

How the executives voted

	1 (10)	2 (9)	3 (8)	4 (7)	5 (6)	6 (5)	7 (4)	8 (3)	9 (2)	10 (1)	Points
Enthusiasm	16	5	8	5	1	5	—	1	—	—	338
Well organized	6	8	11	3	5	5	1	2	—	—	304
Obvious ambition	8	6	5	7	4	3	2	3	3	—	285
High persuasiveness	2	10	3	1	10	4	5	3	1	2	254
General sales experience	3	2	4	6	6	2	8	8	5	4	226
High verbal skill	2	3	3	6	2	7	7	6	4	1	215
Specific sales experience	2	4	2	8	6	1	5	4	4	5	214
Highly recommended	1	—	1	4	3	3	7	2	7	2	149
Follow instructions	—	2	—	3	4	4	2	9	9	8	142
Apparent sociability	—	1	1	2	—	7	6	6	8	10	134

Note: The top numeral in each column is the ranking given by executives, 1-10. The bracketed numerals are point ratings assigned to each rank. Thus 16 no. 1 rankings multiplied by 10 = 160 points.

---

[5] Fred Tibbitts, Jr., "What It Takes to Make It in Selling," *Sales & Marketing Management*, December 13, 1976, pp. 79-80.

[6] Stan Moss, "What Sales Executives Look for in New Salespeople," *Sales & Marketing Management*, March 1978, pp. 46-48.

The account executives in a typical stock brokerage firm are usually expected to have the following characteristics:[7]

Attitude—to be open-minded.

Ability—to learn and continue learning.

Temperament—to withstand the fluctuations of our markets.

Motivation—to succeed and to make money.

Stability—to observe investment opportunities objectively.

Maturity—to accept responsibility for clients' money and to be honest.

Courage—to face themselves and to withstand the rejection of prospects.

Habit plays a prominent part in the successful salesperson's activities. It has been said that successful salespeople form the habit of doing things that unsuccessful salespeople do not like to do. Failures, it seems, would rather adjust themselves to a lower standard of living than endure the hardships and accept the unpleasant tasks that successful methods require.

It has been stated that a large amount of empathy and ego drive are the most important ingredients which a successful salesperson must possess. In fact, it is claimed that these characteristics are more important than experience for successful selling.

Potential salespeople should realize that most companies list qualifications for employment which are somewhat flexible. These qualifications are usually based upon the requirements for an ideal person. Most companies are unable to find the *ideal* person, and therefore they are prone to choose an individual who has the best qualifications, even though he or she does not possess all of the qualifications desired. Companies are more inclined to *overstate* than to *understate* the qualifications necessary for employment.

What kind are you?

Some people are like wheelbarrows—no good unless pushed.
Some are like kites—they'll fly away if you don't keep a string on them.
Some are like canoes—they need to be paddled.
Some are like footballs—you can't tell which way they'll bounce next.
Some are like balloons—full of wind and likely to blow up unless handled carefully.
Some are like kittens—they are more contented when petted.
Some are like tractors—no good unless pulled.

Anonymous

---

[7] "Investment Executive Development Program," Blyth Eastman Dillon & Co., Inc., 1979.

The companies' requirements presented in the following pages show a lack of specific agreement on what is needed to be a success in selling. This is due to the difference in the work to be performed and to the difference in thinking on the part of each company's top management. It should be observed that, while the order of rank of qualities deemed necessary to sell successfully is seldom the same for any two companies, attempts have been made to select a few of the more important traits which are necessary to succeed in most kinds of sales jobs.

In "The Salesman—Ambassador of Progress,"[8] Donald Robinson identifies traits which are important to a selling life. Selling is probably for you if:

> You value independence.
>
> You have ambition, drive, and an independent spirit.
>
> You are sensitive—as interested in the problems of other people as in your own.
>
> You are articulate, with enough command of language to communicate fluently and precisely.
>
> You have an analytical mind, enjoy solving problems.
>
> You are ethical and sincere. There is no place in selling for the con artist.
>
> You are reliable, self-disciplined.
>
> You are enthusiastic.
>
> You are a good administrator, able to draft and implement plans.
>
> You have guts.

It is necessary to realize that, like successful professional people, potentially successful salespeople must be endowed with at least average intelligence, good character, and sufficient maturity. The work of selling, in addition, calls for the individual to possess an *abundance* of human qualities, as well as those qualities which enable him or her to speak well, to present a good appearance, and to be at ease when dealing with people.

A new trend

Typically, considerable weight has been put upon the importance of the art of *persuasion* as a necessary characteristic of good selling. There is no doubt that persuasive ability is important for salespeople who are responsible for moving products through the various distribution channels to the ultimate consumers. There will always be a

---

[8] Published by Sales and Marketing Executives—International.

demand for the salesperson who is known as a persuader; such a salesperson is eagerly sought by many companies.

With the technological and scientific progress of the past decade, however, there has developed a need for the salesperson who is also an expert in communicating information about the company's products. This purveyor of information may well be in a strong position to help create and satisfy needs of prospects.

The abilities to communicate expert knowledge and to educate are essential abilities of this new type of salesperson. High-level persuasive ability is less vital for salespeople who wish to sell for companies which produce many new and changing scientific and technical products or services.

TYPES OF SALES JOBS

Classifying sales jobs

Many attempts have been made to develop a classification of sales jobs which would enable each type of selling to be placed in an exclusive category. This has been difficult to do on any detailed basis.

The National Sales Executives Association (now Sales/Marketing Executives-International, Inc.) developed the following six marketing classifications.

Consumer route.   These sales representatives usually sell and deliver to a regular list of consumers. New customers are solicited, and staple products such as milk, laundry, and other repeat items are sold.

Business route.   These sales representatives call on a predetermined list of business customers to whom they sell familiar supply items. The items could be production materials, office supplies, mill supplies—or other products for resale to consumers. Sales come chiefly from repeat business, and the salesperson may represent a manufacturer, a wholesaler, or a distributor.

Consumer specialties.   Sales representatives in this field contact new prospects constantly and usually do some "missionary work." Products and services must be sold creatively. Typical of sales falling in this category are life insurance, home appliances, insulation, and many other items and services which are sold directly.

Business specialties.   These salespeople do a job similar to that of the "consumer specialties" sales representatives except that they must creatively sell business firms on products and services with which the customer is unlikely to be familiar. They must canvass for a major portion of their business, and they are not likely to have a list of customers supplied to them. Sales may involve such items as business machines, advertising, business insurance, air conditioning, and consultant services.

Retail.   These people sell goods for businesses operating from a fixed place, where the customer comes to the salesperson.

Industrial.   Usually these sales representatives have an engineering background or are technically trained experts on the products and processes which they are selling. The items to be sold may be machinery, product supplies, or services. These items may involve a considerable change in the operation of the customer's business.

The U.S. Department of Commerce classifies sales jobs into four major categories:

1.   The manufacturer's sales representatives.
2.   The wholesaler's salesperson.
3.   The retail salesperson.
4.   The specialty salesperson, including the sales engineer.[9]

This classification is based upon the kind of products and services sold *and* the kind of employer represented.[10]

These classifications and others do not permit the classifying of all selling jobs in any one category to the exclusion of all other categories. For purposes of outlining types of selling jobs, and of showing specifically what is required to fulfill these jobs, an adaptation of the U.S. Department of Commerce breakdown will be used. It will then be possible to answer the questions "What is the salesperson's job?" and "What qualifications are necessary to fulfill the job successfully?"

Examples of sales jobs classified _____

The classification used in the following outline to identify the salesperson's job and qualifications is based primarily upon the people to whom the salesperson sells.

1.   The Manufacturer's Sales Representative.
     a.   A Pioneer-Products Salesperson.
     b.   A Dealer-Servicing Salesperson.
     c.   A Merchandising Representative, Detail Salesperson, Missionary Salesperson.
     d.   Specialty Salespersons—a Consumer Goods Salesperson, a Factory-Office-Goods Salesperson, a Sales Engineer.

---

[9] U.S. Department of Commerce, *Opportunities in Selling*, p. 10.

[10] See also Derek A. Newton, "Get the Most out of Your Sales Force," *Harvard Business Review*, September-October 1969, pp. 130–43, for another frequently used classification.

2. The Wholesaler's Sales Representative.
3. The Retailer's Salesperson.

1. The manufacturer's sales representative. This term includes salespeople who sell to wholesalers, retail dealers, or other middlemen, as well as to the ultimate consumers.

a. A pioneer-products salesperson. This individual's job is to secure outlets for a new product which is unknown to wholesalers, distributors, and dealers.

Success in this field of selling requires self-reliance, aggressiveness, and imagination. The salesperson must be able to find new prospects and to convince them of the advantages of a new product, a franchise, or a dealership.

The financial rewards for these salespeople are high, and jobs will always exist for qualified individuals. They may be selling helicopters, electronic devices, a brand of new cosmetics, or any one of the myriad of new products that American ingenuity produces.

b. A dealer-servicing salesperson. This individual's job is to maintain a regular supply of products for the outlets which represent the company. As a rule, dealers are well established; and while the salesperson may be expected to secure franchises with new dealers from time to time, his or her chief job is to keep an established group of outlets well serviced.

This salesperson will have a well-planned route, will call on customers regularly, and will encourage the use of advertising material supplied by the manufacturer. The use of point-of-purchase displays, for example, must be sold to the dealer, and many times this is difficult because competition for desirable display space is keen. These displays act as a reminder for that large group of people who buy on "impulse."

An important part of the dealer-servicing salesperson's job is to see that the wholesalers, distributors, and dealers are familiar with the company's products, know the selling points for them, and know how to train their salespeople to sell effectively.

Success in this type of selling requires the following qualities: lots of energy, to make numerous daily calls; persistence, to stay on the job and to give advice and counsel where they are needed; enthusiasm, to convince the reseller that the product is good and that the company is friendly and dependable; ability as a teacher, to help employees acquire the product knowledge and the selling techniques necessary to do a good job for the reseller; and integrity, to guide selling activities so that the products sold and the actions taken will contribute to the long-term benefit of the customer, the ultimate consumer, and the company.

This type of selling provides a regular income with more security than exists in many other types of selling and with less emotional and nervous strain than exists in straight-commission selling. Travel is usually restricted to a small area, and long absences from home may be avoided. The products sold might include shoes, hardware, toothpaste, cigarettes, packaged foods, drugs, or any other product which requires constant contact with the dealer.

The following job description in Figure 2-1, used by Colgate-Palmolive Co., gives major emphasis to the company's training program.

c. A merchandising representative. This person differs from the pioneer-products salesperson, and especially from the dealer-servicing salesperson, in that he or she devotes more time and energy to supplying merchandising advice and services. It should be recognized that there is some overlapping of duties between the duties of this classification and those of the dealer-servicing salesperson and the merchandising salesperson. Merchandising salespeople may also be held responsible for the volume of orders taken.

Merchandising, detail, and missionary salespersons are three kinds of merchandising representatives.

A *merchandising salesperson* contacts jobbers, meets with their salespeople, and attempts to encourage greater effort in selling a company's products. Sales promotion is his or her field. Sales can be promoted, for example, by suggesting better advertising and display methods for the dealer's consideration. Merchandising salespersons are prepared to offer sound and unselfish advice on a variety of wholesaler and retailer problems, such as store layouts, displays, special events, store advertising, pricing practices, credit policies, service facilities, and general policies. Their efforts contribute indirectly to greater sales for their companies.

The Procter & Gamble Distributing Company identifies some functions of its sales representatives who call on retailers in the following outline:

Personal selling
—Accounts buying from Procter & Gamble
—Accounts buying from the Procter & Gamble warehouse
Creative merchandising
—Displays
—Promotion support
—Related item sale
Advertising
—Newspaper
—Creative layout
—Promotion tie-in

Figure 2-1

Field Sales Program

Training program:

Each of the Company's major operating divisions, the Personal Care Products and the Household Products Divisions, has a field sales force that is responsible for gaining maximum distribution for the products marketed by the respective division.

To gain the knowledge and skills needed to share in this responsibility, the recruit will participate in an in-depth on-the-job training program of approximately 12 to 18 weeks. This on-the-job program will be administered by experienced sales personnel who began their careers in field sales and who are well aware of the problems faced by a trainee. The training will include instruction in the successful methods and techniques of merchandising, promoting, selling, and distributing our products. The opportunity to observe and participate in buyer presentation, in-store merchandising at the shelf and aisle levels, observation and reporting of competitive activity, and the overall management of a unit or territory will be provided in the unit to which the recruit will be assigned.

In addition to training you in the primary functions of your job, we are also interested in developing you to become a good businessman and grooming you for additional responsibility. Effective management of your territory, plus demonstrated ability to assume greater responsibility, will earn you consideration for promotion to other key jobs. Subsequent advancement may be to the positions of Area Manager, District Manager, Regional Managers and to various Home Office positions.

Location:

Regional Offices are located in seven major cities in the United States:

—New York, New York
—Philadelphia, Pennsylvania
—Atlanta, Georgia
—Dallas, Texas
—Chicago, Illinois
—Columbus, Ohio
—Los Angeles, California

Education:

Bachelor's degree in Business Administration, Arts, or Sciences.

An Equal Opportunity Employer

Shelf improvements
—Shelf space and position
—New brand facings
—Avoidance of out-of-stocks

Records and reports
—Routine reporting
—Special market information

More detailed objectives for a retail store call are spelled out in the Carnation Co.'s list of basic objectives, in order of importance, as:

1. *Secure full distribution of Carnation products.* In a retail chain store this would entail making certain that all Carnation products authorized or available from their supplier or direct account are stocked. If there is a gap in the retail outlet of authorized items, the primary sales goal would be to have the contact write an order in his order guide for the item.

2. *Maintain adequate in-store inventory.* Assuming complete distribution of all Carnation products, all sales efforts should be made to obtain sufficient product inventory both on the shelf and in the back room. If this is not done, an out-of-stock condition occurs, resulting in lost sales. By selling the contact on adequate back room stock in addition to a sufficient amount of shelf space, these out-of-stocks will not occur.

3. *Insure correct pricing.* The unit prices of both Carnation items and competitive items should be checked to be certain that they are in line and competitive with each other. In the case of a chain outlet, the prices of all items are set at headquarters; therefore, your job is to see that all prices on the shelf and on the products are identical to the authorized ones. In an independent outlet you should make certain that the prices of the Carnation products carry the same percent markup as the competitive items.

4. *Obtain best shelf position.* An effort should be made to secure the best possible shelf positions for all Carnation products. In chain stores, sections are frequently set up and authorized by a headquarter merchandising manager, in which case it would be best to contact him regarding merchandising changes. In independent stores changes are always made at the store level. Only by securing the best shelf positions can you be sure of the maximum "off the shelf" movement.

5. *Build displays.* Market research has shown that 76 percent of all the items purchased in retail grocery stores are the result of a store decision made by the shoppers. This points up the importance of creating "impulse purchases," which are most frequently bought from product displays. Developing and presenting ideas for displays (e.g., tie-ins, promotions, etc.) is therefore one of your main objectives for both chain and independent outlets.

6. *Obtain advertising support.* In the case of chains, feature ads are usually set up at headquarters, while independents set them up at the retail

level. Other forms of in-store advertising, such as shelf strips and shelf talkers, should be used whenever possible.

In addition

1. *Know account's distribution.* Know the products stocked by the direct account, especially those products that are in direct competition to Carnation products. When possible, you should find out how well competitive products are selling in the stores which the buyer services. This will, in many cases, reinforce the points in your sales presentation. This communication process is a two-way street since, by giving useful information to the buyer about changing market conditions, you will be building a healthy business relationship based on mutual trust.

2. When a favorable decision is reached or is imminent, be prepared to offer suggestions on the size of the order, the retail shelf price, suggested feature prices for ads, displays, shelf position locations, and any other information that you can anticipate the buyer might request. Try to avoid replying, "I'll have to check on that and call you back." Our customers expect us to be the authority on Carnation products and merchandising ideas.

The *detail salesperson* does much the same type of work as the merchandising salesperson except that considerable time and energy may be required in promoting new products. In the pharmaceutical trade this type of sales representative may spend substantial time calling on physicians, retail druggists, hospitals, public health agencies, and other users of drug products.

An illustration of the duties of a sales representative for Ortho Pharmaceutical Corporation is provided by the job description in Figure 2–2, used to recruit at college placement offices:

Missionary sales representatives are most often employed by manufacturers that do not sell their products directly to the consuming public but supply materials or component parts to other users or manufacturers. The job of these representatives is to provide business indirectly for their company by making certain their outlets prosper. This can be accomplished by suggesting new product uses and new selling methods. These individuals usually spend considerable time with a single customer. It may take days to help with new installations and to handle beginning problems.

All three types of merchandising jobs demand a high type of salesperson. The person should be promotion-minded; experienced in selling, merchandising, and advertising; and highly capable of commanding the confidence of the company's customers. These salespeople may sell such products as groceries, drugs, tobacco, steel, or fabrics. They may be called "factory sales representatives," or "special agents."

d. *Specialty salespersons.* One type of specialty selling—*selling consumer goods*—may require calling at homes to sell such products as sterling silver, books, brushes, home insulation, home

Figure 2-2

Position:

    Sales-Marketing

Duties:

    To promote and sell our products by contacting physicians; pharmacists; wholesale, retail, and chain drug outlets; hospitals; planned parenthood clinics; city, county, and state public health and welfare departments.

Products:

    A wide variety of ethically promoted pharmaceutical specialties, developed through research. Our products are related primarily to the field of obstetrics and gynecology with emphasis on all methods of family planning. We have been the recognized leader in this field for over 30 years.

Requirements:

    A college degree or equivalent in Business, Marketing, Biology or other sciences, Liberal Arts, etc. The ability to get along with people, good poise, appearance, sales experience or sales aptitude.

    Young men and women with demonstrated leadership abilities and a desire to grow in their position and responsibility will be given preference. Due to our policy of promotion from within, we must hire and train our Managers for tomorrow—today.

Training:

    Thorough indoctrination in all phases of company operation and product knowledge. Four to six weeks in division office and field with Manager and Sales Trainer. Followed by two weeks training program in the plant after six to nine months field work. Programmed Instruction Course enables the adept young man or woman to learn technical information rapidly. Continuous self-development program is encouraged. One hundred percent tuition rebate available for those wishing to further formal education.

General:

    For further information pertaining to compensation, expenses, fringe benefits, etc., write to the Director of Employment-Marketing.

An equal opportunity employer M/F

---

furnishings, automobiles, vacuum cleaners, washing machines, refrigerators, sewing machines, and other appliances. The consumer goods salesperson may represent the manufacturer, the distributor, or both. The salesperson's job is to sell the prospect on the acceptance of a demonstration, either in the home or at the store. He or she must be able to demonstrate effectively, answer objections satisfac-

Figure 2-3
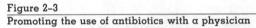
Promoting the use of antibiotics with a physician

Courtesy of Bristol Laboratories

torily, and organize time efficiently to make many calls during the day or evening. Furthermore, a continuous supply of new prospects must be obtained, for *prospecting* is the very essence of this type of selling.

This type of selling requires the salesperson to be alert, well trained, fluent in speech, persistent, tactful, and capable of working without immediate, direct supervision. The rewards are in direct relation to the ability of the salesperson and to the effort expended. Hours may not be regular, and income will fluctuate from month to month. In effect, the salesperson is operating his or her own business.

Another type of specialty selling involves the selling of factory-office goods and services such as the following: office machines, industrial machines, office systems, or a management consultant service.

To succeed in this field the salesperson should have technical training so as to be able to make recommendations to executives, consult with company engineers, and intelligently converse with the company's purchasing agent. The job requires providing service as well as selling a product.

The Business Machines Group of Burroughs Corporation describes the work of a marketing management *trainee* (to be followed by appointment to the position of marketing representative) in the job description given in Figure 2-4.

Figure 2-4

Marketing Management Trainee:

*Marketing Management Trainee, under the direction of a zone sales manager or branch manager, receives formal classroom and on-the-job training in the marketing of Group I products, and learns proven sales techniques covering the more usual marketing situations in preparation for assignment as a marketing representative.

Job requirements:

*This job is normally an entry-level position for recent college graduates with little or no related experience. All must possess the necessary aptitude and ability to undergo intensive training. This position is primarily an orientation period during which the marketing management trainee receives formal and on-the-job training in the operating characteristics and standard applications of Group I equipment.

Typical duties:

*Incumbent undergoes training on the technical aspects of equipment for which he/she has responsibility and its attendant business management systems. Receives formal sales training covering demonstrations, applications, competition, and other techniques of marketing Group I products.

Accompanies experienced sales personnel on sales calls to observe actual selling techniques. May assist in sales presentation, proposal preparation, and demonstrations of equipment to customers. Carries a Group I product quota.

Studies company policies relative to pricing, delivery, and general marketing philosophy. Acquires a knowledge of group and company organizational relationships.

Accountability:

Accountable to assigned manager for acquiring the background and knowledge necessary to market assigned products.

Marketing Representative:

Marketing Representative, under direction of the zone sales manager or branch manager, conducts the sale of assigned products (Group I and Series L) in an assigned geographical territory and/or to lines of business as defined in the individual's contract.

*Upon successful completion of Basic Sales Training School a Marketing Management Trainee is appointed to the Marketing Representative position.

*This position is approximately a six-month period during which the marketing representative sells and installs Group I and Series L equipment.

The factory-office-goods salesperson usually makes fewer sales than one who sells household consumer goods, but orders may be much larger. The time spent in consummating a sale may be as long as several months.

The third type of specialty sales representative is the sales engineer. This salesperson is called upon to solve factory problems and to improve factory operations.

The sales engineer may be expected to have a college degree in engineering or chemistry with perhaps a minor in business. Graduate work in business administration would be advisable. This job requires the individual to be a consultant, a troubleshooter, a salesperson, a teacher, an engineer, and an executive. Some firms use an application engineer to assist the salesperson with the presentation of complete equipment proposals to customers and to provide technical assistance to the sales force, customers, and potential customers.

A current position description as exhibited by the FMC Corporation, manufacturers of food-processing machinery, agricultural machinery, and chemicals, for a "District Sales Representative— Food Processing Machinery" is shown in Figure 2–5.

An engineering background appears to be essential for sales representatives in this field. They will need individuality plus knowledge, and will probably be started on their way to sales jobs by working on the drawing board or in production. Extensive on-the-job training will prepare them to fill highly complex jobs. They may sell elevators, food machinery, printing presses, or other types of industrial machinery.

2. The wholesaler's sales representative. This individual, who functions on behalf of the wholesaler represents companies to the retailer or the industrial consumer. It is not unusual for the wholesaler's representative to sell thousands of items and to supply the retailer with needed merchandise at regular intervals. He or she may sell hardware, drugs, groceries, electrical supplies, or any of numerous other products handled by distributing agencies. If the confidence of the store manager is obtained, the wholesaler's representative may determine the merchant's needs from the store inventory records or by observing the stock on the shelves. Effectiveness in this type of selling is measured in repeat sales over a long period of time.

This type of salesperson need not be highly aggressive, but should be friendly, dependable, and service oriented.

3. The retailer's salesperson. This person is the representative of the retail store and must be able to sell customers who come into the store and in some cases must spend some time prospecting and selling outside the store. Usually the customer has already decided

Figure 2–5

Position Description

Position __DISTRICT SALES REPRESENTATIVE__ Code _____

Reports to __REGIONAL SALES MANAGER__

Division(s), Plant(s), Branch(es) __FOOD PROCESSING MACHINERY__

Purpose of position:

To sell and/or lease all manufactured and agency equipment and parts in the assigned territory and/or to assigned customers, and assist on national account promotions and sales as may be required.

Position responsibilities:

1. Manage territory as an Industry Representative from FPMD to create and maintain an environment for a customer or potential customer to buy, use, and recommend products from FMC and agency suppliers.
2. Call regularly on major, unpenetrated accounts to build future business.
3. Complete studies and quotations, make technical and sales presentations, close sales and leases, draw sales contracts and other sales documents on machinery, and obtain parts orders.
4. Maintain representation between customers and all departments of FPMD, other FMC divisions, and agency suppliers to gain and maintain a high level of acceptance in customers' organizations.
5. Work with the Service and other Departments to insure prompt and adequate service to customers to include using sound business judgment in handling pricing problems, pressures for concessions, and difficult negotiations.
6. Monitor competitive market posture to advise on necessary redesign of equipment, modification of pricing policy, or similar changes as may be indicated.
7. Assist the Credit Department in establishing customer's financial condition.
8. Maintain expenses at a prudent level and evaluate entertainment and conference expenditures to ascertain their potential to generate sales.
9. Implement aggressively divisional product line promotional programs.
10. Manage time and utilize available resources to provide adequate coverage to customers with greatest potential.
11. Assist sales and marketing management in preparing accurate sales forecasts, quotas, and financial reports.

Figure 2–5 *(continued)*

Position requirements:

A. Knowledge and experience
    1. B.S. degree (Engineering, Technical, or Business).
    2. One-three years experience in the food industry (sales, service, plant, application engineering, plus two-five years experience in field sales of capital equipment to food processors).
    3. Willing to relocate.

B. Supervision—not applicable

Positions reporting to you	No. of employees in position	No. of employees reporting to position

C. Supervision (functional)
    1. Service representatives working with customers under the salesperson's jurisdiction.

D. Accountability (see instructions)

    1. Expense control and reporting.
    2. Expense advances.
    3. Maintenance and proper care of company automobile and other company property.
    4. Maintain accurate customer profile.

The above statement reflects the general details considered necessary to describe the principal functions of the job identified, and shall not be construed as a detailed description of all of the work requirements that may be inherent in the job.

---

she needs the product, and she is "looking around" in order to make the purchase. In some stores the salesperson is merely required to wrap the merchandise and make change; in other stores, a high level of selling ability may be necessary.

If the salesperson knows the merchandise and prices and is friendly, patient, industrious, neat in appearance, and tactful, he or she can be successful in most retail selling jobs.

Retail selling experience forms a sound basis for many other selling and merchandising jobs. It is a valuable foundation for those who plan to have businesses of their own; for those whose objectives are to become department heads, buyers, merchandise managers, or other store executives; and for those who plan to enter advertising work.

Some large department stores conduct training programs designed to prepare college graduates, and others who are eligible, for the responsibility of managing a selling department. After spending some time gaining selling experience in various selling departments and in learning to merchandise through observation of superiors and from specialized training classes, qualified candidates may become selling department managers. The position description, provided by The Emporium, San Francisco, illustrates the general duties and requirements for this type of work (see Figure 2-6).

Figure 2-6

POSITION DESCRIPTION

Position title:

Department Manager

Major function:

To develop growth in sales through the proper management and merchandising of the department.

Specific duties and responsibilities:

I. Merchandise planning and analysis
1. To analyze the department's customer to influence the buying staff in planning assortments and stock depth which will develop the proper merchandise mix for your customer.
2. To participate in the development of semiannual sales plans and goals.
3. To analyze and interpret statistical reports and to take action where needed in order to achieve planned sales goals.
4. To identify fast-selling merchandise and to communicate merchandise needs to the central buying organization; to follow through to insure that the requests for stock replenishments are implemented.
5. To identify slow-selling merchandise through analysis of reports, observation, and counts, and to suggest plans for disposition of this merchandise.
6. To shop and analyze the competition in the trade area to evaluate its assortments, prices, and merchandise presentation in order to be competitive in these areas.
7. To review basic stock requirements to maintain the appropriate levels and to determine the needs for additions, deletions, and change of levels.

Figure 2–6 *(continued)*

8. To identify strengths and weaknesses of each department/classification and to develop a plan for increasing sales.
9. To identify, track, and project key items.
10. To make recommendations for needed physical changes and new fixtures in the department.

II. Advertising responsibilities
1. To insure that adequate stock is available for all advertised merchandise.
2. To properly sign and display advertised merchandise.
3. To communicate advertised merchandise to selling personnel.

III. Merchandise presentation responsibilities
1. To present merchandise in a coordinated and exciting manner.
2. To provide direction and merchandise information to display and sales staff.
3. To allocate space according to profitability of merchandise, fashions versus basic merchandise, stock turn, volume, and timing.

IV. Operations and customer service responsibilities
1. To staff the department adequately with sales and stock help in order to achieve planned volume, sales production goals, and customer service standards.
2. To handle customer adjustments courteously and promptly in compliance with the store's standards of customer service.
3. To insure a standard of customer service that is both satisfactory and profitable through supervision and proper staffing.
4. To maintain a clean, neat, and orderly appearance in all selling and stock areas.

V. Shortage control responsibilities
1. To see that all paperwork (price changes, transfers, claims) is completed accurately and promptly.
2. To check incoming merchandise for completeness and pricing.
3. To prepare and take physical inventory.
4. To comply with all store policies regarding shortage control.
5. To insure that merchandise is sold in the correct department at the correct price.
6. To alert sales personnel to problems of theft and shortage.

Figure 2–6 *(concluded)*

VI. Staff development responsibilities
   1. To set an example of selling standards for sales person-
      nel.
   2. To develop staff in selling skills.
   3. To communicate special system procedures and changes
      to staff.
   4. To provide merchandise information to sales staff.
   5. To monitor progress through performance review in terms
      of productivity and customer service.
   6. To identify and develop staff members for additional re-
      sponsibility.*

   * See Chapter 15, Retail Selling, for a further discussion of this field.

CHOOSING A CAREER IN SALES

The foregoing classifications of types of sales jobs point out the responsibilities, duties, qualifications, and rewards for many levels of selling. Prospective salespeople should evaluate themselves in light of the many requirements which have been discussed. Normally, a good procedure to follow in making a tentative selection of a type of selling for career work is:

1. Decide whether a sales career can provide the opportunities for the fulfillment of your own philosophy and goals. You cannot sell unless you have first sold yourself on the desirability of a sales career.

2. Decide whether to sell products or services. The products to be sold may be machines, equipment, supplies, or other tangibles; the services to be sold may be insurance, investments, advertising, or other intangibles. Some people prefer to work with tangible products; others welcome the challenges and opportunities associated with the selling of ideas.

3. Decide whether to sell to customers on a one-call basis or to sell accounts on a continuing basis. Some products are sold once, and there is no need for service or for another contact with the buyer—at least for many years. Such sales may involve real estate or some construction materials. Other products require servicing and replacements, or the users may need advice and help in maintaining, selling, or using the products. These products may include automobiles, industrial machinery, office machines, or merchandise. Some salespersons enjoy the challenge of influencing different buyers to consummate each sale; others prefer to become well acquainted with customers and to serve them over a long period of time.

4. Decide whether to sell to manufacturers, distributors, or household consumers. Manufacturers need parts, supplies, equipment, raw materials, and other products to manufacture their goods. The salesperson who sells to the manufacturer may have relatively few accounts, and the sales volume may be large. The distributor who needs goods for resale may be a wholesaler, a retailer, an independent operator, or a member of a chain group. Individuals selling to distributors may handle many accounts; their work may vary from routine assignments to highly creative selling. Salespersons selling to the household consumer have many accounts and evening appointments, and may need boundless energy.

5. Decide whether to sell in a limited geographic area or to sell wherever the market and the opportunities present themselves. The person who limits job opportunities to a specific county or other small area, and who is unwilling to move as promotions and opportunities become available, automatically narrows, and many times eliminates, a wide range of career selling jobs. For example, a manufacturer's representative whose products are distributed nationally would make little progress if he or she consistently declined new assignments in territories outside the immediate locality.

6. Finally, explore the opportunities, current and potential, and the financial and nonfinancial benefits related to any particular industry and any particular job opportunity.

The salesperson's job and the qualifications will vary, then, depending upon the conclusions reached regarding the aforementioned decisions, and as a result of the standards established by any specific company.

QUESTIONS AND PROBLEMS

1. Do you believe that there are opportunities for women in selling real estate? If so, what advantages do women have in residential saleswork?

2. What reasons, in your opinion, would cause a person to want to become an investment executive or an account executive? Selling stocks, bonds, options, funds, and other investment opportunities are some of the responsibilities of the job.

3. Elbert Hubbard said, "The greatest mistake you can make in this life is to be continually fearing that you will make one." What are the implications of this statement for a salesperson?

4. How would you define the words *empathy, initiative,* and *creativity*? Give your answers in terms of selling.

5. A business executive recently described selling in the following manner: "Selling is the best paid hard work, and it is the worst paid easy work." What is your reaction to this statement?

6. It is commonly accepted that salespeople possess more qualities of the extroverted personality than of the introverted. This does not mean that people must be classified as one type or the other. Most people have some of the personality characteristics of both types of personalities, but tend to have more of one than of the other. Make a list of the personality qualities which you feel are characteristic of the introvert and of those which you feel are characteristic of the extrovert.

7. Assume that you are considering the following sales jobs: (1) a sales representative for a large national prescription drug company; (2) a salesperson for a major department store; (3) a sales representative for a national company which sells sophisticated machine tools and equipment to large manufacturers. List the advantages and disadvantages for each of the proposed job opportunities.

8. How important is "honesty" in the list of moral values? How important is it to the salesperson? Are people becoming more or less "honest"?

9. The Bayview Music Store is a local retail store engaged in the selling of radios, pianos, sheet music, instruments, and music supplies. Mr. Cleff, the owner, would like to have his six salespeople make a self-analysis of their jobs to improve their efficiency in selling. He asks you to draw up a simple checklist, in question form, to enable each salesperson to determine the effectiveness of his or her activities. Prepare a series of questions which would help the salespeople to check on themselves and their jobs.

10. Personality plays an important role in selling. Personality has been defined as "a composite of one's appearance, actions, and speech based upon one's knowledge, attitudes, skills, and habits, which makes one different from everyone else and causes one to be liked, tolerated, or disliked." Identify those personality characteristics which may be classified as "negative" and those which may be classified as "positive" or "constructive."

PROJECTS

1. Make a survey of the materials in your college placement and career counseling office to determine the following:
   a. The number and kinds of firms recruiting at the college for sales positions.
   b. The personal qualifications which the firms are seeking in candidates.
   c. The duties and responsibilities of the salespeople who are hired.
   d. The company training programs which are available to the new salespeople.

   Prepare a statement summarizing the findings.

2. Conduct a survey of selected business organizations in your community. Interview the personnel manager, and collect data on the requirements

for employment in saleswork. Prepare a report summarizing your findings and your conclusions.

3. Application blanks used by many companies contain space for the sales applicant to record a history of participation in college extracurricular activities. Prepare a paper illustrating how the personal qualities companies are looking for may be utilized in student activities.

CASE PROBLEMS

Case 2-1

The Old Paint Company

The Old Paint Company does business on a national scale and has a regular salesforce that calls on independent wholesale and retail paint dealers. The company handles a complete line of nationally advertised paints and paint supplies.

It plans to introduce a new line of insecticides, weed killers, and other nonpaint products during the next year. The sales manager is undecided as to whether the new line should be introduced through the company's regular outlets by the present sales force or whether it should be introduced by a group of specialized missionary sales representatives who will devote their entire efforts to the introduction of the new line.

You have applied for a position with Old Paint, and the sales manager promises to give you the job if you can come up with some recommendations on the pros and cons of using the methods described above.

Questions

1. What are the advantages and disadvantages of each method?
2. What are some other possible methods of introducing the new products?
3. What is your recommendation?

Case 2-2

The Dallas Thermos Company

The Dallas Thermos Company has had considerable success in merchandising thermos bottles, picnic jugs, insulated picnic boxes, and insulated picnic bags.

Sales representatives are expected to perform a variety of jobs. Calls are made on retail drug, hardware, automotive, and grocery outlets.

Recently the Dallas Thermos Company decided to interview at college and university placement bureaus to recruit sales representatives. In arranging for an interview date with a placement office, the company was informed that it would be desirable to file a copy of its job description for sales trainees along with a copy of the personal requirements for the sales job. The sales executive for the Dallas Thermos Company forwarded the following job description to placement officers.

JOB DESCRIPTION

Merchandising-Sales Trainees

Field trainee merchandising-sales representative for the Dallas Thermos Company.

After three weeks of indoctrination training to provide company background, general policies, product knowledge, marketing information, sales procedures, and practices, the sales representative will be assigned to his or her home area, which will be the headquarters city for the Divisional Supervisor (New York, Pittsburgh, Atlanta, Chicago, Dallas, San Francisco).

Fifty percent of the trainees' time will be spent making merchandising calls on retail stores in the drug, hardware, automotive, department, and grocery fields. During such calls survey information will be obtained pertaining to distribution, pricing, product acceptance for our products, as well as competitors; building effective counter and window displays of our products out of stock; establishing sales tests for new products and/or packaging; where possible, selling replacement turnovers orders for handling through local distributors.

Twenty-five percent of the trainees' time will be devoted to assignments by the Divisional Supervisor. These assignments will include checking prospective accounts; inspecting defective merchandise for large customers; assisting Supervisor at dealer trade shows; traveling with Supervisor a minimum of one day per month to observe sales activities in all types of accounts to learn as much as possible about distribution, merchandising, advertising, and selling of our products.

Fifteen percent of the trainees' time will be spent on market and consumer research projects as directed by the home office. This will include trade and consumer interviewing to obtain information pertaining to new products, marketing, and distribution problems.

After proving their aptitude and ability to handle the above activities, the trainees will devote 10 percent of their time to servicing and selling smaller distributor accounts as assigned by Divisional Supervisor.

Approximately 90 percent of all work will be accomplished within the metropolitan trading area of the trainees' home location. Ten percent will be accomplished in smaller towns within a radius of 100 miles. When trainees are working outlying sections, a Supervisor's car will be used and full expenses paid.

Compensation will be on a straight-salary basis, commensurate with background, education, and future potential offered. Out-of-pocket business expenses will be fully paid. No company car will be provided.

Questions

1. Prepare a statement of the personal requirements to fit the job description. This statement is to accompany the job description to be forwarded to college placement officers. Identify each personal requirement (such as age, and so on) which you feel to be important, and write a paragraph explaining each requirement.
2. What success do you believe the Dallas Thermos Company will have in recruiting college or university graduates? Why?
3. Prepare a list of eight or ten factors that are important to you when selecting a career job. Arrange the factors in rank order of importance.

Case 2-3

IBM—The story of Bill Frech—Sales representative, IBM Office Products Division

STORY OF A STORY*

For a representative account of how a person can join and work for the IBM Office Products Division, we reviewed the records of a number of the IBM sales representatives throughout the United States.

This is the story of Bill Frech . . . a young man who has started a rewarding sales career in St. Louis with the Office Products Division

---

* Adapted by permission of the International Business Machines Corporation.

of IBM. Yet, when he was planning his future, he had never even considered sales.

"I never wanted any part of sales."

It was one career he didn't want.

Why Bill Frech changed his mind about IBM selling may also change yours.

Two years ago, Bill Frech was 22 years old and a Liberal Arts major at the University of Missouri. Like many college seniors, Bill was not certain what he wanted to do. He had to choose a career. But what?

He had talked to a number of companies, but nothing aroused his interest. "I want something challenging," he said.

Bill had paid most of his college expenses by waiting on tables, washing dishes, and working in construction. One summer, he had even managed a restaurant. Before that, he had worked part time while attending high school in Columbia, Missouri, and following graduation he had spent six months in the Army. But this experience did not make choosing a career any easier.

And college didn't help either. He had originally enrolled at the University of Missouri as a Business Administration major. But he later changed his major to Liberal Arts. That's when he met Sandy, an art student. At the end of Bill's junior year, they were married, and she took a job as an art teacher while Bill was getting his degree. Together they tried to solve the problem of his career.

"I'm not the selling type. I'm no extrovert."

Three weeks before graduation, an old friend, Russell Rose, dropped in for a visit. He was very interested in Bill's problem. Russ explained that he was now a sales representative for the St. Louis branch of IBM's Office Products Division. He was enjoying his job, working hard, and being well paid.

"I know you've never considered sales, but there's a selling job open in our office, and I think you're the right kind of man for it."

"Who wants to sell?" asked Bill, remembering the despair of Willy Loman in *Death of a Salesman*. "It's the salesman's job to smile—to use tricks and gimmicks. He forces people to buy. And outside of a little money, what does he ever get out of selling?"

Bill spoke of the bad image some salespeople have, the monotony of the work, and the lack of security.

"Besides," he added, "I'm not the selling type. I'm no extrovert."

"Being an extrovert or an introvert isn't the point," Russ said. "IBM selling needs men who are problem solvers. We're not door-to-door drummers. Our aim is to be professionals—to know our prospects' problems and show how our products solve them. The result is my job is satisfying and interesting. The pay is good, and I feel secure."

Bill was not so much persuaded by the words as by Russ's manner. Still he had doubts. Was selling for him? Could he succeed on his own? Would he be compromising his principles?

His wife, Sandy, had a point. "A job doesn't change your principles. You do. I think people with high principles bring more to any job and get more out of it."

"I wasn't sure, but I asked for an interview."

Bill also talked to other sales representatives and to people in other fields. He began to piece together a picture of a salesperson who was totally different. It supported the picture Russ had painted of the IBM sales representative as a professional, someone businesspeople could turn to for advice and help in solving problems and getting their work done more efficiently. And Bill was surprised to learn that a good, hardworking IBM sales representative was usually in higher income groups nationally.

Still, was sales for him? "I wasn't sure, but I asked for an interview." Within a week, he was seated across the desk from "Ship" Atwater, office products branch manager in St. Louis.

Ship is youthful and dynamic. Like all office products branch managers, he has risen through the sales ranks. He understands the doubts and uncertainties that a young man can have about selling.

A formal interview quickly became a friendly conversation.

"A troubleshooter, marketing expert, and executive rolled into one."

Ship asked Bill for his frank opinion of selling. Bill spoke honestly, and as he did, Ship saw many of the qualities that IBM looks for in a young person. Ship then began to explain that today's salesperson is a new kind of individual—a troubleshooter, marketing expert, and executive rolled into one. And to do this effectively, the salesperson has to know and understand the customer's business.

"One of the key concepts in today's approach to selling," explained Ship, "covers the whole area of paper flow—from the origin of an idea to its finished typed form. At IBM we call this 'Word Processing.'

"When someone dictates a report, has it typed, reviews it, changes it, and then has a final version prepared, he's processing words.

"Processing words as efficiently and economically as possible is a real problem. Let me give you some background. During a 12-year period, the number of professional and technical people—idea originators—increased by 87 percent. At the same time, the number of secretaries, stenographers, and typists who support these professionals went up only 49 percent. In terms of words alone, administrative costs have skyrocketed."

"But more paperwork means more business and profits, doesn't it?" asked Bill.

"Yes, if the paperwork flows efficiently. But that doesn't always happen, because people and office equipment have been added without system. Manufacturing, for example, has had to face these problems. For instance, if you are producing cars on an assembly line, and there is a demand for more cars than your line can produce, you don't always build a new assembly line to meet the new demand."

"Why not?"

"Then you're really selling a solution to a problem."

"It may increase the cost per car. So instead, you carefully study your assembly line and expand production by modifying that line with new equipment, new procedures, and new people, at minimum cost."

"So you use this approach in offices?"

"That's right. The cost of processing words can represent anywhere from 40 to 90 percent of administrative time and expense. This is where we come in. We make an analysis of actual versus potential paperwork production, and devise a system integrating people, equipment, and training that can process words more efficiently and economically.

"And when we can prove to top executives that an IBM Word Processing approach gives them the method, the tools, and the training to save them money and do the job better, they listen."

"Then you're really selling a solution to a problem?"

"Exactly. The administrator buys the idea because it's a modern approach to his or her problems. And selling an idea, Bill, is challenging work."

"I had to admit the job sounded challenging."

Still questioning sales, Bill asked, "Do you have a management training program at IBM?"

"Yes, there are a number of management training programs available. But to start, we believe sales is the best management training program we have," answered Ship. "Most of our managers and top executives come up through sales. Starting in sales, you'll be managing your own territory from the beginning, and you'll be getting valuable exposure to other businesses. Managing others is easier after that initial responsibility."

Ship introduced Bill to some of the other people in the office. They went out to lunch together, and Bill felt these were the kind of individuals he would like to work with. "I had to admit the job sounded challenging," he said. His attitude had certainly changed.

Shortly after, when Ship called to offer him a job, Bill accepted.

"At sales school, you begin to get the idea you can be a salesperson."

The Office Products Division Sales School is located in Dallas. It is staffed with instructors who not only have proved themselves to be among the best salespeople in the country, but have the ability to train others. It was established to give all new people the benefit of the best IBM experience.

Bill attended seminars that outlined the marketing programs for the products he would be selling.

He learned how market analysis, product planning, specialized marketing, advertising, sales promotion, and a host of other resources worked together to give him the product to sell and the means to sell it. He learned that, in the entire marketing structure, he and the other sales representatives were the key to the success of the division. Nothing happened unless they did their job.

And they were taught their job. They learned all about the various products, how they were built, and what they were meant to do. They learned to give presentations and make demonstrations to all levels of management.

It was an intensive school, and Bill had never worked harder. But he enjoyed it. "At Sales School, you begin to get the idea you can be a salesperson."

"There are trained selling experts to assist you."

Back in St. Louis, Bill was given a quota and assigned his own territory. As he expected, his first day was a frightening experience. He was not sure he could use his skills. But he soon realized that there was little cause for worry. "There are trained selling experts to assist you," is how Bill puts it.

Ship was there to help—and so were the assistant branch manager and the field manager. They made calls with him.

Afterward, they discussed his calls and made suggestions. He learned a lot watching these professionals work with his accounts, and he learned from the other sales representatives. Soon he gained confidence, and he knew when to turn to other specialists.

The IBM customer engineers were always ready to solve technical problems before a sale or to follow up with service after the sale was made.

Bill also learned to work with the marketing support representative, who usually had business teaching experience and had also been trained in Sales School. They were invaluable in training the personnel who would be using IBM office products. "They very often helped with the actual sale."

Bill had been trained, and he had help. He recognized his problems, and he worked hard. He made his monthly quota.

Bill Frech was on his way.

"Watching those products being built makes a believer out of you."

After he had been in his territory a short time, Bill was sent back to the second part of sales school for further training. The instructors took off some more of the rough edges, but Bill had his confidence now. He had sold more equipment than anyone in the class. Now he was eager for the last part of the course, the trip to Lexington, Kentucky, location of one of the Office Products Division's manufacturing plants.

He was amazed at the size of the plant and the number of products produced. He learned that productivity at Lexington is second— quality and excellence comes first—built by craftspeople, checked by computer. He now understood why IBM products are superior, and how they help with the job he is doing. When it came to engineering, Bill understood the IBM dedication to excellence.

"Watching those products being built makes a believer out of you," Bill added.

"I made my quota. I made the 'Club.'"

He returned to St. Louis once more and went to work. He made his yearly quota. This qualified him for membership in the Hundred Percent Club, which meets once a year in various cities of the United States. There he met and exchanged views with other employees from all over the country. He got to talk to the division's top management, and he attended meetings outlining new developments in his field.

But a good part of the time was devoted to recreation.

It had been a good year for Bill. He put it this way: "I made my quota. I made the 'Club.' I made money." He also sold more new accounts than anyone in the district, and he was named "Rookie of the Year" in the St. Louis office. Best of all, his son Tyler was born.

"I was working smarter, not harder."

In Bill's second year, something happened. "I was working smarter, not harder," he says. He had more time to think. He knew his job and he was more relaxed.

Bill had become more organized. He was budgeting his time and planning his work. His sales and income were far ahead of his first year.

He also got to know the people he was working with much better. "I don't think you could find a finer group of people," he explained. "Each sales representative, with his or her own territory, still realizes that we're all working on the same team."

"Selling is a shared experience," he states.

"A problem solver, a real professional."

The most important change in his second year, however, came in his dealing with customers. He was establishing sound and lasting relationships.

Peter B. Goelz, vice president and controller of United Van Lines, one of Bill's accounts, expressed it this way: "You like to see a young man like Bill develop. He maintains his composure. He has goals and ambitions. You accept him and go out of your way to work with him." Mr. Goelz feels that Bill is helpful. "He keeps us up to date, because he knows our business—what we're doing, how we use our equipment. He analyzes, points out our paperwork problems, and helps us solve them."

Bill also calls on a number of schools. Arthur Langehennig, superintendent for the school district of Hancock Place, likes to have him call. "Bill's a problem solver. . . . He keeps us informed on equipment and techniques that will help us better prepare our business students for jobs."

Bill Frech had become a real professional.

"I'm on the right track."

Today, Bill Frech is extremely pleased with his decision to join the Office Products Division of IBM. His future looks good. The maturity and experience he has gained have brought him respect in his community.

Bill is earning twice as much as many college graduates his age. He is financially secure. His goal is to stay with IBM.

He wants to go as far as he can, enjoy his work and his family.

Looking back over the last two years, Bill smiles at his fears and misconceptions about sales. He realizes he is taking the same road that most IBM management has traveled.

"I'm on the right track," he says.

Questions

1. How do you explain Bill Frech's initial attitude toward saleswork?
2. What has happened to change this original attitude?

SELECTED REFERENCES

America, Richard F., and **Anderson, Bernard E.** "Black Managers: How They Manage Their Emotions." *Across the Board,* April 1979, pp. 80–87.

Chernow, Irving. "Why We Don't Use Sales Reps." *Sales & Marketing Management,* July 9, 1979, p. 32.

Denenberg, Herb. "A Radical Suggestion: America Is Suffering from Low-Pressure Salesmanship," *Sales & Marketing Management,* November 14, 1977, pp. 99–102.

Dowst, Somerby. "Top Salesmen Deliver Service, Expertise." *Purchasing,* August 23, 1978, pp. 48–55.

Fetherling, Doug, and **MacBeth, Mike.** "Top Salesmen and Their Secrets." *Canadian Business,* November 1978, p. 106 ff.

Flarsheim, Henry. "Never Too Old to Sell." *Sales & Marketing Management,* March 17, 1980, pp. 41–42.

Gfeller, John C. "Five Keys to Better Salesmanship." *Nation's Business,* December 1976, pp. 56–58.

Hass, Kenneth B. *Opportunities in Sales and Marketing Careers.* Louisville, Ky.: Vocational Guidance Manuals, 1976.

Have You Considered Insurance? Opportunities for Women Are Expanding. New York: Catalyst, 1976, 46 pp.

Hopke, William E., ed. "Sales Occupations." In *Encyclopedia of Careers and Vocational Guidance.* Chicago: J. G. Ferguson, 1978, pp. 394–433.

Kessler, Bernard M. "New Selling Skills for Today's Changing Marketplace." *Training and Development Journal,* November 1977, pp. 39–41.

Newton, Derek A. "Get the Most out of Your Sales Force." *Harvard Business Review,* September–October 1969, pp. 130–43.

O'Hanlon, James. "The Rich Rewards of the Salesman's Life." *Forbes,* October 16, 1978, pp. 155–58.

Pletcher, Barbara. *Saleswoman—A Guide to Career Success.* Homewood, Ill.: Dow Jones-Irwin, 1978.

Reinhart, Thomas, C., and **Coleman, Donald R.** "Heyday for the Independent Rep." *Sales & Marketing Management,* November 1978, pp. 51–53.

Rosler, Lee. *Opportunities in Life Insurance Sales.* Louisville, Ky.: Vocational Guidance Manuals, 1974.

"Sales Jobs Open Up for Women." *Dun's Review,* March 1978, pp. 86–88.

Scanlon, Sally. "Every Salesperson a Psychologist." *Sales & Marketing Management,* February 6, 1978, pp. 34–36.

"What Does Woman Want?" *Across the Board,* March 1978, pp. 20–61. A series of six articles.

Wilson, Kathy. "Matching Personal and Job Characteristics." *Occupational Outlook Quarterly,* Fall 1978, pp. 2–13.

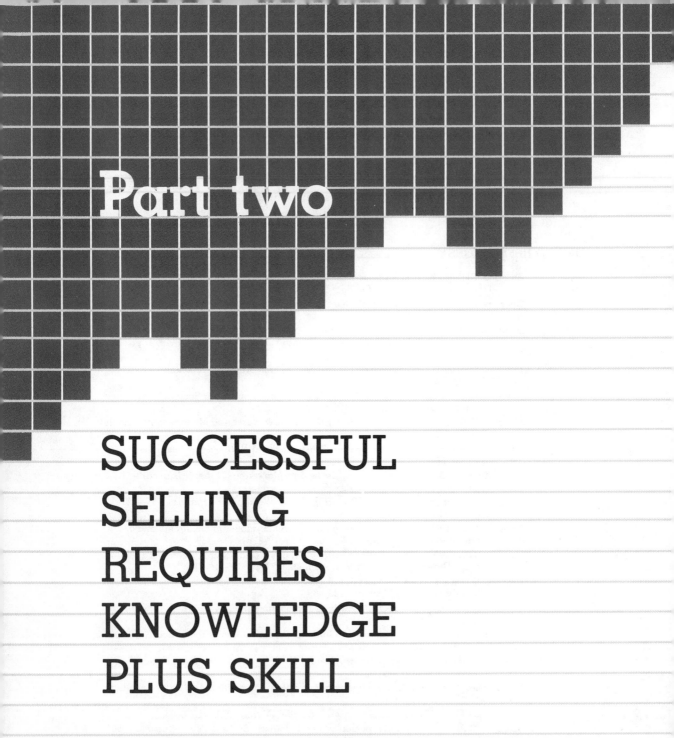

Part two

SUCCESSFUL SELLING REQUIRES KNOWLEDGE PLUS SKILL

This section provides information on buyer characteristics, behavior patterns, and motivation; acquaints the salesperson with the facts which should be known about the company, its products, and its competition; and discusses price, discount, and credit policies and practices, and advertising and sales promotion.

Chapter 3

BUYER BEHAVIOR
AND MOTIVATION

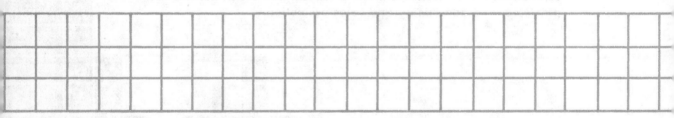

Personal selling requires an individualized approach to the needs, problems, and habits of customers and prospects. In order to plan an effective individualized presentation, the salesperson must acquire facts about people in general and facts of a more specific nature about the prospect's business, habits, and customs.

This chapter answers such questions as the following: Why is it important to study buyer behavior? What are the different types of customers in the marketplace? How do buyers make purchase decisions? What factors affect those decisions? How much and what kind of information about customers are needed to sell effectively? Where and how do salespeople get information about prospective customers?[1]

THE MARKETING CONCEPT—A CUSTOMER ORIENTATION _____

W. Noel Eldred, the late Hewlett-Packard vice president of marketing, stated H-P's emphasis on marketing over selling as follows: "Selling is the technique of getting people to part with their cash, and is short term and selfish because it focuses on the needs of the seller." He preferred the term *marketing*, which he defined as an "integrated effort to satisfy customer needs."[2]

Modern marketing is based on this view that the customer is the key to company success. Called the *marketing concept,* it was stated over 30 years ago by the president of General Electric. He said that "the principal task of the marketing function . . . is not so much to be skillful in making the customer do what suits the interest of the business as to be skillful in making the business do what suits the interest of the customer."[3] The marketing concept replaces a production-oriented approach, which focuses the company's efforts first on manufacturing products and then on selling them. Modern, marketing-oriented companies first find out the needs of customers and then build products to satisfy those needs.

In the marketing-oriented company, all people practice the marketing concept. Engineers design products that customers want, not products that engineers are interested in designing. Production builds products because customers will need them, not because they can be manufactured conveniently. Salespeople sell products that satisfy customer needs, not products that are easiest to sell or that will yield the highest commissions.

To apply the marketing concept, salespeople need to know what their customers are like and how they make purchase decisions. The more salespeople know about their customers, the better able they will be to "help the customers buy." To develop selling strategies, directed toward customer needs, salespeople should have a thorough knowledge of customer buying behavior.

---

[1] For a detailed discussion of sociological and psychological factors in buying behavior, see James Engel, Roger Blackwell, and David Kollat, *Consumer Behavior,* 3d ed. (Hinsdale, Ill.; Dryden, 1978). An excellent shorter treatment of buyer behavior is Peter Bennett and Harold Kassarjian, *Consumer Behavior* (Englewood Cliffs, N.J.: Prentice-Hall, 1971).

[2] Editors of *The Wall Street Journal, How They Sell: The Successful Marketing Techniques of 13 Major American Corporations* (New York: Dow Jones, 1965).

[3] John McKitterick, "What Is the Marketing Management Concept?" in *The Frontiers of Marketing Thought and Action* (Chicago: American Marketing Association, 1975).

TYPES OF BUYERS

Buyers can be grouped in many different ways. One method is to divide them into ultimate consumers, resellers, and industrial customers. This classification is useful because these groups have very different buyer behaviors.

Ultimate consumers

Ultimate consumers purchase products for use by themselves or their families. Clothing, self-improvement lessons, and sports equipment are examples of products that individuals consume. The decision to buy these products is generally made by the persons who will be using them. In such cases, the salespeople need to be concerned only with the needs of these persons.

Many products are purchased to maintain the well-being of a household. Such products include food, shelter (purchasing or renting a house), and risk reduction (insurance). In such cases, all members of the household receive the benefits of the products purchased and several members may be involved in the purchase decision. Thus, the salesperson must consider the needs of each individual in the household.

Resellers

While consumers buy products for their own use resellers buy products with the intention of reselling them. For example, the sportswear buyer in a department store who buys blouses from a manufacturer does not wear the blouses but resells them to ultimate users. Similarly, a buyer for an electronic distributor purchases electronic components for resale to manufacturers.

Resellers are an important part of a channel of distribution that stretches from the manufacturer to the ultimate users. There are many different types of resellers. Among the more common types are retailers, such as department and grocery stores, distributors, wholesalers, and jobbers.

When selling products to resellers, the salesperson must realize that the reseller will buy only those products that ultimate consumers or industrial customers want to buy from them. If there is no demand for products from ultimate consumers or industrial customers, the salesperson will not be able to sell the products to the reseller. Thus, the salesperson must not only satisfy the product needs of the immediate customer, the reseller, but must also be aware of how to satisfy the product needs of the reseller's customers.

When resellers make decisions to buy products, they are usually interested in the services provided along with the products. They would like the manufacturer to help them sell the products by providing advertising assistance, training their salespeople, setting up point-of-purchase displays, and stocking the product on shelves. Often the salesperson provides these services.

Industrial customers

Industrial customers purchase products for use in their design and production efforts, such as machinery and test equipment, and products for use as components in the manufacturer's products. Many people are usually involved in an industrial purchase decision. Engineers examine the product's technical performance; quality control people evaluate its reliability; and purchasing agents consider its price and delivery.

Industrial purchases are often very important to the company. The people who make these decisions spend a long time evaluating alternatives. Formalized decision procedures are often used. These procedures require that specific steps be taken to find and evaluate alternatives. A number of individuals must approve the final decision.

The remainder of this chapter focuses on the buying behavior of individual consumers. The multiple-person decision-making aspects of industrial buying behavior are considered in detail in Chapter 14, Industrial and Trade Selling. However, the information in this chapter is needed to understand industrial buying behavior, because people, not companies, make purchase decisions. Thus, an industrial buying decision can be viewed as a collection of individual buying decisions.

THE BUYING PROCESS

Consumers usually purchase a product only after prior thought or action. Their purchase decisions typically involve several steps. Consider a person's decision to purchase an electronic calculator. First, the person realizes that schoolwork or office work would be easier if a calculator were available. Then the person might talk to friends about their calculators. A trip may be made to the library to read a *Consumer Reports* article on calculators. Several calculators might be examined in a store. Finally, the consumer purchases one. After using the calculator on some problems, the consumer evaluates the degree to which the calculator satisfies his or her needs.

This purchasing scenario suggests that salespeople cannot understand their customers' buying behavior merely by looking at past purchasing decisions. Salespeople must know how and why their customers will make purchasing decisions. What are the customers' needs? What information have the customers obtained? What stores have they visited? What products have they seen? With knowledge of these aspects of the buying process, salespeople can intervene in the process to influence purchase decisions.

The buying process can be represented as a sequence of steps that consumers go through in solving a buying problem.[4] The steps in this process are shown in Figure 3-1.

Figure 3-1

The buying process

1. Need identification.
2. Information search.
3. Evaluation of alternatives.
4. Product selection.
5. Postpurchase evaluation.

Need identification

The buying process is triggered by needs, desires, and wants which give rise to an urge or drive to take some action. Consumers recognize that a need or want is unsatisfied—that their desired level of satisfaction differs from their present level of satisfaction. Tension builds up. It is reduced when the consumers act to satisfy the need.

Types of needs. Needs or buying motives can be classified into two types: (1) functional and (2) psychological. This classification is based on the notion that some products are purchased because of their intrinsic characteristics, while others are purchased because they satisfy psychological needs.

Functional needs are directly related to product performance. For example, a consumer with a need to decorate a wall may purchase paint and a paint brush. The purchase is based on the expectation that these products will satisfy the need. Industrial customers generally make purchases to satisfy functional needs. When salespeople feel that functional needs are stimulating the buying process,

---

[4] A complete discussion of the buying process can be found in James Bettman, л. *Information Processing Theory of Consumer Choice* (Reading, Mass.: Addison-Wesley, 1978).

they will stress the practical and operational aspects of their products.

Psychological needs are associated with the gratification that customers receive from purchasing or owning products. When products are purchased to satisfy psychological needs, functional product characteristics are of secondary importance. For example, a sports car may be purchased to enhance the consumer's self-image as an adventurous, free-spirited person. The functional need of providing transportation may be only indirectly related to the purchase. In this situation, the salesperson might want to emphasize the use of the car by adventuresome people in auto races rather than the car's reliability and dependability.

Frequently, functional needs are referred to as rational, and psychological needs are termed emotional. These labels suggest that people who purchase products to satisfy psychological needs are acting irrationally. Do you think it irrational for people to purchase sailboats so that they can socialize with members of the local sailing club? Are people acting irrationally when they buy expensive clothings to make themselves feel important? Perhaps any action undertaken to improve one's level of satisfaction should be regarded as rational, even if the action only increases psychological satisfaction.

In fact, consumers purchase products to satisfy both operational and psychological needs. A person may buy a sports car primarily to satisfy psychological needs, but the sports car will also satisfy operational needs, such as transportation.

The hierarchy of needs. Another well-known classification of needs was developed by psychologist Abraham Maslow.[5] Maslow's hierarchy of needs is shown in Figure 3-2. The first and most basic needs are such physiological needs as thirst, hunger, and sleep. Satisfying these needs is required for a person's survival. The second group of needs are safety and security. The third group are the needs for love and belongingness—for family and friends. The fourth group are the needs for esteem and status—for self-respect and the respect of others. The highest order needs are the needs for self-actualization. These are the needs of people to achieve everything they are capable of achieving.

Maslow proposed that these groups of needs are hierarchical. That is, people are motivated to satisfy lower order needs before they attempt to satisfy higher order needs. Since physiological needs are the most basic, people will attempt to satisfy them before they attempt to satisfy safety and security needs. People are not interested in love and affection when they are hungry or have no shelter. When

---

[5] Abraham Maslow, *Motivation and Personality* (New York: Harper & Row, 1954).

Figure 3-2
Maslow's hierarchy of needs

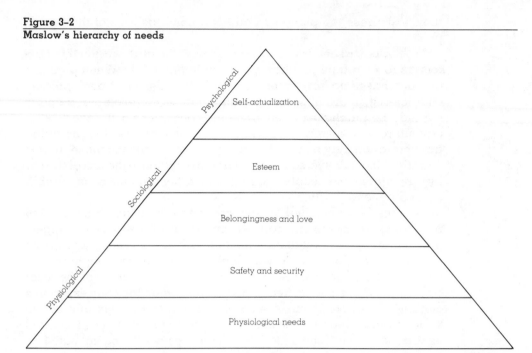

people have satisfied their lower order needs, they will be motivated or driven to satisfy the higher order needs of self-esteem and self-actualization.

Even though needs are hierarchical, Maslow recognized that several groups of needs can motivate behavior at the same time. However, the relative importance of the higher order needs will be related to the degree of satisfaction of the lower order needs. If the lower order needs are largely unsatisfied, their satisfaction will be most important to the person. If the lower order needs are largely satisfied, higher order needs will be more important.

Maslow's theory provides useful guidance for salespeople. It indicates which types of needs might be more important to specific customers. It provides some clue about what the consumer's "hot button" is. Should the clothing salesperson emphasize the warmth or the style of a coat? Should the office supply salesperson emphasize the reliability of a typewriter or its "state of the art" features?

In a postindustrial economy like the United States, the lower level needs of most people are satisfied. The salesperson's focus must shift to a more detailed exploration of their higher level needs. In 1971, Daniel Yankelovich, a well-known social researcher, identified a number of social trends related to consumer behavior. These are listed in Figure 3–3. They reflect the growing sophistication of indi-

Figure 3–3
Social trends

Group 1: Psychology of affluence

1. Toward *physical self-enhancement*—the things people do to enhance their looks.
2. Toward *personalization*—the need to be "a little different" from other people.
3. Toward *physical health and well-being*—what people do to take better care of themselves.
4. Toward *new forms of materialism*—the new status symbols and the extent of de-emphasis on money and material possessions.
5. Toward *social and cultural self-expression*—the "culture explosion."
6. Toward *personal creativity*—the growing conviction that being "creative" is not confined to the artist.
7. Toward *meaningful work*—work that is challenging and meaningful over and above how well it pays.

Group 2: Quest for excitement, sensation, stimulation,
and meaning to counteract the
practical and mundane routines of life

8. Toward the *"new romanticism"*—the desire to restore romance, mystery, and adventure to modern life.
9. Toward *novelty and change*—reaction against sameness and habit.
10. Toward *adding beauty to one's daily surroundings*—the stress on beauty in the home.
11. Toward *sensuousness*—greater emphasis on touching, feeling, smelling, and psychedelic phenomena.
12. Toward *mysticism*—the search for new modes of spiritual experience and beliefs.
13. Toward *introspection*—an enhanced need for self-understanding and life experiences.

Group 3: Reaction against the complexity of modern life

14. Toward *life simplification*—the turning away from complicated products, services, and ways of life.
15. Toward *return to nature*—the adoption of more "natural" ways of dressing, eating, and living.
16. Toward *increased ethnicity*—finding new satisfactions and identifications in foods, dress, customs, and life-styles of various ethnic groups.
17. Toward *increased community involvement*—greater involvement in local groups.
18. Toward *greater reliance on technology versus tradition*—greater confidence in science and technology.
19. *Away from bigness*—the departure from the belief that "big" necessarily means "good."

Figure 3–3 *(continued)*

Group 4: Penetration of certain new values at the
expense of traditional puritanical values

20. Toward *pleasure for its own sake*—putting pleasure before duty.
21. Toward *blurring of the sexes*—moving away from traditional distinctions between men and women and their roles.
22. Toward *living in the present*—straying from traditional beliefs in planning, saving, and living for the future.
23. Toward *more liberal sexual attitudes*—the relaxation of sexual prohibitions.
24. Toward *acceptance of stimulants and drugs*—greater acceptance of artificial agents for mood change, stimulation, and relaxation.
25. Toward *relaxation of self-improvement standards*—the inclination to stop working as hard at self-improvement.
26. Toward *individual religions*—rejection of institutionalized religions and the substitution of more personalized forms of religious experience.

Group 5: Trends which have a direct impact on marketing as well
as on other facets of modern life

27. Toward greater *tolerance of chaos and disorder*—less need for schedules, routines, plans, regular shopping and purchasing, and order and cleanliness in the home.
28. Toward *challenge to authority*—less automatic acceptance of the authority and "correctness" of public figures, institutions, and established brands.
29. Toward *rejection of hypocrisy*—less acceptance of sham, exaggeration, indirection, and misleading language.
30. Toward *female careerism*—belief that more challenging and productive work for a woman is needed.
31. Toward *familism*—renewed faith in the belief that the essential life satisfactions stem from activities centering on the immediate family unit.

Source: Based on Daniel Yankelovich, "What New Life Styles Mean to Market Planners." *Marketing-Communications,* June 1971, pp. 38–45. See pp. 40 and 41. Note that these trends were identified at one point in time, early 1971.

vidual needs. Which of the trends apply to you? Which are now obsolete? How do these trends affect consumers' needs for products?

Conflict of needs. Most consumers find that not all their wants and needs can be gratified. Needs compete for satisfaction. The need to be socially acceptable may conflict with the need to save money. The need for recreation may conflict with the need to study. A consumer may have a very high quality need, a latest-style need, and an economy-price need. It seems improbable that all three needs could be satisfied through the purchase of any one product. The buying decision will be delayed until this buyer can resolve the conflict.

Typically, consumers must make trade-offs among conflicting needs. For example, they may decide to satisfy one need and completely neglect another, or they may satisfy both needs in part. Trade-offs among needs are considered in the discussion of multiattribute models later in this chapter.

Recognition of needs.   Consumers must recognize an unsatisfied need before it can motivate their purchasing behavior. Frequently, consumers do not realize that they have unsatisfied needs. In these situations, a salesperson can help potential customers recognize their needs and then demonstrate how products will satisfy those needs. Salespeople promote need recognition in two ways. First, they can give customers information about products, and the customers can use this information to identify unsatisfied needs. Second, salespeople can examine the customer's situation and demonstrate that unsatisfied needs exist.

However, salespeople and other marketers *cannot* make people buy products they do not want. The potential consumer must recognize the need before any sale can be made. Salespeople can raise the consumer's level of need awareness and perhaps increase the consumer's desire to satisfy needs. But salespeople can only influence consumer behavior; they cannot control it.

Information search

Once buyers recognize a need, they will search for ways of satisfying it. They may conduct the search for information about alternatives rapidly or over an extended period of time. When stock is low, a purchasing agent may simply look up the address of a reliable vendor used in the past. However, when faced with the need for a new vendor, the purchasing agent might initiate an extensive search for new alternatives. A number of vendors might be asked to submit proposals and samples. Other companies purchasing from these vendors might be asked to describe their experiences with them.

Amount of information search.   The search for information is costly. It requires time and effort. How much information is sought depends on the benefits the consumers expect to get from the information. Consumers who have had little prior experience in using or purchasing a product will spend more time searching for information because they will feel uncomfortable about making a quick decision. An extended information search will also be made when the purchase decisions are very important. Consumers who are making a large purchase will spend a lot of time and effort to make sure that they have evaluated all the alternatives. For example, consumers who plan to purchase an automobile spend a lot of time collecting information about different models. They may visit several dealers and talk with friends who own different models. On the other hand, in buying a breakfast cereal, the information search is usually limited to a quick review of cereals that the family has liked in the past.

Sources of information.   Consumers have two major sources of information: internal and external. Internal sources refer to information possessed by the consumer. This is information stored in the consumer's memory, such as the names of different brands, awareness of how members of the family or the company feel about the brands, or the consumer's own attitude toward the brands.

Consumers are exposed to a vast amount of information about commercial products. Each person sees over 500 advertising messages for products each day.[6] In addition, consumers get information about products from friends and acquaintances. One of the most important sources of consumers' information about products is past experience with the products. Even if consumers remember only a small fraction of the information they are exposed to, they have an extensive internal information bank to help them make buying decisions.

There are several reasons why buyers may want to collect additional information. The information stored internally may be out of date. The consumer may have purchased a television set a long time ago and may wish to learn about the alternatives that are now available. The consumer may also feel that the internal information is not adequate. The purchase decision may be so important that additional information should be collected. In some industrial purchasing situations, buyers are required to get additional information. They may be required to obtain bids from three different vendors before they can place an order.

There are a larger number of external sources of information. Some of these sources may be readily available—for example, books, magazines, and department store catalogs. Industrial buyers usually have access to extensive data files. Other external sources of information may require more effort to collect. A consumer may visit the library to look at the *Consumer Reports* issue on the product, or examine the product at several stores, or ask several friends for their opinions. Similarly, industrial customers may request current information from various suppliers.

------

[6] Stewart Britt, Stephan Adams, and Alan Miller, "How Many Advertising Exposures per Day?" *Journal of Advertising Research* (December 1972), pp. 3–10.

Salespeople are an important source of information for ultimate consumers, resellers, and industrial customers. Good salespeople give the consumer the exact information that is needed—information about how a product will satisfy the consumer's needs and what the product's advantages and disadvantages are. But buyers will seek information from salespeople only if they feel the salespeople are knowledgeable and trustworthy. They will not seek information from salespeople who they feel have little knowledge about the products they are selling or the needs of the customers. If customers feel that salespeople do not have their interests at heart, they will not believe what the salespeople tell them. For these reasons, salespeople are effective only if they are perceived as credible sources of information.

Evaluation of alternatives

After collecting information about alternatives, consumers review the information, evaluate the alternatives, and select the alternative that best satisfies their needs. This evaluation process can be represented by a multiattribute model. The model will be discussed in detail because it provides a framework for developing sales strategies.

The multiattribute model is based on the idea that consumers view a product as a collection of attributes or characteristics. Consumers evaluate a product by considering each characteristic and determining how it will help satisfy their needs. Consider a student who is planning to purchase a typewriter. The student narrows her choice to three brands—Alpha, Beta, and Delta. Some of the information collected about these brands is shown in Table 3-1. Notice that the information collected goes beyond the physical char-

Table 3-1
Information about typewriters

	Brands		
Typewriter characteristics	Alpha	Beta	Delta
Purchase price ($)	300	600	900
Consumers Report reliability rating	Very good	Very good	Excellent
Weight (pounds)	9.5	15.3	16.2
Size (cubic inches)	600	975	1100
Maximum typing speed (words per minute)	80	120	100
Appearance of type	Average	Very good	Excellent
Distance to nearest service center (miles)	20	10	2
Warranty (months)	6	12	12

acteristics of the product to include the service provided and the warranty offered. This demonstrates that consumers consider a wide range of characteristics when evaluating a product.

The student mentally processes the "objective" information that she has collected and forms beliefs about the performance of each typewriter on a series of dimensions. Each dimension combines several objective characteristics. Thus, purchase price, warranty, and availability of service are considered when forming a belief concerning economy. The student's beliefs on the various dimensions are represented in Table 3-2 as ratings on a ten-point scale. Because of Alpha's low weight and small size, the student forms the belief that it is a very portable typewriter. This is represented numerically by giving Alpha the best rating—ten—on portability. Beta and Delta have the same poor ratings on portability. Considering price, reliability, and the warranty, the student believes Alpha to be the most economical typewriter. But Alpha is also the most difficult to service because the nearest service center is 20 miles away. These belief ratings illustrate the trade-offs that consumers must make. No one product will have the best performance on all dimensions. No one product will satisfy the consumer's needs on all dimensions. Delta is poor on economy, but the appearance of its typewriting is very good. Beta has a very high rating on typing speed but a low rating on portability.

With this set of beliefs, how does the student select a typewriter to purchase? The eventual purchase decision depends on the relationship between the student's beliefs about performance and the student's needs. Trade-offs must be made. The student needs to consider how important each attribute is to her and the degree to which she is willing to sacrifice poor performance on one dimension for good performance on another dimension.

Product selection

In selecting among the three typewriters, the student forms an overall evaluation of each typewriter. This evaluation is based on

Table 3-2

Beliefs about performance of typewriters

Performance dimensions	Brands		
	Alpha	Beta	Delta
Economy	10	6	2
Portability	10	3	3
Typing Speed	4	9	6
Appearance of typed copy	4	7	10
Ease of service	2	6	9

how important the typewriter's performance on each dimension is in terms of satisfying her needs. Since this particular student has little money, she sees economy as the most important dimension. Portability is also very important because she would like to use her typewriter in the university library and at home. She does not have good typing skills; thus, typing speed is not very important to her.

Each person has a unique set of needs. Thus, the importance of each dimension will vary for different people. For example, the supervisor of a university typing pool is very interested in typing speed. The supervisor's salary and promotion are based on how quickly manuscripts and papers are typed. Since spare typewriters are available, the speed of service is not too important. Portability is unimportant because the typewriters are never moved from the typists' desks. Economy is also unimportant. In this institution, the purchasing agent, not the typing pool supervisor, is concerned with price.

The importance that a consumer places on a dimension can also be represented on a rating scale ranging from ten for very important to one for very unimportant. The importance weights for the student and the supervisor are shown in Table 3-3 along with the beliefs about performance discussed previously. The most important dimension for the student is economy (ten weight), and the least important is typing speed (one weight.) The supervisor places the most importance on typing speed (nine weight). Economy and portability are equally unimportant to the supervisor.

In this example, the student and the supervisor have the same beliefs about the performance of the products. They only differ in terms of their importance weights. In general, consumers will differ on both beliefs and importance weights.

Basis for evaluating products. Frequently, the consumer's overall evaluation of a product is related to the sum of the performance

Table 3-3

Information on which overall evaluations are based

Dimensions	Importance weights for:		Brand beliefs		
	Student	Supervisor	Alpha	Beta	Delta
Economy	10	1	10	6	2
Portability	9	1	10	3	3
Typing speed	1	9	4	9	6
Appearance of typed copy	6	8	4	7	10
Ease of service	5	6	2	6	9
Supervisor's overall evaluation of each brand			100	182	193
Student's overall evaluation of each brand			228	168	158

beliefs weighted by the importance weights. Thus, the student's overall evaluation of Alpha would be the importance of economy times the belief about the brand's performance on economy plus the importance of portability times the brand's performance on portability, and so on. The student's overall evaluation or score for Alpha would be:

$$
\begin{array}{rcr}
10 \times 10 &=& 100 \\
9 \times 10 &=& 90 \\
1 \times 4 &=& 4 \\
6 \times 4 &=& 24 \\
5 \times 2 &=& \underline{10} \\
&& 228
\end{array}
$$

The overall evaluations or scores for the three brands, using the student's and the supervisor's importance weights (needs), are shown on the bottom of Table 3–3. The student evaluates Alpha the highest and would probably purchase it. The supervisor prefers Beta and Delta over Alpha. Since Delta has a slightly higher evaluation, the supervisor would probably select that brand.

In actuality, only a few consumers go through such a mathematically involved process when making purchase decisions. If you ask consumers how they decided on a brand, they will not tell you that they listed the important dimensions, wrote down their importance weights and performance beliefs, performed multiplications and additions, and finally picked the brand with the highest score. However, scores calculated in this manner can be a good indicator of the brands that consumers actually purchase. Thus, although the multiattribute model does not describe the actual purchasing process, it is a good model of the process. Consumers make choices as if they were using multiattribute models.

While consumers may not use multiattribute models in a formal way, industrial customers often do. Industrial customers often develop scores for each vendor they are considering by rating the vendor's performance on the critical dimensions and then weighting the dimensions to arrive at an overall score.

Implications for the salesperson. How can salespeople use multiattribute models to influence their customers? To begin with, the models indicate what information consumers use to make decisions. Thus, salespeople need the following information to influence their customers' decisions:

1. The brands that the customers are considering.
2. The product dimensions or characteristics that the customers are going to consider in making their decision.
3. The customers' rating of each product's performance on each dimension.

4. The importance weights that the customers attach to each dimension.

With this knowledge salespeople can use several sales strategies to influence the customer's decision. First, salespeople must make sure that their product is included in the brands that are being considered. Then, salespeople can try to change the customer's overall evaluations by changing the values in the customer's decision matrices. Some sales strategies for doing this are as follows:

1. Increasing the rating for your product.
2. Decreasing the rating for a competitive product.
3. Increasing or decreasing an importance weight.
4. Adding a new dimension.[7]

The first strategy involves altering the consumer's belief about your product's performance—increasing your product's performance rating. If you were selling the Beta typewriter to the typing pool supervisor, you could base your sales strategies on the decision matrix shown in Table 3-4. From that matrix, you would realize that Delta is your main competition because its overall evaluation is closest to that of your product. Then, you might try to convince the supervisor that your typewriter has greater performance on an important dimension. For example, you might demonstrate that Beta is extremely fast, so that the supervisor should give it a ten rating and not a nine. A small change in the performance belief on a dimension important to the customer will result in a large change in the customer's overall evaluation. In this case, the supervisor's overall evaluation of Beta would go up by nine points. You would not spend

Table 3-4

Typing pool supervisor's decision matrix

Dimensions	Supervisor's Importance Weights	Supervisor's performance beliefs about:	
		Beta	Delta
Economy	1	6	2
Portability	1	3	3
Typing speed	9	9	6
Appearance of typed copy................	8	7	10
Ease of service.............	6	6	9

---

[7] See Harper Boyd, Michael Ray, and Edward S. Strong, "An Attitudinal Framework for Advertising Strategy," *Journal of Marketing,* Summer 1972, pp. 27–33, for a discussion of how multiattribute attitude models can be used in developing advertising messages.

time trying to influence the supervisor's opinion about your type-writer's economy. A one-unit change in the performance rating on economy would change the supervisor's overall evaluation by only one unit because of the low importance placed on this dimension.

Another sales strategy would be to decrease the performance rat-ing for your competitor. This is generally a dangerous strategy. Cus-tomers do not like salespeople who say bad things about the compe-tition. They like salespeople who say good things about their own products.

Altering the customer's importance weight is still another sales strategy. You would want to increase the importance of dimensions on which your product performs better than the competition and to decrease the importance of dimensions on which your product per-forms worse than the competition. For example, the Beta typewriter salesperson might try to convince the supervisor to place more im-portance on economy by demonstrating that more typewriters could be bought if a more economical model were purchased. If the sales-person could get the customer to increase the importance of economy by 3 units (to a weight of 4), the supervisor's overall evaluation of Beta relative to Delta would go up by 18 points. Similarly, the sales-person might try to get the supervisor to place less importance on ease of servicing by emphasizing the availability of a spare type-writer. If the salesperson can reduce the importance placed on serv-icing, the relative evaluation of the Beta typewriter will increase.

In summary, multiattribute models indicate what salespeople should know about their customers. These models also indicate some good sales strategies, such as increasing the performance rat-ing on important dimensions and increasing the importance of di-mensions on which your product performs well.

Postpurchase evaluation

The purchase decision process does not end once customers have selected a product. Customers must still decide whether they have made a wise choice. Most consumers make their postpurchase evaluations informally. They use the product, decide whether or not they like it, and store this information in memory for future use. Often, industrial customers have a very formal postpurchase evalua-tion. The users complete a written evaluation which is distributed to other members of the organization.

After consumers purchase products, they usually cannot return them even if they are dissatisfied with the performance of the prod-ucts. However, dissatisfied consumers can affect salespeople in other ways. They may decide not to purchase products from the same salespeople in the future. Such decisions could have a large effect on the performance of industrial salespeople because they usually have long, continuing relationships with their customers.

Dissatisfied customers can also affect the salesperson by telling other people (for example, friends or co-workers) not to purchase the product.

Salespeople can play an important role in reducing customer dissatisfaction. Part of this effort begins before the sale is made. If salespeople see that customers are fully aware of the capabilities of the products they are purchasing, dissatisfaction will be minimized. With good information prior to the purchase, customers will achieve the level of satisfaction that they expect to achieve.

Salespeople can also minimize dissatisfaction by helping people to use the products they buy. Often, customers become dissatisfied when they do not know how to get the most out of their purchases. Salespeople can help customers realize the maximum possible benefits from the products they have purchased.

BUYING SITUATIONS

For each purchase decision, consumers generally go through the five stages in the buying process shown in Figure 3–1. However, each purchase decision is unique in terms of the time spent and the activities undertaken at each stage. The following three types of buying situations have been suggested:[8]

1. Extensive problem solving.
2. Limited or routine problem solving.
3. Automatic response.

The relative importance of the five buying stages depends on the particular type of buying situation confronting the consumer.

Extensive problem solving

Consumers are faced with extensive problem solving when they feel that a high level of uncertainty or risk is associated with their purchase decision. This condition usually occurs when the purchase decision involves satisfying an important need, when the product is expensive, and when the customer has little product knowledge.

It is important to recognize that risk is subjective. The amount of risk in a purchase decision is the amount perceived by the consumer.

---

[8] John Howard, *Marketing Management*, 2d ed. (Homewood, Ill.: Richard D. Irwin, 1963).

That amount may or may not be related to the risk that actually exists. You as a salesperson may not feel that a given decision is very risky, but if consumers perceive a high risk, they will act as if there were one.

Many kinds of risk may be perceived by consumers. Financial risks are associated with purchases of expensive products. Physical risks can be important if consumers feel that the products being considered may affect their health. Social risks may develop if consumers feel that the product will affect the way others think of them. Psychological risks arise when the product affects the consumer's self-image.

When consumers perceive a purchase decision as risky, they attempt to reduce the level of risk by engaging in extensive problem solving. In such situations, consumers become information seekers. Since they have had no experience with the product class and know little about it, they have not developed a well-defined set of alternative models to consider, or dimensions for evaluating the alternatives. Consumers in such situations will usually consider a number of alternatives. The salesperson can help greatly in reducing the perceived risk by providing consumers with information and by assisting them in evaluating alternatives.

Limited problem solving

Limited problem solving describes the purchasing behavior of consumers who have had some prior experience with the products of interest. The need for information is less than that of consumers engaged in extensive problems. In such situations consumers have a high probability of purchasing a brand they have used in the past. When selling in such situations, salespeople should attempt to reinforce the consumers' buying pattern if the consumers are buying their products. If consumers are not buying their product, salespeople should attempt to introduce new information to break the pattern that the consumers have established.

Automatic response behavior

When the purchasing behavior of consumers is automatic, it is because they have already decided on the specific brand that best satisfies their needs. When the need arises, they automatically purchase that brand. No additional information is sought. No new alternatives are considered. Such decisions are usually of little importance. Advertising is the principal means for marketing products associated with automatic response behavior.

INFLUENCES ON THE BUYING PROCESS _____

Consumers have tendencies to behave in the same way when their situations are similar. These tendencies or predispositions lead to some consistency in consumer behavior. Knowledge of these predispositions will help salespeople predict what their customers will want and what products they will buy. Two major factors that contribute to the predispositions of the consumers are the consumer's characteristics and the influences of the groups with which the consumer is associated.

Consumer characteristics _____

Each consumer has hundreds of characteristics. Some of the characteristics that are useful in determining a customer's predispositions are discussed below.

Demographic characteristics. Demographics are vital statistics describing people, such as sex, age, marital status, number of children, race, education, and geographic location. These characteristics indicate certain buying predispositions. For example, consumers living in New England are predisposed to buy different clothing than is bought by Southerners. Consumers living in the country have a greater need for automobiles than do consumers living in New York City. Married couples with young children have a greater tendency to purchase life insurance than do elderly single people.

It is relatively easy for a salesperson to determine a consumer's demographic characteristics. However, the relationship between these characteristics and buying tendencies is not strong. The salesperson must be careful not to prejudge customers from their demographics. For example, many products traditionally purchased by men are now being purchased by women. The trend will continue as the role of women in society continues to change.

Socioeconomic characteristics. Consumers can be categorized into social classes based on their income, education, and occupation. Typically, consumers with higher incomes are in higher social classes. However, this is not true for certain occupations. For example, college professors and ministers have low incomes but high educational levels and high-status occupations. Thus they are in a higher social class.

In some situations social class can be used as a predictor of a consumer's buying process. Social class is a good predictor of the types of clothing and furniture purchased by consumers. As compared to consumers in low social classes, consumers in high social classes are generally exposed to more information about products and have opportunities to evaluate more alternatives when making a purchase decision.

Personality. Personality is defined as a consistent set of responses that individuals have to their environments.[9] For example, the cautious and the methodical person will react cautiously and methodically in most situations.

There are four basic theories of personality: trait, phenomenological, social behavior, and psychodynamic, or Freudian. Each of these theories proposes different methods for classifying people into personality types. The theory most commonly used in selling is the trait theory. This theory is based on the notion that each individual's personality can be described by the degree to which he or she possesses specific traits. These traits include extroversion, agreeableness, emotional stability, and conscientiousness.

It has been suggested that salespeople should rate the buyer, at least roughly, on an extroversion-interversion scale. However, there is little basis for assuming that buyers can be classified accurately this way. Few attempts to develop accurate measures of personality have been successful.

Buyers can be nervous and agreeable at the same time. They can have characteristics of both the extrovert and the introvert—be poorly dressed, yet have a large bank account; be pleasant, yet buy very deliberately; be cautious and suspicious when buying some products and impulsive when buying others: be procrastinators at one time and enthusiastic and confident at other times; be friendly today and disagreeable tomorrow; and be skeptics when buying products they are well acquainted with and dependent customers when buying products about which they know little.

Psychographics. Psychographics are a way of describing a person's life-style as it applies to his or her consumption behavior.[10] These life-style descriptions include the consumer's activities, values, needs, interests, opinions, purchasing behavior, and personality. Since these variables are directly related to consumer behavior, marketers are placing more emphasis on psychographics than on personality profiles. Advertising agencies often conduct sophisticated national surveys to develop profiles of typical consumers. The

---

[9] See Harold Kassarjian, "Personality and Consumer Behavior: A Review," *Journal of Marketing Research*, November 1971, pp. 409-18, for a more detailed discussion of personality and consumer behavior. A thorough discussion of personality theories can be found in Walter Mischel, *Introduction to Personality* (New York: Holt, Rinehart and Winston, 1971).

[10] For a complete discussion of psychographics, see "Psychographics: A Critical Review," *Journal of Marketing Research*, May 1975, pp. 209-14. For the use of psychographics in advertising, see Peter Bernstein, "Psychographics Is Still an Issue on Madison Avenue," *Fortune*, January 16, 1978, pp. 73-75.

profiles are then used in preparing advertisements. The results of one such survey conducted by Needham, Harper and Steers Advertising is shown in Figure 3–4.

The use of individual characteristics. The success of customer relations depends upon the depth of the salesperson's understanding of customers. Understanding customers is difficult because of the problems involved in placing people into exclusive categories. Much has been written in support of personality and demographic variables, which are supposed to simplify the salesperson's job of classifying prospective buyers. Many of these schemes make unfounded claims. The cause of human reactions are too varied to permit a quick, easy, accurate classification of people as definite types.

Despite all evidence to the contrary, many people still believe that there are shortcuts in the process of analyzing human beings. They think that facial or other body features, handwriting, or the stars will supply keys to the analysis and classification of individual character and personality. Because of this gullibility, phrenologists, physiognomists, palmists, graphologists, and astrologists receive many millions of dollars in fees each year. A glance at the classified advertisements of a newspaper will indicate the extent of this pseudoscientific activity.

Still, companies do provide classifications of customers in order to acquaint their salespeople with various consumer types. Good judgment must be exercised in using these classifications. The salesperson must always be aware of their limitations.

Group influences

The previous discussion has focused on individual consumers. However, individuals do not function as entities independent of those around them. Each consumer belongs to a number of groups. These groups include a family or living group, social clubs and organizations, business organizations, and reference groups.

Groups affect the consumer's buying behavior in two ways. First, they provide information. Members of the group communicate with each other, sharing experiences in purchasing and using products. Second, groups can provide a standard of buying behavior. If buyers do not act in accordance with the standard established by the group, the group can apply social pressure to bring their behavior into conformity.

The family unit. Perhaps the single most important group influence for the consumption behavior of the individual is the family unit. Often, each family member has specific roles in the buying process. These roles usually vary, depending on the type of product being purchased. For example, children may be very influential in

Figure 3-4
Psychographic segments for males

Herman, the retiring homebody (26 percent)

Herman is past his prime and is not getting any younger. His attitudes and opinions on life, which are often in conflict with modern trends, have gelled. And he is resistant to change. He is old-fashioned and conservative. He was brought up on "motherhood and apple pie" and cherishes these values. Consequently he finds the attitudes of young people today disturbing. He realizes he cannot affect any change, and has withdrawn into a sheltered existence of his own within the confines of his home and its surroundings. Here he lives a measured life. He goes to church regularly, watches his diet, and lives frugally. He longs for the good old days and regrets that the world around him is changing.

Scott, the successful professional (21 percent)

Scott is a man who has everything going for him. He is well educated, cosmopolitan, the father of a young family, and is already established in his chosen profession. He lives a fast-paced active life and likes it. He is a man getting ahead in the world. He lives in or near an urban center and seems to like what a big city has to offer—culture, learning opportunities, and people. He also enjoys sports, the out-of-doors, and likes to keep physically fit. He is understandably happy with his life and comfortable in his lifestyle.

Fred, the frustrated factory worker (19 percent)

Fred is young. He married young and had a family. It is unlikely that he had any plans to get a college degree; if he did, he had to shelve them to find work to support his family. He now is a blue-collar worker having trouble making ends meet. He is discontented, and tends to feel that "they"—big business, government, society—are somehow responsible for his state. He finds escape in movies and in fantasies of foreign lands and cabins by quiet lakes. He likes to appear attractive to women, has an active libido, and likes to think he is a bit of a swinger.

Dale, the devoted family man (17 percent)

Dale is a wholesome guy with a penchant for country living. He is a blue-collar worker, with a high school education. The father of a relatively large family, he prefers a traditional marriage, with his wife at home taking care of the kids. His home and neighborhood are central in his life. He is an easygoing guy who leads an uncomplicated life. Neither worry nor skepticism are a part of him. He is relaxed and has a casual approach to many things. He is a happy, trusting soul who takes things as they are.

Ben, the self-made businessman (17 percent)

Ben is the epitome of a self-made man. He was probably not born wealthy, nor had he the benefit of higher education, but through hard work and shrewd risk-taking he has built himself a decent life. He has seen the system work. He believes if you work hard and play by the rules you will get your share (and perhaps some more). Therefore he cannot condone hippies

Figure 3-4 *(continued)*

and other fringe groups whom he sees as freeloaders. He embraces conservative ideology and is likely to be a champion of business interests. He is a traditionalist at home, and believes it is a woman's job to look after the home and to raise a family. He is gregarious and enjoys giving and attending parties. And he likes to drink.

Source: Reprinted from Sunil Mehrotra and William D. Wells, "Psychographics and Buyer Behavior: Theory and Recent Empirical Findings," in *Consumer and Industrial Buying Behavior*, ed. Arch G. Woodside, Jagdish N. Sheth, and Peter D. Bennett (New York: Elsevier-North Holland, 1977), pp. 54–55.

Figure 3-5

These are photographs of professional actors portraying the role of the typical consumer in three of the psychographic segments referred to in Figure 3-4.

cereal purchases but probably have little influence on purchases of automotive batteries. In the past, men assumed a "breadwinner role" and made purchase decisions concerning household items. These distinctions between the roles of men and women in a family are blurring now that more women are working and becoming heads of households.

Marital partners may assume different roles during the buying process. In one study, couples were asked a series of questions about the relative influence of the husband and wife on various aspects of the automobile and furniture purchases.[11] The results are shown in Table 3-5. From this study, it seems that husbands have more influence in purchasing an automobile, while wives have more

Table 3-5

Marital roles in selected automobile and furniture purchase decisions as perceived by wives and husbands (N = 97)

Who decided:	Patterns of influence (percent) as perceived by wives			Patterns of influence (percent) as perceived by husbands		
	Husband has more influence than wife	Husband and wife have equal influence	Wife has more influence than husband	Husband has more influence than wife	Husband and wife have equal influence	Wife has more influence than husband
When to buy the automobile?	68	30	2	68	29	3
Where to buy the automobile?	59	39	2	62	35	3
How much to spend for the automobile?	62	34	4	62	37	1
What make of automobile to buy?	50	50	—	60	32	8
What model of automobile to buy?	47	52	1	41	50	9
What color of automobile to buy?	25	63	12	25	50	25
How much to spend for furniture?	17	63	20	22	47	31
When to buy the furniture?	18	52	30	16	45	39
Where to buy the furniture?	6	61	33	7	53	40
What furniture to buy?	4	52	44	3	33	64
What style of furniture to buy?	2	45	53	2	26	72
What color and fabric to select?	2	24	74	2	16	82

Source: Harry L. Davis, "Dimensions of Marital Roles in Consumer Decision-Making," *Journal of Marketing Research,* May 1970, pp. 168-77.

---

[11] Harry Davis, "Dimensions of Marital Roles in Consumer Decision-Making," *Journal of Marketing Decision,* May 1970, pp. 168-77.

influence in purchasing furniture. However, within a product category, the influence over different aspects of the buying process varies. In furniture purchases, for example, husbands are most influential in initiating the buying process and in determining how much to spend. Wives are most influential in selecting fabrics and colors.

It is very important for salespeople to understand the roles performed by family members. This information can help salespeople to direct their presentation to the appropriate family members at the appropriate stages of the buying process.

Reference groups. The term *reference group* is used to indicate a group of people that an individual uses as "a point of reference" when making judgments. At one extreme, a reference group could be a small number of people in the individual's Bible study group. At the other extreme, a reference group could be a large aggregate of people, such as a political party, a union, a social class, or even a culture.

Reference groups have a substantial influence on consumers. For example, a physician's decision concerning the drug that he or she prescribes may be greatly influenced by the prescribing behavior of the physicians at a leading medical school. The impact of reference group influence is usually most significant for products that are consumed in a socially visible manner. Thus one would expect reference group influence to be greater for clothing than for mouthwash.

INFORMATION NEEDED ABOUT THE BUYER

In order to practice the marketing concept, salespeople must spend a lot of time collecting information about their customers. Instead of developing tricky appeals which may help make sales, good salespeople try to determine what the buyer's needs are. They attempt to obtain action by appealing to customer's needs only when they have made a proper investigation and have full confidence that the product will fulfill those needs. The previous discussion in this chapter indicates that salespeople should collect the following information about their prospects before launching into their presentation.

1. The timing of the purchase decision—the stage of the buying process that the consumer is in.
2. The consumer's performance beliefs—the information that the consumer has collected about the product.
3. The competition—the alternatives that the consumer is considering.
4. The importance of product characteristics—the consumer's needs related to the product.

5. The amount of information that the consumer possesses about the product and the consumer's level of perceived risk in making the purchase decision.
6. Characteristics of the consumer—demographics, socioeconomic characteristics, and personality traits.
7. Influences on the consumer—family roles and reference groups.

WHERE AND HOW TO GET INFORMATION ABOUT THE BUYER

Knowledge about a prospect or a customer is usually obtained over a period of time. First impressions may be quite erroneous. The job of learning about a customer is never-ending, and the good salesperson's ability to size up a customer improves with experience.

Some sources of customer information are discussed in the following paragraphs.

Observe and listen

In some fields of selling the salesperson has to gather customer information chiefly by observing the customer. Sizing up a customer may have to be done on a trial-and-error basis. The customer may give clues, however, as to the treatment expected, and the salesperson learns to recognize these clues through experience.

If the salesperson has no opportunity to gather facts about the customer in advance of the call, it becomes necessary to observe carefully. When calling upon a retail merchant, the following clues may help in sizing up the merchant and the business: the location and appearance of the store, the types of merchandise and the price lines displayed, the brand names featured, the window displays, the types of salesclerks, the selling methods, and the types of customer. In addition, some clues may be obtained by observing the merchant's mannerisms, methods of treating the sales staff, or actions when waiting on customers.

Given the opportunity, most people like to talk about themselves. The buyer, being interested in need satisfaction, is likely to make some wants known through conversation. The good salesperson will listen and will ask questions to bring out the buyer's motives.

In the course of conversation the prospect may say, "Our friends get so much more satisfaction out of their new refrigerator than we do from our old one," or, "Mr. Jones, who plays bridge with us, has a car just like this model." From this the salesperson may be able to conclude that pride of ownership, rivalry, or desire for recognition are dominant motives with this buyer.

The prospect may ask, "Does this car give good gas mileage?" or, "Are repairs expensive on this model?" These questions may indicate that the buyer's dominant need is economy.

The industrial buyer who is interested primarily in dependability or service features may ask, "How long does it take to get repair parts?" or, "Where is your nearest service department?"

Effective listening is an important skill that all salespeople must develop. Listening is an important part of the overall communication process. The lore of personal selling suggests that "if a salesperson was supposed to talk more than listen, he would have two mouths and one ear."

Ask questions

Obviously, the salesperson's opportunity to size up the buyer is enhanced by observing the buyer's reactions to the questions asked. If the proper questions are directed to a purchasing agent, they should yield information on such matters as the purchasing agent buyer's needs, ability to pay, and authority to buy. The conversation will give the salesperson an opportunity to ascertain the purchasing agent's attitude or frame of mind.

Use records

On each call, the salesperson should attempt to gather information about the prospect or customer. These data should be recorded. After a period of time, the information accumulated should serve as an excellent basis for evaluating the prospect or customer.

If possible, an accurate evaluation of a customer and his or her business should be made before the sales call. At least a tentative evaluation should be made, based on facts obtained up to that point.

Data about the customer which may be useful if properly recorded are: the size and frequency of past orders, the status of the customer's credit, the preferences shown for certain price lines, the nature of the company's correspondence with the customer, the adjustments made, the habits established, and the likes, dislikes, and peculiarities evidenced. Companies usually provide their sales representatives with all of the available data on each customer.

Read sales manuals and training materials

Some companies supply their salespeople with sales manuals describing various types of customers and accounts. Such manuals are valuable because the material presented is usually the result of the accumulated experiences with users of the company's products. The manuals include facts about the company's customers which the salesperson could gather only through many years of experience. For example, the manuals will list the common needs of purchasing agents, government representatives, large retail merchants, and various executives of large corporations.

Large retail organizations supply materials on new merchandise and suggestions for selling it. Specific suggestions are given on how to sell various types of customers. Organized discussions may take place at regular or special department meetings. In addition, store training departments may post information sheets on employee bulletin boards.

Obtain experience

There is probably no substitute for experience as a method for learning about people. Good salespeople are students of human nature. They observe people and their reactions whenever the opportunity presents itself. Salespeople soon learn that the reactions of people are endlessly varied; but they also learn that certain habits and reaction patterns are repeated in many customers. While each selling situation is somewhat different, certain similarities will be recognized.

THE SELLING PROCESS

Figure 3–6

The selling and buying processes

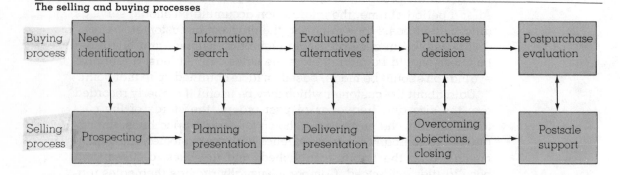

In order to accomplish their objectives, salespeople must move buyers through the five stages of the buying process. Thus, the stages in the selling process are clearly related to the stages in the buying process. This parallel between the selling process and the buying process is shown in Figure 3–6.

Prospecting is the first stage in the selling process. At this stage, salespeople locate customers who have needs that can be satisfied by their products. In some cases, the salespeople have to collect information about the customer, determine that their product will benefit the customer, and then demonstrate how the product satisfies a need that may be unrecognized by the customer. Information about how to identify a good prospect, how and where to locate prospects, and how to get the most out of prospects is presented in Chapter 7, Prospecting and Getting the Right Start.

After identifying potential customers, the salespeople assemble information that the potential customers can use during their search phase. This preparation stage is completed when salespeople have collected all the information they will need to make a sales presentation. They have also provided their customers with enough information to complete an information search. Chapter 8, Planning and Delivering the Sales Presentation, is devoted to this stage.

Having set the stage, the salesperson must make an effective sales presentation. The presentation must cause the prospect to understand, believe, and remember the message. Activities to achieve these goals are discussed in Chapter 9, Dramatizing the Sales Presentation.

During and after delivering the presentation, the salesperson should monitor the customer's reactions, identify the customer's objections and present additional information to overcome those objections. This stage of the selling process is discussed in Chapter 10, Overcoming Objections.

After overcoming the prospect's objections, the salesperson must ask for the order. This crucial aspect of selling is discussed in Chapter 11, Closing the Sale.

Finally, the salesperson must perform postsales functions to insure repeat purchases from the customer and favorable word of mouth. These functions are the subject of Chapter 13, Building Future Sales by Improving Customer Relations.

THE SALESPERSON AS A MINI-MARKETING MANAGER

The steps in the selling process outlined in Figure 3–6 suggest that the salesperson and the marketing manager are alike in a number of ways. Both the salesperson and the marketing manager practice and marketing concept. Marketing managers use their past experience plus specific market research to develop information about the needs of each market segment—each group of consumers. Similarly, salespeople use their past experience plus information collected during the sales interview to determine the needs of their customers.

Both the salesperson and the marketing manager use this information to promote the sale of products. Salespeople make their presentations in face-to-face interactions with their customers. Marketing managers have a variety of means for delivering messages to customers—media advertising, direct mail, and salespeople.

The differences in the quality and the level of the information that salespeople and marketing managers have about their customers affects their influence on purchase decisions. Marketing managers use sophisticated market research techniques, while salespeople use intuitive "market research" methods. But salespeople are able to gather information directly from each individual. Thus they can develop and use the most effective presentations possible for each of their customers. They can monitor the customer's reactions to the sales presentation and make adjustments as they go along.

In contrast, marketing managers must group customers into segments in order to communicate with them efficiently. Although marketing managers collect information more systematically than salespeople do, their information about customers is indirect, filtered by the market research process. They possess abstract description of "typical" customers rather than descriptions of individual customers. Their "presentations" are based on these typical customers. Thus, their communications will be most effective for a small group of customers who resemble the typical customer. Because it takes a good deal of time to monitor customers' reactions to their communications, marketing managers find it difficult to make strategic adjustments based on customer feedback.

Thus salespeople are in an excellent position to practice the marketing concept and to reap its benefits.

QUESTIONS AND PROBLEMS

1. Using Maslow's hierarchy of needs, shown in Figure 3-2, write five statements, one for each group of needs, which could be used by a salesperson to sell a $100 fishing rod.

2. Analyze in detail all the decision steps that you went through the last time you purchased a suit. How do those steps correspond to the five buying stages shown in Figure 3-1?

3. People do things for their reasons, not ours. Do you agree? What are the implications for the salesperson?

4. List psychological dimensions that people would consider when making the following decisions:

   a. Enlisting in the armed forces.

   b. Buying a stereo.

   c. Renting an apartment.

   d. Buying a house.

   e. Buying a calculator.

   How would the importance placed on the dimensions considered in buying a house vary for different groups of consumers?

5. You are a salesperson in a large department store, working in the toy department for the holidays. A customer approaches you and says, "I'd like to buy a toy as a present for my child." What questions would you ask to help the customer reach a buying decision?

6. You have acquired the franchise to sell a portable all-stainless steel home water distiller. The suggested retail price is $135. Why would anyone want a unit that purifies water? Prepare some statements that you might use to appeal to a potential buyer.

7. A new problem in human experience has appeared in our Western world—the rapidly growing proportion of older people in our population. On the whole, however, our society is organized to satisfy the wants of the young, and makes relatively little provision for meeting the needs of the aged.

    The wants of life differ at various stages of life's journey. The young want employment, knowledge, power, honor, and fame. They also have civil, spiritual, and aesthetic wants.

    Identify and discuss the wants and needs of our older population.

8. What are the characteristics of an extroverted person? Of an introverted person? How would you determine whether a person was extroverted or introverted? What differences would this make in your sales presentation?

9. What purchases are most affected by social class? Least affected?

10. For what reasons might a consumer switch from a routine purchase behavior to an extensive problem-solving behavior? As a salesperson, what would you do to alter a consumer's purchase behavior if the consumer was not purchasing your product?

11. In the chapter, it was suggested that salespeople would sell better if they spent less time talking and more time listening. How might salespeople be trained to be good listeners?

12. Assume that as a manufacturer's salesperson you are selling various types of office equipment to dealers? The dealers sell the equipment to business firms. Would you be more successful in the eyes of your firm if you stocked all your dealers to the hilt or if you helped your dealers keep the pipeline clear? Would there be a difference between the short-run and the long-run effects of these two approaches? Why? How could you as a salesperson help the dealers keep their stock moving to their business customers?

PROJECTS

1. Conduct a survey on your campus to determine why college students buy, what they buy, and where they buy. Select one line of goods, such as clothing, cars, sporting goods, books, or gasoline. Summarize your findings, and write up your conclusions.

2. Develop a plan to help you increase your ability to remember names. Use the plan for two weeks, and then write up your conclusions.

3. Talk with a salesperson about a significant sale in which he or she is now involved or has just completed. Use the material in the chapter to understand the situation—both the buying process and the selling process. Describe how that material is helpful in understanding the situation. Also, discuss the limitations of the chapter material.

4. Develop a paper on the college student market. Compare the buying habits and student characteristics of 1970 with those of the current year. Summarize the differences that you find, and state the implications of your findings.

CASE PROBLEMS

Case 3-1

SBS, Inc.

Joe Foote secured a job in direct-sales work, and after a few months he was made a supervisor. He engaged in some selling; but his main task was to hire, train, and supervise his salesforce.

This type of experience, he believed, was valuable in preparing him for saleswork in a different phase of the distribution process. The contacts he made in direct-sales work provided him with a background which was considered desirable in selling office machines, office systems, and office supplies. A large national manufacturer of office machines offered him a job as its sales representative.

Joe decided to accept the job. His progress was slow at first, but he gradually developed selling techniques which enabled him to become a top producer in his class of territory. After spending four years with the company, Joe decided that he would like to operate a business of his own. In direct-sales work and in his work as a company sales representative for the office machines company, Joe observed that there was great opportunity for well-trained salespeople to be of service to businesses and to individual customers. His experience had taught him that too few salespeople took the time to try to understand the customer. He believed he could start in a small way and be of real service to small businesses by setting up tailored business systems and by developing sales promotion programs. Joe organized his own company, which he called, SBS, Inc., for small business systems.

His plan was to contact small business owners and to study their systems problems. The setting up of cash records, accounts receivable and accounts payable records, inventory control records, and credit records was typical of the services to be rendered. In addition, as opportunities presented themselves, Joe planned to help such business owners develop sales promotion plans. This would help them plan sales, move slow-turning merchandise, secure maximum results from advertising campaigns, and obtain desirable results from point-of-purchase displays.

Joe felt that his business would succeed if he could develop some clear-cut method of customer analysis. He was aware that there were advocates of many different systems for building a sales presentation to meet the needs of the prospect.

Joe decided to develop a system of analyzing customers which he could use immediately and which he could eventually teach to his new salespeople as his business grew and prospered. Joe felt that the following three-step system would provide a neat, practical way of sizing up prospects so that the sales approach could be modified and adjusted to fit the needs of each individual:

1. The salesperson should determine how much technical information the prospect had about business operations.
2. The salesperson should evaluate the prospect's ability to grasp and absorb ideas; that is, the salesperson should learn whether the prospect reasoned objectively from the facts presented.
3. The salesperson should determine the buyer's temperament, frame of mind, and moods as they affected the buyer's daily reactions.

Questions

1. What is your reaction to Joe's three-step procedure for making the sales interview flexible? Discuss the desirability of preparing such a plan.
2. Analyze each step, and give several illustrations of how it could be of help in selling more effectively. What specific information should be sought? How could the desired information be secured?

Case 3–2

Casual Clothes, Inc.

Casual Clothes' sales are made directly to more than 1,700 department stores and women's apparel stores through sales offices throughout the United States. Its products include blouses, skirts, sweaters, jackets, shorts, and pants.

Sales representatives are hired who have a real interest in merchandising women's wear. The organization believes in choosing its sales representatives carefully, and after two years of successful experience in the company's regional showrooms, they are assigned specific territories. They are expected to spend considerable time with the buyers and merchandise managers, especially in large department stores and large specialty shops. They are expected to act as sales promotion consultants as well as to secure orders for the company's products.

It is not unusual for the sales representatives to help set up point-of-purchase displays, suggest appropriate window displays, recommend the appropriate size inventory and encourage proper inventory control, train salesclerks, interview retail customers, and engage in some market research activities.

Rather detailed market reports are filed by the sales representatives at frequent intervals.

During the past several months, and from rather scattered geographic locations, sales representatives have intimated that it may be profitable to consider broadening the company's market by making a special appeal to teenagers. They observed that competitors seemed to be successful in selling to both the women's and the teenagers' markets if an intelligent job were done in recognizing the differences in the appeals to the two groups of consumers. The addition of the jackets, shorts, and pants to the company's product lines had come about because of reports which had originated from sales representatives in the Los Angeles area, and hence the company decided that the current recommendations warranted some investigation.

Jay Blow, the sales manager, reviewed the qualifications and performance of the better sales representatives in the organization and decided to assign Paul Wind, sales representative in the Chicago area, to the task of securing additional data on the teenage market. Wind had a flair for writing and was known as a capable salesman who had maintained a close touch with consumers in his area. Wind also had a good background of education and sales experience and enjoyed gathering and interpreting data. He was assigned to the principal offices in Cleveland and was instructed to spend full time during the slack season preparing the report.

Questions

1. What data do you believe Wind should assemble to describe the potential of the teenage market? Analyze and discuss the findings.
2. How do teenagers today differ from the teenagers of 10 or 15 years ago?
3. How do the buying habits of teenagers differ from those of middle-aged women?

4. How do the psychological characteristics that affect spending generally differ between people who belong to the country's middle social class and those who belong to the country's lower social class?

Case 3–3

Buying a mobile home

Shirley and Ray White were thinking about buying a mobile home for use on weekends and vacations. Both Shirley and Ray spent a lot of time on their jobs. They felt that they were not spending enough time with their children, Chris and Carol. Taking family trips in the mobile home would bring the whole family together. One weekend, the entire family visited a large mobile home dealer in Campbell. They approached a salesman seated in the dealer's office.

Ray: Good morning. We're interested in learning more about mobile homes. Can you help us?

Salesman: You've come to the right place. We sell more mobile homes than any dealership in Arizona. I've got some paperwork to fill out on the home I just sold. I am sure we have a model for you. Why don't you walk around the lot and see what you like. Here are some brochures.

Shirley *(walking out the door):* He doesn't seem very interested in us.

Ray: I guess that's a soft-sell approach. Let's look at that brown and white over there. It looks like the right size.

Carol *(inside the third home they had looked at):* Look. This one has a TV. That's fantastic. Dad, how does the TV work in a mobile home?

Ray: I guess it works off batteries. I really don't know how you get all the appliances working when you stop overnight. I hope it's not too complicated to hook up.

Shirley: This really has everything—shower, refrigerator, stove. Looks like there's plenty of room for cooking and eating meals. How do you think the stove works?

Ray: Probably natural gas. I wonder how long a tank of natural gas lasts. I hope you don't have to fill it up all the time.

Salesman *(entering mobile home):* Well, how do you like this one? We really have a good deal on this model. It's usually $15,000, but it's reduced to $14,000 this month.

Shirley: Where do you sleep in this one? How many can sleep in it?

Salesman: You can squeeze in six people, I think. The bed folds down there and there. By the way, we are also giving a full tank of gas with a purchase. That's 50 gallons.

Ray: This home is really big. I bet it's difficult to drive.

Salesman: No. It's a breeze. Have you ever driven a truck?

Ray: No!

Salesman: Oh! Don't worry. You'll get used to it. By the way, this model is really economical to run. It gets ten miles to the gallon. Most mobile homes get only eight.

Ray: I just don't think we're ready for a mobile home yet. I guess we'll just stay in motels on our trips.

Salesman: You really should consider this model more. You can save a lot of money on vacation with a mobile home. No motel costs. Do your own cooking. No restaurants.

Ray: Well, we'll think about it. Thanks for your time.

Questions

1.   What does each member of the family want in the mobile home?
2.   Did the salesman know what the family wanted?
3.   Was the salesman a good listener?
4.   What questions would you have asked if you were selling the mobile home?
5.   Rewrite this interaction as it would have occurred if you were the salesperson.

SELECTED REFERENCES

Belk, Russell. "Structural Variables and Consumer Behavior." *Journal of Consumer Research*, December 1975, pp. 157-64.

Haley, Russell. "Benefit Segmentation: A Decision-Oriented Research Tool." *Journal of Marketing*, July 1968, pp. 30-35.

Hansen, Flemming. "Psychological Theories of Consumer Choice." *Journal of Consumer Research*, December 1976, pp. 117-42.

Kotler, Philip. "Behavioral Models for Analyzing Buyers." *Journal of Marketing*, October 1965, pp. 37-45.

McGuire, William. "Some Internal Psychological Factors Influencing Consumer Choice." *Journal of Consumer Research*, March 1976, pp. 302-19.

Phillips, Lynn, and **Sternthal, Brian.** "Age Differences in Information Processing: A Perspective on the Aged Consumer." *Journal of Marketing Research*, November 1971, p. 444-56.

Schewe, Charles D. "Selected Social Psychological Models for Analyzing Buyers." *Journal of Marketing*, July 1973, pp. 31-39.

Weitz, Barton. "Relationship between Salesperson Performance and Understanding Customer Decision Making." *Journal of Marketing Research*, November 1978, pp. 501-10.

Wells, William, and **Tigert, Douglas.** "Attitudes, Interests, and Opinions." *Journal of Advertising Research*, August 1971, pp. 29-39.

Witt, Robert and **Bruce, Grady.** "Purchase Decisions and Group Influence." *Journal of Marketing Research*, November 1970, pp. 533-35.

Chapter 4

THE COMPANY, ITS PRODUCTS, AND ITS COMPETITION

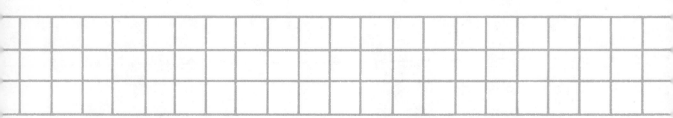

Modern selling is based upon facts. The salesperson cannot depend upon fast talking, a pleasing personality, and a bag of tricks to produce volume and profitable sales.

A thorough knowledge of the buyer's motives, characteristics, and behavior prepares the salesperson who is thoroughly grounded in factual information about the company, the products, and its competition to represent the company effectively.

WHY IS KNOWLEDGE SO IMPORTANT?

Sales production is directly related to the knowledge which the salesperson possesses. As the primary job is to secure orders, any

knowledge that enhances ability to accomplish this task should be
given constant attention. This knowledge will be the basis for supplying customers with the appropriate facts for meeting competitive
claims and for developing a reputation of earning the confidence of
the customer. This knowledge will also give the salesperson confidence and enthusiasm.

Customers demand facts

In most cases, the good salesperson's advice and counsel are requested and the statements of the salesperson are interpreted by the
buyer as those of an expert—an authority. Customers are demanding more and more information about the products they buy. Good
salespeople will have sufficient ammunition to satisfy the needs of
the most demanding types of buyers.

Facts needed to meet competition

Salespeople must know their company and its products to sell
effectively, or competition will force them out of the market. If the
salesperson is unable to explain the merits or construction of a product, there is always a competing sales representative who is eager
and willing to supply another product and to give the buyer all the
facts pertaining to it. Most buyers know they have a choice when
they plan to buy. They want information on how one company's
products or services compare with another's.

As competition becomes greater in many fields, as inventions appear upon the market, and as companies attempt to render greater
and more varied services, products and services become more complex. This condition has caused many sales managers to place
greater emphasis upon the development of well-informed salespeople.

Salespeople who have prepared themselves with full knowledge
of their company, its products, and competitive products do not fear
competition—*they welcome it*. They know that they have the answers.

Buyer has confidence in a well-informed sales representative

The salesperson's job is to supply information which will enable
the buyer to profit from the purchase of the product or service. This in
turn, will earn the buyer's confidence, and a solid business relationship will result.

Even more important to the success of the salesperson's activities is the ability to earn the confidence of the buyer. Later this confidence, established in one area, can be used to reinforce statements made in another area. For example, if salespeople quote interesting and pertinent facts about the company's growth, or the origin of its trademark, they are likely to be evaluated as people who "know what they are talking about." Then, when additional facts about the company's product or about competitive conditions are quoted, the buyer is likely to believe these facts because of the confidence previously established. It is not sufficient to quote facts about the company and its products—these facts must be *believed* by the customer.

Knowledge develops personal confidence

In addition to making selling easier, a thorough background of product and company information enables salespeople to acquire confidence in themselves and their company; it helps to develop a sense of loyalty and a feeling of being a member of a team. A sustained interest in any field is dependent upon a thorough understanding of "what makes the company go" and what company policies are. Enthusiasm and interest cannot be developed if the salesperson has only meager information.

Salespeople must sincerely believe that they have a service or a product which will benefit the user. Knowledge is the basis for this belief. They can have little self-confidence unless they have thoroughly explored the merits of their products or services and those of their leading competitors.

WHAT SPECIFIC INFORMATION IS NEEDED?

The amount and kind of information a salesperson may have to acquire about the company, its products, and its competition will depend on the kind of selling performed, the nature of the product, the characteristics of the customers, and the complexity of the company's organization. In some large companies a long period of on-the-job training and experience in selling are necessary to gain a working knowledge of company information. In some small companies, on the other hand, the salesperson will be expected to secure the information on an informal basis over a period of years.

Company information

The salesperson *is* the company to the buyers. Most company officers have little chance of becoming personally acquainted with the users of company products. The company's name and its reputation will stand or fall on the kind of representation it receives from its salespeople.

Growth and development.   Company histories make interesting reading which salespeople will find useful in their work. Sometimes the biography of a famous man tells the story of a company's development.[1]

Company training manuals usually include the following historical items: when the company was founded, who founded it, why it was founded, the size of the early plants, the principles upon which the company was founded, early experiences in financing and selling, new products and when they were added, the origin of any trademarks or trade names, the expansion that has taken place, and personnel who were responsible for the company's growth.

In many fields of selling, a company can attain an advantage over its competitors by pointing out, for example, that it ranks first in industry sales, plant size, or capital assets. Each company analyzes its competitive position for the purpose of determining the areas of activity in which the company outranks its competitors.

The alert sales representative uses facts about the company's competitive position. The customer may say: "I'm satisfied with my present products. I see no reason for making a change." An effective answer to this comment may be: "Company X is an excellent company. Our company, however, sold three times as many units in 1980 as our nearest competitor. The consumer wants our product. This is shown by a recent survey which shows that our product was requested, by trade name, more than any competing product. Let me show you what this means to you."

Whether the salesperson sells insurance, machines, paints, tools, or other products or services, there will be abundant material in company records to strengthen the sales presentation.

Organization, personnel, policies, and procedures.   Many companies prepare organization charts to show lines of responsibility and authority within their organizations. The completing of the customer's order is dependent upon the activities of many departments in addition to the sales department. The order must be processed by the credit department, the accounting department, and the traffic department, and it may require the attention of other departments. The salesperson should know the routine every order must follow, and who is responsible for each activity in the routine. The salesperson can then make the proper contacts to expedite an order, and explain any situation which involves delay in shipping an order or in adjusting a complaint.

Some companies have relied heavily on outstanding personnel to

---

[1] See articles in *Fortune* and *Forbes* for interesting and informative material on the growth and development of companies.

promote their industry position. They may be inventors, fashion experts, or business leaders. Their names can be used effectively by sales representatives.

To insure uniform action throughout a company, policies may be designed to control channels of distribution, terms of resale, percentage of company profits, methods of financing, treatment of competition, advertising and sales promotion, guarantee on company products, and so on. Any company which is built on a sound philosophy is anxious to perpetuate those actions which will contribute to its long-term success. Therefore, policies are determined in order to guide the action of company personnel. The salesperson must contribute by learning and following company policies.

In a recent *Purchasing* magazine survey of 1,000 U.S. industrial companies' many buyers complained that sales representatives did not know enough about their company policies. Some buyers accused companies of being secretive about their policies with *both* the sales representatives and the customers![2]

The customer may request 90-day terms—the company policy may be 60 days. The customer may request permission to return merchandise within 30 days after it has been received—the company policy may be to limit the return period to 10 days or not to permit the return of any goods after they have been accepted. Such situations require the salesperson to be able to apply company business policies.

Production and service facilities. The salesperson may need a knowledge of plant capacity, production schedules, and other relevant data. Products are of little value to customers unless they can be delivered in appropriate quantities at the times they are needed.

The buyer is often inclined to look to the company's extra services as a basis for buying. The buyer may reason, "If all brands are about equal in construction and performance, what else does this company offer to encourage me to sell its particular product?"

Some companies will help new dealers to determine the proper locations for their stores, to plan store layouts and select store fixtures, to start hiring and training programs, to sell the product, and to maintain necessary records. If a sales representative can say, "We have trained personnel, who are available on call, to service our machines," another selling point may be added to the sales talk.

Additional services, such as supplying advertising pieces, shipping orders from strategically located branches or warehouses, and conducting research studies for customers, lend additional strength to the sales presentation.

---

[2] "The Industrial Salesman: Industrious, but Is He Believable?" *Sales Management*, January 12, 1976, p. 82.

Price, discount, and credit practices. These important topics are covered fully in Chapter 5. At this point, however, it is necessary, to emphasize the relationship between production costs and prices.

While the average salesperson is not expected to have an accountant's command of production costs, a few pertinent figures on changes in costs may be useful. The buyer, of course, is interested only in what these figures mean in relation to the price to be paid.

Company products

One sales representative comments as follows: "I learned early that effectiveness in sales has to start with a thorough knowledge of your own company and *all* of its products. Not just superficial knowledge but knowledge in depth and knowledge about your newest product as well as the old standbys."

An F. W. Dodge Co. survey of 813 of the nation's busiest architects indicated that the architects believed sales representatives could improve their performance by having "better product knowledge." This was the suggestion offered most frequently. In the *Purchasing* survey mentioned above, the buyers rated "knowledge of the product line" as the most important attribute of a good sales representative.[3]

How will products meet the buyer's needs? The proverbial little old lady in tennis shoes, who uses her automobile to run errands in the village, certainly does not need the same kind of tires as the sports fan or the traveling sales representative. The first job, then, is to find out what the buyer's specific needs or interests may be. The second job is to supply the appropriate product information to satisfy these needs.

One field sales manager criticized his sales representatives by saying, "You have what I call the 'salesman's curse': you know your product better than you know how your customers' businesses can use it."[4] This sales manager insists that his representatives must know, among other things, how the *customer's* customers make their buying decisions—how they decide to buy between the customer and the customer's competitors.

The customer's most direct interest in any product is in what it will do. What the product will do is determined by how it is used. It is important that the product be used correctly—in the manner for which it was manufactured. Otherwise, unjustified claims can be expected. The good salesperson, then, must not only inform the buyer of the uses for which the product has been designed, but also of the possibility that the product may be used incorrectly. (See Figure 4-1 for a helpful analysis of a paper product.)

---

[3] Ibid., p. 82.

[4] Mack Hanan, "The Three C's of Selling: A Sure Cure for the 'Salesman's Curse,'" *Sales & Marketing Management*, May 10, 1976, pp. 70-72.

Figure 4-1
Product benefits

Article	Grade used	Reason for use of AirCap	Packing materials replaced
Retail gift items	C-120, TH-120, D-120	Freedom from lint, aesthetic appeal, lightness in weight, transparency	Excelsior, shredded newsprint, cellulosic wadding
Adding machines	D-240	AirCap used as pad on bottom and top of box reduced material costs and breakage	Rubberized hair
Gauges	C-120, D-120	Freedom from lint, lightness in weight, reduced breakage, reduced packaging costs	Cellulosic wadding
Repaired cameras	C-120, D-120	Lint-free, light weight, reduced packing costs through labor savings and smaller containers required, more effective cushioning, reduced breakage	Excelsior, cellulosic wadding, polyethylene bags
Industrial ceramics	C-120, D-120	Extreme flexibility of AirCap, affording use of a single material for packaging many varied shapes, lightness in weight, effective cushioning, reduced packaging costs through labor savings	Newspaper, cellulosic wadding, excelsior
Printed circuit boards	C-120	Freedom from lint, transparency, lightness in weight, more effective cushioning	Polyethylene bags, cellulosic wadding, excelsior pads, corrugated diecuts
Dentures	C-120, TH-120	Freedom from lint, cleanliness, reduced loss of chipped dentures being returned for repair	Cotton

Courtesy of Zellerbach Paper Company

A bulletin supplied to sales representatives for a paper products company explains the reasons for introducing a packing supply called AirCap. The chart shows the type of article, the grade used, what packing materials are being replaced, and the reasons for using AirCap.

The well-trained salesperson is ready with complete knowledge of how the product can benefit the buyer, and that portion of the information is used which is of interest to specific customers.

How are products made? Certain types of buyers may be interested in detailed information about the manufacture of a man's suit. A sophisticated buyer may feel that the job of retailing is easier if information is secured on how the raw wool is processed, how the yarn is prepared, how the fabric is woven, and how the fabric is finished before being made into a suit. The same buyer may be interested in the cutting, sewing, and styling of the suit. Other buyers of the same product may be satisfied that the company name is sufficient to sell the suit.

A car salesperson may want to explain how certain features in the construction of the company's car create greater safety, economy, or convenience for the driver.

Prospects are interested in whether cars have safety glass;

whether hardware tools such as hammers have hickory handles; whether shoes are lined with leather; whether tires or tubes are made of synthetic rubber or natural rubber; and whether power-saw blades are made of tempered steel.

Whether one is selling spark plugs, machine tools, or rifles, only a thorough background of manufacturing or processing information will permit a most effective job.

What service do products need? Any mechanical product will need service of some kind. The purchasers of stocks and bonds or life insurance will expect their investments to be serviced to take care of changing needs or to compensate for changes in economic conditions. Retail dealers expect varying amounts of service from dealer salespeople.

The buyers of such products as typewriters, dictating and transcribing machines, copying machines, and other office machines expect accessible, expert, dependable service. The salesperson must know what services the company is prepared to offer and what the terms and costs will be. The company which can supply dependable, fast service for the users is likely to have an edge on its competitors.

Purchasers of industrial equipment are vitally interested in service. Efficient servicing insures the manufacturer against costly shutdowns of production lines. A food-processing firm cannot wait for service on food machinery which is currently being used to process perishable fruits or vegetables. Nor can the farmer or the trucker afford a delay in the servicing of equipment—time lost means money lost.

In the competition for top salesperson conducted by *Purchasing* in 1978, the winners chosen were selected because of their exceptional efforts to serve the buyer. Among the examples given of services rendered by salespeople were the following: "One salesperson hired a U-Haul and drove all night to keep a customer's plant running." "Digs into *Federal Register* to assess impact of government regulations on his accounts. Came up with uniform unloading procedure that minimizes customer's problems in unloading materials." "Supervises tests in customers' plants—even at 2:00 A.M. Went to bat for buyers to solve winter freeze-up problems."[5] A service-oriented attitude is important, and it can enable the salesperson to solve buyers' problems at any hour of the day.

Some manufacturers operate local service centers, and such centers can be a potent factor in helping to close a sale. Other manufacturers have factory representatives who are available to service their

---

[5] Somerby Dowst, "Top Salesmen Deliver Service, Expertise," *Purchasing*, August 23, 1978, pp. 48 and 50.

accounts. Certified trained service people are becoming a familiar part of the merchandising program of many organizations.

If two competing products will fill the needs of a buyer, the better service program is likely to be the deciding factor when the buyer makes his or her choice.

Are there related products. To those buyers who have successfully used one product of a company, the mere mention that another product is one of the company's family of products may be sufficient to close the sale. It is urgent that the salesperson take advantage of the company's good reputation by making certain that the customer knows where the current product fits into the company's line.

A thorough knowledge of related company products will also help increase sales. If salespeople know that one of their company's products, say adhesive tape, is accompanied by many useful related products—bandages, cotton, and the like—they are in a position to increase their total volume of sales. It is essential that the salesperson know how each of the company's related products will fill a need of the buyer.

Competition

Every product has features which distinguish it from products of the competitors.

Boat salespeople must know how their boat compares with the boats produced by the competition for purposes of water skiing, fishing, racing, picnicking, or just cruising. In addition, they may have to compare their boat on such features as safety and construction, as well as be able to discuss the relative merits of wood, aluminum, cement, and plastics. They may also require detailed comparative data on motor horsepower, gearshifts, electric starters, and remote steering controls.

If a salesperson is selling tractors, comparative data may be needed on such important points as price, service, engine performance, operating and upkeep costs, and ease of maintenance.

Salespeople who are selling dictating and transcribing equipment will probably gather competitive information on the ease of operation, convenience in use, size or compactness, versatility, and dependability of the equipment.

Table 4-1 shows how one large corporation provides a comparison with competition when submitting a written proposal to a prospect.

Salespeople can expect competition in the future to be tough. Laboratories are spewing forth new developments at an unprecedented rate. Consumers are more mobile, more sophisticated than ever, and their most deeply entrenched tastes will be changing.

Buyers are interested in the competitive features of a product only

Table 4-1

Comparison of product features

Features comparison		
Feature	*Present copier*	*Proposed system*
Speed		
Rated speed	10 per minute	40 per minute
Warm-up	None	None
First copy	15 seconds	8 seconds
Flexibility		
Copy on:		
1. Plain cut-sheet bond paper	No	Yes
2. Digital letterhead	No	Yes
3. Gummed labels	No	Yes
4. Transparencies	No	Yes
5. Colored stock	No	Yes
6. Copying bond volumes	Only for volumes up to one-inch thick	Yes, books of any thickness
7. Copying on both sides of paper	No	Yes
Capacities		
1. Paper tray capacity	625 8½ × 11 copies per roll	2,000 sheets
2. Toner capacity	16,000 copies	16,000 copies
3. Productivity*	10 copies per minute; manual feeding and manual sorting	40 copies per minute; automatically feeds originals and sorts finished copies

* Productivity refers to personnel who have increased their output by doing unproductive chores (copying, sorting, changing originals) much more rapidly and then returned to their more productive duties.

Courtesy of Xerox Corporation

to the extent that these features will benefit them. It is not enough to know that a product is novel and different; the differences must be translated into advantages to the user. For example, the airline companies which sell airfreight sell this method of transportation in terms of what it will mean to the shipper. Obviously, speed is of the essence with airfreight. What does this mean to the shipper? It means profits from extra value and extra sales when perishable products are involved; it means more sales and increased company prestige when fashion goods are involved; it means extra sales when newspaper distribution is involved.

For some buyers, price is all-important; for others, service is the primary requirement; and for still others, quality will outweigh price and service.

The salesperson's job in meeting competition is to answer claims which are made by competitors. This task cannot be performed without a complete knowledge of competitive products.[6]

WHERE AND HOW IS INFORMATION SECURED?

CABINET FULL OF COMPETITION'S LITERATURE.

There is no dearth of facts about the company, its products, and its competitors' products. A continuous, well-organized plan for collecting material will keep a salesperson abreast of all new developments.

Information about the company and its products

Information about the company and its products is available from the following sources: work experience, sales training programs, company sales and service manuals, sales meetings and conventions, plant visits, research and testing department bulletins, company employees, company publications and handbooks, company advertising and sales literature, trade association magazines and reports, labels on products or their containers, and customers.

In many of the larger, well-organized corporations, where formal training is considered an important activity, much of the necessary information about the company and its products will be presented during training. Some companies also require their trainees to spend 90 days or more in purchasing operations.

Salespeople, however, cannot learn all they need to know from a training program or from any one source. Learning about the company and its products is a continuous activity—*the process never ends.* Figure 4-2 shows a product analysis in terms of benefits to the buyer.

Most companies use refresher courses, sales conferences, bulletins, and other devices to keep their experienced sales representatives up to date. In addition to the organized training programs prepared by the companies, salespeople are expected to use initiative in adding to their supply of product information. They may insure themselves of a full and complete body of facts by reading association magazines and reports, by observing customers' experiences, and by conversing with company employees. Some companies prepare manuals or handbooks which have information about the company, and sales representatives are expected to keep these publications for ready reference.

The company's annual report provides such information as the

---

[6] For an interesting story on competition between two minicomputer firms, see Bro Uttal, "The Gentlemen and the Upstarts Meet in a Great Mini Battle," *Fortune*, April 23, 1979, pp. 98–108.

Figure 4-2
Selling product benefits

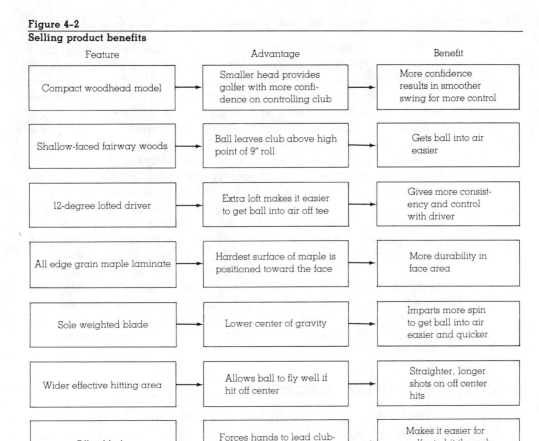

Feature	Advantage	Benefit
Compact woodhead model	Smaller head provides golfer with more confidence on controlling club	More confidence results in smoother swing for more control
Shallow-faced fairway woods	Ball leaves club above high point of 9" roll	Gets ball into air easier
12-degree lofted driver	Extra loft makes it easier to get ball into air off tee	Gives more consistency and control with driver
All edge grain maple laminate	Hardest surface of maple is positioned toward the face	More durability in face area
Sole weighted blade	Lower center of gravity	Imparts more spin to get ball into air easier and quicker
Wider effective hitting area	Allows ball to fly well if hit off center	Straighter, longer shots on off center hits
Offset blade	Forces hands to lead club-head into the shot	Makes it easier for golfer to hit through shot

MacGregor recently advertised its Tourney golf clubs in a manner which effectively showed the clubs' *features*, *advantages*, and *benefits*. A portion of this advertisement illustrates how products should be sold in terms of customer benefits.

I'LL NEVER SEE! THE ANNUAL REPORT.

names of the board of directors, the names of members of the executive committee, the names and titles of the company's officers, and a report on business activities for the past year, as well as a comment on what the future may hold. The report of business activities usually includes such topics as improvement and expansion programs, new plant facilities, product improvements, product demand, current markets, scientific developments, service and supplies, sales and service training, advertising, employee relations, wages and employment, employee welfare, personnel changes, finances, earnings, and future plans. The information in the annual reports is usually condensed and is easily understood. Therefore, this is an excellent source to use.

Information about competitors and their products

Information about competitors' products may be obtained from competitive advertising and sales literature, trade association magazines and reports, company research and testing department bulletins, sales meetings and conventions, customers' experiences with competitive products, and claims of competitive salespeople. Independent laboratories may be sources of competitive data. Material can usually be obtained from testing companies for a fee.

Probably one of the best and most direct ways to gather needed data is to question users of competitive products. Find out what has sold them on the products. If a little initiative is used, observation will also pay dividends. By observing empty containers, it is easy to identify the company's chief competitor; or in a dealer's store, one may observe display advertising, listen to the sales talk of the retail salesperson, or investigate the products on the dealer's shelves.

In some fields of selling, it may be helpful to "shop" (buy or price competing goods or services) at the outlets of competitors to learn the sales features of their products. If the article involved is inexpensive, the salesperson may wish to buy it and to test it in order to have firsthand information that can be used if comparisons become necessary.

HOW TO USE INFORMATION SUCCESSFULLY

Knowledge alone is insufficient to guarantee success. While knowledge is essential, the intelligent and skillful use of knowledge differentiates the average from the superior salesperson. The individual who plans to play golf, for example, can acquire all of the information available about *how* to play golf, but without *practice* he or she will never be able to win a golf tournament. Furthermore, a golfer must not only attain skill in the use of a club but must also know *when to use* each club. A perfectly executed shot with a no. 7 iron will not achieve its purpose if the shot requires a no. 5 iron. Like the golfer, after acquiring information and learning *how* to use it, salespeople must then learn *when* to use it.

While a more detailed description will be presented in Chapter 8, some suggestions on the use of company and product information are appropriate at this point.

Organize

The job has just begun when the salesperson has utilized the sources mentioned above to learn about the company and its products. The information must now be organized so that it may be used effectively in actual selling situations.

It is neither necessary nor practical for a salesperson to try to remember great volumes of facts. However, a salesperson should collect and retain a group of significant facts. This involves sifting the available information so that outstanding facts can be arranged in suitable form. These facts should be collected with a questioning attitude. "What difference does this fact make? Will anybody be interested in it? How can I use it?"

When a suitable set of facts has been collected, they should be organized so that they will be available at the proper stage of the sales presentation. The planning of the sales presentation is discussed further in Chapter 8.

It is obvious that not all of the facts collected will be of interest to any one buyer. Sometimes salespeople may have to use most of the information available to sell the prospect, while at other times they may not find it necessary to tap the bank of facts at all. There is no substitute for judgment in deciding which facts to use. The sole guide will be: "Does this group of facts interest this buyer? Will this group of facts appeal to this buyer's motives?"

Use facts buyers want or need

Many buyers are unable to recognize the merits of a product without some help. Even as they look at a duplicating machine, for example, they cannot see many of its sales features until these are pointed out.

In order to conserve the time of both the buyer and the seller, it is advisable to determine what the buyer already knows about the product. If the buyer has used the product before or has become well informed on it through study or observation, the work is simplified. If the buyer is not acquainted with the product, an attempt must be made to discover what facts are of interest.

When the buyer's motives and the approximate extent of his or her knowledge have been determined, the salesperson is ready to supply whatever product facts are important.

Show buyer benefits

The buyer is not interested in facts about the product or the company except as these facts contribute to the solution of wants or needs. The salesperson's job is to supply the facts and then point out what these features mean to the buyer in terms of *benefits*.

The guide in Figure 4–3 has been prepared for use in selling cars. It shows how product features can be described in terms of customer benefits.

Whatever product is being sold, salespeople's effective use of company and product information is determined by their ability and skill in presenting that information in terms of buyer benefits.

Figure 4–3
Guide for selling cars

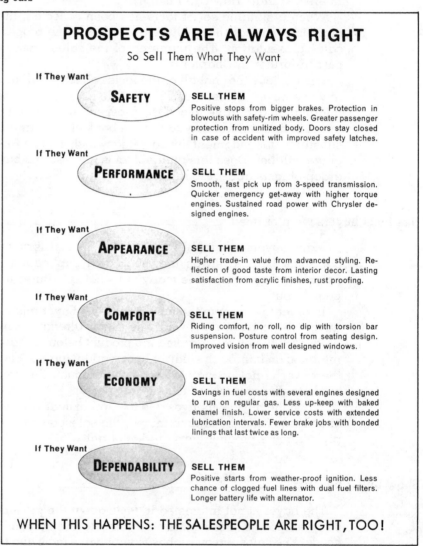

An adaptation—courtesy of Chrysler Corp.

Use the language of the trade

When discussing products with an experienced buyer, the choice and use of words is important. If such expressions as "this thing" or "this gadget" are used instead of the appropriate terms, the failure to use accepted terminology implies that the salesperson is not well informed and is worthy of little confidence. In selling shoes, such terms as *welt, insole, filler, channel, outsole, lining,* and *stitching* are appropriate. In selling water heaters, the experienced buyer would expect to talk in terms of hot-water coils, combustion chambers, boilers, fire tubes, firing units, and insulation.

When selling to uninformed buyers, however, care must be taken not to use highly technical terms which they are unable to understand and which merely result in an unhelpful exhibition of knowledge.

Be specific—Avoid generalities

Specific statements lend authority to the presentation. Generalizations are not only difficult to interpret, but they lack the strength of well-stated specific facts.

"Our airfreight will save you time in transportation" could be stated more specifically: "Airfreight can get your merchandise to San Francisco from New York in one day, while the fastest trucks or trains take from 4½ to 9 days."

Words must be chosen carefully to secure the greatest descriptive power and impact. Avoid words like *pretty, nice, good,* and *fine.*[7] Any good book of synonyms, such as *Roget's Thesaurus,* will provide a wealth of strong, incisive words.

Use positive comparisons

When comparing the company product with a competitor's, present a positive picture. That is, place emphasis on the superior points or features of your product or service rather than on the negative features of the competitor's product or service.

"Company X's machines have a very poor record on maintenance costs" could be stated better in this way: "Our machine has lower maintenance costs than any comparable machine. Records show that our maintenance costs are from 10 to 15 percent lower than our nearest competitor's."

Tearing down a competitor does not add strength to the presenta-

---

[7] Chapter 9, Dramatizing the Sales Presentation, has a section on the use of words.

tion. In fact, it may weaken the presentation and injure the salesperson, the company, and the industry.

QUESTIONS AND PROBLEMS

1. You are selling a replacement product for carbon paper—it won't rip or tear; it won't wrinkle or curl; and it won't strike through like carbon paper. One of these polyester sheets will make 100 copies. List these product features in terms of buyer benefits.

2. The hot tub is usually made of redwood, is either round or oval, and is from three feet to 5 feet high and from three feet to eight feet in diameter. It can be installed indoors or outdoors. A heater is used to keep the water between 104 and 115 degrees. The basic price is $1,500. Optional accessories are available. Why would anyone want to buy such a tub?

3. Mark Twain said, "The difference between the right word and almost the right word is the difference between lightning and the lightning bug." How does this statement apply to selling?

4. As a salesperson in a large department store, where are you most likely to find information on the products you sell? What will a thorough knowledge of your merchandise do for you?

5. Which is more important to the salesperson in making a sale—knowledge of the product or knowledge of the customer? Explain.

6. Henry Downs, a manufacturer's representative, sells footballs, basketballs, volleyballs, and other rubber products to sporting goods dealers. His firm is known throughout the country as the leader in the merchandising of rubber sporting goods. In what facts about the company would the owner of a sporting goods store probably be interested? Identify the facts, and show why the retailer would be interested in them.

7. Jane Harris works for her father in a large appliance store. Sales of refrigerators, disposal units, dishwashers, clothes dryers, and automatic ironers have been featured, but business has been only fair. Jane suggests to her father that she would like to experiment by acting as an outside salesperson in an attempt to sell more home freezers. After securing her father's approval, Jane sits down to organize her sales material. What features about an upright home freezer should she consider for inclusion in her sales talk? Which of the features do you suppose are most important? Why?

8. Why is it insufficient to *describe* the benefits which may accrue to the buyer of a product?

9. Improve the following statement, "Mr. Buyer, our new inventory control system [feature] will assure you of prompt deliveries [benefit]."

10. Describe the features and the benefits which may accrue to a person who buys a citizens band (CB) radio.

PROJECTS

1. Identify the benefits which could accrue to a buyer who purchases any of the following products:

   customized van   home video game
   microwave oven   CB radio
   food machine   solar heating system
   facsimile transmission system   home computer
   smoke detector   laser scanner

2. Select a product which you plan to buy in the near future. Shop for it at four stores that carry the product. Indicate where you plan to buy the product and why you plan to buy the particular brand you have chosen. Be sure to include all the factors which influenced your decision. Submit the analysis, using an appropriate business report form.

3. Write for the latest annual report of a major corporation. Analyze the report, and indicate the information which you believe could be useful when selling the company's product. How would you use that information? Be specific.

CASE PROBLEMS

Case 4-1

Radio PEEK

Bob works for Radio PEEK, which is situated in a city of about 85,000 population. Four stations of a strictly local nature have come on the air in the last three years, and Bob's station is one of this group. The city is only 50 miles from a city of 600,000 population and only 45 miles from one of 400,000 population. The trading area which the local stations hope to reach contains a population of between 300,000 and 350,000, exclusive of the population of the two larger cities.

Advertising over a local station is a relatively new experience for the owners of local retail stores and industries. Bob knows that it will be necessary to sell them on the advisability of using local radio as an advertising medium, and he must also sell them on PEEK as the station to use.

Bob discovers that none of the four stations has been able to collect sufficient data to "prove" to the prospects that it is profitable for them to use the medium. However, surveys are under way to collect the necessary information. The stations have been pioneering in the area, and they have found it difficult to sell time.

Questions

1. What facts about the company or station could be useful in Bob's presentation? What should he say about competitors?
2. What buying motives may be used to convince a merchant that local radio advertising is desirable? Illustrate.

Case 4–2

Handiman

You work in a home building center store that caters to the do-it-yourself market but will also install purchases when requested to do so. Emphasis is currently being placed on "speaking the customer's language."

Are the following statements on product benefits stated in "customer" language? If not, rephrase them.

a. Our aluminum siding has a beautiful finish.
b. This fencing will last longer because it has a heavy zinc coating.
c. This vanity is beautiful.
d. Our tile is easy to work with.

Case 4–3

Forget-me-not

Elsie Fox has decided to look for opportunities to set up a small business. In searching for ideas, she recalled the number of times she had heard people say, "I have a very poor memory" or "I'm so busy I just forgot to remember Susie's birthday."

She decided to research an idea to determine if she could come up with an operation that did not require a lot of capital, that could rely heavily on labor, perhaps even part-time labor, that could be operated out of her home and that would still provide a service for which people would be willing to pay.

After considerable reading and talking with knowledgeable people, Elsie decided to launch her enterprise. She decided on a small business service that would conserve the time of busy people. She planned to start slowly and to sell her service to a limited number of people by offering a *free* "reminder service."

The reminder service would work this way: Ten days before a special occasion—a birthday, an anniversary, or some other special event—Elsie would notify the person that the occasion was approaching. The service could be viewed as a kind of calendar management. It was being offered in order to attract customers who would want other services for which they would be willing to pay.

Questions

1. What services related to the reminder service might busy people be willing to pay for?
2. Where might Elsie get a select list of people to contact?
3. How would you suggest that Elsie reach her prospects?
4. Do you think that Elsie's idea will work? Why or why not?

SELECTED REFERENCES

"The Big Winners in Consumer Sales." *Sales & Marketing Management*, August 2, 1976, pp. 23–25.

Dowst, Somerby. "Buyers Name Top Salesmen." *Purchasing*, November 8, 1977, pp. 48–54.

————. "Buyers Get Tougher on Supplier Quality." *Purchasing*, April 12, 1978, pp. 53–57.

————. "Capital Buying: One Strike and You're Out." *Purchasing*, March 8, 1978, pp. 59–63.

Herndon, Booton. *Satisfaction Guaranteed*. New York: McGraw-Hill, 1972.

Korn, Don. "The Laser, a Beam That's No Longer a Dream." *Sales & Marketing Management*, September 1978, p. 57.

"Middlemen Are Out, Problem-Solvers Are In." *Purchasing*, September 13, 1978, pp. 62–65.

Patty, C. Robert; Haring, Albert; and Vredenburg, Harvey L. *Selling Direct to the Consumer*. Fort Collins, Colo.: Robinson Press, 1973. pp. 45–57.

Snyder, James D. "Selling Sunshine." *Sales & Marketing Management*, April 12, 1976, pp. 55–56.

Chapter 5

PRICE, DISCOUNT, AND CREDIT POLICIES AND PRACTICES

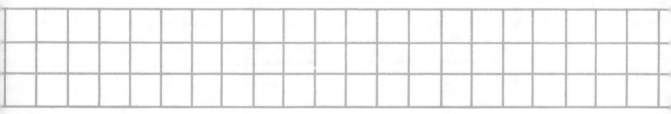

Knowledge of price, discount, and credit policies and practices is more important today than ever before because of new developments in transportation, methods of marketing, and sales control and because of the increasing interest of government in regulating pricing policies and practices. The profitableness of a territory is directly related to the way the salesperson administers the company's financial policies during day-to-day contacts with customers.

In the field of transportation, for example, the increasing use of the airplane has made it possible for the salesperson to cover larger territories, thus necessitating a more thorough knowledge of such factors as territorial price differentials, storage facilities, and shipping methods. To be of greatest service to the customer, the salesperson must be able to provide up-to-date information on comparative freight rates by air, rail, truck, and water.

New developments in mechanized accounting and sales analysis control have made it possible for management to scrutinize more carefully the detailed operations of each salesperson on such items as total sales volume, sales volume by product, profits by product, sales volume and profits for each customer, and ratios of collections to sales. Sales are only one measure of performance. In many companies each salesperson virtually operates his or her own business within the territory. The bonus of the salesperson is based upon total profits. Because of this, the salesperson has a vital interest in prices, discounts, terms of sales, and collections as they affect profits in the territory.

PRICES AND PRICING PRACTICES

The setting of individual prices is generally beyond the exclusive control of the average salesperson. Salespeople do, however, play a part in price determination.[1] Their advice is frequently sought in order to obtain firsthand information on customers' probable reactions to specific prices on various types of merchandise. Most prices are determined after careful consideration of the diverse factors which tend to influence the supply of and demand for particular products. Whether or not the sales representatives have a part in determining prices, they must be able to explain and justify prices to their customers.

The emphasis given to prices will vary by customers and products. Some retail dealers, for example, may carry a line of quality products with well-known brand names. They may be less interested in prices than will dealers who depend primarily on the low-price appeal to sell their merchandise. Distributors who carry a wide range of merchandise may feature price when selling certain products and refrain from price cutting on other products. In general, most companies prefer to have their salespeople stress the *value* of products or services rather than the price.

Prices and profits—Their importance to the sales representative

Normally, the prices quoted to customers depend upon such factors as the nature of competition, the marketing functions being per-

---

[1] See Mack Hanan, "True or False: The Best Way to Approach a Tough Buyer Is to Let Him Set His Own Price," *Sales & Marketing Management*, November 14, 1977, pp. 111–12; and P. Ronald Stephenson, William L. Cron, and Gary L. Frazier, "Delegating Pricing Authority To the Sales Force," *Journal of Marketing*, Spring 1979, pp. 21–28.

formed, the size of the order, and the terms of the sale. Dependence upon price cutting to build sales volume does not build a sound foundation for the salesperson or the company. Most sales executives are acquainted with the statement, "Anyone can give merchandise away, but it takes a good sales representative to sell products at a profit." Reasonable and fair profits are important to the salesperson, to the company, and to the customers.

Definitions of prices

Most companies provide their sales representatives with specific training in the knowledge and use of price terms and price practices. Among the most common expressions used in quoting prices are list price, net price, open price, zone price, postage-stamp delivered price, guaranteed price, FOB price, FAS price, and CIF price. Each of these prices is described below.

List price. A list price is a quoted or published price from which buyers are normally allowed discounts. List prices are used for a number of reasons: (1) The manufacturer or vendor can change prices much more easily by using a supplementary discount list. (2) The use of list prices and discounts facilitates price quotations for different quantities. (3) A list price may serve as a suggested uniform resale price for the merchants and thereby assure them a fair profit and also protect them from excessive price cutting. (4) When list prices are used, it is more difficult for competitors to discover the actual selling prices of the products because the discount sheets can be kept confidential. (5) Through the use of published list prices, the manufacturer may be able to protect the ultimate consumer against overcharges by the retailer or the distributor. Moreover, the final consumer who has access to catalogs will not be able to see what the distributor has paid for a particular product when only the list price is shown in the catalog.

Net price. The net price is the price that the buyer must pay for a product after all discounts and allowances have been subtracted. Many buyers prefer the use of net prices to facilitate comparisons and to simplify the marking up process.

Zone price. In certain industries, equalized delivered prices are established for certain zones or geographic areas. A Chicago manufacturer may divide the market into several zones or territories, one of which is the Pacific Coast zone. Uniform delivered prices are quoted to all customers within the three Western states which make up the company's Pacific Coast zone. Many manufactured food products are marketed through the use of zone prices.

Basing point price. In certain industries, such as the cement and steel industries, a basing point system of pricing has been used.

This may be either a single or a multiple basing point. Under the single basing point plan, a price is established at one given location or base point; the delivered price to a customer includes the price at this point plus freight or transportation charges from the basing point to the delivery point even though the actual shipment is made from a location other than the basing point. Under the multiple basing point plan a similar pricing method is employed, except that a number of basing points are used.

To illustrate, the Apex Corporation, manufacturers of tile, may have plants at Chicago and St. Louis. Chicago may be its single basing point. If sales representatives for the Apex Corporation sell to customers in Lincoln, Nebraska, they will quote these customers a price that includes the FOB price at Chicago plus delivery and transportation charges from Chicago to Lincoln, even though the tile may actually be shipped from the St. Louis plant.

Postage stamp delivered price. This term is used in quoting prices when a company desires to sell its product at identical prices throughout its entire market. The most common use of the "postage-stamp delivered price" is among companies which do national advertising and handle products with relatively low transportation costs, such as chewing gum or packaged drugs. The net result of this price policy is that the freight charges are averaged throughout the market, and all buyers pay the same delivered price for the merchandise whether they are located in Maine or Texas.

Fair-trade price. In 1931, California enacted the first fair-trade law permitting retail price-maintenance contracts between manufacturers and distributors.[2] The objective was to protect trademark owners against injurious practices in pricing articles of standard quality. Most states followed California in enacting fair-trade laws. The Miller-Tydings Act of 1937 and the McGuire Amendment of 1952 legalized price-maintenance agreements in interstate commerce. In December 1975, the president approved legislation repealing the rights of states to pass laws under the Miller-Tydings Act or the McGuire Amendment. When this legislation was passed, 21 states had fair-trade laws. The new law invalidates price-maintenance contracts involving interstate commerce. This has reduced or eliminated the use of fair-trade prices within the states.

"Guaranteed price." During periods of falling prices, buyers may request that the seller protect them against any future price declines which occur prior to the time that the merchandise is either used or resold to the ultimate consumer. In some instances the selling company agrees to a price guarantee of this nature to induce the customer to purchase a large quantity of merchandise or to enter into

---

[2] California repealed its fair-trade law in 1975.

a relatively long-term purchase contract. A price guarantee can prove to be disastrous to the seller in case of an extreme price decline. Consequently, most companies are reluctant to enter into such agreements. Normally, the salesperson does not have the authority to make guarantees against possible future price declines.

FOB price. When an FOB (free on board) price is quoted, the seller agrees to load the goods on board a truck, freight car, or ship at the seller's factory. Such products as coal, lumber, and automobiles are usually priced at FOB mine, mill, or factory. There are a great many variations in the use of the term FOB, including the following: (1) "FOB destination"—the seller assumes the responsibility for transportation costs to the buyer's place and the responsibility for loss or damage while the goods are in transit. (2) "FOB (shipping point) freight allowed"—this term denotes that transportation costs are assumed by the seller, but responsibility for the goods themselves ceases when the goods are delivered to the transportation company. (3) "FOB (shipping point) freight equalized"—this term is used by the seller when a competitor has a more favorable freight cost as a result of being located nearer to the buyer. The seller assumes the difference in the freight rates and thus is able to meet competition.

FAS price. The term FAS (free alongside ship) is used in quoting prices on overseas shipments. The seller agrees to pay the transportation charges necessary to get the goods within the reach of the ship's loading cranes. The title to the merchandise is transferred to the buyer at this point.

CIF price. The term CIF (cost, insurance, and freight) is used in export selling. Such a price quotation includes the cost of the goods to the buyer, all freight and drayage costs to the seaport, ocean freight charges, marine insurance, and fees to land the goods at the foreign port. Unless otherwise stated, the title to the goods passes when the seller turns it over to the common carrier.

WHAT THE SALESPERSON SHOULD KNOW ABOUT PRICE LEGISLATION

Federal and state laws directly affect company pricing policies and practices. Legislation is being introduced constantly to control pricing practices which some legislators believe to be injurious to the public welfare. The salesperson must know what pricing and discount practices are permissible under the present laws and what changes may take place. Normally, the company will provide advice on possible changes. A short description of the most important laws which regulate trade practices and prices should prove valuable to those who plan to enter the selling field.

The Sherman Antitrust Act of 1890

The Sherman Act prohibits all agreements and combinations in restraint of trade and makes it unlawful for groups of merchants or manufacturers to monopolize any part of interstate or foreign commerce. The purpose of the act was to break up the trust agreements and eliminate some of the unfair trade practices which existed when it was enacted.

The Clayton Act of 1914

The Clayton Act reinforced the Sherman Act by outlawing price discrimination in interstate commerce, by prohibiting the acquisition of the capital stock of competitors, by prohibiting interlocking directorates which tend to lessen competition, and by outlawing various types of price discrimination.

The Federal Trade Commission Act of 1914

This act set up the Federal Trade Commission as a policing body to guard against illegitimate competitive methods among business concerns. The Wheeler-Lea Act of 1938 amended the Federal Trade Commission Act by broadening the powers of the Federal Trade Commission. As a result of this amendment the commission no longer had to prove injury to a competitor before it could issue a complaint. The burden of proof now rests with the person, partnership, or corporation which has been accused of unfair trade practices. The amended act also provides possible penalties for violations of its provisions.

The Federal Trade Commission consists of five men who are appointed by the president. The commission has the power to issue cease and desist orders against companies which appear to be using unfair business methods that tend to injure competitors. Specific practices which have been condemned by the commission include the following: giving retail clerks premiums with the purpose of getting clerks to push one company's products at the expense of a competitor's; stealing the business of competitors through unfair practices; adulterating the quality of the product; making false statements about competitors' products; and giving extra discounts or advertising allowances to customers on condition that they do not handle competing products.

The Federal Trade Commission has been very active recently in investigating unfair and discriminatory trade practices.

The Robinson-Patman Act of 1936 _____

This act is an amendment of Section 2 of the Clayton Act; however, it is referred to as the Robinson-Patman Act. During the early years of the New Deal administration, considerable pressure was exerted by independent wholesale and retail groups for additional protection against the aggressive merchandising tactics of chain stores. This led to the passage of the Robinson-Patman Act of 1936.

The major objective of the act is to forbid price discrimination in interstate commerce which will injure competition. The act does not apply to sales within a state. However, a majority of the states have passed similar laws which do apply to intrastate sales.Other types of sales which are not covered by the Robinson-Patman Act include the following: sales in which price differentials do not prevent competition or injure competitors of the seller, the buyer, or customers of the buyer; and sales made to special buyers such as governmental units, exporters, and nonprofit institutions (for example, schools, hospitals, churches, and cooperatives).

Although the Robinson-Patman Act forbids price discrimination, it does not describe in detail what constitutes price discrimination. A number of court decisions, however, have made it clear that illegal discrimination exists when a seller gives unjustified special price or discount concessions or special services to some customers and not to others. To justify a special price or discount the seller must be able to prove that price differentials are the result of (1) differences in the cost of manufacture, sale, or delivery; (2) changes in the quality or nature of the product or in market conditions; or (3) an attempt to meet equally low prices of competitors.

The Robinson-Patman Act is the most basic statute affecting competitive pricing. It is also one of the most complicated and controversial of the antitrust laws. The wording of the original act has not been altered, but the interpretations of the courts and of the Federal Trade Commission have caused a high degree of uncertainty in the minds of many business executives.

The Truth-in-Lending Act of 1968 _____

On July 1, 1969, the Federal Reserve Board's Regulation Z implemented the Truth-in-Lending Act of May 29, 1968. The act and regulations are designed to assure a disclosure of credit terms that will enable consumers to compare the credit terms available to them from various creditors.

The law requires that standard terminology be adopted by all credit grantors, and regulations cover exactly what must be disclosed in writing to customers when a company extends, arranges, or just offers term credit. The law does not set maximum interest rates.[3]

Other recent legislation

Since the passage of the Consumer Credit Protection Act (Truth-in-Lending), other legislative efforts to regulate perceived credit abuses have included the Fair Credit Reporting Act (1970), the Fair Billing Credit Act (1975), the Equal Credit Opportunity Act (1975)[4] and the Consumer Leasing Act (1976).

QUOTING PRICES

The salesperson's responsibility in quoting prices has been increased tremendously during recent years, owing to the complexity of the various federal and state price laws. He or she must be certain that actions in quoting prices will not cause the company to become involved in expensive litigations over price-law violations.

Quality versus price

There probably is no item now being produced that someone cannot produce at a lower price with a poorer quality. It is a well-known fact that over the long pull the consumer gets exactly what he or she pays for. The salesperson has the responsibility of knowing the product thoroughly to provide a quality product which will best fill the needs of the customer at the lowest possible price.

When salespeople sell premium-quality products at a premium price they should never let the customer forget the quality features. Prospects will pay a premium price for premium quality. Customers will not part with their money, whatever the price, until they feel that the value they receive is greater than the price asked.

Price cutting

Purchasing agents do not and should not consider price alone. The general manager of purchasing for a large corporation emphasized this point by saying: "Purchasers who try to beat down price at every opportunity will eventually defeat their own end, because they won't get service when they want it, and they shut them-

---

[3] For more detailed information, see "What You Ought to Know About Federal Reserve Regulation Z," (Washington, D.C.: Board of Governors, Federal Reserve System, 1969).

[4] See *Journal of Marketing*, Spring 1979, pp. 95–104, for an evaluation of this act.

selves off from creative ideas and suggestions that sales representatives might make to them if they were more cooperative."

The Robinson-Patman Act is the basis for decisions by the Federal Trade Commission that "free deals" are a form of price cutting. However, the FTC does not prohibit the use of bonus merchandise, special assortments, and premiums as sales stimulants. It simply insists that all such deals must be offered to every customer on the same terms.

There is a tendency for some sales representatives to succumb to the practice of cutting prices. This is an undesirable practice, and in the long run it can bring nothing but trouble to everybody concerned. It is seldom wise to undercut a competitor's price to get an order. The sales representative must operate on the premise that his or her products are more distinctive, better in quality, more versatile, more durable, or better built, and thus provide plus values over competitors' products.[5] Otherwise, there is no justification for maintaining price levels. Essentially the salesperson should be interested in helping the industrial buyer cut costs, and this is not the same as cutting prices.

When and how to mention price

One of the first questions which many customers ask is, "How much does it cost?" There is a great temptation for the salesperson to get into a discussion of price before actually having a chance to sell the customer on the value of the product. The experienced salesperson, however, avoids mentioning price until the exact needs of the individual customer have been explored. The salesperson is then in a position to recommend the type and quality of product that will provide the greatest long-term satisfaction to the customer. Value and quality are more important than price. The successful salesperson also attempts to minimize price objections by quoting the price in terms that will be meaningful and acceptable to the buyer. At times it will be necessary to negotiate in order to satisfy a buying committee or a challenging purchasing agent. This places a definite responsibility on the salesperson to marshal and organize all material carefully.

An insurance agent who is selling a health and accident policy explains the many features of the policy in relation to the prospect's needs, and then points out that the prospect may receive this valuable protection at a price of only 25 cents a day. A salesperson who is

---

[5] See Mack Hanan. "Can't Bear Telling Customers about a Price Rise? Sell 'em on Value," *Sales & Marketing Management,* August 29, 1977, pp. 96–111; and "New Breed Looks beyond Low Bidders," *Purchasing,* September 13, 1978, pp. 59–61.

selling a product on an installment plan mentions the small monthly payment rather than the total price. Quotations of this kind minimize price objections.

When a prospect drives into a tire distributor's station and asks, "How much will a set of new tires cost me?" the salesperson should avoid an immediate price quotation. An attempt should be made first to find out something about the prospect's driving habits—the ordinary and maximum speeds, the kinds of roads traveled, the number of miles covered yearly, and the people who drive the car. With these facts the salesperson can do a more intelligent job of providing the prospect with the right tires. Such facts will aid in deciding whether the prospect is in the market for top-quality tires. If the prospect drives at high speeds, or if other members of the family drive the car, the prospect is likely to be interested in a quality appeal from the standpoint of safety and convenience. By obtaining this information, the salesperson can defer a price quotation until the prospect has had a chance to consider the many advantages of the top-quality tires as related to his or her own needs.

A successful accounting machine sales representative will refrain from discussing the price of a new machine until what it can do to solve some of the customer's problems has been explored. The salesperson will ask permission to make a thorough study of the present accounting methods and practices in the office. After this has been done, the salesperson will make an analysis of all possible ways of improving these methods through the use of the machine. The salesperson will then make definite recommendations showing the total potential dollar and efficiency savings which will result from the purchase of the machine. When price is finally mentioned, it will be related to the savings that the machine will make.

Most experienced salespeople agree that it is not good policy to begin the conversation with talk about price. Some customers or prospects are embarrassed when the salespeople attempt to qualify prospects at the beginning of the sales process by asking, "In what price level are you interested?" By asking questions about the type of product, the style, the design, and the quality, and by observing the prospect's reactions, the salesperson can usually determine the approximate price range of the goods in which the prospect is interested.

Prices must be understood by customers

Companies may at times desire to use price as the major appeal in selling a particular product or line of goods. In such cases, the salesperson will not hesitate to mention prices early in the sales transaction. No matter what techniques are used in quoting prices, a salesperson should have a thorough knowledge of the company's prices and of competitive prices in the industry. Prices should be quoted to customers so that there will be no doubt in the customers' minds as to the exact price they are paying. A new pricing tool, the option to buy or lease, has become available to many equipment sales representatives. The salesperson can offset purchase objections by reducing the cost to nominal monthly lease payments or payments applicable to lease-purchase agreements.

A good form for submitting price quotations is used by Xerox sales representatives (see Figure 5-1).

The Penn Mutual Life Insurance Company, in a booklet to its new underwriters, emphasizes the importance of knowing how to quote rates:

> The Rate Book is *your* authority, *your* inspiration (if you can see it that way), but it is *not* the authority nor the inspiration of your prospect. YOU, not your Rate Book, are the authority and inspiration of your prospect.
>
> Some underwriters try to get their prospects interested in figures, but except in rare cases, the result is a total failure. They fail because buying is ruled by emotion, as we studied in Motivation. Therefore, *study* your Rate Book, *know* your Rate Book, and *use* your Rate Book, but do not show it to your prospect or try to explain it to him. Consult the Rate Book privately, and tell your prospect what it says in your own language.[6]

Careful quoting of prices will help cut down the number of claims a salesperson will have to adjust. A clear and frank discussion of prices, at the appropriate time, will do much to build customer goodwill and satisfaction.

DISCOUNTS

Manufacturers, wholesalers, and retailers have learned to accept the various types of discounts as important parts of today's system of distribution. Trade or functional discounts are allowed on the basis of the functions they perform. Financial discounts are given to encourage prompt payment of accounts, and quantity discounts are awarded when the selling company can prove that savings have resulted from large-scale orders. Other specialized types of discounts such as territorial, seasonal, advertising, and "early-order" discounts are also common in today's sales transactions. The salesperson, as the official representative of the company, must know how to administer the company's discount policies and must keep up to date on legal developments regarding the discounts that are allowable under the Robinson-Patman Act.

---

[6] *The Rate Book* (Philadelphia: Penn Mutual Life Insurance Co.) pp. 1–2.

Figure 5–1
Cost summary sheet for price comparisons

Cost Summary

Prepared for _____

Location _____

Prepared by _____

Date _____

	PRESENT EQUIPMENT		PROPOSED EQUIPMENT
Description	IBM-II Annual	IBM-II Purchase	3100 Purchase
Volume			
Amortization period			
Rental/purchase price			
MONTHLY COSTS:			
Equipment			
Service			
Supplies			
Other			
TOTAL MONTHLY COSTS			
	SUMMARY OF SAVINGS		
	Per month		
	Per year		
	BREAKEVEN POINT		

Cash or financial discounts

A large percentage of U.S. sales are made on a credit basis, with certain discounts being allowed for early payment. Although discounts vary somewhat from industry to industry and according to the type of product, a common discount is 2 percent in 10 days, net in 30 days. This discount provides that the buyer may deduct 2 percent if the bill is paid within 10 days from the date of invoice. Otherwise the full amount must be paid within 30 days. Buyers frequently request deferred datings on their invoices as an extra form of discount.

The salesperson should encourage customers to take advantage of cash discounts, for in the long run this will benefit both the buyer and the seller. The buyer's financial standing will be improved, and indirectly this will result in increased sales for the salesperson.

Trade discounts

When a manufacturing company sells its product to different types of distributors it will usually allow different functional or trade discounts to the various buyers, depending upon the function performed by these buyers. The manufacturer, for example, may offer the wholesaler a trade discount of 55 percent of the list price to the ultimate consumer. If the manufacturer also sells directly to a large retailer, the retailer may be quoted a trade discount of 40 percent of the list price to the consumer. The theory behind trade discounts is that they tend to provide a sufficient margin to cover the costs of the services rendered by the various middlemen and to provide the middlemen with a fair profit.

Trade discounts offered to wholesalers and retailers vary by trades. They are related to the operating expenses of the particular trade, the turnover of the specific merchandise, and the selling effort needed. For example, trade discounts to the retail druggist may vary from less than 20 percent to more than 40 percent.

Most companies classify their customers according to the trade discounts which are to be allowed. However, certain customers may operate both as wholesalers and retailers. In such cases, it is difficult for the salesperson to determine what trade discount should be quoted. As a safeguard against unlawful price discrimination, the salesperson should make certain that buyers who receive different trade discounts are not in competition with each other or, if they are, that the trade discounts can be justified on a differential cost basis.

Quantity discounts

The purpose of the quantity discount is to pass on to the customer or consumer the savings resulting from the handling, delivering, and billing of large-sized orders. Under the Robinson-Patman Act, quantity discounts are justifiable if the larger orders reduce the seller's costs. If the seller's costs are not reduced, however, a buyer who buys a small quantity and receives a small discount may complain about a competitor who has received a more favorable quantity discount because of large yearly purchases.

Quantity discounts may take the form of single-order discounts or period discounts. A typewriter company, for example, may quote a 5 percent discount on a single order for three typewriters, a 10 percent discount on a single order for four typewriters, and a 15 percent discount on a single order for five or more typewriters. In addition, the company may have a time or period quantity discount plan whereby a discount of 15 percent is allowed on all typewriters purchased during a year or a six-month period. The Federal Trade Commission, which administers the Robinson-Patman Act, however, has always looked upon cumulative quantity discounts with considerable suspicion.

The salesperson should be acquainted with the company's policies concerning quantity discounts to protect the company against possible charges of violating the Robinson-Patman Act. A salesperson should also refrain from overloading customers just because larger orders will qualify the customers for attractive quantity discounts. This practice may result in injurious price cutting to liquidate stocks.

Advertising discounts

Before the Robinson-Patman Act was passed, manufacturers and wholesalers frequently gave rather liberal advertising allowances to dealers and retailers without checking too carefully to see whether the recipients actually used the allowances for advertising purposes. To get business, manufacturers sometimes paid the entire cost of the retailer's window displays, handbills, and newspaper advertising. Many buyers viewed the advertising allowance as a regular type of discount and failed to carry out their agreements to promote the sale of the manufacturer's product.

The Robinson-Patman Act prohibits giving advertising allowances unless they are offered on proportionally equal terms to all competing buyers. As a result, companies have exercised greater care in granting advertising allowances and in following up to see that the allowances are used for advertising purposes.

Salespersons should have a clear understanding of the company's policies concerning advertising allowances. They should know the amount that will be allowed and the exact services or promotional efforts that will be required of the dealer or retailer.

Other discounts

Some companies offer "early-order" discounts to get their customers to place substantial orders early in the season. Another common type of discount is the group discount which is allowed to a number of independent purchasers when they pool their buying. The seller must be able to justify group discounts on the basis of actual cost savings resulting from the joint sales. A popular service to help building-material wholesalers control their inventories is provided by manufacturers in the form of "mixed carlot" quantities. This practice enables the wholesaler to buy smaller quantities and to avoid carrying an excessive inventory caused by buying full truck or railcar lots of one product. The buyer gets a wide variety of products and also benefits by receiving the full-carload price. Additional types of discounts may take the form of special freight allowances, free deals, bonuses, and premiums.

THE SALES REPRESENTATIVE'S RESPONSIBILITY FOR CREDIT

The proper use of credit plays an important part in determining the success of both the buyer and the seller. Many companies have been forced out of business because of huge losses resulting from too liberal or poorly administered credit policies. These experiences, plus the tremendous demand for credit under time or installment buying plans, have caused management to give greater attention to the credit function.

The credit policies of a company are usually established by the credit department after consultation with the sales organization. Some companies delegate the entire credit responsibility to the credit department. Others give the individual salesperson considerable authority in administering the credit policies. The Standard Oil Company of California, for example, emphasizes the importance of the sales representative in administering the company's credit policies as follows: *"The application of any credit policy rests finally with the representative of the Company who actually talks with the customer. The results of these conversations have a direct effect on profitable selling, and the outcome depends not only on what you say but how you say it."*

Even in companies which give the credit department substantial authority in controlling and granting credit, the salesperson will normally be required to discuss credit terms with the customers and to obtain credit information for the credit department.

Credit and profits

When a salesperson's compensation is based upon total sales volume, there may be a tendency to make sales that do not result in a profit to the company. Most companies have recognized this factor and have altered their sales compensation plans so that each salesperson is directly concerned with the profits of the particular territory.

It doesn't take the salesperson long to learn how losses from bad debts affect the profits of a territory. Salespeople find from experience that it is good business to pass up sales to poor credit risks. When a sale is lost, the company sacrifices the potential profit of that sale. When a sale is made to a poor credit risk, however, the company may lose not only the profit on the sale but also the cost of the goods which have been delivered to the customer.

The salesperson's relation to the credit department

Considerable friction sometimes develops between the salesperson and the credit department when the credit department finds it necessary to refuse credit to one of the salesperson's customers. Since salespeople are generally very optimistic, they tend to be somewhat liberal in evaluating a customer's credit position. The credit manager, on the other hand, is usually less optimistic and stricter in the interpretation of the company's credit policies. Differences of opinion are bound to occur from time to time. However, the credit manager and the salesperson should realize that complete cooperation and understanding of each other's problems will result in greater long-term profits for both the company and the salesperson.

Sales management should be certain that salespeople understand the company's credit policies and their duties and responsibilities in carrying out these policies. New sales representatives should be given an explanation of the basic factors, such as capacity, character, and capital, which help determine whether a customer is a good or poor credit risk. The credit department can save the salesperson considerable time and effort by providing advance credit information on present and prospective customers.

Salespeople must be frank and honest in all of their discussions with the credit department, and must do everything possible to keep it informed on conditions in their territories. If salespeople give the credit department complete and factual information on all their customers, they will usually find the credit department equally cooperative in attempting to work out their special credit and collection problems.

The salesperson—A source of credit information

The salesperson is in an excellent position to obtain current information on the financial condition of customers. When this is combined with the information obtained directly by the credit department, the company will have a fairly accurate picture of the credit position of individual customers.

The salesperson usually asks potential customers to send complete financial statements to the credit department. The salesperson also supplies information on such items as the management's ability, the owners' habits and local reputation, local business conditions, the location and identity of the store or plant, bank and credit references, and evidence of the financial status of the business.

When calling on old customers, sales representatives should be on the lookout for danger signals which may indicate unfavorable changes in the customers' credit standing. The New York Credit Men's Association suggests that sales representatives review the following points as a means of discovering credit indicators for the credit department:

a. Are there any indications that the customer has been buying heavily from one house?
b. Have any of the customer's accounts with other creditors been placed in attorneys' hands for collection?
c. Is the customer becoming loose in personal habits? Is the retailer drinking or indifferent in handling customers?
d. Is there any evidence that the customer is getting ready to sell out or close with the intention of quitting business?
e. Is there any indication that the customer is letting business run down—that is, allowing stock to deteriorate?
f. Has the customer guaranteed the paying of obligations incurred by some friend or relative?
g. Is a strike pending in the community's principal plant or industry?
h. Is the customer doing too much credit business?[7]

Through the salesperson's close contacts with customers, information may be obtained from unhappy customers who feel antagonistic toward the company's credit department. The salesperson should attempt to discover the reasons for such feeling. If the company has erred, the credit department should be given the complete facts so that it may take the necessary steps to reestablish cordial relations with these customers.

Credit policy and the customer

Sales representatives must not only have a complete knowledge of their company's credit policies, but they must be able to explain

[7] Research and Survey Committee, *Suggested Outline for Preparing a Credit and Collection Manual for Salesmen* (New York: New York Credit Men's Association), p. 7.

and discuss these policies successfully with their customers. They must think in terms of what will be mutually beneficial to their customers and their company.[8]

Credit terms will vary by industry, by companies, by location of customers, by financial condition of the buyer, and by general business conditions. Short credit terms are usually offered on staple products which turn over fast. Longer terms are common on seasonal and slow-moving merchandise. When a salesperson sells goods to a new customer who does not have an established credit rating, or to an old customer whose credit standing is shaky, he or she is likely to quote one of the following terms: CWO (cash with order), CBD (cash before delivery), COD (cash on delivery), or SDB (sight draft, bill of lading attached).

When a cash discount is allowed, the normal procedure is to figure the discount period from the date of the invoice or from the date of shipment. Frequently, however, the salesperson or the company will agree to special datings. In the dry-goods trade, for example, goods sold and delivered during the first four months of the year may be billed as of May 1. In lines of business where frequent purchases are made during a month, EOM (end of month) terms are often used. These terms provide that the credit period will start at the end of the month in which the goods are received. The customer can thus pay for many purchases at the same time. For example, purchases made on January 1, 9, 12, 18, and 26 are invoiced as of February 1. MOM (middle of month) terms provide that the credit period starts on the 15th and the 1st of each month. Purchases made on February 1, 3, 6, and 12 are invoiced as of February 15; purchases made on February 16, 18, 21, and 24 are billed as of March 1.

The terms ROG (receipt of goods) or AOG (arrival of goods) tend to equalize conditions for nearby and distant customers by providing that the cash discount period, the net credit period, or both, start at the date goods are received. Extra dating provides a specified extra credit period in addition to the regular period. The terms 2/10–60 extra, for example, give the customer a 2 percent discount if the bill is paid within 70 days of the invoice date.

The use of credit cards has increased tremendously since 1950, when the first "third party" travel and entertainment (T&E) credit card was introduced by Diners' Club. It has been estimated that by 1978 two out of three American families used at least one credit card. At that time they owed more than $36 billion to retailers, oil companies, banks, and organizations such as American Express and Din-

---

[8] Buyers also check the vendor's credit rating. See Harold W. Fox, "Credit Matrix Aids Vendor Analysis," *Purchasing*, February 8, 1978, pp. 56–57.

ers' Club.[9] In addition to these organizations Citicorp, Visa (formerly the BankAmerica card), and Master Charge are prominent in the field. Recently savings and loan associations and credit unions have been issuing Visa cards.[10]

Many other types of credit arrangements or terms may be used in specialized fields of selling. Space does not permit a complete description of all these terms. Moreover, the salesperson's company will normally provide the necessary data on special company terms.

When the salesperson discusses credit and collection policies and terms with customers, a high degree of tact and diplomacy must be exercised. At times it is necessary to obtain personal or confidential information. Such information may often be obtained through indirect questions and careful observation, without offending or embarrassing customers. When direct questions are necessary, care should be taken to explain that similar credit information is required of all customers. If salespeople are sincere and honest in all relations with customers, they should have little trouble in winning the customers' confidence and in securing the necessary credit information from them.

Credit policies and terms should be clearly explained to each customer at the time of the sales transaction so that misunderstandings will not arise later. If special credit arrangements are made through the use of trade acceptances, drafts, notes, and installment sales contracts, the salesperson should be certain that customers understand the exact amount of their payments and the dates on which these payments fall due. If a salesperson is to provide maximum service to customers and the company, customers should be made aware of the advantage of taking discounts, even if they must borrow from a bank to secure the necessary funds.

Sales representatives as collectors

If the sales representatives are charged with the collection responsibility, they should not be apologetic about asking for money. Successful salespeople know that most customers will respect a courteous but firm stand on collections. They also know that paid-up customers regard the payment of their accounts to sales representatives as the customary method of paying for purchases. The personal contact of the salesperson makes it harder for the customer to refuse payment than does a company's use of collection letters. In addition, the salesperson is in a position to know all of the details of the bill or

---

[9] "Credit Cards: A Booming Business," *Economist*, September 23, 1978, p. 126.

[10] See also "Non-bank Card Competition: Thrust or Opportunity," *Banking*, October 1978, pp. 146–49.

invoice and hence should be able to make collections with less annoyance to the customer. Finally, the salesperson knows that if collections are not made promptly, customers' orders may be held up and sales may suffer.

QUESTIONS AND PROBLEMS

1. It is always a good idea to encourage the buyer to order a larger quantity in order to get a better quantity price. True or false? Why?

2. The buyer should not necessarily buy the best quality available even though it may be called for on the requisition form. True or false? Why?

3. A new salesperson who represents a manufacturer of quality floor coverings which sell at a premium makes a first call on the purchasing agent of a large governmental institution. After being introduced, the purchasing agent says, "You're just wasting your time here. Your company used to call on me, but we could never get together because your company's prices are too high." How should the sales representative handle this situation?

4. What techniques are being used by purchasing agents in an attempt to secure better prices?

5. What can a salesperson do to secure acceptance by customers or prospects of an increase in the price of the company's products?

6. Determine the annual equivalent rate of interest earned by buyers who qualify for cash discounts on the following terms: 1/10, n/30; 2/10, n/60; 3/10, n/60, 2/15, n/30; 2/20, n/30.

7. What may a buyer actually mean when telling the salesperson that "the price is too high"?

8. Do you believe that the conversion to the metric system will be an advantage to sales and marketing departments? Why?

9. What major factors does a sales representative consider before granting credit to an individual or a company? How do these factors differ? Which is the most important?

10. You represent a reputable food-specialty manufacturer and call on grocers. Your company has built a good reputation because of high-quality products, superior service, and strong advertising. You find out through your customers that a competitor is offering hidden discounts, one-shot extra discount allowances, free merchandise, and even cash for display advantages. How would you meet this type of unfair competition?

PROJECTS

1. Investigate the effects on consumers of the Truth-in-Lending Act. Prepare a report from information secured through a selected survey of businesses and consumers. What are your conclusions?

2. What are the sources of funds which may be borrowed to make consumer purchases? Prepare a chart showing the comparative effective annual rate of interest charged. Include all charges over and above the actual cost of the product or service. Consider that you plan to purchase one of the following: a house, a lot, a car, a boat, a vacation. What are your conclusions?

3. Write a paper on the sources of credit information. Review typical sources for businesses and individuals. Indicate what information would be available if an individual were to seek data on his or her own credit rating. Prepare a summary of conclusions.

CASE PROBLEMS

Case 5-1

Superior Oil Company

The credit department of Superior Oil Company has published a booklet on credit information for the members of its sales organization. The following dialogue, included in the booklet, describes a situation in which Frank Barnes, a sales representative, is calling on Jim Brown, a customer, who owns a large dairy ranch. Brown has been given a temporary extension of credit, and he now wants to stay on a 60-day basis.

Frank Barnes (*area representative*):   Good morning, Mr. Brown. I put that barrel of Animal Fly Spray on the rack where you wanted it.

Jim Brown (*customer*):   Thanks, Frank. I'll be needing it this afternoon, so I'm glad you got here.

Frank: I knew you wanted to use it. That's why I made it a point to stop this morning.

Brown: I've got to hand it to you, Frank. You've never disappointed me on a delivery.

Frank: Thanks, Mr. Brown. By the way, I have your statement here. It's for $230.

Brown: How much is the oldest month?

Frank: It's $125, but could you make the check for both months this time?

Brown: No, just the oldest month like I've been doing. Isn't that OK? I'll bet you'd be satisfied if all your accounts paid in 60 days.

Frank: Well, hardly, Mr. Brown. Our business or any business has to collect promptly to pay its bills just the same as you. That's why we have 30-day terms. Besides, it wouldn't be fair to ask my other customers to pay every month and then let you take two months. You wouldn't like it if we were regularly giving our other customers twice as long as we give you to pay.

Brown: Maybe I wouldn't. But if your company doesn't think I'm good for that much money, I don't know as how I want to keep on trading with them.

Frank: The amount you owe isn't the question at all. It's just a matter of payment in line with our regular terms upon which we sell to all our customers. In fact, I'll gladly deliver to you right now any products you want even though they might add up to several times the amount you now owe for two months' deliveries.

Brown: Why all the fuss today? I've been paying you this way for months.

Frank: That's right—I remember it was some six months ago when you had to lay out some extra money for hay you asked me if it would be OK to skip paying that month. I don't think either one of us had in mind then that it would become a permanent paying plan.

Brown: No, perhaps we didn't. But regardless of that, I can't pay both months now. I could borrow the money, but if you make me do that I'll buy from someone else.

Frank: I'm not asking you to do that, Mr. Brown, but let's go back over this situation. You paid me right on the dot for a long time, and there was never any question about payment. Then one day about six months ago you asked me to let you skip paying that month, and you'll recall I told you the company was willing to help you out with a temporary extension. You really don't mean that as a direct result of my granting you a favor you would buy from some other oil company, do you?

Brown: No, I guess that wouldn't be right. But I can't pay $230 this month, and I don't want to have to borrow from the bank at this time of year, particularly since I'm all clear with them.

Frank: It was a help to you when we gave you the extension. Let's see if we can't again figure out something that will help you. How about this? The 60-day balance is $125—you planned on paying that today. That leaves a balance of $105. Let's set that figure aside as our problem to solve. Suppose we divide it three ways—could you add the one third, $35, to your regular check today and then do the same thing next month and the month after that? I'd appreciate it if you would.

Brown: Yes, I can do that. Milk production will be higher the next three months.

Frank: That's fine. I'll make a note of it on my copy of your statement *(writing on duplicate statement).* "Paid 60-day purchases and one third of balance, $35. Will pay $35 next month, plus the 30-day purchases, and the following month will pay balance on statement." Is that right, Mr. Brown?

Brown: That's OK, Frank. Let me borrow your pen and I'll make out this check.

Frank *(accepting check):* Thanks very much.

Brown: That's all right, Frank.

Frank: By the way, Mr. Brown, I noticed the oil is low in that 30-barrel. Hadn't I better fill it when I bring out gasoline next week?

Brown: You might as well. I really depend on you to see that I have the oil and gas I need around here.

Frank: OK. Thanks again. I'll see you sometime next Tuesday.

Brown: So long, Frank.

Questions

1. Do you have any suggestions whereby Frank Barnes could improve his handling of this situation? If so, what?
2. What sales techniques did Barnes use effectively during the interview? Discuss each technique, and indicate why you believe the technique to be good.

Case 5–2

Pert Drug Company

Jennie Wren is a sales representative for the Pert Drug Company. She calls on a number of customers in Tampa, Florida. One of her customers, Mr. Sparrow, has been in the retail drugstore business for a very short time. He is operating his store on a fairly small working capital.

The Pert Drug Company has established a maximum credit limit of $2,000 for the Sparrow Company. Terms of sale are 2 percent 10 days, net 60 days. Sparrow hopes to develop a strong credit rating.

Ms. Wren is responsible for calling on drugstores to obtain competitive information and to get distribution of all designated Pert products. She is also responsible for making collections and submitting reports on them to the credit manager.

In a recent discussion with Mr. Sparrow, Jennie decided to encourage him to take advantage of the available cash discount terms. Mr. Sparrow's initial response was that he was short of working capital and couldn't see any benefit to him or to her company if he took the discounts.

Questions

1. How would taking the discount help Mr. Sparrow?
2. How would taking the discount help the Pert Drug Company?
3. Make an analysis of whether the Sparrow Company could gain by borrowing the money to take advantage of the discount terms.

SELECTED REFERENCES

"After All Buyers Can Be Choosers," *Sales & Marketing Management*, December 13, 1976, p. 16.

Cole, Robert A. *Consumer and Commercial Credit Management.* Homewood, Ill:, Richard D. Irwin, 1976.

"The Equal Credit Opportunity Act: An Evaluation." *Journal of Marketing,* Spring 1979, pp. 95-104.

French, Warren; Henkel, Jan; and Cox, James, III. "When the Buyer is the Object of Price Discrimination." *Journal of Purchasing and Materials Management,* Spring 1979, pp. 2-7.

Gray, P. J. "The Case for Credit Cards." *Bankers Magazine,* July 1978, pp. 26-30.

Griffin, Al. *The Credit Jungle.* Chicago: Regnery, 1971.

Hanan, Mack. "Can't Bear Telling Customers about a Price Rise? Sell 'em on Value." *Sales & Marketing Management,* August 29, 1977, pp. 96-111.

Hendrickson, Robert A. *The Cashless Society.* New York: Dodd, Mead, 1972.

"Legal Developments in Marketing." A regular section in each issue of the *Journal of Marketing.*

"New Breed Looks beyond Low Bidders." *Purchasing,* September 13, 1978, pp. 59-61.

"That Old Devil Price." *Sales & Marketing Management,* September 17, 1979, p. 28.

Chapter 6

ADVERTISING AND
SALES PROMOTION

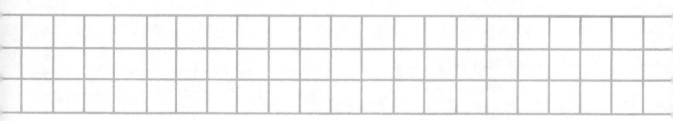

Advertising and sales promotion activities of many companies provide salespeople with valuable assistance in selling new buyers and in helping to create repeat sales. With national and local advertising playing such a dominant role in selling, and with the great variety of sales promotion activities currently being employed, salespeople cannot represent their companies effectively unless they are prepared to talk intelligently in these fields.

While there is no clear-cut distinction between advertising activities and sales promotion activities, for purposes of this discussion the following definitions of the American Marketing Association are used:

> Advertising is any paid form of nonpersonal presentation and promotion of ideas, goods or services by an identified sponsor. It involves the use of such media as the following: magazine and newspaper space, motion pictures, outdoor (posters, skywriting, signs, etc.), direct mail, novelties (calendars, blotters, etc.), radio and television, cards (car, bus, etc.), catalogues, directories and references, programs and menus, [and] circulars.[1]

While this list is not intended to be all-inclusive, it offers an insight into the potentialities of advertising as a selling aid.

Sales promotion activities are sales activities that supplement personal selling and advertising, coordinate them, and help to make them effective. The following activities are included: training the dealer's salespeople, supplying dealer aids, planning sales programs, preparing point-of-purchase displays, supplying management information, and providing special help to the dealer and/or to the ultimate customer in any way which increases sales and makes satisfied customers. For many companies, the use of advertising media is an important part of sales promotion activities.

Selling and advertising—A team

Personal selling and advertising are designed to accomplish the same ultimate objective. Each is important, and one will probably never be able to supplant the other.

Advertising is addressed to the masses, while personal selling represents an attempt to solve the problems of specific individuals. Although the ultimate objective is the same, the immediate objective usually differs. Advertising builds acceptance for a product and lays the groundwork of confidence and respect for the company and its products. It is designed primarily to interest buyers and to help presell them. Personal selling involves the application of the appropriate product features to the individual buyer's needs and to the job of actually closing the sale.

Advertising departments and sales departments must be thought of as a team. Pulling together, they can do a better job of selling than either can do alone. Each has an important function to perform; each is vitally necessary in building a profitable business.

---

[1] Ralph S. Alexander and the Committee on Definitions of the American Marketing Association, *Marketing Definitions: A Glossary of Marketing Terms* (Chicago: American Marketing Association, 1960), p. 9.

Expenditures for advertising

The importance attached to advertising by major companies is shown by media expenditures for 1977 and 1978. The 1978 expenditures are expected to total almost $44 billion (see Table 6-1).

The investment of this amount of money in an attempt to help sell products, services, and ideas attests to the importance of advertising in the plans of businesses throughout the country. Selected company expenditures for advertising and the companies' advertising expenditures as a percentage of sales are shown in Table 6-2.

What, specifically, do these businesses hope to accomplish? How do advertising expenditures help the distributors? How do these expenditures help the sales representatives? What media and sales promotion plans are used? How can the salesperson use company advertising when making sales presentations? These and other questions are answered in the following pages.

ADVERTISING HELPS THE RETAILER

The retailer, the wholesaler, and the manufacturer are interested in advertising and sales promotion plans only to the extent that these plans are designed to help them sell. A logical question for a retailer to ask a manufacturer's representative is, "How will your company's advertising and sales promotion benefit me?" There are at least five good answers to this question.

Increases turnover

Most retailers are interested in securing a maximum turnover of their stock. Any technique which will help them increase their stock turn will command their immediate attention.

A retailer can sell a nationally advertised product more quickly than a product which is not nationally advertised, because the advertising has acquainted the consumer with the product name and its value before the consumer enters the store. This means that the retailer invests money in a product for a shorter time, and can use the money received from its sale to buy more merchandise. The more often the retailer can use the dollars invested, the greater profits will be and the less capital will be needed to maintain business volume.

If a stock of nationally advertised products is sold out four times per year and a stock of nonadvertised products is sold out only twice per year, the dealer secures twice as much business from the investment in the advertised products than from the investment in the nonadvertised products.

While the margin of profit to the retailer may be less on nationally

Table 6-1

Advertising volume in the United States in 1977 and 1978

Medium	1977 $ millions	1977 Percent of total	1978 (preliminary) $ millions	1978 Percent of total	Percent of change
Newspapers					
Total	11,132	29.2	12,690	29.0	+14.0
National	1,677	4.4	1,810	4.1	+ 8.0
Local	9,455	24.8	10,880	24.9	+15.0
Magazines					
Total	2,162	5.7	2,595	5.9	+20.0
Weeklies	903	2.4	1,165	2.7	+29.0
Women's	565	1.5	670	1.5	+19.0
Monthlies	694	1.8	760	1.7	+10.0
Farm publications	90	0.2	105	0.2	+14.0
Television					
Total	7,612	20.0	8,850	20.2	+16.0
Network	3,460	9.1	3,910	8.9	+13.0
Spot	2,204	5.8	2,600	5.9	+18.0
Local	1,948	5.1	2,340	5.4	+20.0
Radio					
Total	2,634	6.9	2,955	6.8	+12.0
Network	137	0.4	160	0.4	+16.0
Spot	546	1.4	610	1.4	+12.0
Local	1,951	5.1	2,185	5.0	+12.0
Direct mail	5,333	14.0	6,030	13.8	+13.0
Business publications	1,221	3.2	1,420	3.3	+16.0
Outdoor					
Total	418	1.1	465	1.1	+11.0
National	290	0.8	310	0.7	+ 7.0
Local	128	0.3	155	0.4	+21.0
Miscellaneous					
Total	7,518	19.7	8,630	19.7	+15.0
National	3,935	10.3	4,495	10.3	+15.0
Local	3,583	9.4	4,135	9.4	+15.0
Total					
National	21,055	55.2	24,045	55.0	+14.2
Local	17,065	44.8	19,695	45.0	+15.4
Grand total	38,120	100.0	43,740	100.0	+14.7

Note: Data reflect final revisions for 1977 and preliminary figures for 1978.

Source: Reprinted with permission from the January 8, 1979 issue of *Advertising Age*, p. 58. Copyright 1979 by Crain Communications, Inc.

advertised products than on nonadvertised products, the increase in sales volume brought about by advertising creates a greater total profit and a higher rate of return on money invested in inventories.

Builds greater store traffic

The retailer is constantly attempting to attract more customers into the store. A well-advertised product can help accomplish this.

Table 6-2

100 leaders' advertising as percent of sales (covering total 1978 ad expenditures, including measured and unmeasured media)

Ad rank	Company	Advertising	Sales	Advertising as percent of sales
Airlines				
73	UAL Inc.	$ 50,624,437	$ 3,890,298,000	1.3
84	Trans World Corp.	37,500,000	3,695,000,000	1.0
92	Eastern Airlines	34,800,000	2,379,564,000	1.5
97	American Airlines	29,000,000	2,735,508,000	1.1
98	Delta Air Lines	28,900,000	2,225,447,000	1.3
Appliances, TV, radio				
21	RCA Corp.	140,000,000	6,644,500,000	2.1
31	General Electric Co.	121,294,400	19,653,800,000	0.6
79	North American Philips Co.	42,100,000	2,184,011,000	1.9
Automobiles				
4	General Motors Corp.	266,346,000	63,221,100,000	0.4
8	Ford Motor Co.	210,000,000	42,784,100,000	0.5
10	Chrysler Corp.	188,900,000	13,600,000,000	1.4
61	Toyota Motor Sales U.S.A.	64,575,700	12,767,840,000	0.5
65	Nissan Motor Co.	61,492,200	10,437,488,000	0.6
69	Volkswagen of America	57,000,000	14,110,000,000	0.4
78	American Motors Corp.	43,444,500	2,585,428,000	1.7
89	Honda Motor Co.	35,000,000	1,639,000,000	2.1
Food				
3	General Foods Corp.	340,000,000	5,472,500,000	6.2
14	General Mills	170,000,000	3,745,000,000	4.5
17	Beatrice Foods Co.	150,370,000	7,468,373,000	2.0
19	Norton Simon Inc.	144,591,000	2,428,797,000	6.0
20	Esmark	141,431,000	5,863,962,000	2.4
23	McDonald's	136,803,000	4,575,000,000	3.0
36	Kraft Inc.	114,166,700	5,669,900,000	2.0
38	Pillsbury Co.	104,000,000	2,165,983,000	4.8
40	Consolidated Foods	91,500,000	4,700,000,000	1.9
42	Ralston Purina Co.	91,000,000	4,058,400,000	2.2
43	Nabisco Inc.	95,600,000	2,197,300,000	4.1
49	Kellogg Co.	79,600,000	1,690,600,000	4.7
52	Nestle Co.	77,919,000	1,306,000,000	6.0
56	H. J. Heinz Co.	74,111,000	2,150,027,000	3.4
58	Quaker Oats Co.	69,312,000	1,685,600,000	4.1
60	CPC International	65,901,700	3,221,800,000	2.0
70	Campbell Soup Co.	56,400,000	1,983,659,000	2.8
74	Borden Inc.	50,000,000	3,802,559,000	1.3
86	Morton Norwich	36,182,000	656,733,000	5.5
94	Standard Brands	34,191,000	2,400,000,000	1.4
99	Carnation Co.	28,500,000	2,576,047,000	1.1

Source: *Advertising Age,* September 6, 1979, p. 8. Copyright 1979 by Crain Communications, Inc. Reprinted with permission. Quotation or reproduction in whole or in part without written permission is expressly prohibited. For further information on advertising expenditures, see "Estimated Advertising Expenditures in Selected Industries," table 1-7, *Sales & Marketing Management,* February 25, 1980, pp. 90–91.

Customers who have developed a preference for a particular brand name are likely to trade where they know that brand is available. When they are attracted to a store to purchase a specific brand name product, the retailer is in a favorable position to sell related products. The customer who prefers Arrow shirts, for example, is likely to need ties, socks, and handkerchiefs.

Store traffic is the basis for great numbers of impulse purchases. It is not unusual for customers to buy on impulse as much as or more than the amount of their planned purchases.

Builds store prestige

The manufacturer's trademark or trade name, in many cases, has become synonymous with quality, style, service, or economy. Value has been associated with the product.

The value attached to a trademark or trade name is likely to be transferred, in the customer's eyes, to the retail store. The customer's only contact with the manufacturer is through the retailer. If the store stocks well-known brands of merchandise, which are considered to be "good buys," then it is viewed as a "good" store. Just as individuals are judged by the company they keep, so a store is judged by the merchandise it carries.

Supplies product information

An excellent way to supply salespeople with the necessary product sales features is through the use of company advertising and sales promotion material.

Catalogs, advertisements, sales literature, manuals, and other effective media are accessible sources of product information. The salesclerk's ability to supply accurate data on the product reflects credit upon the store. Lack of information or inaccurate information will create dissatisfied customers.

Insures more economical selling

The amount of wages a retailer pays the salesforce is a substantial percentage of total expense. The more sales each salesclerk can make, the smaller the share of wages each product will have to bear and the more valuable the employee will be to the store.

Nationally advertised products require less effort and time to sell. This means that the salesclerk can handle more customers per day, thus reducing the cost of selling. Often when customers request a nationally advertised brand, the salesclerk needs only to wrap it up or to supply an appropriate size, style, and color.

During periods of rising costs, retailers look for every available opportunity to reduce expenses. The salesperson must be sure that the retailer is aware of what advertising can contribute to more efficient store operation.

ADVERTISING BENEFITS THE SELLER

The value sales representatives receive from company advertising is in direct proportion to their knowledge of the company program and the skill they exhibit in the use of that knowledge. Advertising programs have been designed to help salespeople sell and not to compete with them. In fact, it has been said that advertising depends upon salespeople for its complete fulfillment.

Advertising increases sales

As an economic force, advertising helps create more sales. Mass production and mass distribution depend upon mass advertising. Creating a demand which will enable more products to be produced at lower prices is one part of the advertising job. While people may eventually learn about a good product without advertising, through effective advertising more people learn about a product's merits in a shorter time.

Advertising reinforces sales points

Salespeople who use company advertising to reinforce their sales talk are taking advantage of a powerful selling force. The prospect is likely to give more weight to the claims made in a sales talk if the salesperson can produce a company advertisement or a testimonial confirming the claims. If the product is nationally advertised, what could be more certain to prove a point than to display current copies of magazine or newspaper advertisements featuring the product?

Advertising secures leads

Some company advertising is designed primarily to secure leads. This type of advertising is frequently used by insurance companies. Free booklets, calendar pads, datebooks, or other gifts are offered to the prospect to return a card with a date of birth or some other information. The sales agent delivers the gift and determines the sender's need and interest in insurance.

Investment companies, book publishers, land developers, and many manufacturers of commercial and industrial products utilize advertising for this purpose.

Advertising presells customers and prospects

Many manufacturers are convinced that their sales representatives can do a better job if the company prepares the way. Some writers compare this advance conditioning of the prospect or customer to the artillery barrage which paves the way for an infantry advance. Obstacles are removed, hazards are eliminated, and sales resistance may be softened. The customer who has read company advertising and has a definite picture of what the product will do requires less selling than the customer who first learns of the product when the salesperson calls.

The use of advertising in preselling customers and prospects saves time, helps eliminate unlikely prospects, and reduces selling effort.

Advertising contacts people who are difficult to reach

A necessary job in selling is to contact not only the person who places the order but also those individuals who may influence the buyer's choice. In many instances the buyer's choice merely reflects the wishes of some other employee or officer of the company. The job of contacting all of the individuals who may influence the purchase of a particular product is a difficult one, and it can seldom be accomplished solely on the basis of personal contact. The job can be simplified by the use of company advertising.

Effective company advertising acquaints prospects, and those who influence prospects, with the company's product and may develop a desire to buy. Help of this kind creates more sales and therefore makes more money for salespeople.

Advertising sells between calls

Salespeople cannot find time to call on their prospects and customers as often as these can be reached through advertising. While the frequency of personal calls will depend upon the value placed on each customer, the product sold, and the territory covered, it is not uncommon for salespeople to cover their territories only two to four times per year. Between calls, advertising can work to make visits more profitable and selling easier.

One advertising executive observed that without advertising help salespeople would have to make more than 60 personal calls a day in order to call on each prospect just once a month.

The combination of personal calls plus advertising between calls makes an effective selling team.

Advertising educates and stimulates the salesperson

A salesperson can use advertising to secure data which can be incorporated into the sales presentation. The sales features which are currently emphasized in company advertising are effective selling points.

The company probably spends much time and money in product, consumer, and market analyses, and its advertising is expected to feature those points which are of interest to the customer and the prospect.

ADVERTISING MEDIA AND SALES PROMOTION AIDS

The advertising media and sales promotion aids utilized by a company can be effective only if salespeople know how to make them effective sales aids. Salespeople should know the principal facts about each advertising medium.

Advertising media

The media which companies are most likely to utilize to supplement personal sales efforts are discussed in the following pages. The advertising expenditures in 1978 of the ten largest national advertisers in the United States are listed in Table 6-3. A standard textbook on advertising should be a part of the progressive salesperson's library.

Newspapers. Newspaper advertising is designed to reach the local public and is usually directed to a relatively small area. Newspaper advertising gives both national and local advertisers an opportunity to change their copy to fit the specific situation in any geographic area. Advertisements can be changed on short notice, and emphasis can be placed where it will do the company the most good.

Table 6-3

Top ten leading national advertisers, 1978 (total advertising expenditures in $ millions)

Procter & Gamble	$554.0
Sears Roebuck & Co.	417.9
General Foods	340.0
General Motors Corp.	266.3
K mart	250.0
Phillip Morris, Inc.	236.8
Warner-Lambert Co.	211.0
Ford Motor Co.	210.0
Bristol-Myers Co.	192.8
Chrysler Corp.	188.9

Source: Reprinted with permission from the September 6, 1979 issue of *Advertising Age*, p. 1. Copyright 1979 by Crain Communications, Inc.

The national advertiser can expect to pay a higher rate than the local advertiser, and this is one reason why the salesperson may attempt to secure a tie-in.

Newspaper advertising by national advertisers may be used to create more sales for local retailers and to keep the company before the public to maintain its position in the field. Most of the newspaper advertising used by local retailers and distributors is designed to create immediate sales.

Magazines. This medium is more suitable for regional and national advertising programs than for strictly local coverage. Magazines are selective in their audiences, since each magazine or group of magazines appeals to readers with a particular interest. Magazine advertisements can be designed to reach farmers, bankers, almost any group of retailers, accountants, engineers, teachers —in fact, hundreds of groups with special interests. Magazines are more selective in their audiences than are newspapers.

Magazines are less flexible than newspapers, because most magazines require advertising copy to be in the publisher's hands several weeks before the publication date. This requirement prevents any extensive use of current events in copy and makes it difficult for the advertiser to make last-minute copy changes. Magazines are often kept and reread, and this practice allows the reader to refer back to advertisements of interest.

The job of magazine advertising is to create and maintain a continuing demand for company products. In most cases, magazine advertising is designed to help the sales of local retailers, although the local retailers may not be mentioned by name. Many successful local promotions have been timed to correlate with the manufacturers' national and regional campaigns. Retailers have found it effective to include copies of magazine advertisements in window and store displays. Salespeople who sell direct to the consumer have also found that magazine advertisements, if used appropriately in the sales presentation, lend strength to the acceptance of their products.

Radio. Radio advertising can provide coverage for a select geographic area, but for intensity of coverage it probably does not compare with newspaper advertising. A certain degree of audience selectivity is provided by the type of program scheduled. However, most radio programs attempt to appeal to the masses, even though only a small percentage of the potential audience listens to any one program. Advertisers can secure national, regional, and local coverage by choosing the appropriate stations and networks.

The nature of radio advertising limits its effectiveness in some ways. Listeners cannot refer back to the advertisement to secure more data. Also, radio listeners often engage in other activities while listening to a program. This impairs the effectiveness of the advertising message. On the other hand, radio combines the powers of speech and sound in putting across a message.

Many companies use national network advertising to promote goodwill and others use it to increase the sales of their products through local retailers by a direct sales appeal. While some local advertisers schedule programs for goodwill purposes, most are interested in directly promoting the sale of specific products or groups of products.

According to the National Association of Broadcasters the overwhelming bulk of radio's growth will come from FM outlets. Projections indicate that whereas revenues of AM stations will advance by only 22 percent between 1975 and 1980 and by only 7 percent between 1980 and 1985, FM outlets will grow 148 percent and 79 percent, respectively.[2]

Television. Television has grown rapidly since the Federal Communications Commission first permitted the commercial operation of television stations in 1941. Television has important advantages over newspapers, magazines, and radio as an advertising medium. Transmitted directly into homes, it combines the effectiveness of pictorial and color presentation, possible in newspapers and magazines, with the advantage of sound, which has been radio's stock-in-trade. And it obtains an even greater advantage from animation—its pictures move.

Ownership of television sets is growing each year. Currently 74.5 million American households are devoting billions of hours annually to viewing television. These television households now amount to 98 percent of the total households in the continental United States.[3]

The A. C. Nielsen Company has estimated that as of 1978 81 percent of all U.S. TV households owned color TV sets, compared to 41 percent in 1970.[4]

Cable television was estimated to be in 18 percent of U.S. TV households as of November 1978. At that time, about 13,400,000 TV households subscribed to a cable service.[5]

Television was originally limited to the larger metropolitan areas, but it expanded rapidly, and smaller communities now provide facilities for advertisers desiring to use this medium. The need to both see and hear a television commercial limits somewhat the effectiveness of television advertising. Furthermore with television, as with radio, it is impossible to refer back to an advertisement after it

---

[2] National Association of Broadcasters, "Radio in 1985," *Sales & Marketing Management*, July 11, 1977, p. 16.

[3] A. C. Nielsen, "1979 Nielsen Report on Television," p. 3.

[4] Ibid., p. 3.

[5] Ibid., p. 16.

has been presented. However, many advertisers use the medium as one part of their advertising and sales promotion campaigns.

Direct mail.   This form of advertising provides a high degree of reader selectivity if the mailing list is well chosen and up to date. The message is planned to go directly from the advertiser to the prospect. The advertiser's opportunity to expand or contract the number of names to be used, and to stop and start the program at will, makes direct-mail advertising highly flexible. Specific territories or markets may be covered, which adds to the selectivity of this medium.

The effectiveness of direct-mail advertising is easily tested. Through proper analysis, costs can be determined to show cost-per-inquiry, cost-per-sale, or cost-per-name on the mailing list. The first two cost figures are of the greatest importance to the advertiser.

Direct mail can be as elaborate or as inexpensive as the user desires. It is commonly used by direct-selling organizations to secure leads, and many companies use it exclusively to consummate the sale.

Other media.   Newspapers, magazines, radio, television, and direct mail are probably the major media used for advertising if importance is measured by total expenditures. Other media are used by producers, manufacturers, and distributors, however, to supplement these media. Also, for some advertisers a minor medium may account for greater expenditures than the major media when the minor medium is designed to accomplish a particular purpose important to the advertisers.

Outdoor posters.   This medium is frequently used along highways and along main thoroughfares within a city. The old term *billboards* is no longer used by advertising people in this field, since the term has been associated with adverse criticism.

The advertiser secures a high degree of geographic selectivity through the use of this medium. Location of the posters within an area can be controlled, and this control allows concentration or saturation where it is most desirable.

Painted displays and electric displays are other forms of outdoor advertising. While a degree of selectivity is possible in the use of these media, they are usually less flexible in use than posters. It is customary to change them less frequently.

Car cards.   This medium is used to appeal to the large group of people who use public transportation to ride to and from work. Car cards are usually changed about every 30 days. The coverage that can be obtained ranges from two cards to each vehicle to as little as one card to every four vehicles. Items of low unit cost, such as candy, cigarettes, chewing gum, household products, and food products, make up the bulk of the goods advertised through this medium.

Miscellaneous. Advertisers use many other forms of advertising. The emphasis placed on the lesser media will vary from product to product and from company to company, and the emphasis of any particular company will vary from time to time.

Sales promotion aids

Sales representatives who plan to provide the most service to prospects and customers must be thoroughly familiar with the sales promotion aids and plans developed by the company. It is difficult to distinguish between advertising and sales promotion. The term *sales promotion* has been used rather loosely, and there appears to be no standard group of activities which all companies classify as sales promotion. The results of one investigation, however, show that most sales promotion departments are concerned with point-of-purchase materials, direct mail, design and execution of premium plans, trade shows and exhibits, demonstrations, sampling, sales meetings, sales training, sales contests, dealer contests, consumer contests, sales bulletins, sales films, house organs, and advertising and sales portfolios. They have a primary interest in some of these areas and a secondary interest in others.

A few of the more important sales promotion activities are discussed on the following pages.[6]

Training aids. Some companies provide retailers and other distributors with considerable help in training retail and wholesale salespeople. This help may be in the form of films, bulletins, publications, manuals, demonstrations, and other sales aids. The training may be accomplished through the company's sales representatives, through special representatives from the company, or by training specialists who conduct programs at the factory or home office.

These aids can become important features which help the salesperson increase the distributor's turnover and hence result in greater sales. Many times the training aids can be an important factor in closing sales and in opening new outlets.

Special sales aids. Some companies provide retailers and distributors with considerable help in planning and conducting special sales promotions. This evidence of interest in the retailer's welfare is a strong selling point for many sales representatives.

This type of aid may be provided through a cooperative analysis of the retailer's sales problems and through the recommending of

---

[6] For a series of excellent articles on sales promotion, see "Marketing and Sales Promotion," *Sales & Marketing Management*, August 1978, special 32-page pullout section.

appropriate sales-stimulating activities. These activities may include the development of a special direct-mail campaign; the development of a special newspaper, radio, or television advertising promotion; the installation of new store signs or other means of identification; the participation in trade shows or commercial and industrial exhibits; the use of demonstrators in the store; the inauguration of a sampling campaign; the development of sales contests and consumer contests; and the utilization of premiums, novelties, stickers, tags, and labels.

Point-of-purchase display aids. There is constant competition among sales representatives to get their company's aids used in the most desirable locations.

Display aids may include charts, graphs, pictures, signs, window displays, counter displays, floor displays, banners, and wall hangers. They may involve the use of baskets, bins, racks, price cards, stands, and other devices for display purposes.

The appropriate shelf display of products is important to manufacturers because of the known relationship between the sale of products and the kind and location of the display provided for them. Salespeople who have attractive display aids can increase the sales of their products substantially if they can convince the retailer that the aids should be used in preferred locations.

Management aids. In addition to the aids previously mentioned, which are usually designed to help secure immediate sales for the retailer or dealer, some companies provide management aids for the dealer. This type of help is designed to engender goodwill through helping the store owner reduce expenses and thus lead to additional sales for the company.

Company aids are available that will help the retailer remodel the store; improve the arrangement of merchandise; improve stock control; employ more efficient accounting, credit, and collection procedures; and improve the procedures and plans used when hiring and compensating salespeople.

USE OF AIDS IN THE SALES PRESENTATION

The use of company advertising and sales promotion aids should be incorporated into the appropriate parts of the sales presentation. Sales are likely to be made more easily and more quickly.

Determine emphasis for each buyer

The salesperson must first determine whether the company's advertising and sales promotions are of particular interest to the buyer.

If they are, the salesperson should be prepared to use pertinent data as one of the sales presentation features. If the buyer's interests are centered on other sales features, good judgment suggests placing the emphasis where it is most likely to result in a sale.

Many salespeople who sell direct to the ultimate user are supplied with portfolios containing full-sized copies of company advertisements which have recently appeared in leading magazines. These advertisements may be shown to the prospect at the beginning of the interview as a technique for starting the sales talk, or they may be referred to as needed to reemphasize some of the product's sales features. To some buyers, the mere fact that a product is nationally advertised lends it prestige.

To other buyers, the sales promotion aids may be of major concern. These buyers may be more interested in the merchandising aids that are available than in the price of the product. A single effective merchandising aid may cause some buyers to decide to do business with the sales representative.

Explain the program clearly

The buyer is entitled to a clear, definite explanation of the benefits of the company's program.

It is not sufficient to say, "We carry on an extensive advertising program in national magazines." The sales representative should point out the company's advertising schedules, quoting the names of specific magazines, their circulation, the date of their appearance on the newsstands, the cost involved, the theme or appeal used, and what this advertising means to the dealer. Actual copies of proposed ads and company-prepared schedules should be shown.

If a national network is to be used for company advertising, or a local station is being employed, the salesperson must be able to answer such buyer questions as: Who listens to the program? How effectively does the program sell? What can I do to cash in on the company advertising? How much will it cost me? What help does the company offer?

Examples of successful promotions with retailers in other cities would be particularly interesting and convincing if the circumstances were similar. Samples of scripts prepared to advertise the store and for use immediately following the company program would be effective.

If the company has prepared store display aids or other dealer helps to increase the sale of the product, these aids should be described in detail, and illustrations and samples should be shown. The factors of cost, appearance, effectiveness, accessibility, installation, and timeliness should be discussed.

Help solve dealer problems

If the sales representative can make appropriate suggestions as to the purpose and relative costs of various media and can offer some profitable sales-stimulating plans, both the sales representative and the company will be enhanced in the eyes of the retailer. A retailer may ask these questions:

1. *"How much money should I spend for advertising?"*

There is no immediate answer for this question. There are, however, some factors which may help determine an appropriate figure. The following points should be considered: Is the retailer new in the business, or is the firm old and established? A retailer just getting started will be required to spend a larger sum than one who is well known. Does the retailer carry wide lines and deep stocks in an attempt to attract the masses, or are the stocks and the appeal limited? How large an area is covered in advertising? What are competitors doing? How are business conditions? Is the store large or small in size? What media are available?

2. *"Which media should I use?"*

After careful consideration of media advantages and disadvantages, it may be decided that several media can do the job. One survey shows that newspapers are the dominant medium, getting about 70 percent of the average budget.[7] Factors which will affect the decision include: What circulation or coverage can be expected from each medium? How much will advertising cost per reader or per sale? Is time a factor in the retailer's advertising? What media are used by competitors? What are the immediate or long-range objectives of the retailer's advertising? Do any peculiar consumer preferences affect the area?

3. *"How can I improve my point-of-purchase displays?"*

This question is easier to answer than the two previous questions. Questions which help point out the requirements for good window displays include: Does your display cause people to stop and look and cause some to come into the store to buy? Is the merchandise clean, well displayed, attractive, popular? Are the items related? Is the window lighting good? Is the merchandise timely? Is the display uncrowded? Have signs or cards been used in the display? Are the profitable items displayed? Is the display changed frequently? Does it tie in with other media advertising?

---

[7] Martin Everett, "Co-op at the Crossroads," *Sales & Marketing Management*, December 13, 1976, p. 41. See also Ed Crimmins, "As Retailers Increasingly Turn to Radio, It's Bound to Attract More Co-op Dollars," *Sales & Marketing Management*, February 6, 1978, p. 48 ff.

Questions which may bring out some of the important factors in good store display include: Do table and counter displays show merchandise of the correct size or sizes? Are the display racks sturdy and attractive? Are the items displayed popular items? Competitive? Timely? Are the displays located so as to provide for the impulse buying of the customer? Are items priced? Are the displays well stocked? Do the displays tie in with window or other media advertising? How often are the displays changed? Are the walls, ceilings, and floors appropriate for displays? Are the display cards neat, readable, attractive, and informative?

4. *"How can I increase sales?"*

The satisfactory answer to this question is the goal of most businesses. At least a part of the answer may be found in the use of a selected group of the sales promotion aids.

Probably the first concern of salespeople is to help the retailer sell more of their company's products. Data such as the following may be reviewed before making any suggestions. Are the products priced right? Are sufficient products on hand to provide a satisfactory selection for the buyer? What has been the turnover rate? How and where are the products displayed? Are the salespeople sufficiently informed to sell effectively? What sales aids are used? What service is available to the buyer after the sale has been made? These and other questions may be used to determine where improvement is necessary.

Some companies have dealers' or merchants' service divisions which will work with retailers in securing answers to promotional and advertising problems. Sales representatives cannot be expected to supply the answers to all retailers' problems, nor can they afford to spend unlimited time with them.

THE SALESPERSON'S RESPONSIBILITY TO THE COMPANY

Encourage use of company aids

The need for a positive effort by company salespeople to encourage the use of available store display aids is shown by the results of several studies. Some studies indicate that when the manufacturer exerts no particular effort to get material displayed only a small percentage of it is used but that with emphasis on how, when, and why to use it, plus help in installation, as much as 80 percent is used. Only when the retailer is convinced that the manufacturer's advertising and sales promotion aids are valuable in increasing store sales will the retailer be willing to supply the time, effort, and space necessary for their effective use.

The purchase by customers of items which they had not planned to buy before they entered the store is called "impulse buying." Many studies show that impulse buying may account for as much as 40 percent of the purchases of some customers. With so many buying decisions being influenced at the point of sale, display is becoming more necessary for volume sales.

Secure a tie-in

A good sales representative will encourage retailers to tie in with company national or local advertising. The manufacturer customarily agrees to reimburse the retailer for a portion of the cost of local advertising when it is used to supplement the manufacturer's program. One large furniture manufacturer incorporates into its franchise agreement with retailers the provision to issue an advertising credit equal to one half of the retailer's advertising and promotional costs. The amount may not exceed 5 percent of the cost of shipments purchased by the retailer during the period.[8]

This practice enables retailers to direct national advertising to their stores by featuring in local advertising the same appeal or theme as is used in national magazines, newspapers, television or radio networks. Direct mail and other media may be used by the manufacturer, and different manufacturers endorse different media for tie-in purposes.

Manufacturers gain from tie-in agreements because in this way they can secure more effective local advertising, and probably at a lower cost than if it were placed from the head office. Newspapers usually quote a lower rate to local advertisers than to national advertisers.

In addition, it is difficult to name local outlets in which a nationally advertised product may be secured unless the local retailer capitalizes on the national advertising. An effective tie-in, then, benefits both the local retailer and the manufacturer, and the sales representative is expected to point out the benefits which accrue to the retailer from this form of cooperation in advertising.

Get dealers' reactions and suggestions

Every manufacturer is interested in what retailers think of the company's advertising and sales promotion aids. If a company's advertising or sales aids are not well accepted, the company wants to

---

[8] For selling smaller stores on co-op programs, see "Marrying Co-op and Classified," *Sales & Marketing Management*, September 17, 1979, pp. 16-21.

know *why* and what can be done about it. It is apparent that unless advertising and sales aids help the dealer, they cannot be effective.

The sales representative is in an excellent position to advise the company on the likes and dislikes of the retailers. Retailers may suggest that display aids are too large or too small, too difficult to install, or not colorful or timely. They may point out that the aids were damaged or soiled in transit. Such comments are valuable to the company.

QUESTIONS AND PROBLEMS

1. It has been said, "An advertisement can be totally truthful, yet sound unbelievable," and "An advertisement can sound totally believable, yet be untruthful." Comment and give illustrations of the latter.

2. In-store sales promotion frequently involves the use of signs. What recommendations would you make to a store owner regarding the use of signs?

3. Co-op advertising is a mutual effort by the manufacturer and the retailer to sell products. To what extent should the retailer establish guidelines for the acceptance of co-op funds from the manufacturer?

4. If a sales representative is to appreciate advertising for what it really is—a help in selling—an understanding of its function is necessary. What are some limitations of advertising?

5. It has been said, "Advertising can do the preconditioning job far better and cheaper than salespeople. And it relieves salespeople of much of the sales burden, so that they can concentrate on the final action: the signed order." Do you agree? Why?

6. Your company has decided to encourage its retailers to conduct a direct-mail advertising campaign to supplement the company's national advertising. On your first dealer contact you get this reply: "Direct-mail pieces are used too often. Customers are getting so they don't pay any attention to them. Besides, what would we use for a mailing list? I'd much rather advertise in our local newspaper. Let's work out a deal on newspaper ads." Assume that your company prefers that retailers use direct mail and is willing to supply the direct-mail pieces for one half the actual printing cost. How would you answer the retailer? Point out five or six advantages of direct-mail advertising.

7. It has been stated that advertising lowers costs to consumers and that advertising forces competition. Comment on these statements, and supply illustrations to support your comments.

8. An advertising executive has said "We are heading for an economy without personal salespeople!" It has been suggested that the need for personal selling is declining and that advertising is slowly taking the place of countless numbers of door-to-door salespeople, counter salesclerks, demonstrators, and jobber salespeople. Do you agree with this reasoning? Why? Do you believe that personal selling is necessary even for products sold from vending machines? Illustrate.

9. What advice could you give an industrial dealer who plans to attract buyers through an exhibit at a trade or industrial show?

10. Suppose you have sold a retailer on the idea of tying in with your national advertising through local newspaper advertising. The retailer then asks you this question: "What can I do in the store to cash in on the ads that I run?" What suggestions would you make?

11. One of the most prevalent problems in merchandising today is getting point-of-purchase displays into retail stores so that they can do the job they were designed to do. What can management do to win retailer cooperation in scheduling merchandising-promotion programs through point-of-purchase displays? What can the sales representative do?

PROJECTS

1. It has been said that "advertising is a poor way to allocate a nation's resources to those consumer wants that can only be satisfied by commercial products and services. Other consumer wants such as education, hospitals, highways, and urban reconstruction—all of which fall in the 'public sector'—are thus neglected. Therefore our economy is not as well balanced as it ought to be."

   Prepare a rebuttal to this quotation, and provide appropriate source references to support your position.

2. Investigate the current role of cable television in today's marketing. Secure information on cost to the user, popularity in your community, and the bases used for marketing the service. Prepare a brief résumé of your conclusions.

3. Collect ten advertisements from magazines, newspapers, and/or direct mail. Evaluate the ads in terms of believability. Try to illustrate both good and bad ads with reasons for your decisions. Summarize your conclusions.

CASE PROBLEMS

Case 6-1

The Heritage Furniture Co.

You are a sales representative for a manufacturer of early American furniture. Your job is to call on retail outlets to sell and promote your company's furniture.

Your company has planned a sales promotion special for retail stores to stimulate sales for a one-week period. The promotion will be called the Early American Festival.

Your company is able to supply retailers with the following items for use in the promotion: displays of early American weapons; small flags; small early American antiques; early American weapons; early American soldiers' uniforms; color catalogs; color postcards, booklets, stuffers, and mailers; a custom room-decorating kit; television scripts, slides, and blowups of advertising reprints; samples of Vermont syrup; and a sound film showing how furniture is made. It will also give retailers the opportunity to rent colonial costumes for one week at a nominal price.

Questions

1. What suggestions do you have for publicizing the promotion?
2. What can be done within the store to capitalize on the Early American Festival promotion?

Case 6–2

Junque Jewelry Co.

The company sells wristwatch bands to jewelers to retail for $24.95, exclusive of taxes. Its two primary competitors are currently budgeting large sums of money for television and magazine advertising.

In 1980 Junque decided to launch a major advertising campaign to meet competition and to increase sales volume.

Color advertisements were run in selected magazines with national coverage. Some of the advertising budget was devoted to radio spot announcements. In selected areas, station break advertising was launched on television.

The company's sales representatives were briefed regarding the objectives of the advertising campaign, and it was generally believed that the advertising effort would pay considerable dividends in sales volume and profits.

One of the sales representatives called on a dealer in a small town to test the value of the new advertising program. The sales representative described in detail the company's efforts to acquaint large groups of consumers with the merits of the premium-quality watchband. After a moment's hesitation, the dealer remarked, "Listen, pal, what difference does it make to me how much money you spend on advertising all over the United States? I'm interested only in my own customers. They live right around here in my own neighborhood. Why don't you fellows quit wasting all that good money on advertising and pass the savings along to your dealers—give us a better margin or cut the price a little?"

Questions

1. How would you answer the statement made by the dealer? Discuss the benefits to the dealer of Junque advertising.

2. What must a sales representative know and what must be done to get the maximum benefits from the advertising of the company? Illustrate.

3. Discuss what the retailer must do to maximize returns on the national advertising.

Case 6–3

The Diamond Hardware Co.

Many salesclerks overlook the opportunity to increase sales because of a lack of training or because of the additional mental and physical effort required to sell more merchandise. One way for salesclerks to increase sales is through suggestion selling. The objective is to sell more than one item of merchandise to each customer whenever the opportunity presents itself. It is recognized that, poorly done, suggestion selling can offend customers. It takes skill to increase the average sales figure. Before a worthwhile suggestion can be made to a customer, the salesperson must learn how to determine what to suggest.

As the sales representative of a manufacturer of a line of hardware products, you call on the owners of small retail hardware stores. You believe that more of your company's products could be sold by the retailers if they used more intensive sales promotion techniques. An opportunity arises for you to suggest to a store owner how to increase sales through the use of suggestion selling.

Give five illustrations of statements that a retail clerk could use to increase the amount of the sale.

SELECTED REFERENCES

"Advertising and Marketing Reports on 100 Leading National Advertisers." 24th annual study. *Advertising Age*, September 6, 1979, pp. 2–160.

Backman, Jules. "Is Advertising Wasteful?" *Journal of Marketing*, January 1968, pp. 2–8.

Cascino, A. M. "There Are Predictable Responses to Advertising." *Sales & Marketing Management*, July 10, 1978, pp. 73–74.

Crimmins, Ed. "Cooperative Advertising." A regular section in *Sales & Marketing Management*.

————. "How Manufacturers' Co-op Funds Can Help Small Retailers Survive." *Sales & Marketing Management*, October 15, 1979, pp. 84–88.

_____. "A Key Co-op Issue between Retailer and Manufacturer: Whose Money Is It?" *Sales & Marketing Management*, September 5, 1979, pp. 57-60.

Dirksen, Charles J., Kroeger, Arthur; and **Nicosia, Francesco M.** *Advertising: Principles, Problems, and Cases.* Homewood, Ill.: Richard D. Irwin, 1977.

Donnelly, R. "Generating Ad Inquiries: 'Go for Quality, Not Quantity'." *Industrial Marketing*, February 1979, pp. 48-49.

Everett, Martin. "Co-op at the Crossroads." *Sales & Marketing Management*, December 13, 1976, pp. 41-46.

"Handling Co-op with Care." *Sales & Marketing Management*, November 1978, pp. 61-70.

Korn, Don. "Co-op Power for the Corner Drugstore." *Sales & Marketing Management*, July 10, 1978, pp. 27-29.

"Marketing and Sales Promotion." *Sales & Marketing Management*, August 1978. A special 32-page pullout section.

Poe, Randall. "Letter from Mad Ave." *Across the Board*, January 1979, pp. 6-17.

Sunoo, D., and **Lin, L. Y. S.** "Sales Effects of Promotion and Advertising." *Journal of Advertising Research*, October 1978, pp. 37-40.

Swinyard, Wm. R. "How Many Ad Exposures Is a Sales Call Worth?" *Journal of Advertising Research*, February 1979, pp. 17-21.

Tillman, Rollie, and **Kirkpatrick, C. A.** *Promotion: Persuasive Communication in Marketing.* Homewood, Ill.: Richard D. Irwin, 1972.

Part three

THE SALES PROCESS

This section explains and illustrates the necessary steps in prospecting and getting the right start, planning and delivering the sales presentation, dramatizing the sales presentation, handling objections, and closing sales.

Chapter 7

PROSPECTING AND
GETTING THE RIGHT START

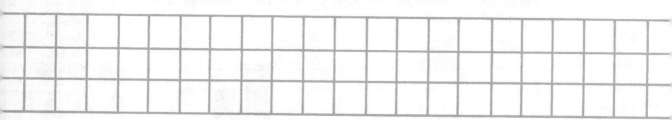

Finding new prospects and obtaining interviews is one of the most important phases of a salesperson's work. An effective plan for prospecting will prevent sales volume from slipping. The normal turnover or loss of customers from transfers, retirement, death, bankruptcy, and solicitation by aggressive competitors will soon rob a salesperson of potential customers unless there is a constant flow of new prospects.

In the following pages mention is made of the characteristics of a good prospect, how and where to obtain prospects, and how to get the most out of prospecting. Attention is also devoted to techniques in making the appointment and to the importance of making a good first impression.

PROSPECTING IS IMPORTANT

Having a list of prospects is critical to the success of experienced salespeople as well as new salespeople. Thus, acquiring prospects is a continuing process. Table 7-1 shows the daily activities of typical salespeople. This survey indicates that salespeople spend more than 30 minutes a day prospecting. The survey also reported that 15% of the calls made by consumer-product salespeople are on new customers, 27% of the calls made by service salespeople are new customers, and 20% of calls made by industrial salespeople are on new customers![1]

In today's environment, extensive changes are taking place in population movements, in the creation of new businesses and products, in the shifting of businesses to new lines, in the expansion of old-line companies, and in the methods or channels of distribution. To keep in step with these changes, many companies call upon their marketing research departments to aid the sales representatives in securing up-to-date prospecting lists. One large company estimates that its annual turnover of customers is approximately 15 percent a year. Unless this company is successful in obtaining a steady flow of new prospects, it will soon be out of business.

Prospecting is more important in some fields of selling than in others. The life insurance or real estate sales representative who does not have an effective prospecting plan, for example, usually does not last long in the business. The New York Life Insurance Company emphasizes the importance of prospecting as follows:

> No one with an ample supply of good prospects ever left the life insurance business. As long as the human heart keeps pumping blood

Table 7-1

A day in the life of a salesperson

Time spent	Consumer (hrs:min)	Industrial (hrs:min)	Service (hrs:min)	Average (hrs:min)
Calling on customers 4:30		4:37	4:25	4:35
On the phone 0:35		1:13	1:40	0:53
Traveling 2:26		2:23	1:25	2:15
On paperwork 0:55		1:31	1:10	1:11
On meals and entertainment 1:22		1:11	0:30	1:14
Prospecting for new customers 0:40		0:41	0:45	0:36
Reading specialized publications 0:24		0:16	0:10	0:32

Source: "A Day in the Life of a Salesman," *Sales Management*, October 16, 1972, p. 40. Reprinted by permission from *Sales & Marketing Management* magazine. Copyright 1972.

---

[1] "A Day in the Life of a Salesman," *Sales Management*, October 16, 1972, pp. 40-41.

through the veins, a person continues to live despite all other infir-
mities. As long as prospecting keeps pumping a supply of names, a
person continues in the life insurance business.[2]

In many types of retail selling, on the other hand, most of the
prospecting is done through advertising. Actually, the salespeople
who have the opportunity to go out and get their own prospects have
a certain advantage over the retail salespeople who must wait for
customers to come into the store. Some retailers, such as appliance
dealers, have recognized the importance of an aggressive prospecting system by having some of their salespeople call at homes to
demonstrate and sell their products.

CHARACTERISTICS OF A GOOD PROSPECT

Some salespeople make the mistake of considering everyone to be
a prospect without first determining whether individuals possess the
necessary characteristics of good prospects.

The importance of qualifying prospects is illustrated in a statement made by a vice president of Emery Air Freight Corporation:

> Most salesreps are sitting in lobbies. They're calling on wrong ac-
> counts. They're calling on accounts that give them all the business that
> they can. They're calling on people that they think can make the buy-
> ing decision when, in fact, they do not or cannot make much of it at all.
> They are efficient in talking about what they do—what their company
> provides—but not in how it fills the customer's needs, because they
> haven't probed to find out what those needs are.[3]

The successful salesperson is a realist and soon determines how
fine a screen should be used in separating the "suspects" from the
prospects. He or she discovers the most profitable way to distribute
time between prospecting and making the sales presentation.
Naturally, the amount of time spent in attempting to answer the
question "Who is a prospect?" varies for different types of selling.
The time spent depends upon such factors as the type of product or
service, the value of the salesperson's time, and the profit per sale.

The following five questions will help determine who the good
prospects are:

1. Does the prospect have a want or need which can be satisfied by
   the purchase of my products or services?
2. Does he or she have the ability to pay?
3. Does he or she have the authority to buy?

---

[2] *Prospecting Guide* (New York: New York Life Insurance Co.), p. 3.

[3] "The New Supersalesman: Wired for Success," *Business Week*, January 6, 1973,
p. 45.

4.   Can the prospect be approached favorably?

5.   Is the prospect eligible to buy?

Does a want or need exist?

Most sales are made on the basis of primary or recognized needs. The salesperson considers such needs as basic in selecting prospects, but also includes as prospects those individuals who may have unrecognized needs for the salesperson's products. The salesperson should always remember the old adage which says, "Sell a product to a customer where the product doesn't come back but the customer does." By using high-pressure tactics, sales may be made to individuals who do not need or really want the salesperson's products. Such sales benefit no one. The buyer will resent making the purchase, and a potential long-term customer will be lost.

Research has not developed infallible answers to why customers buy, but it has established that there are many reasons. Some customers buy products to satisfy basic practical needs. As pointed out in Chapter 3, customers also buy to satisfy intangible needs, such as gaining prestige or satisfying aesthetic desires.

It is not simple, therefore, to select the prospects who need a salesperson's products or services. Life insurance salespeople often use the telephone to determine the needs of a lead or "suspect." Industrial salespeople frequently have an exploratory interview to determine whether a lead has needs that their products can handle. With some product lines, virtually everyone is a prospect. For example, Avon salespeople call on all the homes in their territory because virtually everybody uses their products.

Does the prospect have the ability to buy?

The individual's or company's ability to pay for the products or services separates the "suspects" from the prospects. The real estate agent usually attempts to obtain information on the approximate financial status of each client to determine what price-range house to show. A client with a yearly salary of $20,000 and savings of $12,000 may be a genuine prospect for a house which is selling in the $50,000 to $60,000 bracket. An agent would be wasting time, however, if he or she were to show this individual a house listed to sell at $100,000. The client may have a real desire and need for the more expensive house; the client may have the authority to buy the house; the agent may be able to approach the client on a favorable basis; but the client is still not a real prospect for the higher priced house if he or she does not possess the ability to pay for the product.

Industrial companies may subscribe to a rating service such as Dun and Bradstreet or Moody's Industrial. Salespeople can use this service to determine the financial status and credit rating of a lead. Leads can also be qualified by using information obtained from local credit agencies, noncompetitive salespeople, and the Better Business Bureau.

Does the prospect have the authority to buy?

A "suspect" may have a real need for a product and may have the ability to pay for it, but may lack the authority to make the purchase. Careful advance consideration of who has the authority to buy will save the salesperson much time and effort and will result in a higher percentage of closed sales.

The importance of knowing who does the buying is illustrated by the following experience of a machine tool company. This company planned its advertising and sales efforts on the assumption that its machines were being purchased by production managers. An analysis of coupon and letter inquiries, however, disclosed that only 10 percent of the inquiries came from the production executives; 44 percent came from engineers; 29 percent came from purchasing agents; and 17 percent from others. As a result of this survey, the advertising and sales efforts of the company were directed toward the engineers and the purchasing agents.

Can the prospect be approached favorably?

An individual may possess a need for goods, may have the ability to pay, and may have the authority to buy. Nevertheless, the person may not qualify as a genuine prospect because he or she may not be accessible to the salesperson. To illustrate, the president of a large bank, a major executive of a large manufacturing company, or the senior partner in a well-established law firm normally would not be accessible to a young college graduate who is just starting a career as a sales representative for an investment trust organization. Getting an interview with these individuals may be so difficult and the chances of making a sale may be so small that the sales representative will eliminate them as possible prospects.

Is the prospect eligible to buy?

Eligibility is an equally important factor in determining whether a person is a genuine prospect. A possible prospect for life insurance may meet all of the other requirements of a real prospect but be unable to pass the necessary medical examination. This one factor alone eliminates the person as a prospect.

Similarly, if a manufacturer's representative sells exclusively to wholesalers, the representative should be certain that the individuals upon whom he or she calls are qualified wholesalers. Another factor which may determine eligibility to buy from a particular salesperson is the geographic location of the potential prospect. Many companies operate on an exclusive territorial basis. It is therefore imperative that each salesperson consider the location of a prospect to determine eligibility to buy.

HOW AND WHERE TO OBTAIN PROSPECTS

Prospecting methods and sources vary for different types of selling. A sales representative for commercial chemicals uses a different system of prospecting than that used by the automobile, real estate, or life insurance salesperson. Some of the most common methods of prospecting are described in the following sections.

Inquiries

Most companies receive a steady supply of sales leads from their advertising, telephone calls, and catalogs. The importance of these leads as a source of prospects is illustrated by the following comment:

> The exciting truth is that inquiries generated by advertising, direct mail, publicity, trade shows, etc., can and do produce sales. Our experience at Clayton Manufacturing is that at least 45 percent of our inquiries come from prospects who (1) have a real interest in our products, (2) have the necessary decision-making authority to buy them, and (3) intend to purchase the type of product about which the inquiry is made within about eight months.
>
> More than 30,000 inquiries for our basic product lines have been received and processed, and millions of dollars of sales have been identified and recorded that we can prove are directly traceable to advertising inquiries.[4]

The following example illustrates how a typical company assists its salespeople in finding customers. Beckman advertises its digital multimeter in *Electronic Technician/Dealer*, a trade magazine. A magazine reader sees the ad and requests additional information, using a reader service card in the magazine. The ad and the reader service card are shown in Figure 7-1. *ET/D* forwards information

---

[4] Frank S. Hill. "Why Clayton Loves Its Inquiries," *Sales & Marketing Management*, Special Report 117, November 22, 1976, pp. 5-6.

Figure 7-1
Advertisement and request for additional information

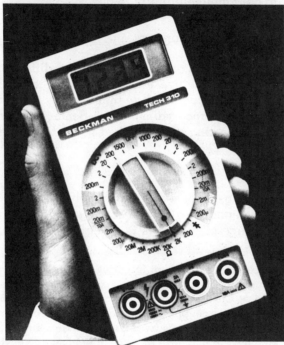

$140 Gets It All.

We just knocked down the last reasons for not going digital in a multimeter. Fast continuity measurement. And price.

Beckman's exclusive Insta-Ohms™ feature lets you do continuity checks as fast as the analogs. And Beckman's superior technology and experience let you own this beauty for such a reasonable price.

Of course you get a lot more. Like 7 functions and 29 ranges including 10 amp ac/dc current capability. 0.25% Vdc accuracy. In-circuit resistance measurements and diode/transistor test function. Two years' typical operation from a common 9-volt battery. In other words, all the features you want in one hand-held unit of exceptional good looks and design.

With 1500 Vdc overload protection, 100% instrument burn-in, plus rugged, impact-resistant case, you're assured of the utmost in dependability and long-term accuracy. You get a tough meter that keeps on going, no matter how tough the going gets.

So visit your dealer today and get your hands on the DMM that does it all. Or call (714) 871-4848, ext. 3651 for your nearest distributor.

BECKMAN

Circle No. 106 on Reader Inquiry Card

Figure 7–1 (continued)

about all people who inquire about the digital multimeter to Beckman. Each inquirer is sent a cover letter and information about the advertised product, and a follow-up inquiry card (see Figure 7–2). A copy of the inquiry is also sent to the appropriate salesperson. Based on knowledge of the territory, the salesperson determines whether a personal follow-up is appropriate at this point. If the inquirer returns the second inquiry card (frequently called a bounceback card), the salesperson is sent a "qualified" inquiry notification.

The leads are printed on a multiple copy of the form. The salesperson is asked to return a copy of the form with information about the follow-up of these leads. Leads from customer inquiries are an important source of prospects for insurance salespeople as well as industrial salespeople.

"Endless-chain" method

When sales representatives use this method of obtaining prospects, they attempt to obtain at least one additional prospect from each person whom they interview. This endless-chain method of prospecting has proven very effective in the sale of such intangible products as educational courses, insurance, and investments. Industrial salespeople also use this method to locate other people in a customer's company who may also need their products.

This simple but effective plan of prospecting produces a continuous supply of good prospects for the salesperson who is skillful in knowing when and how to ask for names. Some people object to having their names used as a means of opening the door to friends or

Figure 7–2

Cover letter, data sheet, and salesperson copy of inquiry

BECKMAN

BECKMAN INSTRUMENTS, INC.
ADVANCED ELECTRO-PRODUCTS DIVISION
2500 Harbor Boulevard, Box 3100, Fullerton, California 92634 • Telephone (714) 871-4848 • TWX: 910-592-1260 • Telex: 06-78413

Gentlemen:

Thank you for your recent inquiry regarding the Beckman Digital Multimeters. Enclosed is a brochure which describes each of the models and their accessories.

To assist you in locating your nearest Beckman Digital Multimeter Distributor, a list of their locations is also enclosed.

Should you need any additional information regarding Beckman Digital Multimeters, please feel free to contact me directly at (714) 871-4848, Ext. 8927.

Very truly yours,

Robert M Buchanan

Robert M. Buchanan
Product Manager

RMB:ds
Enclosures
AI80-2203

Figure 7-2 (continued)

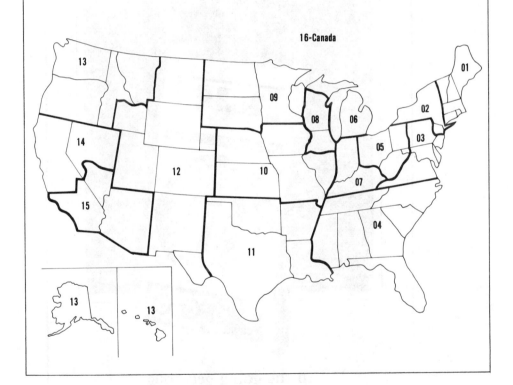

BECKMAN AUTHORIZED REPRESENTATIVES
SERIES 300 MULTIMETERS

Thank you for your interest in Beckman multimeters. The information you requested is enclosed.

If you need additional information or require assistance in locating your local Beckman distributor, contact your nearest authorized Beckman representative. Simply locate the number representing your area from the map below, then contact the representative corresponding to that number listed on the back of this page.

relatives. Others, particularly those who are enthusiastic over the sales representative's products or services, will not hesitate to provide the names of additional prospects. They may write a letter or card of introduction for the sales representative. A prospect obtained in this manner is known as a "referred prospect" and is generally considered to be the highest type of prospect.

Figure 7-3 portrays a case history of how a life insurance sales representative used the endless-chain method of prospecting to pro-

Figure 7–2 *(continued)*

duce $300,000 worth of business within an eight-month period. All of the clients shown in the illustration came directly or indirectly from the first referral from an engineer to whom the sales representative had sold a $20,000 policy. Upon examination of this example, it is interesting to see the wide range of the client's occupational activities. It is also significant to observe how one referral from a lawyer was responsible for $115,000 of insurance sales.

Figure 7–2 *(concluded)*

SALES INFORMATION COPY

BECKMAN'

Beckman Instruments, Inc.
Helipot Division
2500 Harbor Boulevard
Fullerton, California 92634

Max Snowden
AMAC
555 West Culver St.
Denver, Colo. 75436

Telephone Number _____

Product Interest _____Tech 310_____

Salesman: _____

Date Contacted: _____ By: ☐ person ☐ phone ☐ mail

Lead Quality: ☐ excellent ☐ fair ☐ poor ☐ literature collector

Purchase Possibility: ☐ immediate ☐ future ☐ none

Using Competitive Product: ☐ No ☐ Yes

_____   _____
          Company   Model #

Note: Return completed card to: Dan Rime, Beckman Helipot Division; Fullerton, California 92634

"Center-of-influence" method

This prospecting plan is a modification of the endless-chain method. The salesperson cultivates people in the territory who are willing to supply prospecting information. Whenever possible, well-known, influential men or women are cultivated as centers of influence.

In industrial sales situations, the centers of influence are frequently people in important departments that are not directly involved in the purchase decision, such as quality control, equipment maintenance, and receiving. The salesperson keeps in close touch with these individuals over an extended period, solicits their help in a very straightforward manner, and keeps them informed on the sales which result from their aid.

The Penn Mutual Life Insurance Company recommends the following approach for its new sales representatives when calling upon a center of influence:

> Mr. Brown, I have made what I believe to be a mighty fine connection with a real future for me. I am at present taking the training course of the Penn Mutual Life Insurance Company but I am doing no selling as yet. As I expect this to become my life work, I am anxious to build a permanent and substantial clientele.

Figure 7–3
Example of "endless-chain" method of prospecting

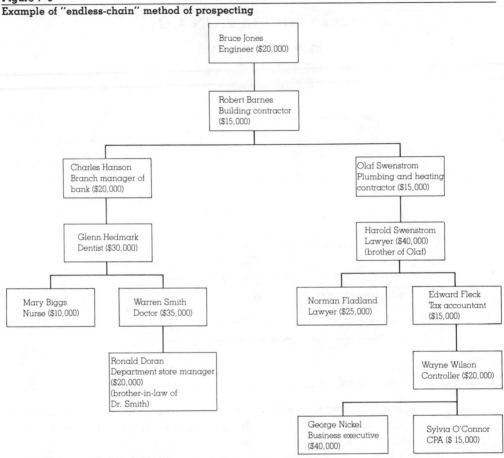

You can help me to this extent, if you will. My job is to get before people in a favorable light. Who is the most promising young married man you know?[5]

Centers of influence can be very productive for the salesperson in a number of ways. They provide information about potential prospects, and they help the salesperson to make appointments by introducing their friends or acquaintances personally or through the use of cards, letters, or the telephone.

The sales representatives who have the greatest success with the center-of-influence method of prospecting are those who provide the right kind of service to their customers. Influential people have little

---

[5] *Prospecting* (Philadelphia: Penn Mutual Life Insurance Co.), p. 9.

use for the sales representative who puts self-interest above the prospect's interest. However, they are happy to assist the salesperson who represents his or her company in a professional manner.

Public exhibitions, demonstrations, and trade shows

Many companies display or demonstrate their products at automobile shows, business machine shows, trade association and professional conventions, and state or county fairs. Sales representatives are present to demonstrate their products to inquiring visitors.

Trade shows are an important source of prospects who are not reached regularly by salespeople. A recent survey found that 83 percent of the people with buying influence who visited manufacturers' exhibits had not been called by the manufacturers' sales representatives during the year prior to the show.[6]

At most trade shows, the salesperson's primary function is to qualify prospects for future follow-up. Typically, the salesperson has only five to ten minutes with a prospect. Thus the marketing manager of Minnesota Rubber instructs his salespeople "to dispense with the small talk used in field selling and get down to the business of qualifying the prospect immediately. To that end, he provides a checkoff form for qualifying buyers."[7]

Lists

Individual sales representatives may develop prospect lists of their own by referring to such sources as public records, classified telephone directories, chamber of commerce directories, newspapers, club membership lists, and professional or trade association membership lists. Secondary sources of information in public libraries can be useful. For example, there are industrial trade directories for most states. Figure 7-4 shows pages from the *New York State Industrial Directory*. The geographically arranged list of companies provides prospects for an office equipment salesperson whose territory includes Nassau County. A salesperson selling small motors could use the list of companies manufacturing electrical household appliances in New York state. Salespeople should become acquainted with the information applicable to their business. A list of some useful secondary sources is shown below:

---

[6] William Mee, "Who Visits Your Booth and Why," *Sales & Marketing Management*, August 20, 1979, pp. 64–66.

[7] "Minnesota Rubber Gets Leads Bouncing," *Sales & Marketing Management*, August 20, 1979, p. 78.

Figure 7–4

Pages from *New York State Industrial Directory*

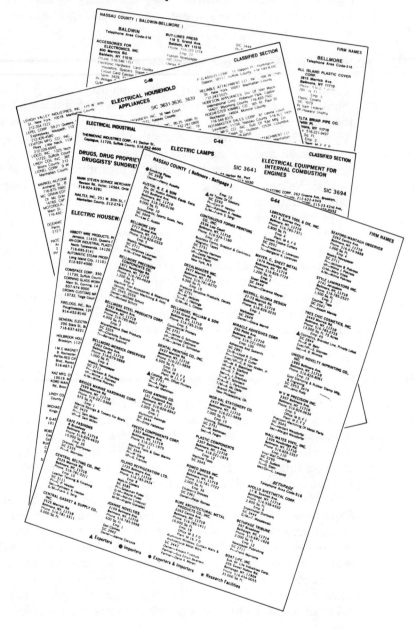

1. *Guides and bibliographies*

Encyclopedia of Business Information Sources. 3d ed. Detroit: Gale,
    1976. 2 vols.
Guide to American Directories. 9th ed. Coral Springs, Fla.: B. Klein
    Publications, 1975.

2. *National directories*

Middle Market Directory. Annual. New York: Dun and Bradstreet.
Poor's Register of Corporations, Directors, and Executives. Annual.
    New York: Standard and Poor's.

3. *Trade directories*

Macrae's Blue Book. Annual. Chicago: Thomas. 5 vols.
Thomas Grocery Register. Thomas. New York: Annual.
Thomas Register of American Manufacturers. New York: Thomas.
U.S. Industrial Directory. Annual. Stamford, Conn.: Cahners. 4 vols.

4. *Trade associations*

Encyclopedia of Associations. Detroit: Gale, 1976.

Friends and acquaintances

In many fields of selling the salesperson's friends and acquaintances will serve as a nuclear source of prospects. This is particularly
true in selling insurance or automobiles. The Guardian Life Insurance Company of America made an analysis of where its successful
agents secured their prospects. The results of this analysis are
shown in Table 7–2.

New insurance sales representatives usually start building their
prospect lists with the names of their friends and neighbors. They
add to this list the names of those to whom it will be possible to
secure a favorable introduction from a mutual acquaintance. Every
possible source of new and old acquaintances is explored. The sales

Table 7–2

Where successful agents secure their prospects

Source	Percent
Old general acquaintances	35
Old associates	4
Recommended or introduced	39
Office leads	11
Newspapers and lists	4
Advertising and circulars	2
Cold-canvass	5

Source: Guardian Life Insurance Company of
America, *The Guardian Training Program for Successful
Selling*, sec. 3, "Prospecting," p. 3.

representatives think back to their school associates; they join social, fraternal, religious, civic, and professional organizations or
clubs; they list the names of persons to whom they pay money—the
milkman, the carrier, the grocer, and the doctor; they try to recall the
names of persons with whom they formerly worked; and they list the
names of persons whom they have met through participation in
sports or recreational activities.

"Cold-canvass" method

A salesperson's product may have a widespread demand among
most of the individuals or companies in a territory. In such cases the
salesperson may resort to the cold-canvass method of prospecting,
whereby calls are made on every individual or company belonging
to a certain group. No advance information as to the needs or financial status of each of these suspects is available. The salesperson
relies upon the law of averages to provide a satisfactory volume of
sales. The past experience of company sales representatives may
indicate that one sale will result from every ten calls. This ratio will
vary, of course, from company to company and from salesperson to
salesperson.

The cold-canvass method has been used extensively for a long
time. The H. J. Heinz Co. was launched in England by cold-canvass-
ing. Henry John Heinz, the company founder, made his first major
sale in England after a cold call on "the largest house supplying the
fine trade of London and suburbs and even shipping."[8]

Prospecting by the cold-canvass method results in considerable
waste of the salesperson's time, as many of the individuals visited
may have neither a genuine want for the product nor the ability to
pay for it. This disadvantage is offset, however, by the complete
territorial coverage which often results in sales to individuals who
would otherwise be neglected.

Some companies use a selective type of cold-canvass which they
refer to as a "cool-canvass." In this plan a complete canvass is made
of each individual within a classification. An automobile salesperson, for example, may secure a list of all the doctors in the community and may then make a complete canvass of these doctors.

One of the commercial airlines has its sales representatives
"blitz" a certain area of a city by calling at every building to solicit
business. During these calls the sales representatives pass out folders and seek the aid and goodwill of everyone in a business concern
from the receptionist to the manager.

---

[8] Robert Alberts, "Those 57 Varieties of Selling Know-How," *Marketing Times,*
May/June 1974, pp. 20–23.

Other sources of prospects

Some other sources of prospects are as follows:

1. *Salespeople for noncompetitive but related products.*
2. *Personal observation.* Many salespeople find prospects by regularly reading trade journals, business publications (such as *Business Week* and *The Wall Street Journal*), and the local newspaper and by just keeping their eyes open when they drive through their territory.
3. *Sales associates or spotters.* In selling automobiles, "sales associates" or "spotters" are sometimes used to do missionary prospecting work. The associate provides information concerning potential prospects. If the salesperson makes a sale, the associate is compensated.
4. *Group prospecting.* Many companies which sell such products as aluminim ware, cosmetics, kitchen utensils, and jewelry rely on group prospecting to stimulate sales. The sales representative might work with women's clubs by providing mass demonstrations to members. Each club receives a premium for its part in arranging the demonstration. Another method is to compensate a person for holding a party in his/her home.

USING DIRECT MAIL FOR PROSPECTING

The use of direct mail for prospecting is illustrated by the sales experiences of the president of a large data entry equipment company:

> Inforex president Mike Harvey's aversion to cold calls began on the first day of his sales career, as an IBM account representative in 1962. "I became interested in marketing," he recalls, "and kept all the secretaries in the branch office busy typing the direct mail pieces I created to screen out the poorest prospects." In his second year he went 400 percent over quota and was made president of the 100% Club, IBM's elite group of supersellers.
>
> Later, he was transferred to a Chicago branch and given the local universities as an account responsibility. "A university is really a hundred separate customers," he notes, "because each department can buy something." Making the rounds in person didn't appeal to him. His solution that time was a weekly newsletter, complete with an inquiry form and eye-catching typefaces, that told department heads what was new in their fields. "It worked beautifully," he claims.[9]

The critical elements of a good direct-mail campaign are shown in Figure 7–5.

---

[9] Thayer Taylor, "New Marketing Input for Inforex," *Sales & Marketing Management,* July 9, 1979, p. 34.

Figure 7–5
Ideal direct-mail plan with all sides equally important

Good product

Preparing the sales message

With so many letters arriving at the prospect's home or the dealer's store, it is important that sales letters be written with skill and extreme care.

Experienced writers of sales letters have found that the following points should be observed.

First, a good sales letter is not too long. While there are no absolute limits on the length of a letter, a busy customer or prospect wants to be able to determine the purpose of the letter in a minimum amount of time.

Second, the letter should be easy to understand. This means that technical jargon and difficult words should be used sparingly. If the prospect has to look up the meaning of some words, the chances are very small that the reaction will be favorable.

Third, a good sales letter tells its story smoothly. The message must flow easily from sentence to sentence and from paragraph to paragraph. The whole story must have continuity to maintain the reader's attention and interest.

Fourth, the sales letter must be personalized. The letter cannot be written to a cold statistic—just anybody. It must be remembered that prospects are people whose likes and dislikes are very much like ours. A courteous, friendly, personal tone is likely to help get a response.

Fifth, a good sales letter is different. That is, the message is stated a little differently from the common, prosaic, standard messages that may appear in some routine correspondence. Imagination and originality in a sales letter help to keep the interest of the prospect or customer.

Sixth, an effective sales letter makes a specific request for some action by the recipient. This requirement is similar to the close in personal selling. Little is accomplished by writing a sales letter which satisfies the requirements identified above and then fails to make the action wanted easy to perform and crystal clear.

An example of an effective prospecting letter is shown in Figure 7–6. The postcard may be used in place of a sales letter, or it may be enclosed with the letter to give the recipient an easy opportunity to take the requested action.

The purpose of the postcard will determine what is put on the card and the physical arrangement of the copy. Figure 7–7 illustrates how postcards may be used to prepare the way for the salesperson or to encourage the customer to call. When enclosed with a letter for return purposes, the postcard must contain all the necessary information to enable the prospect to act even if the letter and the postcard become separated.

If the postcard is used without an accompanying letter, the selling copy must be concise and easily read. To be most effective, the copy must be attractively designed, and the desired action must be featured prominently.

Obtaining a good prospect list

The mailing is likely to be successful only if the prospect list is well selected. Nothing is more perishable than a mailing list. In fact, the process of degeneration begins to take place before the list is completed. Consumer-oriented lists may easily lose their value within a year. The reason is the rapidity of change in society. Women marry and change their names and addresses. People are born, grow up, graduate, move, enlist, change jobs, get promoted, transfer, migrate, and die.

The list may contain the names of old customers who have been inactive; current customers who may be able to buy more; prospective customers who have sent in inquiries; customers who are inaccessible or unprofitable for regular personal calls; and people with whom the company has never done business. The last group poses the biggest problem in preparing a mailing list. Many of the sources for prospects discussed previously are useful in building a mailing list for this group.

PROSPECTING BY TELEPHONE

Telephone prospecting has been used effectively to sell life insurance, hospitalization or accident and health insurance, automobiles, investments, and other products and services. Records show that from five to eight good prospects may be secured out of each 100

Figure 7-6

Paving the way for an interview

Metropolitan Life

Some things you just can't put off.

  Taxes
    Tune-ups for the car
      Doctors
        Dentists
          Utilities
            Rent or mortgage payments

They seem endless, but you can't avoid them.

You can't put off checking your insurance over,
either. Like the car—you want it in good
working order.

You can make sure you're getting the most from
your insurance with Metropolitan's free service,
YOU AND YOUR FAMILY. This service illustrates
graphically how you can use your life insurance,
Social Security, and other assets to put security
in your family's future.

I'll call shortly to explain how YOU AND YOUR
FAMILY can make certain your insurance is working
the way it should.

Cordially

Representative

PAL/aab

Home Office: One Madison Avenue, New York. N.Y. 10010
Head Offices: San Francisco, Calif.; Ottawa. Ontario, Canada

Courtesy of Metropolitan Life

Figure 7–7
Prospecting

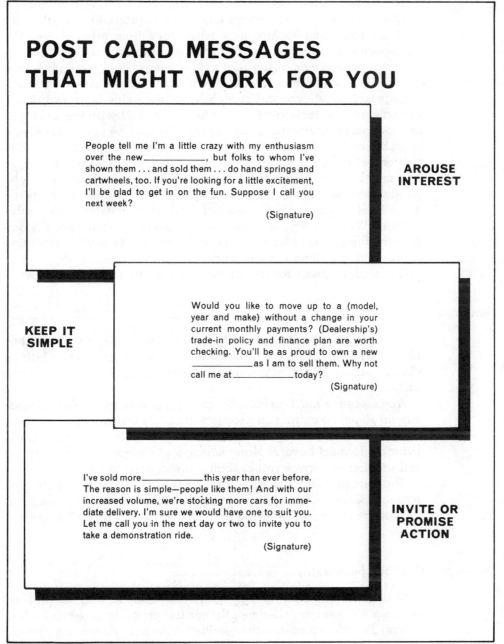

POST CARD MESSAGES
THAT MIGHT WORK FOR YOU

People tell me I'm a little crazy with my enthusiasm over the new_____, but folks to whom I've shown them . . . and sold them . . . do hand springs and cartwheels, too. If you're looking for a little excitement, I'll be glad to get in on the fun. Suppose I call you next week?

(Signature)

AROUSE INTEREST

KEEP IT SIMPLE

Would you like to move up to a (model, year and make) without a change in your current monthly payments? (Dealership's) trade-in policy and finance plan are worth checking. You'll be as proud to own a new _____ as I am to sell them. Why not call me at_____today?

(Signature)

I've sold more_____this year than ever before. The reason is simple—people like them! And with our increased volume, we're stocking more cars for immediate delivery. I'm sure we would have one to suit you. Let me call you in the next day or two to invite you to take a demonstration ride.

(Signature)

INVITE OR PROMISE ACTION

Courtesy of Chrysler Corporation

telephone calls made when prospecting for life insurance and health-and-accident customers. Good salespeople have closed between 40 and 50 percent of the prospects secured in this manner.

One real estate salesperson has found it profitable to call firms that are expecting to hire new employees from other cities. The salesperson secures the name of the new employee and then writes offering the services of the real estate company in locating a new home. This system has paid dividends from contacts with schools, colleges, chain stores, and branches of nationwide organizations. If the salesperson maintains close enough contact with the appropriate sources of information, the information may be secured before it is published in the newspapers and becomes available to competitors. Many such contacts can be made quickly by telephone.

It may be appropriate to try to complete the sales process by telephone when selling some products or services, but most products are more likely to require a personal contact to complete the sales process. With this idea in mind, the salesperson should usually employ the telephone to locate and qualify prospects and then arrange to call and to deliver the sales presentation.

Some suggestions for the effective use of the telephone follow.

Plan the call

Salespeople should know what they plan to say and how they plan to say it *before* the call is made.[10] This requires that a definite plan or pattern be set up to guide the conversation in each telephone call.

Any message must be concise, clear, and courteous. Salespeople may in effect, be calling on people without an invitation. To earn the right to be heard, they must have something to offer, for time is valuable to most buyers. Many salespeople succeed by making the call an offer of service rather than a direct solicitation.

The person contacted should be addressed by name as often as possible. Sellers should also identify themselves and the company, as well as the purpose of the call, at the beginning of the conversation.

Develop a telephone personality

It is important to remember that in telephone selling the prospect can see neither the seller's smile nor the products or services. This means that the voice and the manner of speech must convey friend-

---

[10] American Telephone and Telegraph Co. has numerous publications designed to prepare salespeople for most types of telephone use.

liness and enthusiasm. Telephone communication is different from face-to-face communication because less time is available to make the request or the offer of service and because the salesperson cannot see the effect of the conversation upon the prospect.

Some recommendations for using the telephone effectively are as follows:

1. Move the conversation rapidly. Introduce yourself and your company in one short sentence.
2. Establish rapport by naming a mutual friend, praising the prospect or the prospect's company ("In view of your firm's number one position . . . "), or asking for advice ("We need your help in evaluating a new product").
3. Get to the objective of the call quickly. Brevity is permissible over the phone.
4. Be aggressive without seeming to be so. Short-answer questions which invite a yes answer will help keep the conversation alive.

Tone of voice, inflection, and speed are all important in developing acceptable telephone manners.[11]

HOW TO GET THE MOST OUT OF PROSPECTING

After sales representatives have separated the suspects from the prospects and have obtained the names of prospects for their products or services, they make a careful analysis of the relative value of each prospect. This grading of prospects, or establishment of a priority list, produces increased sales and results in the most efficient use of time and energy.

Qualify and evaluate prospects

Many companies conduct extensive research studies to determine the distinguishing characteristics of good and poor prospects. These characteristics are used as measuring sticks for prospects. The New York Life Insurance Company uses an evaluation formula based upon six factors: age, number of dependents, approximate income, acquaintance, accessibility, and economic status. Each prospect is given a point score on each of the six factors and a composite point rating.

Additional methods of qualifying prospects are used by the sales representatives of other companies. Office machine and equipment sales representatives often qualify their prospects through question-

---

[11] See John P. Moncur and Harrison, M. Karr, *Developing Your Speaking Voice*, 2d ed. (New York: Harper & Row, 1972).

naires. It is frequently necessary to make intensive studies of the practices of certain potential customers. The findings are used to qualify prospects for the specific kinds of machines and equipment which serve their needs.

Countless other methods of qualifying prospects are used in other types of selling. Whatever method is used, it is essential that an effort be made to segregate prospects so that the maximum amount of time can be spent making sales presentations to "live" prospects who are likely to purchase.

Have an organized prospecting plan

The person who does not have an orderly prospecting plan is a slave to confusion, frustration, and chaos. Inexperienced salespeople frequently rattle around in their territories, jump from one spot to another, and waste considerable time between calls. The successful experienced sales representatives, on the other hand, almost always have efficient systems for recording, studying, and using their prospect information.

Keep good records. The information and the type of prospect file needed vary by types of business. Most large companies have developed prospecting systems and standard prospect cards for the use of their sales representatives. The extent to which these systems and cards are used determines the success or failure of individual sales representatives.

The New York Life Insurance Company has an excellent system for organizing and filing its standard prospect cards so that the sales representatives have the necessary information available on each prospect. This system, which the company calls the "Automatic Secretary," divides the prospect file into four sections: (1) the master prospect and policyholder card file, (2) the tickler file, (3) the center-of-influence file, and (4) the district or zone file.

The cards in the master prospect and policyholder card file are filed alphabetically. They contain sufficient information so that they may be used as prospect cards and also as policyholder cards after the prospects have purchased policies.

The tickler file provides the names of prospects and policyholders to be seen each month and the specific days of the month on which they should be seen.

The center-of-influence file helps the sales agent cultivate his or her centers of influence in the proper manner.

The district or zone file cards are used to segregate the names of prospects and policyholders by geographic areas. These cards are very useful for sales agents who cover a number of towns or several well-defined sections of a large city.

Industrial salespeople typically keep a file card for each customer and each prospect. They complete a form after each contact is made. An example of a form used by an electronic distributor is shown in Figure 7-8. The salespeople also put other information into the file that might be useful in converting the prospect into a customer. This information might come from local newspaper or trade magazine articles, annual reports, and data sheets on the prospect's products.

Figure 7-8

Prospect contact form for an electronic distributor

```
                       ELECTRONIC COMPONENT INC

                          Prospect Contact Form


   Date   3/20/80

   Name of Contact  Jack Barry          Telephone Number (714)833-1340

   Company  A & L Labs          Type of Business  Instrument Mfr.

   Address  2305 Campus Dr., Hinsdale, Chicago

   Position  Purchasing Agent

   Contacts Needs  Interested in quick delivery; needs
                   second source for metal film
                   capacitors


   Present Suppliers  Wyle, Hamilton-Avnet



   Credit Rating  AA            Anual Sales  $3M


   Anual Purchases of Components  $200K


   Types of Components Purchased
                  ____ low precision resistors        ____ RAM's
                   ✓  precision resistors              ✓  microprocessors
                   ✓  potiometers                     ____ LCD's
                   ✓  metal film caps                 ____ LED's
                  ____ MOS memory                     ____ bi-polar IC's

   Result of Visit  Still trying to get parts from
                    Wylie

   Follow up  Call in two weeks
```

It is obvious that the records which have been discussed are more detailed than those used in other types of selling. Some kind of prospecting record, however, is essential in every type of selling. In such fields as automobile selling, it is especially important that good prospecting records be kept, for sales commissions are often allocated to the salesperson who files the first prospect card on a customer.

Set quotas.   Most effective prospecting plans include weekly and monthly quotas for new prospects. Goals for obtaining the names of new prospects are, in the long run, just as important as profit and sales goals. The continuous profitable operation of a territory or area is dependent upon a steady flow of new prospects. Quotas remind the salesperson of the importance of keeping a constant lookout for new names to fill the prospect pipeline.

Evaluate results.   One of the greatest dangers in prospecting is the tendency to "ease off" in locating new prospects as soon as the prospect file contains a substantial number of names. Names alone are not enough. Prospect files should be checked periodically to eliminate the deadwood. Additional analysis should also be made frequently to determine whether the best possible factors are being used as measuring sticks in the original qualification or evaluation of prospects.

Experiment with new methods.   Analysis and evaluation may show that the present system is not producing enough prospects or the right kind of prospects. This condition often arises because of an inadequate diversification of prospecting methods. Sales representatives may, for example, depend entirely upon referred names from company advertising or from the service department. These two sources may not supply enough names to produce the sales volume desired. The use of other prospecting methods, such as the cold-canvass, lists, the endless-chain, or the center-of-influence method, should then be considered.

Frequently a new salesperson calls upon potential customers who have never been called upon before. A predecessor may have eliminated these prospects for one reason or another or may never have thought of calling upon them. The new salesperson with new prospecting methods thus uncovers an additional source of sales volume.

Follow-through.   One of the most common complaints from sales managers is that salespeople do not follow through on prospect leads. An insurance company branch manager followed a policy of asking each sales representative to provide a list of 50 of the best prospects at the beginning of each month. The names of these prospects were recorded on visible index cards, and a color-tab system was established to show the action taken on each prospect during the month. Photographs of each sales representative's card file were taken at the beginning and end of the month to show the overall progress which had been made on the 50 key prospects during the month.

The salesperson may call a prospect several times without getting any positive action. He or she must then use judgment as to whether additional time and effort should be spent on this prospect. Too frequent calls may cause the prospect to become resentful and thus may kill all possibilities of a future sale. There is no simple solution to this kind of problem. The salesperson requires judgment, tact, diplomacy, persistency, and ingenuity to know the exact extent to which he or she should follow through. The skill of knowing just how far to follow through on prospects is gleaned from actual selling experience.

TECHNIQUES IN MAKING APPOINTMENTS

Advantages of making appointments

Many sales managers insist that their salespeople make advance appointments before calling on prospects or customers. They have found from experience that working by appointments saves valuable selling time. One large sales organization has estimated that advance appointments increase the effectiveness of their salesforce by at least one third.

Appointments tend to dignify the salesperson. The prospect or customer is more likely to be open-minded toward the salesperson who makes an appointment as compared to the one who "just happened by." Appointments get the sales process off to a good start by putting the salesperson and the prospect on the same level—equal participants in a legitimate sales interview. Appointments also increase the chances of seeing the right person.

How to make appointments

Experienced sales representatives use different methods in contacting individual customers. They have found through trial and error that a certain method of making an appointment works well with a regular customer but may be entirely ineffective with a new prospect. The have also found that a knowledge of many different methods and techniques of making appointments is extremely helpful in obtaining sales interviews. Some of the basic principles and techniques of making appointments are discussed below.

Seeing the right person. Many salespeople have had the unhappy experience of completing an effective sales presentation only to find that they have been talking to the wrong person—someone who does not have the authority to make a purchase. New sales representatives are frequently guilty of this error. Often they are so enthusiastic about their product and so eager to give their presentation that they do not exercise sufficient care in seeing that their appointment is with the person who has the authority to buy.

To illustrate, a paper salesperson for years called mainly on printers. After a careful analysis of sales records and the sales potential, the salesperson concluded that the territory was not producing maximum sales volume. Many sales were lost because the printers lacked the authority to specify the brand of paper used by their clients. The sales representative solved this problem by contacting the printers' sales representatives and finding out from them the names of the persons who normally specified a certain brand of paper when they gave their orders to the printers. The sales representative then contacted these persons and explained the merits of the company's products to them.

Any salesperson whose product or service fills a genuine need of a customer should have no hesitancy about requesting an appointment with the right person—the person who has the authority to say yes or no.

Frequently, however, no one person has the sole authority to buy a product. The salesperson may first be required to obtain the approval of representatives of the line organization or of an operating committee. A forklift salesperson for example, found that he had to see the safety engineer, the methods engineer, the materials-handling engineer, and the general superintendent before he could sell the product to a certain manufacturing company. When such conditions exist, the salesperson should attempt to arrange a meeting with the entire group which has the authority to pass upon the purchase.

Some companies which sell technical industrial products, such as tools, have found it practical to have factory experts periodically accompany salespeople. In advance of the expert's visit to the territory, the salesperson maps out a schedule of interviews with key prospects. It is usually much easier to obtain an appointment with these key people when they hear that a factory expert will be present to explain the new technological changes in the product and the industry.

Calling at the right time.   Much has been written concerning the most propitious time of day for sales interviews. Certain salespeople claim that the best time to see prospects is right after lunch, when they are likely to be in a pleasant mood. Others try to get as many appointments as they can during the early morning hours because they feel that the prospects or customers will be in a better frame of mind early in the morning. There is little agreement on this subject, for obviously the most opportune time to call will vary with customers and types of selling. The salesperson who calls on wholesale grocers, for example, may find from experience that the best time to call is from 9:00 A.M. to 11:00 A.M. and from 1:30 P.M. to 3:30 P.M. A life insurance agent, on the other hand, may discover that the most productive calls are made in the evening between the hours of 7:00 P.M. and 9:00 P.M., when there will be a chance to meet with both husband and wife.

For most types of selling, the best hours of the day are from approximately 9:00 A.M. to 11:30 A.M. and from 1:30 P.M. to 4:00 P.M. This is particularly true for sales representatives who call on business executives, because the executives generally like to have the first part of the day free to read their mail and answer correspondence and the latter part of the day free to read and sign their letters.

Although the above hours may be the most favorable, this does not mean that a salesperson should restrict appointments to these hours. Each salesperson soon learns what hours and what days are most favorable for each customer.

Methods of making appointments. After the salesperson has decided what prospects to see and where and when to see them, he or she then concentrates on the best method of obtaining each appointment. The techniques used in making appointments vary. The door-to-door salesperson may rely upon small gifts to obtain interviews with housewives. The industrial or wholesale salesperson may use the telephone to make appointments with regular customers.

The use of tricky subterfuges in obtaining appointments has no place in modern selling. If the salesperson selects prospects carefully in terms of their product needs, it should not be necessary to conceal the purpose of the visit. At times the salesperson may have to use determination, persistence, and ingenuity in obtaining interviews; but he or she should never resort to deceitful or dishonest tactics.

The salesperson can save many hours by using the telephone to make appointments and can utilize spare moments to call potential prospects. Before making a telephone appointment, the salesperson should know exactly what to say. An example of a telephone approach is shown in Figure 7–9.

Frequently, when a salesperson calls for an appointment, the prospect may ask certain questions concerning the product or service. When this happens, the salesperson should refrain from giving a sales presentation over the telephone. The purpose of the call is to obtain an appointment and not to make a sale.

Some salespeople have their secretaries make their telephone appointments for them. They feel that this practice tends to give

Figure 7-9
Example of telephone approach

Steps	Conversation
1. State the prospect's name; pause for acknowlegment; state your name and your company's name.	Hello, Mr. Walker? *(Pause.)* This is Glen Scott with Gamma Corporation.
2. Check to see if the time is convenient.	Did I call at a convenient time, or should I call later?

3. Attempt to develop a link between the prospect and yourself by:
  a. Identifying a mutual friend.
  b. Indicating the source of a referral.
  c. Demonstrating your knowledge of the prospect's company.
  d. Following up on an advertising inquiry.
	I just read in the *Cleveland Plain Dealer* that your company got a large order from the Navy.

4. State the purpose of the call and ask for an appointment.	I'm calling to let you know about our new office copier. It has more features than the present copiers and could be a real money saver. Could you put me on your calendar for 30 minutes next Monday or Tuesday?
5. Restate the appointment time, or keep the door open for a future appointment.	Thank you, Mr. Walker. I'll be at your office at 9:00 A.M. on Tuesday. or I appreciate your frankness, Mr. Walker. I'd like to get back to you in a couple of months. Would that be allright?

them greater prestige in the mind of the prospect or customer. If the secretary is unable to obtain an appointment, the salesperson may make a second call in which a different approach in requesting the appointment is used.

Confirmation letters are frequently used as a means of verifying the date and time of the appointment and of thanking the prospect for granting the appointment.

Cultivating subordinates. Busy executives usually have one or more subordinates whose function is to plan and to schedule interviews for their superiors. These "barriers," as they are sometimes called by salespeople, often make it rather difficult to see the boss. A secretary usually feels responsible for conserving the superior's time; therefore, she is anxious to discover the true purpose of each salesperson's visit before she grants an interview with her superior.

A salesperson should go out of his or her way to treat all subordinates with respect and courtesy.

A rule for success used by Bob Schiffman, one of the top 100 Cadillac salespeople, is as follows:

To do business with the boss, you must sell yourself to everyone on his staff. I sincerely like people—so it comes naturally to me.

I treat secretaries and chauffeurs as equals and friends. Ditto switchboard operators and maids. I regularly sent small gifts to them all. An outstanding investment.

The little people are great allies. They can't buy the product. But they can kill the sale. Who needs influential enemies? The champ doesn't want anyone standing back throwing rocks.

In many cases, all you do is treat people decently—an act that sets you apart from 70 percent of your competitors.[12]

Waiting for the appointment. Some sales managers instruct their sales representatives that, in normal circumstances, they should not wait for any prospect for more than ten minutes. There are exceptions to this rule, of course, depending upon the importance of the customer and upon the distance that the salesperson has traveled to see him or her.

When a salesperson requests an interview, the receptionist may merely say, "I'll tell Mr. Jones that you are here." After the receptionist has had a chance to check with Mr. Jones, the salesperson should ask the receptionist or secretary approximately how long it will be. If the waiting period is excessive and the salesperson has another appointment, it may be advisable to explain this tactfully and to ask for another appointment. Usually the secretary will either try to get the salesperson in to see his or her superior earlier or will make arrangements for an appointment at a later date.

Every salesperson must expect to spend a certain portion of each working day waiting for sales interviews. Successful salespeople make the best possible use of this time by working on their reports, studying new product information, planning and preparing for their next calls, and obtaining additional information about the prospect.

MAKING A GOOD FIRST IMPRESSION

The first few seconds that a salesperson spends with a prospect often make or break a sale. If the first impression is a favorable one, the prospect is usually willing to listen. A negative first impression, on the other hand, sets up a barrier which may never be hurdled.

A friendly smile is essential when the salesperson meets a customer for the first time. A firm handshake should convey a feeling of confidence and sincerity, and the salesperson should speak clearly and make certain to pronounce the customer's name correctly. Subsequent use of the customer's name during the interview will aid in establishing an attitude of friendliness. The success achieved dur-

---

[12] Bob Schiffman, "Confessions of a Cadillac Salesman," *Marketing Times*, May/June 1979, p. 24.

Figure 7-10
Dress for saleswomen

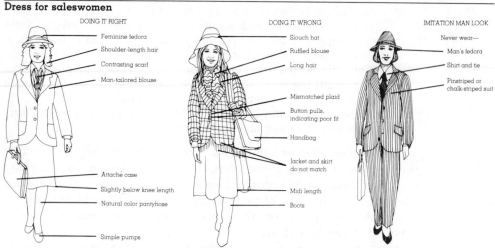

DOING IT RIGHT

- Feminine fedora
- Shoulder-length hair
- Contrasting scarf
- Man-tailored blouse
- Attache case
- Slightly below knee length
- Natural color pantyhose
- Simple pumps

DOING IT WRONG

- Slouch hat
- Ruffled blouse
- Long hair
- Mismatched plaid
- Button pulls, indicating poor fit
- Handbag
- Jacket and skirt do not match
- Midi length
- Boots

IMITATION MAN LOOK

- Never wear—
- Man's fedora
- Shirt and tie
- Pinstriped or chalk-striped suit

Source: From *The Woman's Dress for Success Book* by John T. Molloy, copyright © 1977 by John T. Molloy. Used by permission of Follett Publishing Company, a division of Follett Corporation.

ing the first few minutes of an interview depends a great deal upon the appearance, poise, and ingenuity of the salesperson and upon the sincere interest shown in the prospect and his or her problems.

Appearance and poise

A neat and well-groomed appearance is a most valuable asset to a salesperson. Good taste in dress, knowing what to wear and what not to wear, is a characteristic which every salesperson should seek to acquire. This does not imply that salespeople should be walking fashion models but rather that they should be attired in such a manner that they will make a good first impression with their prospects. If clothing distracts from a sales presentation, the salesperson is overdressed. Proper attire and grooming serve to give the salesperson additional poise and confidence during the first interview with a prospect.

John T. Molloy teaches business people the art of dressing for success.[13] He stresses that clothing immediately establishes the salesperson's authority, credibility, and even likability. The selection of dress style should be based on the salesperson's size; the customer's age, occupation, and social status; and the geographic location. Some recommendations are:

---

[13] See John T. Molloy, *Dress for Success* (New York: Peter H. Weyden, 1975); and John T. Molloy, *The Woman's Dress for Success* (Chicago: Follett, 1977).

Polka-dot or Ivy League ties, pin-striped suits, and pink shirts are unacceptable in the South.

When selling engineers or accountants, a perfectly matched and harmonious outfit is needed.

Lighter colors are better for larger salesmen because they lessen the salesmen's natural look of power and make the customer feel more comfortable.

Smaller salesmen can augment their power by wearing white shirts, pin-striped suits, and heavy framed glasses.

Molloy cautions against pinstripes or pantsuits for women in business. These garments give an "imitation man" effect and reduce a woman's authority when selling to a man. His recommendations for saleswomen are shown in Figure 7–10.

QUESTIONS AND PROBLEMS

1. If you were a salesperson for the following companies, how would you develop a prospect list?

   a. A manufacturer of private light airplanes.

   b. A travel agency specializing in group tours.

   c. A manufacturer of heavy equipment for road construction.

2. Mr. Robert Eppler is a real estate salesperson in a city of approximately 150,000 population. He feels that a successful prospecting plan involves the following three basic steps: (1) an analysis of each property listing to determine the main selling features in which prospects will be interested, (2) a plan for securing an adequate number of prospects, and (3) a system for properly qualifying the prospects with respect to different properties.

   a. What selling features of residential properties, such as size of lot and number of rooms, is Mr. Eppler likely to look for in making his property analysis?

   b. What are some common sources from which Mr. Eppler may secure real estate prospects for homes?

   c. What information should Mr. Eppler obtain on his prospects to qualify them properly?

3. The company you represent carries a full line of sophisticated office equipment, including electronic calculators, word processing equipment, and small business computers. How would you develop a list of business, industrial, and institutional accounts? What information would you collect to screen the prospect list for potential customers?

4. What information should a salesperson collect to qualify prospects for:

   a. A uniformed guard service?

   b. Sponsorship of a Little League baseball team?

   c. Paper for computer output.

5. Salespeople should forget prospects who do not qualify. Comment on this statement.

6. Assume that you are starting a career as a stockbroker. Develop a system for rating prospects. The system should contain several important factors for qualifying prospects, and scales to rate the prospects on these factors. Use the system to rate five of your friends.

7. Assume that you are a sales representative for a national manufacturer which sells a wide variety of business machines. You have heard that the Tanner Manufacturing Company (which employs 3,500 employees and does an annual business of $38 million) is planning to install a new production and cost control plan that includes a complete cost accounting system. Your company has a new machine designed specifically for cost control work. It is being used by a number of large manufacturing companies in your territory. The cost of the machine is $10,000.

   How would you go about making an appointment with a representative of the Tanner Manufacturing Company? Whom would you attempt to see? The president? The controller? The chief cost accountant? The purchasing agent? Why?

8. A paper-products sales representative uses the following approach when in doubt as to whether a certain executive has the authority to buy: "Mr. Smith, my presentation will take approximately 15 minutes of your time. I realize that your time is valuable, and therefore I want to be sure that you are the person with whom I should talk. I would appreciate your frank comments. Are you the one I should see on paper packaging, or does another executive have responsibility for the purchase of this product?"

   What is your reaction to this approach? Why?

9. In industrial sales situations, several people are influential in making the purchase decision. Suppose that you had just completed an interview with an industrial prospect and felt that you should contact other people in the company. How would you raise the subject with the prospect?

10. Suppose that you call by telephone to make an appointment for a personal interview with a prospect. When the secretary answers the phone, you say, "Mr. Welsh, please; Joe Herbert calling." Assume that the secretary says, "What do you wish to talk to Mr. Welsh about?" What answer would you give? Assume that you answer and then are told that Mr. Welsh is too busy to see you. What would you say?

PROJECTS

1. Assume that you have just been appointed advertising manager for your college or university student paper. What would you do to develop the most successful prospecting plan for obtaining advertisers?

2. Write a sales letter designed to induce a prospect to send in an inquiry seeking further information on your product and requesting that a sales-

person call. Prepare a second letter designed to encourage the prospect to call your office by telephone to order the merchandise you are offering. Prepare some guidelines for the persons who will be answering the telephone.

3. Assume that you are a sales representative for the U.S. Steel Corporation and that you call upon industrial companies, engineering construction firms, and large building contractors. Also assume that you are working in one of the following geographic areas: Cleveland, Philadelphia, Atlanta, Chicago, St. Louis, New Orleans, Denver, San Francisco, or Seattle. Review during a one-week period appropriate newspapers, magazines, and other available public information and write a report in which you assess the available information in terms of its value for prospecting purposes.

CASE PROBLEMS

Case 7-1

Cool-Air, Inc.

Two young college graduates organized Cool-Air, Inc., soon after they graduated. The company obtained an exclusive sales agency for a national brand of home air-conditioning units. The units included both portable air conditioners which could be moved from room to room and larger units which could be installed in windows or walls.

The two young owners, Mr. Lewis and Mr. Hall, received their degrees in mechanical engineering. While in school, they became interested in the air-conditioning field and decided to enter this type of business after graduation. Between their junior and senior years in college, they worked to earn money and to obtain some business experience. Lewis worked for a sheet-metal and heating company doing a combination of office work and saleswork. Hall worked for a retail appliance company doing outside saleswork.

During the last semester of their senior year in college, Lewis and Hall spent all of their spare time investigating the air-conditioning business. They talked with the distributors of a number of the most popular air-conditioning units and wrote to several manufacturers to inquire about the possibility of obtaining a franchise for certain territories in Texas.

After considerable negotiation they were successful in obtaining the franchise to sell the Star brand air-conditioning units in El Paso, Texas. The owners put up a limited amount of capital, rented a small combination warehouse and display room, hired a part-time office clerk, and ordered a few units to use for display and demonstration purposes. They decided to concentrate on the sale of units which would be installed in the windows or walls of houses or office buildings. The average home-installation unit was priced to sell for approximately $900.

Lewis and Hall felt that there was a good market for air-conditioning units in the El Paso area but realized that they would have to conduct a hard-hitting sales program if their business was to be successful. One of their first problems was to obtain a list of prospects upon whom they could call.

Questions

1. What prospecting methods should Lewis and Hall use?
2. What factors should they use in evaluating their potential prospects?
3. What methods, if any, may be used to determine whether their potential prospects have the necessary qualifications?

Case 7–2

Joan Leonard—Joseph & Sons

While Joan Leonard attended college she worked full time during the summer and part time during the school year at a large supermarket. After graduation from college, Joan accepted a position as a sales representative for Joseph & Sons, a well-known company that sold a line of delicatessen foods, relishes, preserves, and meat products to retail groceries and supermarkets. Joseph & Sons carried a full line of meat products and also featured a popular brand of TV frozen dinners.

Joan had a successful career as a sales representative for Joseph & Sons and was promoted to a branch manager's position in the central New York region. In this capacity she was responsible for a number of salespeople and she also made calls upon large customers with multistore operations. One of her toughest assignments was to get the Joseph line of products into the National Supermarkets chain, which operated approximately 50 supermarkets in her region. Neil Sundby, vice president of National, was the key person to see in getting the Joseph products into National. Alex Joseph, president of Joseph & Sons, had called on Sundby on several occasions but had never been successful in getting the Joseph line of products introduced into National Supermarkets.

When Joan Leonard called upon Sundby for the first time, Sundby was friendly, but he made it quite clear that National had no intention of stocking Joseph products in its stores. Joan Leonard made several follow-up calls on Sundby but was unsuccessful in convincing Sundby of the advantages of substituting Joseph products for the line now carried by National or of adding Joseph products.

Although somewhat discouraged by her first efforts to "crack" the National account. Joan was challenged by the situation confronting her and was determined to get some of the National business.

Questions

1. If you were Joan Leonard, what plan of action would you follow in an attempt to get your Joseph products accepted by National Supermarkets?
2. Would you continue to call on Sundby, or would you call on someone else at National? If you did call on someone else, what strategy would you use?

Case 7–3

The Carter Company

The Carter Company produces and distributes business forms for almost every office and business need. The company's main office is in Chicago. Its products are sold through regional and district offices located in the United States and Canada. Sales representatives are usually assigned to specific geographic areas. However, in some of the larger cities they are assigned certain key customers.

Alan Beebe, one of the salesmen in the Philadelphia area, has been with the company for 30 years and is planning to retire in six months. In general, he has done a fairly good job in his territory, but his sales during the last year have been somewhat spotty. One of the largest business concerns in Beebe's territory, the United Manufacturing Company, has never given any business to the Carter Company. Beebe has made regular calls on the purchasing agent but has never been able to obtain an order for Carter business forms. The purchasing agent has told Beebe on several occasions that it is impossible to give the Carter Company any business because the company has entered into an exclusive agreement for all printing work with a local concern, the American Printing Company. Beebe has heard indirectly that the sales representative of the American Printing Company is a close personal friend of the purchasing agent.

Ralph Monroe has been a sales representative for the Carter Company for eight years. He has spent three years working for the company in the Chicago area, and during the last five years he has worked in the San Francisco area. Monroe is an excellent sales representative and has a fine background if office systems and methods work. The Eastern regional sales executive has told Monroe to take over Beebe's territory in Philadelphia when Beebe retires. Plans call for Monroe to work with Beebe in the Philadelphia area during the last six months of Beebe's service. When the sales manager told Monroe of his new assignment, he said that he wanted Beebe to introduce him to the regular customers in the new territory. In addition, he said, "Ralph, I want you to concentrate on getting some business from the United Manufacturing Company. There is no reason why we shouldn't be getting some of that business. I told Beebe that I wanted you to spend whatever time was necessary to break that account open for us."

Questions

1. Assume that you are Monroe. What steps would you take in attempting to get some business from the United Manufacturing Company?
2. Whom would you see? If you call on the purchasing agent, how will you get around the objection of the exclusive agreement with the American Printing Company? How can you win the support of the purchasing agent?

SELECTED REFERENCES

Blickstein, Steve. "How to Find the Key Buying Influence." *Sales Management*, September 20, 1971, pp. 51–54.

Chapmam, John. "Get Your Sales Leads by Mail! Here's How!" *Marketing Times*, July /August 1979, pp. 12–13.

Feldman, Laurence P., and Armstrong, Gary M. "Identifying Buyers of a Major Automotive Innovation." *Journal of Marketing*, January 1975, pp. 47–53.

Goodman, Gerson. "Filling Holes with Cold Calls." *Sales & Marketing Management*, February 5, 1979, pp. 46–47.

Molloy, John T. "Clothes Make the Salesman, or, Never Wear Green." *Sales Management*, December 8, 1975, pp. 58–61.

Nanheim, F. *Salesman's Complete Model Letter Handbook.* Englewood Cliffs, N.J.: Prentice/Hall, 1967.

Rosenhein, John. "Telephone Selling's Finest Hour." *Sales & Marketing Management*, January 21, 1974, pp. 43–45.

Roth, Charles B. *How to Find the Qualify Prospects and Get Interviews.* Englewood Cliffs, N.J.: Prentice-Hall, 1960.

Scanlon, Sally. "Striking It Rich with Industrial Ads." *Sales & Marketing Management*, June 18, 1979, pp. 39–44.

"Trade Shows: Where Prospects Call on you: A Special Report." *Sales & Marketing Management*, August 28, 1979.

Chapter 8

PLANNING AND DELIVERING THE SALES PRESENTATION

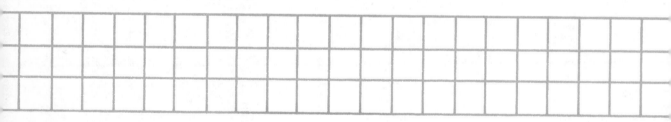

In view of the millions of sales transactions that are completed daily, it is little wonder that various types of sales presentations are being used. In certain types of selling, the memorized canned presentation produces the highest sales volume. In other types of selling, unstructured presentations are more effective.

This chapter describes the basic approaches to personal selling and the type of sales presentation associated with each approach. The chapter also includes some basic techniques for making an effective presentation, such as the art of listening, nonverbal communications, and methods for probing for information.

APPROACHES TO PERSONAL SELLING

The four major selling approaches are (1) stimulus-response, (2) mental states, (3) need satisfaction, and (4) problem solution.[1] These approaches are described in this section.

Stimulus-response approach

Psychological experiments have shown that subjects will respond in a predictable manner when exposed to a specific stimulus. When subjects are rewarded for correct responses, the responses become virtually automatic.

Salespeople using the stimulus-response approach concentrate on saying the right thing (the *stimulus*) at the right time to develop a favorable *response* from the prospect. A standard memorized sales presentation is used to insure that the right points are made at the right time. Knowing how prospects normally respond to certain stimuli enables salespeople to build a sequence of favorable responses.

The major disadvantage of this approach is that people often do not respond in the expected way. When this happens, the salesperson is thrown off track and may not be able to complete the presentation.

The stimulus-response approach is most appropriate in simple, straightforward selling situations such as selling a vacuum cleaner in a home. The approach is also useful when selling time is limited, as in selling (detailing) pharmaceuticals to a doctor.

Mental states approach

The mental states approach is based on a slogan coined by E. St. Elmo Lewis in 1898: "Attract attention, maintain interest, create desire, and get action." This formula suggests that a prospect goes through a logical sequence of mental states in any buying situation. Thus, the salesperson's first task is to present sales appeals that will capture the prospect's attention. Then the salesperson must plan and deliver the sales story with the idea of advancing the buyer from one mental state to another until the sale has been completed.

Although the "mental states" theory of selling is widely accepted, it has certain shortcomings. During a sales presentation it is impossible to know when attention stops and interest starts or when interest stops and desire starts. In fact, most experienced salespeople

[1] See Robert F. Gwinner, "Base Theories in the Formulation of Sales Strategies," *MSU Business Topics*, Autumn 1968, pp. 37–44.

agree that they do not think about the various mental states when they are making their presentations. Another disadvantage of the mental states theory is that it puts the emphasis in the wrong place. Salespeople who follow this four-step plan may overemphasize their side of the story to get attention and interest, instead of adapting themselves to the buyer's desires, needs, and wants.

Despite the weaknesses of the mental states theory, it has the advantage of encouraging salespeople to plan their sales presentations. It has had wide acceptance because of its simplicity.

Need satisfaction approach

The discussion of customer behavior in Chapter 3 emphasizes that people buy products to satisfy needs and solve problems. The need satisfaction approach uses the prospect's need as the logical starting point for the sales presentation. A salesperson utilizing this approach first determines the customer's need. After securing the prospect's agreement that the need exists, the salesperson offers a solution to satisfy the need.

The major advantage of this approach is that it forces the salesperson to practice the marketing concept. The emphasis is on satisfying the customer's needs, not on the product or service being offered. The salesperson must analyze the sales process from the buyer's viewpoint. The presentation is planned and the selling points organized to answer questions such as the following: What are the prospect's real needs and wants? How will my product benefit the buyer? How can I best guide the prospect's thinking so that a decision to buy my product will be made and thus solve the buyer's problems and satisfy the buyer's wants?

The need satisfaction approach is designed for the more experienced and sophisticated salespeople. Salespeople using this approach must understand the psychology of communication and persuasion. They must also spend the time and effort required to determine the prospect's needs and to demonstrate how their product satisfies those needs. Because of the experience and time required by this approach, it is typically used when the product and the customer are rather sophisticated. For example, the need satisfaction approach is often used when selling insurance, stocks and bonds, farm machinery, and industrial products.

Problem solution approach

The problem solution approach combines the need satisfaction approach with the scientific method for solving problems. Like the need satisfaction approach the problem solution approach begins with the salesperson identifying the prospect's need. The salesperson then assists the customer in enumerating possible alternative solutions, helps the customer evaluate the advantages and disadvantages of each alternative, and finally works with the customer to select the best alternative. In using this approach, the salesperson builds a relationship with the customer that resembles a consultant-client relationship.

The problem solution approach places greater demands on the salesperson's time and skills than the three other approaches. It is typically used in industrial sales of technical products and services.

TYPES OF SALES PRESENTATIONS

The three basic types of sales presentations are (1) the standard memorized presentation, (2) the outlined presentation, and (3) the program presentation. The first two types of presentations are used in the stimulus-response and mental states selling approaches. The third type is used in need satisfaction and problem solution selling. The three types are described below.

Standard memorized presentation

The standard memorized sales presentation is a carefully prepared sales story which includes all of the key selling points arranged in the most effective order. The presentation is usually developed after a careful analysis of the sales stories of the most successful salespeople. The best features and sales points from the various presentations are incorporated into a standard sales story which is then committed to memory.

Sixty years ago John H. Patterson, president of the National Cash Register Company, originated the standard sales presentation. He visited the company's sales agencies and had a stenographer take down the sales conversations of the best NCR sales representatives. The talks were then analyzed, and a standard sales story was developed. All sales representatives were then required to use this standard presentation and demonstration. A tremendous increase in sales resulted, and soon many other companies standardized their sales techniques and demonstrations.

There is considerable disagreement among sales managers as to the merits and demerits of the standard memorized sales talk. Many sales managers insist that every salesperson must commit the entire sales talk to memory and deliver it word for word. Other sales managers feel that it is advantageous for each salesperson to memorize a standard sales story, but they believe that each salesperson should be given sufficient leeway to adapt the presentation to his or her own personality. Still other sales managers are bitterly opposed to any type of standard memorized presentation.

Some of the major arguments for and against the standard memorized sales presentation are given below.

Advantages.   The main advantages of the standard memorized sales talk are as follows:

1.   It insures that the salesperson will tell the complete and accurate story about the company's products and policies.
2.   It encompasses the best techniques and methods used by the most successful salespeople.
3.   It aids the new and inexperienced sales representative.
4.   It eliminates repetition and saves time for both the salesperson and the buyer.
5.   It guarantees the most effective presentation by having the sales points arranged in a logical and systematic sequence.
6.   It provides effective answers to all possible objections which may be raised by the prospects and thus gives the salesperson additional confidence.
7.   Most salespeople tend to standardize their sales talks anyway, so why not standardize on the "one best way."

Disadvantages.   The main disadvantages of the standard memorized sales talk are as follows:

1.   It is inflexible and artificial, and it tends to make a robot out of the salesperson. The salesperson thus loses enthusiasm and originality.
2.   It cannot be used in types of selling in which the salesperson makes regular calls upon customers.
3.   It discourages or prevents the prospect from participating in the sales conversation. This keeps the salesperson from finding out the true needs and wants of each prospective buyer, and the sales story tends to become a monologue.
4.   The salesperson who relies on a memorized presentation often finds it difficult to get started again after being interrupted by the prospect.
5.   Its use is not practical when many products are sold.

Conclusions.   The success or failure of a standard sales talk depends to a great degree upon the ability of the individual who is delivering it. A competent person can use a memorized sales talk so skillfully that the prospect does not suspect that it is a canned presentation. On the other hand, an inferior salesperson may sound very artificial.

For certain types of selling, such as door-to-door selling, the standard memorized sales talk has proved very effective. It has also been of great help to beginning salespeople in other types of selling. In many instances individuals memorize a sales story and later modify it to fit their particular personalities or vocabularies. In this way they derive most of the benefits of the standard presentation and are able to deliver their sales talks in a free and natural manner.

Perhaps the chief weakness of the standard memorized sales talk is that it encourages salespeople to talk too much about the products or services without paying proper attention to the wants or needs of prospective buyers. If a product has a universal demand, this may not be a serious objection. However, if the product is such that the needs of the prospects vary, it is essential to consider each buyer's needs and wants. Too many salespeople who use a standard memorized sales talk disregard the interests and desires of their prospects. There is no quicker way to create ill will.

In general, it is not advisable to use a standard memorized sales talk if a person does not possess the ability to adapt the sales story to the prospect and to make it sound informal. The standard presentation should not be used when calling upon professional buyers, when selling a complete line of products, or when making regular calls upon customers.[2]

Outlined presentation

The outlined presentation differs from the standard memorized presentation in that it is more flexible and need not be memorized. It usually consists of a systematically arranged outline of the most important sales points. It may also include the necessary steps for determining the prospect's needs and for building goodwill at the close of the sale.

Frequently sales representatives memorize certain parts of their presentations, such as a standard introduction, standard answers to the most common objections, and a standard close. These memorized portions then become a part of their outlined presentations. Through skillful use of the memorized parts, the sales representatives gain many of the advantages of a complete standard memorized presentation, but they still keep the interview flexible and informal.

Some companies provide their sales representatives with suggested outlines for each product. Others provide general in-

---

[2] See Marvin A. Jolson, "Should the Sales Presentation Be Fresh or Canned?" *Business Horizons*, October 1973, p. 85.

structions on the techniques of developing sales outlines but rely upon the salesperson to develop the individual sales presentation.

Examples of sales presentation outlines.   A manufacturer of electric ranges provides each retail salesperson with an outlined selling guide. The main points in the illustrated selling guide are:

1. *Open your presentation by calling attention to overall beauty, style design, finish and fixtures.*

    Hard, smooth porcelain finish holds its natural luster.

    Easy to keep clean.

    Fiberglass insulation holds oven heat and keeps kitchen cool.

    Sturdy, all-steel, one-piece unit construction eliminates drawer jamming or fixture rattling.

2. *Focus attention on surface units.*

    Surface units are faster, safer, and easier to clean.

    Can depend upon uniform penetrating heat.

    No dangerous fumes or flames.

    No soot on walls or cooking utensils.

    Can prepare entire meal in deep-well cooker—ideal for soups, stews, and french fries—handy at canning time—convenient for sterilizing baby's bottle.

3. *Explain the controls.*

    Efficient controls make cooking a science—always get same results from same recipe.

    Can connect toaster or coffee maker in convenience outlet.

    Special thermostat controls preheating of oven.

    Automatic timer makes it possible to go shopping while dinner is baking.

    Minute minder is handy for fast cooking operations of vegetables, eggs, etc.

    Entire range surface illuminated by fluorescent lamp.

    Pilot light shows when deep-well cooker or surface units are on.

4. *Explain oven and broiler.*

    Each shelf has safety stop to prevent accidents when removing things from oven.

    Oven light comes on when door opens.

    Extra-heavy insulation holds heat in.

    "Positive seal" floating oven door automatically adjusts itself to keep heat in as oven temperature rises.

    No unsightly oven vent—concealed vent takes away excess moisture and fumes.

    Handy waist-high broiler ideal for steaks, chops, and fish—excellent for toasted sandwiches.

    Roomy storage compartments save unnecessary steps.

    Drawers roll easily because they are mounted on roller bearings.

5. *Stress ease of buying through budget plan.*

    Use low-cost slide chart in figuring terms.

The following steps for an outlined sales presentation are recommended by a national stock brokerage firm:[3]

Step	Example
1. Restatement of client's needs	Ms. Blank, last week when we spoke, you emphasized that you're looking for an investment that can provide you with long-term growth and reasonable security.
2. General product reference	One investment that can help you meet these needs is in the communications field.
3. Statement relating general product benefits to the client's needs	The communications industry has a history of stable growth—the kind of history that represents the reasonably secure, long-term growth you want.
4. Reference to specific product	The particular company I have in mind is International Television Company.
5. Probe for client's knowledge and attitudes about the product	How well do you know International?
6. Statement of specific product features	Two factors that attract our analysts to ITV now are its selling price and its strong balance sheet. ITV is now selling for ten times its estimated earnings, well below its typical P/E ratio.
7. Statement relating specific product benefits to the client's needs	With a clean balance sheet, ITV can show profits even in lean years. Its steady growth rate will continue for some time to come. Considering its depressed price now, you can really maximize on your investment.
8. Pause or probe to determine client's acceptance of specific benefit	How does the growth potential ITV offers sound to you?

Advantages and disadvantages. The foregoing illustrations show the great variations in the sales presentation outlines that are being used. Because of these variations it is rather difficult to make an absolute evaluation of the outlined sales presentation. Many of the advantages of the standard memorized sales talk also apply to the outlined sales story. For example, the outlined presentation places the main sales points in the proper sequence; it eliminates duplication and overlapping; it prevents gaps; it forces the salesperson to think of possible objections and to plan appropriate answers; and it serves as a guide for the new salesperson.

The main advantages of the outlined presentation over the standard memorized sales talk are as follows:

[3] Paine Webber, Jackson & Curtis, *Securities Selling Skills*, unit 3: "Presentation."

1. It is more informal and natural.
2. There is less chance for domination by the salesperson, and therefore the prospect's needs, desires, viewpoints, and opinions are more likely to be considered.
3. It is more flexible.
4. It is easier for the salesperson to get back on the track if interrupted.

The main objections to the outlined sales presentation are as follows:

1. The salesperson may not be able to express himself or herself as effectively when speaking extemporaneously.
2. There is a greater chance to be sidetracked from the sales story.
3. The salesperson may not prepare the sales talk as carefully when it is not committed to memory.

Most experienced sales representatives are able to overcome these objections. As they gain experience and confidence, they tend to favor the outlined or program type of presentation over the standard memorized type.

Program presentation

The program presentation usually consists of a complete written or illustrated presentation which is developed from a detailed and comprehensive analysis or survey of the prospect's or customer's needs. This type of presentation is used extensively in trade selling, in the sale of industrial equipment and office equipment and supplies, in management consulting work, in the sale of certain types of advertising, and in many similar types of selling.

A complete program presentation normally includes four basic steps, namely (1) getting permission to make an analysis or survey; (2) making the survey, which includes the gathering and analysis of the facts; (3) preparing the program or proposal; and (4) presenting the program or proposal to the prospect or customer.

Getting permission to make a survey. In order to develop an effective program presentation, the sales representative must first convince prospects or customers of the desirability of making a survey to discover their exact needs or problems. Often the sales representative will refer to similar surveys which have produced substantial savings or gains for other customers. A sales representative of word processing equipment for example, may use case histories to illustrate how surveys enabled certain companies to find inefficiencies in their practices and to effect great savings by installing word processing equipment.

In many instances a sales representative calls in specialists, such as engineers or systems analysts, to assist in making the surveys or analyses. This lends prestige to the proposition, and the prospective customer is thus more likely to authorize the fact-finding survey.

Making the survey. The simplest type of survey consists of a single interview or a short questionnaire which provides the sales representative with a picture of the problems and needs of the prospective buyers. A life insurance sales agent, for example, who is attempting to plan a comprehensive life insurance program for a prospect normally makes no attempt to sell during the first interview. Instead, all the necessary personal information is obtained about the prospect. The sales representative may then spend hours planning a personalized program which is presented during a subsequent interview. Frequently, the computer may be used in developing specific personalized programs.

Some surveys, however, are very complex and require the services of many technical specialists or experts. For example, IBM spends many thousands of dollars in personnel costs alone to get a single proposal ready for presentation to a prospect.

After the fact-finding or initial research work has been completed and all of the facts have been obtained, the sales representative, or in some cases the specialist diagnoses these facts to determine how the company's products or services can best solve the prospect's problems. This analysis serves as the foundation for a definite program proposal.

Preparing the program. After the facts have been carefully analyzed, a written or illustrated proposal is usually prepared for presentation to the prospect. This proposal normally includes a clear statement of the prospect's problem or need, an effective presentation of the proposed solution to this problem or need, and a description of what the proposed program will cost.

Each proposal or program is tailored to the needs of each prospect or customer. Under certain conditions the sales representative will want to dress up the program presentation by using such visual aids as slide or motion pictures, demonstration models, charts, and portfolios. If the presentation is to be given to a group, it is especially important that appropriate visual aids be utilized.

Presenting the program or proposal. The final step in a complete program presentation is the selling of the proposal to the prospect, client, or customer. The success or failure of the entire program presentation hinges on the kind of job the sales representative does in explaining and presenting the proposal. Presentations of this kind demand an unusual amount of advance preparation and practice before the actual interview takes place.

Advantages and disadvantages. The foremost advantages of the program type of presentation include the following:

1. It provides an opportunity to determine the real needs and problems of the prospect. Emphasis is thus put in the right place—the needs of the buyer.
2. It provides sufficient time to gather and analyze the facts and to prepare the most effective solution to the customer's problems.
3. It provides the opportunity to develop a polished and complete personalized presentation.
4. It builds prestige for the sales representative and the company. The prospect or customer thinks of the sales representative as a professional assistant who is helping to solve the customer's problems.
5. It eliminates wasted time caused by an excessive number of interviews. The sales representative normally obtains permission to make the survey during the first interview and presents recommendations during the second interview.

The main arguments against the program type of presentation are as follows:

1. It is time consuming and therefore expensive. The sales representative or a specialist may spend much valuable time surveying the needs or problems of a potential customer without any guarantee of making a sale.
2. The potential customer may object to having the sales representative make a survey on the ground that the sales representative is biased.
3. In the past many sales representatives obtained interviews under the pretense that they were making surveys. Consequently, many customers are suspicious of surveys or studies which are intended to uncover the true needs of the customer.

Conclusions. This type of sales presentation has gained in popularity during recent years. It is used extensively by experienced salespeople, especially where the unit sales are high. Life insurance companies have had very successful experiences with the "programming" type of selling.

Perhaps the greatest advantage of this type of sales presentation is that it emphasizes the problems and needs of the customer. Consequently, there is a greater chance that each sale will result in long-term gains for both the buyer and the seller.

PLANNING THE PRESENTATION

There is a great temptation for a salesperson to call on a prospect without prior planning of what to say and how to say it. It is so easy to depend upon spur-of-the-moment thinking. A few of the most talented individuals may get by with this approach, but most salespeople will benefit from preparing their presentations in advance of their contacts with prospects. Among the aspects of planning discussed in this section are establishing an objective for the sales call and gathering information about the prospect.

Why plan the sales presentation?

Most salespeople agree that advance planning of the sales interview is absolutely essential to success in selling. Such planning has many advantages. It saves the time of the buyer and the seller; it aids the beginning salesperson; it insures an effective presentation; and it increases sales volume. An example of a precall work sheet used by stockbrokers is shown in Figure 8–1.

Saves time of buyers and sellers.   Buyers respect the salesperson who delivers a well-prepared presentation. Purchasing agents want the salesperson to get down to business so that they can function as professional buyers. As James B. Emerson, a marketing consultant, says:

> Your prospect is busy and highly organized. Frankly, he expects you to be equally businesslike. Your presentation should be brief and to the point, your samples geared to the prospect's probable needs: those you discovered during your homework on his company.[4]

The salesperson should remember that the buyer's time is valuable. If the salesperson can make an intelligent analysis of the needs and wants of each buyer and then, through a well-organized and well-planned presentation, show how the company's products or services fill those needs, the salesperson is likely not only to make a sales but to win the respect and confidence of the buyer.

Aids beginning salespeople.   Most salespeople are under a certain amount of nervous tension when they first call on prospects. This tension is especially noticeable when the individual does not know exactly what to say or how to say it. A well-planned presentation will do much to relieve this strain, and it will help to establish the salesperson's confidence.

Many large companies have developed standard sales stories that are based upon the experiences of their most successful salespeople. Considerable time and effort are spent in developing each phase of the sales presentation so that it flows smoothly from one sales point to the next. All customary objections are anticipated, and carefully worded answers are formulated for the salesperson's use. Often en-

---

[4] James B. Emerson, "How to Conserve Your Prospect's Time for Fun and Profit," *Sales & Marketing Management*, March 14, 1977, p. 80.

Figure 8–1
Precall work sheet

Client _____   Needs: Product(s) to be presented:
Investment: ☐ Current income   General _____
   Experience _____   ☐ Short-term growth   _____
   Capital _____   ☐ Long-term growth   Specific _____
   Attitude _____   ☐ Other _____

Initial need statement

I plan to:

1. Restate the client's need(s).   2. Refer to the general product.
_____   _____

      3. Relate a general product benefit to
_____   need(s).

_____   _____

_____   _____

Presentation

I plan to:

1. Refer to the specific product.   2. Probe for knowledge or attitude.
_____   _____

3. Mention specific product features.   4. Relate specific product benefits.
_____   _____

_____   _____

_____   _____

5. Pause or open probe to verify acceptance.

Close

I plan to close by:

1. Restating general product benefits accepted by the client.   2. Restating specific product benefits accepted by the client
_____   _____

_____   _____

_____   3. Requesting a commitment to:
_____   _____

Proof

Sources I could cite about this product are:

_____   _____

_____   _____

Possible objections

My client's objections might be: I'll use these benefits to handle the objections:

_____   _____

_____   _____

_____   _____

_____   _____

gineering or production department representatives are called in to
provide technical information for use in planning the sales story.
This type of sales planning is invaluable to the neophyte salesperson.

Insures effective presentation.   Planning the sales presentation
in advance insures against ineffective interviews and lost sales. If a
salesperson does not plan what to say, he or she is likely to ramble,
backtrack, omit important sales points, or exaggerate. This results in
lost sales and a waste of valuable selling time. In many respects, the
salesperson's job is not unlike that of a public speaker. Anyone who
has had the experience of talking before an audience certainly recognizes the necessity for planning exactly what to say and how to
say it.

Increases sales.   Careful advance planning of what price line to
show first will afford the salesperson the opportunity to trade up to
the higher priced merchandise during the sales interview. To illustrate, if the salesperson's product has three price lines, attention will
normally be focused on the medium-priced line first. It will then be
possible to move up or down, depending upon the needs and desires
of the customer. Generally, it is much easier to trade up to higher
quality and higher priced merchandise than it is to trade down.
Preplanning on this point will usually result in an overall increase in
sales volume.

Setting specific objectives

Objectives should be established for every sales call. These objectives should be specific. Merely stating that the objective is to make
a sale is insufficient. The objectives should also be measurable.
Again, it is insufficient to simply say that the objective is to sell some
of Product A. Finally, the objectives should be aimed at obtaining
action by the customer. The plans should be made in terms of what
the customer should do, not what the salesperson will do.[5]

Evaluate the following objectives in light of the preceding criteria:

Objective 1	Objective 2
Show and demonstrate the entire line of grinding wheels	Have the customer order one-dozen grinding wheels 1001, 4014, and 5511 (specific, measurable)
	Have the customer promise to test our grinding wheels during the next two weeks (customer action).

[5] From Porter Henry, "Who Needs to Plan?" *Sales Management*, June 24, 1974,
pp. 26–27.

Gathering information

Often the difference between making and not making a sale depends on the amount of "homework" done by the salesperson before making the call. The more information the salesperson has about the customer, the higher is the probability of making a sale. However, the salesperson must be aware of the costs involved in collecting information. At some point, the time and effort put into collecting information become greater than the benefits obtained.

A convenient way of organizing information about the customer is shown in Figure 8–2.

DELIVERING THE PRESENTATION

Four basic steps to follow in making a sales presentation are as follows:

1. Establish rapport with the customer.
2. Identify the customer's need or problem.
3. Solve the problem or satisfy the need by linking product features to customer benefits.
4. Make the buying decision easy.

Establishing rapport with the customer

Sufficient time to establish a warm and friendly atmosphere should be allowed at the beginning of the sales process. A warm greeting, a friendly smile, and a sincere attitude help create the right climate for a successful presentation.

Some small talk about current news, hobbies, and the like usually breaks the ice for the actual presentation. Salespeople should use this time to establish links between their customers and themselves. Customers are more receptive to salespeople with whom they can identify—with whom they have something in common. Thus salespeople will be more effective with customers when they establish such links as mutual friends, common hobbies, or attendance at the same schools.

When selling complex, technical products, it is often important to demonstrate product expertise at the beginning of the sales process. The salesperson can accomplish this by telling the customer about his or her special training or education. Salespeople who have established expertise will have more credibility when making their presentations.

Figure 8–2
Method for organizing information about the customer

About competition					About the customer's business	About the customer as an individual
Direct competition	ABC Co.	DEF Co.	RAT Co.	Indirect competition		
Who □ How much □ Trend: up, down, no change □ The salesperson: Call patterns Strategies Entertaining □ The district sales manager: Whom he calls on Frequency □ Location of the nearest office □ Service □ Pricing □ Product				□ Here enumerate the possible alternatives being offered to customer which, if accepted, may decrease his interest in our offering	□ Organizational □ Technological □ Financial □ Marketing □ Policies, procedures, buying patterns	For each customer, individual having any influence on decisions regarding our offerings: □ What is he or she like? □ What are his or her patterns of behavior? □ How does he or she perceive, think, respond? □ What seems to be his set of needs, motives, or personal aspirations? 1. Purchasing agent 2. Chief engineer 3. Plant manager 4. etc.

Source: Adapted from George Downing, *Sales Management* (New York: John Wiley, 1969), p. 108.

Identifying the customer's need or problem

When a sales representative plans and delivers a presentation, it is easy to make the mistake of starting with product information rather than with a discussion of the prospect's needs. The experienced salesperson, however, attempts to find out something about the prospect's needs and problems at the outset of the interview. Attention is then focused on the specific features and benefits that will satisfy those needs.

No matter how strong the temptation is to start the presentation with product information, the salesperson should do so only if he or she is sure of what the prospect's problem or need is. A product-information lead without prior discussion of the problem or need puts the "cart before the horse."

The following introduction to the sales process indicates the right and wrong ways to begin the sales interview.

Real estate prospect

Prospect: I would like to look at some medium-priced houses in this area.

	Wrong method	*Right method*
Salesperson:	That's fine. We have some very nice listings. Now, here's a very good buy that just came on the market . . .	Won't you sit down, Mr. Prospect? We have some very fine listings, and I'm certain that we can show you something that will meet your needs. If you will tell me a little about the kind of house you have in mind, it will be helpful in selecting the right house for you. How many bedrooms will you need?

Probing for information is a useful technique for identifying a customer's needs. Consider the following example. A sales representative for the Paper Mate Company is making an initial call on a purchasing agent for Quaker Foods.[6] Rather than begin the interview with a description of Paper Mate writing instruments, the representative uses the series of probes shown in Figure 8–3. These probes are described below.

Directive probes.   Directive probes or questions usually start with one of the following five words: *who, what, where, how,* and *why.* Probes 1 and 2 in Figure 8–3 are examples of directive probes. The responses to directive probes give the salesperson a better understanding of the prospect, the prospect's business, and the present competition. Directive probes ask for factual information and are easy to answer. It is best to begin with directive probes seeking

---

[6] This illustration and the information in Figure 8–3 come from *Personal Progress through Skill Development—Probing Your Prospect, Course 4.* The Paper Mate Selling Process, The Gillette Company, Paper Mate Division.

Figure 8-3

Probes for information

Salesperson's probe	Customer's response
Directive probe	
1. What brand of pens do you use?	Surewright.
2. Have your office people expressed some concerns about Surewright, such as leakage or skipping?	Not really, although you hear some grumbling.
Reflective probe	
3. You occasionally hear people grumbling?	We have approximately 300 employees at our headquarters office, you know. Our inventory system is reasonably loose. Any employee can go into the stock room and take a handful of supplies . . .
Encouragement probe	
4. I see.	. . . we haven't noticed any abuse of this privilege. Employees are taking one or two pens at a time. However, we have noticed that our pens seem to be running out of ink fast.
Elaboration probe	
5. Can you tell me more about that?	Well, I guess I'm not really sure about the life of the Surewright pens.

general information that is publicly available. Probes that are too personal or too challenging will make the prospect feel uncomfortable.

The responses to directive probes are valuable information that can be referred to when salespeople relate product benefits to customer needs. Frequently, salespeople note down the important comments made by customers. Note taking is in itself a way of showing concern for the prospect's problems.

Reflective probe. The third probe in Figure 8-3 is a reflective probe. Reflective probes are neutral statements that allow the salesperson to dig deeper. These statements stimulate customers to continue their thoughts in a logical manner. By using reflective probes, salespeople can respond to customers without agreeing or disagreeing with them. Reflective probes also allow salespeople to show that they understand what the customer is saying. If the reflective probe is incorrect, the customer will point out the error.

Encouragement probes. These probes encourage prospects to reveal further information. Probe 4 of Figure 8-3 is an encouragement probe. Other verbal encouragement probes are "Really," "Uh-huh," "That's interesting," and "Is that so?" Nonverbal behaviors such as head nodding are also effective encouragement probes.

Elaboration probes. These probes are positive requests for additional information. Probe 5 of Figure 8–3 is an example of an elaboration probe.

Reflective, encouragement, and elaboration probes are examples of neutral probes. The salesperson should continue to use neutral probes as long as they yield pertinent information. However, the excessive use of neutral probes can cause problems. The salesperson's interest may encourage the prospect to invent requirements that the salesperson's offering cannot meet. When this begins to occur, the salesperson should shift to more directed probes.

Disadvantage probes. These probes ask a customer to articulate a specific problem. For example, a salesperson selling a copier which has an advantage in terms of copy quality might use the following disadvantage probe:

Salesperson: The copier you're using to reproduce these sales proposals uses treated paper, doesn't it?

Customer: Yes, it does.

Salesperson: Some of my other customers have indicated to me that treated paper copiers give a gray cast to their copies. Have you experienced that as well?

Customer: Well, yes, the paper the machine uses isn't the best. It's heavy and doesn't look very good.

Disadvantage probes pose questions to which customers will elaborate on problems with their present products. The value of these probes can be seen by comparing the previous conversation with the following conversation.

Salesperson: The quality of the copies you make of these sales proposals must be very poor. Isn't it?

Customer: It's OK.

Consequence probes. When customers realize the disadvantage of their present product, the salesperson can use probes to illustrate the consequences of the disadvantage. Consider the following example of consequence probes:

Salesperson: How does the lack of copy quality affect you?

Customer: Well, we don't like it.

Salesperson: Since the sales proposals go to your customers, is there any chance that the impact of the proposals is reduced?

Customer: Yes, I suppose that could happen.

Salesperson: Then is it possible that a customer may not have bought your product because of the image those copies projected?

Customer: That's possible.

Salesperson: What could the loss of such a customer be worth to you in dollars and cents?

Customer: An average sale is worth $ _____ .

Value probes. Prior to demonstrating features and benefits, value probes can be used to maximize the impact of the product benefits. Here is an example of a value probe:

Salesperson: Would it be of value to you if you were able to reproduce your sales proposals onto ordinary bond paper, perhaps even use your own letterhead?

Customer: Well, that certainly would improve the image of the proposals. Maybe our customers would be more receptive to them.

Solving the problem by linking product features to customer benefits

After attention has been focused upon the prospect's problem or need, the salesperson should make whatever alterations in the presentation are necessary so that the thoughts of the prospect will flow naturally from the prospect's problem to the salesperson's product. The prospect's thinking must be guided to see the salesperson's product as the solution to a problem or need.

The skilled salesperson maintains a "you-and-your-problem" attitude throughout the sales story. He or she knows the product thoroughly and possesses good judgment in knowing the right amount of product information to give to each prospect. The sales presentation has sufficient flexibility built into it to meet the varying problems and needs of all prospects. The sales story is a reflection of honest concern for the customer's point of view.

Every product has certain key points which make it stand out in comparison to competing products. These points should be highlighted in the presentation, and they should be explained in terms of potential benefits to the customer. Customers will buy the products which they feel will provide the greatest benefits. They are interested in hearing about product features only to the extent that these help solve their problems or satisfy their needs.

The example below illustrates the right and the wrong way of stressing key product features.

Selling home insulation

	Wrong method	*Right method*
Salesperson:	Insul-Wool is outselling all other insulation materials by two to one.	Mrs. Nelson, I'm sure you will enjoy Insul-Wool in your new home. With

	Wrong method	*Right method*
Salesperson:	It is treated with a new chemical which makes it absolutely fireproof. Our surveys have shown that as much as 40 percent of the heat in noninsulated homes is actually lost through the ceiling. Insul-Wool will stop 95 percent of this loss.	children in the home I realize how important it is for you to have it warm throughout each room, especially near the floors. Insul-Wool will provide you with a more even temperature throughout because it stops the loss of the heat which normally escapes through the ceiling. You'll also find, Mrs. Nelson, that your ceilings will stay cleaner much longer if you install Insul-Wool. If your ceilings are not insulated, the air and heat goes through the plaster and before long you will notice lines appearing under each ceiling joist. Our fire-proof Insul-Wool will prevent this and thus will indirectly provide you with real savings in reduced painting costs.

Few customers are really interested in the features of a product. Customers are interested in what the product can do for them—the benefits of the product. The salesperson should focus on the benefits and use the features to support benefit statements. Thus salespeople need to know the benefits and features of their product before making a presentation. An example of a benefit-feature relationship is shown in Figure 8-4.

Making the buying decision easy

The decision to buy should be a gradual one. Most people tend to postpone making decisions, particularly if the decisions are of major importance. It is wise, therefore, for the salesperson to encourage the customer to make many minor decisions throughout the sales interview. This procedure eliminates the necessity for piling up evidence and obtaining a definite yes or no answer at the close of the

Figure 8-4

Benefits and features for a brand of chinaware

Benefits	Features
1. Lasts longer and is therefore less expensive	1. Hard leadless glaze Patterns are under the glaze Body fired at 2600° F Cup handles are molded into cup body before firing
2. Stronger	2. Body fired at 2600° F Cup handles are molded into cup body before firing
3. Longer lasting beauty	3. Translucent Hard leadless glaze Patterns are under the glaze
4. Pride of ownership	4. Translucent Patterns are under the glaze Hard leadless glaze

sales interview. Color or model choices can usually be made early in the sales process. If the salesperson observes the prospect closely, he or she is able to determine the points on which the customer is in agreement. Instead of withholding the order blank and pen until the final stage of the sales interview, most sales representatives prefer to write minor decisions on the order blank as they are made. The final decision thus becomes a natural conclusion to a series of small decisions or agreements.

If the customer is given the opportunity to make a series of small decisions throughout the sales interview and if a choice is given when each of these decisions is made, the closing of the sales presentation is simplified greatly.

THE ART OF LISTENING

Many people think that a salesperson just has to be a good talker to be successful. But people in business realize that listening plays an important role in successful selling.

One study has found that participation in most communications is largely devoted to listening.[7] This study found that the time spent in communications is broken down as follows:

Writing 10%
Reading 15
Speaking 35
Listening 40

[7] Harold P. Zelko, *The Art of Communicating Your Ideas* (New York: Reading Services, 1968), p. 3.

People can speak at only 130 to 160 words per minute, but they can listen to over 800 words per minute. Because of this differential, people often get lazy when listening. They do not pay attention and thus typically can remember only 50 percent of what is said immediately after it is said.

Inexperienced salespeople often go into a selling situation thinking they have to outtalk the prospect. They are enthusiastic about their product and company and want to tell the prospect all they know. However, a salesperson who is talking is not thinking. Salespeople who monopolize conversations cannot find out what customers need.

Listening is not just hearing words. If someone says, "Jim, you bum," the words are practically an insult. But the tone of voice may indicate affection. The effective listener must interpret differences in the speaker's voice inflections and body movements. Listening is an active process.

Advantages of being a good listener

There are many advantages to being a good listener. By being good listeners, salespeople get their customers to help them in making a sale. Customers often "tell" salespeople how to sell them. They say what they like and do not like about products, what their problems and needs are, and, in effect, what they want the salesperson to tell them.

In addition to getting information from customers, salespeople who are good listeners build rapport with customers. Listening is a way of telling the customer, "I am interested in what you are saying, and I respect your opinions." It pays a compliment to the customer. Few people listen. So the salesperson who listens effectively has a significant advantage over competition.

Listening skills

A salesperson can listen faster than a prospect can talk. An effective salesperson puts this "spare time" to good use. Some rules for good listening are listed below:

1. Don't waste the "spare time." Don't think about personal problems. Focus on the prospect's words, ideas, and feelings. Don't react emotionally to what the prospect is saying.
2. Try to anticipate the direction the prospect is taking and the conclusions that the prospect will reach. Put yourself in the prospect's place so that you can see what the prospect is getting at.

3. Determine whether the prospect is giving complete support to the position that is being expressed. Look at the prospect's face, mouth, eyes, and hands to detect unspoken feelings. Listen between the lines.
4. Concentrate on the ideas that the prospect is trying to get across and on facts that support those ideas.
5. Periodically summarize (to yourself) the points that are being made. Summarize ideas and concepts, not facts.
6. Give the prospect time to talk. Don't step on the prospect's sentences.
7. Practice listening skills in nonselling situations.

NONVERBAL COMMUNICATIONS

Effective salespeople need to observe their customers as well as listen to what customers are saying. More than two thirds of the communications between salespeople and customers is nonverbal. Nonverbal communications is basically an unconscious language. People are often not aware of nonverbal signals they are transmitting or receiving. Salespeople need to learn how to read and respond to nonverbal signals sent by customers. In addition, salespeople can increase their effectiveness by using nonverbal communications to transmit messages.

It is frequently difficult to interpret nonverbal signals. Those signals vary from culture to culture. For example, Americans typically become uncomfortable if someone invades their personal space, which extends two feet from them in all directions. People engaged in business communications are usually four to seven feet from each other.[8] On the other hand, Spanish people demand less space and like to converse at closer intervals. Because of these cultural differences, an American salesperson might misinterpret the attempt of a Spanish customer to move closer to the salesperson.

In addition to cultural differences, many nonverbal cues can be interpreted only by using other evidence. For example, customers may rub their noses because of an itch or because they doubt the information being presented by the salesperson. When verbal and nonverbal signals provide conflicting information, the salesperson needs to dig deeper into the situation. The whole truth is not being told.

Nonverbal communications includes the space or distance between communications, touching, body messages, and voice char-

---

[8] Edward T. Hall, *The Hidden Dimension* (Garden City, N.Y.: Doubleday, 1966).

acteristics.[9] Body messages and voice characteristics are discussed in the following sections.

Body messages

Messages are sent by body position and posture and by the face, the hands, and body movements. Each of these is discussed in the next section.

Body posture.   An example of a tense, rigid posture is shown in Figure 8–5. The cross-arm position indicates defensiveness or lack of receptivity. Customers who assume this posture may be indicating

Figure 8–5

Customer taking defensive posture

[9] For a more detailed discussion, see Julius Fast, *Body Language* (New York: Evans, 1970), and Albert Mehrabian, *Silent Messages* (Belmont, Calif.: Wadsworth, 1971).

that the sales presentation has been going on too long, that the product does not meet their needs, or that the salesperson is applying too much pressure.

Receptive customers typically assume a more relaxed posture, as shown in Figure 8–6. Posture signals that indicate receptivity include a slightly tilted head, an open-armed stance, and crossed legs pointing toward the salesperson. In addition, when people agree with each other during a conversation, they typically assume the same posture. Thus, if a customer takes the same posture as the salesperson, this can be used as a closing signal.

Body movements. Changes in position typically indicate a change of mind. Customers will change position when they want to end the interview, when they strongly agree or disagree with something that has been said, or when they are ready to accept the salesperson's offer. Customers may "tell" salespeople that they wish to end the meeting by moving backward or cleaning up their desks. When this occurs, the salesperson needs to reinterest the customer, attempt to close, state that he or she realizes the customer is very busy, or terminate the interview quickly.

Figure 8–6
Customer indicating receptivity

Salespeople can use body movements to regain or reinforce customer attention and interest. When a customer begins to show inattention, the salesperson can regain the customer's attention by moving to another place in the room or shifting position in a chair. Moving closer to a customer or tilting the head can be used to indicate interest in what the customer is saying.

The face.   The face contains many small muscles that are capable of communicating innumerable messages. Customers can use their faces to indicate interest, expectation, concern, approval, or disapproval. Through experience, most people have learned to interpret facial expressions accurately.

The eyes are the most important area of the face. When people are interested or excited, their pupils enlarge. Thus, by looking at a customer's eyes, salespeople can determine when their presentations have made an impression. For this reason, Chinese jade buyers often wear dark glasses so that they can be more effective in bargaining by hiding their interest from sellers.

Good eye contact conveys interest and sincerity. Avoiding eye contact conveys insincerity and dishonesty. Thus a salesperson should attempt to maintain frequent eye contact. If direct eye contact is uncomfortable, looking at the bridge of a customer's nose will have the same effect.

The hands.   Hand movements can be used to get attention, convey size and shape, and indicate direction. Tension is revealed when hands are tightly clasped. A clenched fist suggests that strong emotions are being held back. Tapping a desk is a sign of restlessness or lack of interest. As with all nonverbal signals, the salesperson must be careful not to overinterpret these signs because the same signs can have multiple meanings.

Voice characteristics

Good voice and speech habits are quite important for salespeople.[10] The degree to which a customer receives a salesperson's message depends upon the following vocal characteristics of the salesperson: rate of speech, loudness, pitch, quality and articulation.

The normal rate of speech is between 160 and 200 words per minute. A salesperson should vary his or her rate of speech. Simple messages can be delivered at faster rates, while more difficult concepts should be presented at lower rates. The loudness of speech

[10] For a more complete treatment, see Dorothy Sarnoff, *Speech Can Change Your Life* (Garden City, N.Y.: Doubleday, 1970).

should be varied to avoid monotony. Changing the loudness level can also be used to indicate importance.

Articulation refers to the production of recognizable sounds. There are three common causes of poor articulation: (1) locked jaw, (2) lazy lips, and (3) lazy tongue. The best articulation is obtained when the mouth is opened by the width of a finger between the teeth. When the jaw is not opened properly, the movements of the lips and tongue are impeded. When the lips are too close together, the enunciation of certain vowels and consonants will be poor.

QUESTIONS AND PROBLEMS

1. Assume that you are a sales representative for one of the major airlines. Your job is to call on business firms in Chicago to sell them on the advantages of shipping their goods by airfreight. In outline form, list the main sales points around which you would build your sales presentation.

2. Ms. Swanson is a sales representative for a leather-goods manufacturer. She makes regular calls on wholesalers and large retailers, and she carries a fairly complete line of leather products, including such items as luggage, billfolds, briefcases, handbags, and belts. Ms. Swanson has been very conscientious about preparing an effective sales presentation for each of her products. She has found from experience, however, that after she uses the same sales presentation for a certain length of time, she loses enthusiasm and her sales decline. What, if anything, can Ms. Swanson do to overcome this difficulty?

3. Frequently companies utilize a two-person selling team to present their products to the prospective buyers. List typical examples of situations in which two-person teams might be used effectively. What are the advantages and disadvantages of this type of sales presentation?

4. Assume that you are a sales representative for a paper supply house. You sell a number of paper products to retailers and other business concerns. One line of products includes paper napkins and paper drinking cups which are sold to restaurants and soda fountains. Outline the main sales points that you would use in selling paper cups to the owner of a large soda fountain (assuming that paper cups are not now used). What sales points would you emphasize in your presentation? How would you start your sales presentation? What would you say to stimulate wants? Would your emphasis be different if you were calling on the owner of a small retail fountain?

5. An example of a reflective question or probe follows:

   Customer: Look . . . we have been having considerable success with our present supplier for the past three years. Why should we make a change now?

Reflective response: You feel that your present supplier is completely satisfactory?

How would you make a reflective response to the following statements?

a.   "It won't work. I don't think you understand our problem. Our situation is completely different from anybody else's.

b.   "Oh, that. We tried something like that last year, and it didn't work."

c.   "That sounds good in theory, but these things never seem to work out in practice. I don't think that idea will work."

6.   In a selling situation between the salesperson and the prospect, much of what is said is really never heard, and part of what is heard is often misinterpeted by one or both of the parties. What techniques might a salesperson use to improve communication with the prospect?

7.   Prepare a list of features and benefits that could be used in a presentation to high school students. The objective of the presentation is to encourage the students to enroll in your college.

8.   In selling the following products, what would be a good stimulus statement? What would be the expected response?

a.   A retirement investment program.

b.   A $75,000 vacation home in Florida.

c.   A $25,000 foreign sports car.

9.   "The first few minutes in a sales interview may be important to some salespeople, but my selling is different. I only call on a few people whom I know well or have met before." Comment.

10.   Assume that you are a sales representative for a Volkswagen dealer. You have been asked to contribute ideas and sales product information that could be used in preparing a national magazine ad for a Volkswagen panel truck. What theme and what key points would you suggest?

PROJECTS

1.   Outline a presentation to "sell" yourself to a company that has an opening for a salesperson.

2.   Assume that you are a sales representative for an automobile dealer that sells one of the economy cars. You are calling upon the purchasing agent of the Electro Corporation with the purpose of selling Electro a fleet of six cars for use by its sales representatives. Secure the necessary product information from a local automobile dealer, and write a script of a sales interview with the Electro purchasing agent. Write the script so that it can be used in a role-playing demonstration in class.

3.   Observe the selling technique used by a salesperson in a department store. Write a report describing and evaluating the technique.

CASE PROBLEMS

Case 8-1

Ringel Food Service Company

Herb Ringel, president of the Ringel Food Service Company, started in the food service business while he was a student in college. He was house manager of his fraternity, and in this capacity he became aware of the problems that fraternities, sororities, and clubs were having in providing good food to students at a reasonable cost. Ringel talked with other house managers about their food service problems, and he concluded that there was an opportunity to provide better food at a lower cost by having one organization serve several eating units. To accomplish this objective, five fraternities formed a cooperative organization which purchased their food products.

The cooperative organization elected Ringel as its manager and gave him full authority to make its food purchases. Ringel was very successful, and in this capacity he learned a lot about the food service business.

After graduation, Ringel decided to go into the food service business on a full-time basis. In 1960 he established the Ringel Food Service Company, which started by providing limited coffee and sandwich service to a number of industrial plants and offices in Denver. Within five years the company had expanded its service to include a complete food service for schools, colleges, hospitals, office buildings, and factories. The company bought food centrally and operated its own commissary and bake shop. In most instances Ringel employees used the supplies and equipment of the client and prepared, served, and sold the food. Meat was supplied by Ringel in company-owned trucks. Dairy products were delivered to clients from the closest dairy.

Ringel Food Service operated under different kinds of contracts with its clients. Some contracts were called "limited profit and limited loss contracts," and others were subsidy contracts whereby the Ringel company received a guaranteed profit. Contracts ranged in size from a few thousand dollars to over $700,000 yearly. Ringel utilized effective cost control methods and was able to provide food service at a cost substantially below that which the clients could obtain for themselves.

By 1975 the company had approximately 700 employees in all of its operations. Food service was being supplied to many large factories and institutions. Ringel employed two sales representatives who called upon prospective clients to sell the food service. The company also had two food service consultants who worked with the sales representatives and the operating personnel on technical dietary and food problems.

The normal procedure followed by the company was to have the sales representative call upon prospective customers. However, with large accounts Ringel and a food service consultant frequently accompanied the sales representative. In some instances a sales representative would work on a single prospect for over a year before a contract was signed.

One day, during a call on a customer, Dave Corbett, one of the sales representatives, was told that the American Insurance Company was considering the possibility of having an outside food service company take over its cafeteria food service.

The American Insurance Company had approximately 1,500 employees in its building and a modern cafeteria with the latest equipment. Although the company had operated its cafeteria for the past two years, it had never been completely satisfied with the results. Even though the company subsidized the cafeteria, the employees were still dissatisfied with the food and the service.

Questions

1. Assume that you are Dave Corbett, and state what steps you would follow in attempting to obtain the American Insurance Company account?

2. To what extent should the sales presentation to the American Insurance Company be a team effort? Who should be on the team? If Ringel participates in the sales presentation, what part should he play?

3. Write up a sales presentation that would be used in your meeting with the American Insurance Company executives.

Case 8-2

Industrial Conveyor Company

Roger Cope sells conveyor belts and systems for moving small packages. He works for Industrial Conveyor Corporation. The following conversation occurred during a call he made on Mike Lopez, the vice president of a medium-sized warehouse company in Philadelphia.

Cope: Mr. Lopez, I'm Roger Cope of Industrial Conveyor. I would like to discuss our new conveyor system with you. I think the system will be useful in your next warehouse expansion.

Lopez: *(laying out a newspaper on his desk and offering a hand):* Please sit down, Roger. I was reading about the upcoming elections. What do you think about the Democrats and their platform?

Cope: I haven't had a chance to read up on it yet. I'm optimistic that the economy will pick up no matter who is elected. Lots of our customers are thinking about expansion. Do you have any expansion plans?

Lopez: Well, I think we'll be adding 200,000 square feet. We're just in the thinking phase. It really depends on how much space we'll need a year from now. *(Still looking at the paper.)* Say, look at those women at the national NOW meeting. How do you feel about women in politics?

Cope: It depends on who the woman is, I guess. Some have really made some great contributions, and others don't seem to have a long-term viewpoint. Have you made any plans for your expansion?

Lopez: Nothing on paper yet.

Cope: *(pulling some plans out of his briefcase):* Here are some warehouse plans incorporating our new conveyor system. This system reduces the overall cost for a conveyor system by 30 percent. That would be a big savings, wouldn't it?

Question

Evaluate Cope's initial handling of this interview.

Case 8–3

Thomas Hill Publishing Company

The Thomas Hill Publishing Company includes a highly successful textbook division under the direction of a new editor. The new editor has embarked on a new venture that is designed to tap the increasing demand for adult education, continuing education, and other nontraditional forms of education, as well as the increasing market for "practical" courses.

Thomas Hill has developed video courses in the basic business curriculum, including courses in such subjects as accounting, finance, statistics, and economics. The courses are taped lectures by eminent professors and business leaders from around the country, and include colorful and easy-to-understand animated visual materials such as charts and graphs.

Programmed textbooks, cases, and problems accompany the videotapes which can be used in "self-teaching" situations on a flexible schedule. The tapes may be checked out for use in more convenient locations than the administering institution, such as homes, libraries, and high schools. The courses are designed for use by people who wish to continue their education but whose family or work commitments prevent them from attending classes at regular hours or at the university. The technique and content of the courses have been judged excellent by an impartial panel of educators.

The cost for the first tape is $500, with a $50 duplicating charge for each additional copy ordered. It is assumed that the students will buy the accompanying texts.

Make a sales presentation that elicits a buying commitment from the curriculum committee of State University's Business School. Remember, you have the solid reputation of your company behind you. However, you must convince the committee that there is a need for this individualized, flexible, and yet impersonal teaching method. Furthermore, you must convince the committee that your courses will do an effective teaching job for less money than it would cost to have professors teach at irregular hours in many places.

SELECTED REFERENCES

Berne, Eric. *What Do You Say after You Say Hello?* New York: Grove Press, 1973.

Hanan, Mark. "If Your Own Sales Objectives Aren't Working, Try Using the Customer's." *Sales & Marketing Management,* November 12, 1979, pp. 82-85.

Jolson, Marvin A. "The Underestimated Potential of the Canned Sales Presentation." *Journal of Marketing,* January 1975, pp. 75-78.

Kolgraf, R. "Selling and Psychology." *Industrial-Distributor,* October 1978, pp. 37-41.

Reinfeld, George. "Know Where You're Going—Before You Get There." *Inland Printer/American Lithographer,* December 1975, pp. 68-71.

Sokol, G. "The Impact of Consultative Selling." *Training and Development Journal,* November 1979, pp. 34-37.

Spiro, R. L., and **Perreault, W. D.** "Influence Use by Industrial Salesmen: Influence-Strategy Mixes and Situational Determinants." *Journal of Business,* July 1979, pp. 435-55.

Stevens, C. G. "Anatomy of an Industrial Sales Presentation." *Sales Management,* October 1, 1973, pp. 61-62.

Warren, M. W. "Using Behavioral Technology to Improve Sales Performance." *Training and Development Journal,* July 1978, pp. 54-56.

Zelko, Harold P. The *Art of Communicating Your Ideas.* New York: Reading Services, 1968.

Chapter 9

DRAMATIZING THE
SALES PRESENTATION

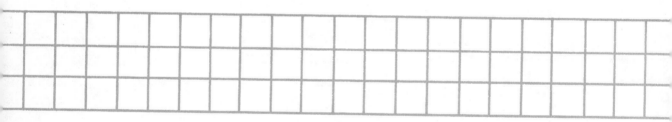

A well-planned sales presentation provides for the necessary organization of material and requires the choice of appropriate product or service sales features and benefits. To insure maximum effectiveness, plans must be made on how best to communicate the sales message.

The next task is to review the material with the idea of breathing as much life and vigor as possible into the communication processes. Sufficient impact must be created to cause the prospect to *understand* the message, *believe* the message, and *remember* the message. The message must be exciting and convincing enough to motivate the prospect to a favorable course of action. Webster's dictionary defines *dramatize* as "full of action, highly emotional, vivid, exciting, powerful—approached from the viewpoint of drama." The series of activities that is designed to facilitate action by the buyer is called "dramatization."

Each salesperson is expected to inject his or her personality into the sales presentation. Actions should be designed to enable the buyer to become aware of the benefits which are in store for the use of the product or service. No two people are likely to use exactly the same techniques and procedures to put their messages across. Salespeople should ask themselves the following questions: "How can I use my imagination and my resourcefulness to make a vivid impression upon my prospect or customer? How can I use my abilities to make my presentation a little different and a little stronger?" With this frame of mind, salespeople are never completely satisfied with their efforts. They are constantly attempting to do a better and more effective job of selling.

Good salespeople are good actors and actresses

Many sales managers have compared good salespeople to good actors. Both salespeople and actors are skillful showpeople; both have parts to play; both live their parts; both dress for their parts; and both attempt to influence an audience. Actors usually have props to help portray their parts more effectively; they practice and rehearse lines tirelessly until they feel that they have mastered every action, every tone or inflection of the voice; they strive for perfection. Successful salespeople likewise use props; they attempt to master their parts; they dress appropriately; and they strive to do a better job each time they deliver a sales presentation. Both salespeople and actors are constantly striving to add a personal touch to their parts which will make them different and more successful in their chosen fields of endeavor.

Good salespeople use multiple-sense appeals

Five avenues may be used to dramatize sales presentations. These avenues are the senses of hearing, sight, touch, taste, and smell—*five* channels to the buyer's springs of action. Appeals should be made to as many of these senses as possible.

Studies show that multiple-sense appeals increase both learning and retention. It is important for sales representatives to recognize that

We *learn* through	And we *retain* of
Taste—1 percent	What we hear—20 percent
Touch—2 percent	What we see *and* hear—50 percent
Smell—4 percent	
Hearing—11 percent	
Sight—82 percent	

Some products can be sold through the use of appeals to all five senses. Others can appeal to a maximum of two or three senses. When selling candy to a retail merchant, the salesperson may describe its merits—this is *hearing* appeal; or show the candy and invite the merchant to taste it—this appeals to *sight, touch,* and *taste;* if certain candies are aromatic, there is the opportunity to appeal to the merchant's fifth sense—*smell.* On the other hand, salespeople who sell machinery are limited to appeals which affect the buyers' senses of hearing, sight, and touch.

THE POWER OF EFFECTIVE DRAMATIZATION

There are at least five good reasons for learning to dramatize sales presentations. Dramatization gets and maintains the interest of the buyer, convinces the buyer, facilitates the buyer's understanding of the proposition, creates a lasting impression, and aids the salesperson.

Dramatizing gets and maintains buyer interest

A touch of showmanship aids in securing the attention and maintaining the interest of the customer or prospect. A prospect can listen to a sales presentation and really not absorb much of the information presented. However, when the salesperson *does* something, interest is likely to pick up immediately.

A salesperson who sells electric globes may pretend to fumble a sample lamp, let it fall, and then pick it up unbroken. A fountain pen salesperson may drive the point of a pen into a piece of wood, and then remove the undamaged pen from the wood and ask the prospect to write with it.

Salespeople who solicit orders for packaged foods from store buyers know that the way to sell them dramatically is to appeal to all five of the buyer's senses. Some use kits to serve hot soup or hot chicken to buyers right in the office or store.

Unless the prospect's interest is secured and maintained, the salesperson has little opportunity to build toward a successful close. Few buyers stay mentally awake long enough to be convinced unless multiple-sense appeals are used.

Dramatizing convinces the prospect

Buyers who are convinced that the product satisfies their needs, and who are really prospects, usually buy. Dramatization is convincing when answering objections and closing sales. Comparatively few products cannot be dramatized in some way.

Pencil and pad are used to draw diagrams, graphs, and rough sketches, and to figure in order to "prove" a point. When roller bearings were first introduced, sales representatives carried sample bearings and a small wooden ruler. The buyer was invited to apply weight to the ruler and push it along the top of the desk. Then bearings were put under the ruler, and the prospect was asked to repeat the experiment. Of course, the almost total elimination of friction was evident. This demonstration convinced many prospects that reducing friction in machinery bearings would save power and reduce equipment depreciation.

An industrial sales representative can create an unforgettable impression when the object is to dramatize the high melting point of an industrial grease by the proof-of-performance technique. Ordinary grease and the company's grease can each be heated in a portable container to show the different melting points. Other product features such as water resistance, rust protection, and noncorrosiveness can also be dramatized.

Colored slides to portray interesting installations of plastic signs have been particularly successful in convincing prospects. Slides are easy to carry, flexible, and inexpensive. Some companies reproduce slides from original shots taken by the salespeople themselves, since it is always of greater interest for salespeople to show installations in their own sales territory.

The salesperson who wishes to convince the prospect or customer may prove claims by dramatizing what the product will do. If the product won't burn, light a match and try to burn it. If the product won't chip, bend or twist a sample piece to show that it won't crack or peel. If the product is unbreakable, drop it or hit it with a hammer to prove the claim. Some type of proof-of-performance demonstration is the most convincing sales technique available to a sales representative, because the demonstration has a simultaneous impact upon several senses.

Dramatizing improves understanding

Many visual-minded buyers actually lack the power to form clear images from the written or spoken word. For these people the most effective sales approach is a dramatization based largely on visual appeals.

Many product benefits cannot be explained adequately in non-technical language. A verbal explanation may be understandable only by buyers with a technical background. But a simple demonstration may *show* other buyers exactly what benefits they can expect through the purchase of the product.

Insurance companies use a graph to show the prospect's needs and how those needs are to be met. The prospect gets a complete, graphic picture of the insurance program on one page. This picture may include provisions for a cleanup fund, an emergency fund, children's education, special funds, monthly income for the family, and guaranteed retirement income.

Sales representatives for a lithography firm added a new selling tool to enable customers and prospects to visualize more clearly the advertising folder to be developed. This tool is a do-it-yourself kit. It enables hotel, motel, and resort operators to produce a colorful brochure with the sales representative's help. Sample layouts are submitted to the operator, who selects the photographs and prepares copy describing the features and services to be emphasized. Sales representatives carry a library of color shots which the operator can use if desired. Once the customer has completed the work-sheet copy of the brochure, the sales representative takes it to the shop for printing. The customer has a complete picture of the brochure before it is printed.

An old Chinese proverb says, "Tell me—I'll forget. Show me—I may remember. But *involve* me, and I'll *understand.*"

Dramatizing makes a lasting impression

When a particular feature of a product is dramatized vividly, a strong impression is created. The customer may almost experience the benefits claimed, will remember the claims longer, and is more likely to tell friends about the product.

Lasting impressions may be created in many ways. One salesperson steps on the rubber plug at the end of a light cord; another kicks the glass in the door of an electric range; still another invites prospects to choose a name or a number from a high stack of cards and then has the electric sorting machine throw out the card wanted. A salesperson may demonstrate by using the pressure of a feather to activate the keys of an electric typewriter or by inviting customers to roll pieces of carbon paper in their hands to prove that the carbon won't come off. Whatever method is used, whether it be melting metal without burning insulation materials or immersing paraffin-treated boxes of raisins in water, the prospect is more likely to remember the sales feature if the dramatization is skillfully presented and well timed.

Dramatizing helps the sales representative

One manufacturer of menswear accessories believes its salespeople benefit from the company's plan of dramatizing through store demonstrations because this forces the salesperson to deliver an orderly sales talk, familiarizes both the salesperson and the retailer with a completely blueprinted merchandising program, and provides an opportunity to kindle enthusiasm in the people who sell to the consumer.

Salespeople find that a good dramatic presentation also builds up their confidence in their abilities and their products. Successful dramatization requires them to plan and to rehearse. They cannot plan and rehearse over a period of time without developing more confidence in themselves and their products.

Dramatization is a time-saver for the seller and the buyer. The sales presentation is reduced to these important points which are necessary to consummate the sale. Pictures, actions, and words tell the story more rapidly than do words alone. Time is money to the salesperson. Every sales aid that conserves time is worthwhile.

Pharmaceutical sales representatives who call on doctors have found that they must tell their story in about five minutes. To get the doctors to think about the product and not about their patients for a few minutes, they rely heavily on visual aids, or sales tools, which keep the doctor's mind and eye on the story.

Dramatizing creates value

Value is suggested by the manner in which a product is handled. Careful handling gives the impression of value even if no words are spoken. Careless handling implies that the product is of little value. A rare painting, an expensive piece of jewelry, or a delicate piece of chinaware "speak" for themselves if the salesperson uses appropriate props, words, and care in handling them.

VISUAL AIDS AND TECHNIQUES FOR DRAMATIZING THE PRESENTATION

In many fields of selling, the company which manufactures or distributes the product supplies effective aids. Xerox, for example, is convinced that using visual aids as a support tool has many advantages. Among the benefits recognized by Xerox are: gains attention, personalizes, simplifies, clarifies, reduces misunderstandings, adds importance and emphasis, heightens interest, reinforces verbal stimulus, and professionalizes your image.[1]

---

[1] Xerox Sales Training Manual.

The following pages show and describe some of the more common visual aids.

Charts and graphs

These aids are particulary helpful in illustrating relationships and trends. Charts may show advertising schedules, some special detail of product manufacture, or illustrations of typical profit margins. Bars, circles, or squares are used frequently to depict relationships.

The slide chart, as the name indicates, is a chart with movable parts.[2] Usually, the parts of the chart are moved to obtain a quick answer to some problem or to point out some pertinent fact. Slide charts have been developed to describe the best method of removing a variety of stains on clothing; to enable poultry farmers to estimate the cost of eggs; to show how much tile is needed for various areas; to determine the right pump for any conditions of gallons, pressure, and depth of well; to calculate Social Security benefits; to compare a company's product with those of leading competitors; to determine profit on selling price or cost; to show the conversion of measurements to the metric system; and for many other purposes.

Realizing that it may cost as much as $5.59 to type a letter, Dictaphone sales representatives use a pocket-size card to indicate the dollar value of the executive's time when selling their Thought Tank machine. (see Figure 9-1.)

Photographs, pictures, and advertisements

These aids may be supplied individually or incorporated into bulletins or portfolios. They are media which permit a realistic portrayal of the product or service and its benefits.

Photographs are easy to prepare and relatively inexpensive. Photographs of people may be particularly effective. Many companies use photographs to illustrate benefits. For example, leisure made possible through savings can be dramatized through photographs of retired people on a ranch, at mountain resorts, or on the seashore. Pictures which are drawn, painted, or prepared in other ways are useful in dramatizing needs or benefits. Real estate brokers rely heavily upon photographs of properties to help qualify prospects and thereby conserve time and reduce inspection tour expenses.

---

[2] The Perrygraf Division of Nashua Corp. (Los Angeles, California) produces great varieties of slide charts and illustrates them in a 36-page booklet along with 16 short case histories.

Figure 9-1

Card used to show value of an executive's time

What's your time worth?

If You Earn	Every Hour Is Worth	In A Year One Hour A Day Is Worth	Save An Hour A Day Leasing Thought Tank™ For Annual Savings Of	Save An Hour A Day And Pay For A Thought Tank™ Within
$2,000	$1.09	$ 266	$ —	40 months
2,500	1.36	332	39	32
3,000	1.63	398	93	27
3,500	1.91	466	107	23
4,000	2.18	532	173	20
4,500	2.46	600	241	18
5,000	2.73	666	307	16
5,500	3.00	732	373	15
6,000	3.28	800	441	14
6,500	3.55	866	507	13
7,000	3.82	932	573	12
7,500	4.10	1,000	641	11
8,000	4.37	1,066	707	10
8,500	4.64	1,132	773	10
9,000	4.91	1,198	839	9
10,000	5.46	1,332	973	8
11,000	6.00	1,464	1,105	8
12,000	6.55	1,598	1,239	7
13,000	7.10	1,732	1,373	6
14,000	7.64	1,864	1,505	6
15,000	8.19	1,998	1,639	5
20,000	10.92	2,664	2,305	4
25,000	13.65	3,331	2,972	3
30,000	16.38	3,997	3,638	3
35,000	19.11	4,663	4,304	2
40,000	21.84	5,329	4,970	2
45,000	24.57	5,995	5,636	2
50,000	27.30	6,661	6,302	2
75,000	40.95	9,992	9,633	1
100,000	54.60	13,322	12,963	1

Based on 244, 7½-hour working days.

PRINTED IN U.S.A.   042

Courtesy of Dictaphone Corp.

General Electric has encouraged dealers to use Polaroid cameras in selling kitchen appliances. Miniature models of kitchens are set up in the home, and then they are photographed to show the prospect how the proposed kitchen will look. Another company has used a similar method to sell furniture for installation in offices and laboratories.

Copies of recent advertisements may be kept in the issue of the magazine or newspaper in which they appeared, or they may be detached and covered with cellophane or another transparent material. It is important that the copies be seen easily and that they be kept fresh and neat.

Sales manuals and portfolios

Some sales manuals are used to reproduce standardized sales talks. These manuals are often illustrated with pictures, graphs, cartoons, drawings, and other visual presentations to insure the use of the right aid at the right time. They are frequently used by direct-to-the-consumer organizations selling such products as cutlery, silverware, and housewares.

Sales manuals are often supplied by the company. Other companies supply their salespeople with ideas and material which they expect the salespeople to organize in an effective manner.

The sales portfolio usually contains only the sales talk, while the sales manual may contain information on many other phases of the salesperson's job. The sales portfolio is usually designed as a guide to the presentation. However, some portfolios are prepared to be read.

Common types of sales portfolios are the easel type, the spiral-bound type, and the binder or zipper-case type.

The easel type is prepared to stand by itself on the prospect's desk or counter. Some larger easel types which are placed on the floor are used when selling to a group. The salesperson turns each page after it has been read or used for illustrative purposes. The pages are arranged logically so that the story unfolds according to plan.

The spiral-bound type of sales portfolio may or may not be of the easel type. Wire or plastic bindings are commonly used. When not constructed to be used like an easel, this type may be referred to occasionally to supply additional sales features, helps, or suggestions to the prospective buyer or customer.

The binder or zipper-case type is in common use. Material may be labeled by tabs and punched to fit the rings in the binder. This type may be referred to often, and it is convenient to carry and to use. For example, Toledo Scale Company sales representatives who sell to retail food stores and restaurants "are supplied with selling kits which are zipper-type portfolios with retractable handles and contain detailed illustrative material readily indexed on all of the items themselves."[3]

One large building contractor improved selling efforts by preparing a visual presentation of the important facts concerning the business. The portfolio, bound in spiral plastic, contained such information as thumbnail sketches of the company's key employees; a financial statement; a list of special equipment; photostatic copies of letters from satisfied owners of various types of buildings; and pictures of completed industrial plants, apartment houses, stores,

---

[3] Quoted by permission from a letter from Toledo Scale Co. (Toledo, Ohio).

supermarkets, and shopping centers. This appeal to the eye tells a story which many words and many minutes cannot equal.

Models, samples, and gifts

These visual selling aids may be one good answer to the problem of getting and keeping buyer interest. Miniature models are carried when the product is too large or bulky for convenient transportation. These may be cross-section models, toy models, or working miniature models. Bearings, industrial equipment, spark plugs, kitchen equipment, and cars are just a few of the products for which models have been prepared.

A large manufacturer of equipment used by such businesses as hotels, meat markets, and restaurants supplied blueprints of layouts for store owners. It became apparent that too few owners could understand blueprints. The company replaced the blueprints with tabletop miniature models of fixtures. The new device proved far more effective than blueprints.

An industrial distributor in Birmingham, Alabama, builds sales to contractors with its Construction Site Service—a four-van fleet in which each van is equipped with an $8,000 inventory and manned by a driver salesperson. The fleet helps the company sell more sophisticated and more lucrative equipment because it enables salespeople to demonstrate on-site the company's line of Phillips Drill Red Head concrete anchors and Black & Decker tools.[4]

Some sales representatives carry samples even when the product is large and heavy. National Cash Register salespeople have found that it pays to carry the types of machines they plan to use. The registers are carried in a station wagon or a passenger car. When the prospect is ready for a demonstration, the register is available immediately. Experience has shown that anything can happen if the salesperson gets the interest of the prospect and then must return to the office to secure a sample register. It may take several more calls to secure an appointment for a demonstration.

Samples of the product make excellent sales aids. Foods, candies, paper products, medicines, and books are among the many products which may be sold through the use of samples. The samples may be arranged in a kit or a case for easy carrying.

Samples are frequently used to maintain the prospect's interest and to serve as a reminder for prospects or customers who do not buy at the time of the interview. In selling ethical drugs, for example, salespeople may use a novel container to demonstrate the delayed

---

[4] "Industrial Newsletter," *Sales & Marketing Management*, September 17, 1979, p. 44.

dissolving action of a drug and then leave the visual with the physician for use as a paperweight. Or an industrial sales representative may use a toy gryoscope to illustrate the quiet performance of a motor and then leave the toy with the buyer as a reminder.

Films, slides, and cassettes

Filmstrips, motion pictures, and slides have become a more common part of the salesperson's equipment. Films are particularly useful when selling to groups, when selling in a showroom, or when showing the operations of complex machinery in the buyer's office. If sound motion-picture films are used, action is combined with sound and sight to make a forceful impression upon the prospect. Motion-picture equipment is heavy and bulky, and motion-picture films are expensive to make. Because of this, filmstrips have been used more extensively.

Films are particularly good for educating distributors and their salespeople. One part of the promotion plan of SKF Industries' (maker of antifriction bearings) included the use of sound-slide films to bring the story of company products to distributors and their salespeople. The company's field representatives are responsible for merchandising the sales promotion plans.

International Harvester Co. has found that selling heavy farm equipment is improved through the use of a sound filmstrip. Sales representatives can take a portable projector, operate it from the car cigarette lighter socket, and bring the sales message to a farmer in the field. The eight-minute message conserves the time of both the salesperson and the farmer.

Many companies and corporations show films at club and organization meetings. Films of this kind must be more than factual. They must be interesting, and the facts presented must be dramatized.

Slides have been effective selling aids for many companies. One large company, a leader in structural timber sales, found that three-dimensional photographs and a viewer convinced prospects that laminated wood treated with waterproof glue was a good substitute for steel. Pictures were taken of construction jobs in which laminated arches were used; slides were made; and sales representatives were provided with three-dimensional viewers to show architects and builders exactly how and where the company's product was used. Each salesperson carries about 60 colored Stereo-Realist slides and a battery-lighted viewer to show product applications.

Sound-slide films have been used effectively in selling mutual investment funds. A typical presentation can be made in about 12 minutes.

Products that are too bulky or too fragile to be carried may be photographed in color and demonstrated at the flick of a finger through the use of a small automatic projector (see Figure 9-2).

For use at retail sales clinics, on a sales call, selling in showrooms, and store demonstrations Technicolor's slide cassette player/recorder and sound amplification system provides the opportunity to put together your own slide and narration show. The equipment is portable and fits under the seat in an airplane (see Figure 9-3).

An even smaller automatic sound filmstrip projector which projects sound filmstrips and standard cassette-loaded tapes is useful for on-the-spot sales activity. It is about the size of a large book and weighs less than nine pounds (see Figure 9-4).[5]

Testimonials

Testimonials are usually in the form of letters written by satisfied users of a product or service. These letters usually commend the product or service and make it known that the writer believes the product or service to be a good buy. Testimonials are frequently used by advertisers in newspapers and magazines, and can be a very effective part of the sales presentation.

Insurance company agents use case histories of claims which report the injuries or disabilities a policyholder has suffered and the

Figure 9-2
Portable unit for visual presentation of sales message

Courtesy of Eastman Kodak Company

---

[5] For information on audiovisual equipment costs, see "Audiovisual Equipment Purchase Costs," table V-1, *Sales & Marketing Management*, February 25, 1980, p. 88.

Figure 9-3
Portable cassette player/recorder

Courtesy of Technicolor Audio-Visual Systems

benefits the company has paid. The case history usually includes a quotation from a letter written by the policyholder expressing thanks and appreciation for the fair and prompt treatment received. These testimonials may cover many different phases of insurance, and may be used in the appropriate spot to prove, support, or illustrate a particular aspect of the presentation.

Company representatives who sell air travel for major airlines have found case histories to be helpful in dramatizing sales points. American Airlines, for example, reproduces cases which are actual experiences of business firms; they show the variety of problems which can be solved by air travel.

Testimonials are used extensively by progressive sales organizations. There are relatively few products or services for which users are not willing to testify. The effectiveness of a testimonial is determined by the skill with which it is used. In some fields, the testimony of a rival or a competitor of the prospective buyer would end all chance of closing the sale; in other fields, this type of testimony may be a strong factor in closing the sale. Discretion is the key to utilizing testimonials.

Figure 9–4

Low-cost, small, lightweight sound filmstrip projector

Courtesy Dukane Corporation

Product demonstration

One of the most effective methods of appealing to the buyer's senses is through product demonstration or performance tests. Customers or prospects have a natural desire to prove for themselves whatever is claimed for the product. Obviously, the proof is much more satisfying and convincing to anyone who is a party to it.

Product demonstrations should not be considered merely an exhibition of how something works. To be effective, demonstrations should prove that your product has the capabilities claimed, enable the prospect to relate those capabilities to the meeting of needs, permit the customer to become familiar with the product, and result in a sale.

A large corporation entering the highly competitive field of plastic covering materials decided to tell its story dramatically. The corporation featured Kalistron, a plastic coating material which was designed for upholstery and wall-covering uses. The product's unique feature was that color was fused to the *underside* of a clear transparent vinyl sheet and then a protective flocking was applied. This process made it impossible to reach the color under ordinary conditions. Using a proof-test copy for its advertising, the corporation invited its buyers to scrape, scuff, rub, and scratch the sheeting which protected the color. To dramatize the fact that the color had a long life and was difficult to mar, the corporation prepared a printed card with a swatch of Kalistron on it, a nail file, and instructions on how to try to injure the material. Customers enjoyed the test, and the invitation to "prove it yourself" convinced many people who would have been difficult to convince solely through the use of words.

It is suggested that Schwinn bicycles be sold by having the prospect try to twist an ordinary rim and then a Schwinn Tubular Rim; by spinning the wheels to see how easily they roll with special roll-bearings; by feeling the fender braces and noting their strength; and by standing on the chain guard to see how strong it is.

An enterprising NCR sales representative was having trouble convincing the buyer for a national retailer that NCR could service all of the retailer's scatterred outlets. On the next trip to the buyer, the sales representative brought along a bag of darts and a map marked with the chain's hundreds of stores and service locations. The buyer was invited to throw darts at the map, then find the nearest stores. It was pointed out that the nearest NCR location for service was always within 50 miles. This helped win the company a multimillion dollar order.

Paper sales representatives sell quality by having prospects hold two sheets of paper to the light and pointing out that in a good grade of paper the fibers are evenly distributed and that in a poor grade uneven distribution produces a mottled effect. To show opacity, they have the customer place a material with black lines on it under the sheet and check for show-through.

A nationally known company manufactures and sells fire extinguishers. Company salespeople—both home-office representatives and distributor salespersons—are trained thoroughly and must become experts in demonstrating techniques for putting out fires. They have little difficulty in arranging for a demonstration because almost everybody from company presidents to purchasing agents likes to see a good fire. *Showing* how the chemical puts out a fire is convincing. Having the prospect take the extinguisher and put out the fire is even more convincing.

Automobile salespeople sell a product which provides many opportunities for demonstrations. They *show* or *demonstrate* as many sales features as possible. Appearance or styling can be shown; comfort and performance can be experienced; and safety can be seen. Power steering, power brakes, air conditioning, and automatic transmissions can be demonstrated effectively. Buyers can *see* or *feel* for themselves, to prove claims about these features. Performance tests provide an opportunity to take the car over rough and smooth roads, into heavy traffic, around sharp curves, and up and down grades. Permitting the prospect to take over the wheel and choose the route adds strength to the demonstration.

While a product demonstration may be used primarily as a closing tool, it can also be used as a prospecting device and a proof. As part of the selling process, it offers such advantages as adding visual impact ("Seeing is believing"), acting as the ultimate proof, providing for customer involvement, saving time for both the prospect and the sales representative, permitting the introduction of related equipment, and serving as evidence of a sound professional approach.

Product demonstration is one of the best forms of dramatization.

Words

The principal ways in which human beings can communicate, as far as we know, are by actual physical touch (we make ourselves understood with a tap on the shoulder, a pat on the back, a slap on the cheek, and the ritualistic handshake); by visible movements of some portions of our bodies (pointing a finger, winking an eye, nodding the head, shrugging the shoulders, and smiling, grimacing or scowling; and finally, by the use of audible symbols—words![6]

An appropriate choice of words adds strength to any sales presentation. Words alone, however, cannot be as effective as words supported by additional sense appeals. Sometimes intangible services must be sold primarily through the use of words and only secondarily through appeals to other senses. When this situation exists, it is even more necessary to choose words which are descriptive and meaningful. Of course, it is important to remember not to talk *more* but to talk *better*—the *quality* of words, not the *quantity*, brings results.

Words are tools. Word artists have the power to be soft and appealing or to be strong and powerful. They can use short words to give strength and force to the presentation or to provide charm and grace. With practice, words may be used like the notes in a musical scale, and the proper mood may be created.

Choose words that have strength or descriptive quality. Avoid such words as *nice, pretty, good, swell,* and *you know.* The salesperson has many choices of words. For example, instead of the word *stingy,* use *penurious, parsimonious, greedy, penny-wise, tight, pinching, scrimping, tightfisted, hardhanded,* or *miserly.* Words of all colors—words soft as fur, hard as steel, and smooth as glass; words that simmer, crackle, or explode; words that sparkle and

---

[6] See *Communications,* Kaiser Aluminum, for a very interesting analysis of problems in communicating.

shine—are available to anyone who spends an extra few minutes in preparing for the presentation.

Creativity in the use of words is as important to the salesperson as it is to the songwriter or the author. Effective communication is necessary for persuasion, and words represent one very important medium of communication. Good salespeople are never completely satisfied with their word power—they are constantly building better vocabularies.

Every sales representative should be able to draw upon a set of appropriate analogies when the significance of a product or service feature can best be understood through their use. The analogy may be a simile, such as "a savings account is like a spare tire"; or a tongue-pleasing phrase, such as "tired old Ford," "modest plenty of thrift," or "miracle of fruit"; or language that conveys a sensory appeal, such as "smooth as silk," "smooth as glass," or "strong as steel."

The sales representative for a duplicating machine may wish to use such expressions as "clean, crisp copies," "library quiet," "at the push of a button," "one-step processing," "standardize your files," "productivity button," and "standardize all your reports."[7]

Some words that are better to use than others when selling real estate are:

Killer words	Better words
deal	transaction
commission	service fee
contract	agreement
sign here	OK or initial
salesperson	counselor
cheap	inexpensive
sell your property	market your property
bid	offer to buy
down payment	initial investment
monthly payment	monthly investment
listing	employment agreement[8]

THE EFFECTIVE USE OF SELLING AIDS

Many of the following suggestions apply to most of the devices discussed in the foregoing pages. However, for illustrative purposes, the "how" of the dramatization is applied primarily to product demonstrations.

---

[7] *Sales Manual*, Xerox Corporation.

[8] "Killer Words," *Better Homes & Gardens Real Estate Service*, November, 1979.

Be prepared

The first requisite of effective demonstration is *knowledge* of the product. Salespeople must *know* to be able to *show*. They must know what the product will do and will not do, how it performs, and what the performance means to the buyer. Only then are they qualified to demonstrate.

Good salespeople are aware that knowledge alone is not enough. Through intelligent practice, skill must be developed in the demonstration techniques. Therefore, those who wish to present a faultless demonstration practice until they become experts. If the machine demonstrated does not perform as it should because of the demonstrator's awkwardness, the customer is likely to conclude that the machine is not much good or that it is difficult to operate. Either conclusion places hurdles in the path of selling.

The car salesperson who cannot find the appropriate controls or switches immediately; the industrial machine sales representative who is not quite sure how a particular lever or button is to be used; the tractor sales representative who cannot shift gears smoothly—all are placing unnecessary barriers in the way of the sale.

Before attempting to demonstrate, the salesperson should check on two additional points: (1) Has a proper place been prepared for the demonstration? (2) Has the equipment been checked to see that it is in good working order?

A good demonstration utilizes effective props and is staged to produce just the right effect. Therefore, tables, chairs, drapes, lights, and other items may be needed. It is much easier to conduct a demonstration in a showroom than in the prospect's office. A proper setting may make the difference between a good and an ineffective presentation.

Salespeople have learned through bitter experience that there is no substitute for a complete personal check of equipment prior to a demonstration. If sound films are to be shown, good judgment dictates that the following be checked: the projector, the cord, the bulbs, and any other parts which can cause trouble. Incidentally, it may be well to make sure that the prospect has electrical outlets available and a room that can be darkened if necessary.

If machines are to be demonstrated, it is important to remember that all machines need to be maintained and serviced. No attempt should be made to demonstrate a machine until the salesperson has operated it personally to see that it is in good working order. A key that sticks, a lever that is hard to shift, a spring that squeaks, a motor that heats up, or a connection which causes static or a shock can ruin otherwise good dramatic presentations.

Control the demonstration

The most effective demonstrations are those in which the customer is encouraged to participate. This helps get the customer emotionally involved. Many product demonstrations are spectacular when performed by the salesperson alone; but the customer should be allowed to prove personally that the claims for the product are sound. The salesperson who becomes an exhibitionist instead of a teacher when demonstrating is likely to find that customers are somewhat resentful when they realize that their skill is far below that of the demonstrator. Not only is it desirable for customers to participate in the demonstration and to experience the results or benefits claimed, but it is necessary that they participate in the manner and at the time deemed to be most propitious. In order to bring about these conditions, the salesperson must have complete control over the demonstration.

It is apparent that to demonstrate effectively salespeople plan exactly what they are to do and exactly what they expect the prospect to do. Generally, when using such selling aids as pictures, illustrations, and graphic materials, the salesperson should be careful not to expose the aids prematurely. It usually proves disastrous to allow the customer complete freedom to peruse visual sales material during the presentation without any guidance or without attention being focused upon the features that the salesperson is discussing. Too often, customers ignore the salesperson's remarks because they have become absorbed in reading captions or looking at pictures which may be unrelated to the remarks.

Many salespeople keep control of visual material by keeping their hands on it and by seating themselves so that it is easy for them to turn the pages at the appropriate times. As each point in the presentation is illustrated, the salesperson may point to the visual aid. If individual illustration sheets are used, it is good to present them one at a time and to remove each one when its purpose has been served. The important point to remember is that the selling aids and the sales talk complement each other and that to be effective they must be coordinated.

Use sound principles and techniques

Successful salespeople make the demonstration an integral part of the presentation. They relate the demonstration to important product features; they appeal to basic buying motives; they *tell*, *show*, and *sell*; they make the demonstration simple, concise, and easily understood; they get commitments from the prospect after each feature has been demonstrated; and they avoid distracting activities.

Demonstration is part of the presentation. No attempt should be made to set the demonstration apart as a separate activity in the mind of the buyer. The salesperson who asks permission to conduct a demonstration may be inviting the answer, "Some other time; I'm pretty busy today," or "I think I understand what the product will do." Most salespeople find that they have little difficulty in conducting a demonstration if they *assume* that the buyer is interested. Of course, this assumption is based upon the fact that the demonstration has been well prepared and the presentation has paved the way.

If it is not possible to get the prospect's full attention and he or she seems busy or preoccupied, it would probably be wise to cancel or postpone the demonstration.

Appeal to basic buying motives. Any dramatization of the product should emphasize the major *benefits* which accrue to the buyer through its purchase. The task is to dramatize, through a demonstration or otherwise, the sales features which are most likely to appeal to the buyer's basic reasons for wanting the product. Dramatizing an interesting sales feature contributes little to the completion of the sale unless the feature will benefit the particular prospect. Figure 9–5 illustrates a method for organizing material.

Automobile salespeople, for example, seldom have sufficient time, nor can they hold the prospect's interest long enough, to dramatize or demonstrate all the sales features of a new model. They must choose the sales features which make the strongest appeal— the brakes, the beauty, the visibility, the automatic transmission, the pickup, the power steering, or the quietness of the ride. Appeals to fear, economy, comfort, and convenience are common when selling automobiles. After the appropriate sales features have been demonstrated, the prospect may be invited to drive the car. The salesperson then guides the demonstration through suggestion by asking the driver to stop quickly to test the brakes, or to step on the gas to test the pickup, or to turn sharply to note the power steering.

Sales representatives for one mutual fund can choose from a library of six sales films. They carefully select the film which focuses on a prospect's specific financial objective. The objective may be a college education, retirement, the needs of career women, current income, long-term income, or a profit-sharing plan. Interest and attention are not difficult to secure and hold when the customer's objective has been identified.

The features which are to be dramatized must be chosen on the basis of each prospect's individual interests. Good judgment and experience help in making a choice of how many and which features to emphasize, and how to proceed.

Tell, show, and sell. This combination of activities results in effective demonstrations. Sales representatives for a large distributor of typewriter ribbons and carbon papers are instructed to spend

Figure 9–5

Method for organizing sales material on tires

Feature	Benefit	Demonstrate
1. Low-profile styling of the future with a wheel sculptured to complement the tire and vehicle.	1. Enhances the beauty of the car—commands admiration and attention.	1. Place tire next to any tire in your line, or better still, next to tires and wheels now on car. Point out increased beauty.
2. Cantilevered construction with four sidewall belts—two on each side.	2. Improved handling, stability, and ride. Also in unlikely run-flat emergency, you have superior control.	2. Use cross section to point out sidewall belts and cantilevered construction.
3. Fiberglass tread belts.	3. Doubles puncture and impact resistance over conventional tires and reduces tread distortions at all speeds.	3. Use cross section and/or your selling department tire construction chart—show customer location of tread belt plies and explain benefit.
4. Rayon cord body with rugged fiberglass tread belts.	4. Over 100 percent more mileage than conventional tires, a smooth ride, and no flat-spot problems.	4. Show customer your cross section of the tire, and point out how the belted construction prevents tread squirming and results in plus mileage.
5. New-concept tread design and more contour featuring more grooves and more siping.	5. Up to 25 percent quicker stopping than conventional tires on wet, slippery pavements.	5. Use cross section or tire itself—point out increased number of lateral grooves and sipes.

only a few moments on the sales talk. Then they are to get a ribbon or a piece of carbon paper into one of the prospect's typewriters or tabulation machines as fast as possible to *show* what the product can do. They keep selling arguments concise and base the strongest appeal upon demonstration—on the customer's own equipment.

A sample demonstration, suggested for use by Frigidaire salespeople, requires the use of a grease crayon, a bottle of iodine, a match, and a soft cloth or cleansing tissue. The objective is to use dramatization to prove the advantages of porcelain on the refrigerator, range, washer, and other products. The demonstration may occur like this:

Salesperson: You know, Mrs. Kerns, if there was ever a product that should be well protected it's a washer—for it is constantly exposed to the rusting and corrosive action of water, soaps, and bleaches. But your

Frigidaire washer always stays bright because it's protected with Frigidaire Lifetime Porcelain, inside and out.

I can smear it with this greasy crayon . . . *(it is smeared).* I can douse it with iodine, one of the most penetrating stains known . . . *(it is doused).*

I can even lay a lighted cigarette on it, or burn it with a match *(a lighted match is put on the washer top).* And even after all this . . .

It will shine as bright as ever, simply by wiping with a damp cloth. I'm sure that's the kind of finish you want on your new washer, isn't it, Mrs. Kerns?[9]

Figure 9–6 shows a portion of a confidential "Money Accumulation Plan" used to help a prospect identify insurance needs. Accompanying the figure shown is a graphic clearly pointing out the amount of money the prospect will earn by age 65 along with figures showing that of

100 men age 25

40 years later at age 65:
  34 are dead
  49 have failed financially
  17 are financially independent

The 17 successes:
  had well-defined goals
  made specific plans to reach their goals
  saved money on a regular basis

A savings margin per month is supplied by the prospect, and then an insurance program is prepared for that amount of premium.

The prospect's needs are fulfilled by appropriate insurance income from assets and Social Security income. The needs and resources are all *visually* portrayed. Separate charts are completed which show in detail the Social Security benefits and returns to be received by the prospect and members of the family; a monthly budget estimator used to help determine the monthly expenses; and a detailed anlaysis of family assets. Specific insurance recommendations are submitted after this fact-finding interview is analyzed.

When selling is done by means of samples and the customer is given a choice of fabrics or colors, it is best to show one sample (or only a few) at a time. Too many samples and too many demonstrations tend to confuse rather than help the buyer.

Make demonstration simple, concise, and easily understood. Long, complicated demonstrations add to the possibility that the buyer will miss the point and that salespeople will do a poor job.

---

[9] *The Prospect Meets the Product* (Detroit: Frigidaire Division, General Motors Corp.), pp. 30–31.

Figure 9–6
A visual approach to determining needs

A Money Accumulation Plan

Name _____ Age _____

Plan _____ For $ _____

1. Your financial goals

Goal

	$	

Money to fall back on in emergencies   Money to start a business   Money for children's education
Financial independence at retirement   Money for a vacation home   Money to buy a home

2. A plan
to help you reach your goals

Your increasing cash values*   After ____ years $ _____

                                                       ____ years   _____

                                                       ____ years   _____

                                                       At 65   _____

                                                Less payments to 65 $ _____
                                                DIFFERENCE $ _____

*Including cash value of dividend additions. The dividend results used in the above figures are merely illustrations of what would be achieved if the latest dividend scale were continued. They must not be considered a guarantee, promise or estimate as to the future. Cumulative figures shown do not allow for any additional interest that might otherwise have been earned.

3. A regular accumulation program

Monthly payments of $ _____ make this plan possible.

OPTIONAL FEATURES: □ **Self-completing feature:** With Disability Waiver your premiums are paid for you (after a 4-month waiting period) if you have an accident or illness that makes you unable to work.
□ **Guaranteed insurability feature:** With Additional Purchase Protection, even if you become uninsurable you may buy additional insurance. This privilege could be exercised at age 25, 28, 31, 34, 37 or 40, or when you are married or have a child.
□ **Inflation-adjustment feature:** The Dividend Addition Plan provides steadily increasing death benefits and cash values to counteract or stay ahead of the effects of inflation. The 5th Dividend Option can be used towards providing increased death benefits.

Financial Service

Courtesy of the Mutual Benefit Life Insurance Company

Simple demonstrations should illustrate some property of the product or enable the prospect to draw a pertinent conclusion about the product. Good demonstrations attract attention to sales features and benefits.

In order to demonstrate the meaning of "silver plate" a salesperson may say, "If I were to take this pencil and dip it into some silver, the pencil would come out coated, wouldn't it? You see, the silver covers this pencil much as silver covers the base metal in a silver-plated spoon." This is a simple, easily understood explanation. It could be used when comparing the merits of sterling and plated ware.

Retail tire salespeople for one large corporation are instructed to use a small screwdriver, a piece of chalk, and a smooth tire section to sell tire safety. To emphasize the danger of driving on smooth tires, they rub the smooth tire section against a table, a smooth surface, or the palm of the hand. Attention is drawn to the fact that no traction is left and that this could cause the car to slide, especially on wet pavement. The screwdriver is used to remove a piece of glass, a rock, or some other object from the customer's tire, and the spot is circled with chalk. The salespeople then explain that the flexing of the tire while driving could enlarge the cut or bruised area and a blowout could result. These demonstrations are designed to show the customer why tires should be replaced. When new tires are shown, the demonstration involves having the customer rub a disc of ordinary rubber and disc of superrubber on a piece of sandpaper to show the difference in chafing and therefore the extra mileage available from the better tire.[10]

Get a commitment.   After *each* product feature has been demonstrated or explained, a commitment should be secured from the prospect. The salesperson may say, "Do you see how the machine works? Isn't that easy to operate?" The objective is to find out how well the demonstration is accepted. If prospects agree that the demonstration has proved several sales features, they may be ready to buy.

If the demonstration has been poorly conducted, or if it hasn't been a natural part of the presentation, the buyer may still be unconvinced. It then becomes necessary to find out exactly why there is some misunderstanding. It is unwise to leave a demonstration until the prospect fully understands.

Avoid distracting activities.   The physical appearance of salespeople is important when demonstrating a product. Customers evaluate the product and the salesperson by what the salesperson does as well as by what is said. The hands, facial expressions,

---

[10] Courtesy of the Firestone Tire & Rubber Co., Akron, Ohio.

posture, and mannerisms, should not be sources of distraction that will weaken an otherwise effective demonstration.

Salespeople should have clean, neat hands and should keep them out of pockets; they should handle the product carefully; and they should use their hands skillfully to enhance the success of the presentation. Facial expressions can help or hinder the demonstration. Interest and enthusiasm can be shown by facial expressions. Good salespeople look the prospect in the eye while demonstrating and do not allow their gaze to wander about the room. A genuine smile should replace any tendency to frown or to wear a constant grin. Posture is important. Alert salespeople do not slump in a chair; nor do they lean on tables, desks, or chairs. Some personal mannerisms are particularly annoying to a buyer. Rattling coins, swinging a key chain, tapping a foot, smoking, or nudging a prospect can detract materially from the effectiveness of a demonstration.

QUESTIONS AND PROBLEMS

1. Effective, easily prepared visual aids are the A-frame, which is placed on the prospect's desk, and the easel, which is the same as the A-frame but is usually placed on a three-legged stand for better visibility to a larger group. Under what circumstances would you select different visual aids? When preparing and using an A-frame or easel chart pad, what can be done to make the tool most effective?

2. J. H. Patterson, of National Cash Register fame, trained sales representatives to "talk with their pencils." What are the advantages of using this type of sales aid?

3. It has been said that "common words do not have meanings—only people do. And sometimes they don't either." Can you give an example illustrating this observation? What are the implications for a sales representative?

4. A prominent psychologist once made this observation on what salespeople should do with a product: "Weigh it; smell it; taste it; pound it; take it to pieces; put it together; listen to it; squeeze it; shake it; roll it; spread it; pour it; bite it; file it; whittle it; burn it; freeze it; soak it; saw it; cook it; kick it; stop it." What are the implications of this statement?

5. Assume that you plan a flight demonstration to prove some of the claims you have made for a new-model airplane. Would the demonstration be any different for each of these three individuals: a nervous person, an economy-minded person, and a performance-minded person? Explain.

6. Traditions and associations unite to establish a "language of color." How important are different colors as they relate to products or to the dress of a sales representative? Illustrate the "language" that different colors communicate to you.

7. Farmers, understandably, like to be *shown* when it comes to making substantial outlays for farm machines. It is obvious, however, that the most enterprising sales representative cannot visit farmer prospects and bring along a selection of hay conditioners, harrows, or other machines. The conventional sales representative relies on word power or on persuading farmers to visit the showroom. Can you think of a better way of making a presentation to the prospect in the home or even in the field where the prospect may be working?

8. Sales aids appealing to the customer's sense of sight are becoming more common. Illustrate the value of eye appeals when contrasted with ear appeals.

9. How would you demonstrate the following?

   a. A water cooler to the owner of a large business who plans to install one for the employees' use. (Assume that the owner is in the store and a model is available.)

   b. The strength of the tray release in a refrigerator. (Assume that the customer is a woman in the store and that she asks if the tray release will work when it is frozen solidly to the shelf.)

   c. The evenness with which the broiler in a range distributes its heat. (Assume that a range is available and is hooked up to operate.)

   d. The ability of an automatic dryer to get clothes dry. (Assume that a machine is hooked up and available and that the customer is a woman.)

   e. The ability of the tube unit (the coil that is electrically heated for cooking purposes) to clean itself if sticky foods boil over. (Assume that the range is connected and available for demonstration.)

   f. The ease of operation of a refrigerator door with ball-bearing hinges. (Assume that you have a model available.)

   g. The lack of heavy vibration of the automatic washer. (Assume that the washer is connected and available for demonstration.)

10. You are a sales representative for a nationally known maker of ball-point pens. You have an appointment with the office manager of a large firm in the food-processing industry. This is your first call.

    After a short wait you are ushered into her office. She appears businesslike and seems pressed for time. You say good morning and introduce yourself.

    Which of the following statements would you select to begin your interview? Why?

    a. I would like to demonstrate to you a Whizzbang product that we are really excited about.

    b. I would like to demonstrate to you a Whizzbang product that offers better quality and color.

    c. I'd like to explore with you how we can reduce the cost of writing instruments. What brand of pens do you currently buy?

PROJECTS

1. Use a book of synonyms and antonyms and see how many words you can identify which are stronger or more descriptive than each of the following: *cheap, pretty, bargain, explain, wonderful, good, neat, swell,* and *nice.* Set up a chart illustrating your findings.

2. Shop several stores for a bicycle, or an air bed, or a smoke alarm for the home or business, or a van, or some other product that is capable of being demonstrated. Write up a report on the demonstration techniques which you encountered. Evaluate the techniques used, and suggest ways which you believe would improve the demonstrations.

CASE PROBLEMS

Case 9–1

Sundown Realty, Inc.

Jimmy Carter owned a real estate office, and he had hired part-time sales agents to sell on a commission basis on weekends. In addition to acting as a broker, Jimmy had qualified for a contractor's license and had built a few homes for speculation purposes. He later invited an insurance agent to join the firm. They soon decided that it would be necessary to hire a full-time sales representative for selling real estate.

An advertisement was placed in the local newspaper, and it was otherwise made known that Sundown Realty was interested in hiring a young licensed real estate agent. In about three months they found the person they were looking for.

The new salesperson was asked to suggest techniques which would be effective in increasing real estate sales volume through a better use of graphics. Jimmy had made no attempt to develop much in the way of selling aids.

Questions

1. What selling aids do you believe the new salesperson should recommend to help dramatize the sale of real estate? Identify what each selling aid is expected to accomplish.

2. How could a sales kit or sales portfolio be used profitably by this real estate salesperson? What records, papers, or materials should be included in the sales kit or portfolio of real estate salespeople so that they can sell intelligently? Assume that the salespeople would utilize the sales kit while in the field as well as at their desks.

Case 9-2

The Smoke Alarm Corporation

A local distributor has offered you the opportunity to sell an early warning home fire safety device called SmokeAlert. A generous commission is provided.

SmokeAlert is easy to install and is run by three batteries. It is mounted on the ceiling. It may be used in mobile homes, apartments, summer homes, camper trailers—wherever fire may strike. Depending upon the size and layout of the unit protected, it may be desirable to have more than one SmokeAlert for adequate protection.

The device operates on the principle of ionization—slight changes in the air caused by fire or even invisible smoke enter SmokeAlert, and the ionization sensor sounds the alarm. The device is "smart" too—it can be set so that heavy cigarette smoke at a party won't cause an alarm, but if a fire starts, SmokeAlert takes over.

Fatal fires in a typical home start in the following areas: living room, den, or family room, 33.8 percent; kitchen, 16.2 percent; basement, 25.7 percent; bedrooms, 12.1 percent; garage, 1.4 percent; and all other, 10.8 percent.

Before you decide to accept this selling opportunity you decide to investigate and learn how the product might be sold and to whom.

Questions

1. What facts can you assemble about fires in homes—what causes them, their frequency, casualties, and any other pertinent facts?
2. Where might you secure prospects?
3. Prepare some statements which you believe will dramatize the need for a SmokeAlert.
4. How can the sales interview be dramatized?

Case 9-3

Sterling Sales Co.

Dolly Deere has planned a sales interview for selling sterling silver by developing a sales talk built around visual illustrations in an easel portfolio. She has placed the easel in front of the prospect, and she seats herself on the right side. She begins her presentation and gets to the second page of the portfolio, and the prospect picks up the portfolio and starts thumbing through it, looking at pictures.

The prospect says, "Go ahead with your presentation. I can hear you while I glance through your portfolio."

What should Dolly do? Explain the reasons for the action you recommend.

SELECTED REFERENCES

"AV Makes the Difference." *Sales & Marketing Management*, February 4, 1980, special section, pp. 49-64.

Battista, O. A. "Color Your World." *Elks Magazine*, February 1979, pp. 4-6.

Bice, D. "Live Presentations Drive Home Point." *Advertising Age*, April 23, 1979, sec. 2: 15-50.

"Bradley Sells Architects, Designers via Film Program. *Industrial Marketing*, September 1978, pp. 48-49.

"Construction Product Demonstrations Go Door-to-Door in Traveling Van." *Telephony*, March 19, 1979, p. 80 ff.

Daiker, Donald. "The Super Sellers." *Audio-Visual Communications*, May 1979, pp. 4-5.

Edlund, Sidney. "Show plus Tell Equals Dotted Line." *Marketing Times*, July–August 1974, pp. 7-9.

"How to Sell Abrasive Products." *Industrial Distribution*, May 1979, pp. 139-41.

"How to Sell Hand Tools." *Industrial Distribution*, September 1978, pp. 73-74.

"Kit Helps Salesmen Overcome Common Ad Objections." *Editor & Publisher*, January 27, 1979, p. 20.

McCall, Chester H. *How to Use the Magic Power of Showmanship.* Englewood Cliffs, N.J.: Executive Reports, 1976.

Scott, Louis. "Is Your Literature a Real Sales Tool—or Just Another Leave-behind?" *Industrial Marketing*, October 1977, pp. 106-8.

"Sound-and-Slide Sales Programs Key Part of Home Manufacturer/Dealer Teamwork." *Professional Builder & Apartment Business*, January 1979, pp. 170 ff.

"Special Report: Choosing the Right Boosters HBA Firms Spend Close to $3 Million." *Product Marketing*, June 1979, pp. 58-61.

Wood, Dean M. "'Back to Basics' Has Garlock O.E.M. Salesmen Flipping over Flip Chart." *Industrial Marketing*, January 1974, pp. 42-45.

Chapter 10

OVERCOMING OBJECTIONS

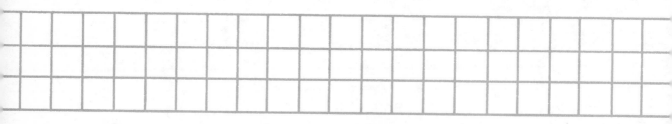

Handling objections and closing the sale constitute the very heart of selling. Many sales executives suggest that selling has not really begun until the prospect voices objections. They believe that many potentially good salespeople prove to be effective only until the buyers object—then they lose heart and consider their efforts to be fruitless.

All salespeople encounter objections during some phase of the selling process. All buyers at some time voice an objection to something that is said or done. In fact, some customers may raise only irrational or nebulous objections that have nothing to do with the product, the company, or the seller. Skill in handling objections is just as necessary as skill in making appointments, in conducting interviews, in demonstrating, or in closing sales. When new sales-people become aware that objections voiced by buyers constitute a *normal* and a *natural* part of the sales process, they treat them as opportunities to sell.

This chapter is designed to answer the following questions: Why do buyers object? What objections can be expected? When do buyers object? What preparation is necessary to answer objections success-fully? And, what are some good methods and techniques to use when answering objections? In addition, illustrations are included of methods and techniques used by major companies when answering objections. A suggested procedure to follow is also outlined.

WHY PEOPLE OBJECT

Negative psychological factors

Every time a prospect expresses an objection he or she is express-ing feelings of insecurity that are common to all of us. As has been pointed out earlier in this text, we all fear punishment, pain, loss, and disapproval, and we try to avoid them. One way to avoid them is by not making a decision to buy—we cannot then lose face or suffer the disapproval of others by making a wrong buying decision.[1] The sales representative's task is to help the prospect overcome these fears.

Simply because they are human beings, most buyers harbor some degree of resistance. Attitudes and emotions play a big role in caus-ing buyers to act the way they do.

People are instinctively afraid of strangers. Perhaps this fear is a carry-over from early tribal fears, from a time when strangers meant danger. Prejudices and biases may be formed by buyers. They may, for example, display an irrational dislike to tall people, short people, conservative people, loud talkers, or other large categories of people. Ego is the basis for the actions of many buyers. The sales-people who do not recognize the need of buyers to express their ego can expect many and varied objections which may seem difficult to understand.

Fear of making a decision because it may be the wrong decision and fear of hurting friends or present sources of supply may be addi-tional negative psychological factors.

---

[1] "Handling Objections, *The PaperMate Selling Process*, (The Gillette Company, Paper Mate Division), p. VI–37.

To get rid of a representative

Some prospects voice numerous objections in an attempt to simply dismiss the salesperson. The prospect may not have sufficient time to devote to the interview, may not be interested in the product or service offered for sale, may not be in the mood to listen, or because of some unhappy experiences may have decided not to face further unpleasant interviews.

These objections may occur when the salesperson is making a cold-canvass or is attempting to make an appointment. The salesperson who is overaggressive, rude, or impolite, or who becomes a pest, can expect the prospect to use numerous devices to keep a presentation from being made.

No money

Persons who have no money to buy may have been classified as "suspects." As indicated in Chapter 7, Prospecting and Getting the Right Start, the ability to pay is an important factor when qualifying a suspect. An incomplete or poor job of qualifying may cause this objection to arise.

When suspects declare that they have insufficient funds, they may be stating a valid objection. If that is so, time should not be wasted and new prospects should be contacted.

Do not need product or service

This objection also may be valid. Expensive machinery may be designed for handling large volumes of work; if the manufacturer operates on a small scale, there may be no need for the product. Or perhaps the salesperson is selling a collection service; if the retail dealer sells for cash, a collection service is not required.

Legitimate objections will arise when prospective buyers have not been qualified on all the essential characteristics of a prospect.

No recognition of need

Salespeople may encounter objections such as "My business is different" or "I have no use for your service." If they have qualified the buyer accurately, these objections are evidence that the buyer is not convinced that a need exists. Buyers may be unaware of the benefits of using the product or service. They may have an "unrecognized need."

It is logical to expect a buyer to object if the salesperson cannot establish a need in the buyer's mind. In pioneer selling, for example, the task of selling the benefits of a new and different product, service, or idea makes the salesperson's task a more difficult one.

Need more information

Some buyers offer objections in an attempt to secure more information. They may not fully understand the presentation, or they may want to receive assurance on points about which they are doubtful.

Buyers who want more information are helping to sell themselves by raising valid objections. They may decide that they want the product or service, but they may wish to fortify themselves with logical reasons which can be used to justify the purchase to others.

There may be a conflict in the buyer's mind. A struggle may be taking place between what emotions dictate and what reason dictates. The buyer may be trying to decide between two competitive products or attempting to choose between buying and not buying. Whatever the struggle, buyers who object in order to get more information are usually interested and there is always a good possibility that they will buy.

Habit or custom

Buyers' objections are not limited to legitimate objections which cannot be overcome. Human beings are creatures of habit. Once they have developed a routine, or once a custom has been established, they are inclined to resist change. Fear or ignorance may be the basis for not wanting to try anything new or different. Many people resist anything new just because it is new and because they have no related experience to guide them in buying. Others are prejudiced; they buy a certain make or kind of product because they have always bought it.

The natural tendency to resist buying a new product or changing from a satisfactory brand to a new one is the basis for numerous objections.

Value does not exceed cost

Most buyers must sacrifice in order to buy. The money spent for the product offered is not available for other expenditures. The choice may be between the down payment on a new car and a vacation trip, or it may be between expanding the plant and distributing a dividend.

Usually, buyers object until they can be sure that the sacrifice they are making is more than offset by the value of the product or services they acquire. The question of "value received" is often the basis for customers' objections.

COMMON OBJECTIONS

Common reasons for not buying may be classified as price objections, product objections, service objections, company objections, time objections, personal objections, and miscellaneous objections.

Price

Regardless of the price asked for a product, somebody will object that the price is too high, "out of line," or higher than that offered by a competitor. Other common price objections are "I can't afford it," "I can't afford to spend that much right now," "I was looking for a cheaper model," "I don't care to invest that much—I'll use it only a short while," "I can beat your price on these items," "We can't make a reasonable profit if we have to pay that much for the merchandise," "We always get a special discount," and "I'm going to wait for prices to come down."

Price objections probably occur more frequently than any other kind of objection and may well be just masks that hide the buyer's real reason for reluctance to buy.

Product

Some common product objections are "The quality is too poor," "I don't like the design," "It seems poorly constructed," "It is the wrong size," "I was looking for a lighter shade," "I don't think it will wear well," "I don't like the material," and "We prefer printed circuits."

Service

Buyers may be critical of the company's method of making adjustments, its delivery policy, its advisory or consulting staff, its maintenance contract, or the speed with which it makes service calls.

The salesperson who sells industrial machinery or office machines to regular customers may encounter such objections as "I can't get my machines repaired," "It takes too long to get a service person on the job," "Your 'experts' don't seem to know much about our problems," "We don't get maintenance help frequently enough," "Our last purchase was unsatisfactory, and we weren't satisfied with the adjustment," "It took a month for us to get our last order," and "Shutdown time is killing us."

Company

Industrial buyers and retail store buyers are vitally interested in the sales representative's company. It is important that they be satisfied with the company's financial standing, personnel, business policies, and products.

Some buyers or prospective buyers may ask these questions: "Isn't your company a new one in the field?" "Is it true that your company lost money last year?" "How do I know you'll be in business next year?" "Your company isn't very well known, is it?" "Who does your designing?" "Can your company give us the credit we have been receiving from other companies?" These questions are evidence that the sales representative has a selling job to do.

Acting now

Objections to making a decision *now* are commonly encountered. In fact, many buyers believe that the postponement of any action is an effective way of saying no.

Salespeople must expect to hear objections like the following many times: "I haven't made up my mind," "I want to think it over," "I'd like to talk it over with my partner," "See me on your next trip," "I'm not ready to buy," "I don't want to commit myself," "I think I'll wait a while," "I want to look around," "I'm waiting till my inventory gets down," "I want to turn in the old unit at the end of the season," and "Just leave me your literature—I'll study it and then let you know what we decide."

These objections are, of course, evidence that the prospect has not been thoroughly sold. The real reason for postponing action may be price, product, or one of a number of other reasons.

Salespeople

Some salespeople's personalities clash with those of their prospects. Everything should be done to adjust manners to please the prospect. However, there are times when it appears impossible to do business with some people. Some prospects object to a presentation or an appointment because they dislike the salesperson.

If these prospects are quite candid, they may say: "I don't like to do business with you," or "You're a pest—I don't have any time for you," or "You and I will never be able to do business." More commonly, the prospect shields the real reason and says? "We don't need any," or "Sorry, we're stocked up," or "I haven't time today to discuss your proposition."

Miscellaneous _____

Objections to price, product, service, company, acting now, and the salesperson's personality are usually the most serious kinds to be raised. However, the objections which may be encountered cannot always be classified into these categories. Some additional objections which may be encountered include the following:

"I always buy from friends."

"My partner must be consulted."

"I'm not interested."

"I'm satisfied with the company with which we now deal."

"I see no reason for taking on another line."

"We have a reciprocity agreement with your competitor."

"We are all stocked up."

"We have no room for your line."

"There is no demand for your product."

"You'll have to see Mr. X."

"My brother-in-law is in the business."

Many of these objections can be handled effectively if the salesperson is prepared to answer them.

WHEN DO BUYERS OBJECT? _____

If the sales process were to be broken down into stages or parts, the salesperson could expect objections to occur at three different stages.

Approach _____

The prospect may object to setting an appointment time or date to allow the salesperson to get started. This is especially true in selling services and ideas. Objections at this stage are not too serious if the prospect has been qualified properly. When using the cold-canvass, the salesperson must expect objections at this stage and be prepared to meet them.

Presentation _____

Objections are usually raised to some points made in the presentation. Such objections may be evidence of the prospect's interest and may actually be desirable. It is easier to sell when the prospects object, because the salespeople know where they stand and they are sure that they have the prospect's attention and active interest. Some buyers permit the salesperson to deliver the entire sales talk without evidencing a reaction of any kind. In these circumstances it may be difficult to judge the effectiveness of the presentation.

Close

Objections may be offered when the close is attempted. Skill in handling objections is more important at this stage than at any other. If salespeople can answer objections satisfactorily in the first two stages but cannot overcome objections in the close, they make no sales. Knowing when objections are likely to occur and what these objections mean enables the salesperson to prepare answers in advance so they will be ready for use when needed.

If too many objections occur, it is likely that significant selling points are being omitted in the presentation.

PREPARATION REQUIRED TO ANSWER OBJECTIONS

In order to overcome objections, some preliminary work can be done which will help guarantee success. There are techniques which have proved successful in handling almost any kind of objection.

Develop a positive attitude

To handle objections effectively, there is no substitute for having the proper attitude. Proper attitude will be evidenced by answering sincerely, by refraining from arguing or contradicting, and by welcoming—even inviting—objections. And by listening!

It is useless to put on a veneer of sincerity. Buyers can see through the veneer with amazing ease. If the buyer once gets the idea that the salesperson is talking for effect, it is almost impossible for the salesperson to regain the buyer's confidence and respect. Sincerity is evidenced as much by the tone of voice and the facial expressions as by the actual words spoken.

A successful advertising agency owner states: "I have always tried to sit on the same side of the table as my clients, to see problems through their eyes." The average buyer wants valid objections to be treated seriously. Buyers want their ideas to be respected, not belittled. They are looking for sympathetic understanding of their problems. Real objections are logical to the prospect, regardless of how irrational they may appear to the salesperson.

The salesperson must have the attitude of a helper, a counselor—and an adviser. To do this it is necessary to treat the prospect as a friend, not a foe. Answering objections should not be an activity which calls for a battle of wits. The objective is not to win an argument. Arguments create much heat and friction, and even when salespeople win an argument they will probably lose the sale and the customer. A lost sale or customer is too big a price to pay for winning an argument.

There is always the temptation to prove that the prospect is wrong, to say "I told you so" or "I'm right and you're wrong." This kind of attitude invites a debate. The salesperson is encouraging, perhaps even forcing, the prospect to defend a position regardless of the merits of the stand taken. Prestige is involved when the prospect finds a position bluntly challenged. Most people attempt to defend their own opinions in these circumstances because they do not want to lose prestige. The sales presentation may then degenerate into a personal duel. The salesperson cannot possibly win. Arguing with a prospect, contradicting a prospect, or showing belligerence toward a prospect is evidence of a negative and unwise attitude.

Real objections are sales opportunities. Ford Motor Company puts it this way, "Objections are signposts guiding you to what's really on the customer's mind.[2] To capitalize on these opportunities, salespeople must show that they welcome any and all objections. They sincerely and convincingly make the prospect feel that they are glad the objection has been raised. This attitude may be shown by remarks such as the following: "I see just what you mean. I'd probably feel the same way . . ." "I'm glad you mentioned that, Mr. Atkinson . . ." "That certainly is a wise comment, Ms. Smith, and I can see your problem . . ." "If I were purchasing this product, I'd want an answer to that same question . . ." "Tell me about it . . ."

The sales representative must convince the buyer that the real objection raised is normal, logical, sensible, important, and deserving of a valid answer.

Truthfulness in dealing with prospects and customers is an absolute necessity for dignity, confidence, and continued relations. Alfred C. Fuller, the original Fuller brushman, says, "It is the truth that makes men free, not only in their business lives but in their business concepts."[3]

Anticipate objections

Salespeople must know that, at some time or other, objections will be made to almost everything concerning their product, their company, or themselves. It is only common sense to prepare answers to

---

[2] *Retail Selling Course* (Dearborn, Mich.: Ford Motor Co.), syllabus.
[3] Alfred C. Fuller, *A Foot in the Door* (New York: McGraw-Hill, 1960), p. 175.

the objections which are certain to be raised. Few salespeople can answer objections effectively on the spur of the moment.

Many companies prepare lists of the objections which are commonly encountered. Effective answers are then prepared, and the salesperson is expected to know the objections and their answers before making sales calls.[4]

Successful sales representatives may keep a loose-leaf notebook and record new objections as they are encountered along with any new ideas for handling them. Experience teaches salespeople which strategies work best with particular types of customers.

When salespeople know that an objection is going to be raised and that they have good answers ready, they do not worry about it. However, objections which are not anticipated or for which no answers are ready can easily cause embarrassment and lost sales.

Forestall objections

Good salespeople, after a period of experience and training, know that certain features of their products or services are vulnerable or are likely to be misunderstood. They may have limited patterns; may have a price which seems to be high; may not be able to grant cash discounts; may have no service representatives in the immediate area; or may represent a new company in the field.

Some salespeople do such a good job of selling those features that appear at first glance to be obstacles to the sale that buyers change their minds without ever having to go on record as objecting to the feature and then having to change their minds. Others approach the problem by saying, "I guess you think this product is expensive, don't you? Well, let me show you how little it will really cost you to get the best." Buyers are more willing to change their thinking if they have not already stated a position which they feel they must defend.

While not all objections can be forestalled, the major ones can easily be spotted and disposed of during a good sales presentation. Buyers are not likely to raise an objection which has been stated and answered.

Evaluate objections

Objections may be classified as *real objections* and *excuses*. There are probably only two real objections to buying—people have

---

[4] See Daniel K. Weadock, "Your Troups Can Keep Control—and Close the Sale—by Anticipating Objections," *Sales & Marketing Management*, March 17, 1980, pp. 102-6.

no immediate need for the product or no money with which to buy it. Even these objections may sometimes be handled effectively. The future may bring about a need, and credit may be used to overcome the lack of money.

Salespeople are likely to encounter more excuses than real objections if they do a good job of qualifying prospects. It is necessary to distinguish between the two because the method of handling them may differ.

An excuse for not buying is seldom stated as "I don't have any reason—I just don't want to buy." It is more common for the buyer or prospect to state a reason for not buying which may appear at first to be a real objection. "I don't have the money" may actually be an excuse. "I can't use your product" may be an excuse. The tone of voice or the nature of the reason may be evidence that the prospect is not offering a sincere objection.

There is no exact formula to use in separating excuses from real objections. The circumstances surrounding the voicing of a reason for not buying will usually be a clue to the answer. In a cold-canvass the prospect may say, "I'm sorry, I don't have any money," and the salesperson may conclude that the prospect doesn't want to hear the presentation. However, if a complete presentation has been made, and data on the prospect have been gathered through observation and questioning, the same reason may be a valid one. Salespeople must rely on observation, questioning, their knowledge of why people buy, and their experience to determine the validity of the reason offered for not buying.

Some buyers agree to everything said or make no comment at all. In these circumstances, if the buyer refuses to buy, the salesperson must uncover the reason for not buying. When objections are stated, the salesperson is in a position to answer them; but when they are not stated, it becomes more difficult to remove the concealed causes for not buying.

The concealed objections may be brought into the open by observing the reaction of the prospect to the sales presentation. Buyers' interest may lag after they have heard the price, or their attention may lessen after they have heard the explanation of some product feature. The experienced salesperson observes these changes in the prospect's attitude, and should stop and review the explanation or go through the demonstration again for reemphasis and clarity.

By the manner in which they handle the product, prospects may give evidence that they are dissatisfied.[5] They may examine it care-

---

[5] J. A. C. Brown, *Techniques of Persuasion* (Baltimore: Penguin Books, 1963), pp. 58-81.

fully and then put it aside. This action may imply, "It doesn't look too strong to me," or "We couldn't sell anything constructed like this," or "It's the wrong style or color."

It may be appropriate to ask questions when these implications exist. Salespeople may say, "Did you notice the leather lining in that shoe?" Retail store buyers may state an objection at this point, or may remark that they did notice the lining. If buyers do not state an objection and there is reason to believe that they are not satisfied, salespeople may ask, "What do you think of the lining of that shoe?" If the answer is, "It looks all right to me," the tone of voice will probably be an indication as to how well satisfied they are. More than likely, if the lining is the source of the real objection, buyers will state their objection. Salespeople should learn to ask information-seeking questions and then stop and listen for both obvious and subtle clues.

Open-ended questions that encourage the prospect to *talk* more may include the following: "Would you like to tell me about it?" "Why is that?" "Can we talk more about that?" "Can we explore that further?"

It is important to remember that sales representatives never sell anybody anything but that they do *help* a lot of people to *buy*. Help is provided by asking the right kinds of questions—questions that customers and prospects have to ask themselves anyway, and answer, before they are going to buy.

Good salespeople find it desirable to get a reaction from buyers by asking if they understand certain phases of the proposition. As an answer is obtained on each phase, they try to secure agreement on that phase. Thereby they accumulate a series of agreements that lead toward a successful close. For example, the sales representative who is attempting to sell the prospect on leasing some industrial equipment asks: "Do you understand the terms of the lease? Let's take it again point by point. First, we agree to service the equipment within 24 hours after we receive your call. However, in most cases we can handle emergency calls in an hour or two. Are there any questions about this point? Will this provision satisfy your requirements? Second, we agree to replace parts without labor cost to you. That's a fair agreement, is it not?" If salespeople can get agreement on each point, they eliminate objections which have not been stated. If they fail to secure agreement, the prospect objects, and then they can answer that objection before going on.

If salespeople try to uncover the real objection and fail, they may admit failure and say to the prospect, "Evidently I have overlooked some aspect in acquainting you with the merits of our products. You still seem to have some doubt in your mind. Do you have a specific question? I believe that I can answer it for you." This procedure may enable salespeople to get the prospect to state the real objection. Normally this procedure should be used only as a last resort.

When making repeat calls, it may be inadvisable to try to uncover the real objection during the initial interview. Succeeding calls may afford the opportunity to discover the true reason why the prospect is reluctant to buy. Persistence is desirable only as long as it is graciously accepted by the prospect.

Time the answer

There are two schools of thought on when to answer the prospect's excuse. Some people think it best to ignore a reason for not buying which is classified as an excuse. That is, such a reason should be ignored unless it is mentioned repeatedly by the prospect. Others believe that any reason for not buying should be answered immediately.

The United States Rubber Company makes this recommendation to its distributor sales representatives who encounter the objection "Your tire is more expensive than other tires":

> From the moment that they [the customers] voice that objection, they want an answer. If you pass over the objection and go on to another portion of your sales presentation, you can be reasonably certain that you have left your customers behind, because they are still thinking of that objection.[6]

Judgment must be exercised in determining whether to ignore an excuse or to answer it immediately. It seems desirable always to *recognize* an excuse, whether or not the answer is delayed. Otherwise, the impression may be given that high pressure is being applied.

If the reason stated is classified as a real objection, it must be answered immediately. The successful closing of a sale is usually the result of a series of approvals by the customer. If a real objection is unanswered, there is no accumulation of positive responses, and consequently a close is difficult.

Under certain circumstances it is advisable to postpone the answer to a valid objection. This may be desirable when price objections occur early in the interview. The technique to be followed is

---

[6] "The Customer Objects," Distributor Training Conference no. 24 (Detroit: United States Rubber Co.), p. 7.

suggested later in this chapter. It is just as important to know when to answer as it is to know what to say.

Build a skill

A large part of the job of selling is built upon skill in the use of techniques and methods. This is true particularly in demonstrating, delivering the sales presentation, answering objections, and closing the sale. Skill can be developed only through much hard work and intelligent practice. The baseball player, the golfer, and the swimmer know that knowledge of what to do is not enough. Practice perfects the skill to the point where it is effective, and it then becomes a natural part of the sale representative's equipment.

Some salespeople develop a skill in answering objections by keeping a list of all the objections they encounter. Each objection is written on one side of a three- by five-inch card, with the answer on the reverse side. They practice the answers until they can state them with ease and conviction. Other salespeople rehearse to develop the right tone, the right voice inflection, and the right emphasis for the answer to objections. The good salesperson invests whatever time and effort are necessary to make answers valid and effective.

EFFECTIVE METHODS AND TECHNIQUES
FOR HANDLING OBJECTIONS

Before discussing specific methods and techniques for overcoming objections, it is necessary to say again that there is no one foolproof method or technique for answering all objections successfully. Therefore, it must be recognized that some prospects are never going to be convinced.

Good methods and techniques are designed to improve the batting average. That is, more objections will be answered satisfactorily if sound techniques are used. Like the baseball player, the salesperson does not expect to bat 1,000; but good techniques can raise the batting average from .200 to .300, which is a 50 percent increase, and may be the difference between a poor producer and a top producer.

In some instances it may not be wise to spend much time trying to convince the prospect. For example, when an insurance underwriter contacts a prospect who says, "I don't believe in insurance," it may be better to spend the available time calling on some of the vast number of people who do believe in insurance.

Salespeople usually attempt to supply answers which satisfy

prospects and thus cause them to buy, or to handle prospect's objections in such a way that a return call will be welcomed.

Relax and listen—Do not interrupt

One word of caution is necessary when employing any technique—*listen first,* then answer the objection. Allow the prospect to state a position completely, Appropriate questions may help the prospect clarify the objection so there is no misunderstanding of the prospect's position. Do not interrupt the buyer to provide an answer even though it may be apparent what objection is to be stated.

Too many salespeople are guilty of conducting conversations somewhat like the following:

You: Mr. Clark, from a survey of your operations, I'm convinced you're now spending more money repairing your own motors than you would having *us* do the job for you . . . and really do it *right!*

Customer: I wonder if we are not doing it right *ourselves.* Your repair service may be good . . . but after all, you don't have to be exactly an electrical genius in order to be able to . . .

You: Just a minute now! Pardon me for interrupting . . . but there's a point I'd like to make right there! It isn't a *matter* of anyone being a genius. It's a matter of having a heavy investment of special motor repair equipment and supplies like vacuum impregnating tanks . . . lathes for banding armatures, boring bearings, turning new shafts.

Customer: Yeah . . . but you don't understand my point. What I'm driving at . . .

You: I *know* what you're driving at . . . and I assure you you're wrong! You forget that even if you own workers *are* smart cookies, they just can't do high-quality work without a lot of special equipment . . .

Customer: But you *still* don't get my point! The idea I'm trying to get off my chest . . . if I can make myself clear on this fourth attempt . . . is this. Our maintenance workers that we now have doing motor repair work . . .

You: . . . could more profitably spend their time on plant *troubleshooting!* Right?

Customer: That isn't what I was going to say! I was trying to say that *between* their trouble jobs . . . instead of just sitting around and shooting the bull . . .

You: Now *wait* a minute, Mr. Clark. Wait jus-s-t a minute! Let ME get a word in here! If you've got any notion that a good motor rewinding job can be done with somebody's left hand on an odd-moment basis, you got another think coming. And my survey here will *prove* it! Now LISTEN!"[7]

---

[7] *Increase Your Selling Skill* (Pittsburgh: Westinghouse Electric Corp.), sec. 3, pp. 4–5.

It is evident that this type of interruption and attitude is likely to cause the interview to be terminated rather quickly.

The following six methods have been used successfully in varied fields of selling.

Agree and counter

This method is often called the "yes-but" method. Its use has been successful because it involves a psychologically sound approach. The edge is taken off an objection by agreeing with the prospect. Prospects expect salespeople to disagree; instead, the salespeople recognize that the objection is offered sincerely and they respect the prospect's point of view. This avoids a direct contradiction and confrontation. To begin an answer, it is good to agree with the prospect to the extent that the agreement does not weaken your position.[8]

After agreeing, then proceed to mention certain points which the prospect either has forgotten or is not aware of. Skill is necessary when introducing the part of the answer followed by *but*. For example, car salespeople may encounter this objection: "I don't like the new automatic transmission on your car." One way to answer is, "You know, Mr. Smith, I felt that way too when I first learned the way it operates, *but* there is really nothing new about it. It is standard for many models which have been on the market for several years." The salesperson has agreed that the reaction of the prospect is logical but then proceeds to contradict by stating that there is nothing new about the transmission. In effect, the answer is, "Yes, but you are wrong. It isn't new." The whole purpose of the yes-but method has been defeated.

A better answer to the same objection might be, "*Yes*, Mr. Smith, I know exactly how you feel. We all need to accept many new ideas, don't we? *But*, did you know that this transmission is very convenient? Think how handy it would be if you had to stop on an upgrade. Now let me show you some other new features you will like . . ."

It is not always necessary to use the words *yes* and *but*. The important features of the method are that salespeople recognize the position of the customer who makes the objection and that they then continue by introducing new evidence or a new thought. For example, the objection may be stated, "I think your machines cost too much." An answer might be phrased as follows: "I know you don't want to pay more for a product than you think it's worth. That's why I'm sure you will see that you are getting your money's worth from

---

[8] For an interesting contrary opinion, see Dan Weadock, "Saying 'Yes . . . but' Is Really No Way to Overcome a Buyer's Objection, *Sales & Marketing Management*, October 15, 1979, pp. 92–96.

our machines. You see, they may cost slightly more than ordinary competitive machines, and this is why . . ."

Some beginning phrases to use with the yes-but method are

"I can understand why you feel that way, Ms. Prospect. On the other hand . . ."

"Mr. Prospect, there is a lot of truth in what you say. However, have you ever considered this angle . . ."

"I would have made that same statement myself two years ago, Mrs. Prospect. Now, let me tell you what I found out . . ."

"You know, a customer made that same statement last week, Mr. Prospect. Let me tell you what we finally agreed upon . . ."

Turn objections into reasons for buying

This method is effective when the prospect offers excuses for not wanting to listen to the presentation. It is sometimes called the "boomerang" method of answering objections.

A sales representative calling on the owner of a restaurant has just made a point of the pennies involved in the use of paper cups instead of glassware when serving customers.

The owner may offer an objection such as, "That penny stuff sounds fine, young fellow—until you add it all up. With all the customers I serve every day I can just imagine my paper cup bill. No, siree!"[9] An effective reply and analysis is provided in the company sales manual of a large corporation.

The suggested reply:	*Analysis:*
1. I know how you feel, Mr. Prospect *(said sincerely, courteously)*.	1–2. Consideration for feelings, and respect for viewpoint.
2. And you're perfectly right.	
3. That cup bill certainly will add up.	3. Repetition of prospect's own words *add up* appeals to prospect's ego.
4. But then so will your dollar volume! *(Enthusiastically.)*	4–6. Turn the objection into a sales point by citing the benefits of your product insofar as it applies to the specific objection made.
5. That is only natural, since a faster service . . .	

[9] Adapted from *Successful Selling* (Toledo, Ohio: Lily-Tulip Cup Division of Owens-Illinois), p. 19.

The suggested reply: *Analysis:*

6. Will help you serve more
    people than ever before.

7. To this increased dollar volume   7. Repetition of more benefits.
    which you'll get from faster
    service, add the savings of
    labor, towels, soap, brushes,
    etc.—savings which come
    about automatically once
    glasswashing is eliminated—
    and I know you'll agree the Lily
    Cups, far from being expen-
    sive, are truly a profitable in-
    vestment.

8. You can begin this week to col-   8. Suggestion that start be
    lect the dividends that Lily   made *now* to collect the re-
    Cups will pay you.   wards of immediate install-
                                                  ment.[10]

 If the prospect suggests, "I'm too busy to see you," the salesperson may answer, "I know you are a busy man, Mr. Smith, and that's the reason I have called. I have a service that is designed for the use of busy executives." If the prospect remarks, "I can't afford it," the salesperson may be able to show how the prospect cannot afford to be without the product or service.

 A prospect may voice this objection, "Your deep freezer is too large—it has too much storage capacity for us." If the salesperson believes the size is appropriate for the buyer's needs, the answer may be: "Yes, Ms. Akin, it would appear that our freezer has some excess storage capacity for your needs. However, I'm sure you realize that one big advantage of owning a deep-freeze unit is that you can store a large supply of frozen foods. You can buy in large quantities, and you can buy during the period of most favorable prices. In other words, what might appear to be extra space is really the feature which provides you the opportunity to save money." To a farmer or a sports enthusiast storage could be an important factor.

 This method, when used skillfully, is effective in overcoming reasons for not buying which are based on the prospect's lack of knowledge.

Ask "why?" or ask specific questions

 This method is often used to separate excuses from real objections. It may also be used to overcome objections.

---

[10] Ibid., p. 20 (adapted).

The inexperienced salesperson may be too quick to answer an objection which seems to be real. If the prospect expresses a major disagreement, the salesperson should ask questions in order to narrow the objection to specific points. Generalized objections are difficult to answer. It is easy to get to the heart of the objection by asking "Why?" Once the objection is concrete and definite, it can be answered.

For example, the prospect may say, "I don't like to do business with your company." A good answer is, "What is it that you don't like about our firm?" The prospect's answer may indicate that there has been a misunderstanding, and the salesperson can then clear it up. Or, in a retail store the prospect may say, "I don't like the appearance of your stoves." An appropriate question is, "Why do you object to the appearance of our stoves, Mrs. Smith?" The prospect's objection may be to some relatively minor point which can be changed.

Another value of the "why" method, especially in cases where the objection is not too serious, is that some objections do not sound very valid once they have been put into words. The opportunity to talk about an objection gives the prospect a chance to evaluate it. The prospect may conclude, without admitting it, that the objection is inconsequential.

Some salespeople use the "why" method to lead prospects to answer their own objection. For example, the prospect for industrial equipment may say, "I can get a machine much cheaper." A good reply is, "Mr. Brown, what is your basis for buying machinery? Do you base you decision solely upon original cost?" The answer is likely to be, "No, of course I am interested in how long it will last and how well it will do the job." The salesperson may say, "Would you say that the machinery you now have in your plant is the least expensive you could buy?" The probable answer is, "No, I guess other makes and models are available at a lesser cost, but we must have machines that will stand up and that will do a job economically and efficiently." Questioning may be continued until the prospect answers his or her own objections. Any attempt, however, to have prospects prove themselves wrong against their will is not likely to result in a sale. People who are *forced* to agree seldom *actually* change their minds.

The question or "why" method has been particularly successful in handling the price objection and in helping to close the sale. When the reason for not buying is, "I think your price is too high," a good answer is, "What do you think is a fair price?" or "How much too high?" It may be possible to show how quantity discounts or cash discounts will bring the price to the level desired; or how a model with fewer or different accessories will cost less. Of course, it would be unwise to imply that prices can be reduced merely because the buyer thinks they are too high. If a price reduction is not possible through the application of discounts, the salesperson must be able to justify the price differential.

Sometimes it may be best to draw out the customer by asking, "I take it that you are concerned over the initial cost of my product because you are not sure whether the cost is justified in terms of what the product can do and, in the long run, how much it can save. Is that a fair statement of your feelings?" This type of question demonstrates a sincere respect for the prospect's objection, and at the same time it offers the sales representatives a smooth, logical opening for strengthening the presentation or restating the benefits of the product.[11]

An appropriate question may help make it easier to close the sale. The question may be, "Is that your only objection to our product?" or "Are you willing to buy if I can satisfy you regarding your price objection?" Of course, the tone and manner of asking the question are important.

Admit valid objections and offset

Certain objections raised by the buyer may be valid. It may be wise to admit such objections and then proceed to show the compensating advantages. This method is similar to the boomerang method.

The car buyer may say: "I'm not interested in an eight-cylinder car. I'm looking for a good six-cylinder or four-cylinder car. Those eights use too much gasoline." A reply may be: "Yes, Ms. Jacobs, eight-cylinder cars often do use more gasoline than six-cylinder or four-cylinder cars. However, just think of these advantages: you get a larger, easier-riding car with more reserve power; you get more storage capacity; you get more comfort; you get a quieter, safer ride; and you are less fatigued on long trips . . . Don't you believe these advantages are worth a larger expenditure for gasoline?"

The insurance prospect may say, "I want straight term insurance to cover my needs on this mortgage. Your company requires me to buy some ordinary life in order to get mortgage protection." If this is true, little can be done to change the company's requirement. Therefore, it is necessary to show the compensating features of the policy. For example: "Yes, Mr. Howard, it is true that we write a policy which includes a base amount of ordinary life insurance. Let me show you what this means to you—you have a cash value at the end

[11] Don Meisel, "Add Salespower! Ask Questions," *Industrial Distribution*, November 1976, p. 64.

of 20 years; or you can borrow on your policy; and you have life insurance when your mortgage is paid for. You will be able to use some money about that time, won't you?"

Almost every product has some advantages and some disadvantages when compared with competing products.

Postpone the answer

In the early part of the sales presentation, objections may arise for which answers are to be given later in the presentation. When this situation occurs, it is good to say, "That's a good point. If you don't mind, let's postpone the answer until later. I have some information that I am sure will satisfy you." The sales representative may then proceed with the presentation until the point is reached at which the objection can be answered best. The prospect will seldom refuse the request if the sales representative is acting in good faith.

A common objection which may suggest the use of this method is, "Your price is too high." Time should not be spent discussing price until product value has been established. The price a prospect is willing to pay is determined by the value expected. Build value to a point at which it is greater than the price asked. This cannot be accomplished, as a rule, during the early stages of the presentation.

If the prospect sees price to be greater than value received, there will be no sale. On the other hand, if the prospect can see value to be greater than price, a sale is a good possibility. Graphically, the situation may be portrayed as in Figure 10–1.

Figure 10–1
Value must be greater than cost

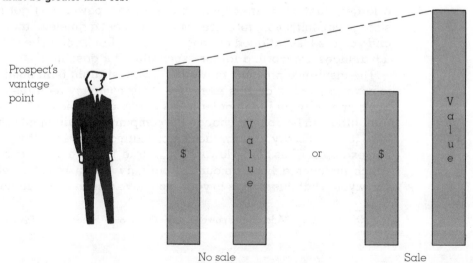

Prospect's vantage point

$ Value   or $ Value

No sale   Sale

Another reason for postponing the answer is that this makes it possible to give a more effective presentation. When too much time is spent in answering the objection, it is difficult to make a coherent presentation. The salesperson who is frequently diverted from the sales talk in an attempt to answer all objections as they arise, cannot make a strong presentation. Some objections can be answered best when they occur; others can be handled best by delaying the answer. Experience is the sales representative's working capital—draw on it!

Where the objection is really an excuse, postponing the answer provides an opportunity to classify the reason for not wanting to buy. If the reason is not stated again later in the interview, it usually may be assumed to have been an excuse.

Deny the objection

The use of this method requires great skill. Seldom is it advisable to meet an objection by making a direct denial. Occasionally, however, this method may be used with satisfactory results when selling buyers who raise objections in order to secure information. Under other circumstances, the buyer may leave the salesperson no other choice.

The buyer may say, "I imagine this cloth will fade when it is washed, won't it?" A good reply is, "No, Ms. Holland, absolutely not. This cloth is guaranteed to hold its color. The reputation of our company is behind this merchandise." Another buyer may say, "I understand your company sells this product to our competitor at a better price than we get. Is that true?" An appropriate answer may be, "Mr. Keen, we faithfully adhere to a one-price policy. You are aware, I am sure, that we cannot afford to discriminate among our competitive customers. In fact, the Robinson-Patman Act prohibits any firm from favoring any one customer. No, sir, Mr. Keen, I assure you that our price quotation is the same to you as to your competitors."

The belligerent buyer who makes false accusations regarding the company or its products may be answered best through the use of a direct denial. Occasionally a buyer in this mood may say, "I know your shoes; cardboard must be used in their construction." The answer may be, "Mr. Smith, there is not a piece of paper of any kind in our shoes. We are proud of the fact that we use only high-grade leather in the construction of our shoes. Perhaps you can show me what appears to be the use of inferior materials." Another buyer may say, "We'd rather deal with Company X; they allow us a 30-day return privilege. If we buy from you, we have no return privileges." If the statement is in error, the salesperson may say, "Mr. Jones, we offer exactly the same return privileges as other companies in the industry. Someone has misled you regarding our policy. We are happy to extend you a 30-day return privilege."

This method must be used with caution. If salespeople become belligerent, or start an argument, they have little chance of getting an order, even though they may win the argument. The tone of voice and the attitude determine the manner in which a direct denial will be accepted by the prospect or buyer. Relatively few companies suggest the extensive use of this method under normal circumstances.

METHODS AND TECHNIQUES USED BY SUCCESSFUL COMPANIES _____

Many of the leading sales organizations prepare procedures which they recommend to their sales representatives. The following illustrations are typical of the methods used when selling a variety of different products.

The Gillette Company, Paper Mate Division—Pens and writing systems _____

This company believes that there are three basic techniques for handling objections. Sales representatives are encouraged to use the technique best suited to a given situation.

Technique I is called *Question Conversion*. This requires getting a clear understanding of the objection by asking questions and then answering it with proof.

Technique II is called *Feel-Felt-Found*. This requires getting in step by understanding the prospect's *feelings*, indicating that many customers have *felt* that way, and pointing out what they *found* after reviewing the latest data.

Technique III is called *Boomerang*. This requires that the objection raised for not buying be used as the very reason why the prospect should buy.

The company believes that the principles common or basic to all of the above techniques are:

1. Listen, analyze, diagnose.
2. Share the prospect's feelings.
3. Condition the prospect to accept logical evidence without losing face.
4. Present evidence and proof supporting your position.
5. Ask for the business.[12]

Sales representatives are trained through a programmed instruction course.

_____
[12] "Handling Objections" *Personal Progress through Skill Development* (The Gillette Company, Paper Mate Division), part 2.

Sperry Remington—Accounting machines _____

This company believes that most objections are necessary to the sale. It believes that there are three basic types of objections—sincere objections, insincere objections, and hidden objections.

Company sales representatives are instructed to prehandle common objections due to claims by competition, hearsay, and bad personal experience, and common product and application objections. These objections are to be prehandled in this manner:

1. Make a written list of the objections most often encountered.
2. With the help of experienced people, write the best answers you can.
3. Incorporate these answers into the logical spots throughout your sales story.
4. Be positive, rather than negative, in your prehandling.
5. Try to turn the objection into a reason for buying.[13]

When answering sincere and hidden objections, the company provides this group of suggestions:

1. Decide whether to answer now or to defer.
2. Consider asking questions. Ask how, or why, or when, or where.
3. Agree—then answer. Use, it *seems* true, but . . . ; it *was* true, but . . . ; it *is* true, but . . . ; the testimony of a third party; comparisons or analogies.
4. Follow through, continue selling. Try for a close.[14]

Westinghouse Electric Corporation—Electrical motors _____

This company trains its sales representatives to answer objections by observing the following rules:

1. Listen before you answer.
   (Salespeople are cautioned not to interrupt buyers and to allow buyers to tell their story completely.)
2. Inquire before you answer.
   (Salespeople are instructed to ask questions about the objections. This procedure allows buyers to get their objections off their chests entirely, and it gives the salesperson additional data on *how* to answer the objections.)
3. Restate before you answer.
   (This makes it apparent to the buyer that the salesperson understands the point the buyer is making.)

_____

[13] Sales Training Department, *Handling Objections* (Blue Bell, Pa.: Sperry Remington).

[14] Ibid.

4. Answer without arguing.
   (This can be done by avoiding any belligerent statements, actions, or words.)
5. Don't do all the talking yourself.
   (Customer participation is necessary in all good sales presentations.)[15]

The company suggests that a good way to stay away from an argument is to introduce evidence which is impersonal—that is, show what has been accomplished by others. Buyers then feel that if they change their minds it is not a personal victory for the salesrepresentative.

New York Life Insurance Company—Insurance

This company prepares its underwriters with these observations: objections are a normal part of the buying process; many objections can be ignored because they are not sincere; requests for assurance and further information often are expressed as objections; and not a single objection is directed toward you, the underwriter, so do not take objections personally.

Underwriters are provided with educational material which spells out a recommended step-by-step procedure for handling the objections they encounter. Detailed illustrations are included. The suggested steps are:

Relax and listen.
Classify the objection.
Ask questions.
Repeat or rephrase the objection.
Turn the objection into a reason to buy.
Help the prospect "save face."
Use the "yes-but" technique.
Never argue.
Tell a motivating story.
Then, close again—and again![16]

Xerox—Copiers

This company's complete sales training program emphasizes the need for developing specific skills in answering objections which

---

[15] Adapted from *Increase Your Selling Skill*, pp. 3–16.

[16] Adapted from *Turn Objections into Sales*, chap. 2, (New York, N.Y.: New York Life Insurance Company), pp. 72–82.

may be encountered on a sales call. Each objection is studied, and an attempt is made to master the correct response.

It is suggested that there are *easy* and *difficult* objections. An easy objection is based upon a customer's misconception about the product or service. To handle this type of objection:

Rephrase it in question form (a confirming paraphrase).

Answer it directly.

Example:

Customer: I can't consider Xerox. I only *buy* office equipment.

Sales representative: Then you're only concerned about having the option to purchase equipment instead of renting it?"

Customer: Yes.

Sales representative: Mr. Customer, I think you'll be pleased to know that Xerox will both rent and sell its equipment. In fact, we encourage you to consider purchase.

A difficult objection is based upon the customer's perception that some aspect of the product or service is a drawback. To handle this type of objection:

Probe to clarify and expand the objection (amplifying paraphrase).

Minimize the objection by stressing other relevant benefits.[17]

Frigidaire—Electric refrigerators

This company identifies the fundamentals of answering and overcoming objections as follows:

1. Learn the real objection, and why it is an objection.
2. Restate the objection, then answer it completely and concisely.
3. Don't evade or minimize objections.
4. Avoid arguments.
5. Discuss objections prositively.
6. Use the yes-but technique.
7. Use the objection as a reason for buying.
8. Don't let the objection throw you off the track.[18]

The company believes that objections provide opportunities to clarify points, review product advantages, offer more sales points, meet competitive claims, and close the sale.

---

[17] Personal Progress through Skill Development, *Handling Objections*, (Xerox), p. VIII-14.

[18] Adapted from "Answering Objections," *Professional Salesmanship* (Detroit: Frigidaire Division, General Motors Corp.), part 4, p. 5.

A SUGGESTED PLAN

Salespeople should develop a procedure which can be followed when answering objections. The following steps can be applied and adapted to needs in most fields of selling:

1. Listen carefully—don't interrupt—let prospect talk.
2. Repeat the prospect's objection. *Make sure the objection is understood.* Ask questions to permit the prospect to clarify objections. Acknowledge the apparent soundness of the prospect's point of view. In other words, agree as far as possible with the prospect's thinking before providing an answer.
3. Evaluate the objection. Determine whether the reason for not buying is a real objection or an excuse. Answer a real objection immediately, if possible. Ignore an excuse, or seek more information to identify the real objection.
4. Decide on the methods or techniques to use in answering the objection. Some of the factors to be considered are the phase of the sales process in which the objection is raised; the mood, or frame of mind, evidenced by the prospect; the reason for the objection; and the number of times the reason is advanced.
5. Get a commitment from prospects. The answer to any objection must satisfy them if a sale is to result. Get them to agree that their objection has been answered.
6. Try a "trial close." If an objection is raised when the close is attempted, try to close immediately after answering the objection to the satisfaction of the prospect.
7. Continue with the sales presentation. If the trial close is unsuccessful, continue the presentation until another close opportunity presents itself.

Whenever possible, objections should be answered briefly, and they should not be built into major obstacles by spending an unnecessary amount of time on the answers.

QUESTIONS AND PROBLEMS

1. A common mistake made by sales representatives is to assume that a customer's question is an objection. Consider the following:

    Customer: What is this going to cost me?

    Sales rep: Then you're concerned about the value you will receive for the dollar you will spend?

    Customer: No, I want to know what it's going to cost!

    What should the sales representative have done differently?

2. If you feel that the prospect isn't giving you the real objection, you may say, "In addition to that, Mr. Prospect, what other reasons have you?

Isn't there something else back of your refusal to buy?" What could an answer to these questions accomplish?

3. Salespeople must decide whether or not to take an objection seriously. If customers make an objection merely because they feel that they must say something, or in order to stall, what action should be taken and what dangers are involved?

4. Sales representatives find it necessary to get to a "screen," such as a receptionist, a secretary, or an assistant, to get to the decision-maker. How would you answer the following objections of a screen:

   a. "I'm sorry, but Mr. Harris is too busy right now."

   b. *"We're cutting back on expenditures."*

   c. "Could you just leave some literature?"

   d. "A representative of your company was by recently."

   e. "I really don't think we can afford your equipment."

5. Illustrate one way to handle each of the following objections:
   a. During a demonstration the customer says, "You know, I really like the model X Company (your competitor) sells."

   b. After a sales presentation the prospect says, "You have a good product. Thanks for your time. If we decide to buy, I'll give you a call."

   c. After the salesperson answers an objection, the prospect remarks, "I guess your product is all right; but—well, I don't think I need one just now. Thanks a lot."

   d. After a thorough presentation the prospect answers, "No, I'm sorry, we just can't afford it."

   e. After the customer says, "Oh, no! That's really too much money. I've been looking at the same product downtown, and I can buy it at a much lower price."

6. The purpose when handling objections is to cause prospects to change their minds without irritating and offending them. Do you believe that there is a difference in handling prospects who present a point of view, an opinion, and a bias or prejudice? How would your technique differ in each case?

7. You have been showing boudoir lamps to a young married couple. The wife wants to replace a lamp that she had before they were married. Company is coming for the weekend, and she wants her guest room to look especially nice. She's particularly interested in one of the dainty lamps which you have shown. Turning to her husband, she says, "Honey, I just love this one." Her husband says, "Well, if that's what you want, OK. How much is it?"

   You reply, "This one is $89.95." The husband exclaims, "For that little thing!!!"

   What should you say or do?

8. Indicate the appropriate action for the sales representative who en-
    counters the following customer attitudes:

    a. "I like the things this copier can do, if it really does them. It's kind of
        hard to believe it'll give me reliable service with all these things
        that could go wrong."

    b. "Let me be plain. Your company's reputation precedes you in this
        office. I've had more trouble with your machines than you would
        care to hear."

    c. "That sounds fine. But there's really no reason to get rid of the
        copier I've got. It works well enough for anything I use it for."

    d. "I see what you're saying. This machine you're talking about could
        end up saving us some time and money."

9. You are planning to work part time and during the summer, gaining
    experience through door-to-door selling. You plan to sell food products
    and will take over a route and sell quality groceries. The company you
    are to represent guarantees its products, offers credit, provides pre-
    miums for buyers, and requires its salespeople to call on customers
    regularly. Make a list of the objections you may expect to encounter.
    What can you do to meet these objections effectively?

10. It has been suggested that objections should be anticipated. How could
    you turn an anticipated objection into a sales point in the following
    circumstances: You are showing a residence to a potential buyer, and
    you anticipate that the prospect will say the kitchen is too small.

11. With more and more opportunities for people to buy products at "dis-
    count," how would you answer prospects who tell you that they can buy
    your product at a discount?

12. It is generally agreed that it is difficult to determine the *real* reason why
    some customers or prospects refuse to buy. Some prospects habitually
    refuse to give the real reason. They offer many reasons, but these are
    advanced merely to disguise the true reason. Before a sale can be
    consummated, the exact reason for not buying must be determined, and
    then it must be answered to the prospect's satisfaction. It does little
    good to answer excuses satisfactorily because they are not the real
    hurdles which must be overcome. If a customer gives you several
    reasons for not buying your product, how can you determine whether
    the real reason has been stated? Suggest a technique which would help
    uncover the real objection.

13. When you make your first sales call on a new prospect, you know that
    one of your major tasks is to reduce the prospect's resistance. Negative
    psychological factors exist in the minds of all prospects, simply be-
    cause they are human beings. A knowledge of these attitudes and emo-
    tions is certain to help improve your ratio of sales to calls. What are
    some negative psychological forces that can be anticipated in most
    buyers? What can be done about them?

PROJECTS

1. Engage in a discussion with fellow students or friends on some controversial topics—politics, religion, the environment, the draft, equal
   rights for women, and so on. Experiment by using a variety of techniques to disagree with the statements they make. Prepare some conclusions as to effective and ineffective techniques. Write a one-page report.

2. Write a 200-word explanation of the need for people to "save face."

3. Select a product that you intend to buy in the near future. Make a list of
   the objections you are likely to raise. List the objections in one column
   and the answers in another column.

CASE PROBLEMS

Case 10-1

Texas Farm Supply Co.

Recently the Texas Farm Supply Co., decided to enter the field of
manufacturing and distributing linings. These will be used to line
crates in which fresh produce is shipped to the market. It is important that fresh produce remain in good condition between the time it
is harvested and the time it gets to the consumer.

Prospective users for the linings are large growers of vegetables
which may be sent to distant markets, such as lettuce, celery, en-
dive, cauliflower, and broccoli. Other potential prospects are packers who buy the produce from growers and repack it and who are
interested in getting the produce to the market in top condition, and
chain-store buying groups which make volume purchases of produce, pack it, and ship it to their warehouses for retail distribution,
and which therefore have a big stake in maximum protection. These
prospects are located in or near the Salinas Valley, the San Joaquin
Valley, and the Imperial Valley in California, and in Arizona, Texas,
and the Northwest.

The Texas Farm Supply Co. has investigated the competition
thoroughly and has found that a real need exists for a lining that will
overcome the difficulties encountered by shippers when using the
standard wet-strength papers and the standard waxed papers. Aluminum foil, produced by foil manufacturers on the West Coast, was
introduced to overcome the difficulties mentioned by the shippers.
However, upon questioning the shippers, Texas Farm Supply Co.

found that the following objections were voiced to the use of foil as a liner: the foil sheets are difficult to separate and to place in the crates when packers work rapidly; the foil sheets tend to tear if they are not handled carefully; and the foil sheets, if punctured by sharp corners when the crates are handled, are likely to lose some of their effectiveness.

The Texas Farm Supply Co. believed that it could manufacture a type of foil sheet that would overcome the difficulties mentioned by the shippers. After considerable experimentation, the company produced an aluminum foil laminated to wet-strength papers. That is, thin sheets of foil were combined with thin sheets of paper to form a lining that would conserve the good features of both the paper and the foil. This combination liner could be printed with iceproof and scuffproof inks to provide the shipper with sales appeal and advertising on the crate liners, as well as provide vastly improved protection.

The following are the main selling features of the new aluminum foil-paper liner:

1. It keeps contents cool. The foil reflects about 95 percent of all the radiant heat it intercepts, as compared with only 7 percent reflection by brown-paper liner.
2. It helps remove heat from the pack. The thermal conductivity of aluminum foil is high.
3. It decreases the collection of moisture on produce. Unloading from cool cars has caused moisture to collect on produce, and this has permitted bacteria to spoil some produce.
4. It prevents the penetration of the sun's rays.
5. It prevents the evaporation of natural moisture from produce.
6. It decreases the chances of bruising produce.
7. Ice does not penetrate it easily.
8. It is colorful, and it can advertise the packer and be used as a point-of-purchase display by retailers.

The company decided to select its prospects carefully and to attempt to sell only shippers who were interested in selling premium-quality produce. The company decided to sell its product through jobbers and, at the same time, to maintain a salesforce of its own to develop and contact prospects and to train and help the jobber sales representatives.

When the company salespeople called on prospects, it became apparent that the major objection which had to be overcome was price. The liner cost was 43 cents per crate, while standard paper liners sold for 24 cents per crate.

Questions

1. As a sales representative for Texas Farm Supply Co., how would you expect prospects to state their objection to the price? What objections are the prospects likely to voice which are really price objections but are not so stated?

2. Suggest some demonstrations, tests, or other selling aids which might be used to overcome the price objection. Illustrate their use.

3. Where should the major emphasis be put when answering the price objection? Illustrate.

Case 10-2

McPherson Business Products

Shari Seller works part time for McPherson Business Products. She sells a variety of items both on the floor and in the offices of prospects in the business community. Shari is paid on a commission basis and has earned considerable supplementary income from her job.

Shari has had some trouble in anticipating and answering objections. Mr. McPherson, the owner, has suggested that Shari classify the objections of her prospects before attempting to answer them. In addition, he has suggested that she attempt to anticipate the objections many customers will raise in order not to be put in the position of having to answer objections on an impromptu basis.

Mr. McPherson has offered to act in a role-playing situation as an office manager and to give Shari an opportunity to practice on him. Shari has agreed to try to improve her skill through this method.

It has been agreed that Shari will attempt to sell dictating equipment and a filing system in two separate practice sessions.

The following statements about the company's automated filing system have been raised as objections for Shari to analyze:

a. "I don't like your visual retriever because I can't be sure I have called the right slide until it arrives."

b. (Making reference to a lever on the device.) "I would probably get calluses from working that thing all day."

c. (After a short presentation.) "I think we'll just stick with the inventory control system we have."

The following objections to the use of dictating equipment are to be raised:

a. "My work doesn't require it."

b.   "I've never used it. Why change now?"
c.   "I'd rather have a secretary take dictation."
d.   "My secretary hates dictating equipment."
e.   "I tried dictating equipment, but I didn't like it."

Questions

1.   How should Shari classify the objections to the automated filing systems?
2.   What suggestions do you have for Shari after she has classified the objections?
3.   Prepare short, effective answers to the objections that will be raised to the use of dictating equipment.

Case 10-3

Easy Flow Company

It is Monday morning. You are a sales representative for Easy Flow Company, located in Dayton, Ohio. You have an appointment with Robina Egge of Quacker Foods, a large user of writing pens in the food industry. This is your first call on Quacker.

Ms. Flair, the receptionist, indicates that there will be a wait. When you enter Egge's office she appears businesslike and seems pressed for time. You say good morning and you introduce yourself.

You start your sales interview by saying, "I'd like to explore with you how we can reduce the cost of writing instruments. What brand of pens do you buy currently?" Ms. Egge indicates that Quacker Foods is using Alwaysright pens.

You proceed to question Egge about her company's needs and about its evaluation of the Alwaysright pen. You take notes, and you provide ample opportunity for Egge to explain what experiences she and the company employees have had with the pen.

It develops that the employees in the Quacker Foods offices have experienced some leakage and skipping of Alwaysright pens. Upon further questioning, and allowing plenty of opportunity for Ms. Egge to talk, you find out that Quacker Foods has 300 employees and that employees can go into the stockroom and take a handful of supplies whenever they wish. This encourages employees to take two or three pens at a time, and the practice could be expensive.

To make certain that you understand the situation you attempt to summarize the key problems that you and Ms. Egge have discussed: orders are being placed more frequently than should be necessary; Alwaysright pens occasionally leak, and they skip quite often; employees are continually picking up new pens, which costs money. Ms. Egge agrees that this is an accurate summary.

Questions

1. Suggest answers to the following objections which occurred at different times during the sales interview:

    a. "Some important things have suddenly come up. Can we make this appointment at another time?"

    b. "I have too much pressure on me to keep costs down."

    c. "Your service has a bad reputation."

    d. "I don't care to do business with your firm now."

    e. "Look, we have been having considerable success with our present pen for the past three years. Why should we make a change now?"

    f. "It won't work. I don't think you understand our problem. Our situation is completely different from everybody else's."

    g. "That sounds good in theory, but these things never seem to work out in practice. I don't think that idea will work."

    h. "Business has been really slow lately."

2. Summarize your philosophy on the best way to answer objections.

3. Distinguish between a "sales interview" and a "sales presentation."

SELECTED REFERENCES

Bigelow, Stanley. "The Art of Active Listening." *Industrial Distribution*, May 1976, p. 129.

Golstein, A. *Secrets of Overcoming Sales Resistance: 386 Tested Replies to Objections.* Englewood Cliffs, N.J.: Prentice-Hall, 1969.

Harrow, Herman. "You Can Disagree without Being Disagreeable." *Sales & Marketing Management*, December 10, 1979, p. 67.

Linkletter, Art. *How to Be a Supersalesman.* Englewood Cliffs, N.J.: Prentice-Hall, 1974, pp. 17–34.

McNutt, George. "Hurdling Toughest Sales Obstacle: State of Prospect's Mind." *Industrial Marketing*, March 1977, pp. 70–73.

Meisel, Don. "Add Sales Power! Ask Questions." *Industrial Distribution*, December 1976, p. 64.

Weadock, Dan. "Saying 'Yes . . . but' Is Really No Way to Overcome a Buyer's Objection." *Sales & Marketing Management*, October 15, 1979, pp. 92–95.

Chapter 11

CLOSING THE SALE

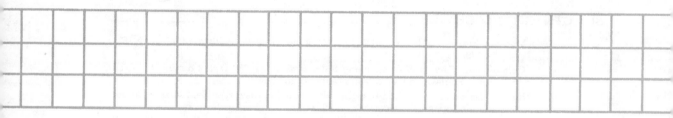

The close is not something apart and distinct from the total sales presentation. In fact, the close actually starts with the *beginning* of the sales presentation.

The close is likely to be successful only when the buyer is convinced that the purchase is desirable. This conviction comes about when the salesperson talks to a qualified prospect, plans the presentation effectively, develops skill in dramatizing and conveying the sales message, treats the buyer as an individual, appeals to dominant buying motives, and recognizes that the close is an integral part of a well-planned procedure.

This chapter is designed to emphasize the importance of securing favorable action, to explore the reasons for unsuccessful closes, to ascertain the factors involved in timing the close, to identify the bases for securing a good percentage of closed sales, to explain methods and techniques that have proved effective, and to review desirable practices for handling closing routines.

THE IMPORTANCE OF SECURING FAVORABLE ACTION

There are at least two good reasons for becoming an expert in the technique of closing sales: first, the close is the ultimate test of sales ability; and second, the income received is usually based upon closed sales.

Test of selling ability

The true test of the selling ability of salespeople is orders secured. Salespeople may spend months in qualifying prospects; may work long hours; may know the product thoroughly; may speak eloquently; may know the customers and their dominant attitudes; but if they do not get orders, their selling careers will be short-lived.

Sales constitute the final yardstick by which salespeople are measured. Sales may be compared with a quota, or may be measured against last month's or last year's figures. Whatever comparison the company makes, it soon becomes evident that success is not determined by the number of interviews secured, by the hours spent in the field, or by the goodwill calls made. The employer must ultimately measure success in terms of the orders received.

The close is the climax of the sales presentation. It is the point at which the buyer agrees to purchase the product or services. This meeting of the minds of the buyer and the salesperson is the result of a carefully planned procedure. The good salesperson determines what the prospect wants or needs; builds value to a point which is higher than the price asked; and climaxes the presentation by securing the order. It takes skill, knowledge, and courage to close sales successfully. The close is a challenge.

Relation of sales closed to income

Some companies pay a basic salary plus a commission; others pay on a straight commission basis. Various plans of compensation are used. However, the salesperson who has the greatest income at the end of the year is almost always the one who closed the greatest number of sales or sold the largest dollar volume.

Companies are constantly looking for men and women who can bring in the orders. After salespeople prove they can close, they are the logical choices for promotion to supervisory or managerial jobs.

WHAT CAUSES DIFFICULTIES IN CLOSING SALES[1] _____

Wrong attitudes _____

Attitude as expressed by speech, mannerisms, body language, or actions may be a hindrance to the completion of a sale. If salespeople build up a great fear that the close is going to be difficult, this fear may be impossible to hide. It is only natural that inexperienced salespeople should be concerned about their ability to close the sale. They know that they must close sales to keep their jobs. If the first few attempts to close are unsuccessful, they may feel that they *must* close the next sale. When salespeople try too hard to complete the sales presentation—when they feel the pressure—they are likely to do a very poor job.

Eagerness to close a sale may be a handicap. Eagerness may be interpreted by the buyer as evidence that there is some doubt about the value of the product, or that the salesperson is inexperienced. These interpretations by the buyer make the close more difficult.

Some salespeople display unwarranted excitement when it becomes apparent that the prospect is ready to buy. This may make it difficult to handle the closing routines effectively. If the salesperson appears to be excited, the sale may be lost even after the prospect has agreed to buy.

Poor presentation _____

Some sales executives believe that the close is merely a point in the sales presentation which arrives automatically after a good presentation has been made. This thought tends to underestimate the need for good closing techniques, but it does point out the need for building up to the close.

Prospects or customers cannot be expected to buy if they do not understand the presentation or are unable to see the benefits which will accrue as the result of the purchase. Failure to make a good sales talk may be caused by haste in making the presentation. Some company executives prepare estimates of the time needed to make a sales presentation effectively. If the salesperson tries to deliver a sales presentation in 20 minutes and it has been planned for delivery in 60 minutes, important sales points may be neglected or omitted entirely.

It may be better to forgo making the presentation than to deliver it hastily. Some salespeople make no attempt to deliver their sales talk

---

[1] See Heinz Goldmann, "The Art of Selling," *Management Today*, September 1977, p. 139, for the results of a survey of training consultants on the major mistakes in closing sales.

if the prospect will not allow them the time necessary to give the presentation effectively.

A sales presentation given at the wrong time, or under unfavorable conditions, is likely to be ineffective.

Poor habits and skills

Closing sales requires skill. Skills are acquired only through constant repetition and intelligent practice. With sufficient repetition and practice, skills become habits. It is evident that poorly developed skills can be the cause of inefficient habits. The salesperson who expects to close a high percentage of sales builds sound habits.

The habit of talking too much and not listening enough often causes otherwise good presentations to fail. It is just as important to know when to quit talking as to know what to say. Some salespeople become so fascinated by the sound of their own voices that they talk themselves out of sales which have already been made. The presentation which develops into a monologue is not likely to retain the interest of the buyer.[2]

WHEN AND HOW OFTEN TO TRY TO CLOSE

Beginning salespeople may ask themselves these questions: "Is there a 'right' time to close?" "How will customers let me know they are ready to buy?" "Should I make more than one attempt to close?" "What should I do if my first close fails?"

When Is the "right" time?

The "right" time to attempt a close is when the buyer appears to be ready to buy. It has been said that there is one psychological moment in the sales presentation which affords the best opportunity to close, that if this opportunity is bypassed, it will be difficult to secure the order. This is not a true picture. Seldom does one psychological moment govern the success or failure of a sales presentation.

Most buyers make up their minds to buy only when they understand the benefits which the purchase provides for them. For some buyers this point occurs early in the interview, during the first call. For others, it may not arrive until a complete presentation and several calls have been made, and all questions have been answered.

Few buyers *ask* to buy. Buyers usually hesitate to make the decision to purchase until they receive help. Salespeople should make it

---

[2] Don Meisel. "Add Salespower! Ask Questions." *Industrial Distribution*, November 1976, p. 64.

easy for them to act. When a salesperson believes that the buyer understands the proposition and *may* be ready to buy, a right time has arrived. The right time usually occurs several times in any interview. Failure to recognize one closing opportunity is usually not fatal. However, consistently failing to reocgnize closing opportunities is unpardonable.

Be alert for closing signals

Customers may indicate that they are or are not ready to buy by their facial expressions, by their actions, or by their comments. These indications, however, are no guarantee that the sale can be closed. They should be interpreted, however, as an opportunity to attempt the close. There are no magic formulas that take the place of good judgment and common sense.

Buyers may not accommodate by registering frowns, quizzical looks, or smiles of satisfaction. Probably the buyer's facial expressions most often serve to indicate that he or she is *not* ready to buy. If buyers appear to be puzzled or frown, this may be evidence that they are not yet thoroughly sold on the product or service.

The actions of the buyer may indicate a readiness to buy. The prospective buyer of a calculator may get a sheet of figures and operate the machine or may place the machine on the desk where it will be used. The buyer who is considering the purchase of insurance may pick up some literature that has been read previously and give it more thorough study. The buyer of paper may take a sample and again compare it with the stock now being used. The woman shopping for a microwave oven may step back and view the oven from a distance. The industrial buyer may refer to a catalog to compare the specifications of the product under consideration with the specifications of similar products produced by competing companies. Any of these actions may be *closing signals*. The buyer may be "extending an invitation" to close the sale.

The customer's comments are often the best indications that a purchase is being considered. A prospect will seldom say, "All right, I'm ready to buy. What terms can be arranged?" Customers may indicate, however, that they are about to make a decision (or that they have already made a decision) by asking these questions or making these statements: "I guess it would be better to get a new roof on this building before it rains." "How would we operate while the changeover of equipment is being made?" "Can I pay for the policy on a monthly basis?" "Do you have any facilities for training our employees in the use of the product?" Do I understand you correctly? Did you say that this machine is guaranteed for five years?"

"How soon would you be able to deliver the equipment?" "How much will you allow me on a trade-in?"[3]

The ability to recognize *closing signals* comes from experience and intelligent observation of buyers' reactions and comments.

How often should the close be attempted?

Some customers make up their minds to buy before anybody calls. They may be sold completely, and they may actually be waiting for an opportunity to buy. However, most customers must be sold, and it is therefore the salesperson's job to plan the presentation so as to *create* closing opportunities.

Figure 11-1 illustrates some of the points at which the salesperson may want to try a close.

Few successful salespeople rely upon the first closing routine. Most sales executives instruct their salespeople to try to close often. *Relatively few sales are closed on the first attempt, even though the customer plans to buy.*

A series of closing routines must be developed. Each routine should be different, because repeating the same routine several times is likely to be unimpressive. Probably a minimum of four or five routines are necessary. Sales manuals have identified four, five, six, seven, or even more closing tries as desirable. A good rule to follow is to attempt the close as many times as good judgment dictates. Of course, persistence is a notable trait, but it is only good selling as long as the salesperson's efforts do not antagonize and irritate the prospect. One buyer may willingly accept five or six attempts to close, while another buyer may lose patience after the third attempt.

If the product being sold is highly technical, and intensive survey work must precede the presentation, it probably will be necessary to make a rather complete presentation before attempting a close. On the other hand, if the advantages of purchasing are rather obvious to the buyer, an attempt to close early in the presentation may be acceptable.

What if the trial close fails?

When the trial close fails, analysis serves as a basis for future actions. There are many reasons why a trial close fails. Salespeople may have attempted to close prematurely; may have misinterpreted

---

[3] For further illustrations of closing signals, see Chas. E. Bergman, "Secrets of the Industrial Close," *Sales & Marketing Management*, 1977, special report.

Figure 11-1

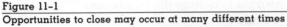

Opportunities to close may occur at many different times

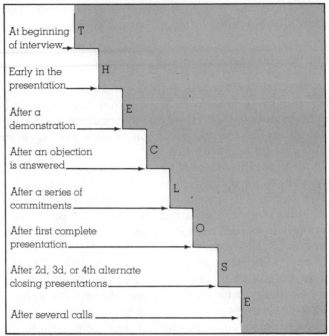

a closing signal; may not have made the presentation clear and forceful; may have appealed to the wrong buying motives; may have failed to answer an objection satisfactorily; or may have been unskilled in the demonstration. Whatever the cause, the real reason must be uncovered. Only then can salespeople proceed intelligently to eliminate the barriers to the sale.

Probably the most important lesson for the inexperienced salesperson to learn is that when a buyer says no, the sale should not be presumed to be lost. A "no" may mean "Not now," or "I want more information," or "Don't hurry me," or "I don't understand." "No" should be a challenge to seek the reason for the buyer's negative response.

When a trial close fails, continue with the presentation and look for another opportunity to close. If the presentation has been completed and several attempts to close have failed it may be necessary to review parts of the presentation or to question the prospect again to determine the cause of failure.

Actually, the failure of a trial close can prove to be of great value. The effectiveness of a sales presentation often can be determined only by testing. The test is the trial close. It tells the salesperson that the customer has been sold and is ready to buy, or *why* the customer is not ready to buy. This testing process may be likened to the activities of a chef who is cooking a steak. Periodically the chef will test the steak to see if it is ready to serve. Maybe it must be cooked slower, or faster, or longer; or it may need more salt, pepper, or other seasoning. The results of the tests suggest what to do to make the steak just right for any specific customer. Certainly, the chef does not throw the steak away because the first two or three tests show that it is not yet ready to serve. The salesperson may be compared to the chef. The salesperson's trial close tells just what to do to make the product or service benefits known and appreciated by the buyer. Neither the salesperson nor the chef quits trying after the first test.

HOW TO CLOSE SUCCESSFULLY

For any closing techniques to be employed successfully the salesperson must be aware of principles which are designed to make the use of a variety of closing techniques more effective.

Maintain a positive attitude

Confidence displayed in the presentation is contagious. Customers like to buy from people who have confidence in themselves, their product, and their company. Any indication that the salesperson thinks the presentation will not be received favorably or that there is little chance of making a sale, is likely to be communicated to the customer. Should this occur, unnecessary barriers are placed between the customer and the salesperson. Enthusiasm and confidence form the necessary background for the effective use of any closing technique.

As the presentation is delivered to each prospect, the salesperson's attitude must be, "I will make this sale." It becomes a question of *"How* or *when* will the prospect buy?" not a question of *"Will* the prospect buy?" Whenever salespeople make a sales presentation, they must sincerely and wholeheartedly believe that they will succeed. This belief must be evidenced by what they say and by what they do.

One successful sales representative describes his attitude as follows: "I approach every interview with the positive attitude that this person is going to buy. I'm not sure what or how much, but I look to every interview ending in a sale."[4]

Is this attitude incompatible with the knowledge that in many

---

[4] Gregory M. Genovese, "Observations on Closing Sales," *NYLIC Review,* January 1977, p. 16.

fields of selling salespeople will lose more sales than they make? How can one maintain this positive attitude when it is known that the ratio of closes may be only one sale out of every two, three, or four presentations? The answer is quickly recognized as sound—we have no prior knowledge indicating which prospects will buy. Experienced salespeople know that they may sell five or six prospects in succession and then fail to sell one, two, or more prospects; or they may sell every other prospect for a period of time; or no pattern may be ascertainable. If we knew in advance which prospects would not buy, it is apparent that we would not waste our time and the time of those prospects.

Any skill is performed best when the individual's attitude is positive. The typist who fears errors will make many; the bowler who fears the tenpin is likely to miss it; the ballplayers who know they cannot hit a certain pitcher are likely to get few hits; golfers who know they will miss short putts usually do. So it is with salespeople. If they fear that the customer will not buy, the chances are good that they will be right.

Keep control of the interview

Control of the interview is necessary in order to create closing opportunities and to permit closing techniques to be used most effectively.

If the prospect takes over and keeps the initiative, closing attempts are likely to be fruitless. If the sales presentation is well planned, it will usually not be difficult to guide the interview along the lines previously planned.

This topic has been discussed more fully earlier in Chapter 8, Planning and Delivering the Sales Presentation.

Let the customer set the pace

Closing attempts must be geared to fit the varying reactions, needs, and personalities[5] of each individual buyer. However, this does not mean that the buyer should be allowed to control the interview.

Some buyers react very slowly, and such buyers may need plenty of time to assimilate the material presented. They may ask the same question several times, or they may give evidence that they do not understand the importance of certain product features. In these cir-

---

[5] Control Data believes that different closing techniques are appropriate for different prospects' personalities. See Sally Scanlon, "Every Salesperson a Psychologist," *Sales & Marketing Management*, February 6, 1978, pp. 34–35.

cumstances, the presentation must be delivered more slowly, and parts may have to be repeated. It would be unwise to attempt a close when it is evident that the customer is not yet ready to buy.

All prospects expect salespeople to supply sufficient information to enable them to arrive at a proper evaluation of the product. The kinds of information and the speed with which the information can be absorbed will vary with different prospects. If salespeople know their prospects and customers, they can make the presentation at the most effective pace.

Give the customer a chance to buy

The only reason for making a sales presentation is to *help the customer buy*. It follows, then, that this goal should be kept in mind constantly.

The salesperson must be ready to close when the customer is ready to buy. The customer who says, "This unit appears to be scratched. Do you have others?" may be providing an opportunity to close. It would be a mistake to continue with additional sales features when it is apparent that the customer is ready to buy. Perhaps the appropriate answer to the question is, "We have the same model in the warehouse. When would you like us to deliver it?"

It is paradoxical that salespeople give sales presentations to make sales and then fail to ask for the order. This failure is explained by the fear that the prospect will say no. Most people do not like to be told no. The salesperson is likely to rationalize, probably unconsciously, "If I don't ask for the order until I am sure the prospect will buy, then I won't be told no." The fear of asking for the order has lost many sales. One sales representative made many calls on a prospect and was finally able to secure the order. Upon securing the order, the store owner was asked why it took so many calls to get the order. The answer was simple. The prospect said, "You never asked me to buy until today."

Keep some selling points in reserve

Sometimes inexperienced salespeople describe and demonstrate all of the product's sales points before making the *first* closing attempt. This is a poor practice. If the closing attempt fails, there is little choice but to review the sales points already presented. One or two sales points kept in reserve can add strength and force to succeeding attempts to close.

Seldom do good duck hunters use all of their ammunition on the first flight of high-flying ducks. If they do they may find, to their disappointment, that succeeding flights offer better targets. However, with their ammunition gone, they have lost their best opportunities to bring home the limit. Salespeople may be compared to duck hunters. To close sales effectively, they keep some sales ammunition in reserve and use it when it is most likely to be effective. One sales manager says, "Hold at least one of the product's advantages in reserve, so that prospects will be pleasantly surprised when they find out about it."

Sell the right item in the right amounts

The chances to close the sale are enhanced when the right product is sold in appropriate quantities.

For example, the life insurance underwriter must be certain that a $50,000 ordinary life policy is what the buyer needs or wants before attempting to sell such a policy. The office equipment sales representative must be certain that two electronic calculators best fit the needs of the buyer's office work. The paper products salesperson selling to a retailer must know that a gross of pencils is more likely to fit the retailer's needs than are 12 gross. The chances to close a sale diminish rapidly when the salesperson is attempting to sell too many units or is trying to sell the wrong grade or style of product.

Salespeople are likely to sell the right product in the right amounts if their attitude is one of service. A large manufacturer of resistance welding machines and equipment, parts, and accessories looks out for its customers' interests by maintaining a production design staff. This staff analyzes the use a customer plans to make of the company's products. Recommendations are then made as to the right number and kinds of machines needed. Sometimes the analysis shows a need for fewer machines than the customer thought were needed. In one instance the company sold a $4,000 machine instead of fulfilling the customer's request for eight $2,000 machines to do exactly the same job.

While the first sale may be smaller if the right product is sold in the right amounts, repeat sales more than make up for a smaller order on the first sale.

EFFECTIVE METHODS AND TECHNIQUES

No method of closing will work if the buyer is not sold on the salesperson, the company, and the product. Closing sales should not require the use of tricky techniques or methods for forcing buyers to do something they do not want to do. Nor should it involve causing prospects to buy something they do not need.

The purpose of studying successful closing methods and techniques is to enable salespeople to *help prospects buy* a product or service for which they have a want or a need. The buyer may have a need or a want and still hesitate to buy a product, even though it will satisfy this want or need.

One of the salesperson's objectives is to help buyers overcome any fear they may have the product is not appropriate. For many types of selling, the salesperson must rely on qualifying techniques to determine the appropriateness of the product for the buyer.

Most sales require a sacrifice from buyers. They must sacrifice money for the advantages which the product or service provides. Making the decision to expend money for any one product may mean giving up other products. The buyer's sacrifice must be more than offset by the advantages that accrue from purchasing the particular product or service.

There is no one method or technique of closing which can be used successfully in all circumstances. The methods or techniques that should be used depend upon the product to be sold, the customer to be sold, and the circumstances of the sale.

Success in applying closing techniques and methods comes from practice. Knowledge alone is not enough. The following methods and techniques are frequently used to close sales successfully.

Assume the sale is made

When assuming that the sale is made, the salesperson is allowing the customer or prospect to follow the line of least resistance. Care should be taken not to create the impression that pressure is being exerted. As is true for all methods of closing, skill in the use of the method is just as important as a knowledge of the method.

The retail salesperson can use this method effectively. The customer may be considering the purchase of a suit. After the sales presentation has reached a point at which an attempt to close is appropriate, the salesperson may say, "Mr. Brown, slip on the trousers too. I will call our tailor to make any necessary alterations." If the customer does not object, the sale is probably closed.

Salespeople for one large distributor of silverware use this method. When the first close attempt is to be made, the prospect is asked this question, "Now, Ms. Smith, which of these four patterns would you choose to set your table?" The prospect usually picks one of the patterns as her choice.

The principles involved in giving the customer or prospect a choice has long been recognized. It is important to note that the choice is between two items or among several items. The choice is never between buying the product and not buying the product. The choice is merely *which one* of the products or units is preferred. The choice may be between ordering one dozen or two dozen, between buying a blue or a red shade, between model Z and model Y, or between the product alone and the product with some accessories. Whichever alternative the customer chooses, the result is an order.

The assumptive technique can be stated in question form. Give the customer a choice: "Would you like to start with 10 gross or 20?" "Would you prefer your order in bulk or packaged?" "Which of these displays do you prefer with your order?" "Would you prefer delivery on the 15th of this month or the 1st of next month?"

A leading manufacturer and distributor of copying machines instructs its sales representatives as follows: "Whenever you ask a closing question, *you must then remain silent!* Remember this always: *the first one to talk loses the advantage.*"[6] This company believes that no pressure that the sales representative can exert will remotely approach the pressure of silence.

In some fields of selling the salesperson inventories the customer's stock and prepares an order for the necessary fill-ins. The customer is then asked to approve the order by signing the order sheet. This practice is followed by some sales representatives of Arrow shirts, for example. In other fields of selling in which regular calls are made, the salesperson may ask for information and begin to fill out an order blank. Unless the prospect refuses to give the information, a sale is assumed. When calling on a regular customer, a good way to close the sale is by asking, "Shall I send this by mail, or do you want me to bring it on my next trip?" or "I'll ship this in the usual manner."

The actual close must represent a meeting of the buyer's and seller's minds. It should not be assumed that the sale has been made until the following conditions exist: the salesperson has a product that the prospect wants; the price is right for the prospect; the prospect believes that this is the time to buy; and the prospect desires to buy from the salesperson's company.

Build a series of acceptances

This method of closing is actually a buildup to the close. However, as has been stated, the close is not something apart and distinct from the presentation.

Prospects and customers find it difficult to refuse to buy if they agree that the product fulfills their need, that the salesperson and the company are reputable, that the value received is fair compared with the price asked, and that now is a good time to buy.

Some salespeople try to build up a series of yes answers as a basis for the close. For example, the manufacturer's representative

---

[6] *Sales Training Manual* (Xerox), p. VII-44.

who is attempting to sell a dealer on a line of products may ask such questions as these:

Salesperson: These advertisements will appear in *Fortune*, and 11 other magazines beginning November 1. They are attractive ads, aren't they?

Customer: *Yes*, they are very attractive.

Salesperson: These ads should help create store traffic for you, especially if you tie in with your local advertising, shouldn't they?

Customer: *Yes*, I suppose they will.

Salesperson: Here is a copy of our franchise. You will note that your percentage of markup is higher than that allowed by our competitors. You can use that extra markup, can't you?

Customer: *Yes*, I certainly can.

Salesperson: You won't need any additional fixtures to display these in your windows. They would make an attractive display by themselves, wouldn't they?

Customer: *Yes*, I imagine they would.

Salesperson: Your main interests are in a fair profit with a fast turnover. Isn't that true?

Customer: *Yes*, it is.

Salesperson: If I can show you how these products will turn fast on a small investment, you would be interested, wouldn't you?

Customer: *Yes*.

This method enables the buyer to make a series of easy decisions. The last decision in the series, of course, should be the buying decision.

Many times a "no" can be the equivalent of a "yes." Prospects who answer no may be committing themselves just as strongly as though they were saying yes. For example:

Salesperson: You want to purchase your equipment as economically as possible, don't you?

Customer: *Yes*.

Salesperson: You don't want to pay any more than you have to for good equipment, do you?

Customer: *No*.

The "yes" and the "no" are commitments. Each answer paves the way for further commitments.

Summarize the selling points

The method of closing by summarizing the main selling features of the product may be used when a buyer wants sound, logical reasons for making the purchase. It frequently is used with the method just described.

The greatest weight in the summary should be upon the selling features which have appealed most to the prospect's buying motives. If economy appears to be the buyer's dominant motive, the review should emphasize the product's economy features. Comfort and style should be stressed for the buyer who exhibits an interest in these product benefits.

When selling to the professional buyer or the purchasing agent, this method may be used to build up to the first closing attempt. The sales representative who sells lighting equipment may review the installation costs, the service and maintenance features, the effects of good light upon office operations, the appearance features, and other points which emphasize values to the buyer or to the company.

Whatever product is being sold, this method may be used to supply a brief, effective review of the product features which are of most interest to the buyer.

Get decisions on minor points

In some fields of selling, decisions on minor points or subordinate points are a good means to a close. Customers are willing to make minor decisions while they may hesitate to make major ones.

The prospect will usually not hesitate to make a choice of color, delivery date, credit terms, method of shipment, or size. However, some prospects may dislike making the actual decision to buy. Recognizing this, allow decisions on minor points to take the place of a major decision to buy.

The car salesperson may obtain a decision on the customer's preference for a two-door or four-door model; for a black or green color; for radio and heater accessories; for cash or credit terms; and for black or white sidewall tires. The insurance underwriter may have the prospect designate a beneficiary. The manufacturer's representative may have the buyer choose a method of shipment.

The important principle involved is to get decisions on minor points, and not require the customer to make a major decision. This method ties in closely with the "assume the sale is made" method.

Use the "what if . . ." or contingent method

A sales representative may say, "Mr. Prospect, if I can show you that our copiers will provide you with more accurate work performed at a higher rate of speed and at less cost than do the machines you are currently using, you will want to take advantage of the savings as quickly as possible, won't you?" Most buyers would readily agree that if these facts are proved they would be willing to buy.

Another approach may be: "You can see from my explanation that our company has a very attractive offer for the right retail store. I am not sure that I can secure an exclusive outlet for your store. However, *if it can be arranged,* shall I draw up the contract?" This close may be used to appeal to some buyers who frequently have difficulty in deciding.

People are inclined to want what they cannot have or what they are not sure they can get. These desires are human weaknesses. If a salesperson takes advantage of these weaknesses to the detriment of the buyers, sound selling practices are being violated. Such action will result in a loss of reputation and a loss of future sales.

Where the contingent method is based upon the existence of a true uncertainty, its use cannot be criticized. For example, insurance agents may qualify prospects to the best of their ability before filling out an application blank for an insurance policy. Later, if it appears that there is some doubt as to the applicant's eligibility for insurance, the agent may say: "The policy we have discussed is exactly what you need. However, there is some doubt that our company will issue the policy. Shall I make an appointment with our doctor for you at 10:00 A.M. tomorrow to see if you can qualify?"

Similar uncertainties may exist when unusual sizes, quantities, colors, or styles are the basis for the close. Sometimes price concessions or special discounts may be the basis for asking for the order.

Try the impending event

Some customers may hesitate to buy *now* unless they feel that a postponement will cause them to suffer a loss. This fear of a loss is a strong motivating force.

The alert salesperson can often close by referring to losses which the buyer may sustain because of some impending event. The life insurance agent frequently uses this method. For example, the annual premium which the prospect is to pay is determined by age. If the prospect's age changes in the near future, it can be pointed out that each $1,000 of insurance will carry a higher annual premium when the new age is reached. Therefore, it is to the prospect's advantage to buy *now.*

When the price trend is upward, sales may be closed by pointing out that price increases are contemplated. The retail store buyer may be particularly anxious to take advantage of an appreciation in inventory value. Some companies notify their sales representatives of price increases several weeks before the increases are to take effect. The chance to obtain now merchandise which will soon cost more is a strong motivating force.

The real estate salesperson often uses this method to sell building sites and homes. The impending event may be a probable rezoning of residential property to industrial property. It may be the possibility that a new school or a new park will be built in the area. It may be the fact that a new subdivision is being planned for an adjacent area. Sometimes the fact that a large national organization is planning to purchase property in an area, or that an urban redevelopment project is under way, will add value to the adjacent property.

Other impending events, such as changes in weather, changes in tax rates, or changes in models, may be of help in convincing the buyer that *now* is the time to buy. When trade-in values on old cars are on the way down, the prospect may lose money by waiting. The chances of an extra dividend or a stock split may make the purchase of stock a good buy *now*. Sometimes the fear of loss caused by waiting to buy causes prospects to purchase such products as roofing, hot-water heaters, refrigerators, and washing machines. The loss may be monetary; or it may be a loss in health, comfort, or convenience to the prospect or the prospect's family.

Obviously, salespeople must be sincere and honest in pointing out the potential losses. They must also be careful not to predict the future on matters which are extremely difficult or impossible to predict. The method is not intended for use as a means of exerting high pressure or as a trick method of closing.

Use the "SRO" method

The "standing room only" method is designed for use when products have sold rapidly and their supply is limited.

This method has proved to be particularly effective in retail selling, although its use is not limited to the retail field. It may be appropriate to use the method in the following situations: if an item is in heavy demand and only a few are left; if the item is a bargain and it cannot be reordered; if the item is a sample or floor model and the price is unusually attractive; or if the item is the last one in stock which will fit the customer.

In real estate selling, the last lot in a popular tract, or the last unsold home in a preferred residential section, or the last piece of property adjacent to a freeway, can be sold effectively through the use of the SRO method.

This method usually implies that the prospects must make up their minds in a hurry, and therefore it must be used with care. To many people, the necessity for a hurried decision is regarded as high pressure or is related to past experiences in which fraud was involved. The salespeople who use the SRO method should be certain of their facts and should give the buyer a reasonable amount of time to make a decision.

When the use of this method is considered desirable, the close may be phrased somewhat as follows: "This is the last piece of property in this area. You have indicated that it is just what you are looking for. Shall we make the necessary arrangements now so that you won't be disappointed?" Or, "This is the only sample we have left. You have agreed that it is an excellent buy. I'm sure it won't be here tomorrow. Shall we put it aside for you, or do you wish to have it sent out?"

Make a special offer

Caution should be exercised in using this method to close, for ~PROPOSAL~ there is a danger inherent in it. The danger lies in creating the impression that the first or second offer is not the best offer that will be made. Customers or prospects may feel that if they put off the purchase a little longer they may be able to get a better bargain. They may never feel sure when they have secured the best terms possible. It is only natural to feel that another customer may have secured better terms. In certain fields of selling, it is important that any concessions be made available to all competing distributors. The company's name and the salesperson's reputation are likely to suffer if it becomes apparent that a "one-price policy" is not being followed. The company may also be charged with price discrimination.

There are companies which promote the sale of their products by offering special inducements to all buyers who will buy on the first call. The inducement, which is often used in selling direct to household consumers, may be a free accessory; or a special price on a container in which to store the product sold; or an extra unit if a certain number of units are purchased. Such inducements are usually offered in an attempt to close the sale immediately. They are usually a part of the regular or standard presentation, and they are offered to each prospect or customer who is contacted.

Other companies offer special introductory terms or special advertising tie-in propositions to help get their dealers to buy in greater volume or in greater variety. The "something extra" or "something-for-nothing" idea is still a strong factor in closing sales.

Try a trial order

As a last resort, or to sell products that are not well known, attempts to close are made by encouraging the prospect or customer to order a small number of units on a tryout basis. If the products are found to be useful, or if their resale is profitable, large orders are to be expected. If for any reason the products prove to be unsatisfactory, the buyer has been subjected to little risk.

Some salespeople are convinced that sales will result if the prospect will only give the product a trial. Trial orders may be helpful in getting a product to be accepted, especially if the product is new.

Certain types of office and industrial equipment are sold on this basis. A unit is installed in the prospect's store or plant and is given a thorough testing under actual working conditions. The trial may be for a few days or a few weeks. At the end of the trial attempts are made to close the sale for one or more machines.

The trial order close is particularly effective when the offer involves no possibility of loss for the buyer. The method may be weak in selling to retailers or wholesalers, because the lack of much investment by the buyer may eliminate the need to promote or push the product. There may be a tendency for the product to receive little or no attention, and therefore its real value may not be determined.

Use the two-person close and the "TO"

Some companies follow the practice of having two people "team up" in an attempt to get the order. This method is effective when help is needed from some member of the company's technical staff. The salesperson and the staff member call on the buyer, and they both participate in the sales presentation. If the buyer has a special problem which can be solved by the staff member, this method may bring results. On the other hand, if the two-person team conveys the impression that its objective is to use pressure, the buyer will be resentful and will resist its efforts. It may be appropriate to use this method when the buyer is considering a large purchase, when the sale is of vital importance to the company, or when the salesperson is confronted with a technical problem which can be handled best by a home-office expert.

In retail selling, some stores encourage their salespeople to "turn over" the customer to another person if the close fails. The customer who cannot be sold by one salesperson and is turned over to the second is called a "TO." The timing of the turnover is important if it is not to offend the customer. Salespeople cannot wait until customers are about to leave the store. They may turn over the customer when they have made a reasonable effort to sell or when they determine that a clash of personalities exists. The introduction may be as follows: "This is Mr. Jones. He is more familiar with the new stock than I am, and I am sure he can find just what you want." Or, "This is Ms. Smith. She has been especially trained to solve problems such as yours." This method must be used skillfully so that the customer is not offended in any way.

METHODS USED BY MAJOR COMPANIES

The following illustrations show the methods and techniques used by typical companies to close sales. Examples are provided in the direct selling of tangible and intangible products and in industrial and trade selling.

Wear-Ever Aluminum, Inc.—Household Products

Wear-Ever Aluminum, Inc., a subsidiary of Aluminum Company of America, trains its direct sales representatives to use minor points as the basis for closing the sale. The company provides a standard close which is to be learned word for word. This standard close, used as the first close attempt, emphasizes the special discount available to prospects who buy on the first call. The cost is broken down into two payments, and the customer is given a choice of the amount of the first payment and a choice of delivery dates.

Two additional closes are provided. These closes include the use of testimonial letters and additional choices on minor points. Some suggested minor points on which to close are as follows:

"Would you want to handle your payment tonight by check or cash?"

"Would you want the same set as Mrs. Jones got, or would you prefer one like Mrs. Johnson's?"

"Which bonus or hostess premium would you prefer? Would you want the small pan or the broiler?"

"How do you sign your name? Is that J. F. or John F?"[7]

The company emphasizes this statement: "Never close on a major point. *Always* use a minor point to write up the order. Always give a choice between something and something."[8]

Life Insurance Agency Management Association—Insurance

The Life Insurance Agency Management Association recommends five standard closes for insurance agents who present a plan of insurance based upon savings of five dollars a week or more. These closes can be adapted or changed to fit any type of policy presentation.

The agent is reminded to try for the close five times by remembering that each letter of the word *close* represents a closing method.

---

[7] *How to Close Sales* (Chillicothe, Ohio: Wear-Ever Division, Aluminum Cooking Utensil Co. of America), pp. 7–8. (Now Wear-Ever Aluminum, Inc.)

[8] Ibid., p. 7.

C —stands for "choice"
L —stands for "lossproof"
O —stands for "obligations"
S —stands for "seek hidden objection"
E —stands for "example or examination"

Two of these methods are reproduced in the following paragraphs. The first illustration seeks to uncover a hidden objection.

"Mr. Prospect, you have told me—

1. That you can, and want to, save five dollars a week;
2. That this is the kind of savings plan you want;
3. That you know of no other savings plan so good.

"Yet you hesitate to go ahead with this. Won't you tell me frankly why?

(If an underlying objection is uncovered at this point, it must be answered, and answered fully, to the prospect's satisfaction. When that has been done, continue.)

"That answers your objection fully, doesn't it, Mr. Prospect? I presume you would want to have the proceeds payable to your wife, in the event that you do not live to 65. What is her full name, Mr. Prospect?"[9]

The second illustration is based upon the assumption that the prospect is having difficulty in making a decision. It also implies that the prospect may be unable to qualify for the policy. It is a method which makes it easy for the prospect to say yes.

"Mr. Prospect, you and I have been carrying on this discussion on the assumption that only one decision is involved, namely your own. However, there are in fact two decisions to be made—yours, and the company's.

"This company's decision rests upon your financial, moral, and physical status. You can well understand my company is vitally interested in your *physical* condition when you stop to consider that it has $_____ at risk on your life. This means that my company is able to make this plan available only to those who are in better-than-average physical condition.

"Now, if you make your decision first, the company's decision remains to be made, and therefore its decision, and not yours, is the final one.

"But since you are undecided on this matter, wouldn't it be a good idea to let the company go ahead and make its decision first? . . . And then *you* will have the last word. We can have the doctor check you over, and if the company sees fit to issue the policy, you can go over it and see that it is as I have represented it in every detail, and *then* you can make your decision at a time when *your* decision will be the final one.

---

[9] Adapted from *The Chassis Plan* (Hartford, Conn.: Life Insurance Agency Management Association), p. 46.

"Which would be better for you—to see the doctor at the office, or to see if we can arrange to have the doctor stop by your home while in your neighborhood?"[10]

Westinghouse Electric Corporation—Industrial products

Westinghouse Electric Corporation trains its sales representatives to close sales to industrial users first by recognizing that sales are *not* closed by using tricky and clever tactics on the prospect at the end of the sales presentation and then by realizing that there is a sound, logical closing procedure which is effective. The company suggests:

1. *"Touch each base."* (Present *all* the good reasons why the product is a good buy.)
2. "Make sure each base you touch . . . is a *benefit base!"* (Convert each product sales point into a buyer benefit before going to the next sales point.)
3. "Ask for the order when you *'head for home'!"* (After a good presentation, ask for the order, not once, but often. It is ineffective to just hint, hope, or plead—the order must be asked for.)
4. "See enough people!" (All people who influence the purchase may have to be contacted—the purchasing agent, technical staff, and sometimes top management.)[11]

In summary, the company believes: "If you do these four simple, basic things you needn't worry about tricks and tactics. You will win orders . . . because you have earned orders."[12]

The Gillette Company, Paper Mate Division—Writing pens

Paper Mate suggests five closing techniques that can be used successfully by its sales representatives.[13] It suggests that the close should be the easiest part of the sale if the interview is handled correctly. Sales representatives are instructed to master the following techniques when selling to the trade:

Assume the sale.   "How many dozen would you like to start with?" Or, "Do you prefer the X or Y deal?"

Benefit close.   A simple summary of benefits. "Jane, in summary it seems that your people are using too many pens because . . ."

---

[10] Ibid., pp. 48–49.

[11] *Increase Your Selling Skill* (Pittsburgh: Westinghouse Electric Corp.), sec. 2, pp. 4–14.

[12] Ibid., p. 15.

[13] "Closing Techniques," *Personal Progress through Skill Development* (Boston: The Gillette Company, Paper Mate Division), course 8.

Comparison close.   This allows the prospect to compare your product's benefits with the benefits of a competitor's product. Paper Mate benefits are written in one column, and competitor benefits are written in an adjoining column, "balance sheet" style. A clear visual comparison is then possible. The prospect is then asked which side weighs more.

Ask his or her opinion.   This is an attempt to find out whether or not the prospect wants the benefits of your product. "Ms. Prospect, we've discussed the benefits you can expect from buying this product [*then summarize them*]. In your opinion, are these benefits really important to you?" Then keep quiet until an answer is given. Silence is important here!

Standing room only.   This should be a low-key approach, so that the prospect is not scared or offended by what may seem to be too much pressure. "During the next two weeks you will have the opportunity of taking advantage of our '2 free with 12' promotion. After that point we will return to our normal deal."

General Telephone & Electronics—Communications

This company believes that closing the sale is highly contingent upon the sales representative's ability to recognize when the prospect is ready to accept the recommendations and buy the service.

The following guidelines have been developed to evaluate the close step:

Ask for the sale.   Use the direct approach. If the presentation has been thorough up to this point, it is logical to ask for the order.

Demonstrate reasonable persistence.   A lack of reasonable persistence indicates to the customer that the sales representative is not enthusiastically convinced that the recommendation is sound. However, a degree of sensitivity to customer reactions is necessary if there is still a lack of understanding.

Recognize, uncover, and answer objections.   The true objections must be uncovered before an agreement can be reached. Thorough preparation and usage prospecting with well-thought-out and well-planned recommendations reduce objections which are difficult to overcome.

Timing and well-chosen words and a summary of parts of the recommendation (selling benefits) are essential in closing the sale.   When the sales representative has acquired customer agreement, it is advisable for him or her to *stop selling*.[14]

These guidelines illustrate a type of low-key closing.

----

[14] Adapted from *GTE Practices, Marketing Administrative Series* (Stamford, Conn.: GTE Service Corporation).

HANDLING CLOSING ROUTINES _____

The closing routines involve getting the signature of the buyer on the order blank, as well as performing those activities which are necessary to terminate the interview satisfactorily.

Getting the signature _____

The signing of the order should be a natural part of well-planned procedure. The order blank should be accessible, and the signing should appear to be a routine matter. Ordinarily, the customer has decided to buy before being asked to sign the order blank. In other words, the signature on the order blank is merely the confirmation of an agreement which has already been reached. The decision to buy or not to buy should not be focused on the writing of the signature. If the close has been conducted properly, the actual signing of the order is not difficult to secure. On the other hand, if the prospect has not decided to buy prior to the attempt to secure the signature, there is little chance that the prospect will sign the order.

It is unwise to ask the buyer to "sign the contract." That is, the suggestion of signing a contract may cause some buyers to feel that they are making a very important decision. If the product has already been sold, this may give the buyer an opportunity to hesitate or to reconsider. The salesperson may say, "Just write your name here the way it appears above," or "While you are writing your name on the line marked by an X, I will be getting together some literature you can use," or "If you will sign right here, I will see that your order is sent by airmail this afternoon."

The important points to remember are: make the actual signing an easy, routine procedure; fill out the order blank accurately and promptly; and be careful not to exhibit any eagerness or excitement when the prospect is about to sign.

Confirm customer's choice _____

In most fields of selling, the close is not considered to be the end of a business transaction. A successful close is merely the beginning of a mutually profitable business relationship. A sale is considered to be closed successfully if it results in repeat sales.

Customers like to feel that they have made a wise choice when they decide to buy. They like salespeople who do not lose interest immediately after the order has been signed. Many customers are not always satisfied in their own minds that their decision to buy has been wise.

Experienced salespeople reassure customers that their choice of products or services has been judicious. They may say, "I know you will enjoy using our office machines. You can plan on many months of trouble-free service. I'll call on you in about two weeks to make sure everything is operating smoothly. Be sure to call me if you need any help before then." Or, "Congratulations, Mr. Jacobs; you are going to be glad you decided to use our service. There is no finer service available. Now let's make certain you get off to the right start. Your first bulletin will arrive Tuesday, March 2." Such remarks as the following may also be appropriate: "You've made an excellent choice. Other stores won't have a product like this for at least 30 days." "This is an excellent model you've chosen. Did you see it advertised in last week's *Time?*" "Your mechanics will thank you for ordering these tools. You will be able to get your work out much faster."

It is important to remember that sales must not only be closed but must *stay* closed. One good way to keep customers from changing their minds and canceling the order or returning the merchandise is to assure them that they have made an intelligent choice.

Show appreciation

All buyers like to feel that their business is appreciated, and this is especially true of the buyers of small quantities. Customers like to do business with salespeople who give evidence that they want the business.

Appreciation may be shown by writing the purchaser a letter. This is good practice, and it develops goodwill when the purchase is large or when it represents the first sale to a new customer. Never forget to thank the purchaser personally. This thanks should be genuine but not effusive.

Cultivate for future calls

If salespeople are to be welcomed on repeat calls they must be considerate of all the parties involved in the buying or using of the product. They learn to pronounce and spell all names correctly; make certain that the buyer or user gets the service which has been promised; make sure to explain and to review the terms of the purchase so that there can be no misunderstandings; and are sociable and cordial to subordinates, as well as to the individual who holds the key position currently.

If the prospect doesn't buy now

In many fields of selling, the great majority of prospects do not buy. The ratio of sales to sales presentations may be 1 to 3, 1 to 5, 1 to 10, or even 1 to 20. There may be a tendency to eliminate the non-buyers from the prospect list after one unsuccessful call. In some cases this may be sound practice. However, many sales are closed on the second, third, fourth, or fifth calls. It is important to prepare for succeeding calls when an order is not secured on an earlier visit.

When a close has failed, regardless of the reason for the failure, take defeat good-naturedly. Be a good loser if you expect to be able to call again. It is good practice to thank prospects for their time. Nothing is gained by engaging in an argument or by showing disappointment.

The salesperson may plan to keep in contact with unsold prospects or customers. This may be accomplished through an occasional telephone call, or through a follow up letter, or by mailing some product literature. In addition, an attempt should be made to analyze the causes for failures to close.

Terminating the interview

Few buyers are interested in a prolonged visit after a sale is closed. Obviously, the departure cannot be abrupt. Take whatever time is necessary to complete the interview smoothly. On the other hand, goodwill is not built by wasting the buyer's time after all business has been consummated. Also, there is a risk that buyers may change their minds if salespeople prolong their visits unnecessarily.

QUESTIONS AND PROBLEMS

1. The most successful salespeople are those who close sales long after they've heard the first, second, and even the third "no." Comment on this statement.

2. Analyze the following statement: "You know that when the prospect says no, he or she is saying no to your proposal—he or she is not rejecting you personally." Why is the understanding of this statement vital to sales representatives?

3. "Next to making the sale, the most important thing to accomplish on a sales call is to *leave the door open*. Seldom is a sale made on a single call. That means we have to come back again and again with more of our story. We should leave a sales call with an imaginary welcome

mat, with our name on it, on the prospect's threshold—and put there by the client."

These are the instructions given to sales representatives by Norelco, manufacturer of a wide variety of office machines.

Evaluate the statements, and indicate how you might "leave the door open."

4. Among the more effective ways to close the sale after an appropriate presentation are (a) to give the prospect a choice between cash and terms or between a large package and small package; (b) to complete the order by beginning to write out the sales ticket and by asking the prospect for the correct initials, name, and address; (c) to prewrite the order and hand the written order to the prospect and ask for approval or an OK; and (d) to concentrate on one main feature and ask the prospect for the order directly.

   If these attempts to close have failed, list at least four contingencies which may motivate the prospect to buy now.

5. If a buyer seems to be wavering, can't make a decision, perhaps help is needed. Suppose you approach the close this way:

   Prospect: I don't think I'm ready to buy now.

   Salesperson: Mr. Smith, you're probably as ready now as you'll ever be. If you need any features clarified, I'll be glad to give you the answers. Otherwise, let's get this thing over with.

   Or, try this approach:

   Prospect: Your company is a little steep in price.

   Salesperson: Oh, if that's all that's bothering you, you can just sign right here. There is no company that can beat our price.

   Evaluate the two approaches. Would you use them? When? Why?

6. Draw an analogy between the activities of a salesperson during the close and a base runner in baseball; between the closing activities of a salesperson and a fisherman.

7. One successful salesperson assumes an attitude of indifference toward whether or not the prospect buys. Do you believe this indifferent attitude is helpful in closing sales? Why? What are the dangers inherent in giving an impression of indifference?

8. Assume that you are planning to earn extra income while attending school by selling automatic washing machines directly to the household consumer. You are to represent a local appliance dealer, and you are to be paid on a commission basis. The appliance dealer requests that you prepare six different closing routines. You are to use your own judgment on the application of each close and on the number of routines to use on any one prospect. What statements do you feel would be appropriate when you ask for the order?

9. A sales representative for a manufacturer of industrial machinery believes that the best way to get an order is to keep in mind constantly

that the order is the goal to be attained. Keep your order book very much in evidence when making a sales presentation, and concentrate on timing the request for a signature "on the dotted line." If the order is asked for at the right moment, the prospect will sign the order blank. Is this good selling? What are the strengths or weaknesses of consistently concentrating on getting the prospect's signature?

10. The following close was used by a new salesperson in an attempt to sell the buyer for a group of stationery stores:

"Joe, our pen is the number 1 pen in the writing instrument field. With our display and advertising allowances you can't go wrong.

"Can we place an order?"

Comment on this close attempt.

11. You are selling copier/duplicators to businessmen and businesswomen in your community for use in their offices. After making a presentation which you think was rather well done, you request the order and get this reply: "What you say sounds interesting, but I want some time to think it over. I'm sure we'll probably go along with you, but I do need some time to think about it."

Your answer to the statement is, "Well, OK. Would next Tuesday be a good day for me to come back?"

Can you improve on this answer? How?

12. The Life Insurance Agency Management Association makes this suggestion for use as a final appeal to get the customer to buy now:

Suppose that I walked into your office this morning and said to you, "Mr. Prospect, I have here a 12-pound package of the finest cork which the world affords, done up in a strong linen container. Notice the fine, even grain. Notice the strength. Sir, this is 12 pounds of the finest Portugal cork that money can buy. It will cost you just ten cents a pound. Wouldn't you like to buy it?"

If I did that, you undoubtedly would say, "What in blazes would I do with 12 pounds of cork?"

And of course you would be certain that you had no use for that cork. But now let us say that you were on the wings of a sinking plane, and I came along and offered to sell you this cork—would you want it then?

Certainly you would. *The trouble is, if you were in such a fix, I would not be there to sell you the cork.*

There is a fundamental similarity between life preservers of the kind they carry on planes and financial life preservers such as this savings plan—and that is that *each must be secured before it is needed.* When the need is desperate, the time is too late.

Let's arrange for your financial life preserver while you are still able to get it!

What do you think of this "cork story" as a final appeal to use in attempting to close a sale? Would you use it? Why?

13. Suppose that you are selling a chain saw in your hardware store to an interested prospect. You are nearing the end of your presentation when the prospect says, "Your saw is fine, and I'd like to buy one, but I don't want to put it on an account unless I can pay for it in 60 days without any carrying charges." Company policy prevents you from giving these terms. What would you say?

14. You are selling a built-in dishwasher to a prospect in your store. The prospect asks, "How soon do you think you could install?" You give the answer, and the prospect says, "What guarantee period do I get?" You answer, "One full year, parts and labor included." Can you think of a better answer than the one given?

15. Do you believe that a trial close is helpful to salespeople, even if it fails? Would you recommend that they wait until they are positive that the customer is ready to make a decision before attempting a close? Why?

PROJECTS

1. Prepare a one-page article on "The Importance of Body Language in Closing Sales."

2. Prepare a scenario for selling tickets to a college or university activity. Include a series of alternative or optional closing routines. Follow the scenario by actually soliciting orders. Write up your conclusions.

3. Visit a number of automobile showrooms. Describe the attempts that are made to sell you a car. Evaluate any closing attempts, and summarize your conclusions.

4. Interview a purchasing agent, and ask for his/her evaluation of the closing routines used by sales representatives.

CASE PROBLEMS

Case 11-1

Economy Cleaning Machinery

Economy Cleaning Machinery has developed a process that will reuse cleaning fluid. This process will enable Economy to market a coin-operated automatic dry-cleaning machine which will clean an eight-pound load of clothing (equal to two dresses, two shirts, and two children's snowsuits) in 45 minutes at a cost of $6.

Economy will have at least four competitors. One competitor is launching a national sales program with a salesforce of 125. The company will offer a complete building which houses up to six machines. The machine sells for $6,600. Construction of the building will cost approximately $20,000, and a typical complete installation, including six dry cleaners, will cost about $75,000. The company has also constructed a specially built mobile demonstration trailer for use by sales representatives when selling to professional dry cleaners. This company will probably offer the stiffest competition.

Economy has been operating six attended centers as a pilot operation. The cleaners are built in banks of eight, costing $40,000, with a common system for recirculating and filtering the cleaning fluid. Plans call for concentrating on selling to present dry cleaners, partly because they already understand the cleaning process and partly to make them allies rather than enemies.

A typical installation for Economy will have 16 dry-cleaning machines, 25 to 30 washers, 10 to 15 dryers, and a pickup station for dry-cleaning work done at the cleaner's main plant on items not suitable for the machines. The company does not believe in either unattended centers or one- or two-unit installations. All operators are required to have a "consultant" on hand during operating hours. The centers will represent an investment of $100,000 to $200,000.

Over 300 distributor sales representatives and four factory field representatives for each section of the country have been appointed to assist in all phases of the selling activities. An advertising schedule has been planned through *The Wall Street Journal, Barron's,* and the *Journal of Commerce.* Ad mats are provided for advertising at the local level. In addition, trade publication advertising has been pointed to the commercial dry-cleaning industry.

Economy will also provide the owner of a center with floor plans and ad mats, design promotion campaigns on a cooperative basis, and other sales aids, and will arrange for a five-year, easy-term plan with a down payment of 10 percent for financing the center.

Steve Wright, a distributor for Economy, is working in a large midwestern city. He has had thorough training on the merits of his company's product and has had the opportunity to participate in demonstrations of the dry-cleaning machine at state and county fairs. He is completely sold on the "center" idea of merchandising his company's products.

Wright has been able to secure the interest of an owner of a dry-cleaning plant and has had several visits with him. Recently, Wright had one of the factory field men accompany him on an interview with the owner.

Questions

1. To what buying motives should Wright appeal in an attempt to close the sale to the owner of the dry-cleaning plant? Why?
2. List the objections which Wright is likely to encounter.
3. Discuss the techniques which Wright might use to close the sale.
4. Prepare one or more closing routines which may be effective.

Case 11-2

Cozy Duplicators

Linda Lean is a part owner of Cozy Duplicators. She spends a good portion of her time contacting industrial offices in the area. In addition to the duplicators she sells filing systems, paper, office supplies, and other office products.

Customarily Linda telephones the office manager or the purchasing agent of an industrial firm and attempts to arrange for an interview. She has been quite successful in getting before the appropriate buyers.

After the sales interview has been completed, she asks for an order. Recently she has found that competition has become heavier and that buyers are less willing to place orders on the first call. This especially is true for the complex and competitive copier/duplicator marketplace.

Linda has been following the structure of a good close by assuming that the sale has been made, summarizing the benefits which are important to the particular customer, and then requesting the order. She has concluded that in selling copiers/duplicators a different type of close will be necessary.

Questions

1. In place of or in addition to asking for the order on the first call, what other types of closing or alternatives might be appropriate?
2. What conditions will determine the options to use?

Case 11-3

Fresh Aire, Inc.

For the past two years Fresh Aire Inc. has been promoting the sale of air-conditioning units for use in homes, offices, and stores. The air-conditioning unit is made by a nationally known manufacturer, and it is considered to be one of the best of the premium-quality units on the market. The company's outside sales representatives have attended the factory school maintained by the manufacturer and are well qualified both to service and to sell the unit.

Pat Fraser, one of Fresh Aire's sales representatives, has developed a portfolio to use when presenting sales talks to prospects. The portfolio contains pictures of the unit, testimonial letters from satisfied users, technical data on the construction of the unit, and data on cost and maintenance. The portfolio has been helpful in keeping presentations brief and to the point, and at the same time it has enabled Pat to give a complete sales presentation.

Fraser recently learned that the owner of a women's specialty shop, Ms. Diderot, was considering the installation of air-conditioning equipment. Fraser gathered as much information as possible on the owner and then made a cold call upon Ms. Diderot. Fraser made little progress on the first call but was able to arrange for a second appointment at a more favorable time and under more favorable conditions. On the second call, after 45 minutes of the interview, Fraser felt that it was time to try for a close, and a portion of the conversation that ensued follows:

Fraser: This clean-cut design and this handsome gray finish certainly blends with your office furnishings, doesn't it, Ms. Diderot?

Ms. Diderot: Yes, it does seem to harmonize with what we have.

Fraser: Not only does it harmonize with your furnishings, Ms. Diderot, but it cools, cleans, and humidifies the air. It will bring in outside air if you wish, provide you with even circulation of air, and all this can be accomplished by the flip of a switch. Best of all, Ms. Diderot, the unit has a very simple mechanism. You'll want good, dependable performance and economy in operation, I suppose.

Ms. Diderot: Why, sure, who doesn't? I want something I can depend upon.

Fraser: Well, I'm sure this unit is just what you want. When would you like to get the installation under way?

Ms. Diderot: Well, I don't feel that I should air-condition my store just now.

Fraser: Ms. Diderot, I know that when you decide to air-condition your store you'll want our unit. The real question, then, is whether to install the system now or at a later date. Is that right?

Ms. Diderot: I suppose so.

Fraser: Now, let's look over the facts and see if we can determine the answer to the question on *when* to make the installation. Let's do this . . .

Suppose we draw a line down the center of this piece of paper and make two columns. We'll head the first column "Reasons for Buying Now," and we'll head the second column "Reasons for Buying Later."

In the second column, let's write all of your reasons for installing later on, and in the first column, let's write all the reasons why it will help your business to install now. Then you can compare the reasons in the two columns and be pretty sure you are making the right decision. How does that sound?

Ms. Diderot: Oh, I don't know. I guess it can't hurt anything. OK.

(Fraser allows Ms. Diderot to state her reasons for installing later, and they are written in column two. Then Fraser completes a much longer list of reasons for acting now and places them in the first column.)

Fraser: We seem to agree that there are many more reasons for you to install now than to wait, Ms. Diderot. When do you feel it would be most convenient for you to have the installation made?

Ms. Diderot: Oh, I don't know. I'm not sure.

Questions

1. Identify the closing techniques used by Fraser. Evaluate the use of the techniques.

2. What additional closing techniques could be used by Fraser? Illustrate the use of each technique by preparing statements incorporating the use of the techniques.

3. Make a list of statements classifiable as closing signals which Ms. Diderot could have made during the interview.

4. Complete the above interview in a manner which you feel would be realistic.

SELECTED REFERENCES

Brown, Steve.   "When to Close." *California Real Estate*, November 1979, pp. 26–30.

"Closing the Sale."   *Sales & Marketing Management*, 1977. A special 20-page report of ten articles by different authors.

Connolly, Robert.   "Courage and Audacity: Keys to Closing Sales." *Marketing Times*, March–April 1973, pp. 24–26.

Cronin, Lawrence D.   "Help Prospects to Do What They Want to Do." *NYLIC Review*, January 1977, pp. 8–9.

Dichter, Ernest.   "Five Ways to Lose a Sale." *Industrial Distribution*, January 1976, p. 83.

Goldmann, Heinz.   "The Art of Selling." *Management Today*, September 1977, p. 139.

Hass, Kenneth B.   "Listen More to Sell More." *Marketing Times*, July–August 1973, pp. 24–25.

"The Ingredients and Timing of the Perfect Close."   *Sales Management*, June 1, 1971, pp. 30–35.

Kahn, George N.   "Nosing Your Way into Extra Sales." *Marketing Times*, September–October 1974, pp. 20–21.

"The Management of Sales Training."   *National Society of Sales Training Executives*. Reading, Mass.: Addison-Wesley, 1977.

Meisel, Don.   "Add Salespower! Ask Questions." *Industrial Distribution*, November 1976, p. 64.

Roth, O. B.   "Secrets of Closing Sales." Englewood Cliffs, N.J.: Prentice-Hall, 1970.

Scanlon, Sally.   "Every Salesperson a Psychologist." *Sales & Marketing Management*, February 6, 1978, pp. 34–36.

Trytten, J.   "Salesmanship: 10 Steps for Boosting Your Sales Right Now." (Sales Builders Division) *Sales & Marketing Management*, 1975.

Wilson, John M.   *Open the Mind and Close the Sale.* New York: McGraw-Hill, 1953.

Yoho, David.   "13 Steps in Closing Sales." *Marketing Times*, September–October 1973, pp. 21–24.

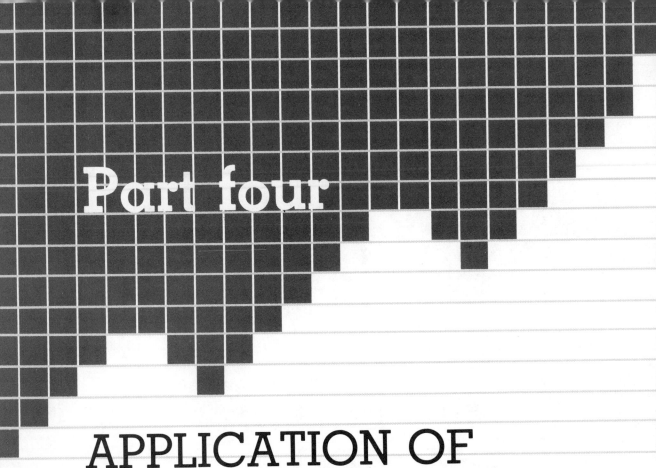

Part four

APPLICATION OF SALES PRINCIPLES, PRACTICES, AND TECHNIQUES

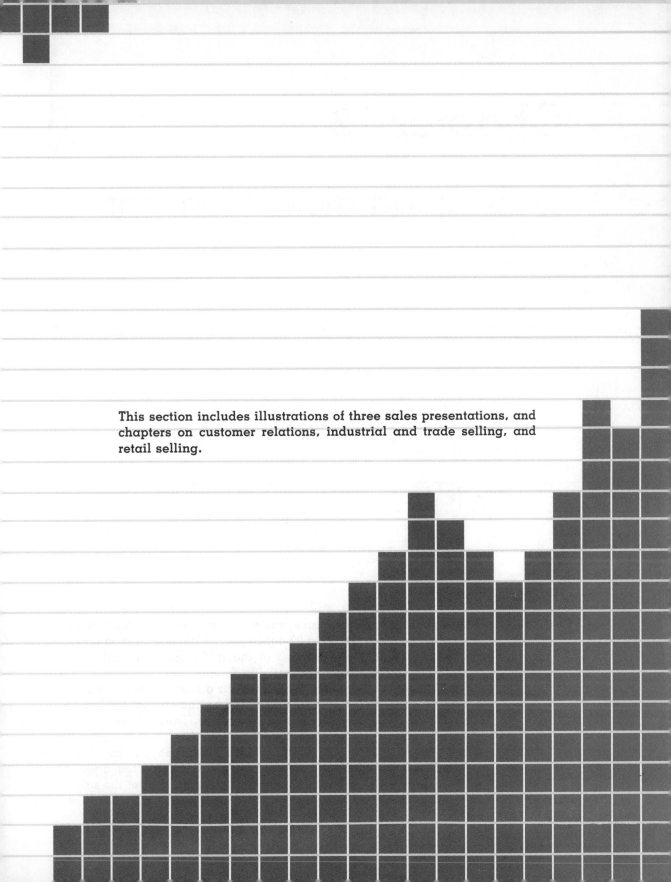

This section includes illustrations of three sales presentations, and chapters on customer relations, industrial and trade selling, and retail selling.

Chapter 12

SALES PRESENTATIONS ILLUSTRATED

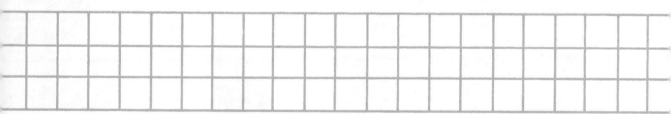

This chapter includes three sales presentations: (1) Carnation Company's presentation of a 22-ounce jar of *Coffee-mate* non-dairy creamer, (2) an IBM presentation of the IBM Copier III, and (3) a presentation of the Lawson Advertising Agency.

The 22-ounce *Coffee-mate* presentation is a presentation in which the salesperson uses a brochure provided by the company. Carnation sales representatives sell to grocery stores. Thus, the sales presentation is based on improving store profitability.

The presentation of the IBM Copier III illustrates the use of an outlined sales presentation made in reply to an inquiry from a prospective customer. This outlined presentation is made after the sales representative has had an opportunity to study the specific needs of the interested customer and to learn what copier equipment the customer has.

The third presentation is a program presentation that the Lawson Advertising Agency has prepared for a particular potential client. This presentation uses charts which provide flexibility so that the presentation can be given to one individual or to a group of people.

CARNATION-22-OUNCE *COFFEE-MATE* PRESENTATION[1]

Introduction

Carnation Company is one of the largest manufacturing and marketing companies in the food industry. Beginning as an evaporated milk company in 1899, Carnation has diversified into many areas of the food industry, including pet foods, canned tomato products, instant products, dehydrated and frozen potatoes, fresh milk, ice cream, and entrée items. *Coffee-mate* non-dairy creamer is included in the family of Carnation instant products, along with such products as *Carnation* Instant Breakfast, *Carnation* Instant Milk, *Carnation* Hot Cocoa, *Carnation* Breakfast Bars, and *Slender* diet foods.

Each Carnation sales representative is assigned a geographic territory. The representative is responsible for selling all Carnation products to supermarkets and wholesalers (jobbers and distributors) in the territory. An important duty of the representative is to get all the grocery stores in the territory to stock new Carnation products. This is a difficult task because shelf space is limited. Large supermarkets can carry only 2,000 to 8,000 of the 50,000 food and nonfood products offered to them by manufacturers like Carnation. Thus, for every new product stocked, the store must discontinue stocking a product.

A few years ago Carnation Company introduced a 22-ounce size of *Coffee-mate* non-dairy creamer. The product was introduced as an extension of the *Coffee-mate* line, joining the 3-, 6-, 11-, and 16-ounce sizes. It was marketed as the most economical size for the heavy user of powdered creamers. The following presentation is an example of a typical new-product sales call.

Background for the sales call

Blair Markets is an independent grocery chain with four stores in Chicago. The chain has been in operation for ten years and has

---

[1] Mary Fishburn, an assistant brand manager, and Jim Heerwagen, director of sales training, at Carnation assisted in preparing this example of a sales call.

developed a loyal, upper middle-class clientele. Blair is planning to open a fifth store in two months.

The head buyer for Blair is Bill Hansen. He is responsible for determining what items to stock, merchandising the space devoted to each product on the supermarket shelf, and conducting promotions. Hansen devotes one day a week to seeing salespeople from the food and specialty goods manufacturers who want to sell their products, promotions, and merchandising ideas to the Blair markets. Jim Jackson has worked for Carnation for one year. He has been calling on Bill Hansen for the past four months. Considering his short tenure on the account, he is pleased with the progress that he has made in selling Carnation's products at Blair. He has developed a good relationship with Bill Hansen. One key to Jim's success on this account has been his ability to provide information about the grocery business. Bill Hansen needs this information but is too busy to search it out himself.

Planning the sales presentation

Jim wants to present Carnation's new promotion on the 22-ounce *Coffee-mate* to Bill. Using this promotion, Jim hopes to accomplish the following objectives:

1. Get the 22-ounce *Coffee-mate* on the shelf in all the Blair markets.
2. Increase the total shelf space that Blair allocates to its coffee creamer section (in which *Coffee-mate* resides).
3. Get a better position for *Coffee-mate* within the coffee creamer section.

Blair currently carries four *Coffee-mate* sizes (3, 6, 11, and 16 ounces). Bill rejected the new 22-ounce size when it was presented five months ago by Jim's predecessor. At that time, he said that he didn't have room for another product in the creamer section. In preparation for his call on Bill, Jim reviewed the details of the new *Coffee-mate* promotion, drew diagrams of Blair's present coffee creamer display section and his proposed reorganization, and pulled together some industry data on coffee creamers. After planning his presentation, Jim made an appointment to see Bill early on Thursday morning. Blair's buyers see vendors only on Thursday from 9:00 A.M. to 3:00 P.M.

The opening

Jim begins his conversations with Bill by discussing an area of the grocery business that allows him to pay Bill an honest compliment and also bring up the purpose of the call. This time he chatted about the new Blair Market that would be opening soon. Then he made an easy transition to *Coffee-mate*.

Jim: Hi, Bill. How are you?

Bill: I'm fine, Jim. Busier than ever, though *(looking at his watch)*.

Jim: I can imagine—especially with all the details of finishing up the new store. I took my boss out to the new location yesterday to show him the site. He was quite impressed.

Bill: Thanks. That store will be a beauty. But like you said, there's still a lot of work left to do. What do you have for me today?

Jim: I want to talk about both our new promotion on the 22-ounce *Coffee-mate* and the overall merchandising of your coffee creamer section. Since you'll be reviewing all your current merchandising diagrams for the new store, I thought this would be a good time to make some suggestions.

Bill: There isn't much more we can do with the creamer section. We've always done as well as can be expected with creamers. I see no reason to change now. Like I told the Carnation sales rep before you, the creamer section is packed. Everything there now is moving OK.

Jim: Well, I've read some interesting material lately about the section that I knew you'd want to hear. In fact, I've got a couple of questions for you—call it a quiz. And I bet you'll be surprised by the answers.

Bill: OK.

Jim: How would you compare coffee to creamers in terms of profit?

Bill: We sell about 20 times more coffee than creamers. So I'd say coffee's about 20 times more profitable.

Jim: That's what most people think. Actually, an independent research agency has found that coffee sales are about 19 times greater than creamer sales. But the profit margin on creamers is three times as high. So coffee sales are only six times as profitable as creamer sales. And creamers are really growing. Look at this chart *(see Figure 12–1)*. Non-dairy creamers are used in almost one quarter of all creamed cups. Dollar sales are increasing 30 percent annually *(see Figure 12–2)*.

Bill: That's news to me. What's the next question?

Jim: What size creamer is showing the greatest growth?

Bill: Well, since you've already told me that you're here for a 22-ounce promotion, I think you've given the answer away. But I would have said the 16-ounce size.

Jim: Right. The 22-ounce *Coffee-mate* was responsible for 90 percent of the industry growth when it was in test market. It got between 10 and 17 percent share in the four test markets *(see Figure 12–3)*. So you really can't afford not to at least examine some alternative approaches for the creamer section.

Bill: OK. OK. I'm convinced I need to listen—but don't get your hopes up too high.

Figure 12-1
Sales growth in product category

Non-dairy powdered creamers
"THE GROWTH INDUSTRY"

Market Penetration

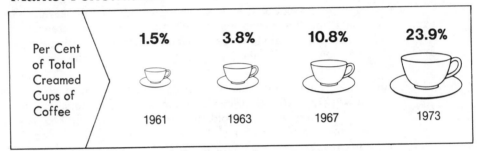

| Per Cent of Total Creamed Cups of Coffee | 1.5% | 3.8% | 10.8% | 23.9% |
| | 1961 | 1963 | 1967 | 1973 |

Sales

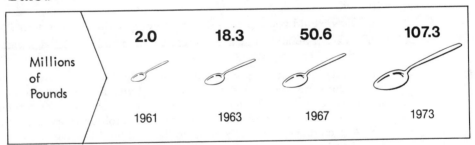

| Millions of Pounds | 2.0 | 18.3 | 50.6 | 107.3 |
| | 1961 | 1963 | 1967 | 1973 |

Grocer Profits

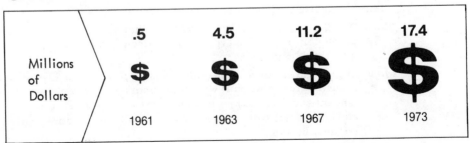

| Millions of Dollars | .5 | 4.5 | 11.2 | 17.4 |
| | 1961 | 1963 | 1967 | 1973 |

Figure 12–2

Growth in *Coffee-mate* sales

Coffee-mate

"THE GROWTH STIMULATOR"

Average Annual Industry Growth + **30**% Annually*

*Average Annual Dollar Increase 1st 10 Years

22 Oz.

16 Oz.

11 Oz.

3 Oz.   6 Oz.

1961
COFFEE-MATE introduced the first non-dairy creamer. Result: A new industry

1963
COFFEE-MATE introduced 11 Oz. nationally. Result: 11 Oz. Coffee-mate captured 38% of the total market by 1965

1967
COFFEE-MATE introduced 16 Oz. nationally. Result: In 1972 16 Oz. Coffee-mate sold more pounds than any other total brand

1973
COFFEE-MATE introduced a 22 Oz. size in selected marketing areas. Result: Coffee-mate presented a balanced line to the consumer. 22 Oz. Coffee-mate alone accounted for over 90% of industry growth for the 6 month period measured in the 4 significant marketing areas.

| **1961** | **1963** | **1967** | **1973** |

Figure 12-3
Test market results

22 oz.
Coffee-mate®

enjoyed immediate success
and achieved the following
market shares:

District	Share
P₁	10.3
J	15.7
C	17.0
P₂	10.1

Coffee-mate

NON-DAIRY CREAMER

NET WT 22 OZ.

WHY?

• **The right size** for all heavy
coffee creaming occasions · For the heavy user
family · For the office · For all social gatherings

• **The right time** to coincide with
increased powdered creamer acceptance and usage

• **The right brand** with demonstrated
consumer preference and maximum grocer
profit dollars

Delivering the presentation

Jim: I've got two areas I want to talk about. First, our promotion on 22-ounce *Coffee-mate*. The promotion is great, and the timing is perfect for your new store. I know that you'll be running all sorts of specials then. I want 22-ounce *Coffee-mate* to be one of them. Second, I want to show you some ideas I have for reorganizing the creamer section.

Bill: OK, I'm listening.

Jim: The *Coffee-mate* promotion is one of our best ever. We have great ad and display allowances, coupons, and even a consumer premium.

Bill: Coupons! Coupons are more trouble than they're worth! They slow down the checkers and are a pain in the neck to administer.

Jim: I thought you might say that, so I took some extra time to find out what they are really worth to you as a retailer. It turns out that the best coupon users are exactly the customers you want to attract to your stores. They are in the 24–49 age group, fairly well educated, and affluent. That describes your clientele. You are presented with a high sales volume opportunity when we blanket an area with coupons— and we'll be using local newspapers for this coupon.

Bill: Tell me more about the promotional allowances. What do I have to do to qualify for the allowance?

Jim: The promotion begins in eight weeks. That's perfect timing for your opening. We will be offering an allowance totaling $2.50 per case of 12 jars of 22-ounce *Coffee-mate*. The allowance has two parts. You will qualify for $1.50 per case if you advertise in your newspaper. The other part of the allowance requires that you display *Coffee-mate*. You'll get $1 for each case displayed during the promotional period.

Bill: That sounds good. Can I make money on this size? Can you give me an idea of what my competitors normally sell this size for?

Jim: No problem. I've already worked up some numbers showing your profit at various suggested retail prices.

Bill: How will the allowances be handled?

Jim: Once I have verified the ad and noted the number of cases displayed, I will write you a check.

Jim: The promotion is one of our best ever. We have great ad and display allowances, coupons, and even a consumer premium.

Overcoming objections

Bill: But displays take a lot of time to set up, and time mean money.

Jim: I'll set up the displays. That's part of my job. But even without my help, a *Coffee-mate* display is well worth the time it takes to build. Displays stimulate impulse buying and reduce out-of-stocks when you've got a special promotion going. And we have found that even when there is no price reduction a *Coffee-mate* display increases sales by 250 percent. A display and a special reduced price will insure terrific sales.

Bill: You said you've worked up some numbers? Let's look at them.

Jim: As you can see, $1.70 is a great price to advertise. Markets around here are charging $1.80. At $1.70, with both allowances taken into consideration, you'll be making over 25 percent net profit on each case you sell. And talking dollars, if you display 100 cases, your profit margin will be $516. *(See Figure 12–4.)*

Bill: The numbers look good. You said that there will also be a consumer premium and national advertising. Tell me about those parts of the promotion.

Jim: I've got a flier on the consumer premium to show you. We'll be offering an eight-cup automatic filter drip coffee maker for $15 less than the regularly advertised price. All your customer needs is a label from a 22-ounce *Coffee-mate* jar. I'll have stack-cards and tear-off pads to use in your stores to illustrate the coffee maker and explain the details. filter drip coffee makers are really increasing in popularity. There should be a lot of consumer interest.

As for our advertising campaign, *Coffee-mate* has always been the leader in creamer advertising. We do about 80 percent of all the industry advertising. We'll be demonstrating that we're the leader again with a new *Coffee-mate* advertisement entitled "Good Coffee." It will be airing soon on local TV. This campaign will keep the *Coffee-mate* name firmly in the mind of the consumer. I have a storyboard of the segments of the commercial to show you. We think it's a winner.

So now you tell me, what do you think of the 22-ounce promotion?

Bill: The promotion looks terrific. It's certainly one of the most complete I've seen in a long time. But I don't think I can get another size of *Coffee-mate* on the shelf. The creamer section is packed. If I put every new product pitched to me in my stores, I'd have to clear the shelves completely every month.

Jim: I know you have shelf space problems. The new 22-ounce size allows Carnation to present a complete selection of sizes to the consumer. For big families the new size offers convenience and economy along with enough product to last a while even if used frequently and in large

Figure 12–4

22-ounce *Coffee-mate* profit review

Regular case cost	$17.74
(packed 12 jars per case)	
Promotional allowances:	
Advertise/price reduction	(1.50)
Display allowance	(1.00)
Net case cost	$15.24
Unit cost (Net cost ÷ 12)	$ 1.27
Suggested retail price	$ 1.70
Case profit margin:	
(Retail price − [Net cost × 12])	$ 5.16
Gross profit:	
([Retail − Unit cost] ÷ Retail)	25.2%

amounts. It's also a popular size for use in offices, coffee-break areas, and other business places where coffee is served throughout the day. Proof of its popularity comes from its success since its introduction. The 22-ounce *Coffee-mate* accounted for over 90 percent of industry growth in the six-month period measured when the product was in test market. And since the 22-ounce size was introduced two years ago, it's captured 14.3 percent of the market. You can't ignore that kind of success, Bill.

Bill: I agree that the product looks like a real winner. But I just don't have room for another creamer. If I take on 22-ounce *Coffee-mate*, I'll have to discontinue something else. I think the creamer section is in pretty good shape now.

Jim: That leads me into the other topic I want to discuss with you, the overall merchandising of your creamer and coffee sections.

First, I think you should seriously consider enlarging the total creamer section by expanding into the coffee section. This would give us room for both the 22-ounce size and increased creamer inventories.

There are several important reasons why you should do this. First, powdered creamer sales have been growing dramatically since the product was introduced. But you have not expanded the creamer sections accordingly. Meanwhile, coffee sales are going down. They have declined 16 percent during the same period.

Bill: I hadn't realized that the creamer increases and coffee declines were so dramatic! Obviously I'm running the risk of creamer out-of-stocks.

Jim: That's my next point. In the four months I've been on the account, you've run out of at least one *Coffee-mate* size on five different occasions. I've taken some snapshots of the section on the Mondays that I do my store checks. You can see for yourself that after the peak creamer buying days of Wednesday through Saturday your sections are a disaster area. You're losing out in two areas: customer satisfaction and profits. There are two reasons why you're running out of *Coffee-mate*. First, as I've already pointed out, your creamer section overall is not large enough to support the product category. Second, within the creamer section, you're not allocating space by market share. Although *Coffee-mate* is the biggest selling creamer in the Chicago area, your shelf allocation does not reflect that fact.

Bill: I guess I haven't been keeping track of the section carefully enough—mainly because it is so small.

Jim: Well, there's still more information to review. We've already talked about the profitability of creamers compared to coffee nationally. Obviously some coffee types are less profitable than others. Supermarket studies have shown that because of consumer resistance to higher prices, consumer demand has dropped off for three-pound cans of coffee. You can probably drop one or more brands of three-pound coffee to make room for more creamer inventories without adversely affecting profit or customer satisfaction. Let's review your sales figures on three-pound coffee to see if your stores show these same trends. What do you say?

Bill:　Agreed. And if you're right, then we will drop some coffee lines and expand the creamer section.

Closing the sale

Jim:　And bring in 22-ounce *Coffee-mate*?

Bill:　And bring in 22-ounce *Coffee-mate*. Let's look at those sales figures now. *(Bill pulls out the sales figures book and turns to the coffee and creamer section.)* You're right about the three-pound coffee pulling its weight. I carry 15 different items, and it looks as if I can drop at least 5 of those without anyone noticing—at least, none of my customers will notice.

Jim:　The next step then is to figure out how much *Coffee-mate* to bring in and to write up an order. My suggestion is that we plan on a 100-case display plus 2 cases of shelf stock in each store. That adds up to 510 cases total.

Bill:　That's an awful lot of *Coffee-mate*.

Jim:　You're going to need that much to insure enough stock to get through the promotion. At $1.70 per jar, you'll make over $500 on each display. That's 25 percent for every jar sold.

Bill:　OK. You certainly seem to be able to back up your suggestions with hard facts, so I'll take a chance on it.

Jim:　Terrific. Bringing in the new size of *Coffee-mate* will mean expanding the creamer section. I'd like to review some merchandising moves with you that will insure your getting the most out of reorganizing the creamer section.

Bill:　OK. Let's see what you've got. *(Jim produces a merchandising diagram of the Blair Markets creamer section as it is now organized.)*

Jim:　Right now you've got the creamers positioned next to the coffees. That works well. But the products are arranged on the shelf by size. That minimizes the impact of the section overall. Research has shown that a section set by size tends to lose its identity. The category gets lost among the thousands of other items in the store. Let me show you a diagram I've drawn for the section. *(Jim produces another diagram.)*

First, set the creamer section horizontally across the shelf by brand rather than size. The majority of shoppers are looking for a specific brand. Setting the section in a block by brand makes it easier for them to find what they want. And the section overall has a better chance of catching the eye of impulse buyers.

Next, set *Coffee-mate* on the eye-level shelf. *Coffee-mate* at eye level increases both its own sales and those of the private label brand you carry. Buyers can see the price differential between *Coffee-mate* and the private label right away. The two brands really aren't in direct competition. *Coffee-mate* attracts users who want the highest quality creamer. Private label purchasers don't believe that the difference in quality is great enough to justify the price differential.

Finally, make sure the number of facings allotted to each brand represents that brand's fair share of the market. [*Facings are the jars or packages on the front line of the shelf.*] This will help insure that enough of each creamer brand is bought. It lessens the chances of out-of-stocks.

Bill: Sounds like you guys are really getting scientific about shelf organization.

Jim: We have to! The grocery business is a big business. If we just guess about things, we could lose millions of dollars. And that loss is not just Carnation's loss. You'll feel part of it, too. Bad shelf placement or product mix causes the consumer to buy elsewhere.

Jim: We've covered a lot of ground this morning. The next step involves your signing this *Coffee-mate* order to your wholesaler. *(Bill signs the order.)* As soon as I get an estimated arrival date for the *Coffee-mate*, we can plan the specific dates for setting up the displays and making the changes in the creamer and coffee sections that we've agreed on.

Bill: Fine.

Jim: Thanks again for the time you've spent with me today. Good-bye.

Questions

1. How would you evaluate Jim Jackson's presentation? What are the strong points in the presentation?

2. Assume that you were the Carnation salesperson and that Bill Hansen of Blair made the following objections. How would you handle each of these objections?
   a. "I don't have enough time to talk to you about rearranging the creamer section."
   b. "I've tasted *Coffee-mate*, and I don't like it. We don't need more of it in the store."
   c. "I don't have the stock clerks available to rearrange the shelves at this time."
   d. "I think my private brand should be at eye level. That's the one I make the most margin on."

3. What would you do if Bill doesn't want to buy on this call?

PRESENTATION OF THE IBM COPIER III[2]

Introduction

Robert Steele, the office manager for Electronic Data Products, received several complaints from his office staff about the poor copies obtained when using the copying machine. He called the manufacturer and had the copier serviced. The complaints continued. Mr. Steele saw an advertisement for the IBM Copier III on television. He called the IBM office in Century City the next morning and left a message for his IBM account representative, Denise Popper. She returned his call after lunch and made an appointment to see him the next morning.

During the sales call, Ms. Popper presented the key features of the IBM Copier III, using the sales brochure. Mr. Steele described some of the complaints he had been receiving. After Ms. Popper assured Mr. Steele that these problems would not occur with the Copier III, she asked him to describe how the copier is used at EDP.

Mr. Steele said that a large number of people at EDP used the copier. The typical application was for three copies to be made of each of three originals. About 32,000 copies were made per month.

Ms. Popper then asked if she could speak to some of the office staff who had been having problems with the present copier. Mr. Steele introduced her to Mary Quaint and Tom Robbins. Mary and Tom described the problems in detail. Ms. Popper then made arrangements to demonstrate the Copier III. She invited Mr. Steele, Mary, and Tom to walk down the street to an account of hers that had a Copier III. Mr. Steel declined the invitation but encouraged Mary and Tom to go with her. Ms. Popper called the account, Sun Battery, and arranged to have its machine demonstrated.

When they arrived at Sun, Ms. Popper introduced Mary and Tom to the people who used the copier. She then demonstrated the unique advantages of the Copier III, stressing the design aspects that improve copy quality. During the demonstration, Mary told Ms. Popper that EDP was a very cost-conscious company. Mr. Steele's supervisor would not spend more for a copier even if it did produce better copies.

After the demonstration Ms. Popper returned to the office and asked Mr. Clifford to help her prepare a proposal for EDP. Mr. Clifford is the copier specialist in the Century City office. In a week Ms. Popper delivered the following proposal to Mr. Steele. She went over it with him page by page, making the following points while directing attention to the numbered spots on the pages of the proposal (Figure 12-5):

---

[2] Jerry Clifford, a copier specialist for IBM, assisted in preparing this presentation.

Figure 12–5

Mr. Robert Steele
Electronic Data Products
10031 Wilshire Blvd.
Los Angeles, California 90024

Thank you for your interest and your evaluation of the IBM Series III Copier/Duplicator. This proposal is designed to assist you with the analysis of your copier needs.

As you know, any copier is significant to your word processing distribution system because your personnel depend on it to produce quality copies quickly. In addition, you've indicated the following considerations to be of major importance in evaluating copiers:

①

    Consistent copy quality
    Simplicity of use
    Versatility
    Productivity
    Simplicity of maintenance
    Low cost

These considerations are discussed in detail in the following proposal. I believe that after you have thoroughly evaluated the IBM Series III Copier/Duplicator, you will accept nothing less than the high performance and versatility it offers.

Thank you for providing the information necessary to prepare your analysis. Prices quoted herein are firm for a period of thirty (30) days from the date of this letter and are subject to applicable taxes.

Sincerely,

Denise Popper

Denise Popper
Account Representative
Office Products Division

DAP/eat
Attachments

Page 1

Page 1
 ① The six advantages of the Series III over your present copier are consistent high-quality copies, simplicity of operation, versatility, productivity, simplicity of maintenance, and low cost.

Figure 12–5 (continued) Feature analysis and comparison

page 2

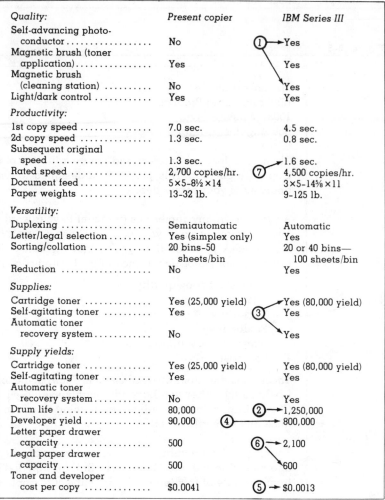

Quality:	Present copier	IBM Series III
Self-advancing photoconductor	No	① →Yes
Magnetic brush (toner application)	Yes	Yes
Magnetic brush (cleaning station)	No	Yes
Light/dark control	Yes	Yes
Productivity:		
1st copy speed	7.0 sec.	4.5 sec.
2d copy speed	1.3 sec.	0.8 sec.
Subsequent original speed	1.3 sec.	1.6 sec.
Rated speed	2,700 copies/hr.	⑦ 4,500 copies/hr.
Document feed	5×5–8½×14	3×5–14⅝×11
Paper weights	13–32 lb.	9–125 lb.
Versatility:		
Duplexing	Semiautomatic	Automatic
Letter/legal selection	Yes (simplex only)	Yes
Sorting/collation	20 bins–50 sheets/bin	20 or 40 bins— 100 sheets/bin
Reduction	No	Yes
Supplies:		
Cartridge toner	Yes (25,000 yield)	Yes (80,000 yield)
Self-agitating toner	Yes	③ Yes
Automatic toner recovery system	No	Yes
Supply yields:		
Cartridge toner	Yes (25,000 yield)	Yes (80,000 yield)
Self-agitating toner	Yes	Yes
Automatic toner recovery system	No	Yes
Drum life	80,000	② →1,250,000
Developer yield	90,000	④ → 800,000
Letter paper drawer capacity	500	⑥ → 2,100
Legal paper drawer capacity	500	600
Toner and developer cost per copy	$0.0041	⑤ → $0.0013

① The IBM Series III has a self-advancing photoconductor and magnetic brushes for both toner application and cleaning. These are patented technologies that guarantee consistent high-quality copies. The self-advancing photoconductor is a method for continuously adjusting the copying drum. This insures that the copying drum will be in adjustment during its entire life.

② Notice that the Series III drum has a lifetime of over one million copies. Your present copier has a lifetime of only 80,000 copies. This means that you have to change the drum in your copier ten times as frequently as you would change the drum of the Series III. Also, without the self-advancing photoconductor, the drum on your present copier probably goes out of adjustment after 40,000 copies. Half of your copies are going to be of less than the best quality.

③ The Series III has a unique automatic toner recovery system. Each toner cartridge lasts for 80,000 copies. That's three times as long as the lifetime of a cartridge for your present copier.

④ The developer yield on the Series III is almost ten times as great as the yield on your present copier.

⑤ That's why the toner and developer costs for the Series III are only 30 percent of the costs for your present copier. The higher yield for toner and developer also means fewer operator interventions, less time waiting for the copier to be serviced.

⑥ The paper bins on the Series III are four times as large as the bins on your present copier. This also reduces the number of operator interventions.

⑦ Notice that the copying speed is much faster for the Series III.

Figure 12–5 (continued) Executive summary of total IBM system

page 3

Hard-dollar savings	32,000 copies
Present copying costs, including supplies	$1,302.90
IBM copying costs, including supplies	$1,190.60
Difference	$112.30 ①
Soft-dollar savings (people costs @ $10/hr.)	
Present copier monthly hours, 16.78	$167.80
Series III monthly hours, 12.34	$123.40
Difference	$44.40
Total hard-dollar difference	−$112.30
Total soft-dollar difference	−$44.40
Total *monthly* IBM system cost difference	−$156.70
Total *annual* cost difference	−$1,880.40

The cost savings are summarized on this page. I have broken down the savings into hard and soft dollars. The hard dollars are out-of-pocket expenses, while the soft dollars are savings in employee time.

① Notice that the savings in hard dollars total over $100 per month. On the next page, the calculations supporting this figure are shown.

Figure 12–5 (continued) Machine cost summary

page 4

		Present copier	IBM Series III
Monthly availability charge .... $		555.00	$ 585.00
Copy allowance		13,800 copies	15,000 copies

	Present copier	*IBM Copier III* ②		
Meters:	6,200 @ $0.0235	15,000 @ $0.018	145.70	270.00
	10,000 @ $0.018	2,000 @ $0.0115	180.00	23.00
	2,000 @ $0.013		26.00	

		Present copier	IBM Series III ①
20-bin collator		105.00	111.00
Suppliers: 32,000 @ $0.0091 32,000 @ $0.0063		291.20	201.60
Monthly total		$1,302.90	$1,190.60
Annual total .... ③		$15,634.80	$14,287.20
Cost per copy		$0.0407	$0.0372

Copy system cost summary

	Monthly	Annual	Cost per copy
Present copy system	$1,302.90	$15,634.80	$0.0407
Proposed IBM Copy System	$1,190.60	$14,287.20	$0.0372
IBM cost savings	$112.30	$1,347.60	$0.0035

① The monthly service charge for the Series III and the rental charge for the 20-bin collator are slightly higher than the charges for your present copier.

② But look at the savings you get in the copying charge.

③ We worked through all the numbers based on your usage rate of 32,000 copies per month. The savings are about $110 per month. That's $1,350 per year in hard, out-of-pocket dollars. In addition, there are savings in less time spent making copies. I have summarized these savings on the next page.

Figure 12–5 (continued) Productivity analysis @ 32,000 copies per month

page 5

		Present copier	IBM Series III
Rated speed		45 copies/min.	75 copies/min.
		2,700 copies/hr.	4,500 copies/hr.
Throughput speed		Yes	Yes
Average three copies, three originals			
1st original	1st copy	6.5	④ → 4.5
	2d copy	1.3	③ → 0.8
	3d copy	1.3	0.8
2d original	1st copy	1.3	1.6
	2d copy	1.3	0.8
	3d copy	1.3	0.8
3d original	1st copy	1.3	1.6
	2d copy	1.3	0.8
	3d copy	1.3	0.8
Total time		16.9 sec.	⑤ → 12.5 sec.

Facts:

Average monthly volume	32,000 copies
Average run length	3 copies ←
Average number of originals per trip	3 copies ← ①
Trips to copier per month	3,555
Average hourly wage	$10 ← ②

	Present copier	IBM Series III
Copying time per month	16.78 hrs.	12.34 hrs.
Soft dollars per month	$167.80	⑥ $123.40

Note: This is not a price quotation. It is an analysis, based upon copier usage assumptions that may vary from your actual circumstances. As a result, minor variations may occur in the price calculations. For an explanation of these variations, contact your IBM Marketing Representative.

① Using your estimates of three originals per trip and three copies per original, we came up with the following estimates.

② We also assumed an average hourly wage of $10 for the people making the copies.

③ The Series III has a much faster speed on the second and third copies.

④ It is also much faster on the first copy of the first original.

⑤ As a result, 25 percent less time is spent on each trip.

⑥ This means about $40 per month in soft-dollar savings.

Figure 12–5 (concluded) Simplicity of key operator maintenance

page 6

> *Elimination of call key operator light*
>
> *Paper misfeeds:*
> Casual users clear most misfeeds.
>
> *Cartridge toner:*
> One cartridge yields approximately 80,000 copies, reducing the frequency of adding toner.
>
> *Other:*
> Add paper (or casual users can add paper).
> Assist casual users when necessary
> Mail meter card.

Thus you can see that the Series III has fewer operator interventions, a cost saving of over $1,000 per year, and a 25 percent increase in productivity. The maintenance costs are also much lower. The toner and developer have a long lifetime. It is so easy to add paper to the Series III that even a casual user can do it. There is no reason to call a key operator.

Questions

1. Evaluate the proposal prepared by Mr. Clifford. Should there be more discussion of the technical design for high-quality copying? Is there too much detail on the financial aspects?
2. How should Ms. Popper follow up the presentation to Mr. Steele?
3. How would you use the proposal when making the presentation to Mr. Steele?

THE LAWSON ADVERTISING AGENCY PRESENTATION

Introduction

The Lawson Advertising Agency is a medium-sized agency located in Oakland, California. It has been in business since 1925 and has successfully handled many large national advertising campaigns for manufacturers of consumer goods, particularly in the food industry.

The Sunnyside Fruit Products Company produces high-quality canned fruits and vegetables under the Sunnyside brand name. It markets products throughout the United States. However, most of its sales are made in the northern half of the country. During the past few years, the company's advertising has been handled by a Philadelphia agency. Recently, however, the company's management decided to change to a Western agency with the idea of obtaining a closer working relationship.

Frank Marks of the Lawson Advertising Agency heard that the Sunnyside Fruit Products Company was contemplating a change; so he made a special call on Felix Hartford, who was chairman of the advertising committee. Hartford said that his company was considering a change. It was planning to have a number of advertising agencies come in to tell their stories before it selected an agency. The Lawson Advertising Agency was invited to give its presentation in about ten days. Marks asked whether the presentation would be given to the entire advertising committee. Hartford replied that he would attempt to have the members of the committee present, but if this were not possible he would transmit the information to them. He indicated that the Lawson Advertising Agency would have about one hour for its presentation.

Robert Lawson, president of the Lawson Advertising Agency, wrote a letter to Hartford thanking him for the opportunity to explain the agency's services to the Sunnyside Fruit Products Company. In this letter, he called Hartford's attention to a few key features of a successful advertising program.

The following sales portfolio was prepared by the staff of the Lawson Advertising Agency. It was used by Lawson when he made his sales presentation. Throughout the presentation he directed Hartford's attention to the portfolio, which featured the major questions and answers that Lawson desired to emphasize. The presentation started with the needs of the client.

PRESENTATION TO SUNNYSIDE FRUIT PRODUCTS COMPANY, INC.
By Lawson Advertising Agency

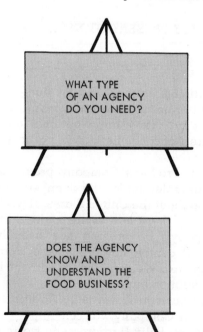

WHAT TYPE OF AN AGENCY DO YOU NEED?

You naturally want an agency that is fully capable of doing the best possible job for Sunnyside Fruit Products. What, then, are the qualifications for such an agency? We suggest that any agency you consider be measured by the following questions.

DOES THE AGENCY KNOW AND UNDERSTAND THE FOOD BUSINESS?

The Lawson Advertising Agency is widely recognized as outstanding for its experience and effectiveness in food advertising.

We Know the Food Business

This, we believe, is due to the fact that over and above food advertising as such, we *know* the food business. We should. It has been our bread and butter for more than 50 years. Many of our most important clients have been food advertisers. The Western Fruit Growers Association (Sunlight), the Poultry Association of Northern California (Freshlaid Eggs), A. B. Jones Packing Company (Serve-U-Soups)—these are only a few of the food accounts which we have served for many years.

Because of the variety of the food accounts we have served and because we work "in depth" with our clients—almost as "members of the board"—we have acquired a very thorough understanding of the food business in all its ramifications.

We know that the great mass of successful food selling, like that of an iceberg, lies below the surface. The consumer advertising which shows is the smallest fraction of the whole. It is the sales organization, the broker, the wholesaler, the chain buyer, the grocer—the whole chain of distribution, in short—that make food sell. And we work with the whole chain of distributors.

Lawson Advertising Agency maintains its head office in Oakland, as does Sunnyside Fruit Products Company. Much of our business, however, is conducted in San Francisco, as is yours.

To that end, we maintain offices in San Francisco, fully staffed as an independent operation, yet providing ample facilities for handling Oakland business when necessary. In fact, several members of our organization divide their time between the two offices.

This provides an ideal working arrangement for an account such as yours. The advantages of the close contact right here in Oakland are obvious. This is where our real "shirtsleeve" work is done. At the same time, our full-scale operation in San Francisco insures metropolitan agency status and the convenience of on-the-spot city service for conferences and technical production.

Lawson Advertising Agency is a member of the INTRA Agency Network, a close-working affiliation of independent, nationally recognized advertising agencies with offices extending coast to coast in the important marketing centers of the United States and Canada.

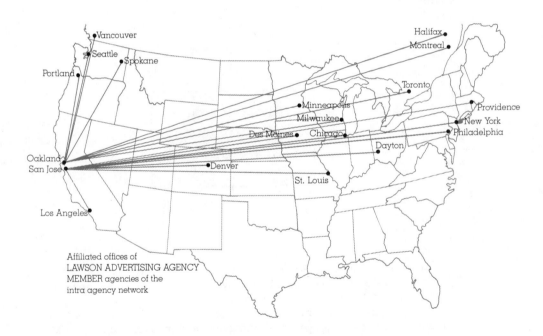

Whereas most so-called national agencies have perhaps five or six branch offices, the INTRA Agency Network provides on-the-spot service in 18 major marketing centers throughout the United States and Canada [see map]. Member agencies in each of these cities serve as local contact offices for their affiliates and continually provide *market data, management information,* and *actual local* service in their special territories.

Our Associates Know Their Markets

Each of these agencies has been established in its respective territory for many years. Most of the principals of the agencies have lived at their present locations for most of their working lives. Hence they are able to offer information that goes far beyond the information available from the typical "branch office," which is staffed by younger people who are frequently moved out. This firsthand knowledge is a valuable asset to the clients of the affiliated agencies.

Service Where You Want It—When You Want It

For example, these agencies conduct consumer and distribution surveys and surveys of market conditions for their affiliates. They advise one another on the best choice of publications or radio and TV outlets. They are able to ascertain the capabilities and responsibilities of prospective selling agents. They are often able to get "high-spot" distribution in localities where it is impractical to send sales representatives. Some members specialize in certain types and fields of advertising. Their special knowledge is available to other agency members for the benefit of clients.

Lawson Advertising Agency thus provides a "doubleheader." It combines the advantages of a local agency working close at hand with the nationwide coverage of 17 strongly established additional agencies which are fully informed on their respective markets. Such coverage is well worth your serious consideration.

The Lawson Advertising Agency is widely recognized as a merchandising agency. It has the experience and the willingness to go beyond mere advertising to become a vital and active part of your sales organization.

In our recent letter to you we stated that short of an expenditure running into millions of dollars, the results of your advertising program rest heavily upon the degree to which the advertising is merchandised to

    Your own sales organization
    Your brokers and their sales representatives
    Wholesalers and their sales representatives
    Retail dealers

Competition between products and brands is increasing every day, and it has already reached a degree that might well be termed "savage." Aggressive advertising is vital for success, particularly in the food field, and aggressive merchandising of the advertising is just as vital.

Often Spells Difference between Success and Failure

Why do we place special emphasis on this phase of our service? Because, despite their extreme importance, merchandising activities (the preparation of follow-up literature, booklets, folders, direct mail, dealer helps, display material, etc.) represent a lot of hard work and often lack glamour. The showy parts are easier and more fun—but the downright spadework represented by the task of merchandising the advertising is what often spells the difference between success and failure—or between only moderate success and the highest degree of success.

IS THE AGENCY
UP TO DATE
ON NEW DEVELOPMENTS
IN ADVERTISING
MEDIA AND METHODS?

Lawson Advertising Agency recognizes the basic value of the forms of advertising which have stood the test of time. They cannot be ignored.

But we are also fully alert to the new. We are well out in front in "depth surveys." Studies of this kind are altogether different from the usual statistical survey. They plumb consumer thinking about products in order to reach consumers with the most effective and resultful appeals. Depth surveys are recognized in the advertising and marketing field as the most advanced research method available today.

These are indications of an alert, active, up-to-the-minute advertising service, with creative imagination as well as solid merchandising knowhow.

IS THE AGENCY
SOUNDLY ESTABLISHED,
FULLY RECOGNIZED,
AND ADEQUATELY STAFFED
TO GIVE YOU
COMPLETE SERVICE?

Lawson Advertising Agency is a nationally recognized advertising agency, with 55 years of experience in agency work and with full advertising and financial credentials.

The agency is a member of the American Association of Advertising Agencies, which is in itself a guarantee of stability.

We are fully recognized by the American Newspaper Publishers Association, the Agricultural Publishers Association, national magazines, the National Outdoor Advertising Bureau, all national radio and TV networks, all transportation advertising companies, and individual media everywhere. A check of our credentials will show them to be the equal of any agency anywhere.

Lawson Advertising Agency has an excellent financial rating, reported to be one of the best on the coast. This can be easily checked through the American Association of Advertising Agencies or the First National Bank of Oakland.

Now, as always, the agency takes advantage of all cash discounts and protects the good name of its clients along this line by protecting its own financial rating with all media. These cash discounts are passed on to our clients.

Perhaps we could give no better picture of the status of our agency and the scope of our work than to list briefly some of the high spots of the *current advertising campaigns* which we are now conducting for our clients.

Right now, as this presentation to you is being given, we are running campaigns in the media summarized in the accompanying list. At times, of course, we have used more of some, less of the others. The current list, however, is representative.

Media in Use in Current Advertising Campaigns

National magazines:
  Ladies' Home Journal
  Family Circle

Good Housekeeping
Better Homes and Gardens
McCall's

Newspapers:
  Newspaper advertising in 134 cities

Trade publications
  Advertisements in 58 trade papers

Radio and television
  Miscellaneous programs, spot campaigns

Farm journals:
  Advertisements in 61 farm papers

Outdoor advertising:
  Poster displays in 226 cities

Minute movies:
  Showings in 345 theaters in 76 cities

Miscellaneous:
  Store displays
  Traveling films
  Sales manuals
  Direct-mail campaigns
  Advertising novelties
  Car cards
  Comic books
  Brochures
  Recipe booklets
  Catalogs, etc.

We believe you will agree that this list indicates a broad scope of agency activity, together with a thorough knowledge and experience in the use of all media on a nationwide scale.

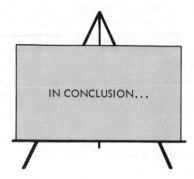

Lawson Advertising Agency

. . . is an advertising agency with years of experience in food advertising and food merchandising.

. . . is an agency with an outstanding record for its ability to merchandise an advertising program so as to extract the last penny in value from every dollar spent.

. . . is alert, creative, fully receptive to new ideas.

. . . is soundly established, nationally recognized, with full advertising and financial credentials.

One More Important Point

Should we be selected as your advertising agency, we are ready to move in fast . . . right now! Your new products are familiar to us. We have been interested in their market possibilities for some time. We have talked with food editors, food distributors, and consumers. In developing a program for you, we would have a running start.

Obviously, a thorough study of the market as well as the products is an essential of good advertising. The more we can do of this, the better we can do the whole advertising and merchandising job. If we can do it at the start, so much the better. If it is important, however, go get the advertising under way at once, we can do that too. We would then follow along with analysis and study as we proceed, so as to coordinate the whole selling job to the best advantage and thus extract the full value out of every dollar invested in the promotion effort.

We believe:

That you have an excellent product with a strong sales potential.

That we have the ability and the facilities to give you first-class advertising and merchandising counsel and service.

That it would be mutually advantageous for us to work together.

We would like to be selected as your *advertising agent.*

Questions

1. Did Robert Lawson follow a sound selling formula in starting his sales presentation? Explain.

2. What major selling points were featured in the Lawson Agency's presentation? Indicate the benefit of each sales point to the Sunnyside Fruit Products Company.

3. How does the Lawson Advertising Agency meet the competition which it anticipates from large advertising agencies with branch offices?

4. Evaluate the "conclusion" of the presentation. What are the strong and weak points?

PROJECTS

1. Obtain the necessary product knowledge and write an outlined sales presentation for one of the following products:

    a. A vacuum cleaner.

    b. A sewing machine.

    c. An automobile.

    d. A lawn and garden tractor.

2. Prepare a standard memorized presentation which will be used to raise money for

    a. A local Children's Home charity.

    b. Scholarships for minority students.

    c. A student center for international students.

3. As a student representative, you have been asked to make a presentation to the board of trustees of your college on the question of whether the student body should elect two students to the board of trustees. In the past, the board has opposed this concept. Assume that in your view students should be represented on the board of trustees. Develop a presentation to convince the board of trustees that this would be in the best long-term interests of the college. In the past, new members on the board of trustees have always been selected by the board members themselves.

CASE PROBLEMS

Case 12-1

KFX Radio Station

KFX is a local radio station in Madison, Wisconsin, a city of 400,000 people. The station was started 25 years ago. James

Wensley, its owner and founder, emphasized public service programming rather than entertainment programming. The station's programming was devoted exclusively to local and national news.

During the past year, Wensley sold the station to Tom Campbell. Campbell reviewed the station's ratings and advertising sales and decided to change its programming format. He also hired four advertising time salespeople.

In designing the new format, Campbell used the following research data on the radio listening habits of Madison residents:

☐ Women listen to the radio four hours a day, while men listen two hours a day.

☐ Radio is preferred to television for coverage of fast-breaking news stories.

☐ The KFX all-news format captured an average of 20 percent of the radio audience.

☐ The average age of radio purchasers is 26.

☐ Car radio owners listen to KFX 40 percent of time when they are driving.

☐ Eighty percent of the cars have radios.

☐ The average car owner listens to the radio 30.2 minutes per day.

☐ Radio listeners like to hear sincere, warm, friendly people.

☐ KFX is particularly popular during the summer and winter vacation.

The new KFX schedule is as follows:

Monday through Saturday

Morning*		Afternoon*	
12:00–4:00	Classical music Host: John Michaels —music host and critic from Los Angeles	12:00–3:30	Popular music Host: Debbie Rudder —host of local TV variety show
4:00–6:00	Call-in question-and-answer format Host: Mike Lupin—recently on a national radio show	3:30–5:00	Rock music Host: Mike Evans—recent college graduate
		5:00–7:30	News Roundup—local and national news Host: George Stein—longtime KFX newscaster
6:00–10:00	Good Morning Show—popular music plus news, weather, and interviews with personalities and local officials.	7:30–10:00	Call-in comments on current events

* Every hour on the hour, five minutes are devoted to national and local headline news.

10:00–12:00   Host: Jim Jackson—
                recently host of a similar
                program on most popu-
                lar station in Minnesota

                Homemaker Show—in-
                formation on such sub-
                jects as cooking and
                child rearing.
                    Host: Jennifer Fiddler
                —recently head of a
                consumer advocate
                group.

10:00–12:00   Host: Ward Baxter—
                host for a similar TV
                program

                Popular music
                    Host: Kamy Lutz—re-
                cently a disc jockey on a
                Chicago radio station

Sunday

Morning

12:00–6:00	Off the air
6:00–10:00	Religious services (non-commercial)
10:00–12:00	Newsmakers—interviews with local and national officials. Host: Jim Taylor—former University of Wisconsin political science professor

Afternoon

12:00–4:00	Sport Event of the Week—a major syndicated event
4:00–6:00	News of the Week Host: Jim Taylor
6:00–8:00	Dance music Host: Debbie Rudder
8:00–9:00	Wall Street Summary Host: Jim Bettman—financial reporter for a local newspaper
9:00–12:00	Opera music Host: John Michael

KFX Rate Schedule

Class	Time for spot	Number of spots purchased			
		1	10	50	100
AAA (Monday–Friday, 6:00–10:00 A.M., 3:30–7:30 P.M.; Saturday, 10:00–12:00 A.M.)	60 seconds	$200	$190	$175	$160
	30 seconds	160	150	140	130
	10 seconds	100	90	80	75
AA (Monday–Friday 10:00 A.M.– 3:30 P.M., 7:30–10:00 P.M.; Sunday, 9:00 A.M.–9:00 P.M.)	60 seconds	120	112	105	100
	30 seconds	100	90	85	80
	10 seconds	60	55	53	50
A (all other times)	60 seconds	85	80	75	65
	30 seconds	72	65	60	55
	10 seconds	45	40	38	35

Develop a presentation to sell advertising to the following:

1. The promoter of a rock concert.
2. The largest automobile dealer in the city.
3. A small sporting goods store.
4. A large discount department store chain.

Chapter 13

BUILDING FUTURE SALES BY IMPROVING CUSTOMER RELATIONS

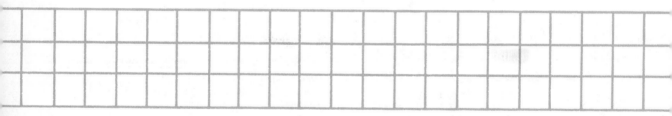

Future business may be affected by elements beyond the control of any one company or its sales representatives. However, one sure way to decrease the uncertainties of the future is to build sound, progressive business relationships with customers. These relationships may be developed through a program of cultivating customer relations.

Building goodwill is an activity that enters into every phase of the selling process. Goodwill is built before the sale is made, during the sales presentation, and after the sale is closed. Goodwill is built when prospecting, when demonstrating, when answering objections, when closing the sale, and after the product or service has been purchased.

This chapter discusses the nature of goodwill and describes methods for developing goodwill and improving customer relations. It gives special attention to the opportunities for building better customer relations by successfully handling customer complaints.

DEVELOPING GOODWILL

The nature of goodwill

Goodwill is the value of the feelings or attitudes that customers or prospects have toward the company or its products. Those feelings and attitudes may change, depending upon customers' reactions to company products and policies. When buyers are satisfied and place more and more confidence in the company, the value of goodwill increases. If the public loses confidence in the company or its products, the value of goodwill decreases and may be wiped out altogether.

Salespeople may view goodwill as the willingness of customers or prospects to give preference to their companies when purchasing products or services of a competitive nature. Goodwill is evidenced by customers when they choose one company's products although several competitors offer similar products on identical or similar terms. Everything else being equal, buyers prefer to buy from the companies they like best.

The importance of goodwill

Goodwill helps make the first sales and secures repeat sales. Customers who believe in the salespeople and their companies will help secure new prospects and new customers. Salespeople should cultivate customers because they benefit directly and indirectly from doing so. The most tangible benefit is increased earnings. Intangible benefits may include the wide circle of friends developed or the satisfaction derived from rendering services to the buyer.

Many salespeople build their prospect lists from the names supplied by satisfied customers. The center-of-influence prospecting method used by insurance underwriters is an example of a method built upon satisfied customers or friends.

Sellers of tangible goods know that word-of-mouth advertising by a satisfied customer is the best recommendation a product, a company, or a salesperson can receive. Some customers will gladly provide letters of recommendation or testimonials, and other may be willing to help demonstrate the product.

Establishing goodwill

Among the general methods for developing goodwill are keeping customers' interests paramount, remembering customers between calls, and developing a personal reputation. Each of these methods is discussed in this section.

Keep customers' interest paramount.   Cunning and shrewdness were once considered essential to selling. Fortunately, both customers and businesses no longer feel that they should be parties to transactions in which trickery is necessary. Both parties in a sales transaction know that subterfuge is not conducive to good business relationships. The buyer and the seller know that they can gain most by placing confidence in each other.

In most fields of selling, it is important to have repeat sales. It takes time to know the customer's wants and peculiarities. Therefore, salespeople who plan to be of the most service to their customers must work with them over a period of time.

The kind of customer relations that builds loyal customers who buy again and again requires a better type of salesperson than is needed to sell on a one-shot basis.

Goodwill is seldom built on one call. Patience and courtesy are necessary if long-term customer relations are to be developed. The customer's attitude toward the salesperson, the company, and the product is the result of actively, positively engaging in the process of cultivating customers goodwill.

Goodwill is much like a person's character or reputation. A person can live an exemplary life for many years, but one major breach of accepted custom and his or her reputation is lost—usually forever. Similarly, salespeople can be trusted, respected, and liked because they treat customers fairly; but once they cheat a customer or give other evidence of being undependable, their chances of further acceptance by the buyer are practically nil. In order to keep a customer's interest paramount a salesperson may have to turn down an order that is likely to prove unsatisfactory to the buyer.

Not only must salespeople keep the customer's interest paramount, but their attitudes toward the customer must be right. Actions alone seldom build friendships if the attitudes behind the actions are unacceptable. The basis for cultivating customers must be rooted in the attitude of service.

A scale to measure the degree to which a salesperson is customer oriented is shown in Figure 13-1. Customer orientation is defined as keeping the customer's interest paramount when making a sales presentation. A salesperson who only thinks of making a sale is a sales oriented rather than customer oriented. Answer the questions, and see how you score.

Remember customers between calls. Keeping a customer in mind between calls can be an effective method of building goodwill. The remembrance must be evidence of a desire to help the buyer, or it may be evidence that the customer is viewed as a friend. Whatever the remembrance, it must be evidence of sincerity.

Some companies use standard forms to congratulate customers on birthdays and wedding anniversaries, upon the arrival of a new baby, or upon other special occasions. The letter illustrated in Figure 13-2 is typical of those used by life insurance agents.

The value gained from such letters depends upon the ability of the salesperson to make the message personal. If the customer feels that the letter is routine and impersonal, it is questionable how much goodwill is engendered. Perhaps a handwritten note on the bottom or margin of the letter can add a touch of personal interest.

The late Thomas J. Watson, founder of International Business Machines Corporation, used to encourage his executives to write notes of congratulations and/or condolence on personal stationery. He knew that such notes meant more than dictated, typed letters.

Some successful methods used by retail salespeople are to telephone customers when new merchandise arrives that they will probably like, to take special orders in order to secure the exact merchandise requested, to set aside merchandise which the salesperson knows the customer wants, and to conduct a follow-up on merchandise which has been sold.

Many retail stores send individual letters or cards to customers who have recently paid their charge accounts. These letters usually remind purchasers that their patronage is appreciated and that the store hopes they will use their accounts again soon (see Figure 13-3.) Special credit ratings are sometimes provided. Menswear stores have found that it pays to send personal letters to recent purchasers of suits to make certain that they are satisfied with their purchases. Figure 13-4 reproduces a good example of this type of letter.

Letters sent at Christmastime to thank good customers for their patronage during the year have proved effective for some companies. The letter used by one company is reproduced in Figure 13-5.

Build a personal reputation. Many salespeople attempt to build a personal reputation with their customers and with the community in which they live.

A good reputation with customers may be built in many ways. Some suggestions follow:

1. *Do not reveal confidential information.* The customer should feel that he or she can place confidence in you.
2. *Speak well of other customers and of competitors.* Salespeople

Figure 13-1

Customer orientation scale

The statements below describe various ways in which a salesperson might act with a customer or prospect (for convenience, the word customer is used to refer to both customers and prospects). For each statement, please indicate the proportion of your customers with whom you act as described in the statement. Do this by circling one of the numbers from 1 to 9. The meanings of the numbers are:

1	2	3	4	5	6	7	8	9
True for none of your customers (never)	True for almost none . . .	True for a few . . .	True for somewhat less than half . . .	True for about half . . .	True for somewhat more than half . . .	True for a large majority . . .	True for almost all . . .	True for all of your customers (always)

For example, by circling 6 below, the salesperson has indicated that *somewhat more than half* of his or her customers are asked a lot of questions.

Never   Always

0. I ask a customer a lot of questions . . . .   1 2 3 4 5 ⑥ 7 8 9

Never   *Always*

1. I try to give customers an accurate expectation of what the product will do for them 1 2 3 4 5 6 7 8 9

2. I try to get customers to discuss their needs with me 1 2 3 4 5 6 7 8 9

3. If I am not sure a product is right for a customer, I will still apply pressure to get him to buy 1 2 3 4 5 6 7 8 9

4. I imply to a customer that something is beyond my control when it is not 1 2 3 4 5 6 7 8 9

5. I try to influence a customer by information rather than by pressure 1 2 3 4 5 6 7 8 9

6. I try to sell as much as I can rather than to satisfy a customer 1 2 3 4 5 6 7 8 9

7. I spend more time trying to persuade a customer to buy than I do trying to discover his needs 1 2 3 4 5 6 7 8 9

8. I try to help customers achieve their goals 1 2 3 4 5 6 7 8 9

9. I answer a customer's questions about products as correctly as I can 1 2 3 4 5 6 7 8 9

10. I pretend to agree with customers to please them 1 2 3 4 5 6 7 8 9

11. I treat a customer as a rival 1 2 3 4 5 6 7 8 9

12. I try to figure out what a customer's needs are 1 2 3 4 5 6 7 8 9

13. I try to have the customer's best interests in mind 1 2 3 4 5 6 7 8 9

14. I try to bring a customer with a problem together with a product that helps him solve that problem 1 2 3 4 5 6 7 8 9

15. I am willing to disagree with a customer in order to help him make a better decision 1 2 3 4 5 6 7 8 9

16. I offer the product that is best suited to the customer's problem 1 2 3 4 5 6 7 8 9

17. I stretch the truth in describing a product to a customer 1 2 3 4 5 6 7 8 9

18. I begin the sales talk for a product before exploring a customer's needs with him 1 2 3 4 5 6 7 8 9

19. I try to sell a customer all I can convince him to buy, even if I think it is more than a wise customer would buy 1 2 3 4 5 6 7 8 9

20. I paint too rosy a picture of my products, to make them sound as good as possible 1 2 3 4 5 6 7 8 9

21. I try to achieve my goals by satisfying customers 1 2 3 4 5 6 7 8 9

22. I decide what products to offer on the basis of what I can convince customers to buy, not on the basis of what will satisfy them in the long run 1 2 3 4 5 6 7 8 9

23. I try to find out what kind of product would be most helpful to a customer ... 1 2 3 4 5 6 7 8 9

24. I keep alert for weaknesses in a customer's personality so I can use them to put pressure on him to buy 1 2 3 4 5 6 7 8 9

The scores for items 3, 4, 6, 7, 10, 11, 17, 18, 19, 20, 22, and 24 are reversed, so for these questions subtract the number circled from 9 to get the score. The score for the remaining items is the number circled. Automobile salespeople typically scored from 150 to 160, while industrial salespeople scored from 175 to 185.

Source: Robert Saxe, "Customer Orientation of Salespeople," unpublished doctoral dissertation, UCLA, 1979.

Figure 13–2

New-arrival letter

Metropolitan Life

Schedules, schedules!

The new baby is home and doesn't know what "schedule" means. Sleeping and eating come at the oddest times.

But before long you'll all be sleeping through the night. Then there'll be the first smile, the first step, the first word—all this and more on a schedule of baby's own.

Right now is when you should give serious thought to another kind of schedule—Metropolitan's insurance rates for children. These rates are low, because your child is young.

You should take advantage of these rates to start the baby out with a sound future. When your youngster grows up, a strong financial asset will be waiting.

I'll call shortly to tell you about the insurance plans we offer for your child.

Cordially

Representative

PAL/cab

Home Office: One Madison Avenue, New York, N.Y. 10010
Head Offices: San Francisco, Calif.; Ottawa, Ontario, Canada

Courtesy: Metropolitan Life Insurance Co.

Figure 13-3
A letter designed to show appreciation for purchases

Ms. Sue Welker   April 21, 1980
114 High Street
Albany, New York

Dear Ms. Welker:

Patronage such as yours is indeed appreciated, and as
we thank you for your recent purchase, may we ask
you also to accept the enclosed certificate of permanent
credit.

This card is issued only to a very selected list of customers
entitled to maximum credit privileges; and we trust that
you will find it useful not only in immediately identifying
your credit rating in our own store, but also in opening
other retail accounts.

Come in to see us often. New furnishing styles are always
arriving and a cordial welcome awaits you whether or not
you plan to buy.

                        Cordially,

                        LEE BROS.

ML:K   Marvin Lee

P.S. Please notify us promptly of any change of address
so that we can give you advance information of any
special events.

Figure 13-4
A letter designed to build goodwill

July 1, 1980

Dr. Walter Jones
508 E. Reedley Ave.
Seattle, Washington

Dear Dr. Jones:

Are you completely satisified with the new suit you recently purchased
at Brown Bros.? Does it feel right? Does its fit please you?

After you wear a new suit for a while you can then tell how it feels.
And we know that sometimes you may have the feeling that it doesn't
fit quite right.

If there is anything at all you don't like about your Brown Bros. suit,
please bring it in. We sincerely want to stand behind our guarantee,
"We won't let you wear it unless it fits."

Out tailors will recheck your suit and make any alterations that are
necessary.

It is the Brown Bros.' policy to guarantee complete satisfaction on
every purchase you make with us.

Sincerely,

BROWN BROS., INC.

R. E. McKay
R. E. McKay
Manager

REM:B

who talk about other customers imply that they will talk about *all*
customers.

3. *Tell the truth even when it hurts.* This may involve stating when
   merchandise can be delivered, or following up on some matter of
   concern to the buyer, or investigating and making recommendations for credit purposes. Implications which are untruths, or
   half-truths, are reflections upon the salesperson.

Figure 13–5
A "thank-you" letter

Mr. Walter Browning   Christmas
2 Ridge Road   1980
Philadelphia, Pa.

Dear Mr. Browning:

One of the greatest pleasures of being in business is the
privilege of saying "Thank You" to good friends like you --
and to wish you a Merry Christmas and a Happy New Year.

If it were not for folks like you, there could be no firm like
ours -- and we are deeply grateful for your patronage.
It has enabled us to grow, and each step forward has been
made possible by friendly customers like you.

So at this Holiday Season may we express our sincere
appreciation for the part you have played in making our
business what it is today. In the years to come we will do
our utmost to merit your continued confidence, and it will
always be a privilege to serve you.

May you and yours have a very Merry Christmas with the
New Year filled with all the good things of life.

                    Sincerely,

                    MOSHER SUPPLY CO.

                    J. Mosher

                    J. Mosher, Sales Rep.

4. *Be dependable, considerate, and courteous.* A good example of how these human qualities develop goodwill and sales is recalled by a sales manager of a large steel company. The sales manager received an order for 25 tons of steel from a buyer who stated that the reason for the order was that the sales manager's company was the only one which was courteous when steel was scarce.

An example of a man who had the ability to sell himself is told by a grateful retailer. The retailer, Mr. Smart, owned a small store and, by way of conversation, informed the salesperson that he was planning to move to another location. The salesperson displayed enthusiasm about the retailer's new location and asked when the move was planned. The salesperson asked to help move the merchandise, and he set up the new department which stocked the merchandise that he carried. Then he helped move and helped set up the remaining departments.

The retailer wrote a grateful note to the company indicating that the salesperson was the company to him and the company should be proud to have him as its representative in the field.

Good relationships are probably built faster and more soundly by the salesperson who does a "little something extra" for a customer—performing services and doing favors which may be considered over and above the salesperson's normal responsibilities.

Because of a willingness to provide extra effort, Loren Kennedy of Bay State Abrasive was selected as a top salesperson by *Purchasing* magazine in 1978. An example of that extra effort occurred when one of Kennedy's midwestern customers was in a bind for grinding wheels because of a trucking strike. "Kennedy flew to his Westboro, Massachusetts, plant and picked up a supply. Then he rented a U-Haul truck, loaded it, and drove straight through the night to keep his customer in operation."[1]

Participation in community affairs will enhance the standing of the salesperson. Some companies place greater emphasis on this activity than do others. If the salesperson sells a limited geographic area, and lives in the area, membership in a service club, a professional club, and the chamber of commerce may be advisable. Participation in United Fund drives or other community activities is evidence of community concern.

People like to trade with people they know, respect, and trust.

---

[1] Somberby Dowst, "Top Salesmen Deliver Service, Expertise," *Purchasing*, August 23, 1978, p. 52.

IMPROVING CUSTOMER RELATIONS

The preceding section discussed some general methods for building customer goodwill. This section focuses on specific activities for improving relations both with customers who place orders and with customers who do not place orders.

If the sale is not made

A salesperson cannot expect to make a sale every time. The best baseball player averages fewer than four hits out of ten attempts. Figure skaters rarely receive 6.0 evaluations. So salespeople must expect to lose sales. However, even when a sale is not made, sales representatives should still try to maintain or increase goodwill of customers.

In these situations, goodwill is maintained by accepting the customer's decision graciously. If a salesperson has attempted several closes and the customer remains uninterested in placing an order, the salesperson should respect the customer's decision. The salesperson should be polite and cheerful even though he or she will probably be disappointed. Parting on a pleasant note will leave the door open for another presentation. Thus, the salesperson should thank the customer for the opportunity to make a presentation and then go on to the next call.

The salesperson who has good rapport with the customer might try to learn or gain something from an unsuccessful call. The customer might be asked to evaluate the presentation, to make suggestions for improving the presentation, or to provide a referral to other prospective customers.

After-sales support

The stages in the purchasing process were discussed in Chapter 3. There it was indicated that the purchasing process is not over when an order has been placed. After an order has been placed, the goods ordered must still be received, installed, and used. When this is happening, the customer will be making a postpurchase evaluation that can affect future orders and customer goodwill.

Since the purchasing process does not end when the order has been placed, the sales process should not end when a sale has been made. The salesperson needs to provide follow-up services to insure that the customer is satisfied with the product. One sales expert says:

> The most important thing I've learned is that selling a man something means doing something for him. Not just describing benefits, but delivering them. In fact, the word I've come to like best is installing: taking out your screwdriver and pliers and actually matching the operating benefit with one of your customer's key processes. This means you don't just take an order; you don't just oversee delivery; you don't just handle complaints. You accept the responsibility for making the benefit happen in the customer's plant. Most important, you make sure the customer realizes he is better off, not because of the benefit per se, but because of you.[2]

The salesperson can insure that benefits happen, and continue to happen, in the customer's plant by seeing that the right product is delivered on time, by assisting during trial periods, and by providing continuing service and information.

Monitor order processing.   It is important for the salesperson to prevent delays in the order cycle. Salespeople should keep track of impending orders and inform buyers when the paperwork is being delayed in the customer's plant. When orders are placed directly with a salesperson, they must be transmitted to the factory immediately. Progress on orders in process should be closely monitored. Customers need to be informed on anticipated delays so that they can plan accordingly.

Delays in shipment often occur when customers use outdated information in placing orders. Salespeople can prevent unnecessary delays and mistakes in orders by making orders accurate, complete, and processible. Customers should be provided with the latest data sheets, product information, and descriptions of ordering procedures. All orders should be reviewed for accuracy and completeness.

Insure proper initial use of product.   Customer dissatisfaction often occurs just after the product has been delivered. If customers are unfamiliar with the product, they may have problems in installing or using it. They may even damage the product by using it improperly. Many salespeople visit new customers shortly after initial deliveries have been made. These visits insure that products are being used properly and that the customer is realizing their potential benefits.

Provide effective service.   Most products require periodic maintenance and repairs. Many mechanical and electronic products need routine adjustments. This condition offers an excellent opportunity to show the buyer that the salesperson's interest has not ended upon delivery of the product. Salespeople should be qualified to make minor adjustments or to take care of minor repairs. If they are unable to put the product in working order, it is their responsibility to see

---

[2] Mack Hanan, "Learn Something New about Selling? Don't Let It Happen Too Often," *Sales Management*, December 10, 1973, p. 40.

that the proper company representative is notified. It is important to follow up on the customer's request to make certain that the service was rendered and that the customer is satisfied. Passing the responsibility for service satisfaction to the company's repair department, and assuming the attitude that service is not their problem, may contribute to the loss of profitable accounts.

Part of the salesperson's job is to visit the customer's maintenance and repair people. The purpose of such visits is to get to know these people, to offer them assistance in expediting parts shipments, and to supply them with up-to-date service manuals. In addition, the names of service people should be placed on the service mailing list to insure that bulletins are received by the proper people. Well-informed, effective service departments in customers' plants can reduce user complaints dramatically.

Provide information on the care and use of products.   A buyer may be satisfied with the operation of a product, but if it is not operating with maximum efficiency, the wise salesperson shows the buyer how to get more profitable use out of it.

Car salespersons may provide the buyer with a guide for getting the greatest satisfaction from the use of the automobile. Suggestions may be offered on how to save gasoline, how to get maximum wear from tires, how to cut down on repair bills, and how to clean the upholstery. Such suggestions may be prepared by the company in booklet form. However, the mere presentation of the booklet does not complete the job. The information must be merchandised so that the buyer understands it. If buyers do not fully understand when to service a new car, for example, they may cause themselves grief for many years. Yet, even though this may be the buyer's own fault, blame will be placed upon the company, the product, and the salesperson.[3]

To be most effective, the salesperson should not wait until the user has had trouble with the product and then point out the remedies. The fewer the difficulties which are allowed to occur, the greater will be the customer's confidence in the salesperson and the product.

Supply help on advertising, sales, and management problems.   This topic was discussed more fully in Chapter 6, but it is appropriate to review it at this point. The industrial buyer or purchasing agent may need help in choosing a proper grade of oil or in selecting a suitable floor cleaner. The buyer for a retail store may want help in developing sales promotion ideas. Whether the buyer

---

[3] Car manufacturers place considerable emphasis on the care and use of the new car in their training programs for dealer salespersons. Retail stores provide information on the care which major items such as rugs should receive.

needs help in advertising, in selling, or in managing, good sales-people are prepared to offer worthwhile suggestions or services.

The salesperson usually prospers only if the buyer prospers. No buyer is in business just to buy from salespeople. Obviously, unless the buyer is able to use the product or services profitably, or is able to resell the product at a profit, there will no longer be a need for buying.

The salesperson who sells to the buyer for retail stores may be required to help in merchandising the products. In some stores the salesperson may be expected to supply answers to the following questions: "What must I sell this product for to realize a 25 percent gross profit?" "How can I improve my window displays?" "Do you have any suggestions for arranging my stock?" "How can I get the most for my advertising dollar?" "Can you help me train our salesclerks?"

The National Cash Register Company is well known for the book-lets it supplies to aid store owners and managers. A few titles indi-cate the variety of subjects which have been covered:

Making People Want to Trade with You
Efficient Management and Store Operation
Controlling Merchandise and Expenses
Profit from Store Records
Buying to Sell Profitably
Making Telephone and Delivery Services Profitable
Pricing Merchandise Properly
Special Sales
Selling Goods through Window Displays and Proper Lighting

Lily, a manufacturer of paper containers, offers a booklet entitled *The Profitable Art of Merchandising Popcorn* to customers and pros-pects. The booklet tells how to select, pop, store, and promote pop-corn.

U.S. Rubber Company recognizes that its sales and profits are directly tied to the performance of the individual retailer, and the company helps the retailer operate at top efficiency. Within the sales area it has set up a separate department composed of business-management supervisors whose full-time job is to help the small independent tire dealer. When field sales representatives uncover poor business practices, they offer to bring in a company business expert to help the dealer iron out the rough spots. The dealer is usually quite happy to accept the suggestion. The company reports that the management supervisory program has more than paid for itself in increased orders from new successful independent dealers.

IBM and Xerox provide a professional product-utilization service to management. The service promotes higher production and lower costs in the office through better utilization of equipment and personnel.

Opportunities to be of help to the buyer are limited only by imagination and judgment. Progressive companies train their salespeople to be of service. Few companies which are after repeat sales fail to supply some aids to the users of their products or services. To be of real service to the buyer and the company, the salesperson should merchandise these aids. The buyer's problems should be the salesperson's problems.

HANDLING CUSTOMER COMPLAINTS

The adjustment of complaints has been singled out for special treatment because of its importance in developing goodwill. The goodwill which has been established through cultivating customers is often nullified by shortsightedness in handling customer complaints. Some firms spend thousands of dollars for advertising, only to have the customer insulted when attempting to secure a satisfactory adjustment.

It is well known that the cost of making the first sale to a customer is higher than the cost of repeat sales. It is good business, then, to make every reasonable effort to keep a customer in whom the company has invested time and money.

Handling claims provides the salesperson with an opportunity to resell the customer. Many customers do not go to the trouble of complaining; so when a customer does make an effort to secure satisfaction from a product or service, this should be viewed as an opportunity to prove that the company is a good one with which to do business. Studies have shown that only about 50 percent of dissatisfied customers register complaints with the retail store or the manufacturer. These studies give evidence that many dissatisfied customers refuse to buy any more products from the company and that they do not hesitate to tell their friends about their unhappiness.

Despite all the care that the manufacturer takes to produce a good product, unsatisfactory products find their way to the ultimate user or to the retailer. This is a natural situation; it should not be viewed with alarm unless the unsatisfactory products become too numerous.

Most progressive companies have learned that an excellent way to adjust customer complaints is through personal visits of sales representatives. This means that the salesperson may have the total responsibility for the company's public relations. The salesperson who carries this burden must be prepared to do an effective job.

Avoiding complaints

The best way to handle complaints is to avoid them. Typically, complaints arise because the company or its products have not lived up to the customer's expectations. This can occur for the following reasons: (1) the performance of a product is poor; (2) a product is being used improperly; (3) the terms of a sales contract were not met; and (4) the customer's expectations were too high. While salespeople cannot improve the performance of the product, they can affect the three other sources of complaints.

Salespeople should make sure that customers have reasonable expectations concerning the performance of the product. To a large degree, customers base their expectations on the sales presentation. If the salesperson exaggerates the capabilities of the product or the company, the customer will be disappointed and will probably lodge a complaint. Telling the customer that there has been a misunderstanding will not satisfy the customer after a complaint has been registered. Complaints can be avoided by making an honest presentation of the product's capabilities and eliminating any misconceptions before the order is placed.

Providing after-sales support as described in the previous section will avoid complaints due to late delivery, the delivery of unexpected merchandise, and the misuse of products.

Complaints cannot be completely eliminated. They can only be reduced in frequency. The salesperson who knows enough about business operations to realize that complaints are inevitable can learn to handle them as a normal part of the job. The following discussion presents a routine and some techniques for responding to complaints.

Encourage customers to tell their story

Some customers become angered over real or imaginary grievances. They welcome the salesperson's visit as an opportunity for getting complaints "off their chests." Other buyers are less emotional in voicing complaints and give little evidence of irritation or anger. In either case, it is imperative that customers be permitted to tell their stories without interruption.

Interruptions will add to the fury and irritation of buyers who are emotionally upset. Reason seldom prevails when a grievance is discussed with an angry person. This makes it almost impossible to arrive at a settlement which is fair to all parties concerned.

The manner in which salespeople treat customers who want to present complaints will determine the ease with which the adjustments can be made. If salespeople get off to a poor start in the discussion, their chances of developing goodwill diminish rapidly. Customers want a sympathetic reaction to their problems, whether these are real or fancied. They want their grievances handled in a friendly manner. An antagonistic attitude, or an attitude which implies that the customer is trying to cheat the company, seldom paves the way for a satisfactory adjustment.

Good salespeople make it evident that they are happy the grievance has been brought to their attention. After the customer describes the grievance, the salesperson may express regret that any inconvenience has resulted. An attempt should then be made to talk about the points upon which there is agreement. Agreeing with the customer as far as possible gets the process off to the right start.

Determine the facts

It is easy to be influenced by the statements of a customer who is honestly and sincerely making a claim for an adjustment. The inexperienced salesperson is likely to forget that many customers make their case for a claim as strong as possible. It is only human nature to emphasize those points which are most likely to strengthen the basis for a request. However, the salesperson has a responsibility to the company as well as to the customer. A satisfactory adjustment cannot be made until the facts of the case have been determined.

Whenever possible, the salesperson should examine, in the presence of the customer, the article which is claimed to be defective. It may be desirable to have the complaining customer tell and show exactly what is wrong. If the defect is evident, this may be unnecessary. In other instances, it is necessary to make certain that the complaint is understood. The purpose of getting the facts is to determine who is at fault.

Experienced salespeople soon learn that there are reasons why products appear to be defective when there is actually nothing wrong with them. For example, a customer may complain that paint was applied exactly as directed but that it was necessary to repaint in a short time. So the customer concludes that the paint is no good. However, the paint may have been spread too thin. Any good paint will cover just so much area. If the manufacturer recommends that a gallon of paint be used to cover 400 square feet with two coats and the user covers 600 square feet with two coats, the product is not at fault if the results are unsatisfactory. Or, if an office equipment salesperson sells a duplicating machine which requires special paper to get desirable copies, the machine is not at fault if the customer gets unsatisfactory results from a low-grade substitute paper.

In some instances a food product may be frozen although the user has been warned that freezing will spoil it; or leather soles may crack because wet shoes have been placed on a stove to dry; or a battery may fail to operate because it has been used for an extended time with insufficient water. It is obvious that complaints about the service received from a product cannot be accepted as a reflection upon its value merely because the customer says so. It must be determined whether the product has been used properly or whether it has been abused.

Salespeople should not take the attitude that when their products or services fail, it is always the fault of the user. It is necessary to have an open mind and to search for the facts in each case. Defective material may have found its way to the dealer's shelves; the wrong merchandise may have been shipped; the buyer may have been overcharged; or the buyer may have been billed for an invoice which had already been paid. The facts in the case may prove that the company is actually at fault.

Investigation of a claim may prove that neither the buyer nor the seller is at fault. For example, goods can be lost in transit or damaged because of improper handling by the transportation company.

The salesperson may sometimes find that both the buyer and the seller have contributed to unsatisfactory results. Perhaps the buyer failed to follow printed instructions accurately and the salesperson failed to instruct the buyer about the precautions to take when using the product.

Sometimes it is almost impossible to determine the reason for a difficulty. Obviously, this creates a problem in attempting to place the responsibility.

In this phase of making an adjustment it is important for salespeople to avoid leaving the impression that they are stalling. The customer should know that the purpose of determining the facts is to permit a fair adjustment and that the inquiry is not being engaged in to delay action.

Provide a solution

After the customer's story has been told and the salesperson has helped place the responsibility, the next step is to take action.

The policies of companies vary, but many companies assign the responsibility for settling claims to the salesperson. Other companies require the salesperson to investigate claims and to recommend to the home office how they should be settled. The proponents of both methods have good arguments to justify them. Some companies maintain that salespeople are in the best position to make adjustments fairly, promptly, and satisfactorily. Other companies feel that when salespeople are only permitted to recommend a course of action the customer is assured of attention from a higher level of management and that therefore the action taken is more likely to be accepted by the customer. Companies holding the latter view also claim that for many technical products the salesperson is unqualified to make a technical analysis of product difficulties. It is probably better procedure to require salespeople to do the job where possible.

Whatever the company policy, it is well to remember that the customer wants action quickly, wants fair treatment, and wants to know the reasons for the action taken.

Nothing is quite so discouraging to a customer as having action postponed indefinitely. While some decisions may take time, the salesperson is expected to expedite action. The opportunity to resell customers, even though action is taken in their favor, may be lost if the time lapse is too great.

Most customers are satisfied if they receive fair treatment. But it is not enough for the treatment to be fair; customers must be convinced that it is fair. Decisions which are fair to the customer and to the company are a potent factor in building goodwill.

Customers are seldom convinced of the fairness of a decision unless the reasons for reaching it are explained to them. It may be necessary for the salesperson to review the guarantee provided with the product. Or it may be desirable to explain the company's policy and to state why it is followed.

Sometimes salespeople are inclined to take the customer's side and to suggest that the customer is being treated unfairly by members of the administrative staff. This is poor procedure. It does not make a friend of the customer as anticipated; it does cause the customer to lose faith in both the salesperson and the company. Moreover, it is poor policy to blame someone else for the action taken. The salesperson who is trusted with making the adjustment or the recommendation for adjustment is expected to shoulder the responsibility. Any disagreement on the action taken should be ironed out between the salesperson and the home office staff. When the action is reported to the customer, it must be reported in a sound, convincing manner.

The action that should be taken varies with the circumstances. Some possible settlements when a product is unsatisfactory are:

1. Replace the product without cost to the customer.
2. Replace the product, and charge the customer for labor or transportation costs only.
3. Replace the product, and share all costs with the customer.
4. Replace the product, but require the customer to pay part of the cost of the new product.

5. Instruct the customer how to proceed with a claim against a third party.

6. Send the product to the factory for a decision.

Occasionally, customers make claims which they know are unfair. They know the company is not at fault, but they believe it worthwhile to try to get a settlement. Fortunately, there are relatively few customers of this type. The salesperson may be tempted to prove that the customer is wrong—to let the customer know that it is quite clear that no fair claim is being made. However, when the customer has been proved a cheat, the salesperson no longer has a customer.

It is dangerous to assume that a customer is willfully trying to cheat the company. The customer may honestly feel that a claim is legitimate even though it is clear to the salesperson that the company is not at fault. It is well, then, to proceed cautiously. If there is any doubt, the salesperson should proceed as though the claim were legitimate. If the salesperson is convinced that a claim is dishonest, there are two ways to take action. First, give the buyer an opportunity to save face by suggesting that a third party may be to blame. For example, if it is apparent that a machine has not been oiled for a long time, the salesperson may suggest, "Is it possible that your maintenance crew neglected to oil this machine?" Most buyers, especially those who are making an unfair claim, would grab at a straw that would place the blame on someone else and thus save face. In these circumstances, it may be possible to refuse an adjustment and still keep the customer. Second, unmask the fraudulent claim and appeal to the customer's sense of fair play. This procedure is likely to cause the loss of a customer. In some cases, perhaps the company is better off without the customer. Obviously, however, the customer should not be alienated if there is any chance of continuing sound business relationships.

Answers to the following questions have a bearing upon the action to be taken.

1. What is the dollar value of the claim?
2. How often has the customer made claims?
3. What is the size of the account?
4. How valuable is the customer?
5. How will the action taken affect other customers?
6. How successful is the salesperson in presenting facts and placing responsibility?

Follow through on action

A fair settlement made in the customer's favor helps to resell the company and its products or services. The salesperson has the chance to prove what the customer has been told for a long time. The time and care devoted to keeping customers satisfied may be emphasized.

When the salesperson has authority only to recommend an adjustment, care must be taken to report the facts of the case promptly and accurately to the home or branch office. It is the salesperson's responsibility to act as a buffer between the customer and the company. After the claim has been filed, contact must be maintained with the customer, to see that the customer secures the settlement promised.

It is the salesperson's responsibility to educate the customer in order to forestall future claims. When a claim has been settled to the customer's satisfaction, an excellent opportunity is provided to make some suggestions. The retail store salesperson may remind the user to keep the tennis racket in a press, or may caution the wearer to follow directions when washing wool socks. The industrial sales representative may provide a new set of directions on how to oil and clean a machine, or may suggest that help in applying the new floor cleaner is available to the maintenance crew. If customers continually have the same kind of trouble with a product, this may be evidence that the salesperson is not doing a good job.

Some big businesses have built great names for themselves by following the slogan "The customer is always right." Within reason, this should be the attitude displayed by salespeople who plan to cultivate customers and to build goodwill for the company and themselves.[4]

A suggested guide

The following suggestions are helpful when a salesperson is expected to handle the claims routine.

1. Listen carefully, sympathetically, and without interrupting.
2. Express regret for any inconvenience suffered.
3. Reassure the customer that the company wants to do what is fair.
4. Talk about those points upon which there is agreement.
5. Inquire, investigate, and examine to get the facts.
6. Place the responsibility for the difficulty.
7. Take action as promptly as possible.
8. Educate and resell to forestall future claims.
9. Follow through to see that the action promised has actually been taken.

---

[4] In a talk, Jack I. Straus, former chairman of the board, R. H. Macy & Co., Inc., said, "I say if we are right and the customer is wrong, but we can't convince her, settle the matter promptly in her favor."

When making adjustments, the salesperson is acting as a public relations representative for the company. Few companies prosper and grow if customer relations are poor.

Complaints and customer satisfaction

Although complaints are always a sign of customer dissatisfaction, the absence of complaints need not mean that customers are happy. Customers probably articulate 1 in 20 of their complaints. Complaints may be made only when dissatisfaction is high. A buyer in a big corporation may not be aware of what is happening until product users blow their stacks. Lower levels of dissatisfaction will have an adverse effect on sales. Salespeople should be continuously monitoring customers' levels of satisfaction and perceptions of product performance.

QUESTIONS AND PROBLEMS

1. How can a salesperson lose by overselling a customer?

2. Explain how the "art of listening" can be applied to the treatment of a customer who makes a complaint. What can the application of this art accomplish?

3. One way to maintain good relations with customers in the service field is to recognize and adjust to the changes that are taking place. What changes do you see taking place in the service field?

4. If the company cannot deliver an item on the date promised by the sales representative who sold it, what should the sales representative do?

5. A solid basis for any business that wishes to build goodwill in a community is to "do more than is expected." Illustrate how this could be done.

6. Suppose that as a sales representative for a manufacturer of industrial supplies you report directly to the branch manager in your district. Your territory is not large, and you can be in the branch office at least every other day. It is customary for you to spend about two afternoons a week in the branch office.

   One afternoon, while you are working in the branch office, the phone rings and an irate customer says:

   "Look, you know how badly we need those supplies I ordered some time ago. Well, this morning I got a flip notice from your outfit in the mail telling me there will be another delay in the delivery date—the *third* such notice, mind you.

   "Frankly, I don't think I can depend on your company's delivery dates any more. And if you think you're going to get any more business from me, you're nuts!"

What action do you believe is required of you as the sales representative? What recommendations would you make to the home office to prevent this type of situation from causing trouble again?

7. Many customers became irritated with the service they receive when they take their cars to a garage for servicing. As the sales manager for a local car dealer, you believe that your service department can help keep old customers and get new customers. What suggestions would you make to the manager of the service and parts department to build g_dwill through good customer relations?

8. It is believed that consumers have become more independent and have been conditioned to almost unlimited expectations with regard to products and services they buy. What reasons can you give for these new attitudes? What are the implications of these attitudes for goodwill development?

9. Should a salesperson handle all complaints so that the customers are completely satisfied? Explain.

10. The soundest philosophy for building goodwill may be summed up in these words: "It's the little things that count." Identify six or eight "little things" that a salesperson could do which will cost little or nothing but may be extremely valuable in cultivating customers.

11. What is your reaction to the statement "The customer is always right"? Do you consider it a sound basis for making adjustments and satisfying complaints? Do you feel that it can be followed literally? Why?

PROJECTS

1. Consider a purchase that you have made. How would you rate the salesperson in terms of postsale activities? Did he or she develop goodwill? Why or why not? What services were provided? Was your level of expectation concerning the product's performance appropriate? Prepare a report.

2. Contact the local Better Business Bureau. Secure copies of its pamphlets, interview the manager, and learn as much as possible about its operation. Prepare a report on the importance of the Better Business Bureau to the merchants and the salespeople in the area.

3. Make a survey of buyers or purchasing agents in the community. Ascertain whether they receive gifts from the companies with which they do business. Get their reactions to the purposes and values of gift giving and receiving between buyers and sellers. Write up your conclusions.

CASE PROBLEM

Case 13-1

The Sunshine Air Lines, Inc.

Sunshine Air Lines, Inc., with headquarters in southern Florida, is one of the oldest U.S. airlines that is engaged in transporting passengers. The corporation is proud of its reputation as a safe, efficient carrier.

A special analysis of plane reservations revealed that some business executives with a long experience of flying with Sunshine were no longer on its reservation lists. Sunshine knows that these executives must be flying with a competitor or using other means of transportation.

In order to win back as many of them as possible, Sunshine's management has instructed its sales representatives to call upon all business executives who travel extensively and who, for some reason, are no longer flying with Sunshine.

Ed Burda, who had been with Sunshine for three years as a sales representative, selected the owner of a small chain of department stores, August Moon, as his first contact. Burda made an appointment with Moon, and the following interview took place.

Burda: Thought I'd stop around to see you, Mr. Moon. Haven't heard your name mentioned lately.

Moon: And you won't hear my name mentioned around your place again either. I'm through traveling with Sunshine Air Lines. I'm sick and tired of being kicked around by your outfit. The last time I flew your line I couldn't locate my baggage for over a week, and when you did return it, it was all bashed in.

Burda: How long ago did this happen?

Moon: The last incident was seven months ago. Sunshine seems to have a complex on baggage. You either lose 'em or crush 'em. I've read your advertisements about having the world's fastest and most modern airlines. I've often thought that you probably have the world's most modern baggage smashers.

Burda: Oh, it can't be as bad as all that!

Moon: You don't think so, eh? You ought to be on the receiving end of a damaged piece of luggage—corners bashed in, skin peeled off, handle ripped away. And you say, "It can't be as bad as all that."

Burda: Well, of course, we are terribly sorry about it, and we are trying to cut down on that sort of thing.

Moon: I've heard that line before, but I haven't enough baggage to keep testing that statement. Moreover, you people just can't get a plane out of here on time. I have six buyers who travel by air at least once a month. I've told them to take your competitor.

Burda: Say, those new L1011's of ours can beat anything they have to offer.

Moon: Says you, Mr. Burda. My buyers take a DC-10 scheduled out of here one hour and a half after your great L1011—and as a rule they beat the L1011 to its destination, usually because of your delayed departures. Hotels won't keep rooms; we miss connections; oh, it's just not worth it.

Burda: Well, Mr. Moon, we are trying to cut down on delays. We are learning more about maintaining our larger equipment, and we feel that we are making headway.

Moon: I'm fed up with Sunshine, and I'm not going to give you any more tries—not until you can really sell me that things are actually different. You haven't done a very good job so far.

Ed Burda concluded the interview by saying that he would certainly appreciate the opportunity to show that Sunshine's service was all that it was advertised to be.

Another Sunshine sales representative, Russ Hodges, was the luncheon speaker for a local Rotary Club when the club celebrated Aviation Day. He talked about the operations of Sunshine Air Lines in particular and about aviation problems in general. After the speech one of the Rotarians, Pete Morley, congratulated him and said he enjoyed the talk. During the conversation Hodges learned that Morley was a former Sunshine Air Lines customer but had become disgruntled and was no longer flying with Sunshine.

Hodges decided to call on Morley at a later date. The following conversation took place about one week later.

Hodges: Mr. Morley, it's kind of you to give me a hearing on your complaints with Sunshine.

Morley: Well, I felt I owed it to you after the way I criticized your company at our club the other day. You made a darn good speech; but when I thought about my experiences with Sunshine, I got somewhat irritated.

Hodges: Tell me about the experience that is making you fly with our competitor.

Morley: It wasn't one experience. It was a lot of the same old stuff over and over again. It was the repetition that got me down. I've used Sunshine since the DC-3s, and I've always thought the world of your management—and to such an extent that I'm a stockholder. And I don't invest my money without thoroughly investigating and knowing the company.

Hodges: I'm sorry that you feel the way you do about our company, Mr. Morley. Specifically, what did you experience?

Morley: Essentially, I'm a short-haul commuter. The last time I flew Sunshine, I had trouble getting a reservation; and although a round trip reservation was finally confirmed, when I checked in at my destination, your agent said they had no record of it at all. I'll bet I spent 20 to

30 minutes at your ticket counter trying to get the reservation straightened out. They never did find any record of it, and finally sold me space on a flight that left an hour later. But an hour with you fellows seems to be very unimportant.

All of which reminds me about the time I was on a short flight of only 35 minutes, but we spent 45 minutes at the airport while your agents ran up and down the aisle counting heads and doing a lot of talking in the rear of the cabin. You waste more time in ticketing and boarding. You ought to be able to solve that kind of problem.

And besides, there're those equipment delays. If you're going to be delayed several hours, tell us. You may lose my business that day, but I'll be back sooner than if you keep stalling me off 15 minutes at a time. There's no point in my taking a plane for an hour's flight if I have to hang around an airport for an hour waiting for a delayed departure.

Hodges: You know, Mr. Morley, if it weren't for the fact that we are getting those problems licked, I'd say you were justified in using other transportation.

Morley: Getting them licked, how—how?

Hodges: In the first place, we have recently installed a new reservations system that is geared to our current needs. Under this setup, we can usually confirm your going and return space immediately. You make only one call. *One call does it all.*

In addition, we have installed a new loading procedure which has been extremely well received. And it's especially pertinent in your case as a commuter. If you have been ticketed before going to the airport, and you have no luggage, you only need to wait for the loading announcement to enplane. That's a real time-saver and a convenience to the commuter passenger, isn't it, Mr. Morley?

Morley: Yes, you're right. That boarding idea sounds great, and your "one call" is an answer to a traveler's prayer if it only works.

Hodges: It works, all right. How about giving us a chance to prove it?

Morley *(laughing):* How about those delays? My sales representatives, unlike me, are long-haul passengers. They are using your competitors whenever possible, and your competition is doing better by them too.

Hodges: Well, I'm not going to deny that we've had delays with our big planes. Naturally, it takes a while for our maintenance personnel to get the know-how of new equipment. When we introduced our DC–7s and –8s we had the same trouble, but we beat the problem. The same holds for our new L1011's, but we are beating that one too. The record isn't perfect yet, but we are way ahead of where we were only three months ago. How about giving us another try?

Morley: And then have another piece of luggage crushed? All airlines are tough on baggage, but Sunshine is near the top.

Hodges: I'll admit we haven't got an enviable record on that score. We have been putting on a campaign all over our system to eliminate damaged baggage. Management is trying its best to clean up that problem. If you will fly Sunshine, I'm sure you will find an improvement on that point too.

Morley: Well, you seem confident things are better. I'll tell you. I'm planning a short trip in about ten days. I was going to use your competition, but I might try Sunshine again. I'll call you as soon as I determine the exact date.

But let me warn you, this is only a trial. I'm not going to advise my sales representatives to travel with your company again until I see some real results. You've told me a good yarn—now we'll see.

Hodges: Thank you, sir. That's a fair arrangement. I'll call you early next week to learn if you have set a definite date for your trip.

Questions

1. What do you believe to be the specific weaknesses and strengths of Burda's interview?
2. What strengths and weaknesses did you observe in Hodges' interview?
3. Which of the two sales representatives did the better job? Why?
4. What do you believe airlines must do to improve their profit patterns?

SELECTED REFERENCES

Berry, D., and **Suiprenant, C.** "Defusing the Complaint Time Bomb." *Sales & Marketing Management,* July 11, 1977, pp. 40+.

Blanding, W. "Customer Service: Believe It or Not, Errors of Omission Do More Damage than Any Other Kind." *Sales & Marketing Management,* September 17, 1979, pp. 112–14.

————. "Customer Service Can Make or Break You in More Ways Than One." *Sales & Marketing Management,* June 6, 1978, pp. 110+.

————. "12 Tips No Salesman Wants to Hear (or Can Afford to Live Without)." *Sales Management,* February 17, 1975, pp. 26–30.

Cron, R. L. *Assuring Customer Satisfaction: A Guide for Business and Industry.* New York: Van Nostrand Reinhold, 1974.

Korn, Don. "Customer Service and the Bottom Line." *Sales Management,* February 17, 1975, pp. 2–4.

"Pulling Sales and Service Together—An Exclusive SM&M Survey." *Sales & Marketing Management,* October 9, 1978, pp. 92+.

Rosenblum, S. "10 Secrets of Better Sales Letters." *Sales & Marketing Management,* May 16, 1977, pp. 36–38.

Sabath, E. "How Much Service Do Customers Really Want?" *Business Horizons,* April 1978, pp. 26–32.

Young, J. R. "Salesperson-Buyer Connection." *Sales & Marketing Management,* May 16, 1977, p. 78.

Chapter 14

INDUSTRIAL AND TRADE SELLING

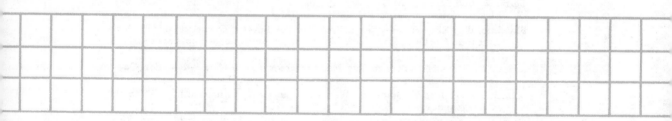

Most consumers have frequent contact with retail salespeople in department stores. Behind each retail salesperson is an army of trade and industrial salespeople. These salespeople are involved in selling the things that go into the products sold in the department store.

For each dollar spent at the retail level, $4.50 is spent by various wholesale and manufacturing companies.[1] The following example

---

[1] *Statistical Abstract of the United States*, 1978 (Washington, D.C.: U.S. Department of Commerce).

demonstrates the size of industrial and trade sales relative to retail sales. Consider a $15 calculator that you might purchase in a store. To make the calculator, the manufacturer purchased $5 of processed materials, such as plastic and electronic components. In addition, capital equipment was purchased to mold the plastic, assemble the components, and test the calculator. The manufacturer sold the calculator to a wholesaler for $10. The retail store purchased the calculator from the wholesaler for $12. In this example, $27 in sales to manufacturers and wholesalers results in a $15 sale at retail.

This chapter concentrates on the specialized skills and knowledge that are needed for industrial and trade selling. Major topics covered are the types of products sold and the purchasing behavior of industrial and trade customers. The skills needed for selling at the retail level are presented in Chapter 15.

NATURE OF INDUSTRIAL AND TRADE SELLING[2]

Who are industrial and trade salespeople?

Industrial salespeople sell goods and services to industrial companies. Traditionally, industrial customers have been defined as manufacturing companies that acquire products and services in order to provide their own products and services. However, this traditional definition of industrial customers is frequently broadened to include governmental and institutional customers. Governmental customers include many municipal, state, and federal agencies. The federal government of the United States is the largest purchaser of goods and services in the world. Institutional customers include hospitals, universities, school districts, utilities, and research laboratories. In this chapter, industrial selling is defined as selling to manufacturing, governmental, and institutional customers.

Trade salespeople sell products to wholesalers and retailers. These middlemen purchase products for resale. The resellers add value to the products by making them readily available, providing credit, and supplying information.

Many firms sell products to both industrial customers and to consumers. Their sales to consumers are made directly or through resellers. A salesperson working for such a company is assigned to one or the two markets. Examples of companies selling to both types of customers are shown in Figure 14-1.

---

[2] For a comprehensive treatment of industrial marketing, see Richard M. Hill, Ralph S. Alexander, and James S. Cross, *Industrial Marketing*, 4th ed. (Homewood, Ill.: Richard D. Irwin, 1975). A more advanced discussion can be found in Frederick E. Webster, Jr., *Industrial Marketing Strategy* (New York: John Wiley, 1979).

Figure 14-1

Examples of companies selling to both industrial customers and consumers

Type of company	Products sold to industrial customer	Products sold to consumer
Fireman's Fund (insurance)	Group insurance plans	Individual life and automobile insurance policies
Cleveland Electric Illuminating Co. (utility)	Energy for manufacturing companies	Energy for private homes
Boise Cascade (wood products)	Lumber for construction	Lumber for do-it-yourself home repair
International Harvester (motorized vehicles)	Fleet trucks to transportation companies	Trucks to individual farmers
Texas Instruments (electronics)	Calculators for office use	Calculators for home use

What are industrial goods and services?

Industrial products are classified as heavy equipment, light equipment, components and subassemblies, raw and processed materials, supplies, and services. The successful seller of these products and services must be both a skilled salesperson and a technical specialist.

Heavy equipment comprises the construction equipment that is used to build roads, buildings, and machinery, such as locomotives, turbines, machine tools, and computers. Such equipment is often designed to meet the needs of a particular customer. Companies usually treat the purchase of heavy equipment as a major investment decision. They often borrow money to purchase such equipment. Thus the purchase of heavy equipment has a significant financial impact.

Heavy equipment is frequently referred to as capital equipment because it is treated as a capital asset. The depreciation of the asset is considered a production cost.

Light equipment includes such equipment as hand tools, cash registers, instruments, and small motors. Both heavy and light equipment are used in the production process. Light equipment has a lower price and a shorter expected life than heavy equipment. It is typically available in standard sizes from several manufacturers.

Components and subassemblies are items that become part of a company's final product. Some examples are gauges, semiconductors, plastic parts, and hardware. The cost of subassemblies and components directly affects the cost of the company's products. Thus companies are very concerned about price when they purchase subassemblies and components. Another important consideration is uninterrupted availability. If companies cannot get the necessary components, they cannot make and sell their own products. To get low prices and assure availability, industrial customers encourage competition among suppliers. Frequently customers will not buy a component unless a "second source," an alternative supplier, is available. The development of new suppliers is an important activity for purchasing agents. Often companies are faced with "make or buy" decisions concerning components and subassemblies. They must decide whether it is best to make parts internally or to buy them from a vendor.

Raw and processed materials are the basic or processed materials of the land and sea. Raw materials include logs, iron ore, crude oil, and fish. Lumber, steel, and chemicals are examples of processed materials. Very few firms sell raw materials. Raw materials are typically traded in markets. Their prices are set by the force of supply and demand. Processed materials are usually available from several sources. The materials themselves are undifferentiated. The suppliers of processed materials compete on the basis of the services they offer such as fast delivery, the available range of sizes and forms, and applications assistance.

Maintenance, repair, and operating (MRO) supplies include cleaning supplies, grinding wheels, paper products, and office supplies. MRO supplies are used by an organization as part of its normal operations. They do not become part of the finished product. The items have a low unit price and are purchased frequently. Often, an annual agreement is negotiated with a supplier. In the agreement the company guarantees to purchase a specific quantity over the contract period. The supplier then provides the item at a reduced price.

Services include all intangibles purchased by an organization, such as insurance, banking, consulting, and shipping. It is very difficult to develop purchase specifications for services. The quality of services is hard to measure. Services depend greatly on the people who deliver them. Thus, the people responsible for delivering a service are often responsible for selling it.[3]

How do industrial, trade, and retail selling differ?

Like all salespeople, industrial and trade salespeople must convince the customer that their products and services will satisfy the customer's needs. Certain characteristics of industrial and reseller

---

[3] Most of this chapter deals with selling products. Information on selling industrial services can be found in Warren Wittreich, "How to Sell/Buy Professional Services," *Harvard Business Review*, March–April 1966, pp. 73–78, and Christian Gronroos, "An Applied Theory for Marketing Industrial Services," *Industrial Marketing Management*, Fall 1979, pp. 45–50.

markets make them different from consumer markets. The following general characteristics are of particular importance to salespeople.

Geographic concentration.   The distribution of consumer product markets and consumer product reseller markets is related to the distribution of the population. In contrast, industrial markets are highly concentrated. There are often great distances between markets in the same industry. For example, companies in the electronics industry are concentrated in Boston, New York City, the San Francisco Bay Area (Silicon Valley), and Los Angeles. Over 50 percent of all U.S. manufacturing is done in seven states: New York, California, Pennsylvania, Illinois, Ohio, New Jersey, and Michigan. Less than 2 percent of the U.S. manufacturing firms account for over 50 percent of industrial sales. Thus, the industrial salesperson usually deals with a few customers in a restricted geographic area.

Derived demand.   The demand for the products sold by industrial and trade salespeople is derived rather than direct. This means that the amount of the purchases made by a customer depends on the demand for the customer's products. For example, the number of Ford automobiles purchased by consumers determines how many tires Ford will purchase from a tire manufacturer. Because demand is derived, the salesperson must understand the needs and buying habits of the ultimate customer as well as the immediate customer. Sometimes salespeople can stimulate the demand for their products by directing their efforts toward the ultimate customer. Thus Procter and Gamble salespeople set up in-store displays so that consumers will buy more of their products. When the consumers buy more, the supermarkets will place more orders with the Procter and Gamble salespeople.

Complexity of the buying process.   The typical industrial sale is much larger in both dollars and units than the typical consumer sale. The purchasing decisions made by industrial companies frequently have a significant effect on company performance. Many people get involved in the decisions. Companies use highly trained, knowledgeable purchasing agents to make the decisions. The purchasing agents work with engineers, production people, and business analysts to evaluate the technical and economic aspects of purchasing decisions. *Factory* magazine found that an average of 11.9 people, not including the purchasing department, are involved in a purchasing decision.

These extensive evaluations and negotiations take place over a long period. The average time required to complete an industrial purchase is over five months. During that time the salesperson must make many calls to gather information and get the order.

The complexity of the industrial purchase decision means that a salesperson must be able to work with a wide range of people. In selling a new packaging material to a food processor, a salesperson might interface with advertising, product development, legal, production, quality control, and customer service people in the customer's company. The salesperson must be knowledgeable about both technical and economic benefits of the product. In addition, salespeople must coordinate all the areas of *their own firm* to assist in making the sale. The salesperson works with engineering to provide the performance needed by the customer, with production to meet the customer's delivery needs, and with the business office to secure appropriate financial terms. Trade salespeople must often coordinate cooperative advertising campaigns in addition to checking on delivery and financial terms.

Long-term customer-salesperson relationships. In industrial and trade selling, the salesperson and the customer are dependent on each other. The salesperson needs the customer's orders to meet sales objectives. However, the customer needs the salesperson to make sure that the product is delivered when it is needed and that repair parts and service are provided. Because of this interdependence, obtaining a specific purchase order is only one point in a long-term relationship between the industrial salesperson and the customer. In contrast, in retail selling the salesperson-customer relationship often ends after the sale has been made.

THE BUYING DECISION PROCESS

Industrial and trade buying decisions are the result of a complex set of activities. Many people in both the salesperson's organization and the buying organization participate in such decisions. This section discusses the phases of the decision process, the types of buying decisions, and the roles of the various participants in the decisions.

Phases of the buying decision process

An important study of purchasing decisions in industrial organizations defined the following eight phases in the process:

1. Recognition of a need.
2. Definition of the type of product needed.
3. Development of the detailed product specification.
4. Search for qualified sources.
5. Acquisition and analysis of proposal.
6. Selection of a supplier.
7. Selection of an order routine.
8. Evaluation of product performance.[4]

---

[4] See Patrick J. Robinson, Charles W. Faris, and Yoram Wind, *Industrial Buying and Creative Marketing* (Boston: Allyn & Bacon, 1967).

The buying process starts when someone realizes that a problem can be solved by purchasing a product or service. This need recognition phase can be initiated by either external or internal stimuli. Examples of external stimuli might include a salesperson's presentation of a new product or a display at a trade show.

When a production manager concludes that his factory is not running efficiently, the buying process enters phase 1, as the result of an internal stimulus. A problem is recognized. But this may not lead to a purchase decision. The manager may find that the inefficiency is due to poor supervision, unskilled employees, or inadequate organization of the production facility.

However, a production equipment salesperson might work with the manager to analyze the situation. This analysis might demonstrate that efficiency could be improved by purchasing some automated assembly equipment. When this occurs, the buying decision goes through phase 2. In the next phase, the salesperson helps the manager develop detailed specifications. The specifications are used by the purchasing department in phase 4. In phase 5 the salesperson works with people in his or her company to prepare a solicited proposal. Then the salesperson attempts to influence the evaluation of the proposals so that his or her equipment is selected in phase 6. If the equipment is selected, the salesperson, in phase 7, finalizes the delivery dates, terms and conditions for the order with the purchasing manager. The salesperson's job is not done when the order has been placed. The salesperson must work with the production department to make sure that the equipment performs well after it arrives. This after-sale support insures that the salesperson's equipment will get a positive evaluation in phase 8, and thus be considered a qualified source in future decisions.

The steps taken by an automobile manufacturer to purchase a test stand for engines are shown in Figure 14–2. Can you relate each step in the test stand purchase decision to the eight phases described above?

Types of buying decisions

It is important for the salesperson to realize that not all buying situations are the same. There are three basic types of buying decisions—a new buy, a straight rebuy, and a modified rebuy. The salesperson must use a different sales strategy for each of these situations.

New buy. A new buy occurs when the customer is purchasing a product that has not been purchased before. An example of a new buy would be a company's purchase of a small computer for au-

Figure 14–2
Steps in purchasing an automotive engine test stand

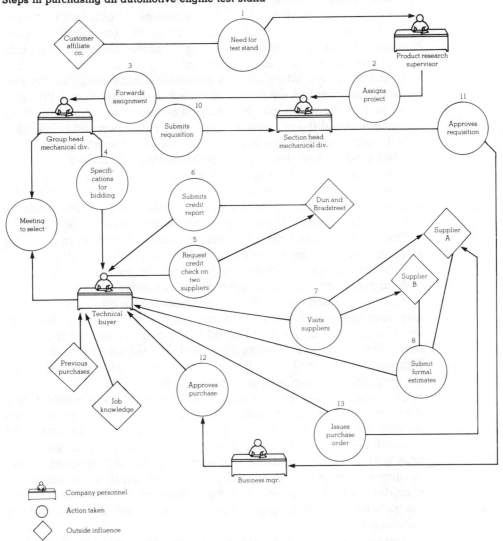

Source: Reprinted by permission of The Motor and Equipment Manufacturers Association from *Marketing Insights*, October 31, 1966, p. 18.

tomating its manual accounting system. Most purchase decisions involving heavy equipment are new buys. The initial purchases of components or even raw materials are also new buys. In such situations, the purchase decision is quite complex. The customer goes through all eight phases of the buying decision. However, the early phases are usually the most important.

In the new buy situation, the customer's knowledge is limited. Since the product has not been purchased in the past, the customer is open to new suggestions. No competitor has an advantage. Such situations afford the salesperson an excellent opportunity. The alert salesperson can help the customer define the characteristics of the needed product and develop the purchase specifications.

The salesperson who works with a customer on these early phases has a significant advantage over competition. Frequently, the purchase specifications can be written so that competitive products are not able to meet all the requirements at a reasonable price.

The postpurchase evaluation phase is also important in new buy situations. Since the buyers are making a new type of purchase decision they are interested in evaluating the results of the decision.

Straight rebuy.   In the straight rebuy situation, the customer has already purchased the product a number of times. In fact, the decision may be so routine that it is computerized. When the inventory level of a part reaches a specified level, a purchase order is automatically rewritten. Typically, straight rebuy purchases are triggered by internal stimuli such as depletion of inventory or the recognition of a supplier's poor performance.

The later buying phases are most important for straight rebuy decisions. The needs are easily recognized; specifications have been developed; and qualified sources are well known. If the price and delivery are in line, the company that provided the product in the past will probably continue to get orders. The salesperson whose company is providing the product does not want the customer to consider another supplier. Thus the salesperson must make sure that the product is delivered on time and meets all the performance specifications.

The salesperson who is trying to break into a straight rebuy situation faces a tough sales problem. It is very difficult to convince a customer to change products when the competition is doing a satisfactory job. In such situations, the salesperson calls on the customer in the hope that the competitor will make a critical mistake. The salesperson can also attempt to create a modified rebuy situation by getting the customer to reassess needs.

A recent study reported that two to three people in the buying company are involved in straight rebuys, while three to seven people are involved in new buys. A straight rebuy takes from one week to seven months, while a new buy takes from seven months to five years.[5]

Modified rebuy. In a modified rebuy situation, the customer has purchased the product in the past but is interested in obtaining new information. This situation typically occurs when the performance of a previous supplier has been unsatisfactory or when new products become available. In such situations, the salesperson needs to convince the customer to alter the purchase specifications or the list of qualified sources.

Who makes the buying decisions?

Even in the smallest company, more than one person is likely to be involved in the purchase decision. The industrial salesperson needs to know the names and titles of all the people who will be involved. Frequently, salespeople have detailed files for each customer, including a complete organization chart of the company and the roles that each person plays in the decision. This section describes some of the people or groups involved in purchase decisions.

The purchasing agent. The person who occupies the formal buying position in a company is the purchasing agent or buyer. The importance of the purchasing agent in a buying decision varies with the type of decision and the company. Generally, purchasing agents are most involved in the latter phases of the decision. They are responsible for placing the order; establishing the price, delivery, and financial terms; and monitoring supplier performance. Because of their involvement in the latter phases, purchasing agents are more important in straight rebuy situations than in new buy situations.

However, purchasing agents may play an important role in all buying situations. They are at the hub of the activities concerning purchase decisions. They know most of the people in the company and what sales opportunities exist. Thus, the purchasing agent can be a valuable source of information. The purchasing agent can also serve as an "internal salesperson" representing the salesperson's product to people in the company. Therefore, the salesperson must cultivate contacts in the purchasing department even if other people in the company have more influence over the purchase decision.

The purchasing agent may also serve as a gatekeeper. In some companies, all contacts must be made through the purchasing agent. The salespeople cannot contact a user directly. The interview must be arranged by the purchasing agent. When the economy is

---

[5] Peter Doyle, Arch G. Woodside, and Paul Mickell, "Organizations Buying in New Tasks and Rebuy Situations," *Industrial Marketing Management*, Winter 1979, pp. 7–11.

depressed and sales are hard to make, salespeople are tempted to bypass the purchasing agent. One agent's comment on this practice is, "I will warn a vendor once. If he continues, we will not do any business with him."[6]

Purchasing agents are professional buyers. They see thousands of salespeople each year. They have heard a lot of sales presentations and have had many two-martini lunches. They cannot be fooled easily. They are interested in hearing about the benefits of a product, but they have no time for idle conversation.

On the other hand, salespeople should not be afraid of purchasing agents. They must remember that purchasing agents have problems. It is often difficult for them to find alternative sources for a product. By proposing new ways of solving problems with products that will reduce costs or increase performance, salespeople can help purchasing agents look good to their supervisors. Purchasing agents appreciate any assistance that will help them save time or effort.

The users.   While the users typically do not make the ultimate decision, they are particularly important in the need recognition, product definition, and final evaluation phases. Thus, the users are particularly important in new buy and modified rebuy situations. The salesperson can trigger a new buy or a reassessment of a straight rebuy by demonstrating a product's new benefits to a user.

The influencers.   In addition to purchasing agents and users, a number of other people in a company influence the purchase decision. Engineers may develop specifications. Frequently, quality control and maintenance personnel determine which vendors are qualified sources. Marketing people may argue that the company's product would sell better if a particular supplier's components were used. The salesperson needs to sell such influencers.

The decision makers.   It is often difficult to determine who makes the ultimate decision in an industrial purchase. For small, routine purchases, the purchasing agent selects the vendor and places the order. However, for important purchases, a number of people influence the selection. Moreover, several people must approve the decision and sign the purchase order.

In purchases involving new tasks, the decision is made by "creeping commitment." At each phase, small decisions are made. These small decisions result in the choice of one supplier. For example, an early decision concerning the type of equipment that will solve the problem eliminates some potential suppliers from consideration. When specifications are developed, manufacturers that cannot meet all of the specifications are eliminated. Some potential suppliers may be eliminated because they cannot meet the delivery require-

---

[6] James Morgan, "Backdoor Selling Is Up—The Economy Down," *Purchasing,* November 21, 1979, pp. 65-68.

ments. Thus successful salespeople involve themselves in decisions made throughout the purchasing process.

FUNCTIONS OF THE PURCHASING AGENT

While many people are involved in the buying decision, the process is usually managed by professional purchasing agents. This section discusses some of the unique activities undertaken by purchasing agents.

Value analysis

Value analysis is a problem-solving method that was introduced by General Electric in the late 1940s. The objective of value analysis is to reduce costs and still provide the needed level of performance. In other words, value analysis is a method for helping the company make the "best buy."

Value analysis is usually performed by members of the purchasing department. When more complex parts or products are examined, technical experts from engineering, production, or quality control may be part of a team making the analysis. The analysis begins with an examination of the product's function. Then questions are asked to determine whether changes can be made in the design, materials, or construction of the product to reduce the product's cost but not its performance. Questions like these are used in a value analysis:

☐ Can the part be eliminated?
☐ If the part is not standard, can a standard part be used?
☐ Does the part have greater performance than is required?
☐ Are unnecessary machining or fine finishes specified?
☐ Can a similar item in inventory be specified?

How can the industrial salesperson use value analysis? A properly planned sales presentation using value analysis is a good way to get a buyer to consider a new product. This technique is particularly useful in straight rebuy situations. In such situations, the purchasing agent will consider a new supplier only if doing so will achieve a significant new benefit. Through value analysis, the salesperson can convince buyers that their needs have changed and that they should consider a new supplier. Customers expect salespeople to make cost-saving suggestions.[7] Such suggestions can trigger a new buy or a modified rebuy decision.

---

[7] See "Suppliers Need Help to Meet the VA Challenge," *Purchasing*, March 28, 1979, pp. 58–63.

Make or buy

Purchasing agents often decide whether to produce a product internally or to purchase it from an outside supplier. This choice is usually made at the early stages of a new buy decision on components and subassemblies. In such situations, the industrial salesperson must show a customer that buying from his or her company is more profitable than making the product internally.

The answer to the make or buy question is not simple. While price is usually the most important consideration, other factors enter into the decision. A company may decide to make a product that could be purchased more economically. This situation often occurs when the company needs assured delivery or an unusually high level of quality control.

Vendor and product evaluations

Many organizations use a formal method for evaluating potential vendors. Typically, each vendor is rated numerically on a number of dimensions. Among the dimensions commonly used are labor situation, quality control, financial condition, plant utilization, spending on research and development, age of equipment, and delivery performance.

For example, National Can uses the following factors and weights to evaluate vendors:[8]

Factor	Weight
Competitive pricing	0.8
On-time delivery	0.9
Quality	0.9
Emergency assistance	0.9
Communications	0.4
Technical service	0.4
Cost reduction suggestions	0.5
Inventory (stocking) program	0.3

A new vendor is then rated on each factor from 0 ("absolutely unacceptable") to 5 ("excellent—top 10 percent of all suppliers"). The rating for each factor is multiplied by the factor weight, and a total score is calculated. A total score of 18 or higher qualifies a vendor as a preferred supplier; a 10–17 score is acceptable; 5–9 indicates a marginal supplier; and 0–5 is unacceptable. Notice that this evaluation technique used by industrial purchasing agents is similar to the

---

[8] Somerby Dowst, "You Can't Rate Vendors in a Vacuum," *Purchasing*, October 10, 1979, pp. 79–84.

multiattribute evaluation model for consumers described in Chapter 3.

Similar procedures are used to evaluate alternative products and proposals. Among the most important criteria for evaluating industrial products are performance, service, and price—generally in that order of importance. However, the importance attached to a factor depends on the phase in the buying process, the type of buying decision, and the type of person who is being sold.[9]

Performance.   A product will be purchased only if it meets the customer's needs. A product that is lower in price but does not provide the necessary performance has no value to the customer.

Service.   Industrial customers expect service. This is particularly true in purchases of heavy equipment. Prepurchase service starts with an analysis of the customer's needs. This analysis should demonstrate to the customer that you understand the problem and are proposing a useful solution.

Postpurchase service includes installation of the equipment, training of operators, and equipment maintenance. A recent survey of purchasing agents reported that of the purchase contracts for heavy equipment 88 percent included installation requirements; 75 percent, operator training; and 38 percent, maintenance.[10]

Another aspect of service is dependability of supply. Purchasing agents must be able to count on the delivery dates quoted by a supplier. If the supplier's delivery is very late, the customer may be unable to produce its products and meet its delivery commitments. A major responsibility of the salesperson is to make sure that the customer is receiving the service needed.

Price.   Obviously, customers are interested in satisfying their needs at the lowest possible cost. They want the lowest priced product that will meet their requirements. However, comparing the prices of alternative products is often complicated. In addition to the basic cost of the equipment, the customer must consider the cost of accessories, installation costs, freight charges, estimated maintenance costs, and operating costs including the cost of energy consumption.

Life cycle costing is an important concept in industrial marketing. Using this method, the cost of the product is calculated over its useful life.[11] The salesperson can often demonstrate that a product with

[9] See William A. Dempsey, "Vendor Selection and the Buying Process," *Industrial Marketing Management*, Spring 1978, pp. 257-67.

[10] Somerby Dowst, "Capital Buying: One Strike and You're Out," *Purchasing*, March 8, 1979, p. 59.

[11] Roger Brown, "A New Marketing Tool: Life Cycle Costing," *Industrial Marketing Management*, Summer 1979, pp. 109-13.

a higher initial cost will have a lower overall cost. An example of life cycle costing is shown in Table 14-1.

Purchasing contracts

Much of today's purchasing takes place under contracts. These contracts reduce the purchase decision to routine clerical activities. In other words, purchase contracts lead to straight rebuy decisions.

Two common types of purchasing agreements are the *blanket purchase order* and the *annual purchase agreement*. The blanket purchase order is often used when low-cost items, such as MRO supplies, are bought frequently.

Under a blanket purchase order, the buyer contracts with the supplier to accept delivery on a specified quantity at a specified price over a specified period of time. A purchase order is issued when the contract is made. When the items are needed, a release form is issued, authorizing the vendor to make a shipment. This type of contract minimizes the number of formal purchase orders.

Under an annual purchase agreement, the supplier agrees to provide parts at a specified discount schedule over the contract period. As the company buys more parts, it qualifies for lower prices.

Purchasing contracts tend to "lock in" organizations to their present suppliers. Thus it is advantageous for salespeople to conclude long-term contracts with customers. On the other hand, it is difficult for salespeople to sell to customers that have made contracts with competitors.

Reciprocity

Reciprocity is a special relationship in which two companies agree to buy products from each other. Such relationships are fairly common in industrial markets. For example, an electronic compo-

Table 14-1
Example of life cycle costing

	Product A	Product B
Power consumption per year	150,0000 kwh	180,000 kwh
Life of machine	10 years	10 years
Initial cost	$ 35,000	$ 30,000
Power cost @ $0.03/kwh for ten years	45,000	54,000
Operating and maintenance cost @ $3,000/year	30,000	30,000
Life cycle cost	$110,000	$114,000

Note: A more thorough analysis would consider the present value of future costs and the tax implications.

nents manufacturer may buy test equipment only from companies that use its components in making their test equipment. There are some good reasons why companies buy from their customers. The interrelationships caused by reciprocal dealings can lead to greater trust and cooperation between their companies.

Attempts at reciprocity can result in ill will between companies. The procedures for monitoring a reciprocity agreement may become very complex. For example, a company may decide to buy from a customer only if the customer's prices are identical to those of competition. In some cases, companies may threaten customers. They may indicate that they will buy from the customer only if the customer agrees to buy from them.

The use of reciprocity varies from informal arrangements to formal agreements that include systems for keeping track of purchases. Formal agreements tend to reduce price competition. For this reason, a large majority of purchasing agents dislike reciprocity.[12] Reciprocity agreements which substantially lessen competition can be illegal. Thus the salesperson must use caution when discussing such deals.

Purchasing policies

Frequently the purchasing agent's activities are governed by formal company policies. For example, a company may require that orders over $10,000 can be placed only after at least two suppliers have made competitive bids. Or it may require that specific people in the company approve purchase orders of specified sizes. Thus an engineer may be able to purchase up to $1,000 worth of equipment. However, the approval of his or her supervisor may be required for purchases of more than $5,000 and the department manager's approval may be required for purchases of over $10,000. The salesperson must know the policies that determine the steps and the people involved in the purchase process.

GROUP BUYING AND SELLING

Industrial and trade salespeople must frequently make sales presentations to groups of people rather than individual buyers. This is particularly true in selling to food retailers. Of all buying decisions for grocery store chains, 90 percent are made by committees.

The principles stated in Chapters 8, 9, 10, and 11 are applicable when an industrial salesperson makes a presentation to one indi-

---

[12] Monroe Bird and C. Wayne Sheppard, "Reciprocity in Industrial Buying and Selling: A Study of Attitudes," *Journal of Purchasing*, November 1973, pp. 26–35.

vidual. This section discusses some special considerations in making group presentations.

Suggestions for group selling

The salesperson initiates a group sales presentation by making a presentation to one person. The purpose of this presentation is to get the person to schedule the group presentation. This presentation is typically made in a conference room in or near the purchasing department.

Before the presentation, the salesperson should attempt to contact each person who will attend. In these pre-meeting contacts, the salesperson attempts to learn each person's needs, interests, opinions, and preferences. The salesperson also tries to determine which participants have the most influence on various aspects of the purchase. If a leader can be identified, the salesperson should try to sell him or her before the meeting. It is very important to have a strong ally when making a group presentation.

The salesperson must be thoroughly prepared for the presentation. In addition to making the presentation, the salesperson needs to encourage and control interactions within the group. These interactions include the salesperson's interactions with each group member and the interactions among the group members. Control of group meetings is accomplished by monitoring and evaluating each member's responses. This can be done by maintaining eye contact, observing facial reactions and body movements, and encouraging comments and questions.

A major problem in group selling is that group members have different technical knowledge and interests and different roles in the purchase decision. The salesperson's presentation must satisfy the needs of each group member. Thus, the presentation should cover a number of product benefits. The statement of a specific benefit should be directed toward the group member most interested in that benefit. When responding to a question, the salesperson should attempt to include group members other than the questioner in the answer. This can often be accomplished by having another member answer the question. However, this technique should be used only if the salesperson knows what the response will be. By encouraging interaction among group members, the salesperson gets the group to sell itself—to recognize that advantages offset disadvantages.

Consider the salesperson who has made a presentation on a digital readout subassembly for an FM tuner. The production manager comments that the readout will be more expensive than the present mechanical dial. The salesperson then asks the design engineer whether the readout will make the tuner more reliable and asks the marketing manager whether the more reliable new feature will justify a higher price. A favorable response from the marketing manager will overcome the production manager's objection.

The group leader presents a difficult problem for the salesperson. The salesperson wants to make sure that the leader is convinced by the presentation. However, the salesperson does not want to offend the other group members by directing too much attention to the leader. It is also important for the salesperson to realize that the leader can be influenced by the group's reactions.

It is very difficult to close a sale at a group meeting. Usually the salesperson must contact some individuals after the meeting to get the order.

Visual aids and demonstrators are particularly important for group presentations. They focus the attention of group members on key points and help the salesperson demonstrate product features and benefits.

It is a good idea to bring another salesperson when making a group presentation. The other salesperson can help by observing reactions to the presentation. Based on these observations, the other salesperson may interrupt to present appropriate information that has been neglected. Such interruptions also give the presenter a break.

Team selling and buying

In many industrial situations, buying and selling are performed by teams of specialists. Both the selling and the buying teams include technical and financial experts.

Team selling is becoming more common in industrial selling. The products are so complex that one salesperson cannot be an expert on all facets of the buying situation. Each member of the selling team works with a member of the buying team. For example, the production specialist of the selling company is matched with the production specialist of the buying company.

Thus team selling brings more expertise to bear on solving the buyer's problems. It also has a psychological impact on the buyer. The buyer realizes that the salespeople are so interested in customer's needs that they are enlisting the aid of a team of experts.

The salesperson responsible for the customer coordinates the activities of the selling team. The purchasing agent coordinates the activities of the buying team. These team leaders are responsible for maintaining a high level of communication between the two groups.

Company experts may provide advice on specific problems, but the salesperson is responsible for all phases of the presentation. It is the salesperson's plan that is implemented.

Figure 14-3
Qualities possessed by top salespeople

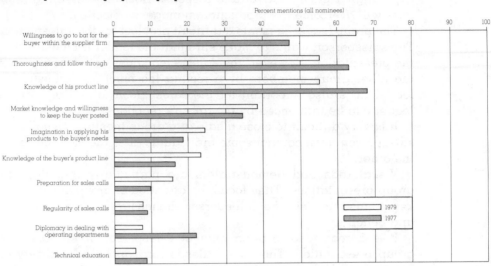

Source: Adapted from *Purchasing*, August 22, 1979, p. 43.

THE SUCCESSFUL INDUSTRIAL SALESPERSON

Each year, *Purchasing* magazine invites its readers—purchasing agents—to nominate salespeople who call on them for its selection of the top ten salespersons of the year. The characteristics of the top salespeople for the years 1977-79 are shown in Figure 14-3. This figure shows that the most important traits of the top salespeople are a willingness to work within their own companies to help the buyer, thoroughness and follow-through, and knowledge of the product line. In other words, the top salespeople practice the marketing concept. They satisfy the customers' needs.

The purchasing agents also list *"the seven deadly sins of selling"*[13]—the things they don't like salespeople to do. These sins are as follows:

☐ *Lack of product knowledge.* Salespeople must know their own product lines and the buyer's products.

☐ *Time-wasting.* Unannounced sales visits are a pain. When salespeople start droning on about golf or grandchildren, it's even worse.

---

[13] Somerby Dowst, "This Year's Winners: All-Around Performers," *Purchasing*, August 22, 1979, p. 43.

☐ *Poor planning.* Even a routine sales call should be preceded by some homework—maybe to see if the call is really necessary.

☐ *Pushiness.* This includes prying to find out competitors' prices, overwhelming and backdoor selling.

☐ *Lack of dependability.* This is evidenced by failure to stand behind the product, to keep communications clear, and to honor promises.

☐ *Ungentlemanly or unladylike conduct.* Knocking competitors, boozing at lunch, unkempt dress, and lack of decorum aren't professional.

☐ *Optimism unlimited.* The honest salesperson is preferred to the "good news bearers" who will promise anything to get an order.

QUESTIONS AND PROBLEMS

1. Compare the sources of product information used by industrial customers with the sources of information used by consumers. How do these sources of information and their importance differ for the two groups?

2. Should a salesperson ever try to change the way in which an individual customer makes a purchase decision? Explain.

3. Assume that you are calling on a customer for the first time. You have just found out that the customer needs a product like the one you are selling. What questions would you ask in order to learn how to sell your product to the customer?

4. If purchasing agents make decisions based on technical and economic factors, do industrial salespeople need to consider what their personality or individual needs are? Why or why not?

5. How might selling to government agencies differ from selling to industrial organizations?

6. Purchasing agents often do not possess the same level of technical knowledge as salespeople or users of the products. This difference in knowledge can create tension between the purchasing agent and the salesperson. What can a salesperson do to reduce this tension?

7. Why does management place pressure on purchasing agents to buy from the lowest priced manufacturer? Why might a purchasing agent ignore this pressure and place an order with a higher priced supplier?

8. The industrial and retail markets differ in a number of ways. What effects do these differences have on the types of sales presentations made in these markets?

9. If you are making a formal presentation to a group, and a member of the

group asks a question that has nothing to do with the presentation topic, how would you handle the situation?

10. How does the selling to industrial agents differ from selling to wholesalers?

PROJECTS

1. Arrange an interview with an industrial purchasing agent. Ask the purchasing agent to describe a recent purchase decision. Analyze the decision in terms of the following factors:

   a. Was the decision a new buy, a straight rebuy, or a modified rebuy?

   b. Who besides the purchasing agent was involved in the decision?

   c. What factors were considered in evaluating the different vendors?

   d. Why was the purchase order given to the specific supplier?

   e. What role did salespeople play in the decision?

2. Write a paper on industrial purchasing agents. In the report, answer the following questions by either interviewing a purchasing agent or consulting a textbook on purchasing:

   a. What are the important qualifications of a purchasing agent?

   b. What are the problems of the job?

   c. What do purchasing agents do during a typical day?

   d. Whom do purchasing agents interact with in their jobs?

3. Locate the purchasing office at your school. Get permission to observe a sales call. Write up your observations concerning the salesperson's presentation and selling techniques and the buyer's reactions.

CASE PROBLEMS

Case 14–1

Dare Drug

Bill Marks is a sales representative for Dare Drug Distribution, a pharmaceutical wholesaler. His customers include all the major hospitals in the Chicago area. One of these is the Metropolitan Hospital, a public institution which is under pressure to cut costs.

Bill has experienced some difficulties in trying to convince Metropolitan's chief purchasing agent that Dare's travel-size toothbrush should be bought in bulk. Bill wants this item to be included in the toilet supply kit furnished to each patient. The kit already contains soap, hand lotion, a plastic pitcher, a tumbler, and a tabletop tub for sponge bathing.

The hospital purchasing agent has argued that the toothbrushes are not essential. Many patients bring their own, and those who don't can ask for a regular-size toothbrush from the hospital pharmacy. The purchasing agent claims that including even this small item would add too much to the patient's bill.

How can Bill convince the purchasing agent that this item should be added in the kit?

Case 14–2

Indiana Steel

One of Indiana Steel's most important customers is the John Elk Company, a small manufacturer located in Mason City, Iowa. Elk buys a special steel alloy in the form of preweighed forgings from the Indiana Steel Company. Elk then casts the alloy into heavy-duty moldboard plough bottoms and sells these to International Cultivator, a large tractor manufacturer.

Unfortunately for Tom Torrance, the Indiana Steel salesman who deals with the Elk Company, a competitor is offering the same forgings at a lower price than Indiana's—$17 as opposed to $19.50. Indiana's price reflects several recent reductions that have been passed on to the customer. These were made possible by technical innovations. At the present price the profit margin for Indiana is rather low. Tom's performance is evaluated on the basis of profits, not just sales. Therefore, he cannot simply undercut the competitor's price. Furthermore, because of recent wage hikes the price of the forgings will be increased to $21 within the next year.

Tom knows that the competitor has never produced this particular alloy to these specifications before. He figures that Elk will probably have to pay the competitor nearly $100,000 for the retooling and additional equipment that would be needed to produce these forgings. Although Elk's buyer has not admitted this, he has expressed some doubts about the competitor's ability to meet the specifications. On the other hand, other materials purchased from the competitor have proved satisfactory in the past.

Since International Cultivator is Elk's largest customer, Elk cannot afford to lose the moldboard contract. International Cultivator is developing a new 24-bottom plough, the largest ever made. In light of the large size of the moldboard contract Torrance feels that Elk may give some of the business to the new competitor, despite the risks involved.

Torrance has called Indiana Steel's vice president of marketing. The vice president ok'd a price cut to $17 if that was the only way to keep the business.

Questions

1. What should Torrance's strategy be in negotiating with Elk's buyer?
2. What factors should he keep in mind?

SELECTED REFERENCES

Doyle, Peter; Woodside, Arch G.; and Mickell, Paul.   "Organizations Buying in New Task and Rebuy Situations."
Industrial Marketing Management, Winter 1979, pp. 7–11.

Finney, F. Robert.   "Reciprocity: Gone but Not Forgotten," *Journal of Marketing*, January 1972, pp. 54–59.

Hass, Robert W.   *Industrial Marketing Management*. New York: Petrocelli/Charter, 1976.

Hakansson, Hakon, and Wootz, Bjorn.   "A Framework of Industrial Buying and Selling." *Industrial Marketing Management*, Winter 1979, pp. 28–39.

Hill, Richard M.; Alexander, Ralph S.; and Cross, James S.   *Industrial Marketing*, 4th ed. Homewood, Ill.: Richard D. Irwin, 1975.

Robertson, Jack.   *Selling to the Government*. New York: McGraw-Hill, 1979.

Sheth, Jagdish.   "A Model of Industrial Buyer Behavior." *Journal of Marketing*, October 1973, pp. 50–56.

Webster, Fredrick E., Jr.   *Industrial Marketing Strategy*. New York: John Wiley, 1979.

————.   "Management Science in Industrial Marketing." *Journal of Marketing*, January 1978, pp. 21–27.

————, and Wind, Yoram.   "A General Model for Understanding Organizational Buying Behavior." *Journal of Marketing*, April 1972, pp. 12–19.

Westing, S. H.; Fine, I. V.; and Zenz, Gary.   *Purchasing Management*. 4th ed. New York: John Wiley, 1976.

Chapter 15

RETAIL SELLING

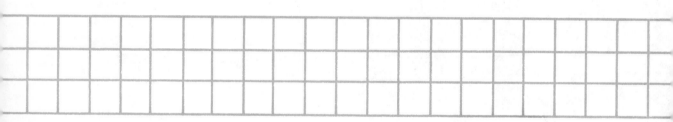

This chapter focuses attention upon the basic concepts of modern personal selling as applied to retailing. Major topics covered include nature and rewards of retail selling, duties and responsibilities of retail salespeople, requirements for success in retail selling, and building goodwill through satisfied customers.

NATURE AND REWARDS OF RETAIL SELLING

Nature and scope

Retail selling differs from other types of selling in many ways. One major difference is that the potential customers normally come to a particular store to shop or to satisfy a need for a product or service. They are perhaps responding to advertising that they have seen in newspapers. The position of the retail salesperson differs from that of the manufacturer's sales representative in that potential customers normally come to the salesperson rather being sought out by the salesperson. A typical retail store selling situation is shown in Figure 15-1. There are some exceptions, such as retail salespeople who sell office equipment, appliances, drapery, or carpeting. These salespeople often seek out customers.

The retail salesperson's job differs from the job of the manufacturer's sales representative in many other respects. Salespeople who do their own prospecting may be more selective in determining how they should spend their time with various prospects after they have qualified the prospects. The retail salesperson must give attention to everyone who comes into the store, even though many of these individuals have no intention of buying or lack the potential to buy. It is important, therefore, that retail salespeople have the necessary skills to determine which individuals are really potential buyers and which are merely "shoppers" or "lookers." The retail salesperson may have several customers to serve at the same time, and this requires unusual tact and skill. In contrast, there are times when there are no customers to serve, which causes some retail salespeople to become bored or frustrated.

Retail selling tends to be more confining than many other sales jobs, but on the other hand it provides security and the opportunity for the salesperson to associate with other employees and to participate as a citizen in community activities.

Retail salespeople represent the largest number of salespeople in the United States. In 1979 there were a total of about 6,163,000 people in the salesforce, and about 3,215,000 of these were retail salespeople. Of the retail salesforce, about 1,605,000 were age 20 or over and about 414,000 were ages 16-19.[1] Openings for retail trade salesworkers far outnumber openings for other salesworkers.

Rewards

There are many opportunities and rewards for individuals who are successful in retail selling. The chances for promotion are very good, and in many instances experience in retail selling provides an excellent background for individuals to go into business for themselves. Recent census figures indicate that there were approximately 1.9 million retail establishments in the United States and about 58 percent of these had two or fewer paid employees.[2]

---

[1] U.S. Department of Labor, "Employment and Earnings," January 1980, p. 172.

[2] See Delbert J. Duncan and Stanley C. Hollander, *Modern Retailing Management* (Homewood, Ill.: Richard D. Irwin, 1977, pp. 3-88, for a description of retailing and retailing opportunities in the United States; and Ian H. Wilson, "Retailing: The Next Ten Years," *Journal of Retailing*, Fall 1977, pp. 5-28.

Figure 15-1
Selling silverware in a large department store

Courtesy of Macy's

Sears, with $17.9 billion in sales, is the leader, followed by Safeway, K mart, and J. C. Penney, all with more than $10 billion in sales volume. There are 44 retail sales companies or retail divisions of nonretail conglomerates which have recorded more than $1 billion in sales in a recent fiscal year.[3]

The normal promotional channels for retail salespeople are through buying and/or sales promotion to assistant department manager, department manager, division manager, store manager, vice president of merchandising, or vice president of branch stores. The channels of promotion vary by types of retail establishments. The opportunities for promotion into executive positions from the field of retail selling have far exceeded those from other areas in retailing.

---

[3] "The $100 Million Club," *Chain Store Age Executive*, August 1979, p. 29. This article provides an excellent review of leading retailers in the United States.

Figure 15-2
Career progression in retail management

CAREER PROGRESSION

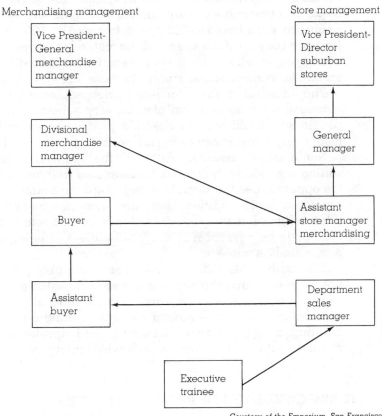

Courtesy of the Emporium, San Francisco

Students who enter retailing on a management training program can expect to move into merchandising management or store management. The career progression in one unit of Carter, Hawley, Hale Stores, Inc., is shown in Figure 15-2.[4]

Financial rewards. The starting salaries for new employees in the retailing field have traditionally been lower than in most industries. For a typical nonmanagement trainee the pay is likely to be close to the government minimum wage. This has often caused the most competent young people to accept positions in industries where they are able to receive higher starting salaries.

However, many young people who are looking for future oppor-

---

[4] See also department manager position description in Chapter 2. Other stores in this chain include Broadway Stores, Weinstock's, Neiman-Marcus, Bergdorf Goodman, and Holt, Renfrew.

tunities rather than high starting salaries recognize the tremendous challenges in retailing for aggressive individuals who are willing to work hard and accept responsibilities. The financial rewards for successful individuals in the retailing field can be very substantial. Department managers, merchandise managers, and store managers frequently earn from $25,000 a year to over $100,000 a year, depending upon the size of the store and the method of compensation. Those young people who reach the top executive level are likely to be paid an annual compensation similar to those shown in Table 15-1.

The financial rewards for retail salespeople who do not go into management positions can also be very substantial. Many salespeople who build a loyal clientele produce sales and profits that justify very satisfactory financial rewards.

Nonfinancial rewards.   Although the financial rewards in retail selling are relatively low for trainees and beginning salespeople, the opportunities for promotion and long-term financial rewards are considerable. In addition, there are many nonfinancial rewards in retail selling. It is an exciting field to be in. The retail salesperson is constantly being exposed to a wide variety of new products, new styles, and new merchandising techniques.

The really professional retail salesperson gets genuine satisfaction from matching the wants and needs of customers with the new products of his or her company. Retail selling also provides other nonfinancial rewards—having security, getting satisfaction out of building a loyal personal following, and developing a personal clientele with a wide range of individual interests.

DUTIES AND RESPONSIBILITIES OF RETAIL SALESPEOPLE

The retail salesperson is the person between the manufacturer and/or wholesaler and the ultimate consumer. In this capacity the retail salesperson must satisfy the specific needs and wants of the consumer and at the same time make a reasonable profit for his or her establishment.

The duties of retail salespeople are as different as the merchandise they sell. In selling such items as furniture, electrical appliances, or clothing, the salesworkers' primary job is to create an interest in the merchandise. They may answer questions about the construction of an article, demonstrate its use, and show various models and colors. In some stores special knowledge and skills may be needed to sell merchandise. For example, in a pet shop the retail salesperson must know how to care for and feed animals.

In addition, the salesperson may be required to make out sales and charge slips, receive cash payments, give change and receipts,

Table 15-1

Remuneration of chief executives of selected retail companies

Company	Annual compensation
Sears	$580,000
J. C. Penney	520,000
Allied Stores	512,000
Federated Stores	478,000
Kroger	380,000
K mart	380,000
May Department Stores	327,000
Macy's	310,000
Woolworth	299,000
Carter, Hawley, Hale	256,000

Source: "Bosz' Paycheck: Who Gets the Biggest?" *Forbes*, May 19, 1978, pp. 86–111.

handle returns, exchange merchandise, and keep the work area neat. In small stores, salespeople may help order merchandise, stock shelves or racks, mark price tags, take inventory, and prepare displays.[5]

The responsibilities of retail salespeople fall into three basic categories, namely responsibilities to the customer, responsibilities to the company, and responsibilities to themselves.

Responsibilities to customers

Today's consumers are the best educated and most sophisticated in history. They expect the store and the salesperson from which they buy to be responsive to their needs. They want to be treated fairly, and they want to be fully informed about the products they buy.

Various consumer groups have recently exerted pressure upon manufacturers and retailers for full disclosure about what the consumer is buying, how it will work, and what the actual finance charges are. Manufacturers have made considerable improvements in their advertising, packaging and labeling so as to provide consumers with accurate product information.

Customers still want to talk to someone about their specific needs and how products will fulfill those needs. The retail salesperson has a responsibility for listening to customers to determine what their needs are and for following up with a full explanation about the products offered. Customers who have the opportunity to be heard

---

[5] U.S. Department of Labor, "Occupational Outlook Handbook," Bulletin 1955, 1978, pp. 242–46.

and who are properly informed by the salesperson are happy customers.

Responsibilities to store management

The retail salesperson is management's representative with the customers. The image created by the salesperson becomes the image of the store in the eyes of customers. The retail salesperson has the responsibility for keeping informed on the store's policies and practices and for keeping management informed as to what customers are buying and not buying. One of the most important functions of the retail salesperson is to provide current information to buyers and department managers concerning the wants and needs of customers.

Personal responsibility

Retail salespeople have a responsibility to themselves to utilize their full capacities at all times. For the person who continues to learn about merchandise, about new selling techniques, about competition, and about new trends in retailing, a career in retailing can be exciting and rewarding.[6]

Successful retail salespeople have a responsibility to themselves to maintain a positive and pleasant attitude at all times, no matter how irritating a customer may be. Personal composure will in the long run provide rich rewards for the individual salesperson.

REQUIREMENTS FOR SUCCESS IN RETAIL SELLING

If individuals are to be successful in retail selling they must be proficient in the following areas: (1) knowledge of company policies and practices, (2) knowledge of company's and competitors' merchandise, (3) human relations skills, (4) selling skills, and (5) conceptual skills. In addition, they should be marketing oriented and should possess the drive and the competitive spirit necessary for success in retailing.

Most large retail stores provide extensive and up-to-date training programs for their sales personnel. These programs contribute a great deal to success in selling.[7]

---

[6] Career information is available from National Retail Merchants Association, 100 West 31 Street, New York, N.Y. 10001

[7] See Alan J. Dubinsky and Bruce E. Mattson, "Consequences of Role Conflict and Ambiguity Experienced by Retail Salespeople," *Journal of Retailing*, Winter 1979, pp. 70–86, for a discussion of the importance of training.

Knowledge of company—its policies and practices

It is important for retail salespeople to have a thorough knowledge of the company's or store's background and of its credit, exchange, and delivery policies.

Knowledge of company or store.   When a customer is making a buying decision, it is very important that he or she know that the company or store will guarantee the quality and performance of the product. If the salesperson is knowledgeable about the company's history, the following comment may be very important to the customer: "We have been in business in Kansas City for 50 years and have always followed a policy of 'satisfaction or your money returned.'"

If the store has established a reputation for leadership in style or fashion, the salesperson should be knowledgeable about this and should convey this message to the customers. If a salesperson is working for a large company with many stores, it may be desirable to refer to the company's advantages in making large-scale purchases which result in savings to the customer.

Salespeople who work in large department stores should have up-to-date knowledge on the location of other departments and on what merchandise is carried in these departments. If special promotions are being featured in other departments, the salesperson should call this to the attention of customers.

Knowledge of policies and practices. Knowledge of credit policies and practices is also an essential requirement for the retail salesperson. If the store provides delivery services, the salesperson should be able to tell customers exactly when their merchandise will be delivered.

Certain products such as appliances and television sets carry a manufacturer's warranty. The salesperson should know what merchandise carries warranties and should inform the customer of what is required to be sure a warranty is in effect.

Knowledge of merchandise

The first principle of selling is to know your merchandise from A to Z so that you can match the values of your products to the needs of your customers. It is not enough to say, "This camera is very good, and the price is low." The customer expects and deserves specific information on the special features of the camera, how it compares with competing products, and what personal benefits it will bring to the customer. The retail salesperson must understand why his or her merchandise is superior to that of competitors. This understanding must be conveyed to the mind of the customer.

If salespeople have a complete knowledge of the merchandise, they will be in a much more favorable position to answer price versus quality questions. Customers are not interested in general statements such as, "This is an outstanding value; we are selling a lot of them." They would prefer to receive specific information about the product and about the benefits it will provide for them.

Salespeople cannot assume that customers will see the true value in merchandise. The salesperson must emphasize the positive points about the merchandise until the value to the customer is greater than the price.

Human relations skills

Successful salespeople normally have a keen perception of the feelings of other people. They possess a high degree of empathy toward the behavior and attitudes of customers and shoppers. They recognize that selling is a two-way operation and that both the customer and the salesperson are human beings. They are aware of the importance of listening to the prospective customer and of asking questions to encourage him or her to talk. In doing this, the salesperson automatically establishes rapport with the customer, so that the customer will pay more attention to the salesperson's presentation.

Greeting the customer. Customers expect salespeople to greet them with a warm welcome and to give immediate attention to serving them. If salespeople are preoccupied with other activities or are talking with other store employees, customers react negatively. Retail salespeople should be constantly aware that the customer is "king" or "queen." Customers should be treated in the same way that you would treat guests in your home.

Determining customer wants. Unfortunately, many salespeople start their sales presentations in the wrong way by placing primary emphasis upon the merchandise. The successful salesperson starts the sales process by finding out what the prospective customer needs and wants. A few questions by the salesperson will provide significant information as to the customer's needs and interests. This will lead to a productive selection of merchandise to show the customer.

Handling complaints. When customers are dissatisfied with merchandise they normally return to the salesperson who sold it to them. If stores have special departments for returns and adjustments, the salesperson involved in the original sale may be included in the settlement with the customer.

When customers enter the store to return unsatisfactory merchandise or to register complaints, they are frequently in unfavorable frames of mind. It is especially important that salespeople handle these customers with tact, diplomacy, and calmness. The salesperson should listen to the customer's complaints and should ask questions to determine the real reasons for the complaints. It may be that a customer has failed to read the instructions on how to use the product. Appropriate education by the salesperson may satisfy the customer.

If merchandise was damaged in delivery or not delivered at the time promised, the salesperson should satisfy the customer promptly, without making derogatory comments about the delivery department or personnel.

Building goodwill. Customers continue to patronize stores in which they have learned from experience that they will be served by friendly and pleasant salespeople who are sincerely interested in how the store's products can best meet the buying needs of customers.

Store and personal goodwill is built in the long run by fair treatment, prompt service, and a high degree of integrity on the part of all store personnel.

The president of one nationally known retail store has attempted to create an understanding of the importance of service by saying,

> I think it is clear that the secret of success in retail distribution is concern for the customer. Anything that detracts from that objective is fatal. Retailing is a service industry. It succeeds or fails depending on how successfully it meets the test of service—above all, the vital point of *personal* contact. If retail contacts are pleasant, easy, and satisfactory, not only will a sale take place but a great many future sales as well. This vital service is a function of retailing that cannot be automated out of existence. *The customer is our business.*"[8]

In certain fields such as women's ready-to-wear, successful retail salespeople build goodwill and a personal following by sending cards or making personal telephone calls when a new item comes in that the salesperson feels would be particularly attractive to a certain customer.

A method of building goodwill when the salesperson is selling cars, appliances, or certain other big-ticket products is to make follow-up calls or inquiries to determine whether the customer is happy with the purchase. This not only builds goodwill but also frequently results in additional sales to the customer and/or prospect referrals.

Selling skills

Separate chapters have been devoted to the special skills required in all types of selling (see Chapter 7 through 11). It is appro-

---

[8] From a speech by the chairman of the board, R. H. Macy & Co.

priate, however, that additional emphasis be given here to selling skills that apply particularly to retail selling. Those skills include approaching customers, selecting merchandise to show, speaking the customer's language, suggestion selling, demonstrating, trading up, serving several customers at once, handling objections, and closing the sale.

Approach. In many types of selling, salespeople can obtain advance information about prospective customers before the initial interviews. This information is helpful in determining the best approach for each individual. In retail selling, however, the situation is often quite different. The prospective customer may be a total stranger to the salesperson, and the salesperson may have only a few seconds to size up the customer. The first few words spoken and a friendly smile are most important in retail selling.

Many customers are naturally warm and outgoing individuals. The approach to such customers is relatively easy. On the other hand, there are many customers who are reserved, quiet, and reluctant to appear to be friendly to strangers.

Retail salespeople must meet and greet all kinds of customers, from the most cheerful and agreeable to the most suspicious and disagreeable. This is why retail selling is interesting and why it is a challenge to each salesperson.

A number of different approaches are used by successful salespeople for different types of customers. One effective method is to open the interview on some neutral subject which is often referred to as "small talk." This "breaks the ice" and gets the prospective customer talking. The small talk may be a comment about the weather, the neighborhood, or some news event.

The "service approach" is often used. It may include such comments as these:

"May I help you?"
"Good morning. May I show you something?"
"Hello. How can I help you today?"

The "customer benefit approach" is used frequently. When using this approach, the opening statements refer to merchandise in terms of customer benefits or interests. If the customer is looking at a piece of merchandise, an appropriate comment may be:

"Colorful, aren't they? They just arrived from Mexico."
"Very attractive, aren't they!"
"What do you think of the style and color?"
"Those are colorfast."
"That guard is a great safety feature."

The benefit approach gets the interview off to the right start because it impresses the customer immediately that the salesperson has the customer's interests in mind. Following the initial comment, a person selling an automatic dishwasher may say: "With this dishwasher you will find that you will have more time for activities that you enjoy more than washing dishes. Your days of having dirty dishes in the kitchen sink will be a thing of the past. You merely rinse the dishes off and place them in the washer." Specific features and other benefits may then be discussed.

After an initial greeting some customers may prefer to "look around" without close supervision by the salesperson. This opportunity should be permitted, but if possible, the salesperson should be available nearby to answer questions when the customer is ready.

Whatever approach is used, its function is to create a friendly atmosphere and to give the customer a chance to talk. The salesperson must remember to *listen*.

Selecting merchandise to show.   Retail salespeople are often perplexed as to what merchandise to show first. This is particularly true in the men's and women's ready-to-wear field. Some salespeople elect to show the medium-priced merchandise on the theory that you can trade up or down from there without too much difficulty. Other salespeople, however, prefer to start by showing the top of the line in the hope that customers will appreciate quality merchandise and will see value before price.

In selling men's suits, an alert salesperson may watch the customer as he approaches the department to see whether he devotes his attention to a particular suit or a specific style. After making an appropriate approach, the salesperson may suggest that he take a measurement and have the customer try on a suit "for size." The customer normally reacts to this suggestion with a positive feeling that the salesperson is interested in his needs. After obtaining the correct measurements, the salesperson then slips on a coat in the right size and asks the customer to step over to the mirror to see whether this is what he wants in fit and style. If the customer is satisfied with the first suit that the salesperson selects, the salesperson has won the customer's confidence.

If the salesperson has shown a high-quality suit to start with and has given an effective presentation on its benefits to the customer, a sale is likely to result. Furthermore, if the customer buys and likes the suit, this will bring him back to the store and to the salesperson for additional purchases.

Another selling skill which is practiced by successful salespeople is to recognize a poor selection immediately when they have asked a customer to try on a garment that does not have the appropriate style or color for the customer. The salesperson comments, "That doesn't really do anything for you. Let's try this one on."

An honest comment of this type convinces the customer that the salesperson is genuinely interested in the customer and not in pressuring the customer to buy something that does not serve her or his best interests.

In selling some merchandise, the correct merchandise to show can be determined only after the customer has explained how the product is to be used and what results are expected. Customers may know the results they expect better than they know what product will give them the desired results.

Sometimes customers ask for a specific brand name or a definite size. If the store does not carry the brand name, or if the size is not currently available, it is important to have the customer explain the use planned for the product. It is quite possible that a different brand or a different size would do the job better. If the customer is not interested in a substitute, no harm has been done. It is too easy to tell a customer of this type, "Sorry, we don't carry that brand. You can get it down the street." Obviously this practice does not represent good selling.

Speaking the customer's language. Because of the limited time that the retail salesperson may have with the customer, he or she must use clear, concise, and powerful language to sell benefits that mean something to the customer. It is not enough to describe product features and their benefits. These benefits must be applied to the customer's needs and environment in terms that the customer understands.

The professional salesperson does not say "This lamp is beautiful." He or she says, "This lamp will look beautiful in your living room. It makes an ideal addition to the furniture and setting that you have described to me."

In selling aluminum siding, the salesperson could say, "Our siding has a beautiful finish." However, a much more professional statement would be, "With our siding, your house would always look better than it would even with a fresh coat of paint." Sales are made by speaking the customer's language.

Suggestion selling. Good selling technique requires that salespeople suggest additional related sales before the original sales transaction has been completed. It is much easier for a customer to add to a sale than to consummate a separate transaction. Customers like new ideas and suggestions that will "go with" what they have already purchased. Many stores provide salespeople with lists of related products.

Accessories, for example, can add variety and interest to a wardrobe. Good salespeople are able to point out that adding the right look in scarves, wearing the right shoe, and/or pinning the right piece of jewelry to a scarf can create that special effect which customers avidly seek each fashion season. Handbags, belts, gloves, and hosiery are other items that could be suggested to complete a purchase.[9]

Care must be taken not to be too aggressive in suggestion selling. Good judgment dictates that suggesting additional or ensemble products should be made only when this is acceptable to the customer. "Specials of the day" can easily be introduced, but an attempt to sell a whole wardrobe when a customer is only interested in a sweater can alienate the customer. When additional suggestions are appropriate, it is important to make them in a positive manner. "Anything else?" is ineffective when compared with "This blue stripe tie matches your new shirt beautifully."

Successful suggestion selling may relate to buying a higher quality product, to buying a larger quantity of the same product at a reduced unit price, to buying tie-in products, or to buying totally different products which are on sale in other departments.

Demonstrating. Retail salespeople have an unusual opportunity to utilize demonstration as part of their sales presentations. Through effective preplanning, merchandise demonstrations can be set up to get maximum results from appeals to the senses of sound, touch, sight, taste, and smell. Appropriate lighting and sound effects can be utilized to emphasize the beauty of products and the customer satisfactions to be hoped for by purchasing the products. Retail salespeople should appeal to as many senses as possible in making sales demonstrations. A picture is better than many words, and the action of a demonstration is usually more effective than still pictures or descriptive words alone.

Customers like to be "shown" as well as told, so demonstrating can be the most effective part of the sales presentation. The demonstration gives the salesperson a chance to make the sales presentation "come alive" as customers see the product perform with their own eyes.

A demonstration offers something else—it is an opportunity to generate customer excitement and enthusiasm as customers get "hands-on" experience with the product and begin to visualize what owning the product will mean to them.[10]

Trading up. Frequently the process of trading up to a higher priced and higher valued product is looked upon as dishonest or shady. This may be true if a store runs major ads for its low-priced product but has a limited supply of the low-priced line and fully intends to use the ads to attract customers in order to trade them up to higher priced products.

[9] Macy's. "Today's Customer."
[10] Zenith, "Techniques of Selling."

In the long run this type of practice will create nothing but ill will on the part of the buying public.

Legitimate trading up involves a recognition that the trading-up process must be of mutual benefit to the buyer and the seller. It is a process whereby the salesperson, after carefully analyzing the customer's needs, sincerely recommends the best product to satisfy those needs.

One large national retail organization contends that there are three basic trading-up areas, namely, an increase in the "quantity" of goods, an increase in the "quality" of goods, and an increase in the "completeness of the product line or the service package."[11] If a customer, for example, is purchasing paint to repaint the garage, a suggestion may be made that a saving could be effected by repainting the entire house at the same time.

Quality trade-ups can be accomplished by stressing the benefits that the customer would derive from "installing a wall-to-wall carpet with a thicker weave."

A "completeness trade-up" may include such suggestions as, "Let's look at the advantages of redoing your entire kitchen instead of just replacing your stove and refrigerator. There are some real advantages to you in doing this. Let me show you some of our combination offers."

Firms with interior decorators emphasize the importance of completing a room or area with compatible furnishings.

Selling several customers at the same time. Handling several customers at the same time is a unique problem of the retail salesperson. An industrial products salesperson may be required to make a sales presentation to a group, but he or she will normally be presenting a single product and will have had a chance to plan the presentation. This is not true with the retail salesperson who is confronted with several customers who may all have different desires and needs. Some of the customers may be slow, deliberate types; some may be in an extreme hurry and want immediate service; and some may merely be shoppers who are passing the time of day.

It is the retail salesperson's responsibility to give attention to as many customers as possible without creating the ill will of any of them. This is not easy. If the salesperson is waiting on a customer who seems to be rather deliberate in making a buying decision, a very aggressive customer who wants immediate attention may come up. The salesperson may continue to serve and give attention to the first customer but at the same time recognize the second customer and indicate that someone will be with him or her in a minute. If other salespeople are near, their assistance should be sought.

Handling several customers at the same time requires a high de-

---

[11] Sears, "Fundamental Selling.

gree of selling skill that usually comes with considerable experience.

Working with people is an art, and keeping customers satisfied comes through sensitivity, empathy, and a sincere desire to please. This art *can be developed.*

Handling objections. The necessary skills for handling objections have been described in Chapter 10. It may be useful, however, to make a few comments on handling objections as applied to retailing. Retail salespeople may be required to respond to a great many objections because of the wide range of products which they sell in certain stores and because of the customer's relative lack of product knowledge.

The important thing for retail salespeople to remember is that objections are a natural part of the sales process. Objections should be answered in a way that does not create an argument. One way of doing this is to turn the customer's statement into a question. For example, if the customer says, "This electric heater is inadequate for the size of our room." The salesperson may reply by saying, "Oh, are you really concerned about the ability of this heater to provide you with sufficient heat for your room?" If the customer replies, "Yes," then the salesperson could say, "Let's take a look at that. How large is your room?"

Usually answering an objection by asking a question will be much more effective than trying to prove that the customer's objection is invalid.

The objective should be to soften the objection by getting on the customer's side. This can be done by saying, "I understand how you feel," or "I can appreciate how you feel—everything seems to cost a lot more these days." Then turn the objection into a question. "What you are really asking is, Should you make this kind of investment for a television set," Right?" Then answer the question. If it is price, translate the price to a low per week or per day cost over a period of time. That will make the expense less intimidating to the customer.

Remember, objections are how some customers ask for more justification to buy![12]

Closing the sale. Of all the steps in the sales process, closing the sale is perhaps the most difficult. (See Chapter 11, Closing the Sale, for a detailed discussion of this step.) This is particularly true in retail selling because the turnover among retail salespeople is normally rather high and most inexperienced salespeople often have difficulty in closing sales. An observant salesperson soon learns to detect customers' closing signals and then takes prompt action to start closing the sale.

When a prospective customer starts asking questions about pos-

---

[12] It may be helpful to review the complete discussion of objections in Chapter 10.

sible delivery dates, about credit terms, or about warranty agreements, the salesperson should recognize that he or she is getting ready to buy.

The following statement may be appropriate to close the sale: "Mr. Customer, we deliver in your area on Tuesdays and Thursdays—which is more convenient for you"? Or after a product demonstration you may say, "May I check in back and see if we have one in stock that you can take with you today?"

In most cases the customers you deal with on a day-to-day basis need a "push" or "help" before they will give the order. Simple ways to do this are as follows: When a customer has indicated a preference, say, "Okay, why not sit down over here, and I'll write up the order!" Or, "What finish do you want—dark oak or light pecan?" Or, "Will this be cash or credit?" Or perhaps, "Do you wish to take this with you today?"

The purpose of every sales presentation or interview you make is to get the order. That's what closing a sale is all about—getting that order! When the customer says that he or she will buy, quit selling and wrap up the order. Overselling can lose the sale.

Especially when big-ticket items are sold, it is wise to reaffirm the customer's good judgment in making the purchase that has just been consummated: "I'm sure you will enjoy your new television." Or, "You will get a lot of pleasure out of this boat." Or, "Be sure to call me if you need any help. I am anxious to hear how the engine performs for you. Here is my card."

Such after-sale comment is an excellent way to build a clientele or what is sometimes called "personal trade." It gives evidence that interest in the customer is not lost as soon as the sale has been made. When customers come to the store and ask for you, you know that you have built a good relationship!

Conceptual skills and promotion

In addition to having human relations skills and selling skills, the retail salesperson who aspires to promotion must possess conceptual skills. He or she must be able to visualize what the future trends in retailing are likely to be. What future changes are likely to take place? Is there likely to be more or less decentralization in retailing? What impact will computers have upon retailing? What impact will computers have upon retailing? What is competition likely to do? What kind of advertising and sales promotion programs will be most effective? How can merchandise be displayed to produce the greatest volume of sales?

If the salesperson is responsible for both buying and selling or is promoted to a buyer's position, conceptual skills become very important. The buyer must be able to analyze past sales and the buying behavior of the store's clientele; must be able to gauge what changes are likely to take place in the economy; and must then order merchandise that will meet the desires of the buying public several months later.

The conceptual skills of buyers, sales promotion personnel, and advertising personnel are essential ingredients to success in retailing. The higher a person rises in the managerial hierarchy of retailing, the more important conceptual skills become.

QUESTIONS AND PROBLEMS

1. You are viewing a display of all kinds of plumbing equipment for the do-it-yourselfer, and you remember that you need an ordinary toilet tank float. You cannot find one.

    A salesperson comes by while you are looking, and you ask

    "Do you have a float?"

    "No."

    "Do you know when you will have some?"

    "No."

    With the final "No," the salesperson walks off into another area of the store!

    Is this an unusual situation? What can be done about it?

2. A customer has just purchased an expensive rug from you, and after getting her to *approve* the order (not *sign* it), you quit selling and want to be sure that you perform whatever after-sale amenities are important. What actions or statements might be important at this point? What is your objective?

3. Assume that you are a salesperson in a specialty luggage store. A well-dressed young woman about 26 years of age comes into the store and looks at several bags in a cursory manner without stopping to examine any of them. You walk over to her and say, "Good morning, may I assist you?" She replies, "No, thanks, I'm just looking." How would you handle this customer? What would you say?

4. Assume that you are a salesperson in the toy department of a large department store and that a woman with two children (ages 6 and 12) looks at a number of toys. Apparently she is shopping for a toy for the six-year-old. While she is looking at some toys for 6-year-old children, the 12-year-old boy wanders over to a counter where some pocket knives are being displayed. He looks around and then picks up a knife and sticks it in his pocket. His mother does not see this, but you do. In the meantime, the customer has picked out a children's book and has brought it over to you to pay for it. Her 12-year-old boy has joined her. How would you handle this situation? What would you say? To whom? When?

5. What are some opportunities for suggestion selling for the following products:

   a. A pipe wrench?

   b. A men's sport coat?

   c. A women's slack suit?

   d. A fishing rod?

   e. A bag of lawn fertilizer?

6. You are working in a shoe department on Saturdays to earn some extra money while going to school. You are paid an hourly rate, and you can earn extra money by selling the last pair of shoes in stock or shoes which are unusual in size. You have been instructed by your supervisor that when you are unable to sell a customer you must "turn the customer over" to another salesperson rather than let the customer walk out.

   What do you think of this procedure? To be effective, how must the "turnover" take place? What are the hazards of the procedure?

7. If you are using a customer benefits approach, what opening statements might you make when the customer is looking at the following products:

   a. A steel tennis racket?

   b. A "see-through" umbrella?

   c. An automatic dishwashing machine?

   d. Steel-belted tires?

   e. A digital watch?

   f. A racquetball racquet?

   g. An air-cushioned mattress.

8. Some people resent having salespeople attempt to trade up to higher priced merchandise. Under what conditions would you consider trading up to be acceptable?

9. What major things should a salesperson remember when an angry customer comes in to make a complaint or to return damaged merchandise?

10. Assume that you are selling Firestone tires. When a prospective customer comes in, what is the first thing that you would do? What additional steps would you take to produce the sale?

11. A woman tries on a $40 pair of shoes in a local retail shoestore. She seems to like the shoes, but she hesitates to buy. While one shoe is being tried on, she remarks, "I like the looks of these shoes, but I don't think they are worth $40." About that time, two women shoppers walk by and one says to the other in a loud voice, "You know, the prices in this store are outrageous. I saw some shoes down the street that are just as good, and they sell for four or five dollars less." You are sure your customer heard the remark. Would you ignore the comment and talk

about the value and the style of the shoes? Would you try to joke about the remarks "some people make"? Would you attempt to justify the price policy of your store? If you would follow none of these procedures, what would you do or say?

12. Merry Chimes has recently obtained a position as salesperson in a local department store. She has been through the company's training program and is beginning to feel more comfortable in helping customers buy. Merry is currently working in the women's bags department.

A husband comes into the department and starts looking at the bags on display. He has decided to buy his wife a gift for their anniversary. He knows that she wants a purse, but he also knows that he knows very little about the product he is looking for. He picks up some of the purses on display, opens them, closes them, and appears undecided what to buy. About this time Merry asks, "May I help you?" He picks up one of the purses and says, "Do you think my wife would like something like this?"

Merry answers, "Oh, I don't know. I like it myself."

How can Merry improve on this answer? What closing principles are involved?

13. Analyze each of the following suggestions on how to close a sale. These suggestions were made by salespeople who sell men's suits.

a. "I always have an 'ace in the hole' . . . one particular suit in which a customer has shown an interest. Or, if I have studied my customer carefully when he first came in (and if I have time I usually have been able to), I go back to the first suit he tried on 'for size,' and very often it is possible to 'close the deal' with that first suit. It is important to keep this suit out of sight and not to bring out this 'ace in the hole' until a sale cannot be made on some other garment."

b. "When a seemingly successful sale bogs down because the prospect is reluctant to take the final step, I simply tell him, *'Take the coat to the door* (or the window) and see how the daylight brings out the character of the cloth.' The psychological reactions are several: it relieves him of the suspicion that any 'high pressure' may be applied to him; his ego is flattered by your apparent confidence in him; the appearance of the fabric is bound to be enhanced by the daylight; the customer is left alone for a minute or so, and with your sales talk bearing fruit, he generally sells himself!"

c. "There's one technique I've found especially effective with 'on-the-fence' buyers: take a tape measure, and as you bend to measure his inseam, ask, 'Do you like to wear your trousers pretty well down on your shoe?' Whatever his answer, it usually gives the go-ahead on the purchase, or at least gives the salesperson a lead as to what may be holding the customer back. This works especially well when the wife is along and she says, 'Yes, I like it, do you?' When that happens, don't wait too long to put the tape on your prospect for complete measurements . . . and the final sale!"

d.   "One of the best ways of helping a customer make up his mind is, surprisingly enough, not to talk about clothing! Discuss current events, sports, his business, or any other subject unrelated to clothing. A few minutes apparently 'wasted' in personal conversation create more customer-confidence in the salesperson, give the customer time to finally make up his mind. In the majority of cases, he will come back to the subject of clothing himself, and will be ready to take the garment about which he couldn't make up his mind just a few minutes before."

e.   "Give your customer a *choice*, for instance, between two colors or two models. Don't hesitate to ask, 'Mr. Jones, which model appeals to you, the green or the brown?' Almost invariably he will make a choice, which is your cue to close the sale by taking the trousers from the rack, starting toward the dressing room with the remark, 'Step over here and slip the whole suit on.' In most cases, the sale will be completed by suggesting that the tailor be called to see if any alterations are necessary."

PROJECTS

1. Visit several stores, and shop for one of the following articles: (1) a portable air-conditioning unit, (2) a TV set, (3) a carpet, (4) a hot tub, (5) a body mitten. Write a report on your experience in terms of the salesperson's knowledge of the store and its policies, knowledge of the merchandise, and human relations and selling skills.

2. Write a report on the advantages and disadvantages of a career in retail selling.

3. Select a person in your class whom you feel would be an outstanding success in retailing. Without divulging the individual's name, write a one-page report describing why you feel that this person would be successful.

4. Shop a discount store and a standard department store for the same items. Write a one-page report on the differences in treatment from salespeople or other personnel. Why do customers patronize both types of stores?

CASE PROBLEMS

Case 15-1

Chatty Gums

Chatty has worked for the Norberg Department Store in the women's ready-to-wear department for the past two years. She is well liked by everyone in the store; she has a pleasant personality; she meets and greets customers with tact and friendliness; she is exceptionally well informed about the merchandise she is selling and about other merchandise in the store; she reads and studies everything that pertains to the products in her department; she knows what competitors are offering, and at what prices.

Chatty's problem is that she has trouble in closing sales. Consequently, she has many friendly customers but her sales performance is below par.

What do you make of this situation? How can Chatty have so many positive qualities and yet have a sales volume which is below what it should be?

Case 15–2

Tom Claw

Tom Claw has been a contractor for about 30 years. Recently he lost his hammer and decided to purchase a new one. He walked into a lumber company which sold hammers and other tools, but he did not buy a hammer! He visited a hardware department of a chain store and looked at its hammers. He did not buy one!

Finally, he looked at hammers in a small hardware store and walked out of the store with a hammer and a smile on his face.

What could have happened? Why do you suppose that Tom refused to buy at the first two stores? Why did he buy at the third store?

Case 15–3

O'Leara's Women's Specialty Store

O'Leara's Women's Specialty Store is located in a relatively small midwestern city. A large percentage of its customers are coeds from the college in the city. The store has an excellent reputation for quality merchandise and service. It has been in business since 1930.

The owner, Barbara O'Leara, is a graduate of the local college and has been very active in alumni and community activities. She has been very successful in buying merchandise that fits the needs and desires of the store's clientele.

O'Leara's major competition is Miller's Women's Specialty Store, which has been in business since 1975. Bob and Mary Miller, who own and operate the store, are very aggressive, and they take particular pride in undercutting O'Leara's prices for similar merchandise.

During August 1980, both stores were having sales and various products were being advertised. The merchandise featured by O'Leara's included handbags and apparel accessories. A product to which O'Leara's gave prominence in its advertising was a South American leather handbag at $27.95. Miller's happened to be offering the same handbag at $32.75. When Bob Miller saw O'Leara's advertisement he decided to drop his price on the bag to $22 and he instructed the salespeople to emphasize the price advantage of buying the handbag at Miller's instead of at O'Leara's. Miller's did not advertise the bag at $22.

Assume that you are a salesperson at O'Leara's and that Mary Cook, who has been a customer of yours for two years, comes in to look at handbags. After you have shown Mary several handbags, she indicates that she is interested in the South American bag at $27.95. You describe the product features of the bag to her, and she says, 'OK, charge it to my account." (Her credit is good).

Just as Mary says this, Miriam, a friend of hers, happens by. Miriam says, "Hi, Mary, what's new?" Mary responds, "Oh, nothing much. I'm buying a new handbag. My old one is really shot." She shows Miriam the handbag she has just decided to purchase, and Miriam says, "It's beautiful, but I was just looking at this handbag at Miller's this morning, and you can buy the same thing there for $22."

Mary looks at you, and you look at her. Miriam looks at both of you. Mary says, "Why should I be paying $5.95 more for the same handbag just because I'm a good customer of O'Leara's?"

How would you handle this situation if you were the salesperson? What are your options?

SELECTED REFERENCES

Berry, Leonard L., and Wilson, Ian H. "Retailing: The Next Ten Years." *Journal of Retailing*, Fall 1977, pp. 5–28.

Duncan, Delbert J., and Hollander, Stanley C. "Modern Retailing Management: Basic Concepts and Practices. Homewood, Ill.: Richard D. Irwin, 1977. Pp. 3–38 and 495–512.

"Executive Compensation: What Works?" *Chain Store Age Executive*, October 1979, pp. 19–22.

Hansen, Robert A., and Deutscher, Terry. "An Empirical Investigation of Attribute Importance in Retail Store Selection." *Journal of Retailing*, Winter 1977–78, pp. 59–72.

Hirschman, Elizabeth C. "Differences in Consumer Purchase Behavior by Credit Card Payment System." *Journal of Consumer Research*, June 1979, pp. 58–66.

"J. C. Penney's Fashion Gamble." *Business Week*, January 16, 1978, pp. 66–74.

May, Eleanor G., and McNair, Malcolm P. "Department Stores Face Stiff Challenge in Next Decade." *Journal of Retailing*, Fall 1977, pp. 47–58.

"The $100 Million Club." *Chain Store Age Executive,* August 1979, pp. 29-60.

"Retailing's Golden Age; or How Long since a Doorman Bowed You into a Department Store?" *Sales & Marketing Management,* August 9, 1976, pp. 41-42.

Touche, Ross. "Retailing: The Consumer and the Future." *Tempo,* November 1, 1974, pp. 1-13.

U.S. Department of Labor. *Occupational Outlook Handbook, 1978-79.* Washington, D.C. Pp. 242-46.

Part five

IMPROVING THE SALES REPRESENTATIVE'S PERSONAL EFFECTIVENESS

This section includes chapters on the legal, social, ethical, and personal responsibilities of salespeople; and material on how to manage yourself, your time, and your territory.

Chapter 16

MANAGING YOURSELF,
YOUR TIME, AND YOUR TERRITORY

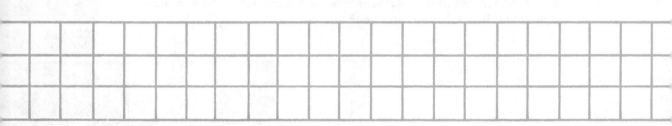

Salespeople have more individual freedom than almost any other type of employee. Their success or failure is largely due to their own efforts. A company assigns them to a territory, and then it is up to them to cover the territory effectively. Because salespeople work away from the office, they must be self-sufficient. No one tells them when to start working or when to quit for the day.

Because salespeople are allowed so much freedom, they need to be good self-managers. Self-management involves using their scarcest resource, time, so that they get the most out of their territory. Techniques for organizing time and territory are discussed in this chapter.

ESTABLISHING GOALS

The first step that a salesperson takes in "sales-managing" the job is to establish *working goals*. These goals are usually based upon the sales quota that has been assigned by the sales manager. They may be expressed in terms of total dollar volume of sales, units of sales, number of customer calls, or number of demonstrations. To meet these goals, the salesperson needs to practice self-discipline by planning and following a working schedule for each day or each week. This will facilitate the realization of overall goals or objectives.

The National Society of Sales Training Executive suggests that the speciality salesperson might plan a schedule which includes the following:

1. A minimum number of hours of work each day in order to get a given result.
2. A minimum number of demonstrations (or "calls" or "contacts"—or whatever the time spent with prospective buyers may be called).
3. A minimum number of unit sales (or volume in dollars—or whatever other measurement of accomplishment is used).

If a salesperson consistently meets the three requirements set forth above, he or she will have little difficulty in realizing the sales quota which has been established.

Achieving minimum goals may limit your long-term growth. Sales production records indicate that many salespeople make the mistake of "freezing" their earnings at a certain level. For example, they may establish an earnings goal of $30,000 per year. As soon as their sales are sufficient to realize this income, they begin to ease off. In other words, many salespeople tend to think of themselves as $30,000-a-year or $35,000-a-year salespeople. When they attain this income they slacken their pace. The salespeople who have this philosophy are seldom promoted into sales management work.

THE VALUE OF TIME

The old axiom "Time is money" certainly applies to selling. A salesperson who works 8 hours a day for 240 days a year will work 1,920 hours during a year. If the salesperson earns $15,000, each hour of time would be worth $7.81. An hour of time would be worth $13.02 if a salesman earned $25,000 a year. Looking at it another way, a salesperson working on a 10 percent commission would have to sell $78 worth of products each hour to earn $15,000 for the year.

That is only part of the story. A lot of a salesperson's time is spent on nonproductive activities. The results of a recent survey of 1,890 industrial salespeople are shown in Figure 16-1. This survey found that, on average, the salespeople worked 9 hours and 22 minutes a day. Many worked through lunch. Only 41 percent of their time was spent in face-to-face selling. The rest of the day was spent in meetings, traveling, waiting for interviews, doing paperwork, or making service calls. This means that the typical salesperson only spends 920 hours each year in front of customers. Thus the salesperson on a 10 percent commission would have to sell $163 worth of products during each hour in front of customers to earn $15,000 for the year.

The lesson from this analysis is clear. The successful salesperson must make every hour count. Time management is particularly important in selling because it is so easy for salespeople not to work. They have little supervision. No one really knows how they spent their time. They can easily waste time by playing tennis, taking many coffee breaks, or engaging in social rather than business conversations with customers.

Figure 16-1
How salespeople spend their time

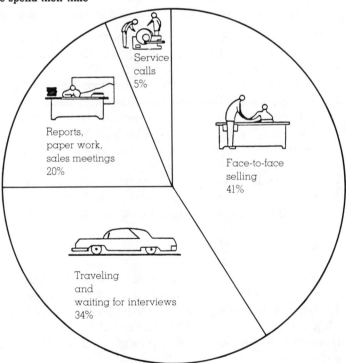

Courtesy of McGraw-Hill Laboratory for Advertising Performance

USING TIME EFFECTIVELY

The steps involved in using time effectively are shown in Figure 16-2. The first step is to list the activities that need to be performed during a period of time. A sales representative might make a detailed list for the next day and a more general list for a longer time period, such as a week or a month. After listing the activities, the salesperson determines the priority of each activity based on its importance. Salespeople who make daily or weekly lists soon become aware of self-deception when they find themselves regularly transferring undesirable activities from one list to the next. A typical list of activities and a priority list for a weekly plan are shown in Table 16-1.

After developing the priority list, the salesperson estimates how much time will be required to complete each activity. These estimates plus the priorities are used to make a schedule for the time period. At the end of the period, the salesperson can compare the

Figure 16-2
Steps in using time effectively

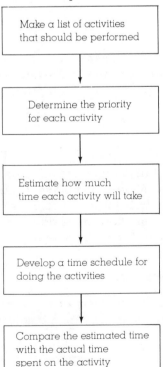

Table 16-1

List of activities and priorities

Activities	Priorities

1. Call on the following prospective customers:
 	
    Flynn Heating and Air Conditioning
    Airtemp Furnaces
    Clayton Plumbing
    Hommell Heating
	1. Daily conference with sales manager.

2. Fill out daily call report form.	2. Complete daily call report.
3. Submit monthly expense report.	3. Be available when delivery is made to Stephenson Electric.
4. Have daily meeting with sales manager.	4. Lunch with Joe Weller.
5. Study new product specification sheet.	5. Cook Plumbing and Heating.

6. Check on customers to see if new heat pumps are working properly:
 	
    Cook Plumbing and Heating
    Bryant Furnace
    South Florida Climate Control
	6. Flynn Heating and Air Conditioning.
	7. Hommell Heating.
	8. Clayton Plumbing.
	9. Study new product specification sheet.
	10. Bryant Furnace.
	11. South Florida Climate Control.

7. Be available when first delivery is made to Stephenson Electric.	12. Monthly expense report.
8. Have lunch with Joe Weller at Miami Heating.	13. Airtemp Furnaces.

estimated time with the actual time spent. Such comparisons allow salespeople to schedule their time better in the future and to check on whether their time is being spent on high-priority rather than low-priority activities.

PLANNING

Planning is the basis for all time organization. Salespeople need to develop both long-range and short-range plans. Long-range plans help salespeople direct their efforts toward customers and activities that will result in the most sales. Short-range daily or weekly plans assist salespeople in using their time efficiently.

Territory analysis and account classification

A first step in planning is an analysis of the territory. Not all customers have the same potential to buy from a salesperson.[1] The salesperson should concentrate on the most profitable customers

---

[1] See Raymond Dreyfack, "A Guide to Profitable Salesmanship," *Sales & Marketing Management*, April 7, 1980, pp. 35–37.

and minimize or eliminate the time spent with customers that offer little opportunity for profitable sales. The proportion of unprofitable accounts is usually greater than one would think. The rule of thumb is that 80 percent of the sales in a territory come from only 20 percent of the customers. Thus it is important for salespeople to classify customers based on their sales potential.

Sales representatives often use a set of account cards to classify customers. Each customer is listed on an index card like the one shown in Figure 16–3. Since the cards are a working tool, information other than the classification is often included. For example, the salesperson may want to list the names of the key buying influences and the hours at which the purchasing agents see vendors.

Sometimes the company will help the salesperson classify accounts, but usually this task is done by the salesperson. Company sales records are a good source of information about existing accounts. However, information on past sales can be misleading. A customer that has placed small orders in the past may have been placing large orders with a competitor. Thus, the salesperson needs to determine the share of business that he or she is getting from each customer. With information about past sales and share of business, the salesperson can determine the potential sales for each customer. Customers with higher potential will be assigned to higher classifications.

For uncalled-on potential customers, the salesperson will frequently have to estimate the sales potential. Such estimates can be made by comparing the potential customer to a present customer of similar size and in a similar business. If an existing customer that purchases $1,000 or more a month is classified as a major account, then a prospective customer with a similar potential is assigned the same rating.

Figure 16–3

Example of account card

Classification: B

Stoppard Plastics Co.
53 Culver Blvd.
Ames, Iowa   Tel.   876-2200

Ms. Susan Blake—Purchasing Agent
Vendor Hours: 9:00 to 4:00 M/W/Th

Sales potential: $300/month.
Buys exclusively from Diamond.

In a typical classification scheme, each customer might be classified into one of three categories—A, B, or C. A accounts are existing or potential customers that are or might be the most profitable for the company. For example, a copier manufacturer might define A accounts as companies that make over 250,000 copies a month. Customers that are growing rapidly might be classified as A accounts even though they do not meet the required minimum. B accounts are existing customers with a lower potential than A accounts, while C accounts are existing or potential customers that are not likely to buy enough to make them profitable accounts.

The salesperson should use the classification in determining the frequency and priority of sales calls. A accounts should be developed first and called on most frequently. Prospecting should be directed exclusively to A accounts. As time permits, other customers can be developed systematically.

A national chemical company classifies its customers as shown below. By adhering to the calling schedule, its sales representatives are able to make the best use of their selling time.

Customer classification	Estimated annual purchases	Required calling period
1st	$30,000	Every month
2d	$12,500–$30,000	Every two months
3d	$ 2,000–$12,500	Every three months
4th	Under $2,000	As time permits

The use of a classification scheme to direct sales efforts helps overcome a natural tendency of new salespeople to concentrate on congenial customers. Research has shown that young salespeople tend to spend most of their time on customers with whom they feel comfortable. Buyers for large companies are often curt and business oriented, while small customers are willing to talk all day. Thus new salespeople have a tendency to spend far too much time with a small portion of their territory's sales potential.

An example of an annual territory sales plan is shown in Figure 16-4. Notice that the allocation of calls is related to the customer potential. This plan serves as a sales goal as well as a method for allocating time.

Key account action plan

Additional planning efforts should be devoted to key accounts in the territory. For each key account, a set of goals should be established. For each goal, a series of activities should be planned to achieve the goal. A form for developing a key account action plan is shown in Figure 16-5.

Figure 16-4

Annual Territory Sales Plan

Salesperson: *Sam Thompson*

Account	*Actual sales ($)* 1978	1979	1980	*Estimated potential*	*1981 forecasted sales*	*Number of calls allocated*
Allied Brake	100	110	90	250	160	48
Zebec	75	75	90	300	115	48
Wright	40	50	60	175	90	24
American Can	20	30	50	150	70	24
Tee Products	10	10	25	100	55	18
Simmons Mfg.	0	0	30	100	80	18
Unilevel	0	0	0	80	75	18
Jackright	0	10	20	75	70	18
Baker Tool	0	5	12	60	60	12
Tool and Die	0	0	10	60	50	12
Castmetal, Inc.	10	8	9	50	40	12

Figure 16-5
Form for key account action plan

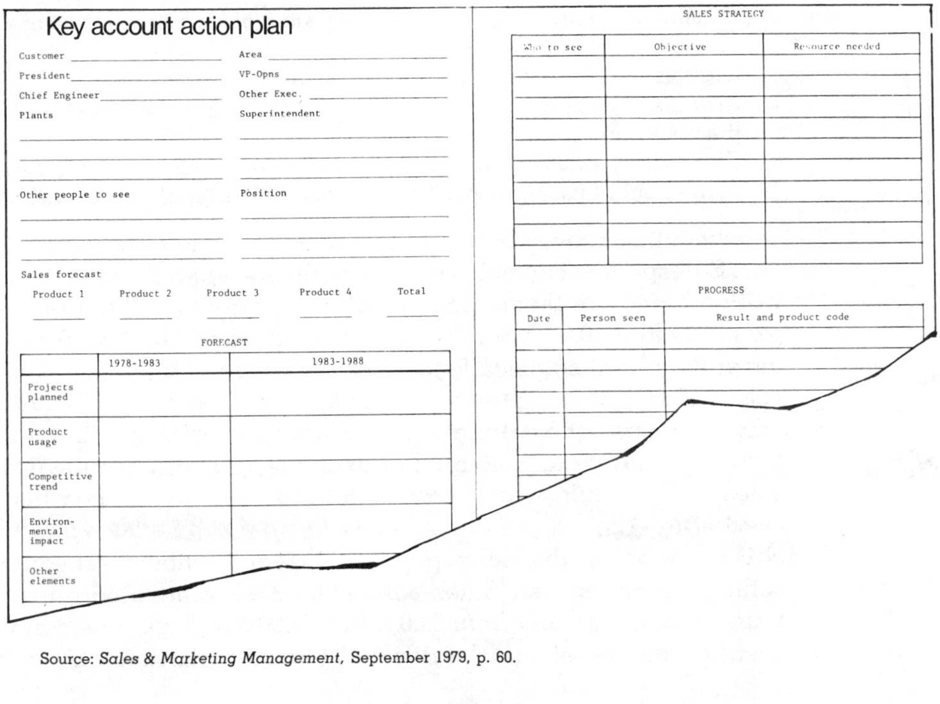
Key account action plan

Customer ____ Area ____
President ____ VP-Opns ____
Chief Engineer ____ Other Exec. ____
Plants ____ Superintendent ____

Other people to see ____ Position ____

Sales forecast
Product 1 Product 2 Product 3 Product 4 Total

FORECAST

	1978-1983	1983-1988
Projects planned		
Product usage		
Competitive trend		
Environ-mental impact		
Other elements		

SALES STRATEGY

Who to see	Objective	Resource needed

PROGRESS

Date	Person seen	Result and product code

Source: *Sales & Marketing Management*, September 1979, p. 60.

Daily planning

Each evening, the salesperson should make a plan for the next selling day. The plan should not be limited to where the first call will be made, but should be an entire schedule for the day. Daily plans include spending a maximum amount of time in essential activities. Calls are routed to minimize travel time. Whenever possible, advance arrangements are made for interview appointments and luncheon engagements.

One company gives its sales representatives the following instructions concerning the daily sales plan:

1. Select your prospects for tomorrow's calls.
2. List the names and locations of each account.
3. Carefully route those calls to save traveling time.
4. Visualize what is going to take place at each call.
5. Organize your data and exhibits to make each call effective.

Procedures to use in planning your sales day include the following:

1. First, consult your tickler file for any customer calls due for the next day.
2. Reread the data on each customer card as a refresher. Determine what stage the sale is in.
3. Plan what is to take place on each call. Establish objectives for the call.
4. Determine whether other business can be attended to between calls, such as calling on prospects in the same neighborhood.
5. Consult the prospect file for the case history of each prospect to be called on.
6. Organize the material you will take with you.
7. Arrange your folders in the order you will wish to use them, and pack them for carrying in your "hot box."
8. Clip a daily sales activity report to a separate folder, and put the folder in the front of your "hot box" so that you may fill in the report as you go.

Scheduling time. Sales calls cannot be made at all hours of the day. Salespeople can only call on customers when the customers are willing to receive them. Many purchasing agents will not see salespeople before 10:00 A.M., during lunch, or after 4:00 P.M. Some customer may limit sales calls to a narrow range of time, such as 10:00 A.M. to 12:00 P.M. on Tuesday and Thursday. Even though a customer may not restrict the calling hours, a salesperson might find it better to visit during certain hours. For example, a pharmaceutical detail salesperson would want to avoid calling on doctors when they are seeing patients.

In developing the daily plan, salespeople should schedule the selling activities first. Sales calls should be scheduled during the prime hours, typically from 9:00 A.M. to 4:00 P.M. Time that cannot be spent on selling should be devoted to such activities as servicing accounts (putting up displays, checking out inventories, handling customer complaints), filling out reports, and making telephone calls to schedule appointments or get information from the home office.

Salespeople must be realistic in developing the daily plan. If they want to make eight calls during the day, they cannot simply schedule a call each hour. They need to consider driving time and what they want to accomplish during the call. Some calls will need 90 minutes, while others will require only 30 minutes.

Flexibility. Although it is important to work out a daily plan, there are times when the plan should be laid aside. It is impossible to accurately judge the time that will be needed for each call. It would be foolish to hastily conclude a sales presentation just because you want to stick to your schedule. The purpose of making sales calls is to get results. If salespeople feel that additional time on a call will yield more results than will other scheduled calls then they should revise their schedule accordingly. However, such rearrangements should be based on new information received while making the call. Salespeople should not rearrange their schedule just because they are enjoying a conversation with a customer.

To plan for the unexpected, the daily schedule should be arranged so that visits are made to the prime prospect first. Then the next best potential customer should be visited. The daily schedule concludes with calls on new prospects. If the day is planned in this manner, unexpected long calls or emergencies will result in canceling the least important calls—the calls at the end of the day.

Routing

Routing plans are used to reduce the nonproductive time spent in going from one sales call to another. Wasting time traveling between customers decreases efficiency and may also increase selling costs through excessive mileage.

There are two basic types of sales call patterns—routine and variable. Routine call patterns are used when a salesperson sees the same customers regularly. For example, when a Procter and Gamble salesperson is assigned a territory, it is expected that each customer will be contacted regularly. Large grocery stores might be visited once a week, while small stores will be visited once a month. Once the Procter and Gamble salesperson develops a routing plan, it can be used over and over. Calls are directed toward customers that have a need for a product at a particular time. The routing plan is built around specific customers and specific locations.

The first step in developing a routing plan is to locate customers on a map. Customers often tend to cluster together. Customer clusters reveal some obvious ways in which the territory can be divided and the routing plan developed. After the customers have been located on a map, the travel time between customers is estimated. At what time of day should the salesperson make calls that are a long distance from his or her home city? Do the expected sales justify the travel costs? How much time can he or she afford to be away from the area?

In planning a sales trip, it is usually best to start working the outlying areas first and to finish at the home area. Typically, the home area is the location of the greatest sales potential. If an emergency brings you back to your home area, you will not have to travel as far to pick up your route again. An example of a four-week itinerary using this principle is shown in Figure 16–6.

Figure 16–6
Routing for large territory

Example of one-week schedule
   Sunday—drive to Albany.
   Monday and Tuesday—calls in Albany.
   Wednesday morning—drive to Schenectady.
   Wednesday—calls in Schnectady.
   Wednesday night—drive to Utica.
   Thursday and Friday—calls in Utica.
   Friday night—drive to Syracuse.

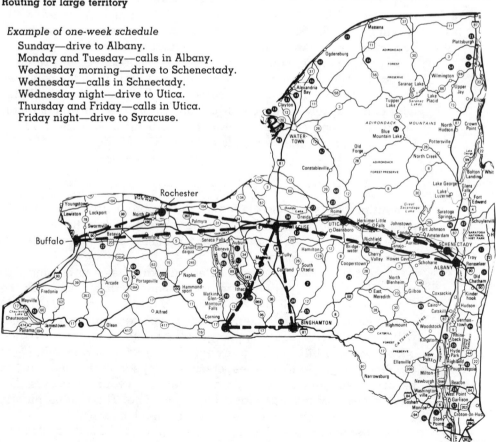

Covering a city or a small territory. When covering a territory within a two-hour radius of your home, it is useful to divide the territory into zones. The zones are worked one at a time. An example of a zone plan is shown in Figure 16-7. The principle of starting with the outermost customer can be used in this situation also. Another way to develop a routing plan for a zone may be to start with a key customer. Suppose that the salesperson keys the routing plan for zone B to a customer at location D. If the customer will see the salesperson only at 3:30 P.M., then the route is developed so that the customer is the last call for the day.

Salespeople often encounter a conflict between developing an efficient routing plan and making calls on the most profitable customer. Typically the most efficient routing plans will include customers with low sales potentials. One approach to this problem is to develop an efficient routing plan for each customer classification. The salesperson can then use the routing plan for the most profitable customer more frequently than the routing plan for the less profitable customers.

Figure 16-7
Routing for compact territory

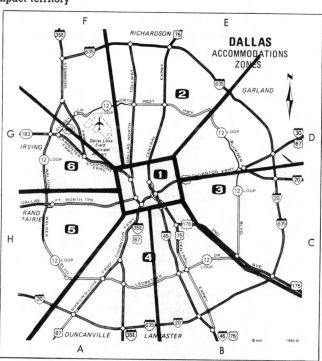

HOW TO MAKE MORE CALLS

Analyzing the territory, making daily plans, and developing efficient routes are important steps toward increasing efficiency. Some other techniques for increasing your productivity are discussed in this section.

Stretching the workweek

Many salespeople who cover large territories develop an "out Tuesday, back Friday" complex. Salespeople can offer a lot of reasons why they need to work in the office or at home on Monday and Saturday. However, this behavior pattern means that the salesperson is making between 20 and 30 percent fewer calls than would be made by spending the whole week on the road.

To get the most out of a territory, the sales representative must utilize all the days available. For example, the days just before or just after a holiday are often slighted. A salesperson might reason that sales effort spent on these days will be unproductive because the customers will be more interested in their holiday activities than in business. However, it is frequently easier to get sales interviews on these days because there is less competition. The same reasoning applies to days when the weather is unpleasant. Bad weather reduces competition and makes things easier for the salesperson who is not interested in finding excuses to take it easy.

Lengthening the workday

The best and easiest way to see more customers is to work smarter and harder. Many salespeople believe that they cannot make calls outside the traditional 9-to-12 and 2-to-4 pattern. But many businesses and professionals are available before 9 and after 4 or 5 in the afternoon. Frequently, people in small industrial and retail businesses work long hours. Many executives pride themselves on being at their desks before their employees arrive in the morning.

These customers are prime candidates for early morning or late afternoon calls. One salesperson brings sweet rolls for his customers so that he can make a sales call while sharing the first cup of coffee in the morning.

It is important to learn which of your customers work long hours so that you can take advantage of these opportunities to make calls during the off-hours. Some customers do not want to talk to salespeople in the early morning. They prefer to use this time to plan their day. However, some early morning calls are possible in almost every sales territory. Once acquainted with their customers' habits, sales-people know where these opportunities exist.

Lunch and dinner offer other opportunities to make sales calls. Customers who are too busy to see salespeople are often willing to take time to eat meals.[2] During these meals, salespeople can talk with customers whom it might be difficult to see at their place of business. However, care must be taken in arranging such appointments. Some customers and companies consider these meetings as entertainment and do not view them favorably. In some situations, the salesperson should refrain from making a presentation during a meal. The meal should be used as an opportunity to develop a better relationship that will be useful in future sales efforts.

Using the telephone and the postal service

The telephone is a valuable tool for saving time and covering the territory more effectively. Probably the most important use of the telephone in selling is to make, confirm, and reschedule appointments. Making appointments in advance eliminates time wasted while waiting in reception rooms or time wasted in traveling to a customer who will not grant an interview. When making appointments, salespeople should remember that securing an interview is just as important and often as difficult as closing a sale. Salespeople need to prepare for telephone calls just as they prepare for personal interviews.

Telephone calls can be used to replace more time-consuming sales calls. Although complete sales presentations cannot be made over the phone, some sales can be concluded over the phone. For example, the telephone can be used to remind regular customers to place routine repeat orders and to inform customers of special discounts and new products. If a salesperson learns that a price increase is anticipated, a telephone call relaying this information to customers will be greatly appreciated. This use of the telephone results in customer goodwill and may even lead to sales.

Some customers in a territory may not have the sales potential to warrant personal sales calls. While effective territory coverage means spending the most time with the larger buyers, small buyers can be contacted by telephone. The telephone is also useful for contacting customers in remote locations that require excessive travel time.

---

[2] For an interesting assessment of the luncheon meetings between salespeople and buyers, see Paul J. Halvorson and William Rudelius, "Is There a Free Lunch?" *Journal of Marketing*, January 1977, pp.44–49.

An example of a typical telephone call to answer a letter inquiry might be planned as follows:

Steps

1. *Identify* yourself and your company. You'll show your customer that this isn't a "routine call" if you use his or her name throughout the call.

2. *Acknowledge* the customer's letter, and explain why you're calling.

3. *Restate* the customer's reason for writing. It will help you understand what was meant. Give the customer a chance to explain if he feels it necessary.

4. *Answer* the customer's questions. Talk customer benefit in the customer's language—not yours. By asking whether the terms are agreeable, you'll help to prevent any future misunderstandings.

5. *Sell.* Your customers' conversation may indicate that they are prospects for an order—or for an "accessory" item.

Comments

"Good morning, Mr. Valdez. This is Bob Sayles of the Wheat Products Company."

"Your letter arrived this morning. I felt I could give you a better answer if we talked it over. It's nice to have a chance to talk with you."

"According to your letter, Mr. Valdez, you wanted the answer to two questions: 1. What delivery could we promise on gross lots of Extra EZs? 2. Would you receive a more favorable price on a 12-gross order?" *(Pause.)*

"Concerning delivery, all orders received by noon are shipped the same day. Since you're within 200 miles, you'll receive your shipment the next day. Does that sound all right?" *(Pause.)*
"You also asked about price, Mr. Valdez. Since it's more economical for us to ship in large quantities, we pass the savings along to you. By buying in 12-gross lots, you'll save 10 percent over single-gross shipments. Does that answer your question?" *(Pause.)*

"Our customers have found the new Extra EZs to be a great income producer, Mr. Valdez. Since you're interested in the savings on a 12-gross order, I'd like to make a suggestion—let me ship you 12 gross. They'll be delivered tomorrow. Joe Service will stop in the next morning and set up some display advertising that'll let your customers know you're handling this new item. He'll also have some sample newspaper ads for your local paper. I know Extra EZs will

6. *Thank* your customers. Let them know that you appreciate them and their business. And that you're there to serve them.

be as successful for you as they've been for our other customers."

"It's been pleasant talking to you, Mr. Valdez. And thanks for your order. If there's every anything else you want to know, just give me a call and I'll do my best to take care of it. Good-bye, and thanks again."

The telephone is an excellent way of handling customer complaints and problems. While it might take days to schedule a service sales call, a quick telephone call placed immediately after a complaint arises can be used to head off future problems.

The mail service can be used to replace costly personal visits. Letters and sales brochures can be used to contact small, "out-of-the-way" customers. It is more efficient to deliver routine information by mail than in person.

Shortening sales calls

A good sales representative does not waste time during a sales interview. Frequently, time can be saved by sending the customer information in advance. During the interview, the salesperson should avoid needless chatter. If a salesperson is not careful, a well-planned sales presentation can degenerate into a casual social conversation. If this happens, both the salesperson and the customer are wasting their time.

Closing earlier and more often can lead to short sales calls. Frequently, the prospect is sold before the salesperson realizes it. Continuing the presentation beyond the appropriate closing time might actually talk the customer out of the sale.

Some customers like to buy in a more leisurely social atmosphere. They will resent any attempt made by the salesperson to rush through the sales call. The salesperson must be sensitive to the needs of such customers. Here, it might be useful to terminate a social conversation by saying, "I realize you're a very busy person and have a lot of things to do, so I'll try to make my presentation as brief as possible.

Finally, it is important to know when to give up. While determination and refusing to take no for an answer are fine qualities for a salesperson, they can be overdone. Investing a great deal of time in making one sale may result in inability to make several less time-consuming sales. The salesperson should continually assess the chances for making a sale. It is often a poor investment of time to continue trying to make a sale to a difficult customer.

ANALYZING YOUR PERFORMANCE

A careful analysis of sales records and reports provides a sales-person with such information as dollar sales per call, dollar sales by products, number of calls made, number of interviews obtained, number of orders lost, miles traveled per day, number of complaints, and new prospects obtained.

Some sales representatives feel that the time spent in analyzing past records is wasted. In many instances, sales representatives pay very little attention to the detailed analyses that they receive from the office. This attitude is most prevalent among the sales represen-tatives of the "old school," who are reluctant to change their old methods.

The younger and more progressive sales representatives, how-ever, realize the importance of analyzing past accomplishments to improve future operations. The information obtained from past rec-ords and reports helps answer the following questions: Am I cover-ing my territory efficiently? Am I concentrating my efforts on the customers with the greatest sales potentials? Am I selling a bal-anced line of products? Am I spending most of my time in actual sales interviews?

Many companies require their sales representatives to fill out daily call reports. An example of a call report form is shown in Figure 16-8. Call report forms are useful in analyzing sales activi-ties. From these forms, statistics such as number of calls per day, sales per call, and percentage of calls made on customers in each classification can be calculated. An examination of these statistics over time might indicate the reasons for a sales slump. For example, a salesperson might find that the number of calls made per day has declined or that too many calls are being made on low-potential accounts.

It is also important for salespeople to analyze their activities dur-ing the day. To make this analysis, some salespeople carry a pocket notebook that is ruled by 30-minute periods. During the day, the salesperson will write down what he or she was doing during each 30-minute period. To be effective, the notebook must be filled in after each hour. The salesperson should not rely on memory to complete the record.

At the end of the week, the salesperson can review the notebook entries and determine how much time was spent seeing customers, waiting to see customers, traveling, planning the day's work, doing paperwork, and so on. This information can help the salesperson determine where improvements in time management can be made. It might be found that too much time was being spent in nonproductive activities such as having lunch or providing extra services to low-po-tential customers.

Figure 16-8

DAILY ACTIVITY REPORT				SALESMAN:				DATE:		
NUMBER OF DEMONSTRATIONS						TOTAL DEMOS	NO. OF PROPOSALS PRESENTED	NO. OF CALLS		
PROD. GR. 1	PROD. GR. 2	PROD. GR. 3	PROD. GR. 5	PROD. GR. 6	PROD. GR. 8				REPEAT	NEW

PROSPECT/CUSTOMER	TRIAL + PLACED - REMOVED DEMONSTRATIONS	COMMENTS
FIRM	TRIAL-STYLE & SER.	
INDIVIDUAL		
	DEMO-STYLE ONLY	
ADDRESS		
FIRM	TRIAL-STYLE & SER.	
INDIVIDUAL		
	DEMO-STYLE ONLY	
ADDRESS		
FIRM	TRIAL-STYLE & SER.	
INDIVIDUAL		
	DEMO-STYLE ONLY	
ADDRESS		
FIRM	TRIAL-STYLE & SER.	
INDIVIDUAL		
	DEMO-STYLE ONLY	
ADDRESS		
FIRM	TRIAL-STYLE & SER.	
INDIVIDUAL		
	DEMO-STYLE ONLY	
ADDRESS		
FIRM	TRIAL-STYLE & SER.	
INDIVIDUAL		
	DEMO-STYLE ONLY	
ADDRESS		
FIRM	TRIAL-STYLE & SER.	
INDIVIDUAL		
	DEMO-STYLE ONLY	
ADDRESS		
FIRM	TRIAL-STYLE & SER.	
INDIVIDUAL		
	DEMO-STYLE ONLY	
ADDRESS		
MILEAGE:	EXPENSES:	
ENDING _____	TOTAL MILES	
STARTING _____		

PRINTED IN U.S. AMERICA   1900537 (REV. 9/77)

HANDLING PAPERWORK AND REPORTS

Preparing reports for management is part of every sales job. All salespeople complain about such paperwork, but it is an important part of the job. In general, salespeople are not known for their interest in shuffling paper. They prefer to be out making calls. But if they want to be successful salespeople, and certainly if they want to be promoted to sales management positions, they must learn how to handle paperwork.

Types of sales reports _____

Some typical reports that salespeople are required to complete are listed below:

1. *Daily work plan.* A list of the customers you plan to see and what you plan to accomplish.
2. *Daily call report.* A daily outline of activities and results. Sales managers can compare the report to the plan to see if you are working effectively.
3. *Weekly summary report.* This report sometimes takes the place of the daily call report. It usually contains a brief recap of activities and results for the week.
4. *Monthly expense report.* This is a list of expenses incurred during the month. The report is used to reimburse salespeople for entertainment and travel costs.
5. *Other reports.* Salespeople may be required to complete reports on the status of potential large orders, prospects for future business, dealer inventory levels, lost accounts, or competitive activity in the territory.

Doing paperwork efficiently _____

Paperwork is unproductive in comparison to time spent selling customers. Thus, it is important that required paperwork get done thoroughly in the least possible time. Some suggestions for handling paperwork are discussed in the following paragraphs.

First, salespeople should think positively about paperwork. Even though paperwork is less productive than selling, it can increase productivity by enabling a detailed review of selling activities.

Salespeople should not allow paperwork to accumulate. Routine reports should be completed daily. They should use nonproductive time during the day to complete reports. For example, call reports can be updated while waiting for a customer.

It is a good idea for salespeople to make notes of things that have to be done and points to remember. If this is not done during the sales interview, it should certainly be done right after the interview. Many salespeople keep a clipboard in their car for holding cards and notes concerning calls made during the day. Clipboards are easy to write on. All notes should be dated so that the salesperson can place them in the correct time sequence when they are needed to write a report.

If a salesperson utilizes waiting time to work on records and reports, more free time will be available in the evenings for rest or

Figure 16-9
Dictating a report

Courtesy of the 3-M Company

recreation. Some companies provide their sales representatives with dictating machines to enable them to make prompt and descriptive verbal reports. New developments in portable recording units and magnetic discs, records, and belts have done much to simplify the sales representative's reporting (see Figure 16-9).

Finally, salespeople should set aside a block of unproductive time to do paperwork. Paperwork can be done much quicker if one concentrates on it and avoids interruptions. A specific time should be scheduled each day for writing brief thank-you and follow-up notes and completing reports.

QUESTIONS AND PROBLEMS

1. After reading the material in this chapter, a salesperson protests, "That's no fun. I like coffee breaks. If I have to hustle every minute of the day, then forget it. I'll get another job." What would you tell this salesperson?

2. What are the benefits of planning?

3. Distinguish between routing and scheduling. Explain how these may interact to complicate the planning of an efficient day's work.

4. Compare and contrast the special problems in self-management for retail salespeople and outside industrial and trade salespeople.

5. How might a life insurance salesperson increase the number of calls made per day?

6. Sales managers know that making more sales calls results in more sales. Does this mean that a salesperson should be encouraged to continually increase the number of calls made each week? Explain your answer.

7. How do sales reports provide useful information for the salesperson?

8. In developing a scheme for classifying customers, what factors would you consider? Why?

9. During the past few years, considerable emphasis has been given to the use of computers and other data-processing equipment in the marketing and sales fields. List the kinds of information that such equipment might make available to the sales representative in the field.

PROJECTS

1. For a typical 24-hour period, keep as accurate a record as possible of how you spent your waking hours. Compare the amount of time spent on achieving basic objectives with the amount of wasted time.

2. Contact a local company which employs a number of salespeople, and request the opportunity to make a survey of how the salespeople spend their time during a specific period. Write a report on your findings in which you break down time utilization by types of activities.

CASE PROBLEMS

Case 16-1

Scheduling sales calls

Sue White, an experienced salesperson, explained her system for scheduling calls as follows:

> My years of experience have taught me that the timing of a sales call is critical. It is very important to catch a buyer in the right mood. One buyer is very hard to deal with on Fridays. Another has a staff meeting every Monday afternoon. If I call on him on Monday morning, I find it difficult to hold his attention. He always seems to be thinking about the afternoon meeting. If you study your regular customers closely, you can determine when they will be most receptive to a sales call.

Questions

1. Do you think White has a good system? Why or why not?

2. How can a salesperson determine whether the timing of his or her calls is significant?

Case 16-2

Northern Farm Equipment Company—A day with a farm equipment salesperson

"We sell a lot of farm equipment throughout this river-bottom area," said Bob Hart, sales representative for Lang Implement Company, the Northern Farm Equipment Company dealer in Quincy, Illinois. Hart's territory lies on both sides of the Mississippi in Illinois and Missouri. He covers it in a Northern pickup truck so that he can go right out to his prospects when they are working in the field. Hart often meets his customers in an open-collar shirt, a leather jacket, and a felt hat that he rarely removes. In fact, Hart frequently dresses more like one of his customers than like a sales representative. He knows the problems of his customers, and he talks their language. He is proud of his ability to "run a tractor around a barnyard and tell pretty well by the sound whether or not the rear end is OK."

Some of Hart's ideas on selling farm equipment follow:

The first thing I do is to get around to enough doors and barn lots to find a person who is interested in buying something. During this time of year, there may be weeks when I'm never in the office except in the morning before I start out on my calls. If you expect to sell farm equipment, you have to go out to the customer. And I usually have plenty of customers on whom to call. I do, however, want to spend some time in the store. If a person tends to business while in the store, he can sell a lot of equipment and get a good many leads for future action.

When you go to some farmers you can sit and talk all day if you want, and then they'll invite you in for dinner. It's a great temptation to waste time this way when you're out in the country. When I drive into a place, I always assume that the customer is just as busy as I am, so 30 minutes is about as long as I stay. I follow a plan of talking business while I'm there, and when I see it's time to leave, I leave. Often I stop at one place and find that my customer is not going to buy anything. But sometimes the customer will say, "Hart, you ought to go down the road and see Albert Fowler. He's planning on buying a new tractor. Now don't you tell him I told you, but I heard that the John Deere people were out there the other day." When I get a lead like this, instead of going directly to Fowler's place, if he's a next-door neighbor, I go down the road, and then maybe the next morning I stop at the Fowler farm. If he doesn't say anything about the tractor deal, I pass the time of day with him for a while. Then our conversation naturally drifts into a discussion about his tractor.

If customers want to buy something that I don't think they should buy because it doesn't fit their needs, I always try to talk them out of buying it. I may lose an immediate sale by doing this, but in the long run I have found that this procedure pays big dividends. The only time I mention anything about a competitive tractor is when the customer brings the subject up first. I prepare myself for such an occasion by studying up on the literature of all competitive machines.

Whenever you try to talk about everything on a tractor, you get your customer confused. I usually stress one or two major features, such as how the torque amplifier works. When I get the customer sold on the TA, then I mention the hydraulic system, which is a special feature on our tractors.

When I drive from one customer's place to the next, I usually listen to the car radio. This is very helpful, as I always pick up the community news and the market information everybody is talking about. Because a lot of fellows will tell you that the price of hogs or cattle dropped off yesterday, and they don't know if they ought to buy anything from you. But if you catch that market news, maybe you can answer right back that they went up 50 cents *today*.

By putting such selling techniques as these into practice, Bob Hart helped the Lang Implement Company stay in the running with the best of its seven competitors in Quincy.

Bob Hart drove 60 miles on March 4, spending the morning across the river in Missouri and the afternoon in Illinois. He made eight calls and talked to two customers at the store. His efforts bore some fruit, but the day also produced its share of blind alleys and frustrations. Arriving at one stop, he learned that the farmer had gone to Quincy to see *him*. Efforts to find another farmer at a grain elevator ended in failure. He found Harvey Ireland ringing pigs and had to talk business with him above their shrill, incessant squealing. Ireland finally decided not to deal.

Right after lunch, Hart drove up to see Glenn Mugdalen, who was in partnership with his brother, Orville, about the possibility of trading for a baler. Glenn's wife, Martha, came out to meet him when she heard the dog bark.

Bob spoke first, "What do you have Glenn doing today?

"Well, he's sowing clover seed."

"What's he doing sowing clover seed—muddy as it is?"

"Well, I tell you, he looked like a mud turtle. But he's sowing clover seed."

"What have Orville and Glenn decided on that baler?"

"You go over and see Orville. Have you been over there?"

"No, I haven't."

"He has all the statistics, and I think when you get over there, you'll get your answer."

"Thank you a lot, Martha. I'll go right over to see Orville to find out what was decided on the baler."

Hart found Orville preparing to go into the fields with fertilizer. They passed the time of day before Bob got down to business.

"I stopped over at Glenn's and talked with Martha. She said you had all the answers about the baler."

"Yes, sir. Well, I wish I did know all the answers about the baler."

"If you go ahead and trade balers with us now, it'll help us to get rid of the used one."

"After thinking it over, we just kind of thought we'd be better off by having this one fixed."

"You want us to pick it up, then?"

"I believe so."

"We can pick it up any time. That's all right with us if you want to fix it and don't want to trade. And while we've got it down there fixing it, you might take a notion you want to trade."

"That's right. I believe that's about as good a way as any to do it."

"Another thing. I want to see what we can do on that tractor deal . . ."

But 15 minutes of earnest talk in Orville Mugdalen's barnyard failed to bring the two men to terms on anything but repairing the baler (although a few days later, Orville *did* buy a new Fast-Hitch for his tractor).

Bob Hart's ratio of sales to calls was considerably less than eight for eight on March 4. But every minute that he wasn't on the road, he was selling.

Bob made two sales on March 4. Both were corn planters. One of the buyers came to him at the store after he had made a sales pitch at the farm. He made the other sale because he went out after it.

Another customer, Bill Adams, owns 400 acres near LaGrange, Missouri, about 12 miles from Quincy. Hart had talked to him before about buying a new four-row planter, using his old John Deere planter as a trade-in. Hart had also agreed to sell Adams' old crawler for him. On the morning of March 4, Hart crossed the river to La-Grange and found Adams at the wheel of his Farmall tractor, hauling feed.

The following conversation ended in a sale:

Hart: You *know* what I stopped for. We're going to trade that John Deere corn planter for that new Northern.

Adams: Just as soon as you sell that crawler.

Hart: They pick it up yet?

Adams: Nope.

Hart: Well, they're *going* to pick it up. Now listen. On that cash part of it. You know we're not worrying about that. But corn planting may be over before we get the crawler sold, and you know you want that new planter. What do you say we trade this morning?

Adams: I have to get some cash—that's all there is to it.

Hart: Your credit is always good.

Adams: You know I never bought anything on time.

Hart: I know you haven't bought anything yet for which you haven't paid cash. But here's our point on the planter. What we're in a hurry for is to get the used one sold because you can wait too long. Then you have to carry it over another year. That's when you lose money. How long would I have to carry you?

Adams: You might have to carry me 'til harvest.

Hart: Aw, I don't think so. You know you're going to buy a planter.

Adams: Oh, I can get by.

Hart: Doggone it, I'd sure like to trade with you . . . I want to look at that planter of yours again.

(At this point, Hart went into a shed to check the trade-in planter. When he came out, Adams waited while Hart returned to his pickup to do some figuring. The conversation began again when Hart finished.)

Hart: Well, here's what I'll do. I'll bring that new planter over here for $402.

Adams: $402. Hmm. Let's see how you figured, Bob.

Hart: That's putting a lot of money in *your* planter.

Adams: You're taking that corn sheller in on that, aren't you, Bob—for $100?

Hart: No. Doggone it, I can't.

(Short pause.)

Adams: You're still asking a lot of money, Bob.

Hart: But that's giving you an awful good deal on a planter, too, you must remember. If you keep yours, you're going to have to put runners on it. Four of them—that's $32. With this new one you'd be getting a high-speed planter that will plant accurately.

Adams: Is that a good hill-drop planter?

Hart: It sure is. It'll hill-drop 211 hills a minute. In other words, if you're spacing 40 inches apart, it'll hill-drop 6½ miles an hour and put 95 percent of the grains in the size of a silver dollar.

(Long silence while Bill Adams thinks it over.)

Adams: That's a lot of money, Bob. It's a good trade, but . . .

(Another long pause.)

Hart: You can see our point. Here it is the fourth day of March, and people are buying this used equipment now. We don't want to wait around too long . . .

(Another pause.)

Adams: Aw, I don't know. You always make me a good deal, Bob . . .

Hart: Sure I do. Why don't you let me write the order this morning? Let's see, that price is $900. I'm giving you $498 on your planter. That's $402 difference.

Adams: By the time this thaw is over, I'm liable to have to put all that money for a planter into gravel for these roads.

Hart: Well, you don't have to pay for that planter today. Tell me when you *would* pay for it.

(Pause.)

Adams: Reckon I can get the job done with that planter?

Hart: I know you can because we'll come out here and start it for you.

Adams: Are you going to get somebody over here to get the governor on this tractor straightened out?

Hart: Sure, I'll get it fixed for you—get somebody out here right away. Can you pay me by the 15th of April? That wouldn't crowd you any, would it?

Adams: Give me 'til the 15th of May. That'll give me a chance to sell some of the bred heifers.

Hart: "OK, let me write it up then and you sign the order.

(At this point, Hart began to write.)

Adams: Better give me $500 for my planter, Bob.

Hart: I'm *giving* you $498.

Adams: Well, I know, but it looks so much better.

Hart: Well, doggone it, OK. That would make $400 even, wouldn't it? Let's see. March 4. I ought to remember that because I was 49 years old yesterday. I'm getting old . . .

Adams: I'll say you are.

Hart: Well, there you are. You just sign here. And thanks a lot to you, Bill. I'm sure you will be happy about it.

"The greatest thing we've got to sell is goodwill," Bob Hart says: "If we can keep the customer's goodwill, we'll keep our fair share of the business. Courtesy calls pay real dividends in this business. About 80 percent of Lang Implement's sales are repeat business. The first sale to a person is a hard one to make. The next one comes easier, and the one after that, even easier. By this time the customers come back because they like the way they are treated."

"Sometimes you can win goodwill by knowing when to walk off a deal." Lang's service manager, Carl Wilson, tells of a case in point:

> Bob Hart and I were out with a customer, and it got to be 11:30 at night when we got through. The sale we were working on amounted to $9,600. The farmer thought we were completely crazy when we walked off and left it over a $21 difference. He thought we'd take it the next day. The only thing he didn't know was that we'd possibly gone $300 too far already. Another dealer took the deal at the farmer's figures. This happened nearly a year ago, and the other dealer still has the same trade-in on his lot. They've long since fallen out over the deal, and we've taken over the service work and sold the farmer another new tractor. The point is, you can cut a deal so close that you're better off not making it. There's a stopping point someplace.

Bob Hart has learned that goodwill can come from a variety of things, as illustrated in the following experience:

> About three years ago, we stopped in where we thought a man had some work to be done on a baler. We caught him right in the middle of mixing concrete. This was just past noon.
>
> A little after nine that night we finished pushing wheelbarrows, shoveling gravel, and mixing cement. The crew was the farmer, his wife, Carl, and myself. The farmer and his wife would never have finished the job by themselves. They invited us to stay for supper, and she cooked steaks for us. An hour later we had sold a tractor and were on our way back to town. The tractor deal was never mentioned in any way, shape, or form until the concrete was finished. Since then, this customer has come back with repeat business. He has bought a new hay baler since, and a 350 Diesel. And he's more than 60 miles away from our store. We still do his service work.

Questions

1. What is your reaction to the way Bob Hart utilized his time on March 4? What, if any, suggestions do you have to improve Hart's sales efforts?
2. If you were Bob Hart, what criteria would you use to evaluate the effectiveness of your sales efforts in your territory?
3. What differences would you expect to find in the planning and controlling of sales efforts for a salesperson who sells heavy construction equipment as compared to a salesperson who sells farm equipment?

Case 16–3

Centerville sales territory[3]

This is the situation:

You are a general-line salesperson for the Great American Corporation. Yours is the Centerville territory. You have worked the territory for several years, and you know it quite well.

You are about to plan your itinerary for the last four weeks of the quarter. Your quota for the quarter is $300,000. Sales for the first two months of the quarter total $280,000, leaving you only $20,000 short of your nut. It is important that you meet your quota because Great American has big plans for you if you do.

You have 14 regular customers for your products in the Centerville territory. You know that among them they have the potential for an additional $27,500 during the remaining month of the quarter.

---

[3] Adapted from Stewart A. Washburn, "Salesmanship: The Time-Is-Money Game," *Sales & Marketing Management*, March 8, 1976, pp. 43–48.

Figure 16–10

List of customers and prospects

		Sales to date	Remaining potential	People to see
Customers:				
1.	Handwound Coil	$75,000	$3,000	Design engineer* General foreman Foreman Purchasing agent
2.	General Dymo	63,000	1,500	Purchasing agent* Design engineer 1 Design engineer 2
3.	Superior Electric	34,000	4,000	Purchasing agent* Design engineer
4.	Herman Transformer	28,000	1,000	Purchasing agent*
5.	Alpha Transformer	24,000	2,000	Purchasing agent* Design engineer
6.	Circle D Contrals	9,500	3,000	Purchasing agent* Design engineer
7.	Easton Motors	8,000	1,500	Design engineer*
8.	Fractional Motors	7,000	3,000	Design engineer* Foreman Purchasing agent
9.	Acme Motors	7,000	2,500	Design engineer* Purchasing agent
10.	Bartlett Transformer	6,500	1,000	Purchasing agent*
11.	Zip Electric	6,000	3,000	Purchasing agent* Design engineer
12.	Taft Electric	6,000	500	Purchasing agent* Design engineer
13.	Macro Electric	5,000	500	Purchasing agent*
14.	Roth Motors	1,000	1,000	Design engineer*
Prospects:				
15.	ABC Transformer	—	3,000	Purchasing agent* Design engineer Foreman
16.	Ace Motors	—	1,500	Design engineer* Foreman Purchasing agent
17.	Air Conditioning Corp.	—	5,000	Purchasing agent* Design engineer
18.	Amp Motors	—	3,500	Design engineer* Foreman Purchasing agent
19.	Eastern Windings	—	1,500	Design engineer*
20.	Holmes Electric	—	3,000	Design engineer* Purchasing agent
21.	Manual Electric	—	1,800	Purchasing agent
22.	Micro Electric	—	2,500	Design engineer* Foreman Purchasing agent
23.	Twister Coil	—	3,000	Purchasing agent* Design engineer
24.	U.S. Lyndon	—	15,000	Design engineer* Foreman 1 Foreman 2 Purchasing agent

Decision maker.

You have also identified ten nonbuying prospects in the territory. They represent an additional $39,800 in potential sales during the remaining month of the quarter. Your job is to plan the itinerary that will generate the most sales for you during the remaining four weeks of the quarter.

For details of your customers and prospects, identified by name and number, see Figure 16–10. A map of the Centerville territory follows showing the location of your accounts and the travel time between them.

1. Available selling time

Sales time is limited to the period from 8:30 A.M. to 5:00 P.M. for five days. Monday through Friday, during the four-week period for which you are to plan the itinerary. Use a planning form like the one in Figure 16–11. You'll need four copies, one for each week.

Sale time is reduced by the following factors:

Travel—the amount of time it takes to travel from one account to another.

Waiting time—the amount of time you must wait to see a prospect or a customer if you do not have an appointment.

Telephone time—the amount of time you spend on the phone making appointments.

Paperwork—each day of selling activity generates one hour of paperwork, which must be completed before the beginning of the next week.

Lunch time—unless the lunch hour is used to entertain a customer or a prospect, effective selling time is reduced by a one-hour lunch period sometime between 11:30 and 1:30.

Don't forget holidays—your territory celebrates them all.

2. Travel time

Travel in the Centerville territory is mostly by car. Facilities for air travel are limited.

North Town Airways has an early morning turnaround flight between Centerville and North Town and a late evening turnaround flight. Service between Easton and North Town and Weston and North Town is quite frequent during the day. The current North Town Airways schedule is shown.

If you travel by air, it will take you one-half hour after your arrival to rent a car and drive to town. For example, if you fly to Easton, it will take you one-half hour to rent a car and drive to Alpha Transformer. However, if your first call after flying to Easton is to be made

Figure 16-11
Territory Planning Form

TERRITORY PLANNING FORM   Week ending_____

DAY	MONDAY			TUESDAY			WEDNESDAY			THURSDAY			FRIDAY		
Hours	Account No.	People To See	%	Account No.	People To See	%	Account No.	People To See	%	Account No.	People To See	%	Account No.	People To See	%
8:30–9:00	24	WAIT	–												
9:00–9:30		DE	5												
9:30–10:00		DE	4												
10:00–10:30		DE	3												
10:30–11:00		WAIT	–												
11:00–11:30		PA	4												
11:30–12:00		PA	3												
12:00–12:30	LUNCH	PA	3												
12:30–1:00	"	"	–												
1:00–1:30	APPTS.		–												
1:30–2:00		TRAVEL	–												
2:00–2:30		WAIT	–												
2:30–3:00	21	PA	5												
3:00–3:30		TRAVEL	–												
3:30–4:00		"	–												
4:00–4:30	6	PA	10												
4:30–5:00		PA	7												
Subtotals	32% for # 24														
	5% for # 21														
	17% for # 6														

on the Air Conditioning Corp., it will take you one-half hour to rent a car and travel through Easton plus one hour of travel from Easton to the Air Conditioning Corp. Except in the case of air travel to North Town, travel to the first call each day may be completed by 8:30.

Hotel or motel accommodations are available within one-half hour's travel of all accounts. It is not necessary to return home each night. See the travel map (Figure 16–12).

3. Making appointments

Calls can be made cold or by appointment. Appointments can be made by phone only on the day before the call is scheduled. Three appointments can be made by phone per half hour. Phone calls to make appointments can be made only during normal selling/business hours, that is, from 8:30 to 5:00. Separate appointments must be made with each individual.

Calls can be made without appointments, but one-half hour of waiting time will be consumed before the person can be seen.

4. Length of each sales call

No sales call on an individual can exceed 1½ hours. However, if lunch is included, a sales call may be extended to 2½ hours.

Figure 16–12
Map of territory

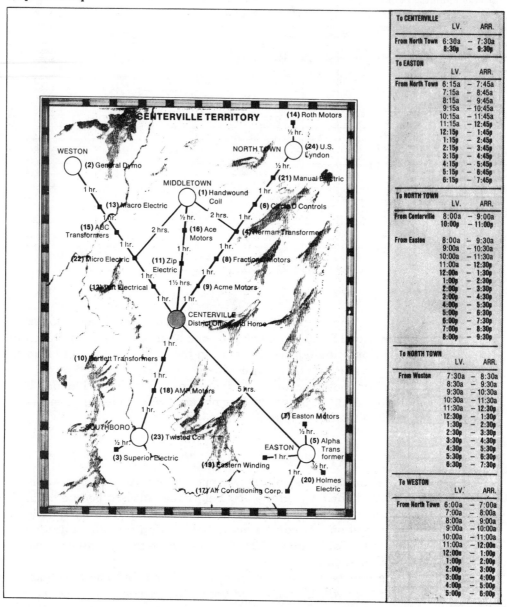

To CENTERVILLE	LV.	ARR.
From North Town	6:30a	– 7:30a
	8:30p	– 9:30p

To EASTON	LV.	ARR.
From North Town	6:15a	– 7:45a
	7:15a	– 8:45a
	8:15a	– 9:45a
	9:15a	– 10:45a
	10:15a	– 11:45a
	11:15a	– 12:45p
	12:15p	– 1:45p
	1:15p	– 2:45p
	2:15p	– 3:45p
	3:15p	– 4:45p
	4:15p	– 5:45p
	5:15p	– 6:45p
	6:15p	– 7:45p

To NORTH TOWN	LV.	ARR.
From Centerville	8:00a	– 9:00a
	10:00p	– 11:00p
From Easton	8:00a	– 9:30a
	9:00a	– 10:30a
	10:00a	– 11:30a
	11:00a	– 12:30p
	12:00n	– 1:30p
	1:00p	– 2:30p
	2:00p	– 3:30p
	3:00p	– 4:30p
	4:00p	– 5:30p
	5:00p	– 6:30p
	6:00p	– 7:30p
	7:00p	– 8:30p
	8:00p	– 9:30p

To NORTH TOWN	LV.	ARR.
From Weston	7:30a	– 8:30a
	8:30a	– 9:30a
	9:30a	– 10:30a
	10:30a	– 11:30a
	11:30a	– 12:30p
	12:30p	– 1:30p
	1:30p	– 2:30p
	2:30p	– 3:30p
	3:30p	– 4:30p
	4:30p	– 5:30p
	5:30p	– 6:30p
	6:30p	– 7:30p

To WESTON	LV.	ARR.
From North Town	6:00a	– 7:00a
	7:00a	– 8:00a
	8:00a	– 9:00a
	9:00a	– 10:00a
	10:00a	– 11:00a
	11:00a	– 12:00n
	12:00n	– 1:00p
	1:00p	– 2:00p
	2:00p	– 3:00p
	3:00p	– 4:00p
	4:00p	– 5:00p
	5:00p	– 6:00p

5. Value of sales time (see Table 16–2)

Each half hour of sales time with a decision maker or a key buying influence increases the probability of making the sale as follows:

If you make a 1½-hour first call on the design engineer of Hand-

Table 16-2

Value of sales time

Calls on present customers

	First call			Second call			Third and succeeding calls		
	1st ½ hr.	2d ½ hr.	3d ½ hr.	1st ½ hr.	2d ½ hr.	3d ½ hr.	1st ½ hr.	2d ½ hr.	3d ½ hr
Decision maker	10	7	5	3	5	2	5	3	0
Key buying influence	6	4	2	5	4	3	4	3	2

Call on prospects

	First call			Second call			Third and succeeding calls		
	1st ½ hr.	2d ½ hr.	3d ½ hr.	1st ½ hr.	2d ½ hr.	3d ½ hr.	1st ½ hr.	2d ½ hr.	3d ½ hr.
Decision maker	5	4	3	6	7	8	10	11	12
Key buying influence	4	3	2	4	5	6	7	4	3

wound Coil and a first call on the general foreman, you will increase the probability of making the sale by 34 percent (10 plus 7 plus 5 plus 6 plus 4 plus 2). You will have consumed three hours of sales time. However, if you make a one-hour first call on both the design engineer and the general foreman plus a half-hour second call on each, you will have consumed the same amount of time, three hours, and you will have increased the probability of making the sale to 40 percent (1st calls: 10 plus 7 plus 6 plus 4; 2d calls: 8 plus 5).

6. Entertainment

You can entertain only one person at a time, only at lunch, and for only one hour. Entertainment increases the probability of making the sale by a percentage equal to the value of the second half hour of the call. You can entertain a prospect or a customer only after spending one-half hour of selling time with him in his office. With entertainment (lunch), a call may extend to 2½ hours, with extra credit for the lunch hour.

7. Scoring

For sales time to count, the probability of making the sale must be greater than 50 percent. To calculate the value of sales time with an account, simply multiply the total probability of making the sale

Figure 16-13

Account	(Remaining potential)	x	(Percent probability)	= Sales income
1. Handwound Coil	$ 3,000	x	_____ %	= $ _____
2. General Dymo	1,500	x	_____	= _____
3. Superior Electric	4,000	x	_____	= _____
4. Herman Transformer	1,000	x	_____	= _____
5. Alpha Transformer	2,000	x	_____	= _____
6. Circle D. Centrals	3,000	x	_____	= _____
7. Easton Motors	1,500	x	_____	= _____
8. Fractional Motors	3,000	x	_____	= _____
9. Acme Motors	2,500	x	_____	= _____
10. Bartlett Transformer	1,000	x	_____	= _____
11. Zip Electric	3,000	x	_____	= _____
12. Taft Electric	500	x	_____	= _____
13. Macro Electric	500	x	_____	= _____
14. Roth Motors	1,000	x	_____	= _____
15. ABC Transformer	3,000	x	_____	= _____
16. Ace Motors	1,500	x	_____	= _____
17. Air Conditioning Corp.	5,000	x	_____	= _____
18. Amp Motors	3,500	x	_____	= _____
19. Eastern Windings	1,500	x	_____	= _____
20. Holmes Electric	3,000	x	_____	= _____
21. Manual Electric	1,800	x	_____	= _____
22. Micro Electric	2,500	x	_____	= _____
23. Twister Coil	3,000	x	_____	= _____
24. U.S. Lyndon	15,000	x	_____	= _____

Scoring Sheet

Total sales volume generated = $ _____

(provided it's greater than 50 percent) by the total remaining potential of the account. Use the score sheet in Figure 16–13.

SELECTED REFERENCES

Allen, Charles C. "A Level-Headed Approach to Increasing Sales Force Productivity." *Sales & Marketing Management,* June 13, 1977, p. 48.

Armstrong, Gary M. "The Schedule Model and Salesman's Effort Allocation." *California Management Review,* Summer 1976, pp. 43–51.

Bliss, Edwin C. *Getting Things Done: The ABC's of Time Management.* New York: Scribner, 1976.

DeBoer, Lloyd M., and **Howard, William.** "Integration of the Computer into Salesman Reporting." *Journal of Marketing,* January 1971, pp. 41–47.

'Fighting the Clock for More Selling Time." *Sales & Marketing Management,* October 10, 1977, p. 27.

Lahein, Alan. *How to Get Control of Your Time and Your Life.* New York: New American Library, 1973.

Lodish, Leonard M. "'Vaguely Right' Approach to Sales Force Allocation." *Harvard Business Review,* January–February 1974, pp. 53–59.

Meyer, Paul J. "Make Every Moment Count." *Sales & Marketing Management*, March 17, 1980, pp. 48–49.

"Time and Territory Management," *Sales & Marketing Management*, May 24, 1976, special report, pp. 33–40.

Whitty, Thomas A. "Focusing the Sales Effort." *Sales & Marketing Management*, September 17, 1979, pp. 57–60.

Chapter 17

LEGAL AND SOCIAL-ETHICAL RESPONSIBILITIES OF THE SALESPERSON

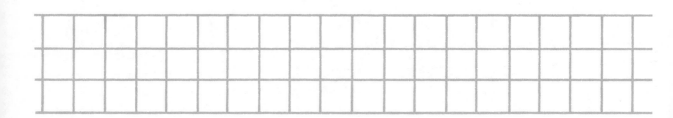

In the last five years, international and domestic bribery and morality in business and government have been common topics in the news. Business activities have been investigated by the Federal Trade Commission, the Securities and Exchange Commission, the Justice Department, and various congressional committees.

Part of this increasing concern over legal and ethical issues is due to the changing nature of the marketplace. Products have become more complex and the terms of sale have become more complicated. Fifty years ago, businesses dealt primarily with their neighbors. Now the bulk of sales transactions are made between strangers. Due to these circumstances, there is a far greater opportunity for honest differences of opinion.

The changes in the marketplace suggest that salespeople need to pay more attention to the legal and ethical issues in selling. Such issues are discussed in this chapter.

LEGAL ISSUES[1]

The activities of American salespeople are affected by three forms of law—statutory law, administrative law, and common law.

Statutory law is based on legislation passed by either the state legislatures or Congress. The principal statutory laws concerning salespeople are the Uniform Commercial Code and the antitrust laws. In addition, there are local laws and ordinances that affect door-to-door salespeople.

Administrative laws are set forth by city, county, state, and federal regulatory agencies. The Federal Trade Commission is the most active agency in developing administrative laws that concern salespeople. However, the Security and Exchange Commission regulates stockbrokers and the Food and Drug Administration regulates pharmaceutical salespeople.

Finally, common law grows out of court decisions. Precedents set by these decisions fill in the gaps where no law exists.

Uniform Commercial Code

The Uniform Commercial Code (UCC)[2] is the legal guide to commercial practice in the United States. The code was initially drafted in 1952 when the high level of interstate commerce necessitated uniform business laws across the states. The final version appeared in 1958. The UCC has been adopted by all the states except Louisiana. Some specific provisions from Section 2 of the code are discussed below.

Agency. An agent is a person who acts in place of his or her company. Typically, salespeople are authorized agents of their company. This authorization to represent the company does not have to be in writing. A salesperson is a spokesperson and a legal representative because the company knowingly and without objection allows the salesperson to act as its agent.

Sales versus a contract to sell. The UCC defines a sale as "the transfer of title to goods by the seller to the buyer for a consideration

---

[1] Some material from C. Robert Patty, *Managing Salespeople* (Reston, Va.: Reston, 1979), was used in developing this section.

[2] Len Young Smith and G. Gale Robertson, *Business Law—Uniform Commercial Code*, 3d ed. (St. Paul, Minn.: West, 1971).

known as the price."[3] Thus, a sale is made only when title passes from the seller to the buyer.

A sale is different from a contract to sell. Anytime a salesperson makes an offer and receives an unqualified acceptance, there is a contract. The UCC also distinguishes between an offer and an invitation to negotiate. A sales presentation is usually considered to be an invitation to negotiate. However, if a salesperson quotes specific terms and the customer accepts, the contract may be binding.

Oral versus written agreements.   Oral agreements between a salesperson and a customer are as binding as written agreements unless the Statute of Frauds applies. The Statute of Frauds, adopted by the English Parliament in 1677, delineates the types of contracts that are enforceable only if they are written. Similar statutes have been adopted by individual states. Typically, written agreements are required for sales greater than $500.

In general, sales agreements should be in writing. However, salespeople must be very careful when signing agreements because they are the legal representatives of their company.

Obligations and performance.   When the terms of a contract have been agreed upon, the salesperson and the customer must perform according to those terms. Performance must be in "good faith." This means that both parties must perform according to commonly accepted industry practices. Even if the salesperson misrepresents the product, his or her company is obligated to meet the terms of the contract.

Title and risk of loss.   A sale is not completed until title passes from the seller to the buyer. The question of title is most important when goods are shipped to the seller. If goods are shipped FOB (free on board) destination, the seller has title until the goods are received at the destination. Any loss or damage during transportation is the responsibility of the seller. The buyer assumes this responsibility and risk if goods are shipped FOB factory. Similarly, the UCC is explicit in defining when title passes for goods shipped COD and for goods sold on approval or consignment.

Warranties and guaranties.   A warranty is an assurance by the seller that the goods will perform as represented. Sometimes a warranty is referred to as a guaranty. The UCC distinguishes between two types of warranties—expressed and implied. An expressed warranty is an oral or written statement by the seller. An implied warranty is not actually stated, but it is an obligation imposed by law. For example, if products are sold using oral or written descriptions rather than samples, there is an implied warranty that the products are of average quality. There is also an implied warranty that prod-

---

[3] Ibid., p. 497.

ucts purchased from a seller are appropriate for the purposes stated by the buyer.

Problems with warranties often arise when selling to a reseller. The ultimate user, the reseller's customer, may complain to the reseller. The reseller, in turn, attempts to shift the blame to the manufacturer. Salespeople are often used to investigate and resolve such problems.

Antitrust laws

The pricing implications of the four laws with antitrust provisions (the Sherman, Clayton, Robinson-Patman, and Federal Trade Commission acts) are discussed in Chapter 5. This section discusses some basic provisions of these laws with regard to sales activities. Figure 17-1 contains a list of rules for avoiding antitrust problems.

Figure 17-1

Rules related to antitrust laws

1. Don't discuss with customers the price your company will charge others.
2. Don't attend meetings with competitors (including trade association gatherings) at which pricing is discussed. If you find yourself in such a session, walk out.
3. Don't give favored treatment to your own subsidiaries and affiliates.
4. Don't enter into agreements or gentlemen's understandings on discounts, terms, or conditions of sale; profits or profit margins; shares of the market; bids or the intent to bid; rejection or termination of customers; sales territories; or markets.
5. Don't use one product as bait for selling another.
6. Don't require a customer to buy a product only from you.
7. Don't forget to consider state antitrust laws as well as the federal statutes.
8. Don't disparage a competitor's product unless you have specific proof that your statements are true. This is an unfair method of competition.
9. Don't make either sales or purchases conditional on the other party making reciprocal purchases from or sales to your company.
10. Don't hesitate to consult with a company lawyer if you have any doubt about the legality of a practice. Antitrust laws are wide ranging, and subject to changing interpretations.

Source: Reprinted from the January 27, 1975, issue of *Business Week* by special permission, McGraw-Hill, Inc.

Tie-in arrangements. A tie-in occurs when a buyer is required to purchase a product in order to purchase or lease another product. For example, a customer who wants to buy a piece of machinery can be required to buy supplies needed to operate the machinery only if it can be shown that competition is not reduced by such a policy.

Conspiracy and collusion. It is illegal for competitors to make an agreement which reduces the level of competition by setting prices or dividing up territories. Thus, two competing salespeople cannot agree to divide up a territory.

Conspiracy covers an agreement made before the sale, while collusion relates to the sale itself. An example of collusion would be two car dealers agreeing not to discount prices on certain models.

Exclusive arrangements. The courts have ruled that exclusive agreements which decrease competition are illegal. Thus, a salesperson cannot demand that a customer not handle competing lines of merchandise.

Unfair trade practices

The Federal Trade Commission has the power to issue cease and desist orders governing unfair trade practices. Some unfair practices related to industrial and retail sales are discussed in this section.

Unfair influence on buyer's employees. One sales practice that is considered unfair is to provide special incentives to induce a reseller's salespeople to push products. For example, salespeople for a cosmetic manufacturer may give cosmetics salespeople in department stores commissions based on sales of their products. Such special incentives are called "spiffs" or push money. They are legal only if the employer of the salespeople is aware that the incentives are being offered. In addition, the same incentives must be offered to salespeople working for all competing resellers.

Another practice that is considered unfair is commercial bribery, or kickbacks. In one case, 30 to 40 salespeople and 6 managers were suspended for 15 days because they kicked back liquor to relatives.[4] It is often difficult to distinguish between a legitimate business gift and a bribe. Is a $15 bottle of liquor to a $5,000-a-year customer a gift or a bribe?

Unfair interference with competitors. Some ways in which a salesperson can interfere unfairly with a competitor's business are as follows:

---

[4] "Punishing Salesmen for Kickbacks," *Sales & Marketing Management*. April 11, 1977, p. 12.

1.   Attempting to get a competitor's customer to break a contract.
2.   Confusing market research studies by buying stock from a store.
3.   Tampering with a competitor's merchandise.

Reciprocity.   The concept of reciprocity—"You scratch my back, and I'll scratch your back"—is discussed in Chapter 14. There is nothing illegal about reciprocal arrangements as long as no coercion is involved.

Fraud and misrepresentation.   The Federal Trade Commission Act states that it is illegal to misrepresent products. Fraud or willful misrepresentation does not have to be shown. Misrepresentation of significant facts can enable the customer to nullify a contract and even sue for damages.

However, the concept of permissible puffery makes it difficult to determine what misrepresentation is. Permissible puffery is defined as an expression of mere opinion by the salesperson. It does not purport to be a representation of fact.

Legal issues related to direct selling

The focus of efforts to legislate or regulate marketing practices is shifting. In the first half of this century, efforts were directed toward protecting competition, under the assumption that keen competition would result in improved consumer welfare. Now, governmental activity is focusing on protecting consumers directly. Some laws regulating the behavior of salespeople who deal directly with consumers in stores and in door-to-door, direct selling are discussed in this section.

Local ordinances.   In many metropolitan areas municipal ordinances have been passed that restrict the activities of salespeople who call on customers door-to-door. These ordinances are often called "Green River ordinances" because the first legislation of this kind was passed in Green River, Wyoming, in 1933.

This first ordinance stipulated that it was illegal to solicit door-to-door without the householder's prior permission. Since the enactment of this initial type of local ordinance, ordinances have been passed restricting telephone solicitations; the time of day when solicitations can be made; solicitation on such holidays as Christmas, Easter, and Thanksgiving; and solicitation at homes which post "No Soliciting" signs.

State constitutional provisions, state laws, local ordinances, and state court decisions related to door-to-door selling vary widely. A salesperson should check the local ordinances of the city in which he or she plans to sell.

Doorstep identification. A common complaint against direct salespeople is that they use deceptive or misleading approaches to get in the door. For example, salespeople may say that they are "conducting a survey," or "taking a poll," or "giving away merchandise to influential citizens."

A number of states have passed laws requiring salespeople to immediately identify the purpose of their call. Some laws even require that a card with the salesperson's name and the company name be handed to the prospect.

Cooling off. In reaction to public dissatisfaction with the tactics used in direct selling, the Federal Trade Commission and most of the state legislatures have adopted "cooling-off" rules. The basic purpose of these rules is to allow buyers to review the decisions they made during a sales presentation that occurred in their homes. These rules state that a notice of cancellation is a privilege. It must be given to the buyer. A sale can be canceled by a written notice mailed to the seller within three business days after the transaction. The FTC regulation requires that the information in Figure 17–2 be included on the first page or next to the signature of any contracts.

Cooling-off rules apply only to retail sales calls made outside the seller's regular place of business. Many statutes exempt sales under $25.[5]

Summary

Most new salespeople just want to make sales calls. They are quite naive about the legal complexities of their jobs. The previous discussion indicates that many legal issues are associated with selling.

Even though there are many legal considerations, few salespeople say or do things that will result in a court suit. A salesperson is not expected to know the fine points of the law. Clearly, salespeople should never set themselves up as experts in legal issues. However, it is important for a salesperson to understand the issues that might arise and to know when to seek legal counseling.

SOCIAL AND ETHICAL RESPONSIBILITIES

The legal issues discussed in the first part of this chapter are prohibitive in nature. The laws and regulations define and penalize sales behaviors that are not in the best interest of society.

---

[5] For an evaluation of the effects of the cooling-off rule, see W. L. Shanklin and H. G. King, "Evaluating the FTC Cooling-off Rule," *Journal of Consumer Affairs*, Winter 1977, pp. 101–6.

Figure 17–2
Cooling-off regulations

You, the buyer, may cancel this transaction at any time prior to midnight of the third business day after the date of this transaction. See the attached notice of cancellation form for an explanation of this right.

The "attached notice of cancellation" form must read as follows:

Notice of cancellation
(enter date of transaction)
_____
(Date)

You may cancel this transaction, without any penalty or obligation, within three business days from the above date.

If you cancel, any property traded in, any payments made by you under the contract or sale and any negotiable instrument executed by you will be returned within ten business days following receipt by the seller of your cancellation notice, and any security interest arising out of the transaction will be canceled.

If you cancel, you must make available to the seller at your residence, in substantially as good condition as when received, any goods delivered to you under this contract or sale; or you may if you wish, comply with the instructions of the seller regarding the return shipment of the goods at the seller's expense and risk. If you do make the goods available to the seller and the seller does not pick them up within 20 days of the date of your notice of cancellation, you may retain or dispose of the goods without any further obligation. If you fail to make the goods available to the seller, or if you agree to return the goods to the seller and fail to do so, then you remain liable for performance of all obligations under the contract.

To cancel this transaction, mail or deliver a signed and dated copy of this cancellation notice or any other written notice, or send a telegram, to *(Name of seller)*, at *(address of seller's place of business)*, no later than midnight of _____
(date)

I hereby cancel this transaction.

_____
(date)

_____
(buyer's signature)

This statement must appear on the first page of the contract or on the receipt.

For many situations there are no laws to govern behavior, but there is some question about what it is right to do. In such situations, philosophies of ethical and social responsibility should provide a higher standard. The Caterpillar Tractor Company's Code of World-Wide Business Conduct says: "The law is a floor. Ethical business conduct should normally exist at a level well above the minimum required by law."[6]

Ethics and social responsibility are not the same. Ethics are the individual's concepts of what is right and what is wrong. Social responsibility refers to the individual's obligations to society in general. For example, some salespeople may believe that it is unethical to offer discounts indiscriminately because their employers trust them to get the highest price possible. On the other hand, it might be argued that offering price discounts whenever possible is socially responsible since this makes products less expensive to society.

Social responsibility and ethics are very important for salespeople. Since salespeople have a lot of freedom in their job, they do not have assistance readily available to help them guide their behavior. They must use their own standards and their own interpretations of societal standards in responding to situations. Each salesperson must set his or her own ethical standards, and there are no easy answers to ethical questions. However, some factors to consider in developing such standards are discussed in this section.

Changing concepts of social-ethical responsibilities

In the early days of American business, some of the tycoons of industry cared little about the impact of their activities upon the public. The statement "Let the public be damned," attributed to Cornelius Vanderbuilt, was widely quoted. For many centuries a large segment of the public looked down upon salespeople and merchants as "fast-buck artists" and "wheeler-dealers." The whole field of business was looked upon by many as an unethical and shoddy activity involving excessive profits and unfair practices by sellers. Some of the unfavorable attitudes toward business, and in particular toward advertising and selling, were justified by the shortsighted behavior of a small number of people who put short-term personal benefits above the long-term mutual benefits of the buyer and the seller.

During the last decade, however, business executives throughout the world have recognized that relying upon the profit incentive

---

[6] Fred T. Allen. "Corporate Morality: Is the Price Too High?" *The Wall Street Journal*, October 17, 1975, pp. 1, 17.

alone is not the most successful way to run a business. Peter Drucker expressed this thought when he commented:

> A . . . more important reason why responsibility for the quality of life is to the self-interest of business is the obvious fact that a healthy business and a sick society are not compatible. Healthy businesses require a healthy, or at least a functioning, society. The health of the community is a prerequisite for successful and growing business.[7]

Negative attitudes of students toward careers in business have awakened many business leaders to the importance of a complete reevaluation of business practices and concepts in the fields of ethics, social responsibilities, and business goals.

The members of the new generation of business people are raising vital fundamental questions about our present and future value systems; they are less materialistic than their parents and grandparents; and they are more sensitive to the social needs of all segments of the community.

Our population today is a young population. Over half of the people are under 30 years of age. This young generation has lived through a period of affluence, technical change, and social upheaval. It is a well-educated and activist group dedicated to change and to high ethical and social ideals in the new phase of growth in our American society.[8]

The salesperson's personal philosophy

Social-ethical responsibilities in the marketplace have their birth in the personal philosophy of each salesperson. His or her behavior is directly related to personal beliefs, habits, and attitudes. No matter how many "codes of ethics" are developed by trade associations and professional organizations, high ethical standards will not be achieved unless each salesperson bases his or her behavior on a sound personal philosophy. That philosophy should include a priority of responsibilities in which the interests of the company are placed above self-interest and the interests of society are placed above the interests of the company.

The personal philosophies of salespeople are built upon specific social and ethical responsibilities to (1) themselves, (2) their custom-

---

[7] Peter F. Drucker, "Business and the Quality of Life," *Sales Management*, March 15, 1969, p. 33.

[8] See Albert H. Dunn, "Case of the Suspect Salesman," *Harvard Business Review*, November–December 1977, pp. 38+ for an interesting case of conflicting values between a young salesperson and an older sales manager.

ers, (3) their competitors, and (4) their company. Each of these areas of responsibility is discussed below.

Your responsibilities to yourself

The salesperson's first responsibility is to abide by his or her own ethical standard of conduct. During selling interactions, salespeople are often tempted to act against their own standard of conduct. The pressure to make a sale may be so great that the salesperson considers being dishonest with a customer in order to close a sale.

Compromising with ethical standards to achieve short-term gains can have adverse effects in the long run. First, salespeople who compromise their principles lose self-respect and confidence in their own ability. They begin to think that they can make sales only if they are dishonest. Second, a short-term compromise makes it difficult to develop a good reputation with customers. Once customers have experienced less than truthful behavior they will be reluctant to deal with the salesperson again. They may even relate their experiences to friends in other companies.

The salesperson's individual responsibility begins with the selection of his or her company. Salespeople should not take jobs with companies whose products conflict with their standards. Before taking a sales job, a person should also investigate the company's procedures and selling technique to see whether they conflict with personal standards. Many companies have articulated ethical policies which the prospective salesperson can consider in selecting an employer. (See Figure 17–3 for an example.)

Relations with customers

During recent years a wave of "consumerism" has been sweeping the country. It is evident at all levels of government and business, including the White House; federal, state, and local governmental bodies; trade associations; and private companies.

Some businesses have viewed consumerism as a threat to business and to our free enterprise system. Others have accepted this new movement as a challenge to business to do a better job.[9] More and more companies are forming consumer advisory panels to consider and take appropriate action on legitimate consumer grievances. Salespeople and/or sales managers are often asked to serve on these panels to provide firsthand information on the needs and desires of consumers.

---

[9] See Frederick E. Webster, Jr., "Does Business Misunderstand Consumerism," *Harvard Business Review*, September–October 1973, pp. 89–97.

Figure 17-3
An ethical policy statement by Johnson & Johnson

1. No corporate or subsidiary funds or assets shall be used for any unlawful purpose. Nor shall any Johnson & Johnson company engage in the practice of purchasing privileges or special benefits through payment of bribes, illegal political contributions, or other forms of payoff.
2. No undisclosed or unrecorded fund or asset of the corporation or any subsidiary shall be established for any purpose.
3. No false or artificial entries shall be made in the books and records of the corporation or its subsidiaries for any reason, and no employee shall engage in any arrangement that results in such prohibited act.
4. No payment on behalf of the corporation or any of its subsidiaries shall be approved or made with the agreement that any part of such payment is to be used for any purpose other than that described by the documents supporting the payment.
5. Any employee having information or knowledge of any unrecorded fund or asset or any prohibited act shall promptly report such matter to the general counsel of Johnson & Johnson.
6. All managers shall be responsible for the enforcement of and compliance with this policy, including necessary distribution to ensure employee knowledge and compliance.
7. Appropriate employees will periodically be required to certify compliance with this policy.
8. This policy is applicable to Johnson & Johnson and all its domestic and foreign subsidiaries.

Source: Reprinted by permission from *Sales & Marketing Management* magazine, May 10 1976, p. 38. Copyright 1976.

In order to discharge fully their responsibilities to customers, salespeople must:

1. Sincerely believe in the modern concept of selling, which includes long-term benefits to both the buyer and seller.
2. Be willing to sacrifice short-term gains for long-term mutual benefits.
3. Treat all customers alike in terms of prices and services.
4. Respect the confidences of each customer when dealing with other customers.
5. Maintain high ethical standards at all times.

Bribes, gifts, and entertainment. Commercial bribery generally goes beyond the normal lunch or entertainment typically given to purchasing agents. A number of specific issues concerning customer relations are discussed in the following sections. As mentioned previously, bribes and kickbacks are illegal under FTC regulations and most state laws. In fact, the Internal Revenue Service does not allow monies paid for bribes to be deducted as a business expense. Ethical issues are involved in determining what is a legitimate gift and what is a bribe. To avoid these problems, many companies have policies forbidding employees to accept gifts from suppliers. As president of Avis, Robert Townsend distributed the following note before holidays:

> There is nothing wrong with having personal friendships with representatives of those companies with whom we do business. However, this cannot be permitted to extend to the giving or receiving of gifts.
>
> It is therefore against our policy for any employee to accept from any company or representative of a supplier company with whom we do business any gifts of value, including cash, merchandise, gift certificates, weekend or vacation trips. This means, of course, returning any such gifts which may be delivered to your home or office.[10]

However, many companies do not have a policy against receiving gifts. In addition, there are unethical employees who will accept and even solicit gifts even if their company does have a policy against receiving gifts. Most sales managers do not view as unethical such traditional gifts as lunch, dinner, or tickets to a sporting event. However, standards vary across industries. Cash, "elaborate" entertainment, vacations, and the provision of prostitutes are generally regarded as beyond the bounds of propriety. Figure 17-4 shows the results of a survey of the attitudes and policies of purchasing managers with regard to certain practices.

A good rule is to provide limited entertainment at most. Bribery is not only poor ethics; it can also be bad business. Lavish expenditure for food, drink, and entertainment is a poor substitute for high-quality selling. Sales won in this manner are usually short-lived. Salespeople who are known as "easy marks" will be subjected to blackmail before being given orders. Customers who base their purchases on bribes are likely to switch their business when a better offer arises. In considering a specific situation, salespeople might use this guideline: When in doubt, do not provide it.

Divulging confidential information. Salespeople must always remember that they are often calling on customers who compete among themselves. During calls, salespeople are exposed to confidential information, such as production schedules, manufacturing costs, and proprietary designs and production methods. There is a great temptation to exchange such information for an order. Succumbing to this temptation can backfire. Once a salesperson develops a reputation for loose talk, no one, not even the customer to whom the confidential information was offered, will trust the sales-

---

[10] Robert Townsend, *Up the Organization* (New York: Alfred A. Knopf, 1970), p. 66.

Figure 17–4

Ethical practices and purchasing managers

Practices	Percent replying "definitely yes" or "probably yes"		
	An ethical problem?	Have stated policy now?	Want a stated policy?
1. Acceptance from a supplier of gifts like sales promotion prizes and "purchase volume incentive bonuses."	83%	71%	89%
2. Giving a vendor information on competitors' quotations, then allowing him to requote.	77	55	86
3. Acceptance of trips, meals, or other free entertainment.	58	70	83
4. Preferential treatment of a supplier who is also a good customer.	65	45	68
5. Discrimination against a vendor whose salespeople try to deal with other company departments directly rather than go through purchasing.	35	38	62
6. Solicitation of quotations from new sources, when a market preference for existing suppliers is the norm, merely to fill a quota for bids.	23	37	59
7. To a supplier, exaggerating the seriousness of a problem in order to get a better price or some other concession.	68	28	57
8. According special treatment to a vendor who is preferred or recommended by higher management.	65	28	56
9. Attempting to avoid a cancellation charge when the cancellation involves an order already being processed by the source.	40	22	52
10. Allowing personalities—like of one sales representative or dislike of another—to enter into supplier selection.	63	24	46
11. Use of the company's buying power to obtain price or other concessions from a vendor.	22	29	46
12. To obtain a lower price or other concession, informing an existing supplier that the company may use a second source.	34	26	42
13. Seeking information about competitors by questioning suppliers.	42	19	34

person. As a result, the salesperson will be unable to get the information needed to develop an effective sales presentation.

Relations with competitors

When Alfred P. Sloan, Jr., was chairman of the board of General Motors, he stated that competition was a "way of life for the corporation and its many divisions. The success of General Motors is testimony to the power of free competition in the marketplace.

If competition is to remain the foundation of our American system, it is imperative that competitive practices be both legal and ethical. Salespeople are on the firing line of competition, and it is therefore important that their behavior reflect ethical practices at all times.

Some salespeople are unable to resist the temptation to make untruthful statements about their competitors' products or services or to start rumors that may be injurious to a competing company. Such unethical practices may win an immediate sale, but in the long run salespeople who resort to them usually find that these practices will result in ill will among customers as well as competitors.

Competition as a "way of life" includes dynamic selling efforts to bring out plus values matched against customers' needs. These values may be presented in terms of comparative quality or quantity of products as related to prices or in terms of unique product uses. Fair and truthful comparisons with the products and services of competitors are desirable to both customers and society. It is through this process that better products and services are created. It is each salesperson's responsibility to accentuate the positive in products or services without engaging in unethical practices concerning competitors.

Relationships to the company

If salespeople are to perform as true professionals, they should put the interests of their company above self-interest. Such behavior may seem to result in short-term sacrifices at times, but in the long run it will bring greater benefits to both the company and the salespeople.

Salespeople are frequently confronted with temptations to cut corners on ethical standards. Their jobs give them considerable freedom while they are in the field. Supervision is usually thin, and their responsibility is extensive. A few of the most common temptations include padding expense accounts, working at less than capacity, faking customer call reports, withholding sales until a sales contest period, entering into agreements with competing salespeople to divide a territory or to fix prices, hoarding information that may benefit other salespeople within the company, failing to use the new tools and techniques provided by the company, and obtaining business through lavish entertainment or gifts rather than effective selling.

Use of expense accounts.   Most companies provide their salespeople with sufficient travel and entertainment allowances to cover the justified expenses of doing business. However, companies sometimes do not provide sufficient funds. In these cases, it is easy for salespeople to rationalize padding their expense accounts in areas covered by the company to make up for inadequate coverage in other areas. Similarly, salespeople may use their expense accounts to supplement what they perceive as inadequate income.

Such use of expense accounts is clearly unethical. If salespeople cannot live within company policies, they have only two ethical choices: (1) to persuade the company to change its compensation or expense policy, or (2) to find another job.

Adequate control of expenses does not mean that the salesperson should be miserly. The following suggestions should help the salesperson to keep expenses in line:

1.   Eliminate unnecessary automobile expenses by planning calls in advance.
2.   When communicating with the home office, do not rely solely on the use of the telephone. An airmail letter, a night letter, or a telegram may do just as well.
3.   Eat plenty of good food, but do not always eat in the most expensive restaurants.
4.   Stay in clean, comfortable, and respectable hotels; however, it is not necessary to have the best room in the very best hotel.
5.   Do a moderate amount of entertaining.
6.   While on the road, maintain the same standard of living and appearance as is maintained at home.

Switching jobs.   A salesperson also has an ethical responsibility to an employer in changing jobs. Companies invest considerable money in training salespeople, and usually the salespeople are given advance information on new products and practices. Over a period of time salespeople also build up customer knowledge and goodwill which they may take advantage of if they change jobs and accept positions with a competitor.

Proselyting has been rather common in the sales field for many years. Recently, however, more and more companies have taken the position that they will not initiate employment negotiations with prospective employees who are still employed by another company.

Successful sales representatives of the leading company in an industry are prime prospects for offers from other companies within the industry that are striving to increase their share of the market.

Figure 17-5

**Statement of Professional Responsibility of
Merck Sharp & Dohme Professional Representatives**

Preamble.   The Merck Sharp & Dohme field organization strives at all times to adhere to the spirit and letter of the law. The following principles express the Merck Sharp & Dohme professional representatives' commitment to a high level of ethical conduct in the service of physicians, pharmacists, and other health care professionals.

Section 1.   Physicians, pharmacists, and other health care professionals should receive as complete and accurate information about Merck Sharp & Dohme products as is appropriate to their role in health care delivery. Professional representatives will discuss product information is strict conformance with the labeling that has been approved or permitted by the Food and Drug Administration. Physicians, pharmacists, and other health care professionals will be offered a copy of the current product circular for each product discussion initiated by the representative.

   Topics covered:
      Use of the product circular
      Physicians
      Pharmacists and other health care professionals

Section 2.   During product discussions, contraindications, warnings, precautions, adverse reactions, dosage, and administration, as well as advantages and usefulness, should be discussed according to the physician's knowledge of the product. Professional representatives must always provide fair balance in their communications with physicians.

IBM, for example, has provided a large number of sales representatives for other companies in the computer and business machines field. This is one of the prices of leadership.

Under certain circumstances it may be highly desirable for a salesperson to change jobs. For one reason or another he or she may be dissatisfied with the company. If such is the case, the salesperson should discuss the reasons for dissatisfaction with a superior before making a change and should give the company a reasonable notice before leaving. When leaving, the salesperson should not take confidential information, such as customer files.

Figure 17–5 *(continued)*

Topics covered:
Elements of a balanced presentation

Section 3.   Discussions about competitive products should not be initiated unless specific instructions are issued by the company; however, when asked, professional representatives may provide such information, limiting their statements to that information contained in the most current product circulars for the products discussed.

Topics covered:
Product comparisons
Sources of information
Nature of comparison
Balance

Section 4.   The privacy of the physician-patient-pharmacist relationship should be respected at all times. Professional representatives may not examine prescription files or other documents that provide information about an individual physician's prescribing practices.

Topic covered:
Right to privacy

Section 5.   Scientific or medical educational materials supplied by Merck Sharp & Dohme may be given to health professionals for information, education, or service. Professional representatives shall not, however, provide gifts, premiums, or prizes to physicians, pharmacists, medical students, or other health care professionals either as a direct or indirect offering in return for the prescribing, use, or dispensing of Merck Sharp & Dohme products.

Topic covered:
Distribution of material

Summary

Ethical conduct is closely related to customer goodwill, discussed in Chapter 13. Both are prime factors in developing long-term relationships with customers. Each individual can adopt unique ethical standards. However, many companies provide detailed guidelines for their salespeople. Figure 17–5 summarizes the guidelines provided by Merck Sharp & Dohme for its pharmaceutical salespeople.

Figure 17-5 (concluded)

Section 6. Samples and complimentary packages of prescription products may be distributed in reasonable quantities to physicians authorized to prescribe drugs. Professional representatives must obtain a signed request for the drugs from the physician.

Topic covered:
  Distribution of samples

Section 7. Proper care must be exercised at all times to keep prescription drugs out of illicit or inappropriate channels of distribution. Professional representatives are fully accountable for the security and proper disposition of all drug samples.

Topics covered:
  Control of samples
  Free distribution
  Transfer of product after purchase

Section 8. The honesty and integrity of professional representatives must not be compromised. They may not, therefore, accept compensation of any kind from any party other than Merck Sharp & Dohme for the distribution and sale of pharmaceutical products.

Topics covered:
  Outside employment
  Conflict of interest

Adherence to these standards by professional representatives supports the safe, knowledgeable, and effective use of Merck Sharp & Dohme products in the practice of medicine and pharmacy.

Source: From Statement of Professional Responsibility of Merck Sharp & Dohme Professional Representatives, January 1, 1976. Provided by Merck Sharp & Dohme.

QUESTIONS AND PROBLEMS

1. What features of the selling job make the salesperson more susceptible to unethical behavior?

2. What effects would the relaxation of antitrust laws have on salespeople? Would this be good or bad?

3. Why do most retail stores disapprove of their buyers' receiving gifts from vendors?

4. Give an example of unethical sales behavior of which you are aware. Why do you consider this behavior unethical?

5. If you believe that a competitor's salesperson has been making unethical remarks about your product to customers, what courses of action are open to you?

6. Some cities have passed ordinances prohibiting door-to-door soliciting or selling. What is your reaction to such ordinances? Under what circumstances would you favor door-to-door selling?

7. What is the best way to eliminate unethical practices in a salesperson's relationship with an employer?

8. What are some ways in which a salesperson can handle a buyer with an outstretched hand?

9. Jim Hanson is a sales representative for a plastics manufacturer. His company has always maintained a policy of uniform prices for all customers. One of his customers, the Hoffman Department Store, always attempts to bargain for special prices because of its large volume of purchases. On several occasions Mr. Hoffman threatened to give his business to a competing plastics company unless Jim Hanson agreed to a special price concession. In one instance, Jim checked Mr. Hoffman's proposal with his sales manager and the sales manager told him to go ahead and make the concession. Jim had previously sold a similar order to another customer at a price which was approximately 10 percent higher than the Hoffman price. What responsibility, if any, does Jim have to his other customer? What are the long-term implications.

10. Assume that you are a loan officer in a bank and that one of your customers has a large balance in an account prior to the date on which personal property taxes are due. If this balance remains at tax time it will be subject to a sizable tax. Should the loan officer suggest that the customer withdraw the money until after tax time? This procedure would not be illegal, and the customer might consider the suggestion to be a service.

PROJECTS

1. Make arrangements to interview a local salesperson. Try to determine the following about the salesperson:

   a. Knowledge of the local, state, and federal laws that govern sales behavior.

   b. Perceived need for new laws or changes in the existing laws related to personal selling.

   c. Perceptions regarding the frequency and nature of unethical behavior by:
      (1) Customers.
      (2) Competitive salespeople.

2. Call the local Better Business Bureau, Chamber of Commerce, or Federal Trade Commission office. Ask for written or verbal descriptions of the local regulations governing the behavior of salespeople.

3. Obtain some recent issues of the *Journal of Marketing*, and read the section entitled "Legal Developments in Marketing." Cite several legal decisions that have implications for salespeople, and describe how these decisions affect sales behavior.

CASE PROBLEMS

Case 17–1

Ethical problems of Earl Wilson

Earl Wilson received his BS in Business Administration from a major Western university in 1967. He was a very personable individual with a tremendous amount of energy and initiative. While he was attending the university, he had a part-time job with a used car dealer. He worked hard in this job and was very successful in producing sales. After graduation he went into the automobile business with the objective of acquiring his own dealership. He secured a position as a salesperson in a dealership located in southern California.

He was determined to be a success in his chosen work. He devoted about 12 hours a day to his job, and before long he was the top-producing salesperson in the dealership. At the end of a year he was promoted to manager of used car sales. After three years with the dealer, he was promoted to manager of both used and new car sales. In this capacity Wilson had 12 salespeople reporting to him.

As sales manager, Wilson was a great believer in building sales volume through special promotional events. Every week was marked by a sales contest or a unique merchandising campaign of some sort. Wilson exerted considerable pressure on his salespeople by establishing volume and profit goals for each salesperson. If salespeople did not produce a sufficient volume of sales, he did not hesitate to replace them.

In order to increase the effectiveness of closing sales, Wilson decided to install electronic listening equipment in each sales booth so that he could listen to the conversations between the salespeople and their customers. Frequently he would telephone the salesperson during a sales interview. The salesperson would then excuse himself or herself and go into Wilson's office, where Wilson and the salesperson would listen to the private conversation of the prospect and his wife. In most instances, useful confidential information was thus made available to Wilson and the salesperson. The salesperson would then return to the sales booth and attempt to close the sale.

Wilson was aware of the ethical problems involved in listening in on the private conversations of prospective customers who were shopping for a car. He justified his actions, however, on the basis that they enabled salespeople to close more sales. He also commented, "By utilizing this technique, we can get a better reading on the true needs and motives of our prospects."

Questions

1. What is your reaction to Wilson's personal philosophy of doing business?
2. How would you like to work for Wilson as a salesperson?

Case 17-2

Tiny Toddlers, Inc.

Ernie Burke received his BA in June 1980. He joined Tiny Toddlers as a sales trainee. He expected to work for six to nine months as a trainee and then to be assigned to a sales territory.

Tiny Toddlers was a large manufacturer of children's wear. Its annual sales were in excess of $20 million. It employed 25 salespeople. The salespeople were paid a straight commission of 6 percent. They all reported to the national sales manager, Susan Hoyt.

In November 1980, Ed Davis, the salesman covering the Atlanta territory, died suddenly. Davis had been a longtime employee of Tiny Toddlers and had a good reputation for selling abilities. When news of his death reached headquarters, Hoyt asked Burke to take over the territory. She went on to explain that she was going on a four-week business trip to Europe and would be unable to introduce Burke to the territory.

After being in the territory for two weeks, Burke visited most of its key customers. He made several sales and opened some new accounts. After this success, he felt confident enough to meet with the buyer for his largest account, Don Black of the Kiddie World chain. Last year, Kiddie World ordered $80,000 in merchandise. Burke arranged a dinner date with Black. He was anxious to present the new spring line and to establish rapport with this key customer.

The dinner meeting went well. After some social conversation, Burke presented the new line and asked Black what he thought of it. Black said that he was impressed but that he was also considering two competitive lines. After Burke explained how Tiny Toddlers' line was superior, Black told Burke that Ed Davis had really taken care of his needs. Davis had given Black a $500 bonus before each season.

Black said, "I hope we can work together the way Ed and I did. There are a lot of good lines and a lot of good salespeople, but Ed was something special."

What would you do if you were in Ernie Burke's position?

Case 17–3

Evaluating ethical aspects of selling behaviors*

1. Mary Kay, a retail salesclerk, uses a sales technique that enables her to increase her sales significantly. When customers are shopping and looking at various items, Mary takes the item that they seem to favor and immediately wraps it up. She then asks the shoppers if they need anything else. Mary has found that most shoppers will buy the item that has been wrapped.

_____ a. If it works successfully, use the idea. The customer can always say no.

_____ b. This is a high-pressure but not an unethical method of selling.

_____ c. This method is clearly unethical and should be discontinued immediately. Mary's supervisor should fire her if Mary continues to use it.

_____ d. Other (write in).

2. A young married graduate of a business school is being seriously considered for a salesperson's job. The sales manager who interviewed him said, "Before we decide to hire you, we'd like to take you and your wife out to dinner. Our vice president likes to meet the wives of our salespeople because they can be a great help in influencing our customers at social events. We like to feel that a salesperson's wife is his helpmate."

_____ a. It is unethical to expect a salesperson's wife to help her husband in influencing customers.

_____ b. The company is right in wanting to meet the wives of its salespeople. Unless the wife supports her husband in his career, he is not going to be very successful.

_____ c. The company has a right to meet the wives of salespeople, but it should not expect them to assist their husbands in their jobs.

_____ d. The company is hiring the salesperson and has no right to be concerned about the wife in any way. The salesperson should decline the dinner invitation.

_____ e. Other (write in).

*Adapted from SELLING: A SELF-MANAGEMENT APPROACH by Ferdinand F. Mauser, © 1973, 1977 by Harcourt Brace Jovanovich, Inc. Reprinted by permission of the publisher.

3. A buyer for an industrial concern lets a salesperson know that his wife is fond of a stereo set manufactured by the consumer division of the salesperson's company. The buyer laughs and says he will make sure that the salesperson obtains a big order if the salesperson gets a stereo for the buyer's wife.

_____ a. The salesperson should pretend that he does not understand the broad hint and should ignore it.

_____ b. The salesperson should pass the information on to his sales supervisor and let him decide whether the company wants to give the buyer the gift.

_____ c. The salesperson should tactfully let the buyer know that he does not like to do business in this manner.

_____ d. The salesperson should get his company to comply with the buyer's wish. This is a good way to tie the customer to the salesperson and his company.

_____ e. Other *(write in)*.

4. A salesperson of industrial processing equipment is selling a new system. The buyer asks, "Does the output from this system pass the state's anti-air pollution specifications?" "Yes," says the salesperson, "the outputs are water-filtered. They are so pollution-free that they will pass any air pollution standards." The salesperson has answered the buyer's question truthfully. However, he has failed to mention that while there is no air pollution problem, there may be a water pollution problem due to the filtering process.

_____ a. The salesperson was unethical in not helping the buyer to explore fully the question of pollution.

_____ b. The salesperson was honest. He cannot be expected to bring up negative factors about his product.

_____ c. It is the buyer's responsibility to know about the drawbacks of the products he is buying.

_____ d. In matters of environmental pollution salespeople should be required to present both the positive and the negative aspects of the products they sell so that customers can make balanced judgments related to their particular situations.

_____ e. Other *(write in)*.

5. A company's top salesperson received a suggestion from a customer. The salesperson thought the idea so good that he did not turn it in to his company. (The company manual states that all customer suggestions should be recorded in the weekly sales report.) Instead, the salesperson resigned to start a company of his own that used the customer's suggestion. The company became very successful and took a lot of business away from the salesperson's former employer.

———— *a.*   The salesperson was unethical. The company policies spelled out in the sales manual were a part of a moral contract. The gathering of customer ideas was part of what the salesperson was paid to do.

———— *b.*   This is how the free enterprise system works. Someone gets an idea, and if he's clever enough to recognize its value, he's got a right to exploit it.

———— *c.*   The customer gave the idea to the salesperson, not to the company.

———— *d.*   A normal business risk that a company has to expect is that not all ideas are going to be turned in. No moral issue was involved.

———— *e.*   Other *(write in).*

SELECTED REFERENCES

Aaker, David A., and **Day, George S.** *Consumerism.* 2d ed. New York: Free Press, 1978.

Everett, Martin. "The Dark Side of Insurance Sales." *Sales & Marketing Management,* February 5, 1979, pp. 25–29.

Decker, R. "Purchasing Law: Supreme Court Puts Tie-in Sales to New Test." *Purchasing,* November 22, 1977, pp. 97+.

Goodwin, James R. *Business Law: Principles, Documents, and Cases.* Homewood, Ill.: Richard D. Irwin, 1980.

"It's Time to Repeal the Right to Do Wrong." *Sales & Marketing Management,* October 11, 1976, pp. 39–42.

"The Law: Getting at the Meat of the Matter." *Sales Management,* February 1975, p. 30.

"Legal Developments in Marketing." *Journal of Marketing,* quarterly.

Levy, Sidney, and **Zaltman, Gerald.** *Marketing, Society, and Conflict.* Englewood Cliffs, N.J.: Prentice-Hall, 1975.

Sturdivant, Frederick D., and **Cocanogher, A. Benton.** "What Are Financial Marketing Practices." *Harvard Business Review,* November–December 1973, pp. 10–75.

"When a Magazine Salesman Knocks at Your Door." *Changing Times,* March 1975, pp. 42–44.

Part six

INTRODUCTION
TO
SALES
MANAGEMENT

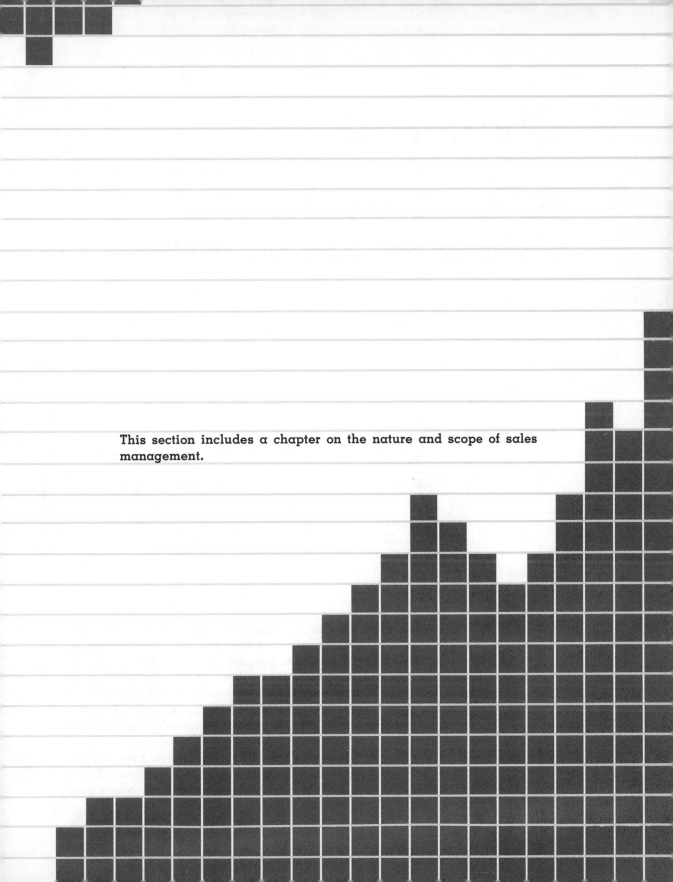

This section includes a chapter on the nature and scope of sales management.

Chapter 18

THE NATURE AND
SCOPE OF SALES MANAGEMENT

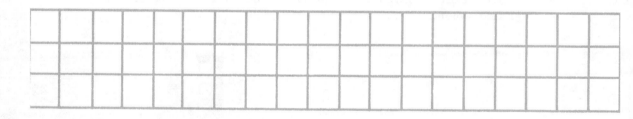

Salespeople who are qualified can look forward to the possibility of becoming sales supervisors or sales managers, and eventually they may have the opportunity to become members of top management. Analyses of the careers of members of top management in business concerns throughout the country show that many of these executives have begun their careers in their companies' sales divisions. It is becoming more common for successful sales managers to be considered for top leadership positions. Early in the text, illustrations were provided of corporation presidents who rose to their positions through successful selling and sales management jobs. It has been estimated that 50 percent of the members of top management got their start in sales.

There is a big difference, however, between selling and sales management. Some individuals would rather continue to work in selling than be promoted to sales management positions. They are able to earn good money and are happier when they are calling on customers and prospects and closing sales.

The objective of this chapter is to acquaint the salesperson with the field of sales management. The chapter discusses the importance of sales management in the firm's marketing program; describes sales management work; reviews the activities of the sales executive and the district sales manager; and presents suggestions for salespeople who aspire to sales management positions.

SALES FUNCTIONS IN THE MARKETING ORGANIZATION

The marketing concept, presented in Chapter 1, emphasizes the need for a coordinated marketing program directed toward satisfying customer needs. The marketing executive is responsible for designing and implementing the marketing program. The elements of such a program are product development, pricing, advertising, personal selling, and distribution. A typical organization chart for a marketing department is shown in Figure 18-1.

The product managers are responsible for developing marketing programs for specific products. They coordinate the advertising, selling, and product development efforts. Although they do not have authority over the sales department, they provide support material for salespeople and assist in training salespeople to sell specific products.

Sales management work is performed at several levels within the organization. The person at the top-level is either a vice president in charge of sales or a national sales manager. The persons in intermediate or middle management include divisional, regional, and district sales managers. The first level of sales management includes branch or unit managers. Middle-level sales managers serve as the connecting links between the policymaking sales executives in the home office and the first-level field sales managers.

Line and staff functions

The sales department shown in Figure 18-1 is a line organization. All of the authority and responsibility for implementing the sales program in an area lies in the hands of the manager for that area. A complete line of authority can be tracked from the sales executive to each salesperson. Communications up and down the organization take place through this line. Decision-making authority is delegated along this line.

Figure 18-1
Organizational chart for marketing department

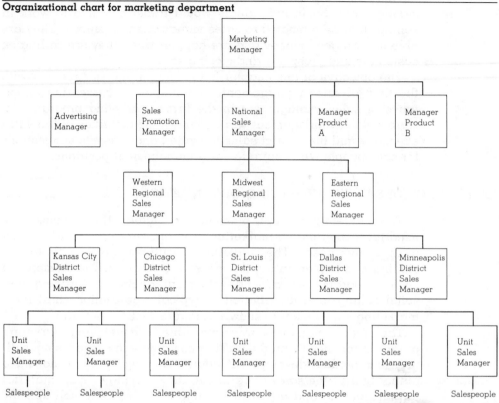

In large organizations the amount of work that must be done by a sales manager is often too great for one person. Specialized skills are often needed to perform some functions. Staff people reporting to the sales managers perform these functions.

Staff people can be used at several levels in the sales organization. A person in charge of sales forecasting may report to the sales executive. This person serves as an assistant to the sales executive. The forecaster may have little or no contact with salespeople. However, even though the forecaster has no direct authority over the salespeople, his or her activities can affect them. Other staff people reporting to the sales executive may be responsible for order processing, sales administration, and training. Middle-level sales managers frequently have staff people who are responsible for hiring and training new salespeople in the field and for providing salespeople with technical support.

Organization of the sales department

Most sales departments are organized into geographic regions. Each salesperson is assigned to a specific territory. The salesperson is responsible for selling all of the company's products to each customer in the territory.

Large companies often find it more efficient to have salespeople specialize in some specific activities within a territory. Such salespeople are not responsible for selling all of the company's products to each customer in the territory.[1] The specialization can be based on sales activities, products, or customers.

Sales activities. A common form of specialization based on sales activities is to have some salespeople develop new accounts and to have other salespeople maintain existing accounts. Developing new accounts is typically more difficult and requires a different set of skills than maintaining an account that has already been sold. Xerox Data Services, a supplier of computer time-sharing services, has two types of salespeople: marketing representatives and account representatives. Marketing representatives are responsible for getting new customers. After a customer has been using Xerox's time-sharing services for six months, the customer is turned over to an account representative. The account representative is responsible for making sure that the customer's needs are satisfied and for encouraging the customer to use additional services.

Products. When companies have a wide diversity of products, it is frequently necessary for salespeople to specialize by types of products. For example, the Johnson & Johnson Baby Products Company has two specialized salesforces: the Disposible Product Sales Force and the Toiletries Product Sales Force. Hewlett-Packard has separate salesforces that specialize in selling computers, electronic test instruments, electronic components, medical test equipment, and analytical test instruments. Each salesforce has its own regional, district, and area sales managers.

In the life insurance field, sales representatives may be grouped by such product categories as (1) individual policies, (2) group policies, (3) business policies, and (4) trusts and estates.

Customers. Customers frequently have different needs for a company's products. When this occurs, salespeople may be organized by distribution channel, industry, or company function. For example, NCR has different salesforces for manufacturing companies, retail institutions, and financial institutions. Some Procter

---

[1] See Alton Doody and William Nickels, "Structuring Organizations for Strategic Selling." *MSU Business Topics*, Autumn 1972, pp. 27–35.

and Gamble salespeople call on central buying offices for grocery store chains, and others call on food wholesalers.

A number of companies are organized in a special manner to deal with large national or key accounts. Typically, national accounts centralize all buying activities in a national or regional headquarters. In some cases, an entire salesforce is developed to service the national account. In other cases, a company executive is assigned to the national account. The executive coordinates all the salespeople who call home offices of the national account.

THE SALES EXECUTIVE'S JOB

The sales executive plays a vital role in determining what the company's future strategies should be with respect to new products, new markets, sales forecasts, prices, and competition. The sales executive is responsible for determining the size and organization of the salesforce, developing annual and long-range plans, and monitoring and controlling the sales efforts. This section discusses some specific activities performed by sales executives. The activities are forecasting, budgeting, setting quotas, and designing a compensation program.

Forecasting

In most companies, long-range planning starts with a sales forecast.[2] The first step in preparing a sales forecast is to make a preliminary forecast based on past and present sales. The preliminary forecast is simply an extension of past sales to predict future sales. This forecast is adjusted based on changes that are anticipated in the company and in the company's environment. For example, the preliminary forecast would be adjusted upward if the company planned to make unusual increases in new-product introductions, advertising, the number of salespeople, or the number of distribution outlets. The preliminary forecast would be adjusted downward if the economy were deteriorating or if competitors were unusually active in terms of product introductions and promotions.

A number of techniques are used to arrive at a sales forecast. These techniques can be divided into two categories: judgmental and quantitative.

Judgmental forecasting techniques. One of the most widely used forecasting techniques is to combine each salesperson's forecast for his or her territory into a forecast for total company sales. Normally,

---

[2] See "Forecasting for Higher Profits," *Sales & Marketing Management*, special report, November 17, 1975.

before the individual salespeople's forecasts are forwarded to head-quarters, each level of field sales management makes adjustments based on its greater experience and broader perspective.

One advantage of this forecasting technique is that it is based on information provided by the people closest to the market—the sales-people. Another advantage is that it places the responsibility for making the forecast in the hands of the people who are responsible for making the sales. However, the sales executive cannot rely exclusively on this technique, because the composite forecast may be biased. Salespeople tend to be optimistic and thus might overestimate future sales. On the other hand, if they know that their bonuses depend upon exceeding their forecasts, they might underestimate future sales.

Other judgmental techniques used by sales executives are collecting expert opinions and surveying customer purchase intentions.

Quantitative forecasting techniques.   The simplest quantitative forecasting technique is fitting a trend line. This technique is illustrated in Figure 18-2. The forecaster attempts to fit a straight line through the points representing past sales. This can be done by sight

Figure 18-2
Trend-line forecast

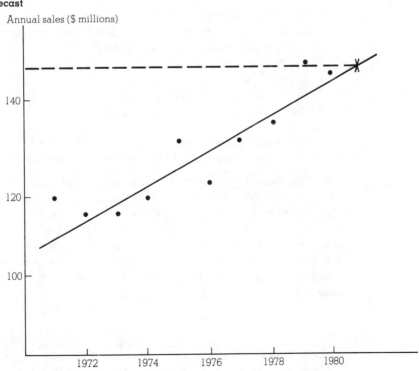

or by using statistical techniques such as regression. More sophisticated trend projections, such as those based on the use of a moving average and exponential smoothing, place greater weight on sales during recent years.[3]

The major problems with quantitative forecasting techniques is that they rely on projections of past sales. They do not explicitly consider what changes are planned or might occur in the future. Thus, the best forecasts combine judgmental and quantitative techniques.

Budgeting

A sales budget is a financial planning guide for the future. It contains both forecasted sales and the costs of obtaining them. Most companies require that budgets be developed on a monthly basis for at least one year ahead.

Budgets for a sales department typically include forecasted sales broken down by territory, product, and salesperson. Expenses are broken down into the following categories:

Salespeople expenses
  Salaries, commissions, and bonuses.

Administrative expenses
  Salaries, commissions, and bonuses for sales managers.
  Traveling expenses for sales managers.
  Sales trainer and trainee costs.
  Secretarial services.
  Sales meetings and conventions.
  Mailing and telephone expenses.
  Recruiting expenses.
  Display and showroom expenses.
  Moving expenses for salespeople and managers.

Management by objectives. It is important that sales personnel participate in the development of plans, forecasts, and budgets. Management by objectives (MBO) is a method for securing such participation by developing goals and objective that are acceptable to management and salespeople. If middle-level sales managers can be persuaded to set realistic goals, they will have greater motivation to achieve the goals and fewer excuses if the goals are not achieved.[4]

---

[3] See Steven C. Wheelright and Darrel G. Clarke, "Corporate Forecasting: Promise and Reality," *Harvard Business Review*, November–December 1976, pp. 50–58.

[4] See Donald W. Jackson, Jr., and Ramon J. Aldag, "Managing the Sales Force by Objective," *MSU Business Topics*, Spring 1974, pp. 53–58.

Control and quota setting

The sales executive is concerned primarily with matching overall performance against predetermined plans and objectives. The challenge of the sales executive is to set up a balanced control system which will encourage each sales manager and each salesperson to maximize results through effective self-control. The sales executive should get involved only when exceptions or major deviations from plans develop.

Quotas are a useful technique for controlling the salesforce. There are many different types of quotas. Quotas based on sales volume represent a simple breakdown of the company's sales forecast. Thus, the total of all the sales quotas equals the sales forecast. Other types of quotas are discussed below.

Expense quotas are used to control costs. An expense quota or budget may be expressed in dollars or as a percentage of sales volume. A regional manager or a salesperson may be awarded a bonus if he or she spends less than the expense budget. However, placing too much emphasis on expenses can lead to lower sales.

Profit or gross margin quotas are used to motivate the salesforce to sell more profitable products or to sell to more profitable customers. Some companies assign a point value to each product based on its gross margin. More points are assigned to products with higher gross margins. Each salesperson must meet a point quota during the specified time period. The salesperson can meet the quota by selling a lot of low-margin products or fewer high-margin products.

Activity quotas are used to control the activities of the salesforce. Activities for which quotas may be established include number of demonstrations, total customers calls, calls on new customers, displays erected, and sales made.

For quotas to be effective in controlling the salesforce, they must be fair, understandable, and attainable. Quotas should be supported by solid information that is accepted by both managers and salespeople. If quotas are unrealistic, people will ignore them.

Compensation and evaluation

An important task of the sales executive is to establish the company's basic compensation and evaluation system. The compensation system must satisfy the needs of both the salespeople and the company. Salespeople need a system that is equitable, stable, and understandable and that motivates them to meet their objectives. The system must base the rewards of salespeople on efforts and results. The compensation awarded salespeople for given efforts and results must be uniform within the company and in line with that received by salespeople who work for competitors.

The company expects the compensation system to attract and keep good salespeople, to encourage salespeople to undertake specific activities, to reward outstanding performance, and to achieve the proper balance between sales results and costs.

Three basic decisions must be made in developing a compensation plan. First, the sales executive must establish the overall or gross level of compensation for each sales job. This decision is based on the experience, education, and ability needed to perform the job; the income of persons holding comparable positions in the company; and the income of salespeople performing comparable jobs for the company.

Next, the sales executive must decide how much income will be based on regular salary versus incentive pay. In other words, what percentages of the salesperson's salary will come from straight salary, commissions, and bonuses. Finally, a decision must be made on the criteria for awarding bonuses and commissions. Performance to quotas is normally used to determine the amount of incentive pay that each salesperson earns.

The four basic methods of compensating salespeople are: (1) straight salary, (2) straight commission, (3) bonus, and (4) combination. Each of these methods is discussed in the following sections. The frequency with which these methods are used and recent trends in sales compensation plans are shown in Table 18-1.

Straight salary. Under this method, a salesperson is paid a fixed amount of money for work during a specific time. This method has the advantages of assuring the salesperson of a steady income and of developing a sense of loyalty toward the customer. It also gives the company more control over the salesperson. Since the salesperson's income is not based directly on results, the company can ask the salesperson to undertake activities that are in the best interest of the company even though they may not lead to immediate sales. The

Table 18-1

Alternative sales compensation and incentive plans

Method	Percent of companies using plans				
	All industries		Consumer products 1979	Industrial products 1979	Other commerce/industry 1979
	1979	1978			
Straight salary	21.4%	23.7%	12.1%	21.0%	34.2%
Draw against commission	6.3	6.1	8.8	6.7	1.3
Salary plus commission	27.8	30.0	15.4	30.6	29.0
Salary plus individual bonus	29.3	28.3	49.4	26.3	19.7
Salary plus group bonus	4.8	4.0	6.6	4.6	4.0
Salary plus commission plus individual or group bonus	10.4	7.9	7.7	10.8	11.8
Total	100.0%	100.0%	100.0%	100.0%	100.0%

Note: Some year-to-year differences reflect changes in the organizations reporting data.
Source: American Management Associations, *Executive Compensation Service.*

principal disadvantage of the method is that it does not provide a financial incentive for salespeople.

Straight salary plans are used when sales require long periods of negotiations (for example, computer sales), when a team of salespeople are involved in making sales, or when other aspects of the marketing mix such as advertising are much more important than the salesperson's efforts in determining sales (trade selling of consumer products). Most sales trainees receive a straight salary.

Commission. The commission plan includes a base and a rate. The base is typically unit sales, dollar sales, or gross margin. The rate is expressed as a percentage of the base, such as 10 percent of sales or 8 percent of gross margin.

Commission plans often include a draw. The draw is money paid against future commissions. For example, a salesperson could receive a draw of $1,000 a month. If the salesperson earns less than $1,000 in commissions during the month, the salesperson will still receive $1,000 in compensation. The difference between earned commissions and the draw will be made up by commissions earned in subsequent months. When the draw is guaranteed, the salesperson does not have to make up insufficient commissions.

The commission plan has the advantage of tying the salesperson's salary directly to results. Thus it provides great financial incentives for the salesperson. However, salespeople under a commission plan have little loyalty for the company. They are basically small entrepreneurs. They are less willing to perform nonselling activities such as writing reports and providing extra services for customers.

Commission plans are typically used by companies that do not emphasize service to customers or anticipate long-term customer relationships (for example, direct selling and life insurance). They are also used when the salesforce consists of many part-time employees.

Bonus. Under bonus plans, salespeople are paid a lump sum of money for outstanding performance. Bonuses may be awarded monthly, quarterly, or annually. They are always used in conjunction with salary and/or commissions, and thus will be discussed under combination plans.

Combination plans. Frequently, two or three of the basic methods are used to create a combination plan. Combination plans offer the greatest flexibility for motivating and controlling the activities of salespeople. They can incorporate the advantages and avoid the disadvantages of salary, commission, and bonus plans.

The principal disadvantage of combination plans is their complexity. Since the plans combine several elements they can be misunderstood by salespeople and misused by sales management.

Salary plus commission plans are used when management wants to motivate salespeople to increase revenues and also to continue to perform nonselling activities. When management is interested in developing long-term customer relations, salary plus bonus plans are used. Bonus plans are also used when the sales effort is made by a team of people.

THE SCOPE OF A FIELD SALES MANAGER'S JOB

The field sales manager's job is similar to that of the sales executive. The same management processes are involved—planning, organizing, directing, coordinating, and controlling. However, the implementation of these processes is quite different in many respects.

Planning

As mentioned previously, the company's sales planning often starts at the grass roots—out in the field—where the salesperson and the customer meet face to face. The field sales manager is responsible for knowing what is really happening in his or her territory. The field sales manager who has good communication with salespeople throughout the territory is the company's most effective source of information with respect to sales forecasts and planning.

In addition to providing information for the company's overall planning, a field sales manager has the responsibility of formulating specific plans in terms of sales and profits by product and by customer throughout the territory; establishing goals; developing specific sales goals and strategies; and establishing policies and procedures to implement those goals and strategies.

Organizing

Field sales managers are in an excellent position to know what kinds of organizations can be most productive in their areas. They know and understand each customer's needs. They recognize special problems involving weather, transportation, and local community culture. They are close enough to the individual salespeople to know what kind of organization will produce the best results for each salesperson.

The key to effective results in the territory is to have a competent field manager and to provide him or her with sufficient flexibility to accomplish territory reorganization with a minimum of red tape.

Directing

The transition from salesperson to sales manager is often quite a traumatic experience. This is particularly true when the new sales manager has been a very successful salesperson. The temptation is strong for the new sales manager to remain too involved in salesperson-customer relations. If the sales manager accompanies a salesperson on a customer call and the salesperson does not appear to be making the sale, the sales manager may succumb to the temptation to take over. This may save the sale, but in the long run it may not be the best strategy for the development of the salesperson.

A new sales manager should realize that his or her primary responsibility is not to make individual sales. It is to direct, to motivate, and to train sales representatives so that they will make effective sales presentations.

Coordinating

The coordinating responsibility of the field sales manager is perhaps not as complex as that of the sales executive. Nevertheless, it is extremely important that the field sales manager perform the function of coordination within the territory and with the regional or headquarters office.

The field sales manager must see that there is effective communication throughout the territory concerning changing conditions in the territory, sales made in the territory, new company developments, new actions being taken by competition, and new governmental regulations. If sales representatives within the territory are having problems in getting delivery on products or in financing sales, the field sales manager should provide the necessary coordination with the home office to resolve the problems.

Controlling

The records and reports submitted by sales representatives play an important role in controlling the sales activities in a territory. However, these reports are not enough. Field sales managers need to make calls with salespeople so that they can directly observe the performance of the salespeople. These observations can be used as a basis for recommendations for improving performance or for commending salespeople who are doing a good job.

LEADERSHIP AND THE FIELD SALES MANAGER

Field sales managers encounter "people-centered" problems. This is natural, as salespeople tend to possess somewhat different personal characteristics and traits than do production or office workers. They frequently tend to be individualists who prefer to do things their own way. Their jobs make it necessary for them to spend a good deal of time alone, away from their homes and families. Extreme emotional reactions may result from the closing of a large and profitable sale or from the loss of a sale which might have resulted in a large commission or bonus. The field sales manager is the individual to whom the salesperson looks for guidance and counsel during periods of stress or discouragement. It is essential, therefore, that field sales managers possess knowledge and skills in the area of human behavior.

The field sales manager is a leader of a group of salespeople. The role of a leader is closely related to the role of a salesperson. Salespeople attempt to influence customers to purchase their products or services. Similarly, leaders attempt to influence members of the group to work toward a set of goals or objectives.

Dimensions of behavior

There are two basic dimensions for categorizing how a leader behaves. These dimensions are: (1) authoritarian versus participative and (2) relations-oriented versus task-oriented.

Authoritarian versus participative. Authoritarian managers make all of the decisions for the group. They use the authority of their position to get salespeople to do what the managers think they should be doing.

Participative managers are more democratic. They share information and power with subordinates. Salespeople are treated as equals and are allowed to participate in decision making. However, participative managers are not passive. They attempt to direct salespeople by using influence rather than authority.

Task-oriented versus relations-oriented. Task-oriented managers are primarily concerned with getting sales. Salespeople are important only because they can produce sales. On the other hand, relations-oriented managers are concerned with the welfare of the salespeople working for them. They are considerate of each salesperson's feelings and strive to provide a supportive atmosphere for the salesperson.

Leadership styles[5]

Psychologists have identified a number of different styles or behavior patterns used by leaders. Some of these styles are shown in

---

[5] Adapted from Thomas F. Stroh, *Managing the Sales Force* (New York: McGraw-Hill, 1978), pp. 408-14; and Robert Tannenbaum and Warren H. Schmidt, "How to Chose a Leadership Pattern," *Harvard Business Review*, May–June 1973, pp. 162–80.

Figure 18–3. Each style is related to the amount of authority used by the sales manager and the amount of freedom that the salespeople have.

Over the last 50 years, psychologists and managers have searched for the one, best leadership style. Now people have come to realize that there is no one best style. Each leadership style is appropriate in some situations and inappropriate in others. The effective sales managers will use all of the styles over time. For example, a sales manager might be autocratic with a new trainee and give free rein to an experienced sales manager. The remaining portion of this section discusses each style and the situations for which it is appropriate.

Autocratic.   The sales manager using an autocratic style makes all of the decisions. The results of these decisions are presented to the salespeople for implementation. The salespeople are given no opportunity to participate in the decision making. The sales man-

Figure 18–3

Leadership styles

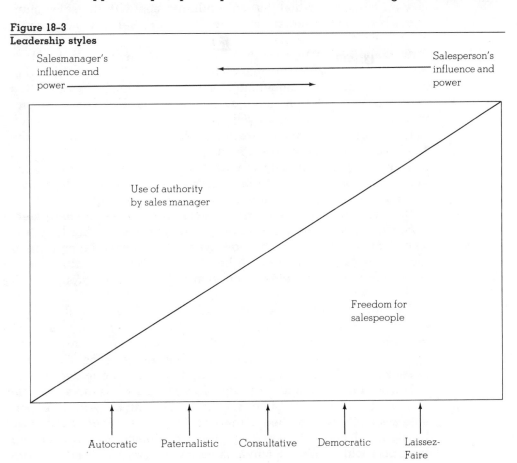

ager uses his or her authority, rather than persuasion, to get salespeople to do their jobs.

The autocratic style is most appropriate for new sales representatives for sales representatives who have become complacent and lazy, and when an emergency arises precluding the use of a more participative style. The autocratic style is inappropriate for use with experienced salespeople or in situations requiring teamwork and group effort.

Paternalistic. When using the paternalistic style, the sales manager assumes the role of father or big brother. While the sales manager still establishes the goals for the salespeople, he or she attempts to persuade the salespeople that the goals are in their best interest. Participation is not stifled completely, but it is limited to minor issues.

The paternalistic style works best for managers who are not in a strong position of authority. This may occur when a sales manager is new on the job or when the real authority lies with the sales manager's boss. A paternalistic style does not work well with mature and independent salespeople.

Consultative. The consultative sales manager solicits the ideas and beliefs of the salespeople before making a decision. For example, a consultative manager might say the following: "We are getting a lot of complaints from headquarters about the service we are providing customers. What do you think is going wrong? How do you think this problem can be corrected?" After getting opinions from the salespeople, the consultative sales manager makes the decision.

This style of leadership is useful when salespeople are experienced, mature, and well trained. It is not suitable for independent salespeople who are not interested in working as a group.

Democratic. The democratic style represents a movement toward more freedom for the salespeople and less authority for the sales managers. Democratic managers are interested in implementing the views of a majority of the salespeople who work for them. Such managers encourage discussion and accept the group's decision.

The democratic style is most suitable when dealing with a small group of knowledge sales representatives. It is difficult to use the democratic style when the number of salespeople is large, when decisions must be made quickly, or when the salespeople do not possess enough knowledge or training to participate in decisions.

Laissez-faire. The laissez-faire or free rein style is at the passive end of the leadership-style spectrum. This style permits expert salespeople to control their own work. The sales manager exercises little control and acts primarily to assist salespeople in achieving their personal goals. This style is very appropriate in dealing with the most experienced salespeople.

SPECIFIC DUTIES AND RESPONSIBILITIES
OF A SALES MANAGER _____

Brief mention has been made of the types of problems encountered by the sales executive and the field sales manager. The higher the sales manager is in the organizational structure, the more likely it is that he or she will be concerned with broad management problems. If the sales manager is responsible for sales in a small territory, district, or branch, his or her most immediate concerns will be with such activities as recruiting, training, stimulating, and motivating salespeople. The following pages are devoted to a description of typical problems that arise in working with salespeople. It is impossible to cover more than a few selected activities. However, the activities described will give the student some insight into the field of sales management.

Recruiting _____

Most organizations have a constant problem of recruiting and maintaining a competent sales staff. The major responsibility for the replacement and addition of salespeople usually rests with the field or district sales managers. Sales managers have become increasingly aware of the value of developing a recruiting and selection program in cooperation with personnel specialists.

Many large companies with comprehensive staffing plans follow a standard procedure which entails; (1) an analysis of the essential elements in the sales job and a determination of the qualifications necessary to perform this job in a satisfactory manner; (2) an analysis of the present salesforce to find what distinguishes the superior salespeople from the inferior salespeople; (3) the setting of standards, norms, or profiles based upon the characteristics or qualities of the successful salespeople; (4) the location of sources to provide the types of sales applicants desired; and (5) the measurement of the qualifications of sales applicants to permit comparisons with the norms which were based upon the characteristics of the company's successful salespeople.

How to recruit.   While no single technique of recruiting and hiring will apply equally well to all types of businesses, certain fundamentals are essential to most effective recruiting programs.

Ordinarily, the sales manager recognizes that a well-organized sales structure is built from the bottom up after determining what a salesperson must do to sell prospects. The number of salespeople needed in the future can be estimated only after sales-job descriptions are written and sales forecasts made. The sales manager knows that some salespeople will resign, some will be transferred, and some will prove unsatisfactory. In other words, provision must be made for replacement. In addition, in most companies there is a constant need for recruiting new salespeople to sell new products and to cover additional territories. After the preparatory steps have been completed and the number and types of salespeople to be recruited have been determined, the sales manager will proceed with the actual recruitment.

From company experience, certain standards are determined with regard to such factors as age, education, experience, marital status, and minimum test scores. Critical profiles based upon these standards may then be utilized as a measuring device to evaluate candidates for sales positions. While the profiles may show the characteristics of ideal employees, the sales manager should be knowledgeable enough to recognize that a certain amount of flexibility is desirable in selecting individuals for sales positions.

After acceptable standards have been set, the next problem is to locate sources of desirable applicants. An important part of a sales manager's job is to locate and cultivate good sources of competent salespeople.

Where to recruit.   University and college placement offices are excellent sources. Many sales managers contact individual professors for leads on outstanding graduates before visiting the placement offices.

Present employees of the company are sometimes solicited for recommendations. Members of the sales staff may have friends or acquaintances who are ideally suited for saleswork. However, it is wise to be aware that friends may be recommended who do not possess the desired qualifications.

Employees working in another department of the company are sometimes qualified for saleswork. An employee currently engaged in accounting, credit, or traffic work, for example, may be interested in transferring into saleswork.

Customers or clients are often able to recommend qualified applicants. From their dealings with company salespeople they are in a position to know what types of persons will probably succeed.

Well-prepared advertisements in newspapers, magazines, and trade publications may bring good results. For sales jobs requiring a minimum of qualifications, newspaper advertising is likely to bring numerous inquiries. However, unless the necessary qualifications are stated, many unqualified candidates may apply. For sales jobs requiring highly qualified individuals, trade publications are likely to reach more acceptable candidates.

Sales representatives for competing companies or sales representatives who are selling related lines are sometimes available for a new sales job. Of course, the practice of pirating employees from competitors can work both ways.

Public and private employment agencies have supplied qualified sales applicants for certain kinds of work. Influential friends and voluntary applicants are sources for additional names.

The sources for new employees are numerous. The sales manager who is to maintain an efficient sales staff is continuously looking for potential sales representatives. No one source can be relied upon to supply company needs. Good sales managers constantly evalute their sources to determine which ones are providing the greatest number of successful candidates. There is no easy way to get good sales representatives; it takes time and an organized plan to attract capable people. However, it is less expensive to take the time and effort to hire good people than to hire subpar candidates who fail after the training investment has been made.

Selecting

In recent years, considerable progress has been made in improving the process of screening and selecting salespeople. Most companies have discarded the myth that there is a "sales type" who will be successful in any type of selling, whether it is routine behind-the-counter selling or creative outside selling of intangibles.

It is generally recognized today that an effective sales recruiting and selection plan should start with the development of realistic specifications for the different sales jobs. These job descriptions are used to screen potential recruits. Each applicant's qualifications are matched against requirements in a job description. Some important sources of information about recruits are (1) the application form, (2) references, (3) tests, and (4) personal interviews.

Application form. This is a preprinted form that the candidate completes. The form collects factual information about the candidate and is often useful in structuring a personal interview.

References. Consulting with people who know the applicant is a useful method for validating the information on the application form. References are also helpful for amplifying the information on the application form with personal observations. The most frequently contacted references are former employers. Other references are co-workers and leaders of social or religious organizations to which the applicant belongs.

An experienced sales manager generally expects to hear favorable comments from an applicant's references. The most useful information is contained in unusual comments or gestures, such as ambiguous remarks, faint praise, hesitant responses, or inconsistent facial expressions.

Tests. Intelligence, ability, personality, and interest tests are designed to provide information about a potential salesperson which cannot be obtained as readily from the use of other selection tools. The intelligence test, for example, provides information on the individual's native ability. This information can be used effectively in training and supervising a particular salesperson. Tests also serve to correct the misjudgments made by sales managers who feel that they can spot a good salesperson at first sight.

Most companies are attaching less importance to test results in the selection process because these results have not been good predictors of sales performance.[6] Candidates can fake responses to personality tests or can "freeze up" when taking ability tests. In addition, many tests discriminate against minorities. Women, blacks, and first- or second-generation Americans often do not share the experiences and values of the white middle-class males who design the tests.[7]

Interviews.   More attention is being given to the use of multiple interviews in the selection process. This seems appropriate because selling is based on interpersonal communications. An interview also emphasizes that the selection process is a two-way street. The sales manager needs to know more about the applicant, and the applicant needs to know more about the company.

Interviews are generally conducted in the later stages of the selection process. Applicants are asked questions about their background, experience, and objectives. The interviewer frequently poses a hypothetical situation to get the candidate's reactions.

There is no one sales selection plan that is used by all companies. The selection methods differ, depending upon such factors as the following: size of the sales organization, nature of the product, geographic location, status of the labor market, and personal characteristics of management. The sales selection plan tailored to meet the specific needs of a given company will, in the long run, prove to be the most beneficial.

Training

The training program in a large organization is devised to educate the beginning salesperson and to provide refresher training for the experienced salesperson. The sales manager is concerned with what to teach and how to teach. The discussion here is designed to explore some methods which may be used for training salespeople. The amount of money expended on training a salesperson is shown in

---

[6] See Barton A. Weitz, "Effectiveness in Sales Interactions: A Contingency Framework," *Journal of Marketing*, Winter 1981, pp. 16–24.

[7] See Hal Lancaster, "Job Tests Are Dropped by Many Companies Due to Antibias Drive," *The Wall Street Journal*, September 3, 1975, pp. 1, 19.

Table 18-2

Average cost of sales training per salesperson

Type of company	Training cost* including salary		Percent increase	Median training period (weeks)	
	1979	1978	1978-79	1979	1978
Industrial products	$19,025	$15,479	22.9%	26	24
Consumer products	13,173	11,338	16.2	16	16
Services†	9,918	8,828	12.3	9	8

*In addition to salary, this covers such items as instructional materials prepared, purchased, and rented for the training program; transportation and living expenses incurred during the training course; instructional staff; outside seminars and courses; and management time spent with the salesperson when it is a part of the training budget.

† Includes insurance, financial, utilities, transportation, retail stores, etc.

Source: *Sales & Marketing Management* survey.

Table 18-2. Table 18-3 summarizes the amount of time spent on training a new salesperson.

Training the new salesperson.   Typically, these programs include a combination of the following: centralized instructional meetings; assignment to production and/or other departments to obtain product and company knowledge; and on-the-job supervised sales practice in a sales territory. The nature and length of the training program for new salespeople vary considerably. Companies in highly technical industries, such as the computer, chemical, and paper industries, usually have very comprehensive training programs for new salespeople.

IBM, for example, has an educational and training budget which is as large as the educational budget of many major universities. The corporation utilizes all of the most modern tools and techniques in training its new sales representatives.

Table 18-3

Length of training period for new salespeople

| Time period | Type of company | | | | | |
	Industrial products		Consumer products		Services*	
	1979	1978	1979	1978	1979	1978
0 to 6 weeks	14%	16%	27%	25%	31%	36%
Over 6 weeks to 3 months	7	9	24	16	33	28
Over 3 months to 6 months	30	42	39	42	25	27
Over 6 months to 12 months	49	33	7	9	9	9
Over 12 months	0	0	3	8	2	0
Total	100%	100%	100%	100%	100%	100%
Median training period (weeks)	26	24	16	16	9	8

* Includes insurance, financial, utilities, transportation, retail stores, etc.

Source: *Sales & Marketing Management* survey.

The Dow Chemical Company also has a very comprehensive training program for new sales trainees (see Figure 18-4).

The Hewlett-Packard Company has a training program as modern as its electronic products. A school is maintained at the home office the year around to give Hewlett-Packard sales representatives initial training and refresher training.

The new sales representative at Hewlett-Packard attends five weeks of intensive product information classes. After this initial

Figure 18-4
Dow Chemical sales training program

GENERAL TRAINING

ORIENTATION
    DURATION   1 week chemistry course
                  4 weeks general orientation

    PURPOSE   to gain knowledge of the chemical industry with emphasis
                  on Dow's products, plants, and people

SALES OFFICE EXPERIENCE
    DURATION   1 week in office
                  3 weeks traveling with various salesmen

    PURPOSE   to obtain first hand information
                  to learn the functions of the sales office and its
                  relation to the overall organization
                  to learn what the job of a field salesman involves

PRODUCTION TOURS
    DURATION   8 to 10 weeks

    PURPOSE   to acquaint men with our research labs, production
                  facilities and raw material picture

SALES CLINIC
    DURATION   4 weeks

    PURPOSE   to develop actual sales tools to be of use to the salesman —
                  help him gain insight and sharper judgment

PRODUCT END-USE TRAINING
    DURATION   1 to 5 months

    PURPOSE   to give specific information on uses of products, markets,
                  competitive materials, etc.

ON-THE-JOB TRAINING
    DURATION   6 months to 1 year

    PURPOSE   to increase job skills and to familiarize the salesman
                  with his territory and customers

Adapted courtesy of Dow Chemical Co.

schooling, the sales representative serves a year's apprenticeship as a staff engineer, taking phone orders, handling customers' calls for information, and becoming generally familiar with the products. Then the new sales trainee works for another year as a field engineer making sales calls under close supervision before being given a territory.

The sales manager's role in training a new salesperson is extremely important. Where a selling skill must be developed, the practice method is very effective. The salesperson can watch a skilled person (the sales manager or the sales supervisor) make a presentation. The salesperson can then practice until the presentation becomes effective.

The sales manager's function, then, is to train the new sales representative through individual instruction, coaching, and evaluation. One sales manager has listed the following "five steps to successful coaching":

1. *Tell* the salesperson what you are going to do on the call. For instance, "I am going to explain three reasons why our transformer runs cooler," or, "I am going to show how we can get by the receptionist into the prospect's office," or, "I am going to tell the buyer why it's to his or her benefit to place an order three times larger than before."
2. *Demonstrate* your plan by making the call in the role of a sales representative, with your associate standing by silently.
3. *Have the sales trainee do it* when he or she feels ready. People learn by doing. This step is where sales training really begins. Let the salesperson handle the call. Don't come to the rescue.
4. *Constructively correct* between calls. Compliment for things done right. Invite analysis of things done wrong or left out.
5. *Habituate*—continue coaching until better performance becomes habitual.

Training the experienced salespeople. Frequently it is more difficult to train experienced salespeople than new trainees. The experienced salespeople may have acquired ineffective techniques or bad habits. They may resent outside advice and may want to "do their own thing." If they have been reasonably successful and have reached an economic earnings plateau that is satisfactory for their way of life, additional training becomes less attractive to them.

The sales manager is responsible for analyzing the training needs of each salesperson in the territory and for taking the necessary steps to jar the experienced, but reluctant, salespeople out of their "comfort zones."

Experienced salespeople may receive refresher training as individuals or in groups. The group method of training has many advantages, and the sales manager can choose from several methods when conducting sales training meetings—the lecture method, the demonstration method, the practice method, or the conference or discussion method. Any one method or combination of methods may be desirable, depending upon the objective to be accomplished.

Stimulating and motivating

One of the most difficult tasks of sales managers is to keep their salespeople in a positive frame of mind. It is not uncommon for new sales representatives to begin their selling careers with great enthusiasm and with a determination to set sales records. However, personal problems, failure to meet quotas, changes in economic conditions, and many other factors may cause them to become discouraged. Unhappy sales representatives are usually ineffective representatives of the company.

Motivating cannot be accomplished solely through the personal contact of the sales manager or through contests and sales promotion schemes. The product must be of high quality and properly priced; the territory must be appopriate; the salesperson must be properly trained and must have the proper selling tools; and the company's compensation plan must be fair. Otherwise, maintaining morale is a difficult assignment.

The successful sales manager knows that the sales staff is composed of individuals who differ in their likes and dislikes. He or she knows that certain methods are effective in stimulating some salespeople and ineffective with others. In other words, individual differences must be considered. In large organizations, it is impractical to develop a different method for each salesperson and a variety of plans are generally used in an attempt to interest the greatest possible number of salespeople. Personal contacts with each salesperson, however, enable the sales manager to take individual differences into consideration.

The alert sales manager knows how to best motivate each salesperson in his or her territory. Some salespeople can be motivated only through prospects for increases in salary, bonuses, or commissions. Others strive for promotion in the company or for public recognition of their performance at a sales meeting. Some salespeople just want a pat on the back from the sales manager. Salespeople have different needs and thus must be motivated in different ways.

HOW TO PREPARE FOR SALES MANAGEMENT WORK

Opportunities

Opportunities for sales management work are available for the student who wishes to train for the responsibility directly upon graduation from college and for the experienced sales representative who wishes to engage in management work after having proved himself or herself as a successful salesperson.

One large life insurance company recruits at the college level by selecting sales management trainees. Figure 18-5 shows the announcement prepared by one company to recruit college graduates. The company believes that some sales experience is necessary but that a particular kind of management skill must be learned. This skill may be exercised, the company believes, by people who have not had many years of top sales production experience.

Other companies will consider as candidates for sales management persons who have had considerable experience both in selling and in management work.

Sales management opportunities are available in all types of industries. For the capable salesperson who has the desire to manage and the characteristics required, there will always be opportunities to manage a salesforce.

How to prepare for management responsibility

Advancement to sales management work does not just happen. Advancements are awarded only to salespeople who are qualified and ready when the opportunity presents itself. Salespeople who desire advancement do not wait until the opportunity arrives to get ready to assume a new responsibility—they prepare in advance.

What can the salesperson do to get ready for more responsibility? How far in advance can a salesperson prepare? How long does it take? Obviously, there is no one answer to these questions. However, a few helpful suggestions follow.

While a college education in itself guarantees nothing, it can be helpful in preparing for management work. Education, however, does not end with a college degree—it is what is learned after the degree is obtained that earns progress and advancement. Students who have evaluated themselves, have identified their strengths and

Figure 18-5

Announcement from a college placement bureau

> **Sales Management Trainee:** This interview has as its purpose the selection and training of men and women for a sales management career rather than for a purely sales career. Graduates of this program will be placed in the company's sales offices as managers, assistant managers, or supervisors. Training will be in Los Angeles or in an agency city under the supervision of the resident manager. $12,000 to $15,000 to start, annual increases.

weaknesses, and have found that they have the necessary qualifications, can improve their chances of success by obtaining a sound education. In addition, work experience while attending college pays dividends in both getting and keeping a job.

In addition to obtaining an education and securing work experience, the potential sales manager looks for opportunities to be a leader at school. He or she participates in clubs, sports, and organizations to gain confidence.

On the job, the salespeople who want to manage others must first prove that they can manage themselves in their own territories. Answers to the following questions may be a clue to efficient self-management activities: Is the ratio of sales calls to sales favorable? Are lost accounts replaced with new accounts? Have any ideas for improvement of operations been passed along recently? Are sales calls and territory coverage planned efficiently? These and similar questions can help point to evidences of good self-management.

Ambitious salespeople also prepare for advancement by trying on the boss's job for size. That is, they attempt, in their own minds, to solve the problems with which the sales manager is faced. The salesperson compares his or her decision with that made by the executive and attempts to evaluate the results. Of course, these decisions are not volunteered unless they are requested. Self-confidence is built if the salesperson finds that he or she tends to arrive at conclusions which resemble those of the successful sales executive.

Frequently, salespeople can visualize the activities in which they would engage if they were responsible for sales management. They may ask themselves: "How would I recruit? Where?" "How would I get more sales?" and "How would I cut expenses in the territory?" The potential sales manager would be expected to have ideas on these and other problems.

A good procedure is to try and make a self-evaluation from the viewpoint of the current sales manager. The salesperson may place himself or herself in the sales manager's position and ask: "Is this salesperson doing his or her best?" "Would I be glad to recommend this salesperson should an opening occur?" "Is the salesperson growing or just standing still?" Answers to these questions can help determine a salesperson's fitness for promotion.

It is desirable to study the decisions which are made by management at the policy level. How many were good decisions? How many were poor decisions? What were the probable causes of the poor decisions? What can be done to insure right decisions most of the time?

Sales management ability is not a gift; it is an ability which is developed through study, experience, and willingness to work. If salespeople have the right attitude, if they plan and organize their efforts, they can look forward to working in this challenging management field.

QUESTIONS AND PROBLEMS

1. Robert R. Smith, director of sales, film department, E. I. du Pont de Nemours and Co., made the following statement concerning the problem of remotivating older salespeople:

    This is no ordinary day-to-day problem of motivation we're talking about. This is a special case—and it could well be a lasting one. We're talking about the problem of motivating a person who has come face-to-face with a sobering realization that comes to all of us. We're talking about a person who has had to face squarely the knowledge that he or she has gone as far as he or she can go. Depending upon the individual, this can be a bleak and deeply disturbing realization—particularly if the person has lived for years not only with ambition for higher attainments but with an unrealistic appraisal of his or her own potential. It can, and often does, produce a protracted period of rationalizing. It can, and often does, effect a change in a person's personality. It stalls the sales engine, and when the engine stalls, we don't move goods.

    What can be done to remotivate the older salespeople who have started to coast? How should it be done?

2. Surveys show that there is tremendous waste in current methods of hiring and training new salespeople. Make a list of some questions a good sales executive should ask to determine whether there is room for improvement in hiring and training techniques.

3. Assume that you are the sales manager for the western district of a manufacturer of trucks, tractors, and farm machinery. A dealer in your district is eager to increase the sale of parts for this equipment. He asks you to help him determine the potential market for machine parts in his area. To what sources would you refer him to get the needed data? Justify each source or method recommended.

4. How would you feel about having your sales manager travel with you as a part of your regular evaluation? Do you feel that the sales manager has anything to gain *personally* from such visits?

5. Write a job description for a salesperson in the men's clothing department of a department store.

6. Good salespeople do not make good sales managers. Explain why you agree or disagree with this statement.

7. What leadership style would you recommend for sales managers of door-to-door salespeople selling encyclopedias? For managers of computer salespeople? Should the styles be different? Why?

8. To what extent should salespeople be allowed to manage themselves? What are the advantages and disadvantages of self-management?

9. The Emporium is the largest department store in San Francisco. For many years this concern has operated a very successful training program for new employees. A new applicant fills out a preliminary appli-

cation form and is given a screening interview by the supervisor of the trainee program. The trainee supervisor gives the applicant a training program brochure; briefly outlines the training program, store policies, and benefits; and answers questions. If the candidate appears to have good potential, a longer application form is filled out and an appointment is made to return for a battery of aptitude tests and a patterned interview. The tests and interview last about two hours. The applicant is then given some booklets so that he or she may learn more about the store before returning for the tests and interview. Assume that you are interested in entering the Emporium's training program. What kinds of tests would you expect to take? What kinds of questions would you expect the interviewer to ask you during the patterned interview?

10. Should new salespeople be trained by the sales manager and the regular sales representatives or by specialized company instructors who teach full time? What are the advantages and disadvantages of each method as far as the new salespeople are concerned?

PROJECTS

1. Make a survey of three local sales organizations, and obtain information on the kinds of incentives that are being used to motivate their salespeople. Evaluate and contrast the incentive plans of each organization.

2. Assume that you are a sales manager for a company which sells typewriters and dictating machines. Design a patterned interview blank which you could use when interviewing candidates for sales positions with your company.

3. Compare the ads for sales positions that appear in the Sunday classified section of your local newspaper and in "The Mart" (classified advertising) section of *The Wall Street Journal*. Write a report describing the differences in the ads. Explain why these differences exist.

CASE PROBLEMS

Case 18-1

Robertson's Clothing

Don Moore is a store manager for Robertson's Clothing, a nationwide chain carrying quality men's clothing and accessories. He is having considerable problems with his salespeople.

Two of the salespeople reporting to Paul Stevens are Jim Miller and Walter Carter. Stevens is the assistant store manager. Moore hired him because he wanted to spend more time on planning and merchandising. He was also interested in developing Stevens into a store manager, so that he could have a ready replacement when an opportunity for promotion in the corporation arose.

Unfortunately, Stevens has not turned out the way Moore expected. Stevens, who is in his late 30s, has had considerable difficulty in getting along with Miller and Carter. He finds it nearly impossible to give them orders. When he does, they always reply with a sarcastic comment. Miller and Carter are always playing practical jokes on Stevens. They hide his order pad and put tags on his back when he is not looking.

Stevens has not taken these problems to Moore. He is afraid that Moore will see the problems as a sign of poor management ability. However, the situation has resulted in a decrease in sales. Customers are being neglected. Some customers have been offended by the practical jokes. When Moore asked Stevens why sales had declined, Stevens responded that there were not any customers.

Finally, Moore heard about the situation through complaints from regular customers. When these complaints were presented to Stevens, Stevens blamed Miller and Carter. He said that they were immature. Moore said that he had never had problems with either Miller or Carter.

Questions

1. What kind of leader is Stevens?
2. What should Moore do about the situation?

Case 18–2

Ad Special Company

The Ad Special Company produces and sells approximately, 1,000 leather, paper, plastic, and metal advertising specialties on a nationwide basis. Most of its advertising specialties are remembrance advertising items, such as calendars, matches, executive datebooks, pencils, pens, and pocket business cards.

The company employs 1,000 salespeople who earn an average income of $19,000 after one year of employment. During 1980, about half of the salespeople earned over $20,000. The top 15 salespeople earn from $60,000 to $80,000 a year. The average order is about $300. The salespeople study the specific needs of their clients and recommend remembrance advertising that will appeal to the customers of each client. Ad Special sales representatives are taught to consider carefully what their prospects need to make them better known, better liked, and better patronized. The sales representatives must be alert to opportunities that others do not see, and they must have very keen imaginations. The company sells remembrance advertising to about 120 different kinds of businesses, so the sales representatives must be flexible and astute.

Past experience shows that many sales representatives fail during the first year with the company because they are not able to sell specialized remembrance advertising. Once the sales representatives become established, however, they seldom leave the company. The company's experience indicates that the best sales applicant is about 30 to 35 years of age; is married, with one or two children; and possesses life insurance, a car, and equity in a home.

The company has always placed major emphasis upon recruiting new salespeople through the present field personnel. Sales aptitude tests have never been used because management feels that such tests do not meet the needs of the Ad Special Company. The responsibility for recruiting, selecting, and training new sales representatives rests primarily with the district managers.

Questions

1. Assume that you are a district manager for the Ad Special Company. What sources would you depend upon in securing sales applicants?
2. If you used newspaper advertising as one of your sources, what kind of advertisement would you run? What kind of copy?
3. What, if any, training aids and help would you expect from the home office in training the salespeople in your district?

Case 18–3

The Wilkes Office Supplies & Equipment Company

The Wilkes Office Supplies & Equipment Company employs 25 sales representatives who sell office supplies and equipment directly to business and industrial users in the metropolitan Atlanta area. In addition to hundreds of office-supply items such as carbon paper, pencils, rubber bands, paper clips, blotters, erasers, ink, and stencils, the company sells typewriters, safes, adding machines, desk lamps, posture chairs, filing cabinets, desks, calculators, and many other office-equipment products.

The company's sales representatives are required to spend one day each week on the floor at the company's downtown retail outlet. The remainder of the workweek is spent outside the store contacting and selling buyers who have a need for almost any type of office supplies or equipment. The sales representatives have small drawing accounts or guarantees to provide them with an adequate minimum income during their learning period, and they are paid on a straight commission basis after the learning period ends.

Each individual is assigned a specific territory, and all sales in this territory are credited to his or her account exclusively for commission purposes. The company's sales representatives are required to concentrate their selling of certain products periodically in order to guarantee that the complete line of office products is merchandised. At some periods the emphasis is on adding machines; at other times, on typewriters; at other times, on checkwriters; and so on.

Quotas are assigned for various families of products, and contests are held frequently to help stimulate sales and meet quotas. New business is important, and detailed records of activity are required. Considerable emphasis is also placed upon the cultivation of old customers.

The company's sales manager plans to award a "Sammy" each year to the company's outstanding sales representative, and appropriate ceremonies are to accompany the presentation of the award. In order to select the outstanding sales representative, the sales manager asks each sales representative to submit a scoring sheet identifying ten areas in which a rating should be made.

Questions

1. Identify ten areas and list four or five appropriate questions in each area to point out the important success factors to be considered. For example, areas may be "personal habits and qualities": (a) Is the person neat in appearance? (b) Can he or she be depended upon to complete what is started? (c) Is the person enthusiastic about work? (d) Does the person constantly strive to improve selling ability? (e) Can the person express himself or herself effectively? Prepare the material in the form of a rating sheet.

2. Which of the areas listed do you feel should be given the greatest weight in the total evaluation of the salesperson? The least weight? Why?

SELECTED REFERENCES

Abernathy, Paul L., Jr. "Setting Performance Objectives Requires Lots of Give and Take." *Sales & Marketing Management*, May 19, 1980, pp. 86–91.

Archibald, Dale. "S&MM Spends a Day at Josten's New Man's Sales School." *Sales & Marketing Management*, April 7, 1980, pp. 46–50.

Dobbs, John H. "Hiring: Sales Force Turnover Can Make—or Break You." *Sales & Marketing Management*, May 14, 1979, pp. 53–55.

Falvey, John J. "Myths of Sales Training." *Sales & Marketing Management*, April 3, 1977, pp. 81–83.

Henry, Porter. "Managing Your Sales Force as a System." *Harvard Business Review*, March–April 1979, pp. 85–95.

Patty, C. Robert. *Managing Salespeople.* Reston, Va.: Reston, 1979.

Robertson, Dan H., and **Bellenger, Danny N.** *Sales Management: Decision Making for Improved Profitability.* New York: Macmillan, 1980.

Stanton, William J., and **Buskirk, Richard H.** *Management of the Sales Force.* 5th ed. Homewood, Ill.: Richard D. Irwin, 1978.

Still, Richard R.; Cundiff, Edward W.; and **Govoni, Norman A. P.** *Sales Management Decisions, Policies, and Cases.* 3d ed. Englewood Cliffs, N.J.: Prentice-Hall, 1976.

Walker, O. C., Jr.; Churchill, G. A.; and **Ford, N. M.** "Motivation and Performance in Industrial Selling: Present Knowledge and Needed Research." *Journal of Marketing Research,* May 1977, pp. 156–68.

Author Index

Company Index

Subject Index

This book has been set VIP in 10 and 9 point Memphis Medium, leaded 2 points. Part numbers are 48 point Memphis Bold. Part titles and chapter numbers are 36 point Memphis Bold, and chapter titles are 20 point Memphis Medium. The size of the type page is 32 x 48 picas.